Music an

Music and the Mind
Essays in honour of John Sloboda

Edited by

Irène Deliège

Jane W. Davidson

OXFORD
UNIVERSITY PRESS

OXFORD
UNIVERSITY PRESS

Great Clarendon Street, Oxford OX2 6DP

Oxford University Press is a department of the University of Oxford.
It furthers the University's objective of excellence in research, scholarship,
and education by publishing worldwide in

Oxford New York

Athens Auckland Bangkok Bogotá Buenos Aires Cape Town
Chennai Dar es Salaam Delhi Florence Hong Kong Istanbul Karachi
Kolkata Kuala Lumpur Madrid Melbourne Mexico City Mumbai Nairobi
Paris São Paulo Shanghai Singapore Taipei Tokyo Toronto Warsaw

with associated companies in Berlin Ibadan

Oxford is a registered trade mark of Oxford University Press
in the UK and in certain other countries

Published in the United States
by Oxford University Press Inc., New York

British Library Cataloguing in Publication Data

Data available

Library of Congress Cataloguing in Publication Data
Library of Congress Control Number:
2011920659

Typeset in Minion by Glyph International Bangalore, India
Printed in Great Britain
on acid-free paper by
CPI Antony Rowe, Chippenham, Wiltshire

ISBN 978-0-19-958156-6

10 9 8 7 6 5 4 3 2 1

Whilst every effort has been made to ensure that the contents of this book are
as complete, accurate and up-to-date as possible at the date of writing,
Oxford University Press is not able to give any guarantee or assurance that
such is the case. Readers are urged to take appropriately qualified medical
advice in all cases. The information in this book is intended to be useful to
the general reader, but should not be used as a means of self-diagnosis or for
the prescription of medication.

Prelude

In 1985, Oxford University Press published what was to become the seminal text in the then young field of psychology of music. *The musical mind*, written by the relatively unknown John Sloboda, made ground-breaking inroads into raising crucial questions relating to music's status as a form of human expression. The scope of the book was impressive: from music perception to production, embracing topics as diverse as music's origin and the circumstances that encourage its skill acquisition. Musical structure, grouping, and perceptual processing, including memory, were key areas where John had made early empirical investigations. Discussion of emotional responses and creative processes were far more inductively written, based on John's personal experiences. What made *The musical mind* so significant was that John laid a research agenda in asking those crucial how and why questions that have since occupied a growing body of researchers from all over the world for the intervening 25 years.

Over John's career, not only has he pursued many of the questions emergent from the research agenda established in *The musical mind*, but he has also worked alongside undergraduates, master's and doctoral students, and post-doctoral researchers from all over the world to stimulate and develop the field. This volume draws upon the work of John's collaborators, to illustrate how John Sloboda's foundational input has led to many fruitful inquiries and key discoveries in the field of music psychology.

Of course, a commitment to a research domain does not end at researching and writing. John was also crucial in stimulating discipline-related societies and allied research networks. Over his career, John has had significant involvement with the British Psychological Society (BPS), the Society for Education and Music Psychology Research (SEMPRE), and the European Society for Cognitive Sciences of Music (ESCOM). As a scholar, in 2004, John was elected to the Fellowship of the British Academy, and as of 2008, he became Emeritus Professor of Psychology at Keele University, and an Honorary Professor in the School of Politics and International Relations at Royal Holloway, University of London, having previously worked at Keele through the ranks from junior lecturer to professor over a period of some 30 years.

More latterly, John has taken up the executive directorship of Oxford Research Group, an organization which works to promote a more sustainable approach to security for the UK and the world. The group facilitates constructive dialogue between policy makers, academics, the military, and civil society. John undertakes regular speaking engagements for the group, and is an occasional author for *openDemocracy*, an online publication committed to human rights and democracy.

This book's genesis stems from the membership of ESCOM wishing to offer John a tribute and celebration of the past 25 years of thought, research, and achievement in the advancement of knowledge about 'the musical mind'. But also, and most significantly, the book lends insights into key areas of research in the field at the present time, written by world-leading authors in the field, each making a significant and original academic contribution. In sum, the book offers a perspective on how the field of psychology of music exists today and also reflects on how that work has been—in significant measure—stimulated by the influential work of John Sloboda.

Contents

Part 5 **Musical achievement and expertise**

Part 6 **Examining musical performance**

Part 7 **Music and cultural integration**

About the authors

The editors

Irène Deliège obtained her qualifications at the Royal Conservatory of Brussels. After a 20-year career as a music teacher, she retrained in psychology and obtained her PhD in 1991 from the University of Liège, where she was responsible for the Unit of Research in Psychology of Music. A founding member of ESCOM, she has been its permanent secretary since its inception and also the Editor of the journal *Musicæ Scientiæ* since its initiation in 1997. She is the author of several articles and has co-edited books dedicated to music perception including:

- *La musique et les sciences cognitives* (1986). Pierre Mardaga, Liège, Belgium (with Steve McAdams)
- *Music and cognitive sciences* (1987). Contemporary Music Review, UK (with Steve McAdams)
- *Naissance et développement du sens musical* (1985). Presses Universitaires de France (with John Sloboda)
- *Musical beginnings* (1986). Oxford University Press (with John Sloboda)
- *Perception and cognition of music* (1987). Psychology Press (Taylor & Francis group) (with John Sloboda)
- *Musique contemporaine: perspectives théoriques et philosophiques* (2001). Pierre Mardaga, Liège, Belgium (with Max Paddison)
- *Musical creativity. Multidisciplinary research in theory and practice* (2006). Psychology Press (Taylor & Francis group) (with Geraint Wiggins)
- *Musique et évolution* (2010). Pierre Mardaga, Wavre, Belgium (with Oliver Vitouch and Olivia Ladinig)
- *Contemporary music: theoretical and philosophical perspectives* (2010). Ashgate, Aldershot, UK (with Max Paddison)

Two issues of *Musicæ Scientiæ* are published per year (Spring and Fall) with several special issues and discussion forums.

The special issues published to date are:

- 1998—*Wagner, Tristan and Isolde, 'cor anglais' solo*
- 1999/2000—*Rhythm, Musical Narrative, and Origins of Human Communication*
- 2001/2002—*Current Trends in the Study of Music and Emotion*
- 2003/2004—*Musical creativity. ESCOM Special 10th Anniversary Issue*
- 2005/2006—*Interdisciplinary Musicology*
- 2007—*Performance Matters*

- 2008—*Narrative in Music and Interaction*
- 2009/2010—*Music and Evolution*

The discussion forums published to date are:

- DF I (2000)—*L'Afrique et l'Europe Médiévale*
- DF II (2001)—*Nicholas Cook. Music: A Very Short Introduction* (Oxford University Press, 1998)
- DF III (2004)—*Aspects of Time in the Creation of Music.*
- DF IVa (2007)—*Similarity Perception in Listening to Music*
- DF IVb (2009)—*Similarity Perception in Listening to Music*
- DF V (2010)—*Lerdahl and Jackendoff: A Generative Theory of Tonal Music, 25 years after*

Jane W. Davidson is the current Callaway/Tunely Chair of Music at the University of Western Australia. She has published extensively within psychology of music with research topics including expressive body movement, collaborative performance, music learning and ability, and singing. Her first academic appointment was at University of Keele between 1991 and 1993, where she worked as a post-doctoral fellow with John Sloboda and Michael Howe on an innovatory study of the biographical determinants of musical abilities. This led to more than 20 joint peer-reviewed publications. She has edited the following books:

- *The music practitioner* (2004). Aldershot: Ashgate.
- *La purpura de la rosa: the staging of an opera* (2007). Durham: Durham University Modern Languages Series (with Anthony Trippett).

The authors

Mario Baroni, Emeritus Professor, University of Bologna, Italy
Mario Baroni has taught musicology and music education at the University of Bologna, Italy, He was the president of ESCOM and the main organizer of ICMPC-ESCOM Conference held in Bologna in 2006. He is associate editor of *Musicæ Scientiæ* and consulting editor of *Music Perception*.

Arild Bergh, University of Exeter, UK
Arild Bergh completed his PhD on the topic of music and conflict transformation at the SocArts group at the University of Exeter in 2010, with fieldwork in Norway and Sudan. He instigated and is an editor of the journal *Music and Arts in Action* (www.musicandartsinaction.net). He has previously worked as a music journalist, and has researched and written on topics ranging from immigrant music in Europe to cassette music culture and underground music in communist countries.

Roberto Caterina, Associate Professor of Psychology of Music, University of Bologna, Italy
Roberto Caterina's main interests concern the relationship between music and emotional communication, and he has done several empirical studies on this topic and which have been published in a number of international journals.

Roger Chaffin, Professor of Psychology, University of Connecticut, Connecticut, USA
Roger Chaffin teaches courses in cognition, consciousness, history of psychology, and music psychology at the University of Connecticut, Connecticut, USA. His research on musical memory has appeared in journals such as *Psychological Science*, *Music Perception*, and *Music Psychology* and in the co-authored book, *Practicing perfection: memory and piano performance* (2002). His work on memory and language appears in numerous journal articles and two books: *Memory in Historical Perspective* (1988) and *Cognitive and Psychometric Analysis of Analogical Problem Solving* (1991).

Eric F. Clarke, Heather Professor of Music, Oxford University, Oxford, UK
Eric Clarke has published widely on various issues in the psychology of music, musical meaning, and the analysis of pop music, including *Empirical musicology* (2004, co-edited with Nicholas Cook), *Ways of Listening* (2005), and *Music and Mind in Everyday Life* (2010, with Nicola Dibben and Stephanie Pitts). He is an Associate Director of the AHRC Research Centre for Musical Performance as Creative Practice, is an associate editor for the journals *Musicæ Scientiæ*, *Music Perception*, *Empirical Musicology*, and is on the editorial boards of *Psychology of Music* and *Radical Musicology*, and was elected Fellow of the British Academy in 2010.

Nicholas Cook, 1684 Professor of Music, University of Cambridge, Cambridge UK
Nicholas Cook is the author of articles and books on a wide variety of musicological and theoretical subjects, and his *Music: a very short introduction* has been translated into 12 languages. His latest book is *The Schenker Project: culture, race, and music theory in Fin-de-siècle Vienna*. Until 2009 he directed the AHRC Research Centre for the History and Analysis of Recorded Music (CHARM). A former editor of *Journal of the Royal Musical Association*, he was elected Fellow of the British Academy in 2001.

Rossana Dalmonte, Professor, University of Trento, Italy
Rossana Dalmonte has been full professor of musicology since 1986 at the University of Trento, where she worked in the field of music history. She organized the second European conference of music analysis in Trento in 1991 and has published articles on the relationships between music and verbal language and on the perception of musical style.

Angelika Dorfer, University of Graz, Austria
Angelika Dorfer studied musicology in Graz and wrote her masters thesis on the role of music in cultural integration under the supervision of Richard Parncutt.

Alf Gabrielsson, Professor Emeritus, Uppsala University, Sweden
Alf Gabrielsson earned his PhD with a thesis on musical rhythm from Uppsala University in 1973. His research areas include musical rhythm, music performance, music experience, music acoustics, and audiology. His present research focuses on strong experiences of music and on expressive performance in music. He has published numerous papers in scientific journals and books. He edited a volume on action and perception in rhythm and music (1987) and recently summarized his research on strong experiences in a comprehensive book (*Strong experiences with music—music is much more than just music* (2008). He is consulting editor for *Psychology of Music*,

Music Perception, *Psychomusicology*, and *Musicæ Scientiæ*. Until his recent retirement in 2001, Gabrielsson held a professorship and taught general psychology and music psychology in the Department of Psychology at Uppsala University and at the Royal University College of Music in Stockholm. He is a member of the Royal Swedish Academy of Music. He was President of the European Society for the Cognitive Sciences of Music (ESCOM) between 1997 and 2000. He organized the Third Triennial ESCOM Conference in Uppsala in 1997 and has been awarded Honorary Life Membership of ESCOM.

Jane Ginsborg, Centre for Music Performance Research, Royal Northern College of Music, Manchester, UK
Jane Ginsborg has degrees in music and psychology from the University of York and the Open University, respectively, an advanced diploma in singing from the Guildhall School of Music and Drama and completed her PhD in 1999 under the supervision of John Sloboda at Keele University. She undertook post-doctoral research at the University of Sheffield, was a lecturer in psychology at the University of Manchester and a senior lecturer in psychology at Leeds Metropolitan University. She became a research fellow at the Royal Northern College of Music in 2005 and has been Associate Dean of Research and Enterprise there since 2009. She won the British Voice Association's Van Lawrence Award in 2002 for her research on singers' memorizing strategies and is currently Managing Editor of the on-line journal *Music Performance Research*.

Michel Imberty, Professor of Psychology, Université Paris X-Nanterre, and Director, Centre de Recherche en Psychologie et Musicologie Systématique (Psychomuse)
Michel Imberty has a multidisciplinary background in philosophy, musicology, and psychology. Two-time President (Chancellor) of his university, Michel Imberty is the author of more than 200 articles and books on the musical development of children, musical semantics, music and the unconscious, Debussy, Mahler, Wagner, Berg, Berio, and Boulez. His most recent book '*La musique creuse le temps. De Wagner à Boulez: musique, psychologie, psychanalyse*' (2005) is considered to be one of the most important works on musical time in the twentieth century.

Antonia Ivaldi, Department of Psychology, Aberystwyth University, UK
Antonia Ivaldi completed her MSc in Music Psychology, and her PhD on adolescents' famous musical role models, at the Unit for the Study of Musical Skill and Development at Keele University. Between 2006 and 2010, Antonia worked as a Research Fellow at the Royal Northern College of Music, Manchester, in the Centre for Music Performance Research during which time she continued her research into adolescent music engagement. Antonia moved to Aberystwyth University in September 2010; her current research interests are in identity and social interaction in a musical context.

Patrik N. Juslin, Professor of Psychology, Uppsala University, Sweden
Patrik Juslin teaches courses on music, emotion, perception, and research methodology at the Uppsala University, Sweden. He completed his PhD in 1998 under the supervision of Alf Gabrielsson, with John Sloboda as the opponent at the examination. Juslin has published numerous articles in the areas of expression in

music performance, emotional reactions to music, music education, and emotional speech, including articles in journals such as *Psychological Bulletin*, *Behavioral and Brain Sciences*, *Journal of Experimental Psychology*, *Emotion*, and *Music Perception*. In 2001, he co-edited the book *Music and emotion: theory and research* with John Sloboda. The two recently edited the *Handbook of Music and Emotion*. Juslin is an associate editor of the journal *Musicæ Scientiæ*. He is a member of the International Society for Research on Emotions (ISRE) and received a Young Researcher Award from the European Society for the Cognitive Sciences of Music in 1996. Alongside his work as a music researcher, he has also worked professionally as a guitar player.

Reinhard Kopiez, Professor of Music Psychology, Hanover University of Music, Media, and Drama, Germany
Reinhard Kopiez has a degree in classical guitar, and a master's and PhD in musicology. From 2000 to 2003 he was vice-president of ESCOM and organizer of the 5th Triennial ESCOM conference in Hanover, Germany in 2003. From 2001 to 2004 he was president of the German Society for Psychology of Music. His main research area is performance research (e.g. Satie's *Vexation* and sight reading) and music and emotion.

Alexandra Lamont, Senior Lecturer in Psychology of Music, Keele University, Keele, UK
Alexandra Lamont joined Keele's School of Psychology in 2001 and led the MSc in Music Psychology for its last seven years. She currently directs masters programmes in social development and health and wellbeing. Her research spans infancy through to adulthood and explores why people are motivated to engage with music, as listeners and performers. She has published widely in the fields of music psychology and education, and is associate editor of the journal *Psychology of Music*.

Andreas C. Lehmann, Professor for Systematic Musicology and Music Psychology, University of Music, Würzburg, Germany
Andreas Lehmann received his PhD in musicology after completing a degree in music education (both from the School of Music and Drama in Hanover, Germany). During an extended post-doctoral stay with K. Anders Ericsson in the psychology department of the Florida State University, Tallahassee, he grew especially interested in questions on skill acquisition and expertise. Andreas Lehmann is associate editor of the music cognition journal *Musicæ Scientiæ*, president of the German Music Psychology Society, and (co-)author of a number of chapters, journal articles, and books (e.g. co-authored with John Sloboda and Robert H. Woody, is entitled *Psychology for musicians: understanding and acquiring the skills* Oxford University Press, 2007).

Geoff Luck, Academy of Finland Research Fellow, Department of Music, University of Jyväskylä, Finland
Geoff Luck obtained his PhD from the Unit for the Study of Musical Skill and Development at Keele University, UK, under the supervision of John Soboda. He then moved to the University of Jyväskylä, Finland, and is currently an Academy of Finland Research Fellow within the Finnish Centre of Excellence in Interdisciplinary Music Research. His research focuses on music and movement, such as temporal and

expressive aspects of conducting gestures, synchronization processes, movement therapy, and listeners' spontaneous movements to music.

Daniel Müllensiefen, Goldsmiths, University of London, UK
Daniel Müllensiefen studied systematic and historical musicology and journalism at the universities of Hamburg and Salamanca, graduating to PhD, summa cum laude, in 2004, at Hamburg. His work combines interests in music analysis, statistics, and experimental and cognitive psychology. This work has applications in the fields of music psychology and music information retrieval. He lectured at the Institute of Musicology at Hamburg University on music psychology from 2004 to 2006. From 2006 to 2009 he worked on the EPSRC-funded project Modeling Melodic Memory and the Perception of Melodic Similarity at Goldsmiths, University of London. Since 2009 is a lecturer in Psychology and co-director of the MSc in Music, Mind and Brain at Goldsmiths.

Adam Ockelford, Roehampton University, UK
Adam Ockelford has had a lifelong fascination for music, as a composer, performer, teacher and researcher. While attending the Royal Academy of Music in London, Adam started working with children with special needs—a number of whom, he noticed, had special musical abilities too—and he became interested in how we all intuitively make sense of music, without the need for formal education. Adam pursued this line of enquiry, and gained a PhD in music at Goldsmiths College in London in 1993, in which he set out his 'zygonic' theory of musical understanding. This theory has proved a valuable tool in music theory and analysis, in investigating musical development, and exploring interaction in music therapy and education.

Susan A. O'Neill, Simon Fraser University, Canada
Susan O'Neill began her career at Keele University with the Unit for the Study of Musical Skill and Development, where she later became Associate Director. Together with John Sloboda she was co-founder of the M.Sc. in Music Psychology and co-director of the 6th International Conference on Music Perception and Cognition (ICMPC). In 2001, she was awarded a two-year fellowship at the University of Michigan, and she is currently an Associate Professor at Simon Fraser University's Faculty of Education. Her research focuses on the way young people value music-making and the impact of youth music engagement on motivation, well-being, identity, creativity, and innovation.

Richard Parncutt, Professor of Systematic Musicology, University of Graz, Graz, Austria
Richard Parncutt's research lies mainly in music psychology and addresses musical structure, performance, modelling, origins and interdisciplinarity. He holds degrees in music and science from Melbourne University and an honours degree in physics and a PhD from the University of New England. He founded the series 'Conference on Interdisciplinary Musicology' and is academic editor of the *Journal of Interdisciplinary Music Studies*.

Frederick A. Seddon, Northampton University, Northampton, UK
Frederick Seddon is a researcher at the Northampton Business School, Northampton University, where he conducts research into musical communication, the training of music teachers and the use of technology in music education. He is a member of the international advisory board of the journal *Music Education Research*. He has published several articles in international peer-reviewed journals, contributed chapters to edited books on collaboration, technology and music education and presented his research at international conferences during the past 10 years.

Geraint A. Wiggins, Professor, Goldsmiths, University of London, UK
Geraint Wiggins was educated at Corpus Christi College, Cambridge and at the University of Edinburgh. He holds PhDs in artificial intelligence and music, as his work is interdisciplinary between these subjects. In computational music cognition, he has published on music representation, automated composition and analysis, interactive performance, musical meaning, melodic perception, and musical similarity and methodology. A recent development is the study of new methods for musicology involving the application of cognitive models. He is an associate editor (English) of *Musicæ Scientiæ* and a consulting editor of *Music Perception*. From 2000 to 2004, he chaired the Society for the Study of Artificial Intelligence and the Simulation of Behaviour. From 2001 to 2007, he was founding editor-in-chief of the *AISB Journal*.

Part 1

John Sloboda and his contribution

Chapter 1

Music, linguistics, and cognition

Michel Imberty

Abstract

The work of John Sloboda has marked the psychology of music both by providing it with a solid scientific grounding based on the most up-to-date findings in neuroscience and the cognitive sciences and by ensuring that a scientific approach to understanding musical phenomena is not disconnected from the real world of musicians. An excellent pianist himself, he has been sensitive to the more dynamic aspects of musical cognition as well as to little studied aspects of the role of emotion and affect in music listening and performance. He has set out the bases of a psychological theory of musical performance. This chapter highlights these highly original aspects of John Sloboda's work and discusses some of their implications by showing how musicological analysis can be revised in the light of a dynamic psychology of situated cognition.

Since its publication over 25 years ago, Lerdahl and Jackendoff's *A Generative Theory of Tonal Music* (1983a) has been at the centre of every comparison drawn between music and language, and also at the heart of the epistemological conflicts between musicology and linguistics. A close re-reading of John Sloboda's *The Musical Mind*, which appeared shortly after *A Generative Theory* (1985), highlights the limitations of the generative approach for music and also brings into sharp relief the propositions formulated by Sloboda, at a time when this was not a dominant focus in psychology. In this chapter I undertake such a re-reading of generative approaches to music and highlight several channels of research that have resulted from this stimulating activity.

All research drawing on generative hypotheses has adopted the same perspective. Following models borrowed from either visual perception or the psychology of language, perception is regarded as a collection of procedures for processing sound and musical data. From this starting point, research has mainly focused on the construction of abstract representations of musical structure and how these representations are stored in memory. In cognitive music psychology, studies have treated listeners' cognitive strategies as a way of reducing the complexity of real music to such abstract representations, from which can be identified cognitive universals that might go far beyond the issue of musical ability.

However, there are at least two concerns that have not yet been addressed by the above perspective of cognitive psychology of music. First is the issue of musical universals, when considered in relation to the diversity of cultures on the one hand and contemporary trends in music on the other, since psychological research has remained entirely focused on Western tonal music. Second, and more important, is the issue of the dynamic and temporal organization of a phrase or a piece of music—that which might be called its 'movement' or its unfolding in real time. This second issue is closely related to the problem of temporal continuity and discontinuity in the sense that these terms reflect the listener's ecologically valid musical experiences during the course of listening, or the composer's intuitions during the creative act. I will consider these concerns in turn, highlighting issues that John Sloboda had prefigured in an innovative way in his book in relation to generativity.

Musical grammar

The Generative Theory of Tonal Music

The cognitivist agenda of the 1980s aimed to formulate, in as coherent and general a manner as possible, a theory of human behaviour in terms of systems of *competences* which are more or less specific to a given domain but whose structures and rules of operation are identical. Moreover, these competences, which are specific in terms of content but constitute a substantial and coherent collection of functions, are also innate. This belief can clearly be seen to have been inspired by Chomsky, in his first proposal of 1957, the well-known *generative grammar*. From that point onwards, Chomsky has influenced many fields of psychology—initially psycholinguistics, then the psychology of intelligence and thought, and currently the psychology of music. In this respect, Lerdahl and Jackendoff's work has cast a new light on our approach to musical analysis and raised many new hypotheses in the wider field of psychology. Specifically, their work has contributed to a more general trend in psychology to return to concepts and experimental paradigms derived from Gestalt theory.

I will not give a full account of Lerdahl and Jackendoff's theory here but will provide some points that are essential for my argument. The theory is presented as a hierarchical description of the tonal system, or the structures of the tonal phrase, which are also assumed to be a description of how musical memory functions more generally. The theory implies that the strong hierarchical nature of tonal music is both a property of its cultural and historical origins and a psychological necessity, that is, a general property of the human mind. Thus there should be a relationship between the ways in which tonal music and musical memory operate, and the rules of tonal grammar should constitute a specific example of more general cognitive rules.

Lerdahl and Jackendoff's primary hypothesis is that in order to understand and memorize a musical phrase, the listener identifies the most important elements of the structure, reducing the musical 'surface' to an economical and strongly hierarchical schema. The idea is thus that the listener carries out mental operations of simplification in order to understand the complexity of the surface. In addition, the performer can reconstruct that complexity based only on this memorized and simplified schema, and can even produce different musical phrases of the same type by reactivating this structure.

The Generative Theory of Tonal Music (GTTM) posits that any piece of music can be analysed in terms of four hierarchically structured levels. The *grouping structure* translates a hierarchical segmentation of the piece or the sequence into demarcated units during listening or while analysing the score. These units are of varying size (motive, phrase, or section), and can themselves be combined into longer units at higher levels. The *metrical structure* establishes a hierarchy of regular rhythmic and tonal accents where the smallest unit is the alternation of strong and weak beats. Within the series of grouping and metric structures, the *timespan reduction* is the location of important events for the listener. This is no longer a direct segmentation of the musical surface, but a reduction of the apparent complexity of rhythmic units or pitch group-ings into an essential schema or structure that underlies the segmentation—its weft, to use the literal meaning of this word in a weaving context. Lastly, the *prolongational reduction* delineates the succession and progression of tension and relaxation within or between time periods. This relates to the underlying structure of the series of temporal reductions, namely the most abstract and fundamental organization of the piece of music. Moreover, each of the elements of tonal grammar described by each of these levels of the hierarchical structure consists of three types of rule: *well-formedness rules*, which set out the conditions of hierarchical structure at each level; *transformational rules*, which permit a limited set of modifications of the surface and enable certain phenomena of elision or of synthesis to be understood; and *preference rules*, which determine for a given piece the potential formal structures that can be perceived by the listener. In sum, the well-formedness rules and the transformational rules describe formal conditions, while the preference rules relate these formal conditions to specific musical surfaces.

Cognitive implications of GTTM

Following on from Lerdahl and Jackendoff's work, many psychologists have attempt-ed to find empirical support for the 'rules' elaborated in GTTM, particularly those relating to the grouping structure. Deliège (1987) initiated the first of a long series of systematic empirical studies on this issue. It is important to remember the links between GTTM and Gestalt theory, since we know that Lerdahl and Jackendoff devel-oped their ideas from at least three basic principles deriving from the first 'grand the-ory' of scientific psychology (as this is understood in the physical sciences) and the work of Köhler, Gottschaldt, Guillaume, Lewin, and others. These three principles have important consequences for any type of psychology drawing on Gestalt approach-es, and they have particular consequences for our understanding of human beings (Imberty, 2005, p. 27 onwards). These principles are as follows:

1 Forms are innate and their laws operate from birth.

2 Forms are universal and independent of culture or context.

3 Forms respond to a general principle of isomorphism such that the laws of physical, physiological, psychological, and sociological forms all correspond to one another.

In sometimes widely differing modalities, cognitive theories of language and music have adopted these three principles as follows:

1 There are abilities or 'competences' specific to language or music which operate in the form of what can be described as 'grammars', namely systems capable of 'generating' linguistic or musical sequences without the need for any training. For our purposes, musical competences comprise an original collection of aptitudes or innate abilities whose successful operation is barely affected by experience with the environment from early childhood through to adulthood. This might be conceived of as a return to the psychology of musical 'talent'.

2 There are linguistic and musical universals which are elements of human thought. These universals can be expressed by 'basic rules' that comprise a 'core' grammar common to all languages or musical systems and generate sequence-types or 'forms' which are found in every culture. In terms of music, collation of different musical grammars should gradually lead to a better delineation of the universal 'elementary forms' which are found in all musical cultures, are entirely structured by the psychological systems that produced them, and by virtue of this are assumed to be common to all humans.

3 Grammatical systems, inasmuch as they are a formalization of psychological competences, should be paralleled in the internal functioning of the brain, meaning that competences should correspond to defined and independent neuronal systems. Here again, a range of hypotheses have been developed for music to explain how these might relate to modular neuronal systems.

Let us briefly examine each of these points to understand their philosophical and epistemological implications.

Universalism, innateness, and historicism

Gestalt theory and generativity

One of the strongest and thus most limiting hypotheses of generative theory, whether in linguistics or music, is the notion of the innateness of competences. This hypothesis can rapidly lose all meaning depending on how carefully it is defined. One argument in favour of the notion of innateness is that language, like music, is an activity that is limited to humans and not found in the animal kingdom. However, this argument does not address the degree of specificity of these corresponding competences. In other words, how generally can one define universal competences? In the domain of language in nearly every case studied, it has been shown that deep structures are built on identical generative rules and on identical functions. Yet to date in music the only serious attempt to define any kind of general structures produced by innate capacities has been the GTTM proposed by Lerdahl and Jackendoff. Moreover, their attempt is clearly presented as a theory of *tonal* music, and it is impossible to clarify precisely how this limits it. The authors are careful not to overextend themselves. While they may show that certain rules established for the tonal corpus could be generalized to non-tonal repertoires (in non-Western modes), Lerdahl and Jackendoff are not in a position to state whether these phenomena, by merit of their generality, truly refer to an innate cognitive competence. In contrast to the case of language, it is not possible to falsify any of the examples that the model generates except in a limited and unconvincing manner. For example, how can one define a melodic sequence as 'good'? More importantly, how can one falsify it—in other words, how can one determine the element(s) that would transform any 'good' melody into a musically unacceptable melody in the mind of a listener or a musician? Any modifications can only bring about changes at the surface, and the listener will not judge the new sequence to be 'melodic' or 'unmelodic' (as the speaker judges a phrase in his or her own language to be 'grammatical' or 'ungrammatical'), but rather more or less melodic, novel, or well organized. If musical competence could be defined in the same way as linguistic competence, on listening to a sound sequence the subject should be able to say 'This is music' or 'This is not music'. Even if such a judgement could be made, this could only be with reference to a given cultural and historical context, and not with reference to the universality of musical structures and musical thought in general.

The above argument highlights a fundamental difference between language and music. Musical grammars, whether those of Lerdahl and Jackendoff or the *Ursatz* theory of Schenker that inspired them, move from the surface to the 'fundamental' in a series of reductions which preserve only the 'skeleton' of the phrase—its simplest tonal expression that remains entirely correct from a musical point of view. In short, this simplified sequence appears banal and largely devoid of any aesthetic value (as illustrated in the numerous examples given by the authors). In contrast, the successive rewritings in Chomskyan grammar lead to deep structures that are not phrases, and bring into play processes that generate surface phrases.

There are thus two problems in defining the innateness of musical competence.

First, through successive reductions, musical grammars can, or at least can have the potential to, evoke so-called elementary and simple forms (and not functions), *prototypical schemas* (which Lerdahl and Jackendoff term *grouping structures* of pitch and duration) that give place to surface developments by a process of extension and amplification (which the authors term 'elaboration' of the strong hierarchical element). In this sense, musical competence can be reduced to the ability to produce variations and developments, and every sequence has the potential to appear as an amplification, a simplification, or an elaboration of another without any repetition. For example, through tightly specified rules one could transform a tonal musical phrase of Bach into a musical phrase of Boulez, illustrating the infinite potential for transformation through a sequence of hierarchical rules that enable anything to be derived from anything else. However, in natural languages, transformations cannot generate ungrammatical phrases which do not belong to that particular language. In other words, theoretically possible transformations are impossible in reality.

Second, leaving aside any philosophical and anthropological arguments, the innateness of musical competence is only *inferred* on the basis of the supposed *universality* of these simple forms, prototypical schemas or *patterns*. This implies that it is not the generative processes which come first (as in the case of language, where the phrase is generated from syntactic functions), but rather these so-called 'natural' groupings which can be said to relate to fundamental psychological or physiological states of equilibrium (which themselves are elements of human thought). This refers back to the third Gestalt principle.

As a consequence, the problems of innateness and universalism can be seen to be closely linked in psychological theories of music. This link is more marked than in theories of language because the definition of musical competence is itself more fluid and linked to the inventory of the structure of objects. Thus GTTM implies that musical competence is of the same type and operates in the same way as all other human cognitive competences, and therefore universally applicable and biologically determined. Many cognitive scientists currently consider tonal music (although they never explicitly refer to it as 'tonal') as a privileged site for studying the human brain: after mathematics and language, music has become an important focus.

As early as in 1985, John Sloboda clearly set out in his book the limitations of Lerdahl and Jackendoff's initiative. He began by demonstrating that generativity implies the notion that the deep structure reflects not only thought mediated by human language but also the pre-linguistic structure of human thought itself. This means that for music the question is 'whether there is any entity which bears the same relationship to a musical sequence as a thought bears to a linguistic sequence' (p. 20). In other words, if an idea or a representation can be translated into linguistic propositions but exists nonetheless independently from language, which is only a tool for thought, the question arises whether there are ideas which could be translated or 'expressed by a musical sequence' (p. 20), whether these sequences be a nursery rhyme or a Tibetan chant. These 'pre-musical' ideas could be the universal forms that are found in the deep structures of musical grammars, such as the Schenkerian *Ursatz*, which Sloboda notes 'is likely to have a close resemblance to the underlying thought representation of music' (p. 21). Sloboda's innovative suggestion was to locate this 'pre-musical' thought at the level of the schema of tension and relaxation which alternates more or less regularly throughout the general pre-linguistic organization of a story. I will return to this important argument below.

The other issue arising from applying generativity to music, as Sloboda noted, is that of the musical corpus which the syntax is able to explain, and its definition is much more fluid than that of language. Most people have only one language—their mother tongue. Yet there is no musical mother tongue, and most people's musical experiences are much more complex and affected by context, education, and cultural background. One argument that Sloboda put forward to clarify the nature of this problem was that 'syntax is a vehicle for communicating knowledge about the world' (p. 38), which foregrounds the stability of syntax as a means of improving communication. In contrast, in music syntax fulfils a primarily aesthetic purpose 'and the pressures for novelty invite diversity and change' (p. 38). This observation means that generativity in music proceeds along a different path: without a given limited corpus (a period of history in a musical culture or the works of a composer), it does not take the form of a language extending over very long periods of history and across a substantial number of speakers.

Stability, variability, and historicism

Sundberg and Lindblom's (1976) proposal, as examined in detail by Sloboda and more recently by Baroni, Dalmonte, and Jacoboni (1999) in their notable book,

Le regole della musica. Indagine sui meccanismi della comunicazione. It is an alternative path to resolve potentially the impasse of generativist psychology, at least in terms of the analysis of musical structures.

At the outset Baroni *et al.* note that most musical grammars, and particularly those based on a corpus of arias by Legrenzi, comprised rules which are more like *transformational rules* than *rewriting rules* for the deep syntactical structure in Chomskyan generative grammar, 'since [these musical rules] are always specific to particular musical traditions, repertoires or styles, and they do not have that element of psychological universalism which gives rise to the comparisons with Chomskyan deep syntax' (1999, p. 47). Cognitive psychology has gathered data on musical thought processes, yet musical grammars still remain dependent on the particular repertoires on which they are based. Moreover, as argued above, the question of the innateness of the listening processes that form the rules of GTTM is far from resolved. As they argue 'the comparison between the structures of language and music is still highly problematic. Specifically, it can be argued that the deep universal syntax of language does not seem to have any straightforward equivalent in the grammatical structures which can be discerned in music' (Baroni *et al.*, 1999, p. 47).

They first considered that any musical grammar must be culturally determined (as they note, the notion of a rule possesses a social and thus conventional value), and its rules can change over time in theoretically infinite ways. They wrote: 'nevertheless, beyond the modifications which are contingent on certain stylistic structures, there exists a type of continuity underlying several syntactical rules' (1999, p. 48). This clearly applies for tonal harmony which, despite numerous variations and considerable development, is founded on a small number of rules or principles that have remained unchanged over several centuries. Through their construction of the rules of a grammar of Legrenzi's melodies, they also discovered more general principles which they verify in relation to repertoires which are very diverse and far removed stylistically from Legrenzi (such as the pre-tonal monody of Gregorian chant or medieval polyphony, eighteenth-century melodies, romantic music, Debussy, Ravel, Messiaen, etc.). Their basic idea is that every melody has a 'simple' form, on which variations, ornaments, amplifications, and developments can be overlaid to give it its actual form. Although again not strictly based on the Chomskyan linguistic distinction between 'deep' and 'surface' structure, this does show how some rules in the model based on Legrenzi's airs can be transposed and transformed by different historical and aesthetic settings while still retaining their relevance to make sense of compositional structure. For example, in Schoenberg we can see that the scalar form is often transformed in a 'stimulating' way by applying octave transposition of certain notes, a transformation that masks the scalar schema at a perceptual level but maintains it in a grammatical sense. In other instances, in contrast, transforming the rules of the model can lead to mutations in the system itself. To consider this historically, while the 'simple form'[1] of the melody had been based on scalar functions for a long time, the nuclear cell being

---

[1] The authors use 'simple schema' in a melody to refer to a type of core structure where the articulations of sections of the melody are found, as in Lerdahl's tripartite symmetrical structure: a structural beginning, a development, and a final structural event.

an expression of the polarities of the scale, since the beginning of the twentieth century the core itself has been transformed, seemingly in a very restricted manner, and sometimes even consisting of a single note that 'polarizes' the shapes (as in Debussy, for example; Addessi, 2000).

Hence Baroni and colleagues proposed an alternative to the notion of (psychological) universality by arguing for historical or temporal stability, which could be described as *diachronic stability*. 'Musical grammar exhibits a dialectical continuity between two opposing principles: between elements of marked variability (which are linked directly to the variability in styles and cultures) and more marked elements of stability. These two principles are intrinsically linked, but are probably diverse in nature and origins' (1999, pp. 48–49). In summary, while the authors accept the notion that rules which are common to a number of composers, styles, and periods might constitute a core grammar of Western music, they do not seek its foundations in universal cognitive mechanisms. There is merely a coincidence between certain stable rules and structures and certain perceptual laws, but it is difficult if not impossible to explain how the latter might determine the former. If a definition is absolutely necessary, one might consider it as a 'diffuse' or 'weak' kind of determinism, which illustrates the dialectical ideas of the authors. On the one hand it is impossible to predict based on these few principles the innumerable diversions linked to culture and history, but on the other these same principles guarantee that throughout and despite all its transformations, music can retain 'several properties that we can define as "requirements of good listening", namely the properties of being clearly perceived, readily elaborated at a cognitive level, more efficiently memorised, and so on' (p. 49).

Thus any musical grammar is first a grammar of the musical work, melody, or song, before it can model the listener or the composer, and in the first instance it concerns the analysis of the neutral level, as defined by Jean Molino and Jean-Jacques Nattiez as the level of the text (Nattiez, 1987, p. 32 onwards). In this sense it is primarily an ordered system of rules. Yet it is more than this, as in certain cultural and historical contexts it also provides the composer with *potential choices*, which remain relatively free and which provide the function of 'giving meaning' to the composition. This resonates with the underlying principles of the *preference rules* in Lerdahl and Jackendoff's generative grammar, although in the process of studying Legrenzi's melodies it goes much further than that. Choices made by the composer depend both on highly generalized cognitive laws and on the cultural context and contemporary state of the musical system, and Legrenzi is sometimes seen to make 'choices' that clearly violate a recurring 'rule' with the aim of 'giving meaning'.

Sloboda made a similar point in relation to Beethoven's Piano Sonata op. 14, no. 1: 'The rules for the introduction of ambiguity, if rules there are, lie outside the set of rules which describe legal moves within tonality. When psychologists and others talk of a musical syntax they are usually talking of rules for the construction of music which is intended to be *un*ambiguous' (1985, p. 45 [original emphasis]). However, ambiguity often arises as a consequence of the desire of the composer to create an expressive effect or tension outside the syntax in the corpus of rules. Such an ambiguous construction is in many instances seen as an innovative stylistic development, and an important factor in the evolution of music history.

Giving meaning is a fundamental motivator of this diachronic stability, which is constantly in a dialectic state as a result of infinite possibilities and historical variations. Meaning is born out of deviation from the rule, and in order for there to be meaning, there must also be some small-scale unpredictability and an enduring 'core of continuity'. As the deviations become more and more distant from the basic principle, history unsettles the system and turns it upside down. This is what happens, for example, when the most general and stable rules of melodic grammar found in Legrenzi's arias 'force the morphological foundations of the tradition to the point of destruction (as in the case of certain 20th century music which eliminated the concept of melody), or requires new morphological structures to be defined (as in the 17th century with the introduction of figured bass which provided a historic change to the course of the grammar)' (Baroni *et al.*, 1999, p. 61). Baroni and colleagues emphasize here the complexity of the relationships that come into play between grammar and hermeneutics: 'Grammar can be seen as a device which has the goal of constructing meaningful or expressive musical contexts, in others words of creating clusters of sound which present themselves to listeners to be *interpreted*, to evoke emotions, and to generate meaning and appreciation. Grammar can thus be understood as a functional device for generating meaning in the sense that one of its most important motivators lies in its capacity to enable the construction and interpretation of clusters of sound endowed with meaning' (1999, p. 32 [emphasis added]). These are thus the choices left open by the grammatical system itself, which enable meaning and expression to be generated, but here again, for these choices to be meaningful they must take place within the framework of a more general and stable system, within which each of the two principles (variability and stability) constitute a type of 'intrinsic motivation' for the other, 'the rules "incorporating" their motivations in that they impose certain structural characteristics on the music in order to achieve certain goals' (p. 51). However, hermeneutics is not inferred from grammar, as it is an entirely different undertaking which begins at the point where the grammatical system as constructed by researchers permits a multitude of different variations, each of which is 'logically' explicable even if they sometimes appear surprising on the part of the composer.

Semantics and narrativity

Tension and relaxation

As I have already suggested, following the parallel between music and language and between theories of language and music to its logical end begs the question, as raised by Sloboda, of whether there exist forms of thought that can be expressed by music independently of language, pre-linguistic thoughts that could be manifested in musical sequences, for non-musicians as well as for professional musicians.

Sloboda's hypothesis has only more recently been tested and developed in the scientific literature. This highly heuristic perspective is presented next, and merits a lengthy quote:

> One suggestion is that the mental substrate of music is something like that which underlies certain types of story. In these stories a starting position of equilibrium or rest is specified. Then some disturbance is introduced into the situation, producing various

problems and tensions which must be resolved. The story ends with a return to equilibrium. The underlying representation for music could be seen as a highly abstracted blueprint for such stories, retaining only the features they all have in common. (1985, p. 20)

Sloboda's view is interesting in that it provided an opening for a range of different lines of enquiry developed over the last 10 years. First, the notion of tension and relaxation as the basic force of the temporal progression of a piece provided Lerdahl (1989) with a basis for understanding atonal and dodecaphonic music in terms of his generative model (Imberty, 2005, p. 42 onwards). Lerdahl and Jackendoff had already argued for the importance of the phenomena of tension and relaxation in an overview of their work back in 1983: 'One of the most important types of intuition that a listener can have relates to the way in which movement tenses and relaxes between important notes' (1983b, p. 234). They continue: 'If two events are experienced in the connection of a prolongation (at the musical surface or an underlying level) and if the second event is experienced as less stable than the first, the succession will be experienced as "in tension". If the second event is more stable than the first, it will be experienced as "in relaxation". Moreover, the degree of tension or relaxation will depend on the perceptual contrast between the two events. The more significant the contrast, the more the dynamic alternation will be noticeable for the listener, and conversely the less marked the contrast, the stronger the *prolongation*, reinforcing the perception of continuity and stability' (pp. 234–235 [original emphasis]).

The eventual underlying structure of a piece of tonal music is thus a hierarchy of tension and relaxation, of alternating stable and unstable events, and it converts the listener's intuitions about the progression of the music beyond delineations of groups and patterns into temporal frameworks. It is also a kind of dynamic structure presented by the composer in order to create surprise, resolving the listener's expectations. I myself have developed the concept of perceptual macro-structure of a musical work to illustrate how the hierarchies of tension and relaxation operate during the listening process and also as a guiding schema of the compositional framework of musical time (Imberty, 1981, 2005, pp. 63–71). The parallels with the concept of a story are clearly evident. However, as Sloboda has illustrated, and Baroni and colleagues have established, as a consequence this means that musical grammar, and generative grammar in particular, is not an explanation for the compositional activity. On the contrary, that has the function of creating tension by deviating from the grammar (whether melodically, rhythmically, or harmonically) in order to provide resolutions later by returning to the rule, after a shorter or longer time period during which the listener will have been in a state of uncertainty.

In highlighting the importance of the concept of *implication*, the work of Meyer (1973) and later Narmour (1992) has fleshed out this hypothesis. In his 1973 work *Explaining Music*, Meyer developed the idea that one of the functions of a melodic line is to create implications which will provide an orientation for future events, or, in other words, that its internal structure creates at every stage for the listener the expectation of a given 'next event' or 'continuation' in a given direction which is the most likely at any moment in the given context. Yet in reality no implication is ever unique, and every melodic form embodies many potentialities, sometimes contradictory. *Deviations* (or secondary implications) from the initial pattern are always possible, leading the melodic process in unexpected directions that the composer can play with before returning to the initial position. According to Narmour, who has taken up Meyer's ideas in a more systematic fashion in two substantive works (1990, 1992), implications are tendencies of the deep structure of melodies, which he defines in the form of psychological 'rules of implication', while the contextual choice of one or another particular implication by the composer (or listener) is based on 'stylistic rules', which are conventional and historical. In their work on melody, Baroni and colleagues suggest, perhaps rightly, that these rules of implication should be described as 'pre-grammatical rules' (1999, p. 236) comprising a 'theory of listening' rather than stylistic grammars. 'We can see that Meyer's and Narmour's approaches are not really grammars but analyses of certain fundamental elements which can contribute to the understanding of the origins and uses of rules of grammar' (p. 236), which the authors had previously termed 'motivations' of the rules of melodic grammar. All these arguments and observations clearly apply to tonal music, and partially to non-tonal music. Thus I agree with Sloboda in saying that we can propose a 'deep universal' which has the function of 'creation and resolution of motivated tension' (Sloboda, 1985, p. 22).

Narrativity in music

The notion that 'universals' in music have something to do with a story, or at least certain elements of a story, is echoed in more recent work which can be described as concerning *human musicality*. The idea is that a narrative is above all a temporal line, a melodic and rhythmic contour with affective and emotional content, which is not derived from verbal language (or not only, in the case of songs with words) but from the body, body movements, and postures, and is founded on a communicative intention. Several authors have demonstrated how, from the earliest exchanges between mother and infant and between infant and other humans, human interactions are structured in the voice, motor actions, looks, facial expressions, and other non-verbal means (Gratier, 2003, 2007; Gratier & Trevarthen, 2008; Malloch, 1999; Trevarthen, 1999, 2008). For example, Trevarthen (1999/2000) and Malloch (1999, 2000) see narrativity as the fact that when we connect short temporal sequences together, out of these short sequences of behaviour or subjective internal experience we gradually make larger and more extensive time periods, which take form with a beginning, a development, and an end. As a result a temporal unity appears, delimited in the sense of a cognitive and affective segmentation of the infinite temporal flow of life. This unity is a unity of memory, a part of the subjective and intersubjective experience of exchanges between human beings. In memory, it unfolds as a story with or without words, namely as an expansive temporal form containing different episodes of tension and relaxation leading to a conclusion.

This form not only exists in narrative and in the stories that we tell, but also exists in non-verbal behavioural sequences. These are the forms of narrative in action and in affect. It also relates to intentionality, as these forms give meaning to any collection of behaviours which are goal-directed. Having reached the goal, the sequence comes to an end. Narrativity is thus a property of exchanges between human beings, beginning with exchanges between mother and infant.

These exchanges are arranged in a proto-narrative, meaning that the sequence is organized with a beginning and an end, and the narrative is without words but involves the exchange of meaning, emotions, and feelings. Malloch (1999) shows that most maternal utterances resemble songs which begin with a calm introduction, followed by an animated phase which is enhanced following the infant's response, leading to a peak where vocalizations are rapidly exchanged, and finally a slow and calm conclusion organized by a longer central duration. In our research group, Maya Gratier (1999/2000, 2003, 2007; Gratier & Trevarthen, 2008) has studied many examples that share these characteristics.

This structure corresponds to Stern's (1985) 'proto-narrative envelope', which is a contour of sensations, perceptions, emotional, and cognitive experiences distributed over time with the coherence of a *quasi-plot*. Stern writes: 'The basic idea is that continuous interpersonal experience is interrupted due to the capacity of narrative *thought*. It is assumed that narrative thought is a universal mechanism by which everyone, including newborns, perceive and reflect on human behaviour' (1998, p. 182). Narrative thought is arranged around two interdependent aspects, *intrigue* on the one hand, which is 'the unity which connects the "who, where, why, and how" of human activity. This focuses on perception of human behaviour as motivated and goal-directed'; on the other hand, we have 'the line of dramatic tension … [which] is the contour of feelings as they emerge at the present moment' (p. 182).

The voice and vocal exchanges between mother and infant play a central role in the construction of proto-narrative structures. Lévi-Strauss had already written in 1971: 'every melodic phrase or harmonic development puts forward a new opportunity' (p. 590). More generally, as Gratier and Trevarthen (2008) note, everyone who sings, recites poetry, or speaks in order to convey information makes a departure which is in essence an opportunity. This implies that song, words, and all forms of human expression are fundamentally musical and potentially cultural phenomena. The authors also provide a good definition of what is in play in the voice and vocal exchanges, whether this be at birth, in early infancy or much later in adult life: 'Human vocalisation is constructed around the need to tell a story … The voice can tell stories of intention and reflect experiences of the past by reproducing a "narrative" of intention … This is how members of a group share their experiences of the world and their intentional actions' (p. 132). The voice, with its intentional contour which is not yet language, provides the foundation for the thread of our personal individual life story, which later we will know how to put into words, but without which we would not be able to begin telling.

This concept is fundamental, providing the basis for the communicability of personal experiences between people by using language and signs, the comprehensibility of behaviour in interactive situations, and the expressive capacity of individuals in the realm of social or private imagination. It also provides the basis for the enormous expressive power of music alongside the fact that it is a kind of universal pre-language of 'refigurations' of experience in art, this art 'beyond language' being the ideal type so sought after by its creators. Art 'refigures'[2] (in Ricoeur's sense) the Proustian experience

---

2 '*Configuration* is the capacity for language to configure itself in its own space, and *refiguration* … the capacity for the work to restructure the world of the reader by unsettling, challenging, and remodelling his or her expectations … herein lies the creativity of art, penetrating into the world of everyday life to rework it from the inside' (Ricoeur, 2001, p. 260, emphasis added).

which was extensively discussed in the preceding chapter. As Proust so elegantly described at the start of *Remembrance of Things Past*, the temporal contour of the mother's voice forms this *link* between the intense desire of the young Marcel to 'be with Mother' and the mysterious and musical proto-narrative that this voice forms in the novel, thereby giving meaning to the future life of the author. In this context, it is unsurprising that music has the power to create stories without words.

Conclusion

Music may be the translation or representation of the origins of every symbolic form and form of language, that is, every form of structured time, because its origins are found in the earliest human exchanges from the very start of life. As Sloboda concluded, 'Because our instincts for music are rooted in the conditions that prevailed in the infancy of humanity [and, I would add, as we have just seen, the conditions prevailing in early infancy and the start of inter-subjective communication], the *forms* that were available to early people [and, I would add, to infants] have a primal and inescapable influence. In particular, it is the *voice* and the human body in rhythmic movement which forms the motivational mainspring of music. If music departs too far from this mainspring, it will cease to have deep meaning and power for us' (1985, p. 268 [original emphasis]).

There is no society without language, and no society without music. The two are necessarily intertwined. Herein lies the source of every form of expression: like language, music takes its power from its dual nature as biological and also deeply social. The temporal matter of music is provided by modes of being in the world which we have constructed from early infancy, and which further guide our modes of being at the present moment, in our culture, with our perception, body, emotions, and feelings. Beyond different musical systems and the ways in which these are used, it is possible that the anchoring of life from its beginnings in the sound world, in duration, rhythm, time and movement, provides the basis for the universality of music as an expression of human subjectivity. And this may be why the precocity of specific musical capacities enables us to develop behavioural and social musicality in order to develop our personalities in the fullest and richest ways possible.

Acknowledgement
Translated by Alexandra Lamont.

References
Addessi, A. R. (2000). *Claude Debussy et Manuel de Falla. Un caso di influenza stilistica.* Bologna: CLUEB.

Baroni, M. Dalmonte, R., & Jacoboni, C. (1999). *Le regole della musica. Indagine suimeccanismi della communicazione.* Torino: Edizioni di Torino (EDT).

Chomsky, N. (1957). *Syntactic structures.* La Haye: Mouton.

Deliège, I. (1987). Grouping conditions in listening to music: an approach to Lerdahl and Jackendoff's grouping preferences rules. *Music Perception, 4*(4), 325–360.

Gratier, M. (1999/2000). Expressions of belonging: the effect of acculturation on the rhythm and harmony of noter-infant vocal interaction. *Musicæ Scientiæ, Special Issue*, 93–122.

Gratier, M. (2003). Expressive timing and interactional synchrony between mothers and infants: cultural similarities, cultural differences and the immigration experience. *Cognitive Development*, *18*, 533–554.

Gratier, M. (2007). Musicalité, style et appartenance dans l'interaction mère-bébé. In M. Imberty, & M. Gratier (Eds.), *Temps, geste et musicalité* (pp. 69–100). Paris: L'Harmattan.

Gratier, M. & Trevarthen, C. (2008). Musical narrative and motives for culture in mother-infant vocal interaction. *Journal of Consciousness Studies*, *15*(10–11), 122–158.

Imberty, M. (1981). *Les écritures du temps*. Paris: Dunod.

Imberty, M. (2005). *La musique creuse le temps. De Wagner à Boulez: musique, psychologie psychanalyse*. Paris: L'Harmattan, Univers Musical.

Lerdahl, F. (1989). Structures de prolongation dans l'atonalité. In S. McAdams, & I. Deliège (Eds.), *La musique et les sciences cognitives* (pp. 103–135). Bruxelles: Mardaga.

Lerdahl, F., & Jackendoff, R. (1983a). *A generative theory of tonal music*. Cambridge, MA: MIT Press.

Lerdahl, F., & Jackendoff, R. (1983b). An overview of hierarchical structure in music. *Music Perception*, *1*(2), 229–247.

Lévi-Strauss, C. (1971). *L'Homme Nu*. Paris: Plon.

Malloch, S. (1999/2000). Mothers and infants and communicative musicality. *Musicæ Scientiæ, Special Issue (1999/2000)*, 29–58.

Meyer, L. B. (1973). *Explaining music: essays and explorations*. Berkeley, CA: University of California Press.

Narmour, E. (1990). *The analysis and cognition of basic melodic structures. The implication-realization model*. Chicago, IL: University of Chicago Press.

Narmour, E. (1992). *The analysis and cognition of melodic complexity. The implication-realization model*. Chicago: University of Chicago Press.

Nattiez, J. J. (1987). *Musicologie générale et sémiologie*. Paris: Ch. Bourgois.

Ricoeur, P. (2001). *La critique et la conviction*. Entretiens avec François Azouvi et Marc de Lunay. Paris: Hachette, Littératures.

Sloboda, J. A. (1985). *The musical mind*. Oxford: Oxford University Press.

Stern, D. (1985). *The interpersonal world of the infant*. New York: Basic Books.

Stern, D. (1998). Aspects temporels de l'expérience quotidienne d'un nouveau-né : quelques réflexions concernant la musique. In E. Darbellay (Ed.), *Le temps et la forme. Pour une épistémologie de la connaissance musicale* (pp. 167–185). Geneva: Droz.

Sundberg, J., & Lindblom, B. (1976). Generative theories in language and music descriptions, *Cognition*, *4*, 99–122.

Trevarthen, C. (1999/2000). Musicality and the intrinsic motive pulse: evidence from human psychobiology and infant communication. *Musicæ Scientiæ, Special Issue*, 155–215.

Trevarthen, C. (2008). The musical art of infant conversation: Narrating in the time of sympathetic experience, without rational interpretation, before words. *Musicæ Scientiæ, Special Issue*, 15–46.

Chapter 2

'What are the important questions?' a reflection

Eric F. Clarke

Abstract

The psychology of music occupies what has sometimes seemed an uncomfortable position between musicians' practical concerns, and the more abstract academic concerns of psychological research. For most of the time, research in the psychology of music (as in many other subject domains) simply gets on with its immediate concerns, seldom looking up to consider the larger horizon within which it works. But on at least three occasions, John Sloboda has addressed—in different ways—what the 'important questions' are in music psychology, and whether and how research is making any headway towards those larger aims. This paper critically reflects on Sloboda's own assessment of 'the important questions', and considers alternative perspectives on what those might be—from different standpoints, at different times in the developing history of research in the psychology of music, and as the relationship of the subject to its institutional contexts changes.

Introduction and take 1

It is one thing to carry out important and influential research in the psychology of music, and another to have the capacity to stand back from the immediacy of that engagement with your own research domain and consider what the pressing questions are, or should be, and whether the discipline is tackling them. On at least three published occasions John Sloboda[1] (JAS) has had the foresight, and sense of purpose and academic responsibility, to do just that, and this chapter is a reflection on his analysis of how he saw the situation on those three occasions.

The three pieces of published writing are collected together in the book *Exploring the Musical Mind. Cognition, Emotion, Ability, Function* (Sloboda, 2005), but were

---

[1] Avoiding both the over-formality of 'Sloboda' and the potentially off-putting chumminess of 'John', I will refer to John Sloboda with his initials (JAS) throughout this chapter.

originally published in 1986, 1992, and 2005. The first, entitled 'Cognition and real music: the psychology of music comes of age' (Sloboda, 1986), reflects on the progress of research in the psychology of music from its somewhat disparate origins to its emergence as a properly constituted discipline in the mid-1980s. The philosopher of science Thomas Kuhn, to whose work (Kuhn, 1962) JAS refers, distinguished between the (1) pre-scientific, (2) normal science, and (3) revolutionary science phases of a discipline. The pre-scientific phase is characterized by informal and unsystematic observation and experimentation, and is unstable and unpredictable in its development and progress. In the circumstances of normal science, agreed concepts and methods are established whose primary functions are to explain and assimilate previously unsolved problems to the dominant paradigm, thus expanding its explanatory power. In revolutionary science, the range and seriousness of the phenomena inexplicable within the paradigm (or the internal contradictions in the central framework itself) reach a crisis, and a new paradigm, whose aim is to embrace both all the old and the new phenomena, is adopted. JAS asserts that there are five characteristics for a healthy paradigm:

> An agreed set of problems; agreed methods for working on these problems; agreed theoretical frameworks in which to discuss them; techniques and theories which are specific to the paradigm; research which is appropriate to the whole range of phenomena in the domain being studied. (Sloboda, 1986, p. 199)

Until the mid-1980s, JAS asserts, these conditions were not met. Research in the psychology of music, though demonstrating some of these characteristics and on occasion constituting significant and admirable work in its own terms, was fragmented and dispersed, and failed to identify agreed objectives. In the context of this chapter, it is the first of JAS's five characteristics (the agreed set of problems) on which I want to focus, since it is this that captures 'the important questions' that should be the focus of psychology of music research. JAS supplies his proposal half a page later:

> There seems to be a growing consensus that a central problem for the psychology of music is to explain *the structure and content of musical experience*. (Sloboda, 1986, p. 200 [original emphasis])

He is then in no doubt about the historical moment that signals the 'coming of age'— or perhaps the 'coming into normal science'—of the psychology of music: the publication in 1983 of Lerdahl and Jackendoff's *A Generative Theory of Tonal Music*. The basis for this confident assertion on JAS's part is the particular combination of attributes that Lerdahl and Jackendoff's book demonstrated: its breadth and ambition, the centrality of the structure of musical knowledge, its explicitness and detail, its empirical orientation, the expertise of its author team, and the keen interest with which it was awaited and then devoured on its appearance.[2] Even as JAS celebrated the

---

[2] It is worth noting that there were significant symposia assessing and reassessing its continuing impact 10 years on (at the Third International Conference on Music Perception and Cognition, held in Liège in 1994) and 25 years on (at the 'Music, Language, and the Mind' conference at Tufts University in 2008), which was explicitly billed as 'A conference in celebration of the 25th anniversary of Fred Lerdahl and Ray Jackendoff's *A Generative Theory of Tonal Music*'.

importance of GTTM (as it soon became known), he recognized that it was not without it own shortcomings; but what was vital about the book was the boldness and explicitness with which it set out its stall, inevitably laying itself more open to criticism and attack than a more provisional or evasive account would have been.

> Lerdahl and Jackendoff are to be congratulated for making themselves so explicit that criticism of them is relatively easy and fruitful. By seeing what they do not do, we should be able to make rapid progress in developing better theories. … We may have come of age, but we still have a long way to go. (Sloboda, 1986, p. 206)

In summary, then, JAS's assessment of 'the important questions' in 1986 can be understood as a concern that the psychology of music should agree on the structure and content of musical experience as its central concern, tackled with agreed methods, and understood within a broadly applicable conceptual framework that is expressed in maximally explicit terms. And having arrived at something close to that paradigmatic position, JAS already pointed to some of the areas that were ripe for an invigorated research effort: composition and improvisation, communication in ensembles, the experience and cognitive characteristics of extended listening, and performers' memorization skills.

Take 2: 1992

JAS's second stock-taking was published in 1992, and demonstrates a characteristically 'Slobodan' quality. 'Psychological structures in music: core research 1980–1990' was a chapter that in its approach embodies JAS's commitment to what might be termed 'accountability' (of which more below). The aim of the chapter was to identify the most significant and influential strands of research in the psychology of music during the decade from 1980 to 1990. It would have been all too easy to launch into either an unapologetically personal account of the 'big hits' of the decade, or a concealed version of the same masquerading as an 'authoritative survey', but JAS did something significantly different from either of these, attempting an appraisal of the field that is founded 'on explicit and rational bases, rather than on personal whim' (Sloboda, 1992, p. 803). His method is to identify the 10 most frequently cited publications in the first five volumes of *Music Perception*, spanning the years 1983–1988, which he identifies as the most important psychology of music journal. These 10 key publications (KPs; and GTTM comes out as equal top in this initial ranking) then act as a 'filter' with which to identify a larger number of publications that in turn cite a minimum of three of the KPs. In essence, the 10 KPs are treated as a quantitatively justified reference point around which a larger collection of 19 'core articles' (CAs) is assembled on the basis of common reference.

What, then, do these KPs and CAs tell us about the preoccupations of the psychology of music in the target decade—and what is JAS's perspective on those preoccupations? Interestingly, the KPs consist of three music theory publications (GTTM, Schenker's *Free Composition*, and Meyer's *Explaining Music*) relating to the organization of tonal/metrical music, and seven scientific publications—all of which are concerned with tonal pitch. As JAS points out, this narrow focus can be understood as the concern of psychological investigation to tackle 'historically and culturally pervasive aspects of music before looking at forms that inhabit a more prescribed and closed domain' (Sloboda, 1992, p. 808)—though he also recognizes that it may reflect the conservatism or populism of psychologists' own musical preferences. Taken together, the body of work represented by the KPs and CAs shows that the target decade was dominated by a concerted effort to investigate, and try to model explicitly, the perceptual and cognitive processes that are involved in listeners' abilities to pick up and understand the organization of musical materials at a variety of levels and scales. Tonal organization emerges as the most intensively studied property, for the possible reasons already given, and for the related reason that as the most widely theorized aspect of Western music it arguably offers up a more significant body of hypotheses that might be tested empirically. But other aspects of structural organization (more generalized aspects of hierarchical structure, including its impact on performance; the linear dynamics of melody) also feature in the literature, bringing with them the development of new and different experimental methods.

As JAS suggests, one of the achievements of this decade of research was the establishment of robust and systematic methods with which to tackle significant issues in music in explicit terms. Carol Krumhansl's work—which dominates the 'core research'—is cited as the paradigmatic case: 'not necessarily the most adventurous or far-reaching research', since it is essentially an experimental verification of traditional theoretical ideas about tonal relationships, it nonetheless 'represents a secure platform of scientific achievement which has undoubtedly raised the general standards and expectations of the field to new levels, and against which any new developments must be compared' (Sloboda, 1992, p. 808). If this seems a little like damning with faint praise, it is certainly not intended to be—as a reference back to JAS's 1986 paper makes clear: if the theoretical explicitness of GTTM, and its amenability to being 'operationalized', were the principal signs of music psychology's coming of age, the development of agreed working methods, and of specific techniques appropriate to the paradigm, were of equal importance in establishing music psychology's scientific credentials. And in this respect, Krumhansl's work with her associates was absolutely crucial—quite apart from her own theoretical contributions.

With the benefit of hindsight, JAS's 1992 stock-taking, understood as an overview of what 'the important questions' seemed to be in the 1980s, captures conflicting tendencies in a fascinating way. There is a genuine enthusiasm for the manifest advances that had been made, and for the new confidence and stability that the discipline had begun to enjoy. But at the same time there are already the signs of an impatience to tackle issues that were somehow more directly connected to people's sense of why music is psychologically important, and why so many people willingly give up such enormous amounts of time and energy to pursue their musical enthusiasms. At a methodological level, getting a handle on this might involve developing less obvious and more 'back door' approaches that could 'yield a richer picture of what is known than a direct judgement would suggest' (Sloboda, 1992, p. 834); and at a more programmatic level it might involve tackling some of the questions of which psychologists, and music theorists, had largely fought shy. As JAS remarked, impressive thought they are in their own terms, the studies described in the selected 'core research' from the 1980s give very few clues as to why people are motivated to develop the intense involvement with music that is observed in such a wide range of human cultures. One part of that story would require a better understanding of the musical development of children and young adults; and another, the kinds of psychological functions that music is able to fulfill. As JAS put it, despite a considerable volume of theorizing 'What we have lacked is any really convincing empirical work on, for instance, the links between musical structure and emotional response' (Sloboda, 1992, pp. 835–836).

Responding to, or in parallel with, his own identification of these gaps in the research—and a little like those TV chefs who right on cue reveal 'one that I prepared earlier'—JAS had started to publish work on these issues at exactly the time that the 1980–1990 survey was published. The first of a number of papers on music and emotion (with a title that mirrors his own perspective on how such work should be framed: 'Music structure and emotional response: some empirical findings') appeared in 1991 (Sloboda, 1991), as did the first papers in what was to become one of the major preoccupations of JAS's work in the 1990s—the factors that determine differential success and perseverance in music (e.g. Sloboda & Howe, 1991). Both of these research directions demonstrate a concern to engage directly with issues that loom large in people's musical lives (the intensity of their reactions to music, and why it is that there are such sharp differences in people's musical achievements), about which there were widespread mythologies that JAS was keen to address and perhaps dispel. In the case of music and the emotions, it was the attitude that people's responses are too idiosyncratic and mysterious to be understood empirically; and in the case of musical achievement, it was the myth of musical talent.

Take 3: 2005

The third, and most challenging, of JAS's discussions of what 'the important questions are' appears as the final chapter—and the only chapter specially written for the volume—of *Exploring the Musical Mind* (Sloboda, 2005), which otherwise consists of work published elsewhere and brought together into a single volume. This chapter, entitled 'Assessing music psychology research: values, priorities, and outcomes', could hardly be more direct in challenging readers to consider what the important questions in music psychology might be, whether in the face of an increasingly dangerous and unstable global context the pursuit of such research can be justified at all, and whether there is any rational basis on which to tackle such fundamental questions. As JAS states right at the start of the chapter:

> in exploring them [these questions] it will be necessary to address broader questions, to do with the social responsibilities of scientists, academics, and educated citizens. How do we decide where to devote our energies? Can we make such decisions in rational ways, which optimize both our own personal fulfilment, and our need to earn a living, but also address the needs of society? (Sloboda, 2005, p. 395)

A first step in addressing these questions might be to ask whether music itself—or perhaps more appropriately Christopher Small's word 'musicking' (Small, 1998)—is a benign human manifestation, something to celebrate and encourage, as well as understand. We could compare it, for example, to another widespread human capacity, such as fighting.[3] Like musicking, fighting takes place in informal ways (between school kids in the playground, and angry adults at home) as well as in more formalized, organized, even aestheticized contexts (between professional soldiers, in boxing and wrestling, and in martial arts). My guess is that most people would recognize that at root fighting is essentially a 'negative' human capacity, and one that should not be celebrated and encouraged, while recognizing that in some of its manifestations, admirable human attributes can be demonstrated: the skill and physical beauty of an exponent of Aikido, for example; or the courage and commitment of a person who has no option but to fight to defend someone against a crazed attacker. It is, however, still something that we should want to understand, not only because to understand fighting might shed important light on the nature of human aggression and the wider question of 'what it is like to be human', but also for the more obviously applied reason that it might help to find ways to reduce the incidence of fighting in all kinds of contexts.

Musicking, by contrast, is widely regarded, or assumed, to be a positive human capacity—and particularly so (not surprisingly) by those who are involved with it—despite that fact that we also know that musicking can be used for negative or destructive purposes: as a means of torture (Cusick, 2006), or to persuade or goad people to prejudice, antagonism, and even violence against others (jingoistic, inflammatory or deliberately violence-inciting music). The widespread background assumption of the positive virtues of musicking,[4] however, means that most people believe that to be involved with music is a 'good thing'. If music has social benefits, then it might be hoped that psychology of music research would help to reveal what those social benefits are, and recommend ways in which those benefits might be more widely and effectively realised. And in essence, this is the challenge raised by JAS's next question in direct and uncompromising terms:

> A question which I have posed repeatedly to anyone who will listen is: suppose all the music psychology in the world had never been written, and was expunged from the collective memory of the world, as if it had never existed, how would music and musicians be disadvantaged? Would composers compose less good music, would performers cease to perform so well, would those who enjoy listening to it enjoy it any less richly. (Sloboda, 2005, pp. 395–396)

If the psychology of music is broadly concerned with understanding the human capacity for musicking, and if musicking has social benefits, then it is not unreasonable to think that research should lead to a demonstrable increase in social benefits. But a search by JAS of two relevant research databases (carried out in 2003) revealed vanishingly little research with an avowed focus on social benefit (just 14 examples over a 20-year period), against an overwhelming preponderance of what might be termed 'pure research'.

---

[3] While musicking does seem to be a specifically human attribute, fighting of course is not.

[4] To start to list these positive virtues would take me too far from the main focus of this chapter, but they include cognitive, social, aesthetic, cultural diversity, creative, economic, political, personal development, educational, and therapeutic benefits.

Against a background of increasingly pressing global problems, encompassing the environment, economics, security, poverty, intolerance, food and health, how can psychology of music research continue to be justifiable? If, as observed earlier, JAS demonstrates his commitment to 'accountability' in his method of assessing the 'significant achievements' of psychology of music research in the 1980s, then it is an 'accountability' of an altogether different order that lies behind these questions that he asks:

> How can I allow myself the luxury of researching music psychology, when half the world's population lives below the poverty line, when millions of children die of malnutrition and avoidable disease every year, when the activities and consumption patterns of the rich world are destroying the ability of the planet to sustain human life into the long term future, and when violence between people grows increasingly dangerous as the means to inflict violence become ever more lethal and large-scale. (Sloboda, 2005, p. 406)

And if there is even the possibility of a positive answer to this somewhat rhetorical question, JAS then asks the following 'secondary' question:

> If I can allow myself the privilege of conducting music psychology research, how is that privilege best and most responsibly exercised so as to be more than 'harmless' …, but actually contributing in a direct way to the greater human good. (Sloboda, 2005, p. 407)

These are appropriately tough questions that demand JAS's readers to consider in what way, and to what extent, their work can be considered to be socially engaged. His own response to the challenge has been both to make a fundamental change in his own working life,[5] and in the more immediate context of his own chapter to propose a four-levelled template aimed at working towards increased and improved social engagement. Level 1 ('Sensitivity to historic academic norms') identifies as a minimum commitment that research should abide by its own socially agreed 'good practices', including such principles as honesty, openness, ethical conduct, and academic freedom. Levels 2 and 3 ('Sensitivity to applicability' and 'Focus on applicability', respectively) recognize the potential for researchers to contribute to social change either by being sensitive to the applicability of their research 'after the fact' (level 2); or by making deliberate choices designed to lead directly to applicable research (level 3). Level 4 ('Focus on values') seems to undermine the apparent gains of levels 2 and 3 by pointing out that 'applicability' is not necessarily socially beneficial, and turns instead to the more fundamental matter of values, proposing that this highest level enjoins researchers to find ways to ensure that the work that they do reflects their own core values.

Music and transformation

Having raised the question of whether musicking is unfailingly benign, and offered some rather obvious examples of its failure to be so, I am now going to argue—perhaps uncontroversially—that musicking is overwhelmingly an extraordinary

---

[5] In 2005, when *Exploring The Musical Mind* was published, John was in the middle of making the transition from full-time academic to full-time director of the independent non-governmental Oxford Research Group, the aim of which is to foster international peace and security. See also footnote 11.

human asset, even if it brings with it the potential to turn that asset to repressive or destructive purposes, just as language has the capacity to enslave, conceal, and destroy. From the earliest Greek writing on the subject (see Strunk, 1998) it has been recognized that musicking has considerable psychological and social power, both constructive and destabilizing, a topic that has been discussed and researched from a huge variety of perspectives in more recent writing. Among many others, Theodor Adorno's writings can be understood as a profound exploration of the ways in which music is both a 'seismograph of reality', as he memorably expressed it, and (less passively) as a significant form of social praxis (e.g. 1976, 1997). The abstractness of Adorno's perspective has been a source of both frustration and opposition for many, but Tia DeNora (2003) argues persuasively for what can still be valued in Adorno's work, even as she advocates a much more concrete and empirically inclined sociological approach (DeNora, 2000, 2003) that makes a direct connection with some of JAS's own work on the use and impact of musicking in people's lives (e.g. Sloboda, 2008; Sloboda, O'Neill, & Ivaldi, 2001). Equally, Nicholas Cook has argued that music offers important insights into other cultures and subcultures, just as others have drawn attention to its power to shed light on, and even afford the experience of, other subjectivities (e.g. Clarke, 2005; Cumming, 2000; Kramer, 2001). And a sizeable body of research has investigated, and argued for the importance of musical and proto-musical skills and capacities in infant development (see e.g. Malloch & Trevarthen, 2008) and in biocultural evolution (Cross, 2003).

Without, I hope, drawing disparate elements together in too pat or simplistic a manner, these diverse research strands all point to the crucial role that musicking plays in people's lives, to its transformational capacity, and to the insights that it can afford. There is no single window onto 'what it is like to be human', but musicking seems to offer as rich, diverse, and globally distributed a perspective as any—and one that engages people in a vast array of experiences located along dimensions of public and private, solitary and social, frenzied and reflective, technological and bodily, conceptual and immediate, calculated and improvised, instantaneous and timeless. At a time when the importance of mutual understanding could hardly be more crucial at a global scale, anything and everything that helps us to understand other human beings and their passions and perspectives must be hugely important. It seems like an enormous gulf between, say, the continuing conflict in the Middle East, and an understanding of the relationship between rhythm and emotion, but as the Simon Bolivar orchestra, and the Venezuelan music education system ('El Sistema')[6] of which it is an expression have shown, musicking does have the capacity to change people's lives—and the more we are able to understand why that is, why people are prepared to dedicate such enormous amounts of time and effort to it,[7] and what kinds of change it can elicit, the more likely it is that we will find ways to develop that capacity.

David Huron (2008) has argued for the urgency of trying to document and understand the rapidly disappearing diversity of 'musical minds in culture' that can still be found around the globe, but which in his view are terminally threatened by the rapid

---

[6] See http://fesnojiv.gob.ve

[7] See, for example, the research reported in Green (2001) and Pitts (2005).

and far-reaching circulation of a much more narrowly circumscribed dominant culture—for all its apparent subcultural diversity. Huron claims that never before has humanity been so well equipped (technologically, and perhaps conceptually) to undertake such a documentation and investigation—just at the time when those same technological and cultural forces threaten to wipe out the very phenomena that they enable us to tackle. There is, in his opinion, not much more than a 10-year window of opportunity for such an enterprise, before a significant number of those particular kinds of musical mind will be lost forever. The consequences for our understanding of global humanity, and its long-term psycho-cultural 'health', could be as disastrous as is the accelerating loss of species of flora and fauna for an understanding of biodiversity, our biological health, and the integrity of our environment.

Returning, then, to JAS's rhetorical question about the consequences for people's capacities to compose, listen to, or perform music of all music psychology research being eliminated, I am in little doubt that the answer would be 'little or nothing'. But I have also never thought that the main aim of music psychology research should be to change how people do their musicking, since after all they've been refining those ways of doing it, through the pervasive methods of formal and informal cultural practices, for millennia. Indeed, it might be unrealistic or naive to think that the activities of a comparatively tiny number of well-intentioned researchers over a period of a few decades could possibly have a significant practical impact on such a deeply embedded human attribute. The aims of music psychology research are to understand this remarkable and in some ways perplexing human capacity, not only out of simple and benign curiosity, but also because of the deep connection between music and human subjectivity, and as a significant step towards the larger goal of understanding, and learning to live with, other human beings better. In a 2005 interview with James Powell, largely concerned with his own political aims and motivations,[8] JAS observed:

> I think being able to feel empathy is hugely important to how much we care about other people and act in their interests. … [W]e define 'other people' too narrowly. Those for whom we are prepared to put ourselves out may be confined to family, locality, or country. It is very difficult to see and act on the notion that 'other people' means everyone on this planet.

Anything that can help us to feel that empathy is vitally important, socially and politically, as well as individually—and anecdote and intuition, as well as research, suggest the incredibly important part that musicking can play in that.

There's the danger, of course, of finding a suitably grand way to dress up arcane research in the clothes of spurious social relevance to defend a position that at root is indefensible. Given the importance of the global questions to which JAS draws our attention, it's hard to avoid the implication that we should all find ways to move from whatever it is that we do (as academics, musicians, researchers, or whatever) into socially engaged political work. You could argue that the world might be a duller place if we all gave up this fascinating psychology of music work and used our energies to campaign for peace and social justice—though my hunch is that there would be

---

[8] Available at: www.oxfordmuse.com/selfportrait/portrait57.htm (accessed 1 June 2009).

many millions who would gladly exchange the poverty, danger, or oppression in which they live for a little of that 'dullness'. But not everyone has the skills and capacities to do that work effectively, and even for those who do, the opportunities to live by that work are relatively few and far between. More positively, in subtle but important ways people may make more of a difference in less obviously politically engaged activities (in which they can make a living) than it seems at first sight. JAS's 30 years of teaching and collegiality in the psychology department at Keele University, may not seem an obvious platform for social change, but through his influence over generations of students, collaborators, and colleagues, his values have permeated a complex and widespread network of individuals. An obvious expression of this is that when, in 2003, in response to the build up to the Iraq war, JAS, with Hamit Dardagan, founded the Iraq Body Count[9] (dedicated to counting the cost of the war, and subsequent occupation, in civilian lives), more than half of the volunteers who constituted that group were current or former psychology of music colleagues of JAS's, or their close relatives, many of whom continue to be actively involved. Education isn't a bad place to start if you want to 'make a difference'.

To conclude, I will be rash enough to propose that for those doing research in the psychology of music the important questions[10] are: to try to understand human subjectivity, intersubjectivity, and empathy through musicking; to do so in the full context of music's complex embedding in everyday life (Clarke, Dibben, & Pitts, 2010, DeNora, 2000; Sloboda, 2008) to rise to David Huron's (2008) challenge to document and comprehend something of the global diversity of musical-minds-in-culture; and to demonstrate that neither a science nor a humanities approach has a monopoly on the insights that we seek. But equally, behind or above these discipline-specific questions there lurks or hovers the pressing and uncomfortable question about where our core priorities lie, how we direct our energies, and how we continue to justify what we do. John Sloboda's outstanding contribution to the psychology of music can be demonstrated with the usual (albeit blunt) methods of citation, professional recognition, honours, and awards. Less easy to measure, but arguably of still greater importance, are the uncomfortable questions that he asks—and we will all have our own responses to them—and the example through action that has been his own resonant answer.[11]

References

Adorno, T. W. (1976). *Introduction to the sociology of music* (E. B. Ashton, Trans.). New York: Continuum.

Adorno, T. W. (1997). *Aesthetic theory* (R. Hullot-Kentor, Trans.). London: Athlone Press.

Clarke, E. F. (2005). *Ways of listening. An ecological approach to the perception of musical meaning*. New York: Oxford University Press.

---

[9] See www.iraqbodycount.org.

[10] Though none of them is a question!

[11] John Sloboda took early retirement from the psychology department at the University of Keele, in the autumn of 2007, to work full-time on peace and security issues, as Director of the Oxford Research Group (www.oxfordresearchgroup.org.uk/).

Clarke, E. F., Dibben, N. J., & Pitts, S. E. (2010). *Music and mind in everyday life.* Oxford: Oxford University Press.

Cross, I. (2003). Music and biocultural evolution. In M. Clayton, T. Herbert & R. Middleton (Eds.), *The cultural study of music: A critical introduction* (pp. 19–30). London: Routledge.

Cumming, N. (2000). *The sonic self. Musical subjectivity and signification.* Bloomington: Indiana University Press.

Cusick, S. G. (2006). Music as torture/music as weapon. *Transcultural Music Review, 10.* Available at: www.sibetrans.com/trans/trans10/cusick_eng.htm (accessed 21 September 2010).

DeNora, T. (2000). *Music in everyday life.* Cambridge: Cambridge University Press.

DeNora, T. (2003). *After Adorno: Rethinking music sociology.* Cambridge: Cambridge University Press.

Green, L. (2001). *How popular musicians learn: A way ahead for music education.* Aldershot: Ashgate Press.

Huron, D. (2008). Science and music: Lost in music. *Nature, 453*(7194), 456–457.

Kramer, L. (2001). The mysteries of animation: History, analysis and musical subjectivity. *Music Analysis, 20,* 153–178.

Kuhn, T. S. (1962). *The structure of scientific revolutions.* Chicago, IL: University of Chicago Press.

Lerdahl, F., & Jackendoff, R. (1983). *A generative theory of tonal music.* Cambridge, MA: MIT Press.

Malloch, S., & Trevarthen, C. (2008) (Eds.). *Communicative musicality. Exploring the basis of human companionship.* Oxford: Oxford University Press.

Pitts, S. E. (2005). *Valuing musical participation.* Aldershot: Ashgate.

Sloboda, J. A. (1986). Cognition and real music: the psychology of music comes of age. *Psychologica Belgica, 26,* 199–219.

Sloboda, J. A. (1991). Music structure and emotional response: some empirical findings. *Psychology of Music, 19,* 110–120.

Sloboda, J. A. (1992). Psychological structures in music: core research 1980–1990. In J. Paynter, R. Orton, T. Seymour & T. Howell (Eds.), *A compendium of contemporary musical thought* (pp. 803–839). London: Routledge.

Sloboda, J. A. (2005). *Exploring the musical mind.* Oxford: Oxford University Press.

Sloboda, J. A. (2008). Science and music: The ear of the beholder. *Nature, 454*(7200), 32–33.

Sloboda, J. A., & Howe, M. J. A. (1991). Biographical precursors of musical excellence: an interview study. *Psychology of Music, 19,* 3–21.

Sloboda, J. A., O'Neill, S. A., & Ivaldi, A. (2001). Functions of music in everyday life: an exploratory study using the Experience Sampling Methodology. *Musicæ Scientiæ, 5,* 9–32.

Small, C. (1998) *Musicking: the Meanings of Performing and Listening.* Hanover: University Press of New England.

Strunk, O. (1998) (Ed.). *Source readings in music history.* New York: Norton.

Part 2

Motivating musical lives

Chapter 3

Developing a young musician's growth mindset: the role of motivation, self-theories, and resiliency

Susan A. O'Neill

Abstract

This chapter examines the role of motivation, self-theories, and resiliency in the development of a young musician's growth mindset. To provide some background information and contextualization for these concepts, the chapter begins with an overview of several motivation and music learning studies conducted during the early 1990s. These studies were influenced by John Sloboda's research contributions to the precursors of musical expertise and Dweck's (1986) theory of achievement motivation. Over the past two decades, Dweck and her colleagues have made significant progress in developing and testing a meaning system approach to the development of young people's beliefs about their abilities (self-theories or conceptions of ability). According to Dweck (2006), positive self-theories are necessary for developing a growth mindset as a means of achieving successful performance outcomes. There is growing evidence to suggest that a growth mindset serves as a protective factor that may promote resiliency, which sustains motivation and reduces the negative effects of adversity, failure, and stressful life events (Wang, Haertel, & Walberg, 1997). The chapter concludes with some educational strategies that may help young musicians achieve their full potential, as well as suggestions for future research.

Background and context

It is a great pleasure to be part of this Festschrift honouring John Sloboda's contributions to the field of music psychology. In preparing this chapter, I was asked by the editors to make clear how my work is connected to and influenced by John Sloboda. I first met John nearly 20 years ago when he agreed to be my Ph.D. supervisor. We later became colleagues in 1995 when I joined the psychology department at Keele University and the newly established Unit for the Study of Musical Skill and Development. Over the course of my eight-year appointment at Keele, I had the opportunity to collaborate and work with John on a number of teaching and research initiatives. We established and each served several years as director of a master's degree in music psychology. In 2000, we were co-directors of the 6th International Conference on Music Perception and Cognition (ICMPC). We were also co-investigators on a number of studies involving motivation and music learning (O'Neill & Sloboda, 1997), the functions of music listening in everyday life (Sloboda & O'Neill, 2001; Sloboda, O'Neill, & Ivaldi, 2001) and a large-scale study of music engagement known as the 'Young People and Music Participation Project', which was funded by the Economic and Social Research Council (O'Neill, Ryan, Boulton, & Sloboda, 2000; O'Neill, 2001).

In the beginning stages of my Ph.D., John and I would meet once a week and talk through my research ideas. I must have tested his patience (although he never showed it) as I explored everything from behavioural analysis to ethnography in my attempts to find a suitable method for quantifying or systematically accounting for the differences in motivation and achievement that can be found among young people who are learning to play a musical instrument. I was interested in why some children persevere at the task, while others with seemingly equal levels of ability or potential make little progress or even abandon music learning altogether. Why is it that among highly competent children there are some who deteriorate in the face of difficulty and avoid challenge, perhaps not realizing their full musical potential? Conversely, among less proficient children, why is it that they seem to thrive on challenge and attain levels of musical skill that one might not have predicted from their initial musical behaviour?

Although many commonsense explanations for these apparent differences had been put forward, they tended to encompass broad perspectives ranging from genetic endowment to teacher behaviour and the educational environment. Few empirical studies on motivation and the development of musical skills had been undertaken, and theoretical conceptualizations of motivation in terms of music learning were poorly understood. As such, music educators had little concrete evidence that could be used to inform and increase the effectiveness of their practice. In addition, explanations for how motivational processes influence music learning relied heavily on (often erroneous) implicit assumptions about the role of success, praise, and self-confidence. Since motivational problems create considerable barriers and constraints on young people's music learning opportunities, particularly within formal music education contexts, my aim was to explore theoretical frameworks and empirical evidence that would increase our understanding of motivational processes in the development of young musicians.

My early research was inspired in part by an exploratory interview study that John Sloboda and Michael Howe carried out at the beginning of the 1990s into the biographical precursors of musical expertise (Sloboda & Howe, 1991). They interviewed 42 exceptionally 'gifted' young musicians at a specialist music school in England and asked them why they started learning to play an instrument. The most common reasons were: it was part of their normal school routine; their parents instigated it for its general educational benefits; they were interested in music; they wanted to emulate an older sibling. Most of the children gave non-musical reasons for beginning an instrument, for example, 'I began recorder with my dad. I think it was probably his idea, you know parents always like to introduce all sorts of things to their kids.' There were also some musical reasons, such as 'I heard the sound of the flute on the radio or something and I just really loved the sound of it.' However, only one young musician in their sample began as a result of having parents who recognized some special musical ability in their child. We now have further evidence to suggest that high achievers in music do not necessarily show more initial music aptitude than those who make far less progress (O'Neill, 1996, 2001).

An intriguing finding from the Sloboda and Howe (1991) exploratory study was that many of the young musicians believed that their musical achievements were made possible because they had a special, inherent musical talent or ability. John and his colleagues became interested in the origins of this widespread 'folk psychology' belief in innate musical talent and its impact on the development of young musicians. Their research culminated in two seminal target articles that were followed by a series of invited peer commentaries: 'Is everyone musical?' (Sloboda, Davidson, & Howe, 1994); and 'Innate talent: reality or myth?' (Howe, Davidson, & Sloboda, 1998). In these articles, Sloboda and colleagues argue that the notion of innate 'talent' has been overemphasized in Western cultures and music traditions. Research suggests that rather than some fixed prior ability, musical talent is really a form of developing musical expertise through *deliberate practice* (Ericsson, Krampe, & Tesch-Römer, 1993; Sloboda, Davidson, Howe, & Moore, 1996). Deliberate practice involves two main factors: (1) engagement in activities designed specifically to improve an individual's performance, and (2) amount of time spent in solitary practice during musical development (typically 10 000 hours by the age of 20). Because an expert musician's performance may appear natural and effortless, people tend to attribute it to a special or innate talent even if they are also aware of the many hours of practice that are necessary to develop high levels of expertise. Other arguments for the notion of innate musical talent focus on child prodigies and the young age when their talent emerges, and the fact that many young people try hard but often fail to develop their musical ability (see also Winner, 1996; Gagné, Blanchard, & Bégin, 2001; Lehmann, Sloboda, & Woody, 2007).

Around the same time as the Sloboda and Howe research was taking place, an influential edited book was published entitled *Competence Considered* (Sternberg & Kolligian, 1990). Contributors to this book reviewed a number of motivation studies from developmental, educational, and social psychological perspectives. These studies demonstrated strong links between the development of competence and motivational criteria in different contexts, such as school achievement (e.g. Eccles, 1983; Stipek, 1984), creativity (Amabile, 1983), and performance-related activities (e.g. Nicholls, 1984). What captured my interest was the idea that motivation is associated with multiple pathways to success, as well as complex interrelationships between social-cognitive processes, behavioural outcomes, and achievement-related contexts. While exploring the links between motivation and music learning during one of our Ph.D. supervision meetings, John Sloboda and I reviewed a paper by Carol Dweck (1986). Dweck used a series of ingenious experiments to investigate the motivational processes that influence children's learning in relation to academic performance achievement situations. Children are given a series of tasks in which success is assured, followed by tasks designed to prompt failure. It has been demonstrated, for example, that children respond with two different patterns of behaviour when failure trials begin (Dweck & Leggett, 1988). When some children begin to fail at tasks, they display adaptive behaviour and continue to employ effective strategies that maintain or improve their performance. They have a positive outlook and view the difficulty they encountered as a challenge to be mastered through effort; this is referred to as *mastery motivation*. Mastery children will remain high in their persistence and continue to employ effective strategies even in the face of failure. They display psychological and emotional resilience, often not recognizing failure as negative and something to be avoided, but instead viewing it as part of the learning process or as a challenge that can be mastered through increased effort.

Conversely, other children show maladaptive behaviour and a marked decline in their performance following failure. They begin to chat about irrelevant topics and view their difficulty as a sign of low ability; this is referred to as *helpless motivation*. When confronted with a potential failure, helpless children will begin to engage in irrelevant task behaviour, such as attempting to alter the rules of the task, devaluing the task (e.g. 'this is boring', 'this isn't fun anymore'), or boasting of their talents or prized possessions in an attempt to divert attention away from their poor performance towards their more praiseworthy attributes. In addition, helpless children report negative feelings and views of themselves when they meet obstacles, whereas mastery children maintain positive views of their competence and enjoy challenges.

What is particularly interesting is that some of the brightest, most skilled individuals exhibit the helpless pattern. In other words, a helpless motivational pattern is not related to intelligence or ability. Rather, it is a way of viewing oneself and one's capacity to be effective in a particular achievement situation. Immediately prior to failure situations, when mastery and helpless children are both experiencing success, their performances are equal (Dweck & Leggett, 1988). Numerous investigations have shown that differences in children's motivational patterns following failure are not related to their demonstrated pre-failure ability as measured by prior skill on a task, grades, or standardized intelligence tests (e.g. Dweck & Reppucci, 1973; Dweck & Licht, 1980; Smiley & Dweck, 1994). Based on the results of these studies, John Sloboda and I decided to explore the extent to which the study of motivation in the domain of academic learning might contribute to our understanding of motivation in the domain of music learning.

Early studies of achievement motivation and music learning

In order to investigate mastery and helpless motivational patterns in a music learning situation, we conducted a study with 51 children (aged 6–10) using a specially designed music task (O'Neill & Sloboda, 1997). We began by administering a standardized melodic direction test. Then, the children were taught to perform a similar melodic direction test where they encountered success followed by a failure condition. After both conditions they were asked to self-evaluate their performance and predict how well they thought they would do on subsequent tests. We found that, following failure, over half the children experienced deterioration in their test performance and displayed the helpless pattern, whereas the test performance of the other children either remained the same or showed improvement as they displayed the mastery pattern. We also found that the children who reported low confidence following failure experienced the most performance deterioration. We found no differences in their test performance on the standardized test that was taken at the beginning; however, helpless children scored even higher than mastery children on the success condition. Although our testing procedure may have increased the emphasis placed on evaluation and performance achievement, these are nevertheless common factors associated with many formal music learning contexts.

Our study found maladaptive motivational patterns for some children after exposure to only a very brief obstacle or learning challenge. It is therefore possible that exposure to frequent setbacks or adverse situations may well have devastating effects on those who lack resilience and those who are vulnerable to helpless patterns. However, an important question remained. If helpless children are able to perform equally as well as mastery children initially, how long does it take before we begin to see negative effects on their overall levels of motivation and performance? According to Dweck (1986), during the early school years, good students in particular may not experience very much difficulty or failure. This is similar to the way formal instrumental music instruction may structure tasks in such a way that young children in particular are ensured a great deal of initial success. Thus, helpless patterns may not influence children's long-term musical achievement until much later when obstacles and difficulties become more pronounced. It is at this point that helpless children may begin to avoid challenges or even withdraw their efforts towards formal music education altogether.

To investigate the longer-term impact of motivational patterns on children's musical performance achievement, my Ph.D. research involved a short-term longitudinal study of 51 children (aged 6–10) during their first year of learning to play a musical instrument (O'Neill, 1994a, 1996). Prior to their involvement in the study, the children had no prior formal instrumental music lessons but they were about to start lessons with an experienced music teacher. Before their first lesson and again at the end of their first year of lessons, they were interviewed individually and given a variety of measures that included a general IQ test, a musical skills test, and a problem-solving task designed to measure mastery and helpless patterns. At the end of their first year of formal instrumental lessons, the children were asked to prepare for a performance that was videotaped. The performance included a preparatory test used by the Associated Board of the Royal Schools of Music, an 'own choice' piece that they thought they could play well, and several simple aural tests that required no special preparation by the teacher. The videotaped performances were then evaluated by four experienced Associated Board examiners, who produced ratings that indicated a good level of agreement with correlations ranging from 0.70 to 0.82.

The results showed no relationship between the amount of performance achievement the children displayed and their prior measures of intelligence or musical skills. There were, however, a number of other significant effects, which included motivational patterns. Children who showed mastery patterns on the non-musical problem-solving task prior to their first music lesson made more progress than children who displayed helpless patterns. However, when the amount of time spent practising (the children used practice diaries to record their practice) was compared between helpless and mastery children, the findings indicated that helpless children were doing roughly twice as much practice as the mastery children to reach the same level of performance achievement (O'Neill, 1997). This suggests that although some helpless children were spending large amounts of time practising, they were using their time less effectively. The interviews revealed that these children spent most of their time playing pieces that they could already play well, or making up their own pieces. They tended to avoid practising pieces that they found difficult. This was in stark contrast to the mastery children who tended to report that they liked the challenging pieces the best and were often trying to learn pieces that were far beyond their technical ability. Although helpless children were (at least initially) spending more time than mastery children playing their instruments, they did not appear to benefit as much as mastery children from the same approaches or practice strategies used in formal instrumental music education. These early studies also indicate that mastery and helpless behavioural responses are inextricably linked to an individual's self-beliefs, such as confidence in one's ability to succeed. A complete account of motivational process is therefore not possible without a concomitant understanding of an individual's internal belief systems or self-theories.

Self-theories and achievement motivation

After investigating the mastery and helpless behavioural responses of children who are confronted with difficulty or failure situations, Dweck began to focus her attention on the beliefs or *meaning systems* that individuals hold when thinking about their own and others' abilities. She referred to these meaning systems as implicit theories of ability, conceptions of ability, or *self-theories*. During the 1980s and 1990s, Dweck and colleagues demonstrated that young people tend to conceptualize and hold different self-theories about the nature of their abilities (e.g. Diener & Dweck, 1980). Self-theories manifest themselves by constructing different psychological worlds and identities that influence children to think, feel, and act differently in identical situations (Dweck, 1999). Dweck referred initially to young learners who hold a fixed view of their intelligence (or other abilities such as athletic or musical ability) as *entity theorists*. These learners are highly concerned about outcomes that show what their 'true' abilities are. According to Dweck, entity theorists are more likely to use outcome traits (e.g. grades, number of goals scored in a game, number of instruments played) as evidence in support of their judgement of abilities. For learners who endorse an entity belief system, musical ability is viewed as something that you either have or you don't have. Entity theorists evaluate whether someone has the requisite amount of musical ability by seeking opportunities to display and make judgements about their own and others' musical performance.

A distinctly different self-theory of ability is endorsed by children with an incremental belief system. These learners, initially referred to by Dweck (1986) as *incremental theorists*, hold flexible beliefs about the nature of ability as something that can be improved through effort. They seek challenges and opportunities to learn new strategies that will help them solve problems and overcome obstacles and difficulties.

By the age of 8 years, children can distinguish between abilities in different domains, apply different self-theories to different domains, and use their self-theories to make judgements about the abilities of others (Bempechat, London, & Dweck, 1991). For example, in a study of 172 children (aged 6–11 years), I found that over 65% of children endorsed an incremental theory of academic and musical ability, compared with over 87% who endorsed an incremental theory of sport (O'Neill, 1994b). I also found that children's self-theories of musical ability were related to their involvement in music. Children who were learning to play an instrument were more likely to endorse an incremental theory than children who had never learned to play an instrument. One interpretation of this finding is that having the experience of learning to play an instrument, even for a short time, helps to foster an incremental belief system about the nature of musical ability as something that can be improved through effort.

Dweck does not claim that it is always beneficial for individuals to believe they are capable of mastering all tasks; indeed, one needs to have an objective diagnosis of one's strengths and weaknesses in order to pursue one's goals effectively. However, incremental theorists manage to coordinate performance and learning goals better than entity theorists. For example, an over-concern with proving oneself may lead a music learner to ignore, avoid, or even abandon potentially valuable learning opportunities. As such, young people who hold predominantly an entity self-theory of musical ability are at an increased risk of maladaptive motivation that does not promote learning.

Fixed and growth mindsets

In her most recent book, Dweck (2006) provides a synthesis of her achievement motivation research that incorporates self-theories into the concept of mindsets. A mindset is a set or system of assumptions, beliefs, and values that once established informs the goals we pursue, the decisions we make, and the way we come to view ourselves and others in our world. According to Dweck, a growth mindset encompasses an incremental self-theory or belief system. It is the hallmark of successful individuals and the development of a growth mindset is a crucial component of achieving positive motivation and successful performance outcomes. A growth mindset is characterized by a passion for learning, the active seeking of challenges, a valuing of effort, and the resiliency necessary to persist in the face of obstacles or adversity.

Contrastingly, a fixed mindset encompasses an entity self-theory or belief system that constructs the world and self-identities in ways that compel individuals to seek constant validation of their abilities and achievements. To emphasize this point,

Dweck quotes from McCall's (1998) book *High Flyers*: 'Unfortunately, people often like the things that work against their growth. … People like to use their strengths. … to achieve quick, dramatic results, even if they aren't developing the new skills they will need later on. People like to believe they are as good as everyone says. … and not take their weaknesses as seriously as they might. People don't like to hear bad news or get criticism. … There is tremendous risk in leaving what one does well to attempt to master something new.' According to Dweck (2006), a fixed mindset is associated with the idea that your abilities are fixed attributes that are 'carved in stone', and this 'creates an urgency to prove yourself over and over' (p. 6). In other words, a musician with a fixed mindset views his or her musical ability as evidence of talent rather than a starting point for future development.

Young 'gifted' musicians may be told from an early age that they have a special talent or ability. They begin to believe that this special ability will enable them to achieve great success. They are given constant 'proof' of their special talent in the form of winning competitions, achieving high grades on music performance examinations, auditioning successfully and gaining places among highly respected music performance ensembles and schools. However, at the same time these young musicians are achieving great success, they are developing a fixed mindset that reinforces the idea that their continued success is inevitable or even a right that they deserve because of their special talent. To ensure continued success, they may avoid taking risks or situations where they might not succeed—because failure would harm their self-image as one of the best, brightest, and most talented. When they do fail or produce a poor performance, they may deny it or apportion the blame and responsibility to anyone or anything except their shortcomings. They tend to avoid or deny accurate assessments of their abilities, and they are not very good at identifying their strengths and weaknesses. They also tend to have great difficulty dealing with setbacks and only continue to thrive when 'things are safely within their grasp' (Dweck, 2006, p. 22).

In an interview study that examined the self-identity of young musicians, we found evidence of a fixed mindset among our interviewees (O'Neill, 2002; O'Neill, Ivaldi, & Fox, 2002). For example, a 17-year-old girl described herself as follows: 'I see myself as a musician. That's all I can see myself as. Um, I think a musician isn't something you kind of develop over time … it's something that's there at the beginning and although you can appreciate—learn to appreciate music and what have you, but you can never really become a musician.' The implication is that being a musician is a fixed attribute that relatively few people possess. Indeed, it is not uncommon for highly skilled and successful young musicians to interpret their ability through a fixed mindset, or as Dweck (2006) suggests, there is a tendency for them to 'live in a world of personal greatness and entitlement' (p. 122).

Although individuals with a fixed mindset may thrive provided they continue to encounter validations of their ability, it is unlikely they will be able to avoid indefinitely problems and obstacles that may challenge or shed doubt on their self-evaluations. Numerous educational and social conditions make it difficult for many learners to achieve their full potential. There is, however, growing evidence that a growth mindset serves as a protective factor that is capable of reducing the negative effects of adversity, failure, and stressful life events (Wang *et al.*, 1997). Resilient children who experience failure seem to bounce back faster and display the characteristics associated with mastery motivation and incremental self-theories—in other words, they display a growth mindset.

Resiliency and music learning

The pathway to musical expertise is often turbulent and characterized by challenges and obstacles that must be overcome if individuals are to reach their full potential (MacNamara, Holmes, & Collins, 2006). To what extent do we prepare young musicians for the challenges they may face during their formal music education and after they leave their disciplined educational environments? According to Subotnik, Jarvin, Moga, and Sternberg (2003), many gate-keepers such as parents and teachers take the notion of persistence for granted despite the fact that 'major professionals will have endured and overcome rejection and other setbacks by the time they have acquired management and sufficient career recognition to be considered for [prestigious] venues' (p. 6). Subotnik and colleagues found that many music performance students view persistence as a major characteristic of being a musician, since these are 'the values of their early teachers, who socialized them into believing that a true musician will be prepared to suffer for his or her art' (p. 6). Nonetheless, in order to overcome adversity and be successful, a musician must be more than persistent; he or she must also be resilient (see also Subotnik, 2000).

The concept of resiliency or resilience has grown exponentially over the past decade in psychology and education through studies involving children and adolescents who are considered vulnerable or 'at risk'. Resilience derives from the Latin verb *resilire*, meaning 'to rebound' or 'jump back'. The origins of resiliency date back to at least the 1600s when Henry More wrote in his *Divine Dialogues*: 'strong and peremptory Resiliency from this sordid Region of Misery and Sin' (as cited in Napoli, 2007). The terms resilience and resiliency are often used interchangeably, however there is a tendency for the term *resiliency* to refer to the capacity or tendency to rebound from adversity and for the term *resilience* to refer to the act of rebounding. One of the most widely used definitions of resiliency in education is 'the heightened likelihood of success in school and other life accomplishments despite environmental adversities brought about by early traits, conditions, and experiences' (Wang, Haertel, & Walberg, 1994, p. 46).

Resiliency is associated with inquisitiveness, optimal optimism, active coping and problem-solving, effectiveness despite fear and anxiety, emotional self-regulation, bonding for a common mission, positive self-concept, internal control, desire to improve oneself, altruism, social support, the ability to turn traumatic helplessness into learned helpfulness, humour, and meaning (Napoli, 2007). Within the framework of positive psychology (Seligman & Csikzentmihalyi, 2000) and positive youth musical development (O'Neill, 2006) resiliency is viewed as an active concept, similar to the notion of a growth mindset; this being in contrast to the notion of resiliency as merely the capacity to rebound or the act of rebounding from adversity.

In education, the concept of resiliency is not seen as a fixed attribute; rather, it is something that can change as young people improve their social competence, problem-solving and decision-making skills, autonomy, and sense of purpose (Benard, 1993). Parents and teachers can do a great deal to foster resiliency by providing social skills training, and by teaching students self-monitoring, self-evaluation, and self-regulation strategies (Bruce, 1995). According to Good & Dweck (2006), different self-theories lead to different levels of resilience. An entity self-theory or a fixed mindset can undermine resilience, while an incremental self-theory or a growth mindset can promote resilience and increase learning opportunities. Because it is possible to influence young people's self-theories, it is also possible for educators to intervene in order to optimize the learning potential of students. For example, by fostering a growth mindset that emphasizes an incremental belief in one's musical ability, teachers can help students overcome the difficulties that they will inevitably encounter in their learning careers. This can help to improve students' resilience and increase their resistance to the influence of negative stereotypes about their abilities.

Educators can also help students through direct instruction about self-theories by encouraging them to reflect critically on their self-theories and goals. In addition, teachers can examine the messages that are inherent in their own pedagogical practices to ensure that they are conveying a growth mindset about learning to their students. For example, when referring to a musician as a 'genius', teachers may inadvertently send the message that a musician is born and not made, and that musical ability is a fixed trait. A more productive approach is to encourage students to focus on identifying the characteristics of a growth mindset for the musicians they admire in terms of their dedication, hard work, and the resiliency they displayed when overcoming problems, obstacles, or barriers to their success.

The way that teachers and parents praise their children can also send messages that foster either entity self-theories that encourage the development a fixed mindset or incremental self-theories that encourage the development of a growth mindset (Mueller & Dweck, 1998). As Good and Dweck (2006) point out, 'after children experience a success, many teachers, in an effort to boost their students' confidence and self-esteem, lavish praise upon them by telling them how smart they are. This well-meaning approach sends the unintended message that intelligence [or musical ability], per se, is the important and valued thing and that it can be measured by performance' (p. 53). It is this sort of 'trait' praise that promotes a fixed mindset. Whereas students who are given 'process' praise for their effort or strategies (and not constant praise for the things they do easily or quickly, either through luck or shortcuts), are more likely to develop a growth mindset that will promote resiliency thereby increasing their learning potential. Failures or setbacks also offer important opportunities for giving 'process' praise that does more than just offer 'a simple encouragement to try harder. Rather, teachers should use the failure as an opportunity to explore with their students new strategies and approaches that could lead to a better outcome in the future' (p. 54). To enhance their educational practices, teachers need to reflect critically on their specific assumptions, beliefs, values, and expectations in order to scrutinize consciously existing practices to promote the development of a growth mindset among their students.

The development of a growth mindset may also foster the resiliency necessary to help young people overcome negative outcomes that result from a perceived mismatch between their developmental needs and their educational environment (Eccles & Midgley, 1989; Newell & Van Ryzin, 2007). For example, studies have demonstrated that as young adolescents make the transition from elementary to secondary school, they want more autonomy and input into the decision-making that impacts on the function and structure of their education (e.g. Eccles & Midgley, 1989; Eccles, Lord, & Roeser, 1996; Eccles, Lord, Roeser, Barber, & Hermandez Jozefowicz, 1997). Negative motivation is associated with a mismatch between an adolescent's needs and an educational context that is not able to meet those needs. The development of a growth mindset may act as a buffer against negative influences on motivation and performance achievement.

There is increasing evidence that motivational problems often result from a mismatch between the developmental needs, beliefs, and values of music learners and their educational context. For example, North, Hargreaves, and O'Neill (2000) describe the mismatch that may occur between young people's musical preferences and the music curriculum of schools. This mismatch can have negative consequences for motivation and interest in music learning at school. In a study of 1205 young people's music participation, we found that those who continued learning to play instruments following the transition from elementary to secondary school, reported feeling more self-directed and autonomous than those who gave up playing instruments (O'Neill, 2001, 2005). When asked to expand on their experiences during an interview, the young people who gave up playing instruments reported that they had fewer opportunities to take responsibility for various aspects of their music education, particularly following the transition to secondary school. There was also a mismatch between the instruments that many young people wanted to learn to play and the instruments they actually played. Those who were most likely to continue playing reported valuing the instruments that they played and identified positively with adult role models who played similar instruments (see also Ivaldi & O'Neill, 2009, 2010).

McPherson and O'Neill (in press) recently examined the competence beliefs and valuing of music compared with other school subjects according to 24 143 students (11 909 females and 10 066 males, aged 9–21 years) from eight countries (Brazil, China, Finland, Hong Kong, Israel, Korea, Mexico, and USA). The results indicate that the majority of students across all eight countries tend to rate their competence and valuing of music lower than other school subjects. This widespread belief that music is less important than other school subjects suggests that there are many misconceptions about the short- and long-term benefits of engagement in music (see further Robinson, 2009). Helping young people develop a growth mindset towards music learning, which is characterized by a passion for learning, the active seeking of challenges, a valuing of effort, and the resiliency necessary to persist in the face of obstacles or adversity, may help increase the factors that initiate and sustain what Sternberg (2005) refers to as *purposeful engagement* in music. According to Sternberg (2003), 'the main constraint in achieving expertise is not some fixed prior level of capacity but purposeful engagement involving direct instruction, active participation, role modeling, and reward' (p. 71). Future research is needed to explore the relative importance and influence of these factors on motivation and music learning.

Directions for future research

Dweck's (2006) notion of a growth mindset provides an interesting framework or lens from which to examine motivation and the development of young people's music performance skills. However, more research is needed into the personhood and musical lives of music learners if we are to increase our understanding of the single, cumulative, and interdependent strengths of developing a young musician's growth mindset. We need to increase our understanding of the benefits, processes, and development of a growth mindset, including research that focuses on the role of self-theories and resiliency. Recent studies in the area of educational resilience, for example, have focused on the characteristics that differentiate between resilient and non-resilient students in terms of their academic abilities. Similar research is needed in relation to the development of musical abilities. There is also a need for longitudinal studies that examine a range of motivational predictors. Mixed methods approaches are needed that include teacher self-reports together with student interview data, as well as survey and observational data. According to Waxman, Gray, and Padron (2003) 'such data could help us understand, from different perspectives, the complexity of issues surrounding the educational improvement of students' (pp. 14–15). Research is also needed that can inform music educators and musicians about how to develop positive motivation, adaptive self-theories, and resiliency at different ages and phases of music learning and over the course of a musician's performing life.

Increasingly, school–family–community partnerships are viewed as offering protective factors that foster educational resilience in young people (Christenson & Sheridan, 2001; Waxman *et al.*, 2003). These protective factors are associated with caring and supportive adult relationships and opportunities for meaningful youth engagement in schools and communities (Benard, 1995, 1997; Wang *et al.*, 1997). For example, Herbert (1999) conducted a study with 18 culturally diverse, high-achieving students in an urban high school. The results showed a positive influence of several factors on students' resiliency. Among these factors were supportive adults at home, at school, and in the community; extracurricular after-school, Saturday, and summer enrichment programmes; challenging educational experiences; a network of achieving peers; and a strong belief in and sense of self. School–family–community partnerships offer the potential for collaborative initiatives or relationships whereby all partners involved work together to coordinate and implement programmes and activities aimed at the increased success of all students. Although school–family–community partnerships are not a panacea for solving all motivational problems that students encounter, they can foster the protective factors and resiliency that mediate these problems. Future research might examine some of the benefits that young musicians derive from increased resiliency and the development of a growth mindset. For example, young musicians may be less impacted by the effects of obstacles or barriers that they come in direct contact with compared with young musicians with fixed mindsets.

It is also necessary to explore the various conditions and contexts that promote, sustain, and enhance music engagement, particularly in relation to specific obstacles or barriers that young people encounter. Both short- and long-term influences on motivation need to be identified, as well as the different pathways, factors, and strategies that foster adaptive self-theories and resiliency among music learners. There is a tendency to view musical ability, self-identity, and character as separate or distinct aspects of a young musician. However, growing evidence suggests that there is a common underlying influence that can shape these attributes, particularly when they relate to achieving a successful outcome such as a musical performance. If we accept the premise put forward by Good and Dweck (2006) for achieving success in non-musical achievement-related domains, future research should focus on the reasoning skills that contribute to the development of musical skills, the resiliency that constructs identity in a particular way, and the responsibility that helps to define the character and long-term development of young musicians.

References

Amabile, T. M. (1983). *The social psychology of creativity*. New York: Springer-Verlag.

Bempechat, J., London, P., & Dweck, C. S. (1991). Children's conceptions of ability in major domains: an interview and experimental study. *Child Study Journal*, *21*(1), 11–36.

Benard, B. (1993). Fostering resiliency in kids. *Educational Leadership*, *51*, 44–48.

Benard, B. (1995). *Fostering resilience in children*. Urbana, IL: ERIC Clearinghouse on Elementary and Early Childhood Education. (ERIC Document Reproduction Service No. ED386327.)

Benard, B. (1997). *Turning it around for all youth: From risk to resilience* (ERIC/CUE Digest, No. 126). New York: ERIC Clearinghouse on Urban Education. (ERIC Document Reproduction Service No. ED412309.)

Bruce, M. A. (1995). Fostering resiliency in students: Positive action strategies for classroom teachers. *The Teacher Educator*, *31*, 178–188.

Christenson, S. L., & Sheridan, S. M. (2001). *Schools and families: Creating essential connections for learning*. New York, NY: The Guilford Press.

Diener, C. I., & Dweck, C. S. (1980). An analysis of learned helplessness: II. The processing of success. *Journal of Personality and Social Psychology*, *39*(5), 940–952.

Dweck, C. S. (1986). Motivational processes affecting learning. *American Psychologist*, *41*, 1040–1048.

Dweck, C. S. (1999). *Self-theories: Their role in motivation, personality, and development* (Essays in Social Psychology). Philadelphia, PA: Psychology Press, Taylor and Francis.

Dweck, C. S. (2006). *Mindset: The new psychology of success*. New York, NY: Balantine Books.

Dweck, C. S., & Leggett, E. L. (1988). A social-cognitive approach to motivation and personality. *Psychological Review*, *95*, 256–273.

Dweck, C. S., & Licht, B. G. (1980). Learned helplessness and intellectual achievement. In J. Garber & M. E. P. Seligman (Eds.), *Human helplessness: Theory and applications*. New York, NY: Academic Press.

Dweck, C. S., & Reppucci, N. D. (1973). Learned helplessness and reinforcement responsibility in children. *Journal of Personality and Social Psychology*, *25*, 109–116.

Eccles, J. (1983). Expectancies, values, and academic behaviours. In J. T. Spence (Ed.), *Achievement and achievement motives: Psychological and sociological approaches* (pp. 75–146). San Francisco, CA: Freeman.

Eccles, J., Lord, S., & Roeser, R. (1996). Round holes, square pegs, rocky roads, and sore feet: The impact of stage-environment fit on young adolescents' experiences in schools and families. In S. L. Toth & D. Cicchetti (Eds.), *Adolescence: Opportunities and challenges, Vol. 7* (pp. 49–93). Rochester, NY: University of Rochester Press.

Eccles, J., Lord, S., Roeser, R., Barber, B., & Hermandez Jozefowicz, D. (1997). The association of school transitions in early adolescence with developmental trajectories through high school. In J. Schulenberg, J. I. Maggs, & K. Hurrelmann (Eds.), *Health risks and developmental transitions during adolescence* (pp. 283–321). New York, NY: Cambridge University Press.

Eccles, J., & Midgley, C. (1989). Stage-environment fit: Developmentally appropriate classrooms for young adolescents. In C. Ames, & R. Ames (Eds.), *Research on motivation in education, Vol. 3: Goals and cognitions* (pp. 139–186). New York, NY: Academic Press.

Ericsson, K. A., Krampe, R., & Tesch-Römer, C. (1993). The role of deliberate practice in the acquisition of expert performance. *Psychological Review, 100*(3), 363–406.

Gagné, F., Blanchard, D., & Bégin, J. (2001). Beliefs about the heritability of abilities in education, music, and sports. In N. Colangelo, & S. G. Assouline (Eds.), *Talent Development IV: Proceedings from the 1998 Henry B. and Jocelyn Wallace National Research Symposium on Talent Development* (pp. 155–178). Scottsdale, AZ: Great Potential Press.

Good, C., & Dweck, C. S. (2006). Motivational orientations that lead students to show deeper levels of reasoning, greater responsibility for their academic work, and greater resilience in the face of academic difficulty. In R. J. Sternberg & R. F. Subotnik (Eds.), *Optimizing student success in school with the other three Rs: reasoning, resilience, and responsibility* (pp. 39–58). Charlotte, NC: Information Age.

Herbert, T. R. (1999). Culturally diverse high-achieving students in an urban school. *Urban Education, 34*, 428–457.

Howe, M. J. A., Davidson, J. W., & Sloboda, J. A. (1998). Innate talent: reality or myth? *Behavioural and Brain Sciences, 21*(3), 399–442.

Ivaldi, A., & O'Neill, S. A. (2009). Talking 'privilege': Barriers to musical attainment in adolescents' talk of musical role models. *British Journal of Music Education, 26*(1), 1–14.

Ivaldi, A., & O'Neill, S. A. (2010). Adolescents' attainability and aspiration beliefs for famous musician role models. *Music Education Research, 12* (2), 179–197.

Lehmann, A. C., Sloboda, J. A., & Woody, R. H. (2007). *Psychology for musicians: Understanding and acquiring the skills.* Oxford: Oxford University Press.

MacNamara, A, Holmes, P., & Collins, D. (2006). The pathway to excellence: the role of psychological characteristics in negotiating the challenges of musical development. *British Journal of Music Education, 23*(3), 285–302.

McCall, M. W. (1998). *High flyers: Developing the next generation of leaders.* Harvard Business School Press.

McPherson, G. E., & O'Neill, S. A. (in press). Students' motivation to study music as compared to other school subjects: A comparison of eight countries. *Research Studies in Music Education.*

Mueller, C. M., & Dweck, C. S. (1998). Intelligence praise can undermine motivation and performance. *Journal of Personality and Social Psychology, 75*, 33–52.

Napoli, J. C. (2007). Resiliency, resilience, resilient: A paradigm shift? Available at: www.resiliency.us/media/Resiliency,%20R,%20R_%20A_%20Paradigm_Shift_08-22-07.doc (accessed 11 September 2009).

Newell, R. J., & Van Ryzin, M. J. (2007). Growing hope as a determinant of school effectiveness. *Phi Delta Kappan, 88*(6), 465–471.

Nicholls, J. G. (1984). Achievement motivation: Conceptions of ability, subjective experience, task choice, and performance. *Psychological Review*, *91*, 328–346.

North, A. C., Hargreaves, D. J., & O'Neill, S. A. (2000). The importance of music to adolescents. *British Journal of Educational Psychology*, *70*(2), 255–272.

O'Neill, S. A. (1994a). Factors influencing children's motivation and achievement during the first year of instrumental music tuition. *Proceedings of the Third International Conference on Music Perception and Cognition*. Belgium: University of Liège.

O'Neill, S. A. (1994b). Children's beliefs about ability in academics, sport and music. *Proceedings of the Third International Conference on Music Perception and Cognition*. Belgium: University of Liège.

O'Neill, S. A. (1996). *Factors influencing children's motivation and achievement during the first year of instrumental music tuition*. Unpublished doctoral thesis. UK: Keele University.

O'Neill, S. A. (1997). The role of practice in children's early musical performance achievement. In H. Jørgensen & A. C. Lehmann (Eds.), *Does practice make perfect? Current theory and research on instrumental music practice* (pp. 53–70). Oslo: Norges musikkhøgskole.

O'Neill, S. A. (2001). *Young People and Music Participation Project: Practitioner Report and Summary of Findings*. UK: Unit for the Study of Musical Skill and Development, Keele University.

O'Neill, S. A. (2002). The self-identity of young musicians. In R. A. R. MacDonald, D. J. Hargreaves & D. Miell (Eds.), *Musical identities* (pp. 79–96). Oxford: Oxford University Press.

O'Neill, S. A. (2005). Youth music engagement in diverse contexts. In J. L. Mahoney, R. Larson, & J. S. Eccles (Eds.), *Organized activities as contexts of development*: *Extracurricular activities, after school and community programs* (pp. 255–273). Mahwah, New York: Lawrence Erlbaum Associates.

O'Neill, S. A. (2006). Positive youth musical engagement. In G. McPherson (Ed.), *The child as musician: A handbook of musical development* (pp. 461–474). Oxford: Oxford University Press.

O'Neill, S. A., Ivaldi, A., & Fox, C. (2002). Gendered discourses in musically 'talented' adolescent females' construction of self. *Feminism and Psychology*, *12*(2), 153–159.

O'Neill, S. A., Ryan, K. J., Boulton, M. J., & Sloboda, J. A. (2000). Children's subjective task values and engagement in music. Winchester, UK: Proceedings of the *British Psychological Society Annual Conference*.

O'Neill, S. A., & Sloboda, J. A. (1997). The effects of failure on children's ability to perform a musical test. *Psychology of Music*, *25*(1), 18–34.

Robinson, K. (2009). *The element*. New York: Viking.

Seligman, M. E. P., & Csikzentmihalyi, M. (2000). Positive psychology: An introduction. *American Psychologist*, *55*(1), 5–14.

Sloboda, J. A., Davidson, J. W., & Howe, M. J. A. (1994). Is everyone musical? *The Psychologist*, *7*, 349–364.

Sloboda, J. A., Davidson, J. W., Howe, M. J. A., & Moore, D. G. (1996). The role of practice in the development of performing musicians. *British Journal of Psychology*, *87*, 287–309.

Sloboda, J. A., & Howe, M. J. (1991). Biographical precursors of musical excellence: an interview study. *Psychology of Music*, *19*(1), 3–21.

Sloboda, J. A., & O'Neill, S. A. (2001). Emotions in everyday listening to music. In P. Juslin, & J. A. Sloboda (Eds.), *Music and emotion: theory and research* (pp. 413–429). Oxford: Oxford University Press.

Sloboda, J. A., O'Neill, S. A., & Ivaldi, A. (2001). Functions of music in everyday life: an exploratory study using the Experience Sampling Method. *Musicæ Scientiæ, 5*(1), 9–32.

Smiley, P. A., & Dweck, C. S. (1994). Individual differences in achievement goals among young children. *Child Development, 65,* 1723–1743.

Sternberg, R. J. (2003). *Wisdom, intelligence, and creativity synthesized.* Cambridge: Cambridge University Press.

Sternberg, R. J. (2005). Intelligence, competence, and expertise. In A. Elliot, & C. S. Dweck (Eds.), *The handbook of competence and motivation* (pp. 15–30). New York, NY: Guilford Press.

Sternberg, R. J., & Kolligian, J. (1990). *Competence considered.* New Haven: Yale University Press.

Stipek, D. J. (1984). Young children's performance expectations: Logical analysis or wishful thinking? In J. G. Nicholls (Ed.), *Advances in motivation and achievement: Vol. 3. The development of achievement motivation* (pp. 33–56). Greenwich, CT: JAI Press.

Subotnik, R. F. (2000). Developing young adolescent performers at Juilliard: An educational prototype for elite level talent development in the arts and sciences. In C. F. Van Lieshout, & P. G. Heymans (Eds.), *Talent, resilience, and wisdom across the lifespan* (pp. 249–276). Hove, UK: Psychology Press.

Subotnik, R. F., Jarvin, L., Moga, E., & Sternberg, R. J. (2003). Wisdom from gate-keepers: Secrets of success in music performance. *Bulletin of Psychology and the Arts, 14*(1), 5–9.

Wang, M. C., Haertel, G. D., & Walberg, H. J. (1994). Educational resilience in inner cities. In M. C. Wang & E. W. Gordon (Eds.), Educational resilience in inner-city America: Challenges and prospects (pp. 45–72). Mahwah, NJ: Lawrence Erlbaum.

Wang, M. C., Haertel, G. D., & Walberg, H. J. (1997). Fostering educational resilience in inner-city schools. *Children and Youth, 7,* 119–140.

Waxman, H. C., Gray, J. P., & Padron, Y. N. (2003). *Review of research on educational resiliency.* Santa Cruz, CA: Centre for Research on Education, Diversity & Excellence.

Winner, E. (1996). *Gifted children: myths and realities.* New York, NY: Basic Books.

Chapter 4

Negotiating music in the real world: development, motivation, process, and effect

Alexandra Lamont

Abstract

This chapter explores how people learn to negotiate their use of music in everyday settings. I draw on theory and research within the social approach to music psychology, which argues that music listening is active, social, and critical. I explore the developmental processes involved in responding to music and learning to make musical choices, and consider how this changes across the lifespan. I review a range of recent research studies addressing three key questions. First, how do people learn to negotiate their music uses in the real world, and how is this process shaped by others? Second, is the music itself important? This highlights an ongoing tension in music psychology between an emphasis on the music or the listener. Third, just how important is the element of choice? I review a complex set of findings which address these questions and illustrate the considerable challenges that research in everyday settings presents. Throughout I include the effects that musical engagement can have on many areas of life: musical, personal, cognitive, and social.

In this chapter I will consider the important issue of how people learn to negotiate music in the real world. How do we learn to engage with music listening across the lifespan? What motivates us to listen to and make use of music in different situations? How does it happen, where, when, who with, and most importantly, why? Finally, what effects does it have on us? The chapter aims to shed light on these key questions, and to propose a new contextual framework for studying music in everyday life. My focus is on engagement with music in terms of listening; other chapters consider related issues in relation to playing and performing music (cf. Chapters 3 and 11).

The issue of what music can do for its listeners as a collective or social group has a long and distinguished pedigree in other disciplines, notably ancient and modern philosophy (Kivy, 1990; Langer, 1942; Stamou, 2002) and sociology (Adorno, 1976; DeNora, 2000; Willis, 1978). From a psychological perspective, however, music psychology did not start out by considering the social dimension of responses to music. Some isolated moves towards the 'social' to provide real-world answers to real-world questions about musical engagement and the processes of listening to music began in the 1980s (e.g. Behne, 1986; Konečni, 1982). However, it was not until the 1990s that empirical research in music psychology began to address this in a more systematic manner, and even by the start of the twenty-first century it was still being argued that the social was receiving less attention than the cognitive and emotional domains in music psychology (e.g. Hargreaves, Miell, & MacDonald, 2002). A more social approach to music psychology has characterized a great deal of recent research in the UK, and John Sloboda's research at Keele has been a major inspiration for this new and fruitful direction. The current chapter considers the theoretical underpinnings of this type of research and illustrates its impact through a review of more recent studies focusing on the important issues of listeners' engagement with music in everyday life.

Theoretical concepts: music as leisure

Engagement in leisure activities has been seen by some sociologists as providing a way of understanding social stratification (Bourdieu, 1984), since in many ways society reproduces its cultural distinctions in leisure time. The everyday has also been theorized as having the potential to be a critical arena within capitalist culture. For example, Lefebvre (1958/1991) discusses how individuals can achieve a critique of everyday life through their engagement with leisure activities, such as music listening and music-related activities. Leisure provides an arena whereby individuals can challenge the social stratification of their work-related life, overthrow the dogmas of corporate culture, and fulfil their own personal and emotional needs. More extreme views might suggest that engagement with leisure pacifies the need for revolution, quelling potential revolutionary tendencies by providing a safe outlet for them. In any case, this view posits that the social representation of society can be understood by its modes of behaviour—the tactics that people use to take control of their own everyday lives (de Certeau, 1984).

Leisure in this view is far from passive. This resonates with the social-psychological approach to leisure activities which show them to fulfil important functions. The psychology of happiness (e.g. Maslow, 1943) illustrates how engagement in various 'projects' can help achieve the goal of self-actualization in the process of exploring personal fulfilment. Seligman (2002) defines three components of happiness: pleasure (a hedonic route achieved through increasing positive emotion); engagement (the pursuit of gratification through absorption); and meaning (using strengths in the service of something larger than oneself). Evidence suggests that the pursuit of engagement and meaning contribute more to life satisfaction than the pursuit of pleasure (Seligman, Parks, & Steen, 2005), suggesting the importance of activity and agency.

Within the engagement route to happiness, Csikszentmihalyi and Csikszentmihalyi (1988) developed the concept of *flow* to explain how rewarding difficult tasks could be: providing a suitable balance of challenge and skill leads to the individual experiencing a state of flow where they lose all sense of time and conscious awareness. Csikszentmihalyi (2002) identifies a list of different activities which are likely to induce flow in participants, including active participation in dance, theatre and the arts, reading, sex, eating, and even vandalism or joyriding. He also includes live concert audiences and, under the appropriate concentrations of active engagement and focus, home music listeners. These listeners must 'begin by setting aside specific hours for listening. When the time comes, they deepen concentration by dousing the lights, by sitting in a favourite chair, or by following some other ritual that will focus attention' in order to be in a position to potentially experience flow (2002, p. 111). Similarly, Argyle's (1996) research on motivations to engage in leisure activities (including listening to music) indicates that some active involvement or engagement in leisure is important in order for it to be personally beneficial.

This active approach to leisure corresponds to Small's definition of 'musicking' as paying attention in any way to music, which, he argues, 'covers all participation in a musical performance, whether it takes place actively or passively, whether we like the way it happens or whether we do not, whether we consider it is interesting or boring, constructive or destructive, sympathetic or antipathetic' (1998, p. 9). Music listening can thus be understood as an important leisure activity which provides the potential for personal fulfilment. However, music presents its own challenges in that there is a tension between the individual and the social elements of music. While music can be argued to be a 'fundamental channel of communication … something we do with and for other people' (Hargreaves, MacDonald, & Miell, 2005, p. 1), listening to music, while it has an implicit social dimension (Davidson, 2004), also has considerable potential to be highly personal.

The key theoretical underpinnings of recent research into the social psychology of musical engagement can thus be summarized as: considering music listening as an active, social, and at times critical process; recognizing the power of music in its own right as well as to serve particular functions; and, most fundamentally, the critical importance of exploring music listening in everyday contexts in order to further understand this active and dynamic process.

Research into everyday life engagement with music

The starting point for the current chapter is the focus on musical engagement in everyday life that has been a feature of music psychology research at Keele since the 1990s. In one early study with the Sussex Mass-Observation project (Sloboda, 1999), respondents were asked to 'tell us all about you and music', and their responses were analysed in terms of self-chosen music and music in public places. This preliminary study showed that music fulfilled a number of functions for listeners. Although the single most frequent function was listening to music as a reminder of a valued past event (50%), a combination of mood-related responses (mood change, mood enhancement, mood matching, catharsis, and calming) totalled 52% of all functions, indicating that music listening fulfils both cognitive and emotional functions most often. (Responses could be categorized as fitting more than one function). In terms of activities, the most common categories were housework and travelling (driving/running/cycling), at 22% each, with music also frequently accompanying desk work (14%) and eating (12%). Chosen music thus accompanies overwhelmingly solitary activities and its functions are mainly self-referential. Sloboda's findings also indicate ambivalence towards music in public places. Non-chosen music was more likely to be liked if it was street music as opposed to music in shops, and older respondents and men were more likely to dislike music in public places.

This approach relies heavily on the autobiographical method, and assumes that people are able to reliably report on their own experiences of music and what functions and effects it has on them (cf. DeNora, 2000). There were some individual differences in the data, however. Sloboda (1999) found that women provided more detailed descriptions of mood-related functions than men, and older respondents tended to report fewer activities that were accompanied by self-chosen music. A different approach and one which provides a great deal of inspiration for the research described later in this chapter was adopted in a highly novel study a few years later. Sloboda, O'Neill, and Ivaldi (2001) explored everyday musical engagement in a small sample of university staff and students using the experience sampling method. This seminal paper was the first to attempt to engage with musical experiences as they took place in real time. It drew on the technique first developed in the context of flow-related research (Csikszentmihalyi & Lefevre, 1989) to sample slices of everyday life by randomly alerting participants who were free to go about their normal lives for the duration of the study. Sloboda et al. (2001) paged their eight participants seven times a day for one week, and on being paged, participants completed a response form detailing whether or not they were listening to music (or had been during the past two hours), and if so, details of the listening context. In addition they were asked to note their mood states (using 11 bipolar scales) before and after listening to the music, and to answer questions relating to the impact and choice of the music.

The findings indicated that there was a 44% chance that music would be heard in any two-hour period, with 23% of episodes having music being heard at the time of paging and a further 21% in the preceding two hours. Participants were mainly at home or at work, although transport, shops and entertainment-related venues were more likely to have music than not. Music tended to have effects on mood, mostly in terms of increasing positivity, arousal, and attention, and these effects were stronger when participants had high levels of choice over the music that they heard (which tended to also be when participants were alone). One of the most important findings from this study was that listening to music as a main activity was very rare, at only 2%. Subsequent studies using similar methods have found slightly higher estimates (e.g. 11% by North, Hargreaves, & Hargreaves, 2004), but these findings suggest that the kind of focused listening necessary for attaining a state of flow is extremely unusual in most adults' everyday lives.

Three key questions arise from this existing literature on the uses of music in everyday life. First, how do people learn to negotiate music in the real world? Negotiation is used here as an active verb indicating an interaction between listeners and music—'how we do things to music and how we do things with music' (DeNora, 2000, p. 7). All the studies reviewed indicate that adults generally have high levels of conscious awareness of the music they choose to listen to and the effects that it will have on them, but it is important to consider the origins of such awareness. Second, is the music itself important? Although not reported on explicitly by Sloboda *et al.* (2001), other studies have indicated a vast diversity of different music in studies with adults as having similar effects (e.g. mood regulation, time filler, enjoyment; DeNora, 2000). Third, how important is the element of choice? Sloboda *et al.* (2001) found positive mood change to be greatly enhanced in high choice contexts, and other work has shown that non-chosen music can have negative effects on listeners (DeNora, 2000). These issues will be used to structure the remainder of this chapter, which presents a synthesis of existing research and novel empirical findings addressing these questions.

Developmental processes: learning to negotiate

It is now well known that exposure to music begins before birth, and music is an intrinsic part of infants' lives. Even mothers who lack confidence in their own singing will readily sing to their infants (Trehub *et al*, 1997), and music accompanies many early caregiving rituals (Custodero, Britto, & Xin, 2002; Young, Street, & Davies, 2006). In terms of infants' motivations to listen, live singing produces hormonal changes that reduce arousal and stress, helping the infants regulate their own state (Shenfield, Trehub, & Nakata, 2003). Listening to music in general thus has powerful physiological effects even for infants. However, even immediately after birth, infants respond differently to different kinds of music. For example, 2-day-old infants of deaf parents (thus without extensive prior exposure to music) showed a preference for an infant-directed version compared with non-infant-directed version of the same song sung by the same singer (Masataka, 1999). These findings indicate that very subtle preferences for music are present very early in development and may not require extensive experience to develop (Trehub, 2009).

In the first years of life, musical exposure tends to be determined by parents and thus the music that young children are familiar with will be dictated by their family situation. As children become more independent throughout early childhood, the range of contexts open to them increases exponentially, and this is a fruitful time for exploring the listening behaviours children might adopt in different settings. I adapted the experience sampling method used by Sloboda *et al.* (2001) to investigate the musical experiences of 3.5 year olds (Lamont, 2008). Parents were loaned a mobile telephone for a one-week period and asked to pass it to whichever adult was responsible for the child (including other family members, childminders, nursery staff, and friends). Calls were made at random intervals and the adult answering the call responded to a series of questions based on Sloboda *et al.*'s (2001) earlier response sheet concerning the music, situation, and effect. The detailed mood scales used in the earlier study could not be employed here since these data were 'second-hand', but the child's observable emotional response to the music was asked about.

Results from 32 children indicated a greater incidence of musical exposure among this age group than for adults, with a total of 81% of music episodes (38% at the time of the calls and 43% in the preceding two-hour period). What was particularly striking about these results was that despite the age of the participants, the children themselves chose the music or the activity that involved music independently most often (40.2% of all episodes, compared with 20% for mothers). A great deal of this choice focused on children's television programmes or videos which include a great deal of music, and which are a great deal more interactive than much adult-oriented television (cf. Marsh, 2004). Related to this, the children's choices were more likely to be for music at the foreground of the activity, whereas adults' choices were more often for background music to accompany another activity, such as mealtimes. Despite the prevalence of music, the opportunities for focused listening were rare, except for those accompanying television programmes (where arguably attention is divided between the visual and auditory and between the storyline and the music) and only two occasions out of 353 music listening episodes took place when the child was alone.

Thus the ability to negotiate and interact with music, even in recorded format, is apparent from early childhood. The process of learning what music works in given situations is likely to be a gradual one, progressing from an implicit awareness (enhanced by physiological changes) of the power of music to structure basic caregiving situations in early infancy, which becomes more deliberate and conscious in early childhood. For example, all but one of the car journeys with young children were accompanied by music mainly of children's choice, and the only 'silent' car journey was the result of a faulty car stereo (Lamont, 2008). At this point, children are becoming aware of the fact that certain music fits certain situations, although most of them have not yet developed a sensitive understanding of what to do if the music does not fit. The first response in infancy is to show displeasure through crying, fussing, and fidgeting. In early childhood it becomes possible to remove oneself from the situation if the music is not liked. For example, one child who experienced a great deal of music in his everyday life was recorded in one episode running between two rooms at home, one playing loud pop music on television and the other with soft soul music on the radio, because he was unsure about which kind of music he wanted (Lamont, 2008).

Only later does it become possible to make active choices about music listening by manipulating the source of the sound and choosing one's own music for specific functions. However, beyond the early childhood stage, research has not yet explored how children might learn the functions and purposes of music through childhood. Behne (1986) found that children younger than 13 years did not seem aware of the different ways in which they could engage with music, but from age 13 onwards a number of different listening styles can be found, such as compensating, distancing, sentimental, associative, and vegetative. Interestingly, some listening styles seem to be associated with particular problems in adolescence (Behne, 1997). For example, adolescents with family problems and boredom at school were characterized as having a 'stimulative' listening style, while depressed adolescents who were worrying about the future and had health problems preferred more 'sentimental' listening. This suggests that adolescents are developing an awareness of how to use music to fulfil their own personal needs. Other research has explored adolescents' music preferences focusing on the *non*-musical functions of group identification within a process of identity formation (Tarrant, North, & Hargreaves, 2002), highlighting that use of music at this stage in life can be more than just musical. The emphasis given to music listening at this stage in life reflects important changes such as a shift from time spent with parents to time spent with peers (Larson, Kubey, & Colletti, 1989). While important in describing how musical uses change at different stages, none of this evidence sheds light on *how* the process of developing engagement takes place, and more research is needed that looks at everyday experiences in the real world with these age groups.

Later in life, adults are able to reflect in considerable detail about the ways in which they 'use' music in the real world (Greasley, 2008; see further below), and seem adept at choosing music in particular situations to fit the context (DeNora, 2000; North & Hargreaves, 1996). However, their discourse does not prioritize *developmental* processes. The one exception to this is the effect of other people. When describing how they compiled their music collections, adults of all ages referred to the importance of the period of early adulthood, after leaving school or college, as one which helped to broaden their musical tastes (Greasley & Lamont, 2006). Here again more research is needed to explore the process of learning that might take place at different phases in life.

In sum, while adults seem to be adept music 'consumers' in the sense of knowing how to engage with music to serve their own purposes, little is known about how this process might develop. What is clear from the evidence reviewed here is that while there are certain general musical predispositions that exist from a very early age (e.g. fast music 'fits' infants in energetic moods or adults in exercise classes), more subtle patterns of interaction with music emerge more gradually. The key influence at each phase of development seems to be other people. For instance, friendship groups are important for establishing a sense of identity during adolescence (Tarrant *et al.*, 2002) and adolescents share music (Brown & Sellen, 2006). As social circumstances change, different social influences open up people's musical tastes, such as in the transition from school or college to university or work (Greasley & Lamont, 2006). This points towards a *social* motor for development, although more research is still required to disentangle other influences and to explore this process across the lifespan.

Does the music matter?

There is an ongoing tension in the field of music psychology in terms of emphasis on the music or the listener. Much of the work in everyday contexts has tended to focus on the music as a 'stimulus', prioritizing the outcomes and effects it has on the listener rather than exploring intrinsic features of the music itself. This line of research adopts a socio-constructivist approach in that the meaning is in the listener's mind, and the music becomes somewhat irrelevant. For example, arguably any kind of music can be the 'tune' in the 'Darling, they're playing our tune' theory of musical associations (Davies, 1978) and its effects in evoking a personally significant episodic memory should be the same. While details are often gathered of the music being experienced in such everyday life situations (e.g. Sloboda *et al.*, 2001), these are typically not reported in analyses which tend to emphasize the functions, effects, and emotions of music listening in a more general sense. Part of this lacuna stems from methodological procedures for participants to report and researchers to categorize the music being experienced (Juslin, Liljeström, Västfjäll, Barradas, & Silva, 2008). However, methodological problems notwithstanding, this begs the question of whether it really matters what music is experienced.

A different line of research has focused on the intrinsic properties of music as being somehow responsible for engendering particular effects, and this corresponds to Frith's (2003) call to explore properties of the music as well as the functions that it can serve. Cooke's (1959) theoretical study of the features of measured music of the harmonic period attempted to identify the structural elements of music that should evoke particular responses, such as time, melodic, and tonal tension. Following on from this, Sloboda (1991) found that listeners could recall and pinpoint particular structural moments in pieces that evoked emotional responses in them, and that these tended to have some commonalities. For example, melodic appoggiaturas tended to induce tears, while new or unprepared harmonies evoked shivers. This kind of intramusical expectancy first described by Meyer (1956) has not been much studied, although in a laboratory setting Steinbeis, Koelsch, and Sloboda (2006) recently found that more and less expected harmonic cadences evoked different subjective and physiological responses.

As argued above, a focus on the music itself has not typically been present in research exploring everyday music listening settings, and generalizations about the types of music that tend to be liked come from laboratory contexts or from non-chosen music settings. For example, as illustrated earlier, in the laboratory very young infants prefer live music, particularly singing that is directed towards them, and older infants seem to prefer music which is consonant, lively, familiar, and eventually (by the age of 12 months) which complies with the musical system of their native culture (Trehub, 2009). However, experimental research with this age group tends to rely on overt attentional measures such as directional looking or head turning which may bias responses in favour of attention-capturing stimuli. Similarly, for adults in exercise settings, music which has a tempo that fits the pattern of the exercise (thereby enabling entrainment) tends to be preferred by exercise participants (DeNora, 2000; Karageorghis, Jones, & Stuart, 2007). In such structured settings it does seem possible to make generalizations about particular musical styles and how they may fit the situation.

In real-life settings, however, musical preferences are more varied. Although 'Itsy Bitsy Spider' is reportedly the favourite song of infants and young children in the USA (Johnson-Green & Custodero, 2002), there are also substantial individual differences in the music experienced and responded to in early childhood (Lamont, 2008). While real-time music exposure is mainly centred on child-oriented music (nursery rhymes, playsongs, and music accompanying children's television programmes and films) and popular music, individual children were sampled listening to a diversity of music. In early adulthood, similar differences are observed. From a free response item about preferred music listening in a survey of 119 university students (Greasley & Lamont, 2006), a total of 99 different musical styles and sub-styles were listed, and most respondents chose three or more styles. Some chose considerably more: for example, one 21-year-old listed his main preferences for listening to 'hip-hop, r 'n' b, alternative, indie, rock, drum 'n' bass, 80s slow jazz, classics, dance, ambient chill-out, and electric beats'. Within this, individuals also reported diverse combinations of preference, such as a liking for rock, metal, classical, and musicals, indicating that it is not possible to do justice to listeners' musical tastes by reducing them to a single category such as 'likes jazz'.

Even within styles, there is also a considerable diversity of pieces heard. For instance, the same children in my earlier study of preschoolers (Lamont, 2008) often experienced the same piece of music several times during the week, yet there were remarkably few overlaps in specific pieces between children (with the exception of young children's television theme tunes). In a study asking university students to nominate daily favourite pieces of music (Lamont & Webb, 2010), nine participants were exhaustively sampled over two separate weeks. Between them, they mentioned 96 different daily favourite pieces of music, with only five overlapping pieces nominated by two participants. This was despite the fact that all participants were in the same year group and were all acquainted with one another, and four of them lived in the same student house. Similarly, free-report data gathered from 67 students over a three-year period about their single strongest experience of music (Lamont, in press) did not reveal any overlapping artists or songs. Many respondents selected a music festival or a live concert as having evoked their strongest experience of music, but none of them reported on the same event in the same year, and none of the music overlapped.

So does the music matter? The notion of 'high' culture as being the only way to evoke strong or valued responses (Adorno, 1941) has long been left behind in research into everyday engagement with music. For example, Chrissie, a 48-year-old interviewee, talked at length about getting to know the 'teenage' band Hanson when she was 44, and how she had broadened her experiences (both musical and non-musical) through her love of this music (Greasley, 2008). Across styles, some generic features of music appear to be recognized and appreciated by many listeners. For example, in free interviews exploring music preferences across the lifespan, Adam, aged 22, explained that he liked Queen songs because 'they go through a sequence, and it's not all the same throughout, and you have ups and downs and usually there's a big crescendo ending or something' (Greasley, 2008, p. 122). This discourse refers to the patterns of tension and relaxation that have been explored in more traditional laboratory settings outlined earlier. Similarly, Willis's in-depth exploration of bikeboys' patterns of musical engagement reflects the importance of tempo in generating an active response to music: 'if you hear a fast record you've got to get up and do something, I think' (Willis, 1978, p. 73).

As well as these features of music already identified by earlier work, listeners describing their strongest experiences of music often also referred to particular instruments or sound qualities as evoking strong responses (Lamont, in press). For instance, a description of an experience of Les Misérables prioritized the sound quality: 'The chorus was so loud, it was rumbling through my chest ... I think the atmosphere increased the intensity but it was the way the voices reverberated around the room ... I could not just hear it but feel it'. Another participant described a live performance by Björk in terms of instrumental qualities:

> I was already hyped and having this totally immense experience, but it was when she played Joga that it hit me. It's one of my favourite songs. I had never heard it played with brass instead of strings. It sounded beautifully, the brass made it sound quite harsh and in your face too. Then when she sang, 'and push me up to, a state of emergency', this strong

and almost tribal beat kicked in. It didn't feel like we were dancing, but instead marching as a whole unit, all together. It's originally quite a slow and moving song, but now it was this full blown marching band with trumpets and rough saw-like synths. (Lamont, in press)

It could be hypothesized that any kind of music that embodies such intrinsic patterns or elements has the *potential* to move its listeners. The question then becomes why music does not always work in this way. As has been emphasized throughout, the listener and the listening situation also have significant contributions to make to the impact of music (cf. Hargreaves *et al.*, 2005). This in part explains why The Pixies can move a listener to tears at a festival when she has been waiting all day to hear the band, but leaves her unmoved when overheard on the radio (Lamont, in press). As DeNora has argued (2000), music partly has meaning and emotional power because as listeners we want and expect it to. However, some important experiences can come from unexpected situations. For example, one student reported a strong experience at a music festival when a familiar band played an unknown song. He explained the cause of the experience as follows: 'The atmosphere at the festival. But mainly the sound experience and also the fact that they played a song I never expected' (Lamont, in press). Thus expectancy may operate at the level of the listener's expectations, as well in its more common intramusical sense.

Further research exploring a wider range of listener types, types of music and listening situations may help uncover whether there are any generalities across styles and situations beyond the fundamental features already identified of tempo, loudness, timbre/instrumentation, and patterns of expectation. A focus on the musical materials as a resource rather than a cipher for musical affect (DeNora, 2000) will be valuable in helping achieve this aim.

Whose music? The importance of choice

Choice in music listening is beginning to emerge as a very significant influence on the effect that the music can have. Choice operates in two main ways: first, at a general level, choosing to listen to music or not, and second, the specifics of the music that is chosen. Within each, context is important. Technological changes have made it possible to listen to music in many more contexts than was previously possible (Bull, 2006), but there are many situations where music listening is still not acceptable (such as, for example, a doctor's appointment or a university lecture hall). Specific music choices also operate within constraints, again dependent on context, such as how much music can be stored on a personal music player. However, the degree of choice is very influential. For instance, studies using music for non-musical outcomes such as pain relief, both in clinical settings and in everyday life, find many beneficial effects of music listening (e.g. Batt-Rawden & DeNora, 2005; Mitchell & MacDonald, 2006; Mitchell, MacDonald, Knussen, & Serpell, 2007). In such settings, music generally tends to provide some benefit, and self-chosen music tends to have maximum effect. However, introducing an element of choice by giving participants several selections to make a choice from has a greater impact than music listening under entirely experimenter-chosen conditions (Siedliecki & Good, 2006). This corresponds to other findings in everyday life that where choice is entirely dictated by others, listeners often respond more negatively (e.g. Gavin, 2006).

Early in life, music heard by infants is selected by adults. However, the 'audience' is still involved in giving their reactions to the music, and mothers adapt their choices of music to fit their infant's mood and the situation (Young, 2008). As noted above, even 3.5 year olds have considerable autonomy in their listening situations, particularly in the home and in family settings (Lamont, 2008). When children make choices, they tend to opt for children's music, while adults tend to choose other kinds of music including pop and classical more frequently. Children also tend to be more engaged with the music episodes that they have chosen themselves, confirming earlier findings with adults (Sloboda et al., 2001). In the early years there appears to be a kind of 'commodification' of young children's music (including specially designed toys with music, music accompanying television programmes and children's websites) which most infants and young children appears to respond to positively (Young, 2008). However, at this stage in development little can be inferred about the nature of choices, and the options for children to choose music that they would not have previously encountered in their everyday lives are very limited.

Apart from controlled environments, many everyday contexts for adult listeners enable them to choose a very broad range of music, both from what they have personally available to them in their music collections and from external sources such as the radio and the internet. However, technology and expertise both have an impact on the degree of choice. When listening to music while travelling, depending on the capacity and technological specifications of portable music players, listeners can make a range of choices which are found to depend on their mood and the purpose of their journey (Heye & Lamont, 2010). In this case the overall choice is listener-constrained as the music comes from the listener's own music collection. Listeners tend to report choosing at the level of an artist but then selecting a particular song using features such as track skipping to accompany their journey. Those travelling by bus tended to use the random/shuffle mode of playing music to help pass the time more effectively, thereby introducing an element of surprise into a situation which is broadly constrained by their own previous choices of what to put on the music player. Similarly, listeners described building their music collections with assistance from technology such as downloading, finding the technology acted as a filter for choice (Greasley & Lamont, 2006). Finally, choice for most listeners is broadly limited by their access to recorded music or to live concerts. While this has indubitably increased exponentially in recent years, trained musicians also have the ability to consciously recall music they are familiar with and listen 'in their heads' (Bailes, 2007), and thus choice is also somewhat limited by expertise.

When reflecting on music choice, those listeners who are more engaged with music have more conscious awareness of how much choice they have (Greasley & Lamont, 2006). For example, Karl, aged 27, in describing his music collection, explained 'there's a different mood attached to all of them, there's a different feeling attached to all of them, erm, I know every single one of them inside out, so I know what I want and where it'll be and I always have a choice' (Greasley, 2008, p. 94). Less engaged listeners use music in similar ways to affect their mood and make them feel a particular way, but seem less aware of how they do this, as Adam, aged 22, elaborated: 'I can put that on and it would help me change my mood and stuff, and I have done that in the past, I've never really thought about it in that kind of way' (p. 94).

In an in-depth study focusing on the moment-to-moment process of listening to music, Greasley (2008) used experience sampling to study a group of young adults over the period of one week, exploring whether there were differences in listening behaviour according to participants' level of musical engagement (previously defined as self-rated importance of music and musical enjoyment). As well as some differences in behaviour according to level of musical engagement, Greasley also found differences according to choice. Each listening situation was rated for the degree of choice over hearing the music on an 11-point Likert scale. In most episodes listeners reported having at least a moderate degree of choice over the music they were hearing (67% of episodes). Listeners who had higher levels of choice were more likely to report having chosen the music for the purposes of enjoyment and mood regulation, and when they had low levels of choice, listeners not only reported music as having helped pass the time and distracted them, but also reported enjoying the music less and sometimes it having annoyed them. Highly engaged listeners were significantly more likely to be hearing self-chosen music (around 60% of the time) than less engaged listeners (around 33% of the time).

It is also important to consider the reasons behind choices to listen to music in given situations. Here again there is a distinction between choosing music in general and choosing specific music. In some situations, such as travelling, listeners seem to be choosing music in general as a matter of routine or habit, although the specific music is nonetheless chosen according to its fit with the listener's mood and situation (Heye & Lamont, 2010). Most commonly, reasons cited for choosing to listen to a given piece of music at a given moment emphasize enjoyment, mood-related variables, relaxation, and enhancing an activity or creating an atmosphere (see also Greasley, 2008; Lamont & Webb, 2010). Listeners very rarely report choosing to listen to music to feel less lonely (see also Greasley, 2008), which suggests that the level of communication between music (artist, composer) and individual listener is not a sufficiently powerful motivator to engage in music listening. Across a number of different situations (Greasley, 2008), in many cases listeners' reasons for choosing music typically matched the actual outcomes of the music listening, but in some instances music also had a number of unexpected effects (mainly for high choice situations). For example, Vikki, aged 29, reported that she had chosen to listen to music in her office at work for enjoyment, to help her pass the time and to listen to the lyrics; she went on to note that the music had also distracted her, accentuated a mood and made her feel less alone.

The most important factor to bear in mind when considering musical choice is that despite the fact that listeners have considerable awareness of the effects particular music will have on them, they sometimes behave in seemingly paradoxical ways. For instance, as reviewed earlier, there is a wealth of evidence suggesting that music listening, particularly to one's favourite music, can reduce pain and anxiety. Yet a colleague undergoing chemotherapy told us how she actively refused to bring her favourite music with her into hospital to accompany the treatment, as she did not want to set up further negative associations with it that would carry forward into the future (Lamont & Greasley, 2009). This powerful example serves to remind us not to lose sight of the listener's agency and autonomy in creating a meaningful music listening experience.

A contextual approach to understanding musical engagement

We have seen that listening to music is both intensely personal and entirely social, and almost always active. From the evidence to date, it appears that people are born with certain predispositions to respond to certain features of music, such as tempo, which can have relatively direct influences on the body in terms of entrainment. Choices about music are apparent from early infancy. Through immersion in a particular musical culture in the normative process of enculturation, listeners also acquire the conventions of this culture such that they can respond to additional features of music such as intramusical expectancies and patterns of tension and release. Listeners also have specific individual experiences with particular musical styles, artists, and pieces which become part of their musical autobiographies as well as their listening libraries, and they develop both these collections and their abilities to engage with it through a range of experiences over time and with input from other people.

All of this research illustrates how ubiquitous music listening has become in the early twenty-first century in industrialized societies, and the importance of music in people's lives is indisputable. All the evidence emphasizes an active use of music. Moreover, reflective interview data point towards the importance of engagement and of meaning, which are key components of happiness (Seligman, 2002). Conversely, on a moment-to-moment basis, listeners report choosing to listen to music overwhelmingly for enjoyment, following what Seligman identifies as the (less effective) hedonic route to happiness, and the opportunities for focused music listening as outlined by Csikszentmihalyi (2002) are relatively rare.

This leads to a new conceptualization of the processes involved in learning to negotiate music in everyday life (Figure 4.1). Unlike earlier static models which separate listener, context, and response (cf. Hargreaves *et al.*, 2005), this is a seen as a diachronic process, with the cyclical interactions between listener and music continuing across the lifespan. Neither the listener nor the music is considered to be in a vacuum, but rather to have fundamental interactions with other listeners and other musics. The listener–music relationship is fluid, with the listener negotiating the listening context by exercising motivations to listen, choosing music, and generating expectations about the listening situation and the music itself; the music affects the listener through the hedonic route, through engagement and through the generation of meaning, which in turn affects future listening experiences in an ongoing cycle. Finally, and most importantly, the listening context is not treated as a separate interaction but encircles the entire process, as a medium rather than a variable (cf. Cole, 1996; Lamont, 2006). In this schematization of everyday life, music listening contexts also have an intimate relationship with other everyday contexts, which again encircle them.

This contextual approach to understanding musical experience still has some way to go. Different methodologies tend to emphasize different aspects of the ways in which

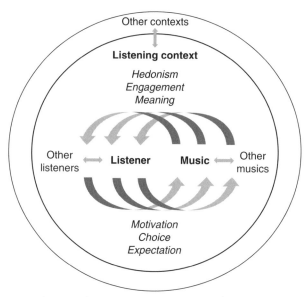

Fig. 4.1 A contextual approach to negotiating music.

music can affect listeners. As indicated above, interviews highlight engagement and meaning while moment-to-moment methods prioritize enjoyment. More real-life research meshing and linking methods in an integrative way to ask questions about connecting parts of these experiences (cf. Mason, 2006) is needed to uncover why people choose to listen to particular pieces at any given moment. This might provide opportunities for listeners to demonstrate the sense of engagement and meaning that they offer in more reflective interview settings in research contexts which are closer to the experiences themselves.

More attention is also required on the musical experience itself and how this might differ for different types of listener, exploring the cyclical interactions in Figure 4.1 more fully. Evidence so far highlights that music is found to accompany other activities almost all the time. As noted above, solitary focused music listening accounts for less than 10% of all everyday music listening occasions across the studies presented here, and in many cases for much less than this. This means that the potential for strong experiences of music and for achieving a state of flow through listening to music is also relatively rare. Certain conditions, such as live musical events, seem to predispose listeners to these intense experiences which are often described as being life-changing; however, just as it is not possible to predict the specific outcomes of a chosen listening situation it is also not possible to predict which situation, music, and listener would coincide to generate such a strong experience. Listeners have considerable autonomy in the ways in which they choose to engage with music at foreground or background level, and different types of listener, such as those with high levels of musical training, may have different listening strategies to the 'background' approach which is found in many studies. More research is required to explore how this might vary from context to context (cf. Sloboda, Lamont, & Greasley, 2009).

In conclusion, the research reviewed here, grounded by the move towards the social in psychology of music and inspired by the work of Sloboda and colleagues, illustrates the importance of engaging with everyday contexts in the goal of understanding the complexities of meaning-making that guide music listeners. These contexts present considerable methodological challenges as well as theoretical tensions, which I have given a flavour of here. However, in the pursuit of understanding the kinds of musical experiences that most people have, and which can change people's lives in such far-reaching ways, it is vital to devote more effort towards meeting these challenges.

References

Adorno, T. W. (1941). On popular music. *Studies in Philosophy and Social Science, IX*, 17–48.

Adorno, T. W. (1976). *Introduction to the sociology of music* (E. B. Ashby, Trans.). New York, NY: Seabury.

Argyle, M. (1996). *The social psychology of leisure*. Harmondsworth: Penguin.

Bailes, F. (2007). The prevalence and nature of imagined music in the everyday lives of music students. *Psychology of Music, 35*(4), 1–16.

Batt-Rawden, K., & DeNora, T. (2005). Music and informal learning in everyday life. *Music Education Research, 7*, 289–304.

Behne, K.-E. (1986). *Hörertypologien*. Regensburg: G. Bosse.

Behne, K.-E. (1997). The development of 'Musikerleben' in adolescence: How and why young people listen to music. In I. Deliège, & J. A. Sloboda (Eds.), *Perception and cognition of music* (pp. 143–159). Hove: Psychology Press.

Bourdieu, P. (1984). *Distinction: A social critique of the judgement of taste*. London: Routledge.

Brown, B., & Sellen, A. (2006). Sharing and listening to music. In K. O'Hara, & B. Brown (Eds.), *Consuming music together: Social and collaborative aspects of music consumption technologies* (pp. 37–56). London: Springer.

Bull, M. (2006). Investigating the culture of mobile listening: From Walkman to iPod. In K. O'Hara, & B. Brown (Eds.), *Consuming music together: social and collaborative aspects of music consumption technologies* (pp. 131–149). London: Springer.

Cole, M. (1996). *Cultural psychology: a once and future discipline*. London: Harvard University Press.

Cooke, D. (1959). *The language of music*. Oxford: Oxford University Press.

Csikszentmihalyi, M. (2002). *Flow: The classic work on how to achieve happiness*. London: Rider.

Csikszentmihalyi, M., & Csikszentmihalyi, I. S. (1988). *Optimal experience*. Cambridge: Cambridge University Press.

Csikszentmihalyi, M., & Lefevre, J. (1989). Optimal experience in work and leisure. *Journal of Personality and Social Psychology, 56*, 815–822.

Custodero, L. A., Britto, P. R., & Xin, T. (2002). From Mozart to Motown, lullabies to love songs: A preliminary report on the parents' use of music with infants survey (PUMIS). *Zero to Three, 23*(1), 41–46.

Davidson, J. W. (2004). Music as social behavior. In E. Clarke, & N. Cook (Eds.), *Empirical musicology: aims, methods, prospects* (pp. 57–75). Oxford: Oxford University Press.

Davies, J. B. (1978). *The psychology of music*. London: Hutchinson.

de Certeau, M. (1984). *The practice of everyday life* (S. Rendall, Trans.). Berkeley, CA: University of California Press.

DeNora, T. (2000) *Music in everyday life*. Cambridge: Cambridge University Press.

Frith, S. (2003). Music in everyday life. In M. Clayton, T. Herbert, & R. Middleton (Eds.), *The cultural study of music: a critical introduction* (pp. 92–101). London: Routledge.

Gavin, H. (2006). Intrusive music: The perception of everyday music explored by diaries. *The Qualitative Report, 11*(3), 550–565.

Greasley, A. E. (2008). *Engagement with music in everyday life: An in-depth study of adults' musical preferences and listening behaviours*. Unpublished Ph.D. thesis, University of Keele, UK.

Greasley, A. E., & Lamont, A. (2006). Musical preference in adulthood: why do we like the music we do? In M. Baroni, A. R. Addessi, R. Caterina, & M. Costa (Eds.), *Proceedings of the 9th International Conference on Music Perception and Cognition* (pp. 960–966). Bologna: University of Bologna.

Hargreaves, D. J., MacDonald, R. A. R., & Miell, D.E. (2005). How do people communicate using music? In D. E. Miell, R. A. R. MacDonald, & D. J. Hargreaves (Eds.), *Musical communication* (pp. 1–25). Oxford: Oxford University Press.

Hargreaves, D. J., Miell, D. E., & MacDonald, R. A. R. (2002). What are musical identities, and why are they important? In R. A. R. MacDonald, D. J. Hargreaves, & D. E. Miell (Eds.), *Musical identities* (pp. 1–20). Oxford: Oxford University Press.

Heye, A., & Lamont, A. (2010). Mobile listening situations in everyday life: The use of MP3 players while travelling. *Musicæ Scientiæ, 14*(1), 95–120.

Johnson-Green, E., & Custodero, L. A. (2002). The Toddler Top 40: Musical preferences of babies, toddlers, and their parents. *Zero to Three, 23*(1), 47–48.

Juslin, P. N., Liljeström, S., Västfjäll, D., Barradas, G., & Silva, A. (2008). An experience sampling study of emotional reactions to music: listener, music, and situation. *Emotion, 8*(5), 668–683.

Karageorghis, C., Jones, L., & Stuart, D. P. (2007). Psychological effects of music tempi during exercise. *International Journal of Sports Medicine, 28*, 1–7.

Kivy, P. (1990). *Music alone: philosophical reflection on the purely musical experience*. Ithaca, NY: Cornell University Press.

Konečni, V. J. (1982). Social interaction and music preference. In D. Deutsch (Ed.), *The psychology of music* (1st ed.) (pp. 497–516). New York, NY: Academic Press.

Lamont, A. (2006). *Review of Musical Communication*, D. Miell, R. MacDonald, & D. J. Hargreaves (Eds.). *Musicæ Scientiæ, 10*(2), 278–282.

Lamont, A. (2008). Young children's musical worlds: Musical engagement in 3.5-year-olds. *Journal of Early Childhood Research, 6*(3), 247–261.

Lamont, A. (in press). University students' strong experiences of music listening. *Musicæ Scientiæ, Special Issue*.

Lamont, A., & Greasley, A. E. (2009). Musical preferences. In S. Hallam, I. Cross, & M. Thaut (Eds.), *The Oxford handbook of music psychology* (pp. 160–168). Oxford: Oxford University Press.

Lamont, A., & Webb, R. J. (2010). Short- and long-term musical preferences: What makes a favourite piece of music? *Psychology of Music 38*(2), 221–241.

Langer, S. K. (1942). *Philosophy in a new key*. Cambridge, MA: Harvard University Press.

Larson, R., Kubey, R., & Colletti, J. (1989). Changing channels: Early adolescent media choices and shifting investments in family and friends. *Journal of Youth and Adolescence, 18*(6), 583–599.

Lefebvre, H. (1958/1991). *Critique of everyday life* (J. Moore, Trans.). London: Verso.

Marsh, J. (2004). The techno-literary practices of young children. *Journal of Early Childhood Research, 2*(1), 51–66.

Masataka, N. (1999). Preference for infant-directed singing in 2-day-old hearing infants of deaf parents. *Developmental Psychology, 35*, 1001–1005.

Maslow, A. H. (1943). A theory of human motivation. *Psychological Review, 50*, 370–396.

Mason, J. (2006). Mixing methods in a qualitatively-driven way. *Qualitative Research, 6*(1), 9–26.

Meyer, L. B. (1956). *Emotion and meaning in music.* Chicago, IL: Chicago University Press.

Mitchell, L. A., & MacDonald, R. A. R. (2006). An experimental investigation of the effects of preferred and relaxing music listening on pain perception. *Journal of Music Therapy, XLIII*(4), 295–316.

Mitchell, L. A., MacDonald, R. A. R., Knussen, C., & Serpell, M. G. (2007). A survey investigation of the effects of music listening on chronic pain. *Psychology of Music, 35*(1), 39–59.

North, A. C., & Hargreaves, D. J. (1996). Responses to music in aerobic exercise and yogic relaxation classes. *British Journal of Psychology, 87*, 535–547.

North, A. C., Hargreaves, D. J., & Hargreaves, J. J. (2004). Uses of music in everyday life. *Music Perception, 22*(10), 41–77.

Seligman, M. E. P. (2002). *Authentic happiness: using the new positive psychology to realize your potential for lasting fulfillment.* New York, NY: Free Press.

Seligman, M. E. P., Parks, A. C., & Steen, T. (2005). A balanced psychology and a full life. In F.A. Huppert, N. Baylis, & B. Keverne (Eds.), *The science of well-being* (pp. 275–304). Oxford: Oxford University Press.

Shenfield, T., Trehub, S. E., & Nakata, T. (2003). Maternal singing modulates infant arousal. *Psychology of Music, 31*, 365–375.

Siedliecki, S. L., & Good, M. (2006). Effect of music on power, pain, depression and disability. *Journal of Advanced Nursing, 54*(5), 553–562.

Sloboda, J. A. (1991). Music structure and emotional response: Some empirical findings. *Psychology of Music, 19*, 110–120.

Sloboda, J. A. (1999). Everyday uses of music: A preliminary study. In S. W. Yi (Ed.), *Music, mind, and science* (pp. 354–369). Seoul: Seoul National University Press.

Sloboda, J. A., Lamont, A., & Greasley, A. (2009). Choosing to hear music: Motivation, process and effect. In S. Hallam, I. Cross, & M. Thaut (Eds.), *The Oxford handbook of music psychology* (pp. 431–440). Oxford: Oxford University Press.

Sloboda, J. A., O'Neill, S. A., & Ivaldi, A. (2001). Functions of music in everyday life: An exploratory study using the Experience Sampling Method. *Musicæ Scientiæ, 5*(1), 9–32.

Small, C. (1998). *Musicking: The meanings of performing and listening.* Middletown, CT: Wesleyan University Press.

Stamou, L. (2002). Plato and Aristotle on music and music education: Lessons from Ancient Greece. *International Journal of Music Education, 39*(1), 3–16.

Steinbeis, N., Koelsch, S., & Sloboda, J. A. (2006). The role of harmonic expectancy violations in musical emotions: evidence from subjective, physiological, and neural responses. *Journal of Cognitive Neuroscience, 18*, 380–393.

Tarrant, M., North, A.C., & Hargreaves, D. J. (2002). Youth identity and music. In R. A. R. MacDonald, D. J. Hargreaves, & D. E. Miell (Eds.), *Musical identities* (pp. 134–151). Oxford: Oxford University Press.

Trehub, S. E. (2009). Music lessons from infants. In S. Hallam, I. Cross, & M. Thaut (Eds.), *The Oxford handbook of music psychology* (pp. 229–234). Oxford: Oxford University Press.

Trehub, S. E., Unyk, A. M., Kamenetsky, S. B., Hill, D. S., Trainor, L. J., Henderson, J. L., & Saraza, M. (1997). Mothers' and fathers' singing to infants. *Developmental Psychology*, *33*(3), 500–507.

Willis, P. (1978). *Profane culture*. London: Routledge.

Young, S. (2008). Lullaby light shows: Everyday musical experiences amongst under-two-year-olds. *International Journal of Music Education*, *26*(1), 33–46.

Young, S., Street, A., & Davies, E. (2006) *The music one2one project: Final report*. University of Exeter, UK. Available at: http://education.ex.ac.uk/music-one2one/ (accessed 30 September 2006).

Chapter 5

Musical participation: expectations, experiences, and outcomes

Jane W. Davidson

Abstract

This chapter draws together important strands of work in my own research output and that of John Sloboda: ideas about musical skill, expertise, cultural belief, and social opportunity. It contends that many of us are fearful of musical participation in Western cultures because of a lack of exposure to these strong musical experiences. The experiences themselves fulfil psychological needs for competency, social relatedness, and personal autonomy, which can offer the sufficient and necessary conditions for positive experiences of wellbeing and health. The work relates to singing groups created for social opportunity and therapeutic benefit for maginalized members of society.

I began working for John Sloboda as a post-doctoral research fellow, joining his newly created Centre for the Study of Musical Skill and Development at Keele University, UK, in 1991. I took the position having trained in classical singing, school teaching, and psychology of music research that had focused on expression in performance. During the three years I worked with John I also collaborated with Michael Howe, a highly productive and influential researcher on giftedness. Together, we investigated how children acquired musical performance skills, in particular those individuals on a trajectory for professional career involvement. In parallel to that research, I continued my freelance opera singing, even performing for a choral ensemble John directed. During the same period, John was beginning his research on the relationship between music and emotion.

In selecting a topic for the current volume, I have decided to focus on a project I have been running since my arrival in Australia in 2006 which concerns the forming and monitoring of a programme of group singing activities for adults with no previous musical experiences. It is relevant to and reflective of my relationship with John in many ways: it links to our previous projects where we examined individual biography and the impact of motivation and attributions on participant belief and development in music; it is about singing, something both John and I love to do; also, the work has a strong social motivation, for it aims to assess the impact of the singing experience on participants, and is aimed at investigating individuals who have faced social difficulty. Addressing social disadvantage has increasingly become part of John's agenda in his work seeking non-violent approaches to security and human rights issues.

Overview

This chapter is deliberately broad-ranging, beginning as Sloboda, Davidson, and Howe (1994) had done by exploring how reflections on cultural practices outside one's own everyday experiences facilitate investigating questions about how certain human behaviours are formed and why the beliefs underlying them are developed. It goes on to discuss how in contemporary Western contexts music participation can be employed as a means of offering motivation for learners from young children through to older people. Literature is investigated which indicates that positive engagement leading to wellbeing outcomes can be achieved in many musical experiences, but that these are particularly immediate in group singing contexts where there are few barriers to participation. Data are then discussed which are drawn from detailed interview studies with participants of singing groups founded to work with socially marginalized people: the very old and a group of socially disadvantaged people. The chapter concludes with a discussion of practical applications of the findings.

Reflecting on cultural practices and outcomes

Insights from Africa

Sloboda and colleagues (1994) wrote a piece for the British Psychological Society's publication *The Psychologist* entitled: 'Is everyone musical?'. This paper elicited many responses and heralded a series of publications by the team focused on musical skills development, most of the work emerging from biographical studies of children who were learning musical instruments in Western contexts (see Davidson, Howe, Moore, & Sloboda, 1996, 1998, and Davidson, Howe, & Sloboda, 1997, for an overview of this research).

In the writing, we (Sloboda, Howe, and myself) observed that different cultures had starkly contrasting musical practices with varied opportunities for musical engagement and these affected level of engagement, attainment, and overall quality of experience. John Messenger's work from the 1950s to 1990s with the Anang Ibibo tribe of West Africa (Nigeria) was used as an example where music was highly valued. He noted that try as he might, he could not find a person who was not musical; that is, everyone in the tribe demonstrated an understanding of their specific musical practices, being able to generate appropriate manipulations of musical dynamics, tempo, pitch, and phrasing in performances, thus demonstrating a culturally sensitive musicality; also all members of the community were competent as players, singers, and dancers (Messenger & Messenger, 1992).

Similar examples of extensive musical prowess were discussed in the fieldwork of John Blacking who lived with the Venda people in the north-eastern part of

South Africa, in what is now called Limpopo Province (the research is published most notably in Blacking, 1962, 1964, 1965, 1969, 1973). The Venda thrilled Blacking with their fine musical arts practices, which were used for ceremonies such as initiation rites as well as accompanying everyday activities such as undertaking manual work, in familial contexts such as engaging in playful social songs, and in improvised drinking songs and dances. The musical arts practices offered opportunity for personal expression, social communication, and sharing. This social function of music was especially evident in children's songs and the communication of crucial cultural knowledge: songs informing how girls and boys should relate to one another, how children should deal with family and work responsibilities, and songs for educational purposes (counting, names of body parts, etc.). So, not only was the musical practice an integral part of expression and regulation, it was also a communicator of cultural knowledge that might not otherwise be expressed.

Sloboda and colleagues (1994) used these different African examples to draw contrast with contemporary Western culture—UK, USA, and Australia in particular—where musical opportunities are comparatively limited, with the majority of people having limited experience of musical participation. Music listening, by contrast, is widespread and the broad spectrum of musical media afford frequent listening and viewing across the globe. As Sloboda (2005) notes, this voracious consumption of music is used for self-administered mood regulation, social sharing, and cultural goals—indeed, belonging to the 'right' music-listening group can be used to denote social identification and status. But the separation of musical engagement means that listening has become associated with non-musician engagement and performance has been regarded as a more specialist and demanding activity—a musician's activity—where the potential expressive benefits are not widely experienced.

A model of elite-level musical skills acquisition persuasively shows that in order to learn a complex instrument such as the Western violin or piano, thousands of hours of accumulated task-focused practice (technique, repertoire, etc.) is necessary to reach professional competence (Sloboda, Davidson, Howe, & Moore, 1996; Davidson *et al.*, 1997). On that basis alone, it is easy to see why so many individuals raised in a contemporary Western cultural context might not engage with musical learning long enough to achieve performance competency: it takes a lot of time and requires considerable degree of focused engagement to achieve the skills necessary to perform music with competence. We know that the majority of those who learn a musical instrument, for instance, do indeed terminate within a year of starting, before they are confidently able to play a piece of music (McPherson & Davidson, 2006). Although switching on a CD or watching a live concert does offer expressive and communicative possibility, anecdotes relating to the increased intensity of experience achieved through active musical participation attest to the powerful function of performance (Clarke, Dibben, & Pitts, 2010). This chapter presents a study that aimed to investigate how adults with no former musical performance exposure experience participation, especially when they are required to devote time and effort to practice and overall involvement.

Thus far, it has been shown that we are all affected by music, with music listening having a crucial role across cultures in its use for self-regulation, and social and cultural practice, especially communication and sharing. Participation through music performance is enjoyed by many in cultures such as the Venda, but in Western contemporary practice, performance opportunity has become very uneven and piecemeal, and experienced only by a minority.

Music and motivation for engagement

Research by Davidson and colleagues (1998) and McPherson and Davidson (2006) indicates that specific environmental conditions favour the development of musical skills in Western contexts: supportive parents, siblings, friends, teachers, and ample formal and informal opportunity for engagement. While opportunities are different in Africa, it is possible to see that people engage in music in the context of a highly supportive environment: it is a far more inclusive environment than that found in the West as everyone who participates is highly motivated so to do. But, in order to persist, develop, and grow in desire for musical engagement, it seems that more than environmental factors need to be satisfied. Surveying theories of how and why humans thrive, Deci and Ryan (2000) have noted that just as we have physiological needs such as food and water, we require psychological fulfilment. Three psychological needs are proposed: *competence*, the need to be effective in one's efforts; *relatedness*, the need to be connected socially and integrated in that social group; and *autonomy*, the need to feel that one's activities or pursuits are self-endorsed, self-governed, and of free will. While other psychological needs have been proposed, such as meaningfulness and self-esteem, Deci and Ryan argue that all of these can be explained as subsets or combinations of *competence*, *relatedness*, and *autonomy* (Ryan & Deci, 2002; see Evans, 2009, p 21). When psychological needs are met, human behaviour and experience is enhanced. The relevance of this theoretical proposal for musical engagement is obvious: if we feel able, included, and in personal control of that engagement, enjoyment, progress, and satisfaction are highly likely experiences. Moreover, Deci and Ryan propose that when psychological needs are met, feelings of wellbeing ensue. That is, a sense of happiness, comfort, security, safety, and positive health is promoted (Deci & Ryan, 2002). Evidence of the different cultural approaches to wellbeing and emotions is borne out in Africa where, for example, even though physical needs may be barely met, psychological needs are often fulfilled. For instance, research by Barley (1997) into death and bereavement across the world shows that in African contexts, owing to strong family bonds, the cathartic experience of grief through group mourning using music seems to helps people to recover and accept loss more quickly than Westerners in similar bereavement situations.

Research on competence in Western music learning contexts has revealed that learners experience greater satisfaction of psychological needs when they are most engaged, and less satisfaction at the time they cease musical engagement (Austin & Vispoel, 1998). Indeed, at the time of ceasing to learn a musical instrument, they feel less capable and less autonomous, and also relate less to the people with whom they are engaging: teachers and peers (Austin, Renwick, & McPherson, 2006; McPherson & Davidson, 2002). The musical environment becomes less relevant, and divorced from positive and satisfying conditions for participation. Examining each psychological need as defined by Deci and Ryan, it becomes apparent why Western musical learning for performance has not been widespread (thanks to Paul Evans for detail presented, pages 68–70).

Competency

Competency beliefs and values are influential in approaching any learning situation: we need to believe we can attain competence (Deci & Moller, 2005). In the African music examples, it would seem that music is a means through which people easily pursue and attain competence because everyone is appropriately motivated. Music is valued and believed to be for all, each person assuming that she or he has the capacity to achieve competence. In the West, the story is different, with the expert model for engagement predominating. It would seem that to generate positive conditions to encourage sufficient engagement to achieve perceived as well as actual competency, a shift in Western goal orientation for participation may be necessary. There has been a tendency for those who have not received encouragement to learn an instrument in early childhood to regard musical capacity as something that is fixed, with musical potential being regarded as something that cannot be improved incrementally (McPherson & Davidson, 2006). So, it would seem that if the learning environment can encourage a belief in incremental skills acquisition—with minimal indicators of accomplishment being regarded as sufficient conditions for competency rather than expert fluency—motivation for engagement and a belief in the attainment of competence could potentially be increased.

Relatedness

Humans are highly social beings, with behaviour being dependent on strong forms of connectedness, social expression, and relatedness. The need for relatedness encourages organization of the self within larger social groups to offer mutual protection and sharing and forms a basis for the transmission of knowledge (see Evans, McPherson, & Davidson, under review). According to psychological needs theory, people will tend to choose activities that are conducive to integration and success in their social world, and reject activities that prevent or stifle such integration (Deci & Ryan, 2000). Evidently, with musical arts being central to everyday social engagement in some traditional African contexts, relatedness is strongly experienced in musical practices, thus enhancing feelings of connection. Such outcomes have been recently reported by contemporary Venda fieldwork (see Emberly, 2009, in press; Emberly & Davidson, in press). We cannot deny that relatedness is a strong component of engagement with Western music, especially in popular music listening and concert attendance and dance responses. As a form of cultural practice, pop music offers opportunity for peer identification, social bonds in subcultural practices for generational and trans-generational connection; it is highly pervasive in mass media, bringing a focus for social discussion, if not participation (Clarke *et al.*, 2010). But for Western classical music, the numbers exposed to and involved in its practices are far fewer, and thus the potential for relatedness is restricted to those in a classical music-enriching environment. Indeed, research has demonstrated that in Western classical music, successful learning occurs where there is parental, peer, and teacher engagement to feed a sense of relatedness to others, the sense of connection being strongly mediated by identification to the group (Davidson, Faulkner, & McPherson, 2009). Thus, enhancing the sense of relatedness seems crucial for people to engage with music as participants. Moreover, investigating the role of relatedness in singing for those new to musical experiences will be important to explore the degree to which the activity brings group cohesion and relevance even where the activity is novel.

Autonomy

Autonomy is regarded as being important in all human learning situations because it influences the satisfaction of competence and relatedness. Self-regulation is closely linked with autonomy, since the more individuals internalize regulation, the more they are intrinsically motivated, and therefore more likely to feel as though their actions are self-endorsed and self-governed (Evans, 2008, p 47; Deci, Ryan, & Williams, 1996). Feelings of autonomy facilitate intrinsic motivation and promote the internalization of regulation. Venda culture promotes the development of autonomy with requirements such as entry to performance groups for display or competition being permitted only once certain basic skills have been achieved, and so youngsters are left free to explore through trial and error at the margins of the everyday musical environment, being able to enter the performance group once their learning challenges have been met. It is common to see young children playing alongside a musical group, standing at the border, trialling songs and dances, working autonomously, highly internally motivated, to attain the level necessary to join the troupe or team (Emberly, 2009). Of course, such autonomy can occur in Western music contexts, with some of the greatest performers in history being highly autonomous in their learning. For instance, jazz trumpeter Louis Armstrong learned within the highly musical environment of New Orleans, and through repeated self-stimulated exposure to music and plenty of opportunity for individual practice, he was able to acquire the skills necessary to learn the trumpet with limited instruction (Collier, 1983).

The examples of highly self-regulated musical engagement tend to commonly occur in popular forms of music learning such as jazz or pop music, where there is a strong interface between group and individual learning—pop musicians learning together, motivating one another as they develop sufficient and necessary skills to fulfil their creative and performance needs (Green, 2002). This does not happen that often in classical music. Indeed, in learning Western musical performance skills it is common for the learner to report feeling incapable, owing to the adoption of few or inappropriate strategies to engage in certain kinds of work such as individual practice (McPherson & Davidson, 2006). So, finding ways to facilitate ownership and self-motivation for engagement is important, and it will be necessary to investigate this approach in the current study.

In summary, psychological needs must be met for successful learning and sustained engagement with music. Western cultural practices around classical music learning have tended to restrict both access to and the perceived potential for engagement. It is not surprising that many adults in Western contexts have never had performance opportunities and feel that music-making could never meet their psychological needs requirements. Indeed, those who have tried and failed to engage with practical music-making often have poor self-perception owing to poor learning experiences.

An aim of the research described in this chapter was to understand what factors were necessary to engage adults to committed musical practice where they had never previously been involved in music-making, with the goal of understanding which opportunities would facilitate the satisfaction of psychological needs. Another aim of the investigation was to explore the extent to which wellbeing could be achieved through the music-making opportunity, noting that Deci and Ryan (2000) argue that if psychological needs are met, then the conditions for good mental health and wellbeing are achieved.

Music, emotional experience, and healing

When relating wellbeing to musical experience it is known that musical listening and performance can elicit physiological responses such as shivers down the spine or palpitations (Sloboda, 1991). Since different pieces of music elicit different physiological responses, it seems that there is a psycho-physiological basis for discrimination of emotional responses to music: crying or laughing as a result of listening or participation, which are themselves contingent on factors such as who we are with, or what we are doing or thinking when exposed to the musical experience. In Chapter 7, Patrik Juslin presents a theoretical explanation that provides the bases for the mechanisms through which music might induce emotion. These mechanisms range from rhythmic entrainment (an external rhythm in the music influences some internal 'bodily rhythm of the listener so that the latter's rhythm adjusts toward and eventually "locks in" to a common periodicity', p. 122) to musical expectancy ('a specific feature of the music violates, delays or confirms the listener's expectations about the continuation of the music' p. 123) as well as contagion (i.e. 'where the listener "mimics" the emotional expression of the music internally').

Whether these mechanisms stand up to empirical testing is still to be investigated, however, it is certain that music can offer a profound emotional experience. Indeed, the modern Western discipline of music therapy has explored ways in which musical interventions can assist in promoting both physical and psychological wellbeing in a range of contexts (Bunt, 1994). Examples of such therapeutic work are: a mentally ill individual being presented with musical opportunity to play out emotional expressions of anxiety and anger through to regulate and calm mood; a terminally ill patient using music to express their grief and sense of loss; an opportunity for individuals with restricted movement or movement control problems to synchronize and coordinate with others using musical stimuli (see Ansdell, 1995, and Pavlicevic & Ansdell 2004, for more details); and group work using music to explore feelings of empathy and emotional transference (Odell-Miller, 2005; Robarts, 2006). Strong emotional affect through music clearly offers huge potential for physical and cognitive stimulation as well as the evocation of collective experience. It was with these potentials in mind that the current project was developed.

In the West, outside the specialist domain of music therapy, benefits of participation in music have been promoted in a series of arts and health initiatives, e.g. the National Network for the Arts in Health (UK), and the Music in Healthcare Partnership Project (Ireland). Preliminary evaluations (Windsor, 2005) suggest that such arts programmes engage people, eliciting immediate responses that can subsequently lead to positive 'knock-on effects' (Greaves & Farbus 2006, p. 141) for longer-term psychological and physical wellbeing. In one study, older adults who participated in a short-term theatre training programme showed significant improvements on measures of cognitive performance and psychological wellbeing (Staricoff, 2004). The activities parallel the types of engagement observed in the Venda and Anang contexts and they remind us that musical facilitation is perhaps something whose needs are better represented in contemporary Western society, in other words, finding ways to offer musical experiences in order for people to optimize their potential for musical engagement.

Given that for most musical instruments, it does take time to learn the basic skills for playing, and an aim of this research was to investigate participants who were new to their music-making activity, it was decided to focus the current research on singing activity. Singing is a particularly immediate form of engagement for those new to music-making experiences as it has few skill barriers to participation. In essence, we can all open our mouths and sing, whereas we can spend weeks just learning how to generate a musical tone from a reed instruments such as the oboe.

Singing

Cohen, Perlstein, Chapline, Kelly, Firth, and Simmens (2006) found that older people with mood disorders who engaged in choral participation, in contrast with a comparison group who undertook different activities, reported improved general health and morale, reduced loneliness, had fewer visits to doctors, and reported a reduction in the number of over-the-counter medications taken. Betty Bailey and I (Bailey & Davidson, 2005) demonstrated that homeless men benefited from a singing group formed in their soup kitchen in Montreal, with the singing experience leading to feelings of personal pride in achievement. In the light of these previous studies, singing groups seemed to offer good potential for the current project.

The needs of older people and the socially disadvantaged in Western society

Surveys reveal that while many older people enjoy good health, more than half have some disability that restricts everyday activities. A proportion of these people are likely to experience high or very high levels of psychological distress, as they are typically adults who live alone (Flood, 2005). There is evidence that older people are significantly more likely than other members of society to lose family members and friends, and be more vulnerable to loneliness and social isolation. Berkman and Glass (2000) cited evidence that socially isolated people have between two and five times greater risk of dying from all causes compared with those who maintain close ties with family, friends, and the community.

Homeless people are clearly a vulnerable sector of Western society, with many finding themselves in marginalized life situations owing to mental health problems. Finding strategies to offer social and emotional support is crucial. We should be prepared and able to develop care and life satisfaction strategies to address people's concerns and cope with their situations.

It is a sad reflection that Western society has evolved in a manner that permits vulnerable individuals to remain on the margins of society (see Bailey & Davidson, 2005). Of course, although poverty is a huge issue in Africa, people are generally socially supported within their village communities by extended family networks, with older and socially vulnerable people being cared for (Emberly, 2009). It is not the intention here to continue a comparison between Western and African social structures, but rather to explore how participation in singing Western music can be used in Western contexts for socio-emotional benefit and greater wellbeing through the satisfaction of psychological needs.

In the section that follows, I explore the experience of group singing participation by interviewing a sample of participants from two very different community singing groups.

Case study groups

Note: to preserve confidentiality, identifying characteristics of the participants have been anonymized. The work reported here was subject to the University of Western Australia's human ethics procedures.

The Sound of Song

This group, hitherto referred to as SOS, was formed within the past few years for recruiting people coming from backgrounds of homelessness, long-term unemployment, social exclusion, histories of substance abuse, and mental illness. The group is supported by charity workers and is led by an experienced male community musician (referred to as Y below). The choir has approximately 30 members who range in age from young adults to older people.

The Senior Singers

This group, hitherto referred to as TSS, has recruitment targeted around people over the age of 70 years who live alone and are in receipt of home-help care. It was created by the University of Western Australia and has been co-sponsored by a health promotion organization, and is directed by an experienced female community musician (referred to as X below). The group comprises some 35 members, with an ever-growing base. The oldest participant is 94 years of age.

Data collection

Data were collected by carrying out informal semi-structured interviews with a cross-section of singers. Questions asked included topics relating to motivation for joining, ongoing experience, positive and negative aspects of involvement, and impact of experience on each participant's self-confidence and social connection; in other words, issues related to the underlying psychological needs. The types of question were developed from Evans and colleagues (under review). The interviews were transcribed for analytical purposes and subjected to interpretative phenomenological analysis techniques (see Smith, 2003, and Smith, Flowers, & Larkin, 2009).

Participants

A total of 16 people were interviewed: eight members of SOS (four women and four men) and eight members of TSS (four women and four men). These people are identified by gender and choir codes only (e.g. male SOS1, female SOS2; female TSS1; female TSS2, etc.)

Analysis

The key themes identified are discussed below and focus on the following areas:

1 The challenges of joining a new social group: getting started
2 Approaching the challenge of the activity: being a singer; being a performer; being a musician
3 Structure and freedom in the workshops
4 Therapeutic experience
5 Social opportunity
6 Role of the facilitator
7 Complexities of psychological needs
8 Expansion.

The challenges: getting started

As might be expected, the idea of joining a new group for adults who have experienced loneliness and personal difficulty was challenging.

> *Female (TSS1)*: 'It was very difficult turning up to the first session. I did not know a soul. I couldn't have gone alone. The home-help service sent me a leaflet about joining and then provided me with a lift to the first eight sessions. When the car turned up on the first morning, I had to go. It would have been easier to stay inside, but I went. Looking back, it was nerve-wracking, but now, I couldn't imagine my life without the choir.'

> *Male (SOS1)*: 'Going along in there with Y there, well that was hard. I wouldn't say I'm shy, but going along to join a whole bunch of strangers is tough.'

> *Female (TSS2)*: 'Going in the room on the first day was very hard for me. Walking in with a group of strangers was something I'd not done for years and years. As you get older, you tend to lose confidence in yourself. That was hard.'

> *Female (SOS2)*: 'Something inside me said: "Have a go, because if you don't do it now, you'll never do it." So, I did, and I've never regretted it for a second. I plucked up the courage to go and I did it. It is none of those scary things I thought it could be.'

Finding ways to encourage people to cross barriers to joining a new group is important, especially with older people who face a growing lack of social confidence when their social networks are diminished as partners and friends start to die as they move into the final stage of life. As evident from the cases above, TSS was formed to encourage people to get out of the house and have new experiences and meet new social contacts; the potential participants were provided with lifts and their home-helps proactively encouraged them to join the group. For SOS, the charity workers recruited the members. The crucial element for both groups was that there was someone assisting the members to make the journey from their own world into this new socio-musical one. Once there, none of the people interviewed ever felt like dropping out.

> *Male (TSS3)*: 'At the start, it was tense, but the leader cracked a joke and that was it: the ice was broken. It took a while, but little by little the people would chat. It got better and better.'

> *Female (SOS3)*: 'We're not one big happy family, but in the context of the group, may be we are. From that first meeting, I thought: "This will be ok as they're an ok bunch of people."'

For recruitment to both groups, information had been widely distributed to people who never answered an advert or attended, so as to understand what prevented engagement and thereby gain insights into barriers to participation. For those who joined, besides making that initial effort to attend, they had to tackle many matters such as what it was like to be a singer and a musician.

Approaching the challenges

Being a singer

None of the people interviewed had ever imagined themselves joining a singing group, and none had ever experienced previous formal singing experience.

> *Male (SOS)*: 'Sing, me? I thought it was a crazy idea. Weird, not and not for my sort of world: "Former druggie meets Luciano Pavarotti." Now that's a joke!'

Yet, all had interviewees had engaged in singing in their early lives.

> *Female (SOS4)*: 'I used to sing all the time as a child: in the playground, with my Mum at the park. But, that is different to being in a proper choir. I mean, being at home isn't really proper singing—you know, being able to sing scales, harmonies, hold a line.'

The view that 'proper' singing was something for which you had to be skilled or refined or special was common. Yet, all of the participants from both groups had somehow managed, despite highly negative views about themselves as potential singers, to join the group and involve themselves in the singing experience.

> *Female (SOS3)*: 'I'm no singer, but I thought: 'Well, it is a group so no one will be able to hear me. In a group you can vanish a bit. It took me a while to really sing out. But now, I do and I can.'

> *Male (SOS5)*: 'I would never have considered myself a candidate for a singing group: voice like a fog-horn. These days I think everyone can and should do it. It is not so hard. I really belt it out and no one tells me to shut up or anything. I sing because that's what I'm there to do and everyone else seems to be doing the same.'

> *Male (SOS6)*: 'When I was in my "out there" phase as a real alcoholic, I would have never joined anything like a singing group that performs classical music

in Latin! But, you reflect on life and you think: "Why not give it a go, you've got nothing else to lose!" When you sing with the others there is a discipline to it. I didn't realise how precise it has to be: come in together; blend in together; pronounce your words clearly; try to sing that high note stronger or softer; watch your tuning. There's a precision and beauty to it. Being a singer is not easy, but it is better and more enjoyable that I imagined. Being a singer also means you've got to be a team player. Team-building can be challenging' [*smirks*].

Thus the data clearly reveal that singing sets new challenges and provides new opportunities. Performing added considerably to these novel experiences.

Being a performer

Female (TSS4): 'My grandchildren thought it was brilliant that I was going to be performing in a concert. Of course I go and see them at swimming events and in school concerts, but when all the family came to see and hear me in a concert, now that was something special! I've never been one for the spotlight. Getting applause and being praised in public is important recognition. It gives you worth. I don't think I've ever had applause for anything else I do.'

Male (SOS7): 'On the streets no one takes notice of you—apart from moving you on and shouting at you because you're homeless. When you get up in a concert and all those eyes are looking at you, then applauding you and praising you; well it is fabulous.'

The value of performance evidently offered a sense of pride in the achievement; it was also apparent that the performance activity itself contributed to feelings of self-worth and being valued by others.

Male (SOS7): 'In the group, I've become the rock figure. I didn't think I had a good voice and then Y asked me if I'd try a solo. I panicked, but did it and everyone though I had this real great and gravelly voice. Then, I started practising along to rock CDs and stuff. Now, I get up there and sing solos for anyone. I have something good to offer: I sing and people like me in a different sort of way. Performing gives another side to my sense of who I am. I feel good at what I'm doing. I'm no trained musician, but I can do the job and other people tell me that.'

So, revealing that performance puts a person into special role, the respondent also noted that he was not a musician, which was a view expressed across the interviews, though all did come to recognize that they had found new skills that could be improved with practice: a view that was evidently quite alien to some of the participants.

Being a musician

Female (SOS8): 'I never knew I'd be able to do that: Ha! [*laughs*]. But, I can and I'm getting better at the music the more we do. When I was younger I thought music was something you could either do or you couldn't. I now see it is about how you regard yourself and how you face its challenges.'

Male (TSS): 'Well, it is a singing group, isn't it. We're not musicians like X, I mean she can read music, be precise about the counting. I do try to express what she tells me about interpretation. I like it all because I'm learning something new in music. But, musicians really understand the technical things and they play musical instruments as well.'

Male (SOS1): 'We're not really musicians: we don't play from music or anything. But, we can be musical in what we achieve. We perform with emotion and the spirit. This means we're musical.'

Although most interviewees believed they were not musicians owing to a lack of technical competency, they could see they had the capacity to express themselves musically—in other words, they had the capacity to be appropriately expressive with the musical materials. In fact, of all interviewees, only two women could read music. Both ladies had learned the piano as children, but then had not done anything active for some 60 years. Both felt that the singing group was of an appropriate standard for them now. They did not want to reintroduce the stress of having to read music and work in a technical manner, but like the others, they wanted to experience the 'beauty of the music itself'.

In summary, having musical experiences were vital to all participants. While musicianship offered new and different types of opportunity, their goals were not to become musicians, indeed, in some cases, they were happy to select TSS because it had been specifically promoted as not requiring any former experiences.

Structure and freedom in the workshop

All choristers noted how important it was that the sessions offered a clear structure. Not only did it give them a sense of 'knowing what you're doing and where you're going', but it also helped them both physically and mentally with the singing task itself. The sessions ran by the two different leaders followed a similar outline: a warming up element, work on repertoire and a summarizing ending.

Male (SOS5): 'Warming up gets me going. Going over what we've learned makes me leave feeling I've achieved something and it helps me to remember the tune so that I can practise it for next time. The middle bit of the session is always the most work: trying to learn new songs. But, knowing where you've got to be [in] the tea break is always encouraging.'

But, perhaps most important was the repertoire.

Female (SOS3): 'We've written our own stuff, we do covers, we sing what we like and what we know. On that basis, we know others will like our stuff too.'

Female (TSS6): 'I love the songs: old time and newer ones, but most of all mainly ones I know. We did a concert for a charity event and we had to learn a song to sing with the other choirs. In the end, it was brilliant to learn a new song, but while we were learning it I hated it until I got to really know it. I think we prefer ones we already know.'

Getting the balance between familiarity, liking, and new and challenging repertoire was something both leaders worked at in each session. The requirement showed a fine balance of skills and evidence of the leaders being highly sensitive to the therapeutic potentials of their work.

Therapeutic potentials

The singing experience itself

Participants were aware of quite profound impact of the experience.

> *Female (TSS4)*: 'It had an astonishing effect on me. I realized that as much as I like music (I listen a lot) I don't sing. I'm now singing in the car all the time, something I haven't done before [*laughs*]. ... [the singing group] is an hour and a half of forgetting any sorts of troubles and worries, it really is. It's a sort of physical high, it's amazing.'

So the group facilitated a new sort of identification with musical experience, a new experience that did lead to a strong physical impact, as another member commented:

> *Female (TSS6)*: 'You let yourself loose sort of ... and it makes you get a buzz out of it afterwards. You feel very happy and it elates you afterwards ... it's a nice overwhelming thing ... and it does help with your breathing and you see with swimming it's the same sort of thing ... and you come out actually exhausted but very ... well what is it the endorphins or something running around and you feel very elated. They say the same with singing. I mean for all you know the standing and sitting, but your breathing ... Sometimes you can feel the stinging at the back of your throat with just you know ... the hard work. And then we'd come home and have a cup of tea and the pair of us would both be asleep' [*laughs*].

A member of the SOS added:

> *Female (SOS8)*: 'I go into a different place when I sing: I'm flying, better than any drug. That high makes you feel as though you've run a marathon. You know: exhausted but satisfied.'

It seems that the physicality of the activity was crucial to the experience and this was perceived by all the interviewees to have a tangible wellbeing impact. For example, in both groups, physical and vocal warm-ups were done at the start of each session and many participants commented as follows:

> *Female (SOS4)*: 'Warm-ups make you aware of your body, and that helps you feel alive: sensing every bit of yourself. Sometimes we dance and stuff and that is real fun. Singing and dancing is what it is about: getting yourself in contact with your life, and energy! It makes you feel better, uplifted, fitter and healthier.'

Many commented on the importance of memory stimulation, and the significance of the repertoire to them and their past lives.

> *Female (TSS2)*: 'I wouldn't say I got teary, but when you haven't heard those songs for so many years and your memory goes back ... to when you sort of ... family company and that.'

> *Male (SOS7)*: 'Man, I think about those bad times and those sad times and those good times with the songs we sing. It brings me to a good place. Before I did the singing group I used to get stuck in my mood and in one of those times. Singing helps to remember and see that life isn't so bad.'

Female (TSS2): 'Expressing through being in the music is very powerful. It is another way of being. It permits you to be together with everyone in the music—part of the harmony, like one whole thing. But, you're also independent. So, in music you can be small and big, contributing in different ways to the whole. May be that's particularly true of singing groups?'

This participant's notion of 'being in the music' is a key concept in Nordoff–Robbins music therapy (see Nordoff & Robbins, 1971, 1983, 2007, for details). It highlights the role of musical material operating on the individual, with emotional responses being elicited by the musical structures (see Chapter 7), and these are regarded as being central to the experience. From this perspective, it is evident that skilled music therapists manipulate musical material for mood affect.

The approach of Nordoff-Robbins does contrast with some other music therapy philosophies. Some psychodynamic approaches work more fundamentally on the premise that there is 'music in therapy'. Their belief is that music accompanies a therapeutic process, with elements such as interpersonal exchange through talk and other social processes being equal partners in the experience (see Robarts, 2006). It is evident from music therapy outcomes that a combination of processes are in fact likely to shape outcome: in major part, the emotional impact and regulation of the musical material physiologically as well as cognitively; and in a purely social manner, offering companionship.

From the interviewee's (TSS2) response above, it is apparent that being part of the group experience influenced her. A significant comment is that in the group singing experience she can be part of a musical whole as well as an individual having a personal experience. This is clearly the case that in most group behaviours you make a significant individual contribution. The notion of being part of a musical whole or an individual within a whole is worth further consideration, because it can help to explain the specific experience of relatedness. It makes people feel close emotionally and physically.

Female (TSS6): 'Singing makes you feel happy. Also, close physically and emotionally to the group.'

Male (SOS5): 'Singing, I've discovered feelings of closeness again. After the bad stuff I've been through and put my family though, it feels so good to "belong".'

Female (TSS6): 'The truth is that as you get older, you're less attractive and there are far fewer opportunities for intimacy. When your husband dies, well you don't get that sort of physical reassurance. I've found with singing that you get close to the people emotionally and physically, you know I can feel the hairs on the back of my neck stand up when the men sing those lower harmonies.'

Consonant with the literature explored at the start of this paper, it seems that the group singing links physical, emotional, and social factors for the participants.

Male (SOS7): 'Singing helps me feel good and strong physically and inside my head. I do it to lift my spirits. I like being with the other people, sharing in the sound together.'

This therapeutic link to relatedness can be best explained by considering social opportunity (see next section).

Social opportunity

While the previous examples demonstrated the importance of social interactions, some of the participants found this experience to have quite independent musical and non-musical components.

> *Male (TSS7)*: 'The tea break is great fun. You catch up on the news and share some cake you've made and things like that. I found the baking stressful at first because I had never really used the oven for cakes. When you're alone you don't bake or even cook much, especcially when your wife used to do all that. But, the idea is that we bring food to share and that's good. It makes every week like a special party or something.'

There is evidently space for social sharing and offering which not only links back to former skills and experiences, but which also demonstrates that members want to contribute to the whole experience in a range of ways.

> *Male (SOS6)*: 'I don't have a car or anything—no money for that. I haven't really got much money for the bus either. So, I walk everywhere. Nowadays some of the others come with me, or some of them give me a lift. They look out for me.'

So, the group has also provided a network of support. This was very evident among the TSS members, who had been offered a volunteer driving service when the singing group was initially formed, but over time, this support ceased.

> *Female (TSS4)*: 'At first the home-help service provided me with a lift to the group, but after the eighth session, that all stopped. So, we had to organize ourselves. This very nice lady, [gives name], picks me up and two others, so we have a carful. I look forward to it. I couldn't go if it wasn't for the lift. Actually, we've been doing this for two years now, so when the driver celebrated her eightieth birthday a couple of weeks ago, the three of us who take the lift all went out for breakfast with her. It was so nice. I never thought I'd be able to make three new and dear friends at my age. We all just get along so well. We all met at the singing.'

The programme for TSS has incorporated a tea break for social purposes; it had also aimed to develop the group to such an extent that it would become self-sustaining.

> *Male (TSS7)*: 'We're going to manage the group between us: you know, organize the venue, fix concerts, even apply for our own funding. We've now got our own committee and everything.'

Having a plan for the future in mind was certainly the case of TSS. The other group had been set up much more casually. But, it was evident from the respondents comments that leadership offered by the facilitators was crucial to the success of the two groups.

The positive social experiences, inevitably linked to musical ones, were heavily shaped by the singing group leaders. All interviewees were incredibly positive about the leaders and the challenges they presented the choristers.

Leadership and social facilitation

While the facilitators in the two groups described above did not have a formal training in how to work therapeutically, both had experienced leadership roles with many different music groups. Their experience and extensive knowledge enabled them to generate a positive social ambience as well as gauging what could be attained with their respective groups. They selected and used the material for a range of effects.

Male (SoS7): 'Y is fabulous. He knows what sort of thing we'd like to do: an old 1960s rock number or a quite interesting classical piece. But, he also helps us to create our own songs. A few of us have helped him and we sing one of our own songs as our anthem. It's great. Y is a very good guy. He knows when to tell us to pull into line and he also knows when to encourage us. Sometimes we talk about all sorts of stuff.'

Male (TSS8): 'X she's a classic. She's just so funny. The way she introduces every session with a joke to get our diaphragms working is just great. She sets a tone. She won't let anyone change that mood. She's very clever. One of two can be a bit awkward at times, but she just encourages them and you know, she works it all out. The songs are lovely. *Non nobis domine* is my favourite. It is classical, but easy to remember.'

These specific leadership characteristics seemed to encourage feelings of autonomy among the singers. That need to feel that one's activities or pursuits are self-endorsed, self-governed, and of free will, was experienced in both group contexts, but very much more verbalized by the membership of SOS, and this clearly had a strong relationship to their backgrounds.

Female (SOS2) comments: 'I get to say what I think and what I want. I do things just as I like. We all do. Some of us have been like running for years. Try to ties us down and we're like caged birds. Y let's us fly in the music. I feel like I'm me.'

Male (SOS7): 'The group makes me feel strong. It is really up to me whether I go or not, because nobody's forcing me to do it, but I go because Y and the guys are good and I feel like they want me too.'

Female (SOS4): 'Y's a great bloke—just a cool musician. He let's me try out songs and helps me get the right notes.'

Male (TSS8): 'She was a delight … she could entertain me 23 hours a day! I thought she was A1. I went because I wanted to. But, I also went to hear her.'

Male (TSS3): 'She makes it, she treats everybody the same … She is very nice and I get along well with her and she's a good teacher.'

Female (TSS6): 'She's so beautiful and sometimes when we make a mistake! [*laughter*] … she's so beautiful and funny with us.'

The facilitators themselves knew how important their own previous experiences were and how their own skills shaped the groups. After these interviews and initial analysis, they were both asked to comment on their roles:

X (TSS): 'I always believe in fun, but I challenge them a bit too. Not too much though, as I want them to feel safe. You begin with simple things like breathing, then a bit more technique and them eventually, you can vary the repertoire from very straight forward unison songs, to parts and rounds. It takes a long time to build their confidence and develop the dynamic in a way that they will rise to the new challenges that I set. You learn to follow a routine to give people a structure and a formula. Sometimes I get complaints if I don't do things the same as usual.'

Y (SOS): 'We talk about all sorts of things from social through to musical and sometimes very personal stuff, but we keep moving, and getting through the singing too, because I need to balance up all their needs with the central role of the group: to sing. It seems that all the other stuff happens too, quite naturally, but I've got to keep my material in the session. We try to work on creative work too: bringing some lyrics, writing a new tune and that sort of thing.'

The two facilitators reveal the role of experience. But they also illustrate that there is a need to balance and be flexible with their groups. As the next section reveals, a range of psychological approaches needed to be balanced in order for the groups to have impact on the individuals and this was a responsibility as much falling with the participant choristers as each facilitator.

The complexities of the psychological factors

Respondents relayed something of the complex interaction of factors necessary for these groups to offer some wellbeing benefit: the experience facilitated autonomy, yet relatedness, indeed, delight in being entertained and challenged and taught by the facilitator, and also the need to be connected to the others in the group. A sense of competency was perhaps always less certain, but sufficient to sustain a committed involvement, in part the result of a socio-emotional fulfilment related to the musical material itself.

Female (SOS2): 'It is within my range and I'm improving: we're all getting better together.'

Male (TSS8): 'You're dealing with a really specialized age group … and they need company, they need interactions with other human beings … With the singing group, it fitted exactly what they were looking for. That's why they came, they enjoyed you know, it was tailor-made it for a group of people … This group was for people whose voices are on the way out and who haven't got time to learn about point and counterpoint and harmony and all the rest of the music. The people went not for hard work, they went to enjoy music with a minimum of [music technique] mental exertion … It was a perfect balance with a great leader. You felt good, challenged and you were happy. There is no other thing to think about when you are there … It is a special place.'

Male (SOS1): 'I sometimes have to think less about myself and sometimes about others. Sometimes I don't want to do the songs nor the exercises, but I do them for everyone else. You have to try to balance between what you want and need and what the others want and what Y has time to do in the sessions.'

All the interview data point towards the singing groups being particularly successful in offering positive impact because of their structures (sharing group experiences) and the materials they deal with (music for emotional affect), with these collective conditions fulfilling the participants' psychological needs. Singing is perhaps the most significant and useful medium for group musical engagement with Western adults because the barrier to participation are minimal (no instrumental skill is required, nor capacity to read music). Singing also has strong physical and cognitive components which make the participants feel both exercised and challenged. Furthermore, the individual contribution to the group is crucial, yet the group sound and feeling is more significant than the individual exposure, thus group singing is a safe as well as challenging context.

But, besides the responses that one might have anticipated given the theoretical contextualization offered at the start of the chapter, these singing groups perhaps reveal that it is the opportunity for personal expansion and ever deepening emotional satisfaction that gives a clue as to how and why such music groups can offer ongoing levels of positive opportunity for wellbeing. One of the most significant aspects of the singing group process to emerge during the interviews was the idea of each individual being on a new trajectory, one in which they experienced personal growth through an expanded sense of what they could achieve and what they had experienced.

Expansion

For one member, it was noted how singing led to him to making a new kind of social contact with a friend outside the choir:

> *Male (TSS7)*: 'In between sessions, I'm going around recording all the songs … I made a copy for a friend of mine … we sit at her place and we put the tape on and we sing together.'

Thus, the participatory musical experience offered new kinds of emotional expression, self-satisfaction and social opportunity with a friend. Similar experiences were reported by many and one woman, TSS1, re-evaluated her love of music to be a love of musical participation through singing. Prior to the singing group, she had considered her radio listening to be her only musical pleasure, but joining the group, she realized that she loved to sing, and that was a crucial part of her Sunday church worship which she had virtually overlooked, not having regarded herself to be a singer.

Expansion of horizons also included wanting to learn new repertoire and face new musical challenges.

> *Male (TSS3)*: 'We like our familiar stuff, you know: songs from the Second World War and all that, but we're trying to learn new music: music my kids listened to when they were teenagers. We even did some quite high brow classical stuff.'

This sort of expansion resonates strongly with Cohen's (2005) notion of the liberation phase he had observed among old American adults. He argues that older people are in fact more open to new experiences that younger people, even though they are perhaps intimidated by social challenges and overwhelmed by loneliness and shyness; their desire to try something before their time runs out is evident in many of the statements above and suggests how the personal, social and feelings of competency resonate with Deci and Ryan's psychological needs theory needs.

Concluding comments

The background literature discussed at the opening of this chapter proposed that we can and should all benefit from musical participation. It seems that African cultural opportunities are rich in artistic practices that offer psychological needs satisfaction and wellbeing benefit through active participation. Westerners have impoverished access to musical participation through performance, even though evidence in Western contexts is beginning to reveal the important social, musical, and personal benefits simple activities such as group singing can afford. The chapter then explored case study data from two socially marginalized groups in Western culture to demonstrate the wellbeing effects of singing participation, especially benefits related to social contact and the singing experience itself. Data from the participants revealed emotional, physical, and cognitive benefits. The group leader was shown to have a major role in facilitating the social processes and also provided a significant motivation for the participants to attend. Participation was an emotionally powerful experience many of the group members had not anticipated. The study also revealed that many participants, especially the very old people, were open to the new challenges of singing. This point was discussed in relation to Cohen's (2005) focus on a liberation phase which he has observed to develop in the final stage of life.

Taken together the literature explored and the data discussed revealed that singing programmes can offer effective means of providing social connection, musical, physical, and emotional experiences, all of which satisfy the needs of the participants and so lead to a positive impact on wellbeing. It is also important to note that these singing programmes can be offered at little cost and that a simple and effective programme can be developed along basic principles of introductory exercises to warm the voice and establish good group relations; then working on repertoire; and finishing with summarizing work for memorization and closure of the session.

Finally, in terms of developmental process and conditions for learning, it seems that given the desire for expansion and liberation experienced by the participants in the singing programmes described in this chapter, we could and should be working towards expanding conceptions of human development as a lifelong process. Whilst some skills are perhaps more difficult to acquire in later life owing to some of the degenerative conditions associated with ageing—arthritis being a difficult challenge to overcome if trying to learn the piano or guitar, for instance—singing and other instruments such as the harmonica, flute, some percussion, and drums are instantaneous providers of new opportunity. The quick progress in learning and potential for group integration and experience can assist in finding liberation and developing new interests and opportunities for an all-round positive musical experience.

Acknowledgement

The author wishes to thank all participants and sponsors of the current research programme. Special thanks to John Sloboda for encouraging the author to develop her studies and practical interests in music and psychology.

References

Ansdell, G. (1995). *Music for life*. London: Jessica Kingsley.

Austin, J. R., Renwick, J. M., & McPherson, G. E. (2006). Developing motivation. In G. E. McPherson (Ed.), *The child as musician: a handbook of musical development* (pp. 213–238). Oxford: Oxford University Press.

Austin, J. R., & Vispoel, W. P. (1998). How American adolescents interpret success and failure in classroom music: Relationships among attributional beliefs, self-concept and achievement. *Psychology of Music, 26*, 26–45.

Bailey B. A., & Davidson J. W. (2005). Effects of group singing and performance on maginalized and middle-class singers. *Psychology of Music, 33*(3): 269–303.

Barley, N. (1997). *Grave matters: a lively history of death around the world.* New York, NY: Henry Holt and Company.

Berkman L., & Glass T. (2000). Social integration, social networks, social support and health. In L. Berkman, & I. Kawachi (Eds.), *Social epidemiology* (pp. 137–173). New York, NY: Oxford University Press.

Blacking, J. (1962). Musical expeditions of the Venda. *African Music 3*(1), 54–72.

Blacking, J. (1964). *Black background: the childhood of a South African girl.* London: Abelard Schuman.

Blacking, J. (1965). The role of music in the culture of the Venda of the Northern Transvaal. In M. Kolinski (Ed.), *Studies in ethnomusicology* (pp. 20–52). New York, NY: Oak.

Blacking, J. (1969). Songs, dance, mimes and symbolism of Venda Girl's initiation schools, Parts 1–4. *African Studies, 28*(1–4).

Blacking, J. (1973). *How musical is man?* Seattle, WA: University of Washington Press.

Bunt, L. (1994). *Music therapy: an art beyond words.* London: Routledge.

Clarke, E. F., Dibben, N. J., & Pitts, S. E. (2010). *Music and the mind in everyday life.* Oxford: Oxford University Press.

Cohen, G. (2005). *The mature mind.* New York, NY: Basic Books.

Cohen, G. D., Perlstein, S., Chapline, J., Kelly, J., Firth, K. M., & Simmens, S. (2006). The impact of professionally conducted cultural programs on the physical health, mental health, and social functioning of older adults. *Gerontologist, 46*(6):726–734.

Collier, J. L. (1983). *Louis Armstrong: an American genius.* New York, NY: Oxford University Press.

Davidson, J. W., Faulkner, R., & McPherson, G. E. (2009). Motivating musical learning. *Psychologist, 22*(12), 1026–1029.

Davidson, J. W., Howe, M. J. A., Moore, D. M., & Sloboda, J. A. (1996). The role of parental influences in the development of musical ability. *British Journal of Developmental Psychology, 14*, 399–412.

Davidson, J. W., Howe, M. J. A., Moore, D. M., & Sloboda, J. A. (1998). The role of teachers in the development of musical ability. *Journal of Research in Music Education, 46*, 141–160.

Davidson, J. W., Howe, M. J. A., & Sloboda, J. A. (1997). Environmental factors in the development of musical performance skill in the first twenty years of life. In D. J. Hargreaves, & A. C. North (Eds.), *The social psychology of music* (pp. 188–203). Oxford: Oxford University Press.

Deci, E. L., & Moller, A. C. (2005). The concept of competence: A starting place for understanding intrinsic motivation and self-determined extrinsic motivation. In A. Elliot & C. Dweck (Eds.), *Handbook of competence motivation* (pp. 579–597). New York, NY: Guilford Press.

Deci, E. L., & Ryan, R. M. (2000). The 'what' and 'why' of goal pursuits: Human needs and the self-determination of behavior. *Psychological Inquiry, 11*, 227–268.

Deci, E. L., & Ryan, R. M. (Eds.). (2002). *Handbook of self-determination research.* Rochester, NY: University of Rochester Press.

Deci, E. L., Ryan, R. M., & Williams, G. C. (1996). Need satisfaction and the self-regulation of learning. *Learning and Individual Differences, 8*, 165–183.

Emberly, A. (2009). '*Mandela went to China . . . and India too': musical cultures of childhood in South Africa*. PhD dissertation. University of Washington, Washington.

Emberly, A. (in press). Venda children's musical cultures in Limpopo, South Africa. In T. Wiggins, & P. Campbell (Eds.), *Oxford handbook of children's musical cultures*. Oxford: Oxford University Press.

Emberly, A., & Davidson, J. W. (in press). From the kraal to the classroom: Shifting musical arts practices from the community to the school with special reference to learning tshigombela in Limpopo, South Africa. *International Journal of Music Education*.

Evans, P. (2008) *Psychological Needs and social-cognitive influences on participation in music activities*. PhD dissertation. University of Illinois at Urbana-Champaign.

Evans, P. E., McPherson, G. E., & Davidson, J. W. (under review). Psychological Needs and Motivation to Continue or Cease Playing a Musical Instrument. *Psychology of Music*.

Flood, M. (2005). Mapping loneliness in Australia. Manuka, ACT: The Australia Institute; Report No.: *Discussion Paper Number 76*.

Greaves, C. J., & Farbus, L. (2006). Effects of creative and social activity on the health and well-being of socially isolated people: Outcomes from a multi-method observational study. *Journal of the Royal Society for the Promotion of Health, 126*(3), 134–142.

Green, L. (2002). *How popular musicians learning*. Aldershot: Ashgate.

McPherson, G. E., & Davidson, J. W. (2002). Musical practice: mother and child interactions during the first year of learning an instrument. *Music Education Research, 4*, 141–156.

McPherson, G. E., & Davidson, J. W. (2006). Playing an instrument. In G. E. McPherson (Ed.), *The child as musician* (pp. 331–352). New York, NY: Oxford University Press.

Messenger, J. C., & Messenger, B. (1992) Sexuality in folklore in a Nigerian society. *Central Issues in Anthropology, 3*(1), 29–50.

Nordoff, P., & Robbins, C. (1971). *Therapy in music for handicapped children*. London: Gollancz.

Nordoff, P., & Robbins, C. (1983). *Music therapy in special education*. St. Louis, MO: MMB Music.

Nordoff, P., & Robbins, C. (2007) *Creative music therapy: a guide to fostering clinical musicianship* (2nd ed.), Revised (with 4 CDs). Gilsum, NH: Barcelona Publishers.

Odell-Miller, H. (2005). *Why provide music therapy in the community for adults with mental health problems? Voices, 5*(1), mi40005000172. Available at: http://www.voices.no/mainissues/mi40005000172.html (accessed 21 September 2010).

Pavlicevic, M., & Ansdell, G. (Eds.). (2004). *Community music therapy*. London: Jessica Kingsley.

Robarts, J. (2006). Music therapy with sexually abused children. *Clinical Child Psychology and Psychiatry, 11*(2), 249–269.

Ryan, R. M., & Deci, E. L. (2000). The darker and brighter sides of human existence: Basic psychological needs as a unifying concept. *Psychological Inquiry, 11*, 319–338.

Ryan, R. M., & Deci, E. L. (2002). Overview of self-determination theory: An organismic dialectical perspective. In E. L. Deci, & R. M. Ryan (Eds.), *Handbook of self-determination research* (pp. 3–33). Rochester, NY: University of Rochester Press.

Sloboda, J. A. (1991). Music structure and emotional response: some empirical findings. *Psychology of Music, 19*(2), 110–120.

Sloboda, J. A. (2005). *Exploring the musical mind*. New York, NY: Oxford University Press.

Sloboda, J. A., Davidson, J. W., & Howe, M. J. A. (1994). Is everyone musical? *Psychologist, 7,* 349–354.

Sloboda, J. A., Davidson, J. W., Howe, M. J. A., & Moore, D. M. (1996). The role of practice in the development of expert musical performance. *British Journal of Psychology, 87,* 287–309.

Smith, J. A. (Ed.). (2003). *Qualitative psychology: a practical guide to research methods.* London: Sage.

Smith, J. A., Flowers, P., & Larkin, M. (2009). *Interpretative phenomenological analysis: Theory, method and research.* London: Sage.

Staricoff, R. L. (2004). *Arts in health: a review of the medical literature.* London: Arts Council England.

Windsor, J. (2005). *Your health and the arts: a study of the association between arts engagement and health.* London: Arts Council England.

Part 3

Music and emotion

Chapter 6

How do strong experiences with music relate to experiences in everyday listening to music?

Alf Gabrielsson

Abstract

People's experience of and reactions to music have recently received increased interest in music psychology research. Several reports (books, articles) have dealt with 'music in everyday life', that is, how people perceive and use music in their daily life. In such circumstances music is often no more than a background to other activities and listening is somewhat absent-minded. However, there are also reports that demonstrate focused listening and indicate that music serves important personal functions, for example, to evoke pleasant memories, relieve distress, or enhance or change the present mood. Another line of research has dealt with particularly strong experiences related to music (SEM). In such cases music is in definite focus, nothing else matters. Analysis of strong experiences has resulted in a comprehensive descriptive system (Gabrielsson & Lindström Wik 2003; Gabrielsson 2008) that may serve as reference for comparison of different kinds of music experience. In the present chapter this descriptive system is used to reflect on similarities and differences in 'music in daily life'—experiences and exceptionally strong experiences. Although there are of course obvious differences between the experiences, it turns out that the limits between them are fluid.

While there are numerous studies on the perception of expression in music (reviewed in Gabrielsson, 2005, 2009; Gabrielsson & Juslin, 2003; Gabrielsson & Lindström 2001, 2010), there has been less research on listeners' reactions to music. Furthermore, such research has usually taken place in the laboratory. Recently, however, an increasing number of studies have been devoted people's reactions to music, especially with regard to everyday listening. Their purpose is to investigate how, when, where, and why people listen to music—in other words, to explore the uses and functions of music in everyday life. Another, less common approach focuses instead on instances of particularly strong experiences with music. Such experiences happen only now and then but may leave long-lasting impressions. The purpose of this chapter is to compare these different approaches—everyday listening to music (ELM) and instances of strong experiences with music (SEM)—with regard to the kind of reactions that are involved and the conditions in which they occur. The comparisons are based on a limited number of recent papers and the findings should be considered as preliminary.

As shown in the following sections, John Sloboda has made important contributions to both the ELM and SEM areas. He has initiated and conducted several studies on uses and functions of music in everyday life as well as on personally significant experiences with music, and furthermore has conducted research surveys in these areas. This inspired me to undertake the comparison between ELM and SEM which is presented in this chapter. It is still an exploratory and incomplete study, but I hope it will evoke both John's and other readers' curiosity and encourage to further research.

Everyday listening to music

Within the 'mass-observation project' run at Sussex University, which recorded aspects of people's everyday lives, Sloboda (1999) conducted a study on the uses and functions of music. Data from a random sample of 76 people (45 women, 31 men) demonstrated a number of different functions of music for these respondents. The most common was 'Reminder of valued past event' (reported by 50% of the subjects), followed by 'To put in a good mood' (16%), 'Moves to tears/catharsis/release' (14%), 'Mood enhancement'(8%), 'Calms/soothes/relaxes/relieves stress' (8%), 'To match current mood' (6%), 'Source of pleasure and enjoyment' (6%), 'Spiritual experience' (6%), 'Source of comfort/healing' (4%), and 'Evokes visual images', and 'Excites' and 'Motivates' (2% each). Furthermore, 'Tingles/goose pimples/shivers' were reported by 10% of the respondents.

Many of the above functions refer to mood and/or positive emotions, and it may be assumed that the most frequent function, 'Reminder of valued past event', also includes positive feelings. Women mentioned mood altering or enhancing functions more frequently than men, and women in general gave more articulate and detailed descriptions of music for mood-related functions than men. Similar gender differences appear in other papers as well (e.g. Gabrielsson, 2008; Juslin, Liljeström, Laukka, Västfjäll, & Lundqvist, in press; North, Hargreaves, & O'Neill, 2000, pp. 263, 269). Music was reported as being used in connection with various activities, such as driving/running/cycling, on public transport (Walkman), during housework or desk work, while having a meal, to get to sleep or to wake up to, while exercising, as background while socializing, and to accompany sexual/romantic events.

Similar results concerning musical functions and activities are reported in later studies. Juslin and Laukka (2004), who interviewed 141 music listeners, identified the same music accompanied activities as Sloboda—music during housework, when socializing, while driving/cycling/running, while exercising, working or relaxing, as background to romantic company, etc. The motives for listening to music were also similar: to express, release, and influence emotions (47% of the subjects), to relax and settle down (33%), for enjoyment, fun, and pleasure (22%), as company and background sound (16%), 'It makes me feel good' (13%), 'It's a basic need, I can't live without it'(12%), 'Because I like/love music'(11%), to get energized (9%), and to evoke memories (4%). By and large, the same activities and motives recurred in Laukka's (2007) study with older adults (aged 65–75 years); however, the highest rated motive was that 'music is beautiful', furthermore 'interest in music itself' also belonged to the highest rated motives. Factor analysis reduced the motives to four fundamental factors: identity and agency (e.g. 'to express my personality', 'it makes me feel competent'), mood regulation (e.g. 'to enhance positive moods', 'it evokes memories'), relaxation and company (e.g. 'to relax and calm down', 'to reduce feelings of loneliness'), and enjoyment (e.g. 'for entertainment', 'music is beautiful').

North *et al.* (2000) found that teenagers reported that they mainly listened to pop and various kinds of dance music for reasons such as enjoyment, to be creative/use their imagination, to relieve boredom, to help get through difficult times, to be trendy/cool, to relieve tension/stress, to create an image for him/herself, to please friends, and to reduce loneliness. Girls were more concerned than boys with how music listening could help with their emotional needs, while boys were more concerned with the external impression created by their music listening. Laiho (2004) reviewed studies on the psychological functions of music in adolescence and summarized the findings in a model with four basic themes: emotional field (enjoyment and emotion regulation), interpersonal relationships (belonging and privacy), identity (construction and strengthening of identity and conception of self), and agency (control, competency, and self-esteem). The emotional field was considered the most central theme and was investigated further in group interviews with eight adolescents (Saarikallio & Erkkilä, 2007). The different strategies used for emotion regulation were found to be 'revival' (feelings of reviving, relaxing, getting energy), 'diversion' (forgetting about current negative mood), 'discharge' (music gives form to the expression of current negative mood), 'solace' (feeling understood and comforted), 'entertainment' (lifting up spirits, maintaining positive mood), and 'mental work' (music promotes imagery, insights, clarification, and reappraisal of experiences).

DeNora's studies (2000) seem so far both broadest in scope and most penetrating in the description of how people use music in everyday life. Her ethnographic investigations included in-depth interviews with 50 women in metropolitan areas and small towns, as well as participant observations in aerobic exercise classes, karaoke evenings, and music therapy sessions, as well as unobtrusive observation of music in the retail sector, and interviews with personnel in all these settings. Her subjects were usually aware of what music was needed to have desired effects on themselves or on others in different situations. They provided ample concrete information on how they used music for mood regulation or, more generally, 'as an ordering device at the personal level, as a means for creating, enhancing, sustaining, and changing subjective, cognitive, bodily, and self-conceptual states' (2000, p. 49). Headings such as: 'Musically composed identities', 'Music in the neonatal unit', 'Music and bodily security', 'Music and intimate culture', 'Music and collective occasions', 'Music in public spaces', and 'Music's social powers' illustrate the rich contents of this volume.

Most of the preceding reports relied on subjects' memories or judgements of experiences in the past, and so were liable to possible biases of various kinds. In order to study everyday reactions to music as directly as possible, researchers have applied the so-called experience sampling method (ESM). In ESM, subjects are contacted (by mobile phones, electronic pagers, small handheld computers or palmtops) at random times during a certain period (say, one week) and then immediately, or as soon as possible, they answer questions concerning where they are, what they are doing, if they are alone or with others, if there is any music present, and, if so, how they react to this. This technique has been used by Sloboda, O'Neill, and Ivaldi (2001), North, Hargreaves, and Hargreaves (2004) and Juslin, Liljeström, Västfjäll, Barradas, and Silva (2008). Music was present in as many as 37–44% of the random episodes. However, it was rarely the main factor, it was present while the subject was involved in other activities, such as travelling, doing physical work, mental work, or emotional work (mood management).

In a review including most of the above studies regarding self-chosen exposure to music in daily life, Sloboda, Lamont, and Greasley (2009) (see also Sloboda & O'Neill, 2001) concluded that music is usually not the primary focus of attention or concern but may serve as a distraction (e.g. reducing boredom), to energize (e.g. by maintaining arousal and attention), as entrainment (synchronizing movements with musical pulse/rhythm), and as meaning enhancement.

Strong experiences with music

The study of particularly significant experiences, 'peak experiences', was pioneered by Maslow (1968, 1976), who identified a number of characteristics of such experiences. Many of them are reflected in the four fundamental factors found by Panzarella (1980) in a study of intense experiences with music and art: (1) *renewal ecstasy*, an altered perception of the world; (2) *motor-sensory ecstasy*, various physical and quasi-physical reactions (e.g. shivers, 'floating'); (3) *withdrawal ecstasy*, loss of contact with both the physical and social environment; and (4) *fusion-emotional ecstasy*, merging with the aesthetic object.

Sloboda (1990) obtained reports from about 70 subjects regarding musical memories from the first 10 years of their lives. The reports indicated that significant musical experiences were most likely to occur in connection with relaxed, informal listening when the person was not being evaluated and in the company of family or friends. Such positive experiences may have long-lasting effects on musical behaviour and involvement in the future. However, musical memories associated with school and/or teachers had a much lower occurrence of positive significance.

At about the same time the first results from our own project on SEM were published (Gabrielsson, 1989; Gabrielsson & Lindström, 1993). Subjects were asked to describe, in their own words, the strongest experience with music that they ever had. Content analysis of their reports showed about 150 different reactions, which have been sorted into a descriptive system with seven basic categories: (1) general characteristics, (2) physical reactions and behaviours, (3) perception, (4) cognition, (5) feelings/emotion, (6) existential and transcendental aspects, and (7) personal and social aspects. Each category has several subcategories, which in turn contain a varying number of reactions (Gabrielsson, 2008; Gabrielsson & Lindström Wik, 2003). A condensed version of the descriptive system is given in Appendix 6.1. So far this is the most comprehensive and detailed study of reactions during SEM. A general review of research on peak experiences with music is given in Whaley, Sloboda, and Gabrielsson (2009).

Comparison of ELM and SEM

Studies of ELM usually focus on its uses and functions rather than on subjects' direct reactions to it; however, some studies have provided ample evidence of emotional reactions to music. Conversely, studies of SEM focus on respondents' own reactions. Since such experiences occur more rarely and often unexpectedly, questions concerning use and function have less relevance.

Before going into more detailed comparisons, let us first state the most fundamental difference between ELM and SEM. In ELM the music itself is usually secondary; it is there as accompaniment or background to other activities. In SEM, however, the music is unambiguously the primary event. The listener is absorbed by the music, nothing else matters—one is neither aware of one's surroundings, nor of time or body. One may feel as if filled by the music, as if merging with it.

The comparisons that follow are limited to recent studies which included at least 30 subjects and provided data that allow quantitative comparisons. Two types of comparison are made, one dealing with studies of single musical episodes, another with 'long-time reactions' to music. Data from SEM are used as reference in both cases. (These data refer to experiences in listening to music; data regarding SEM in connection with own performance of music are omitted in this context.) It should be noted that the studies cited may have had different purposes; moreover, only selected parts of them are used in the following comparisons.

Single musical episodes

These include the following cases:

1. SEM that may have occurred 1–82 years back in time (Gabrielsson, 2008; Gabrielsson & Lindström Wik, 2003);

2. The most recent musical episode (EPI) when the subject experienced an emotion while listening to music (Juslin *et al.*, in press);

3. Use of the ESM to study an immediately preceding experience (Juslin *et al.*, 2008; North *et al.*, 2004).

The cases under (2) and (3) may be said to mainly represent ELM. Data on subjects in these studies are given in Table 6.1.

The SEM and EPI studies were similar with regard to the number and composition of subjects; however, SEM subjects were self-selected, while EPI subjects were a random sample. SEM episodes were from 1908 to 2004, while the EPI occasions were recent: 35% within the last 24 hours, 42% within the past four weeks, and 14% more than four weeks ago. Both the ESM studies differed markedly from the SEM and EPI studies with regard to the mean age and occupation of the subjects.

Table 6.1 Subject demographics in selected studies of musical episodes

	SEM (Gabrielsson & Lindström Wik, 2003; Gabrielsson, 2008)	EPI (Juslin et al., in press)	ESM (North et al., 2004)	ESM (Juslin et al., 2008)
No. of subjects and method of selection	782, self-selected	706, random sample	346, self-selected	32, self-selected
Gender	Females 62%, males 38%	Females 57%, males 43%	Not given	Females 66%, males 34%
Mean age; range	44; 13–91	41.5; 18–65	26; 13–78	24; 20–31
Occupation	Mixed	Mixed	Many students (48%)	Students

Note: self-selected subjects were volunteers, subjects who have accepted to participate in the respective studies.
SEM, strong experiences with music; EPI, recent musical episode, ESM, experience sampling method.

Types of music

The music in both the SEM and the three ELM studies belonged to many different genres. Table 6.2 shows the distribution of the most common genres. There was much more classical and religious music in SEM than in the other studies, which show more pop and 'mixed' (various genres in popular music) than in SEM.

In making these comparisons one should consider the age of the subjects as well as the time when the experiences occurred. As a rule, old people listen more to classical music than young people do, and young people listen more to pop, rock and other 'popular'

Table 6.2 Percentage of music of different genres in SEM, EPI, two ESM studies, and in SEM occurring after 1980

Genre	SEM	EPI (Juslin)	ESM (North)	ESM (Juslin)	SEM (1980)
Classical	43.8	11.0	3.0	4.0	30.4
Religious	12.8	–	–	0.7	14.1
Folk	5.2	–	0.8	5.0	6.0
Jazz	5.0	–	1.1	3.3	4.9
Rock	7.1	19.0	4.7	5.0	12.5
Pop	5.0	41.0	47.2	53.0	8.1
Mixed	4.3	8.0	10.9	10.0	7.9
Dance	1.0	–	5.3	2.0	1.1

Note: Folk music also includes world music, jazz also includes blues. 'Mixed' means any of several genres in popular music, such as rhythm and blues, soul, reggae, hip hop, trance, techno, disco, house, jungle, rave, techno, indie.
In the EPI Juslin column, the 11% classical music also includes jazz and traditional music, and the 41% pop music also includes country and Swedish 'danceband' music.
(Where percentages do not add up to 100% this is due to omission of some genres and/or missing values.)
EPI Juslin: Juslin et al., in press; ESM Juslin: Juslin et al., 2008; ESM North: North et al., 2004.
SEM, strong experiences with music; EPI, recent musical episode, ESM, experience sampling method.

genres than old people. It is thus not surprising that the subjects in the both ESM studies, much younger than the subjects in the SEM and EPI studies, show much higher percentages for 'popular' music than for classical and religious music. Moreover, many of the popular music genres did not appear until relatively late in the 20th century.

In order to adjust somewhat for these differences in listeners' age and time when the episode occurred, SEM data may be limited to include only subjects who had their SEM after 1980 (n = 384; mean age 33.8 years, median age 29 years, range 13–82 years), see the last column in Table 6.2. In comparison with the total SEM material, there is now (after 1980) less classical music but more rock, pop, and mixed genres. However, the proportion of classical and religious music is much higher in SEM than in any of the other studies. More details of musical genres in SEM as well as their distribution, depending on gender, age, and time of the experience, are given in Gabrielsson (2006, 2008, 2010).

Place of the experience

Both ELM and SEM may occur in a variety of places. Most of them are shown in Table 6.3. SEM mostly occurred in concert halls (including various assembly halls), at home, outdoors, and in churches (all together 81.4%), only now and then in schools, restaurants, or while travelling (more data in Gabrielsson, 2008). In the other studies the experience occurred mostly at home and relatively often when travelling (driving or being transported), in restaurants and shops.

All four studies show a high frequency of episodes at home, especially the three studies representing ELM. SEM occurred often in 'formal' settings, such as in concert

Table 6.3 Percentage of SEM/EPI/ESM episodes in different places

Place	SEM	EPI (Juslin)	ESM (North)	ESM (Juslin)	SEM (1980)
At home	21.9	50.0	50.1	60.0	14.4
Other home	3.5	–	4.6	8.0	3.1
Concert hall	32.1	–	0.3	<1.0	31.1
Outdoors	13.8	–	–	10.0	18.1
Church	13.6	–	0.2	<1.0	12.9
School	2.2	–	–	5.0	1.8
Restaurant	2.4	–	8.6	1.5	3.6
Travelling	1.9	–	13.6	5.0	2.3
Shop	0.0	–	5.8	2.0	–
Party	–	–	–	1.5	–
Gym	–	–	0.9	1.0	–

Concert hall also includes opera, theatre, and assembly halls. Outdoors also includes outdoor concerts. Church also includes other places for religious worship. School also includes other work places. Restaurant also includes pubs, cafés, and night clubs.

Places in EPI (Juslin) were only given as 50% 'at home' and 50% 'not at home' due to lacking information in the subjects' open-ended responses.

EPI Juslin: Juslin et al., in press; ESM Juslin: Juslin et al., 2008; ESM North: North et al., 2004.

SEM, strong experiences with music; EPI, recent musical episode, ESM, experience sampling method.

halls and churches, also outdoors (including outdoor concerts), whereas the ESM episodes relatively often occurred in 'informal', everyday settings, such as while travelling, in restaurants and shops. Data for SEM after 1980 are similar to the total SEM data, except for a decrease in episodes at home and an increase in outdoor episodes, mainly referring to attendance at outdoor concerts.

Live or reproduced music?

Most SEM episodes (68.8%) included live music heard in concert halls, churches, and at outdoor concerts, for example. Reproduced music (on the radio, on tape or disk, or on television) was heard in 31.2% of the episodes.

In the ESM study by Juslin *et al.* (2008), live music was heard only in 7% of the episodes; the remaining 93% involved hearing of reproduced music, with the subjects utilizing stereo equipment (32%), personal computer (31%), television (10%), Walkman/MP3 (9%), radio (8%), and public loudspeaker (2%). There are no data on this issue in the remaining two studies, but in consideration of where the experiences occurred (Table 6.3) it seems obvious that most episodes included reproduced music. There is thus a dominance of live music in SEM but of reproduced music in ELM. There is simply not as much live music available in everyday situations, and with the increasing use of portable equipment for music listening (iPods, MP3 players, etc.) the dominance of reproduced music in ELM can be expected to increase still more.

It seems probable that, beside the music itself, the visual impressions of the performing musicians and the surroundings, the acoustical conditions, and the atmosphere associated with live music, are factors that contribute to SEM (Gabrielsson, 2008). Conversely, it is notable that many SEM episodes (21.9%) occurred in listening at home. There are, for instance, several reports describing how music in the background suddenly took over and led to an SEM during routine housework, desk work, or while driving or other travel (Gabrielsson, 2008).

The social situation

The nature of social situation in which the experience occurs may be divided into three types: being alone, being with acquaintances, or being with strangers (Table 6.4). In all studies most experiences occurred when the listener was in the company of people they knew well (friends, spouse/partner, family members, work colleagues, boy/girlfriend). Listening alone was more common than listening with strangers.

Table 6.4 Percentage of SEM/EPI/ESM episodes in different social situations

Social situation	SEM	EPI Juslin	ESM North	ESM Juslin	SEM (1980)
Alone	20.2	44.0	26.3	41.0	18.2
Acquaintances	64.4	–	42.8	49.0	64.6
Strangers	15.4	–	2.5	10.0	17.2

Note: EPI Juslin included only two categories, 'alone' 44%, and 'not alone' 56%. There are much missing data in ESM North. Data in ESM Juslin refer to all episodes (musical and non-musical).
EPI Juslin: Juslin *et al.*, in press; ESM Juslin: Juslin *et al.*, 2008; ESM North: North *et al.*, 2004.
SEM, strong experiences with music; EPI, recent musical episode, ESM, experience sampling method.

Comparisons of SEM and long-time listening

Another comparison between SEM and ELM makes use of data from studies on how often people listen to various types of music and/or what type of music they prefer. Such data do not refer to single episodes but to a kind of 'average' of experiences across long periods of time, thus relying on semantic memory rather than on episodic memory. The comparisons included the following studies:

1 SEM as above

2 Teenagers' preferences for different musical styles, included in a study on the importance of music to adolescents (North *et al.*, 2000)

3 A questionnaire study of everyday listening to music (Juslin & Laukka, 2004)

4 The use of music among elderly persons (Laukka, 2007)

5 A survey study of emotional reactions to music (Juslin *et al.*, in press).

Studies in alternatives (2–5) may be seen as mainly representing ELM. For details about the subjects see Table 6.5. Comparisons between these studies were limited because data on musical genres, location, and social situation do not appear in all of them. However, the main differences between SEM and ELM are still obvious.

Types of music

Available data on musical genres for the comparative study are given in Table 6.6. Again, these refer to percentages of music of different genres, except in the studies by

Table 6.5 Subject demographics with regard to SEM and in selected studies on long-time listening

	SEM (Gabrielsson & Lindström Wik, 2003; Gabrielsson, 2008)	ELM (North et al.,2000)	ELM (Juslin & Laukka, 2004)	ELM (Laukka, 2007)	ELM (Juslin et al., in press)
No. of subjects and method of selection	782, self-selected (volunteers)	2465 (72% of intended population)	141, self-selected (convenience sample)	280, random sample of persons aged 65–75 years	762, random sample
Gender	Females 62%, males 38%	Females 51.4%, males 46.6%	Females 55%, males 45%	Females 49.3%, males 46.8%	Females 57%, males 43%
Mean age, range	44; 13–91	13–14 years	Females 36, 18–74; males 33, 17–70	Females 69.3, males 69.1	41.5; 18–65
Occupation	Mixed	Pupils in Year 9 in secondary school	Mixed	Mixed	Mixed

Note: Where percentages do not add up to 100%, this is due to missing data.
SEM, strong experiences with music; ELM, everyday listening of music.

Table 6.6 Percentage of music of different genres (SEM, ELM Juslin) and ratings of liking (ELM North, ELM Laukka)

GENRE	SEM	ELM North	ELM Laukka	ELM Juslin
Classical	43.8	1.44	4.1	20.0
Religious	12.8	–	3.6	6.0
Folk	5.2	1.28	3.6	4.0
Jazz	5.0	2.71	4.0	6.0
Rock	7.1	3.61	2.5	19.0
Pop	5.0	8.59	3.1	30.0
Mixed	4.3	9.25	3.3	7.0
Dance	1.0	9.25	4.0	8.0

Note: Data in ELM North and in ELM Laukka are ratings of liking for different types of music, on a scale from 0 to 10 (North) or from 1 to 6 (Laukka). Data from Laukka's study do not appear in his original paper (Laukka, 2007) but were given to the present author in a personal communication. Data in ELM Juslin are percentages for types of music with which the participants were most inclined to experience emotions.
Folk music also includes world music, jazz also includes blues. 'Mixed' means any of several genres in popular music, such as rhythm and blues, soul, reggae, hip hop, trance, techno, disco, house, jungle, rave, techno, indie.
ELM North: North *et al.*, 2000; ELM Laukka: Laukka, 2007; ELM Juslin: Juslin *et al.*, in press.
SEM, strong experiences with music; ELM, everyday listening of music.

North *et al.* (2000) and Laukka (2007), in which data are ratings of liking for different musical styles. The SEM and ELM Juslin studies are similar regarding number, gender, age, and occupation of subjects (Table 6.5). With regard to musical genre SEM shows a higher percentage for classical and religious music than ELM Juslin, while the latter shows a higher percentage for 'popular' genres (rock, pop, mixed, dance) than SEM.

Teenagers and elderly people's preferences differ markedly. Teenagers (ELM North, scale 0–10) like popular music, especially pop, mixed, and dance music, much more than classical, folk, and jazz music, while elderly people have the opposite preferences (ELM Laukka, scale 1–6). Juslin and Laukka (2004, not included in Table 6.6) used a mixture of conventional genres (classical music 29%, popular music 47%) and other categories, such as happy music 8%, sad music 8%, calm music 22%, arousing music 11%, magnificent and/or solemn music 4%, and music 'that one recognizes and likes' 14% (non-mutually exclusive categories).

Place; live or reproduced music

In the ELM studies there are in general no specific data regarding where music listening took place. However, considering that music listening often occurs in combination with other activities, it is obvious that ELM may take place in a variety of different places, however, usually *not* in concert halls, assembly halls, or churches—that is, places where the music itself is in focus.

Table 6.7 Percentage of SEM/ELM listening in different social situations

Situation	SEM	ELM North	SEM teenagers
Alone	20.2	60.0	23.1
With family/friends/colleagues	64.4	30.8	71.1
With strangers	15.4	5.7	5.8

SEM, strong experiences with music; ELM, everyday listening of music.

For the same reasons it can be concluded that most ELM is associated with reproduced music, as there is not so much live music available for everyday listening. For example, among the teenagers participating in the study by North *et al.* (2000) 61% listened to music at least once or twice a day, and the average listening time per day was 2.45 hours. Likewise 64% of the elderly persons in the study by Laukka (2007) listened to music once or several times a day, and in the study by Juslin and Laukka (2004) 64% of the subjects listened to music several times a day.

The social situation

Among the teenagers (13–14 years) in the study by North *et al.* (2000) a majority (60%) reported that they listened to music when they were alone (Table 6.7). Predominance of listening in privacy has also been reported in other studies of adolescents (Zillmann & Gan, 1997, p. 162). However, data for the teenagers in SEM (n = 96) show the same result as for the whole SEM material, that is, predominance of listening with family, friends, and colleagues.

Juslin and Laukka (2004, p. 230) and Juslin *et al.* (in press, Table 6.4) asked their subjects in which situations they were especially prone to experience emotions to music. A variety of situations were mentioned, including listening while alone.

Listeners' reactions in SEM and ELM

The reference for this comparison is the descriptive system for SEM shown in Appendix 6.1; for a full description, see Gabrielsson and Lindström Wik (2003) and Gabrielsson (2008). The system contains seven basic categories: (1) general characteristics, (2) physical reactions and behaviours, (3) perception, (4) cognition, (5) feelings/emotion, (6) existential and transcendental aspects, and (7) personal and social aspects. There is so far no comparable descriptive system for ELM. However, some of the studies cited above have presented extensive data on emotional reactions in ELM or similar situations. Comparisons are therefore limited to emotional reactions in SEM and ELM. The data were supplemented by the findings of two more studies:

1 Janata, Tomic, and Rakowski (2007) studied cognitive and affective properties of music-evoked autobiographical memories. The students (n = 329; 52% females, 48% males; mean age 20.6 years, range 18–29) listened to music excerpts from the Billboard Top 100 Pop and R&B lists, a total of 1515 different songs. Each subject listened (in the laboratory or online) to 30 musical excerpts, selected randomly from the Billboard charts in the years during which the participants were between 7 and 19 years old, and completed various questionnaires and ratings. Figure 2D in

Janata et al.'s article (2007, p. 852) displayed the average proportion of autobio-graphically salient songs that evoked any of 34 different emotions, covering a range of positive and negative reactions including both basic and more complex emo-tions. These data are used in the comparisons below (Table 6.8).

2 Zentner, Grandjean, and Scherer (2008) reported four interrelated studies on music-induced emotion. In one of them, study 3, a total of 801 subjects (55% females, 42% males, 3% unknown; mean age 44.8 years, range 12–88) listened to concert performances of music—mostly classical, but also rock, world, and jazz—and immediately afterwards indicated which emotions out of a total of 66 they had felt somewhat or a lot. The selection of the 66 emotion terms was based on various surveys of emotion terms and on extensive pre-tests of their relevance for description of emotional responses to music from different genres. The percent-age of listeners reporting to have felt any of these emotions were given in Table 2 in their article (p. 504), separately for each of the four genres and across all genres (column 'Total', part of which is reproduced in Table 6.8). Since the rat-ings were completed immediately after the concerts, this approaches an ESM procedure.

Data concerning emotional reactions in seven studies are summarized in Table 6.8. As there is still no general agreement on which and how many emotion terms should be used, researchers have adopted different approaches, referring to any of the com-peting emotion theories (e.g. categorical or dimensional), and/or to terms used in earlier research, or to results from pre-tests. There are thus many gaps in the table. Terms that were used in only one of the studies have been omitted; 69 remain. The terms are given in English, but most of them were originally given in other languages (Swedish, French). Translation into another language always poses a risk for change of meaning in relation to the original terms. All these issues should be kept in mind when looking at the results.

The first two data columns in Table 6.8, ELM Juslin (from Juslin et al., in press) and ELM Laukka (Laukka, 2007) show ratings of how frequently subjects tended to have felt each of 45 emotions—selected from a survey of the literature on emotion and complemented with emotion terms often used in musical contexts—in response to music. The rating scale extended from 1 ('Never') to 4 ('Always'). These data represent a kind of long-time average of emotional responses to music and may be seen as mainly referring to ELM. Data in these two studies (columns) are extremely similar, $r = 0.98$. As the data originate from two independent and large random samples (see Table 6.5, the two rightmost columns), they may suggest the existence of a common and stable structure of average long-time emotional responses to music. As would be expected, positive feelings have received high or relatively high ratings, while negative feelings appear towards the lower end of the scale.

In the next three studies (columns) data refer to the percentage of subjects who felt the respective emotions when they actually listened to music, thus representing musi-cal episodes in the present time. (In Janata's study the percentage values actually refer to the proportion of songs that evoked various emotions). Janata et al. (2007) used 34 emotion terms, while Zentner et al. (2008) included 66 emotion terms. In the ESM

Table 6.8 Ratings of frequency (ELM Juslin, ELM Laukka; scale 1–4) and percentage of subjects who felt the respective emotion (all other columns); see text for further explanation

Emotion	ELM Juslin	ELM Laukka	Janata	Zentner	ESM Juslin	EPI Juslin	SEM
Happy	3.06	3.10	58.4	43.2	25.0	53.8	18.8
Joyful			20.8	33.0			18.2
Euphoric				17.7			1.8
Enjoying	2.97	3.02			5.3		13.0
Sweet				20.0			11.2
Relaxed	2.94	2.86	0.3	40.6		10.4	4.0
Calm	2.92	2.84	18.7	32.7	37.0	10.0	9.2
Amused	2.83	2.78	0.3	17.0			
Moved	2.82	2.82		32.3		1.9	18.7
Touched				40.2		1.9	18.7
Enchanted	2.23	2.53		34.8			6.4
Excited			25.6	10.6			6.6
Nostalgic	2.73	2.94	27.2	30.3	6.5	9.3	0.3
Bittersweet			11.1	5.5			
Longing	2.52	2.27			6.5	9.3	0.5
Dreamy				37.1			1.3
Meditative				25.2			0.3
Sentimental				26.0			0.2
Wonder				31.3			0.8
Loving	2.68	2.58	21.2	15.7	3.0	2.2	2.9
Tender	2.38	2.41		23.1	3.0	2.2	2.9
Interested	2.59	2.73			9.5	1.7	6.3
Content	2.46	2.54	21.4		37.0	10.0	1.4
Hopeful	2.46	2.31	15.9				2.0
Inspired			16.6	18.6			7.7
Free				26.3			3.7
Mellowed				17.0			4.5
Strong			11.8	14.3			6.6
Energetic			23.7	24.5			6.6
Relieved	2.33	2.22					3.1
Admiring	2.32	2.61					0.9
Expectant	2.31	2.33			9.5	1.7	26.6
Curious	2.22	2.21			8.9	1.6	6.3
Emphatic	2.17	2.13					0.1
Sad	2.12	1.94	16.2	11.5	3.7	13.1	5.2

(continued)

Table 6.8 (continued) Ratings of frequency (ELM Juslin, ELM Laukka; scale 1–4) and percentage of subjects who felt the respective emotion (all other columns); see text for further explanation

Emotion	ELM Juslin	ELM Laukka	Janata	Zentner	ESM Juslin	EPI Juslin	SEM
Melancholic					3.7	13.1	2.0
Depressed			7.3	3.2			
Solemn	2.11	2.44		13.0			1.0
Proud	2.10	1.85	8.0	6.7		1.4	0.3
Desiring	2.00	1.90					11.1
Ecstatic	1.86	1.71					2.2
Spiritual	1.84	2.04	8.0	19.0			8.3
Transcendent				16.4			11.3
Lonely	1.79	1.82	13.4				0.5
Honoured	1.71	1.81					0.1
Bored	1.66	1.56			2.6		
Surprised	1.62	1.55			0.2		5.2
Angry	1.60	1.30	3.2	2.7	3.0	2.9	0.5
Disappointed	1.58	1.53					0.5
Tense	1.51	1.36		7.5			0.1
Nervous				5.6			0.5
Indifferent	1.50	1.52		4.0	2.6		0.0
Frustrated	1.47	1.26					0.6
Irritated			1.0	6.5	3.0	2.9	
Anxious	1.43	1.24		4.6	1.8		1.1
Confused	1.37	1.23	6.1				0.5
Regretful	1.37	1.19	7.0				
Jealous	1.34	1.24	1.5				0.4
Contemptuous	1.28	1.17			0.2		
Afraid	1.22	1.12			1.8		1.0
Guilty	1.21	1.12	1.2		0.7		
Disgusted	1.21	1.18			0.2		0.1
Ashamed	1.16	1.09	3.1		0.7		0.8
Humiliated	1.13	1.09					
Aroused						3.5	6.6
Light				23.1			1.2
Floating				16.2			5.5
Thrills		2.21	1.4	14.4			8.1
Goose bumps				12.5			5.0

ELM Juslin, Juslin *et al.*, in press; ELM Laukka, Laukka, 2007; Janata: Janata *et al.*, 2007; Zentner, Zentner *et al.* 2008; ESM Juslin, Juslin *et al.*, 2008; EPI Juslin: Juslin *et al.*, in press.
SEM, strong experiences with music; EPI, recent musical episode, ESM, experience sampling method; ELM, everyday listening of music.

study by Juslin *et al.* (2008) responses were given immediately or as soon as possible when the subjects were contacted at random times during two weeks, selecting among 14 emotion terms representative of the two dominant conceptualizations of emotions (categories/basic emotions and dimensions, valence/arousal) and terms particularly relevant to music.

In the remaining two studies (rightmost columns) the subjects' answers also refer to musical episodes—however, episodes in the past. These episodes were fairly recent, from the same day to more than four weeks ago, in the study on musical episodes included in Juslin *et al.* (in press), and more distant in SEM episodes, from one to 82 years. In both cases, subjects labelled the felt emotion using their own words (free description). Juslin *et al.* then sorted these emotion labels into 10 common emotion categories, for example, happy-elated, sad-melancholic, and nostalgic-longing.

Comparisons among the studies on musical episodes are restricted due to many gaps in the data. Like in the first two columns on long-time listening, values (percentages) are much higher for positive feelings than for negative feelings. However, there is considerable variation in values for the same emotion. It is particularly notable that the percentages are usually higher for the three studies on present musical episodes (Table 6.8: Janata, Zentner, Juslin ESM) than in the studies on musical episodes in the past (Table 6.8: EPI Juslin, SEM), especially in SEM episodes. While this might reflect a difference between present and past episodes, a more plausible reason is that subjects in the three studies on present episodes were provided with lists of emotion terms, whereas subjects in the two studies on past episodes had to use their own vocabulary to describe their experience (free descriptions). It is much easier for subjects to make use of given terms—they may even feel compelled to use all of them—than to try to verbalize the experience oneself.

Correlations between the different studies are positive throughout, varying from $r = 0.21$ to $r = 0.98$ (Table 6.9). This mainly reflects the fact that positive feelings received higher values than negative feelings in all studies. As could be expected, the correlation between the two studies representing averages of long-time listening (ELM

Table 6.9 Values of the correlations between all the reviewed studies

	ELM Juslin	ELM Laukka	Janata	Zentner	ESM Juslin	EPI Juslin	SEM
ELM Juslin	1.00	0.98	0.57	0.82	0.60	0.46	0.50
ELM Laukka	0.98	1.00	0.58	0.87	0.60	0.42	0.50
Janata	0.57	0.58	1.00	0.54	0.51	0.86	0.58
Zentner	0.82	0.87	0.54	1.00	0.74	0.47	0.50
ESM Juslin	0.60	0.60	0.51	0.74	1.00	0.40	0.32
EPI Juslin	0.46	0.42	0.86	0.47	0.40	1.00	0.21
SEM	0.50	0.50	0.58	0.50	0.32	0.21	1.00

ELM Juslin, Juslin *et al.*, in press; ELM Laukka, Laukka, 2007; Janata: Janata *et al.*, 2007; Zentner, Zentner *et al.* 2008; ESM Juslin, Juslin *et al.*, 2008; EPI Juslin: Juslin *et al.*, in press.
SEM, strong experiences with music; EPI, recent musical episode, ESM, experience sampling method; ELM, everyday listening of music.

Juslin, ELM Laukka; $r = 0.98$) is higher than their correlation with any of the studies on single episodes. It is also higher than any of the correlations among the various studies of musical episodes.

As there are many gaps in Table 6.8, the correlations in Table 6.9 are based on a varying number of cases, extending from only 10 common emotion terms, as for the studies by Zentner and ESM Juslin, up to 44 common terms for the ELM Juslin and ELM Laukka studies. In fact, only six emotion-related terms appeared in all studies—happy, calm, nostalgic, loving, sad, and angry (see Table 6.8)—including both basic emotions (happy, sad, angry) and emotions representing all four quadrants in a dimensional space formed by valence and arousal (Russell, 1980). Correlations based on only these six cases are still higher ($r = 0.43$–0.99) than the corresponding correlations in Table 6.9, thus demonstrating high agreement among all studies regarding these six emotions.

The most striking difference between the two correlation calculations is that the correlation between EPI Juslin and SEM was only 0.21 (Table 6.9), but was 0.91 when calculated on only the six emotion terms common for all studies. This example, then, highlights the problems with interpreting correlations between studies that use different emotion terms. There is a high need for establishing a common set of emotion terms as discussed by many researchers (e.g. Juslin & Västfjäll, 2008; Zentner et al., 2008). Of course, there are also many other factors that contribute to higher or lower correlations among the studies, such as differences in the type of music, characteristics of subjects (e.g. age, musical preferences), and methods for response (e.g. ratings versus free descriptions). This is left for future investigation.

The importance of emotional reactions to music is beyond question. For instance, in the comprehensive study by Juslin et al. (in press), participants were asked to rate how frequently they experienced emotions to music on a scale from 1 ('Never') to 5 ('Always'). The mode value was 4, corresponding to 'Often'. Generally positive feelings occur much more frequently than negative feelings, both in ELM and SEM. However, some specific differences may be mentioned. While nostalgia is relatively frequent in ELM, it has few appearances in SEM (at least so far). As noted already in the study by Sloboda (1999), music in ELM was often used as a 'Reminder of valued past event', which may include feelings of longing and nostalgia. As SEM occurs rarely and often unexpectedly, it cannot be 'used' in such a way (possibly afterwards as commented below). On the other hand, feelings mentioned only in SEM reports are gratitude (for having had such a happy experience), beauty, and perfection; they reflect the focus on the music itself, unlike in most ELM settings. Other feelings appearing only in SEM (thus not appearing in Table 6.8) are omnipotence ('everything is possible'), humility, insignificance, and awe as in front of something great and overwhelming.

Fairly common negative feelings in SEM are being tired, even exhausted, due to the overwhelming experience. One may feel embarrassed because of being unable to conceal one's strong reactions, especially tears, in front of others. There are single instances of very strong negative reactions as feeling threatened, persecuted, or even panicked due to frightening features of the music or in the performance of it. SEM reports also often describe mixed or conflicting feelings, or feelings that change from negative to positive; such reactions cannot be captured by simple rating scales but require free descriptions.

The main difference between SEM and the other studies concerns the compass of reactions. Emotional aspects are undoubtedly important in any musical circumstances, and we are generally always in some kind of affective state. However, when subjects are asked to provide free descriptions of strong experiences with music, their reports reveal a much more multi-faceted pattern of reactions, as displayed in the SEM descriptive system (see Appendix 6.1). They extend all the way from physical reactions to experiences that are existential or transcendental in character and with far-reaching consequences on a personal level, bringing new insights, confirming and strengthening identity, and increasing self-confidence.

Further comparisons and discussion

ELM and listening in SEM differ in many ways. Most respondents in studies of ELM reported that they listened to music once or several times a day (Juslin & Laukka, 2004; Laukka, 2007); teenagers may spend several hours a day in listening music (North *et al.*, 2000). In ESM studies, music was present in 37–44% of the occasions on which the subjects were contacted (Juslin *et al.*, 2008; North *et al.*, 2004; Sloboda *et al.*, 2001). Such a wide presence of music in everyday life is nowadays a well-known phenomenon among Western listeners, especially in urban settings. In contrast to this, SEM is a rare phenomenon. Respondents in our investigations reported that SEM may appear about once a year (44% of the subjects) or a few times in life (32%; Gabrielsson, 2008).

Studies of ELM may therefore be said to have much higher ecological validity than studies of SEM. Why, then, devote so much work to SEM? There are two main reasons. One is that in order to uncover as completely as possible what components may be contained in the experience of music, there is a need to investigate the most extreme examples of such experiences—a principle stated long ago by William James (1902/1985, p. 39) and often mentioned in textbooks on research methods. Another reason is that, although SEM occasions are relatively rare, they may have far-reaching consequences for the individual, not only in his or her views on music but also on questions regarding identity, relationships with other people, changed views on life and existence, and other matters of great individual importance (see Section 7: Personal and Social Aspects in Appendix 6.1). A single SEM occasion might mean more than a life-long 'average' listening to music.

Of course, ELM and SEM studies differ with regard to their aims. ELM studies aim at investigating the uses and functions of music in people's everyday life; what reactions occur is of secondary importance (at least so far). In SEM the purpose is just the opposite—to uncover the reactions as completely as possible; it is less meaningful to discuss the uses and functions of such rare and often unpredictable experiences. However, many subjects reported that their SEM has led them to 'use' this experience, especially in somehow critical situations, in order to affect their mood. They try to revive the positive feelings from this occasion by listening to the same music or just thinking of how it felt (Gabrielsson, 2008). SEM becomes a resource available for use when needed.

In ELM music is usually secondary, in SEM it is primary. Of course, this difference is a matter of degree and not an absolute difference. Everyone can remember an ELM situation in which music was in fact present but not noticed at all; one was unaware of the music due to total absorption in some other activity—a kind of 'inattentional deafness' (Koreimann, Strauss, & Vitouch, 2009). On other occasions—as when one chooses to listen to certain music to affect one's mood, or to maintain an appropriate level of activity, reduce boredom, or get reminders of past events—one is well aware of the music, at least to start with, but it is not the primary ingredient, it is there to achieve something else. In SEM music is the primary ingredient but even here to a varying degree. Not all SEM occasions are equally intense. In the most explicit SEMs the absorption is total: nothing else matters—one is not aware of the surroundings, nor of body or time, one is overwhelmed by the music, merges with the music. The music is not a figure with something else in the background, it occupies the whole of awareness—'as if it were all there was in the universe, as if it were all of Being' (Maslow, 1968, p. 74). In less intense experiences such a state of total absorption may come and go, attention vacillates just as concert attendants may vacillate in their attention to the music. Moreover, if the music in SEM happens to be connected with personally significant associations or memories—such as of loved persons, beautiful nature, historical events, religious conversion, funerals—the absorption is due to a kind of symbiosis between the music and the associated component, in which the latter may be as important as the music itself, or even more.

We have observed differences between ELM and SEM regarding musical genres— relatively more classical and religious music in SEM, relatively more of various 'popular' genres in ELM; differences in place—relatively more often in concert halls, churches, and other 'formal' settings in SEM, more at home and in various 'informal' settings, such as in cars, restaurants, and shops in ELM. SEM is in most cases associated with live music, ELM with reproduced music. SEM seems to occur more often when one is together with other people, especially with acquaintances, than alone; data on ELM varies in different studies but it seems than listening alone is more common than in SEM. Generally, however, one must take other factors in consideration, such as the subjects' gender, age, and musical preferences, see discussion in connection with Table 6.2 above. Far more detailed analysis, then, may be conducted than that reported here. Perhaps this chapter can serve as inspiration to further exploration of the relations— similarities and differences—between everyday listening to music and single strong experiences with music as well as to exploration of their relevance in different phases and conditions of our lives.

Acknowledgements

I am grateful to Petr Janata, Patrik Juslin, Petri Laukka, and Marcel Zentner for providing supplementary information concerning their studies and to two anonymous reviewers for valuable suggestions.

References

DeNora, T. (2000). *Music in everyday life*. Cambridge: Cambridge University Press.

Gabrielsson, A. (1989). Intense emotional experiences of music. In *Proceedings of the First International Conference on Music Perception and Cognition* (pp. 371–376). Kyoto, Japan: The Japanese Society of Music Perception and Cognition.

Gabrielsson, A. (2001). Emotions in strong experiences with music. In P. N. Juslin, & J. A. Sloboda (Eds.), *Music and emotion: Theory and research* (pp. 431–449). New York, NY: Oxford University Press.

Gabrielsson, A. (2005). Aspekte expressiver Gestaltung musikalischer Aufführungen. In T. S. Stoffer, & R. Oerter (Eds.), *Enzyklopädie der Psychologie. Musikpsychologie Bd 1. Allgemeine Musikpsychologie: Allgemeinpsychologische Grundlagen musikalischen Handels* (pp. 843–875). Göttingen: Hogrefe.

Gabrielsson, A. (2006). Strong experiences elicited by music—What music? In P. Locher, C. Martindale, & L. Dorfman (Eds.), *New directions in aesthetics, creativity, and the arts* (pp. 251–267). Amityville, NY: Baywood Publishing Company.

Gabrielsson, A. (2008). *Starka musikupplevelser—Musik är mycket mer än bara musik* (Strong experiences with music—Music is much more than just music). Hedemora: Gidlunds (under translation).

Gabrielsson, A. (2009). The relationship between musical structure and perceived expression. In S. Hallam, I. Cross, & M. Thaut (Eds.), *Oxford handbook of music psychology* (pp. 141–150). Oxford: Oxford University Press.

Gabrielsson, A. (2010). Strong experiences with music. In P. N. Juslin, & J. A. Sloboda (Eds.), *Handbook of music and emotion* (pp. 547–574). Oxford: Oxford University Press.

Gabrielsson, A., & Juslin, P. N. (2003). Emotional expression in music. In R. J. Davidson, K. R. Scherer, & H. H. Goldsmith, (Eds.), *Handbook of affective sciences* (pp. 503–534). Oxford: Oxford University Press.

Gabrielsson, A., & Lindström, E. (2001). The influence of musical structure on emotional expression. In P. N. Juslin, & J. A. Sloboda (Eds.), *Music and emotion: Theory and research* (pp. 223–248). Oxford: Oxford University Press.

Gabrielsson, A., & Lindström, E. (2010). The role of structure in the musical expression of emotions. In P. N. Juslin, & J. A. Sloboda (Eds.), *Handbook of music and emotion* (pp. 367–400). Oxford: Oxford University Press.

Gabrielsson, A., & Lindström, S. (1993). On strong experiences of music. *Musikpsychologie. Jahrbuch der Deutschen Gesellschaft für Musikpsychologie, 10,* 118–139.

Gabrielsson, A., & Lindström Wik, S. (2003). Strong experiences related to music: A descriptive system. *Musicæ Scientiæ, 7,* 157–217.

James, W. (1902/1985). *The varieties of religious experience*. Harmondsworth: Penguin.

Janata, P., Tomic, S. T., & Rakowski, S. K. (2007). Characterisation of music-evoked autobiographical memories. *Memory, 15,* 845–860.

Juslin, P.N., & Laukka, P. (2004). Expression, perception, and induction of musical emotions: A review and a questionnaire study of everyday listening. *Journal of New Music Research, 33,* 217–238.

Juslin, P. N., Liljeström, S., Laukka, P., Västfjäll, D., & Lundqvist, L.-O. (in press). A nationally representative survey study of emotional reactions to music: Prevalence and causal influences. *Musicæ Scientiæ, Special Issue.*

Juslin, P. N., Liljeström, S., Västfjäll, D., Barradas, G., & Silva, A. (2008). An experience sampling study of emotional reactions to music: Listener, music, and situation. *Emotion, 8,* 668–683.

Juslin, P. N., & Västfjäll, D. (2008). Emotional responses to music: The need to consider underlying mechanisms. *Behavioral and Brain Sciences, 31,* 559–621.

Koreimann, S., Strauss, S., & Vitouch, O. (2009). *Inattentional deafness under dynamic musical conditions*. Paper given at the 7th Triennial ESCOM conference. Jyväskylä, Finland.

Laiho, S. (2004). The psychological functions of music in adolescence. *Nordic Journal of Music Therapy*, *13*, 49–65.

Laukka, P. (2007). Uses of music and psychological well-being among the elderly. *Journal of Happiness Studies*, *8*, 215–241.

Maslow, A. H. (1968). *Toward a psychology of being* (2nd ed.). New York, NY: Van Nostrand Reinhold.

Maslow, A. H. (1976). *The farther reaches of human nature*. New York, NY: Penguin.

North, A. C., Hargreaves, D. J., & Hargreaves, J. J. (2004). Uses of music in everyday life. *Music Perception*, *22*, 41–77.

North, A. C., Hargreaves, D. J., & O'Neill, S. (2000). The importance of music to adolescents. *British Journal of Educational Psychology*, *70*, 255–272.

Panzarella, R. (1980). The phenomenology of aesthetic peak experiences. *Journal of Humanistic Psychology*, *20*, 69–85.

Russell, J. A. (1980). A circumplex model of affect. *Journal of Personality and Social Psychology*, *39*, 1161–1178.

Saarikallio, S., & Erkkilä, J. (2007). The role of music in adolescents' mood regulation. *Psychology of Music*, *35*, 88–109.

Sloboda, J. A. (1990). Music as a language. In F. R.Wilson, & F. L. Roehmann (Eds.), *Music and child development* (pp. 28–43). St. Louis, MO: MMB Music.

Sloboda, J. A. (1999). Everyday uses of music listening: A preliminary study. In Y. I. Suk Won (Ed.), *Music, mind, and science* (pp. 354–369). Seoul: Seoul National University Press.

Sloboda, J. A., Lamont, A., & Greasley, A. (2009). Choosing to hear music. Motivation, process, and effect. In S. Hallam, I. Cross, & M. Thaut (Eds.), *The Oxford handbook of music psychology* (pp. 431–440). Oxford: Oxford University Press.

Sloboda, J. A., & O'Neill, S. A. (2001). Emotions in everyday listening to music. In P. N. Juslin, & J. A. Sloboda (Eds.), *Music and emotion. Theory and research* (pp. 415–429). Oxford: Oxford University Press.

Sloboda, J. A., O'Neill, S. A., & Ivaldi, A. (2001). Functions of music in everyday life. An exploratory study using the Experience Sampling Method. *Musicæ Scientiæ*, *5*, 9–32.

Whaley, J., Sloboda, J. A., & Gabrielsson, A. (2009). Peak experiences in music. In S. Hallam, I. Cross, & M. Thaut (Eds.), *The Oxford handbook of music psychology* (pp. 452–461) Oxford: Oxford University Press.

Zentner, M., Grandjean, D., & Scherer, K. R. (2008). Emotions evoked by the sound of music: Characterization, classification, and measurement. *Emotion*, *8*, 494–521.

Zillmann, D., & Gan, S-L. (1997). Musical taste in adolescence. In D. J. Hargreaves, & A. C. North (Eds.), *The social psychology of music* (pp. 161–187). Oxford: Oxford University Press.

Appendix 6.1

Descriptive system for SEM

Note: This is a condensed version; for the original version, see Gabrielsson and Lindström Wik (2003), Appendix.

1 General characteristics

    1.1 Unique, unforgettable experience

    1.2 Hard-to-describe

2 Physical reactions, behaviours

    2.1 Physiological reactions, e.g. goose flesh, chills, heart race, changed breathing, tears, feel dizzy

    2.2 Behaviours/actions, e.g. laugh, sing, shout, jump, dance, become immovable, withdraw

    2.3 Quasi-physical reactions, e.g. feel weightless, as if floating, as if leaving one's body, as if being carried away by the music

3 Perception
Auditory, visual (impressions of musicians, audience, surroundings, etc.), tactile, kinaesthetic, synaesthetic, intensified, multimodal.

4 Cognition

    4.1 Changed attitude, e.g. special openness, receptivity, expectancy, focused attention, complete absorption

    4.2 Changed experience of situation, body and mind, time and space, wholeness, e.g. unaware of body, time and space, experience of unreality, experience of wholeness

    4.3 Loss of control, e.g. be surprised, moved, hit, shaken, spellbound, fascinated, overwhelmed, music goes straight in

    4.4 Changed relation to the music, e.g. feel embedded in the music, become one with the music, merge with the music, feel directly addressed by the music

    4.5 Associations, memories, thoughts, e. g. of earlier experiences, people, situations; expectations, recognition of music (or not), reflections, wishes

    4.6 Imagery, e g. inner images of landscape, nature, situations, dream oneself away, inner music

5 Feelings/emotions

   5.1 Intense/powerful emotions

   5.2 Positive emotions, e.g. calm, humility, wonder, admiration, solemnity, contentment, gratitude, enjoyment, sweetness, beauty, joy, happiness, elation, excitement, love, perfection, pride, grandeur, rapture, euphoria

   5.3 Negative emotions, e.g. feel lonely, abandoned, longing, melancholy, sadness, confusion, nervousness, disappointment, embarrassment, shame, jealousy, fear, anger, horror, panic

   5.4 Different feelings/emotions, mixed feelings, change of feelings

6 Existential and transcendental aspects

   6.1 Existence, e.g. meaning of life, intense feeling of living, pure being, changed view of life/existence

   6.2 Transcendence, e.g. trance, ecstasy, out-of-the-body experience, cosmic experience, experience of other worlds

   6.3 Religious experience, e.g. vision of heaven, a life after this, feeling addressed by a spiritual message, meeting with the divine, religious confirmation

7 Personal and social aspects

   7.1 New possibilities, insights, needs, e.g. reach one's innermost, healing experience, feel free, inspired, get comfort, hope, power, relief, catharsis

   7.2 Music: new possibilities, insights, needs, e.g. changed view of music, want to learn performing music, choose music as profession, use music to affect one's mood, as therapy

   7.3 Confirmation of identity, self-actualization, e.g. feel chosen, the music reflects one's own person, increased self-esteem

   7.4 Community: communication, e.g. among listeners, performers, with the whole of humankind

Chapter 7

Music and emotion: seven questions, seven answers

Patrik N. Juslin

Abstract

The study of music and emotion has never been in a healthier state. Yet the field is marked by considerable disagreement regarding several issues. In this chapter, I address seven questions that currently define the field. I offer preliminary answers to these questions based on the best theory and evidence available. The aim is to show that researchers have made some progress in answering these questions since John Sloboda's pioneering early work, and that the answers, even those that come from basic as opposed to applied research, could have important implications for broader society.

From a lay person's perspective, few issues in music psychology are more important than explaining how music evokes emotions in listeners. This is because such experiences are one of the primary reasons for engaging with music. Perhaps it may be a surprise to learn, then, that systematic efforts to understand emotions to music are quite recent (Juslin & Sloboda, 2010). Shaped by its origin in late nineteenth century general psychology, with its focus on psychophysics and experimental control, music psychology mostly came to explore more 'basic' perceptual and cognitive processes involved in music listening (Deutsch, 1999). Sloboda was one of the driving forces in establishing 'music cognition' as a thriving research field in the 1980s. Yet, by the time his influential book, *The Musical Mind* (Sloboda, 1985), began to have an impact on the field (for a discussion, see, e.g. Parts 1 and 5 of this volume), Sloboda, always the restless scholar, had already moved on to another field that would blossom in the early 1990s: music and emotion. Still, in reviving Leonard B. Meyer's (1956) classical theory about musical expectations, Sloboda (1991) showed that 'cognition' and 'emotion' might not be as far apart as one would think. Indeed, emotional responses to music *require* cognition (broadly defined). Sloboda would later be one of the researchers who helped to bring 'music and emotion' to the forefront, as a primary topic in music psychology (e.g. Thompson, 2009).

However, while being an enthusiastic contributor to, and patron of, music and emotion research, Sloboda also posed the greatest challenges for the field. For instance, in his commentary on a special issue on the 'Currents trends in the study of music and emotion' (Juslin & Zentner, 2002), Sloboda raised the question 'to what extent the research reported in this issue points to, explicates, and encourages an understanding of diversity and complexity in musical experience' (Sloboda, 2002, p. 242). And in the closing chapter of his most recent book, he urged scholars to consider the social benefits of their work, and underlined the need to provide 'better answers' to important questions (Sloboda, 2005). What is good about such challenges is that they may indeed motivate researchers to look for 'better answers'.

In this chapter, I shall address seven questions that currently define the field of music and emotion. The goal is to demonstrate that the field has made some progress in answering these questions since Sloboda's early work, and that the answers, even those that come from basic as opposed to applied research, could have important implications for broader society.

Does music arouse emotions in listeners?

It seems generally accepted that music is often perceived as expressive of emotions, and some progress has been made in mapping the musical factors involved in this process (Juslin, 2005, Table 5.1; Juslin & Laukka, 2003). But does music also arouse felt emotions? The answer to this question might seem obvious to the reader. Yet this question is to some extent still debated in the field, and it is not trivial, because it raises important issues about the *definition* and *measurement* of emotion. In regard to the first of the issues, note that whereas lay people tend to consider emotions mainly in terms of the phenomenological *feelings* they engender, researchers tend to define emotions in terms of a wider range of phenomena: emotions can increase our heart rate; activate certain brain regions; make us cry, laugh, or trash furniture; make us more prone to remember certain memories than others; and change our perception of the world—however momentarily. A working definition of emotion that adopts this broader view may look like this:

> Emotions are relatively brief, intense, and rapidly changing reactions to potentially important events (subjective challenges or opportunities) in the external or internal environment—often of a social nature—which involve a number of subcomponents (cognitive changes, subjective feelings, expressive behaviour, and action tendencies) that are more or less 'synchronized' during an emotional episode.

Given this definition, it becomes pertinent to ask: to what extent may listening to music produce reactions in the various components of emotion? The most obvious form of evidence concerns *subjective feeling*. Listeners have repeatedly reported that they experience 'feelings' during music listening in experiments (Pike, 1972), survey studies (Gabrielsson, 2001), diary studies (Juslin, Liljeström, Västfjäll, Barradas, & Silva, 2008), and qualitative interviews (DeNora, 2000). Although it may seem unlikely that people are mistaken about their own feelings (Griffiths, 1997), some researchers have claimed that verbal self-reports of musical emotions[1] may be unreliable—either because listeners confuse the emotions *expressed* in the music with their *own* emotions, or because the listener is reporting an emotion simply because this is expected by the experimenter, so-called 'demand characteristics' (Orne, 1962). Therefore, several researchers have attempted to obtain other types of evidence, which cannot be explained (away) in such ways.

One emotion component which is far less subject to demand characteristics than verbal self-report of feelings—because it is not usually possible to control by will—is *physiological response*. Several experiments have shown that music listening can give rise to physiological responses very similar to those shown to other 'emotional' stimuli, including changes in heart rate, skin temperature, skin conductance, breathing, and hormone secretion (see Hodges, 2010, for a recent review). Different pieces of music can produce different patterns of physiological response (Krumhansl, 1997), such that it is possible to discriminate among emotions based on psychophysiological variables by using multivariate techniques (Nyklíček, Thayer, & Van Doornen, 1997). More intense subjective feelings tend to involve more pronounced physiological reactions (Rickard, 2004), which may include 'chills' (Panksepp, 1995).

Independent support for emotional reactions to music also comes from recent studies of *brain activation*. Listeners' responses to music involve many brain areas that are known from previous studies to be implicated in emotional responses. These include both subcortical and cortical areas (e.g. the thalamus, the hippocampus, the amygdala, the orbitofrontal cortex, the insula, and the nucleus accumbens; see Blood & Zatorre, 2001; Brown, Martinez, & Parsons, 2004; Koelsch, Fritz, von Cramon, Müller, & Friederici, 2006).

Further evidence of emotions to music comes from *expressive behaviour*. Music listening makes people cry, smile, laugh, and furrow their brows—as indicated by observations and electromyographic (EMG) measures of facial muscles. Such responses have been documented under controlled laboratory conditions (e.g. Witvliet & Vrana, 2007), but may, of course, also be observed informally during concerts where facial, vocal, and bodily expressions of emotion are common. Crying to music seems to occur frequently (Frey, 1985), and may begin within a few seconds of hearing a piece of music. Expressive behaviour is usually a distinct indicator of an emotion: as observed by Sloboda (1992), 'it is very difficult to be mistaken about whether you cried or not to a piece of music' (p. 39).

Music may also influence people's *action tendencies*, such as the tendency to help other people (Fried & Berkowitz, 1979), to buy certain products (North & Hargreaves, 2010), or to move, whether overtly or covertly (Harrer & Harrer, 1977). Some musical contexts encourage overt actions in the listener (e.g. rock concerts, music in shops), whereas other contexts force the listener to listen 'respectfully', that is, still and silently (e.g. symphony concerts).

One final component of emotions involved in listening to music is *regulation*. Listeners regulate their own emotional responses to music with regard to what are deemed 'appropriate' responses in the social context (Becker, 2004; Gabrielsson, 2001). For instance, a listener may become embarrassed if he or she is moved by a piece of music and starts to cry, and may thus attempt to regulate this emotion (e.g. by breathing slowly).[2]

It could be argued, perhaps, that several of the above studies have looked at only one of the components, and that this should not count as evidence if an emotion involves *all* or *most* of the components. Thus, Scherer and Zentner (2001, p. 363) proposed the quite conservative criterion that an emotion to music should involve 'evidence of a synchronized response of all or most organismic subsystems' (or components).

Such synchronization in response to music has recently been demonstrated. An experimental study measured self-reported feeling, facial muscle activity (EMG), and autonomic activity in 32 subjects while they listened to pieces of pop music that were composed with either a 'happy' or 'sad' expression. The results revealed a coherent manifestation in the experiential, expressive, and physiological components: thus, for instance, 'happy' music produced more zygomatic facial muscle activity (smiling), greater skin conductance, lower finger temperature, more felt 'happiness', and less felt 'sadness' than 'sad' music. Furthermore, the effects of the music were generally large, suggesting that music can be a rather potent elicitor of emotions (Lundqvist, Carlsson, Hilmersson, & Juslin, 2009).

Such evidence of a synchronized reaction in multiple emotion components obtained from focused music listening in a controlled laboratory environment, is difficult to explain (away) for those who argue that music does not evoke emotions: if such a reaction is *not* an emotion, what is it? Synchronization is most easily observed during intense emotions, and seems to be stronger between feelings and expression, than between feelings and physiology (Mauss, Levenson, McCarter, Wilhelm, & Gross, 2005). Still, its presence may help us to distinguish arousal of emotions from mere perception, which is still a problem in the field (for a discussion, see Gabrielsson, 2002).

Which emotions does music arouse?

To the extent that we can agree that music arouses emotions (and most researchers do), the next question is *which* emotions music arouses. This is the issue of *prevalence*—that is, the relative frequency of occurrence of a phenomenon, such as emotional reactions to music, in the population of interest. This issue is commonly debated in the field, yet few studies have actually addressed it. Prevalence data are important, since they describe the phenomena that any theory of music and emotion must be able to explain. Sloboda (1992, Table 1) provided some seminal findings (see also Wells & Hakanen, 1991): Seventy-six college students were asked to indicate which of 25 emotions they had experienced to music. *Sadness* and *joy* were the two emotional states experienced by most listeners (96.2% and 93.4%, respectively).

As interest in music and emotion has increased, more attention has been devoted to this issue. Recent evidence from a handful of survey studies suggests that music can evoke quite a wide range of affective states. Among the most frequently felt musical emotions, according to these survey studies, are: *happiness*, *calm*, *nostalgia*, *love*, *sadness*, *interest*, *hope*, *excitement*, and *longing*, as well various synonymous emotion terms (see Juslin & Laukka, 2004; Sloboda, 1992; Wells & Hakanen, 1991; Zentner, Grandjean, & Scherer, 2008).

However, the above studies share certain limitations. First, they relied on retrospective and aggregated estimates, which are subject to certain biases (e.g. Robinson & Clore, 2002). Second, the studies did not use a representative sample of participants—and it is well known that precisely who participates in an investigation might have a profound effect on the results. Finally, the data were based on ratings of terms selected by the researcher. It could be argued that this issue should ideally be investigated using an open-ended response format, so that the participants are not influenced by the researcher's preconceptions.

Of particular interest then are findings that are not subject to such limitations. In a large-scale survey study (Juslin, Liljeström, Laukka, Västfjäll, & Lundqvist, in press), based on a randomized and statistically representative sample of the Swedish population, over 700 participants reported their most recent emotional experience of music. They could describe their *feelings* in their own words rather than using a pre-selected list of terms. This unique set of episodic data revealed several notable tendencies. First, 84% of the episodes referred to positive as opposed to negative affective states. Second, 92% of the episodes referred to *specific* emotions as opposed to broader (positive or negative) affect states. Third, of the specific emotion episodes, 89% featured 'single' emotions, whereas 11% featured 'mixed' emotions (e.g. happiness and sadness). Figure 7.1 presents the prevalence of specific emotions, in terms of the 10 most frequently reported emotion categories. As seen, music aroused a fairly broad range of emotions. The five most frequent emotions were *happy elated*, *sad-melancholic*, *calm-content*, *nostalgic-longing*, and *aroused-alert*. It can further be noted that affective states such as *wonder*, *awe*, and *chills* seem to be experienced rarely in response to music in everyday life, as previously suggested by Huron (2006).

In sum, the findings from studies so far suggest that music listeners experience anything from mere arousal, chills, and 'basic' emotions (e.g. *happiness*, *sadness*) to more 'complex' emotions (e.g. *nostalgia*, *pride*), and even 'mixed' emotions. This, then, is what any satisfactory theory of musical emotions must be able to explain. Prevalence data from open-ended formats (such as those presented in Figure 7.1) may be

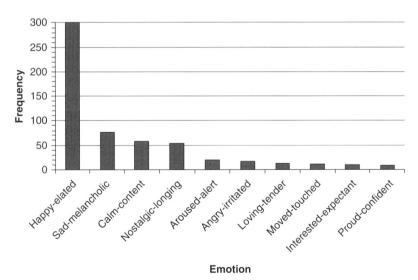

Fig. 7.1 Prevalence of freely reported emotions to music from a randomized and statistically representative sample of the Swedish population. (*N* = 706) (From Juslin *et al.*, in press.)

especially useful to develop new reporting schemes for this domain (see Nielsen & Kaszniak, 2007). Indeed, several authors have proposed novel self-report scales specifically for musical emotions (e.g. Bartel, 1992; Juslin & Laukka, 2004, Table 5; Zentner *et al.*, 2008). Although these scales are interesting and may be quite useful, it may be premature to commit ourselves to specific response formats until we have more prevalence data from different contexts. This is because the prevalence of specific emotions varies depending on the precise *context*, which leads us to consider the next question.

In what contexts do musical emotions occur?

Why is this issue important? If there is anything we have learned, it is that emotions to music can never be predicted from musical characteristics alone. Different listeners react differently to the same piece of music. And even the same listener reacts differently to the same music in different contexts. All musical emotions occur in a complex interplay between the listener, the music, and the situation. This interplay is obviously difficult to capture in a laboratory. Hence, to understand musical emotions, we must study them as they naturally occur in everyday life.

When the 'social psychology of music' blossomed in the early 1990s (e.g. Hargreaves & North, 1997), it helped music psychology move away from the typical 1980s paradigm of laboratory-based experiments concerning cognitive processes to a broader exploration of the ways in which music is utilized and experienced in everyday life. Again, Sloboda's research was at the centre of a new trend (Sloboda, O'Neill, & Ivaldi, 2001) that would offer novel opportunities for exploring 'when' and 'where' musical emotions actually occur, for instance using the experience sampling method (ESM).[3]

Preliminary results (e.g. Juslin *et al.*, 2008; see also North, Hargreaves, & Hargreaves, 2004; Sloboda *et al.*, 2001) indicate that music in some form occurs in approximately 30–40% of the episodes sampled randomly in everyday life by means of the ESM. However, music does not *always* evoke an emotion. Preliminary estimates indicate that we are only 'moved' by the music in 55–65% of the episodes featuring music; further, musical emotion episodes are most prevalent in the *evening* (followed by the *afternoon*, and the *morning*). Emotions to music are also more frequent during *weekend days* than during *workdays*. These patterns largely reflect patterns of work versus leisure, with music occurring more often during leisure.

Moving on to the question of 'where', it is clear that musical emotions occur in a wide range of settings in everyday life. The settings have been characterized in terms of activities, physical locations, and social conditions. Both survey (Juslin *et al.*, in press) and ESM data (Juslin *et al.*, 2008) indicate that the most common activities during musical emotions are focused music listening, travel, movie or television watching, work/study, social interaction, and relaxation. Note, however, that in a random sample of 573 musical emotion episodes from everyday life, only a minority (15%) of the episodes featured focused music listening (Juslin *et al.*, 2008). It further seems that attending a concert is a rare activity, even among people who are interested in music. Therefore, 'live' music is rarely the source of musical emotion in everyday life.

The most common sources of music heard are instead: stereo equipment, personal computers, television, Walkman/MP3 players, and radio. The most commonly heard (and preferred) musical genre in emotion episodes in everyday life is 'pop/rock', suggesting that more research should focus on this musical genre in order to have ecological validity (Juslin *et al.*, 2008, in press—the latter study featured a statistically representative sample of listeners from the Swedish population).

The settings in which emotions to music occur have also been analysed in terms of the location. A few studies have shown that listeners are especially prone to experience emotions to music 'at home' and 'outdoors' (Juslin *et al.*, 2008; North *et al.*, 2004; Sloboda *et al.*, 2001). However, in at least one of these studies (Juslin *et al.*, 2008), the emotions were most frequent at home and outdoors mainly because participants spent most time there. Yet musical emotions can occur in a variety of locations, indicating that they are not really dependent on a particular location, with the exception of special concert experiences.[4] This may seem to suggest that the context is not important after all. However, as noted earlier, the context might influence *which* emotions are evoked. For example, consider the influence of social condition (i.e. if other people are present or not in the musical event). Although music often occurs in social settings (e.g. with partner or friend), a significant proportion (approximately 40%) of musical emotion episodes seem to occur when the listener is alone. Moreover, the social condition (alone versus with others) seems to influence which emotions are induced. Some emotions, such as *happiness-elation*, *pleasure-enjoyment*, and *anger-irritation*, often occur in 'social' settings (during social interaction, among friends). Others, such as *calm-contentment*, *nostalgia-longing*, and *sadness-melancholy*, often occur in 'solitary' settings (listening alone). That the prevalence of specific emotions varies depending on the context—activity, location, and social condition—highlights the need to use representative samples of situations in order to obtain valid estimates of prevalence (Juslin *et al.*, 2008). Yet, claims about the prevalence of specific emotions to music are frequently made on the basis of data that do not involve representative samples of either listener or situations.

If the context affects which emotions are aroused by music, we might be tempted to ask: Can musical emotions even be *predicted* based on the context? Many scholars have noted that musical emotions may be 'too subjective' to be predictable (Gutheil, 1952, p. 11). Fortunately, data from a survey study indicate that musical emotions *can* be predicted to some extent from information about the context. Fifteen predictors were featured in a discriminant analysis, five for each of the main factors (i.e. listener, music, situation). The analysis focused on predicting three common emotion categories in a representative sample—*happy-elated*, *sad-melancholic*, and *nostalgic-longing*. Results revealed that these emotions could be predicted with an overall accuracy of 70% correct (compared to an accuracy of 33% that would be expected by chance). This success, however modest, suggests that musical emotions may not be too subjective to be modelled, in principle. However, the prediction was far from perfect, even though this analysis included many predictors in the music, the listener, and the situation (Juslin *et al.*, in press). Why is that? Is it perhaps because the analysis neglected another important variable: the underlying mechanism responsible for the arousal of the emotion. This leads us to the next question.

How does music arouse emotions?

Lay people are frequently puzzled by musical emotions, and so, it seems, are philosophers of music: 'Music provides neither the objects nor, therefore, the belief-opportunities that would make it possible for musical works to arouse such emotions as anger, sadness, joy ...' (Kivy, 1990, p. 165). How, then, can music evoke these emotions, as well as numerous other states? To me, this is the most important question in the field. And it is an issue that indirectly holds the key to many other issues currently debated (see below).

How emotions to music are caused has been addressed in two different ways. One way has been to map those factors (in the listener, the music, and the situation) that, in some way, influence emotions. Another way has been to develop a theory about the specific mechanism that mediates among musical events and experienced emotions. I shall consider each of these approaches in turn.

The most common approach has been to explore causal factors. Research has revealed a number of factors in the *individual* that could potentially affect emotional responses to music, such as the listener's age, gender, personality, musical training, music preference, and current mood (Abeles & Chung, 1996). Similarly, Gabrielsson (2001) suggested several factors in the *situation* that may potentially influence emotions, such as 'physical factors' (e.g. acoustic and visual conditions, time and place), 'social factors' (e.g. listening alone versus with others, type of audience), and 'special occasions and circumstances' (e.g. a vacation). However, most studies have focused on causal factors in the *music* itself. In Sloboda (1991), 83 participants aged 16–70 (most of them musicians) were asked to mention specific pieces of music, to which they could recall having experienced various physical manifestations associated with experiencing emotions. Having identified such pieces, which came mostly from classical music, they were then asked to specify the exact location within the music that provoked these reactions. Most participants reported whole pieces, movements, or sections of movements, which suggests an emotional response to the 'overall' character of the music (Table 3 in Sloboda, 1991). Such a response might reflect 'emotional contagion', based on the emotional expression of the piece (discussed below). However, about a third of the participants were able to locate their reaction within a theme or smaller unit. The data showed that musical events associated with 'tears' (i.e. crying, lump in the throat) commonly contained melodic appoggiaturas and melodic or harmonic sequences; events associated with 'shivers' (i.e. goose pimples, shivers down the spine) usually contained a new or unprepared harmony; and events associated with 'heart reactions' contained syncopations or prominent events occurring earlier than prepared for. What is particularly interesting about Sloboda's study is that unlike most other studies, it does not *only* point to links between musical factors and emotional responses, it also attempts to relate these links to a possible mechanism. The results are related to Meyer's (1956) notion that schematically based *musical expectancies*, and violations of these, play an important role in emotional responses to music (discussed below). Hence, Sloboda's early interest in the role of musical expectancy may be seen to have foreshadowed more recent approaches to emotion causation in music that focus on underlying mechanisms (Juslin & Västfjäll, 2008a, 2008b).

Understanding the important role of underlying mechanisms in accounting for emotions to music requires a broader consideration of the issue of how, precisely, emotions are evoked. General research on emotions and stress soon discovered that it was difficult to find objective situation predictors that would (invariably) affect different people in the same way: different persons tend to react in different ways to the 'same' stimulus. This realization forms the basis of theories of emotion causation (for an overview, see Moors, 2009): to be able to explain the individual differences among people, it becomes necessary to describe what happens *between* objects and emotions. The term *psychological mechanism* refers to this mediation, the type of 'information processing' in the brain that leads to the arousal of an emotion.

The most commonly discussed mechanism is *cognitive appraisal* (e.g. Scherer, 1999). Cognitive appraisal refers to a process whereby an emotion is evoked in a person because an event is interpreted as having important implications for the person's goals (in terms of goal congruence, coping potential, or compatibility with social norms). The problem is that music as such rarely has implications for life goals. Indeed, preliminary data indicate that cognitive appraisal is rarely the cause of musical emotions in everyday life (Juslin *et al.*, 2008), casting serious doubts on Scherer and Zentner's (2001) argument that componential process theories (appraisal theories) are 'better suited to provide the theoretical underpinnings for research on the specific emotions produced by different types of music' (p. 381). Quite to the opposite, it seems necessary to study other mechanisms that are more relevant in the case of music. Several scholars have discussed possible mechanisms, typically focusing on one or a few possibilities (e.g. Berlyne, 1971; Dowling & Harwood, 1986; Juslin & Sloboda, 2001; Scherer & Zentner, 2001), but the most comprehensive attempt to delineate the various mechanisms that underlie musical emotions is the BRECVEM model (Juslin, Liljeström, Västfjäll, & Lundqvist, 2010), which postulates no less than seven mechanisms (besides cognitive appraisal) through which music might induce emotions: namely *brain stem reflexes*, *rhythmic entrainment*, *evaluative conditioning*, *contagion*, *visual imagery*, *episodic memory*, and *musical expectancy*.

The point of departure is an evolutionary perspective on the emotion induction process. Mechanisms of emotion induction are regarded as information-processing devices at various levels of the brain, which use distinct types of information to guide future behaviour. As Patel (2008) notes, humans are unparalleled in their ability to make sense out of sound—including music. The mechanisms are conceived of as based on a number of more or less distinct brain functions that have developed gradually and in a specific order during evolution. Because the mechanisms depend on functions of different evolutionary origins, each mechanism will have unique characteristics that influence its functioning. Some mechanisms operate at lower 'subcortical' levels: their processing is largely subconscious, automatic, and independent of other psychological processes (this is so-called 'modularity'). Other mechanisms operate at higher cortical levels: their processing is more available to consciousness, can be influenced by will to some extent, and is easily 'distracted' by competing stimuli or processing. The mechanisms may interact to some extent, leading to conflicting outputs under certain circumstances, hence the occurrence of 'mixed emotions' in response to music (see above).

None of the mechanisms evolved for the sake of music, but they may all be recruited in interesting (and perhaps unique) ways by musical events. Each mechanism is responsive to its own combination of information in the music, the listener, and the situation. The mechanisms do not necessarily treat 'musical' events as distinct from other events, which can explain why music can evoke even emotions that do not appear to 'make sense' in a musical context. Each mechanism has a tendency to arouse some emotions rather than others, but between them, the mechanisms can account for a wide range of emotions. The seven mechanisms featured in the BRECVEM framework may be described as given below (for a detailed discussion and references, see Juslin & Västfjäll, 2008a, 2008b; Juslin *et al.*, 2010).

Brain stem reflex refers to a process whereby an emotion is induced by music because one or more fundamental acoustic characteristics of the music are taken by the brain stem to signal a potentially important and urgent event that needs attention. In music, this may involve sounds that are sudden, loud, dissonant, and feature fast or rapidly changing temporal patterns. Brain stem reflexes are quick, automatic, and unlearned. A response to an auditory event suggesting 'danger' can be emitted as early as at the level of the inferior colliculus of the brain stem. (An example of a musical stimulus that could evoke a brain stem reflex is the kettledrum stroke in Joseph Haydn's Symphony No. 94.) This mechanism, however, will primarily evoke *arousal*, and surprise.

Rhythmic entrainment refers to a process whereby an emotion is evoked by a piece of music because a powerful, external rhythm in the music influences some internal bodily rhythm of the listener (e.g. heart rate), such that the latter rhythm adjusts toward and eventually 'locks in' to a common periodicity. The adjusted heart rate can then spread to other components of emotion such as feeling, through proprioceptive feedback. This may produce an increased level of arousal in the listener. Musical properties that can contribute to such reactions are a strong pulse (e.g. 'techno music'), preferably one that is relatively close to the natural heart rate or respiration of the listener, and a tempo *accelerando* that may help to 'drive' the pulse. Since 'oscillators' (autonomous rhythmic processes) do not synchronize instantaneously, the entrainment mechanism is a slower induction process than a brain stem reflex. However, the entrainment-inducing qualities of music might produce feelings of arousal, communion, and perhaps even trance-like altered states of consciousness (e.g. shamanic rituals, rave parties).

Evaluative conditioning (EC) refers to a process whereby an emotion is induced by a piece of music simply because this stimulus has often been paired with other positive or negative stimuli. For example, a particular piece of music may have occurred repeatedly together in time with a specific event that always makes you happy, such as meeting your friends. Over time, through repeated pairings, the music itself will eventually evoke happiness even in the absence of the friendly interaction. EC may occur even if one is unaware of the contingency of the two stimuli. Which element of the music best serves as the 'conditioned stimulus' and its degree of generalization and discrimination remain to be explored—though the melody or theme of the music could be especially effective, as illustrated for instance by Wagner in his *Leitmotif* strategy. EC depends on unconscious, unintentional and effortless processes which can be subtly influenced by mundane musical events in everyday life.

Emotional *contagion* refers to a process whereby an emotion is induced by a piece of music because the listener perceives the emotional expression of the music, and then 'mimics' this expression internally. Why would listeners react in such a way to music?

The answer lies in the fact that music often features acoustical patterns similar to those that occur in emotional speech. One might thus hypothesize that that we get aroused by voice-like features of music because a brain module responds quickly and automatically to certain stimulus features *as if* they were coming from a human voice conveying emotion—presumably through some kind of 'mirror neuron' system involved in empathic responses. Instrumental teaching often aims for the voice as an ideal, and most music today includes vocals, making a contagion reaction even more plausible. However, this could also involve 'voice-like' instruments, like the cello or the violin. Indeed, I have theorized that a 'contagion module' in the brain might treat such instruments as 'super-expressive voices': they are reminiscent of the human voice and yet go much further in terms of their expressive features (e.g., wider pitch range).

Visual imagery refers to a process whereby an emotion is evoked in the listener because he or she conjures up inner images (e.g., of a beautiful landscape) while listening to the music. The listener appears to conceptualize the musical structure via a metaphorical, non-verbal mapping between the metaphorical affordances of the music and 'image-schemata', grounded in bodily experience. For instance, in listening to a piece one can hear a melodic movement as 'upward' and then visualize oneself 'flying higher'. Listeners may presumably respond to these mental images much in the same way as they would to the same stimuli in the 'real' world. Note that the listener may influence the imagery to a considerable extent. Although images might come into the mind unbidden, in general a listener may conjure up, manipulate, and dismiss images at will. Yet, certain musical features (e.g. repetition; predictability in melodic, harmonic, and rhythmic elements; slow tempo) may be especially effective in stimulating imagery. It should be noted that there are wide individual differences between listeners regarding imagery: some experience it regularly, whereas others hardly experience it at all.

Episodic memory refers to a process whereby an emotion is induced in a listener because the music evokes a personal memory of a specific event in the listener's life. Music often evokes episodic memories (the 'Darling, they are playing our tune' phenomenon), and some of these can be strongly emotional, perhaps because the physiological reaction patterns to the original events are stored in memory along with the experiential content. Episodic memory appears to be one of the most common sources of emotions to music, judging from ESM data. Listeners actively use music to remind them of valued past events, which suggests that music serves an important *nostalgic* function in everyday life. Episodic memories associated with music from young adulthood seem especially vivid, perhaps because many self-defining experiences tend to occur at this stage of life development, with music playing a prominent role in establishing a self-identity. Through episodic memories, music can truly be the 'soundtrack of our lives'.

Musical expectancy refers to a process whereby an emotion is induced in a listener because a specific feature of the music violates, delays, or confirms the listener's expectations about the continuation of the music. However, this concept does not involve *any* unexpected event that can occur in relation to music.[5] It only refers to musical expectancies that involve *syntactical* relationships between different parts of the musical structure. Such expectations are based on the listener's previous experiences of the same musical style, as suggested by Leonard Meyer. Emotional reactions to music are usually evoked when the listener's musical expectations are somehow disrupted, for instance by unprepared or unexpected harmonic changes, as shown in Sloboda's seminal research. Syntactic processing in language and music may share a common set of processes for syntactical integration (Patel, 2008).

What, then, are the essential characteristics of these seven psychological mechanisms? By synthesizing theory and findings from various domains mostly *outside* music, Juslin and Västfjäll (2008a) provided the first set of hypotheses that can help researchers to distinguish between the proposed mechanisms. An updated version of these hypotheses (from Juslin *et al.*, 2010) is provided in Table 7.1. The crucial point is that each mechanism has some unique characteristics, and that failure to distinguish between the mechanisms in studies may lead to seemingly inconsistent findings. Most studies in the field have looked for simple one-to-one relationships between music and emotion. This is essentially a 'behaviourist' approach, since it focuses on stimulus–response relationships, while ignoring intervening psychological processes. The problem is that when you play a piece of music for a listener, any of a number of mechanisms can be activated, and depending on which one, the results (e.g. feelings, brain regions involved, process characteristics) may be quite different (see Table 7.1).[6]

If the above reasoning is correct—that musical emotions reflect general mechanisms of emotion induction activated by music—this raises another recurring question in the field.

Are musical emotions different from other emotions?

In my estimation, there is no simple 'yes' or 'no' answer to this question, because the answer depends on what we mean: 'Different' in what sense? Indeed, the question can be approached in a number of ways.

One approach to the question is to ask whether there are types of affective states which music cannot evoke, but that occur in other contexts. Thus, for example, some scholars have argued that music cannot arouse proper emotions, it can only arouse moods. However, there are several findings suggesting that what music listeners experience are emotions rather than just moods. Besides the fact that the induction process involves a specific 'object' (the music or, more specifically, certain information in the music processed in relation to individual and situational factors), the states last for only a brief duration (e.g. Scherer, Zentner, & Schacht, 2002); they have a relatively strong intensity (e.g. Juslin *et al.*, 2008, in press); and they include autonomic responses (Krumhansl, 1997). All these features are believed to be associated with emotions, rather than moods (e.g. Beedie, Terry, & Lane, 2005). Hence, the notion that music can only arouse moods appears to be without merit.

Another approach is to argue that music can only arouse certain emotions. For example, some scholars have suggested that music does *not* arouse emotions of the 'garden variety', or 'basic' emotions (see Kivy, 1990; Scherer, 2003). As should be apparent, this notion has been disconfirmed by a large number of studies which clearly suggest that music can arouse 'basic' emotions—such as *happiness*, *sadness*, and *anger*—in listeners (e.g. Juslin & Laukka, 2004; Scherer *et al.*, 2002; Sloboda, 1992). Juslin *et al.* (2010) argued that the notion that music does not induce 'basic' emotions rests on the mistaken assumption that such states can only be aroused by cognitive appraisals in relation to life goals (Kivy, 1990), which is not the case, as we saw above (see Table 7.1). 'Basic' emotions can be aroused by both music and non-musical stimuli through mechanisms other than cognitive appraisal (e.g. contagion).

Table 7.1 Hypotheses for seven mechanisms through which music may evoke emotions in listeners.

Mechanism	Survival value of brain function	Information focus	Ontogenetic development
Brain stem reflex	Focusing attention on potentially important changes or events in the close environment	Extreme or rapidly changing basic acoustic characteristics	Prior to birth
Rhythmic entrainment	Facilitating motor coordination in physical work tasks	Periodic pulses in rhythms, especially around 2Hz	Prior to birth (perception only)
Evaluative conditioning	Being able to associate objects or events with positive and negative outcomes	Covariation between events	Prior to birth
Contagion	Enhancing group cohesion and social interaction, e.g. between mother and infant	Emotional motor expression	First year
Visual imagery	Permitting internal simulations of events that substitute for overt and risky actions	Self-conjured visual images	Pre-school years
Episodic memory	Allowing conscious recollections of previous events and binding the self to reality	Personal events in particular places and at particular times	3–4 years
Musical expectancy	Facilitating symbolic language with a complex semantics	Syntactic information	5–11 years

Mechanism	Key brain regions	Cultural impact/ learning	
Brain stem reflex	Reticular formation in the brain stem, the intralaminar nuclei of the thalamus, the inferior colliculus	Low	
Rhythmic entrainment	Networks of multiple oscillators in the cerebellum and the sensorimotor regions	Low	
Evaluative conditioning	The lateral nucleus of the amygdala, the interpositus nucleus of the cerebellum	High	
Contagion	'Mirror neurons' in the pre-motor regions, right inferior frontal regions, the basal ganglia	Low	
Visual imagery	Spatially mapped regions of the occipital cortex, the visual association cortex, and (for image generation) left temporo-occipital regions	High	

(continued)

Table 7.1 (*continued*) Hypotheses for seven mechanisms through which music may evoke emotions in listeners.

Mechanism	Key brain regions	Cultural impact/ learning	
Episodic memory	The medial temporal lobe, especially the hippocampus, and the right anterior prefrontal cortex (applies to memory retrieval)	High	
Musical expectancy	The left perisylvian cortex, 'Broca's area', the dorsal region of the anterior cingulate cortex	High	
Mechanism	**Induced affect**	**Induction speed**	**Degree of volitional influence**
Brain stem reflex	General arousal, unpleasantness vs. pleasantness	High	Low
Rhythmic entrainment	General arousal, pleasant feelings of communion	Slow	Low
Evaluative conditioning	Basic emotions	High	Low
Contagion	Basic emotions	High	Low
Visual imagery	All possible emotions, although especially relaxation and pleasure	Low	High
Episodic memory	All possible emotions, although especially nostalgia	Low	Medium
Musical expectancy	Surprise, awe, pleasure, 'thrills' disappointment, hope, anxiety	Low	Low
Mechanism	**Availability to consciousness**	**Modularity**	**Dependence on musical structure**
Brain stem reflex	Low	High	Medium
Rhythmic entrainment	Low	High	Medium
Evaluative conditioning	Low	High	Low
Emotional contagion	Low	High	Medium
Visual imagery	High	Low	Medium
Episodic memory	High	Low	Low
Musical expectancy	Medium	Medium	High

For further discussion and supporting references, see Juslin & Västfjäll, (2008a) and Juslin et al., (2010). Reproduced from Juslin and Sloboda, *Handbook of music and emotion*, 2010 with permission from Oxford University Press.

Some scholars have argued that music—or 'art' more generally—might arouse 'unique' emotions not experienced in everyday life. Swanwick (1985) proposed that 'emotions in "life" … and emotions we might experience as a result of engaging with music are not the same' (p. 29). However, so far, no one has been able to present any convincing evidence of such 'music-unique' emotions. Proposals have involved states that either occur in other realms of life (e.g. *pleasure, wonder, nostalgia, awe, feeling moved*) or cannot seriously be regarded as emotions (e.g. *cognitive irony*).

However, although music may not evoke 'unique' emotions, it could involve a specific frequency distribution of emotions. Juslin *et al.* (2008) were the first to provide estimates of prevalence of specific emotions in response to both musical and non-musical events using a representative sample of everyday situations. There were both similarities and differences in the results. The overall trend was similar for musical and non-musical emotion episodes. For instance, *calm-contentment* and *happiness-elation* were the most frequently felt emotions and *shame-guilt* and *disgust-contempt* the least frequently felt emotions, regardless of the type of episode. Further, positively valenced emotions were more common than negatively valenced emotions in both types of episodes. But there were also some differences: *happiness-elation* and *nostalgia-longing* were more common during musical emotion episodes than during non-musical episodes. Conversely, *anger-irritation*, *boredom-indifference*, and *anxiety-fear* were more common during non-musical episodes than during musical emotion episodes. Moreover, and as hypothesized, musical emotions involved a larger proportion of positive emotions than did non-musical emotions. Hence, it might be the case that, although music evokes several of the same emotions as other stimuli in life, music has a characteristic frequency distribution of emotions that is skewed towards positive emotions. This could be just one example of a more general phenomenon—that there are different frequency distributions across the spectrum of emotions as a function of the precise context sampled (e.g. music, sports, politics).

In addition, it seems likely that musical emotions could have some other characteristics. For instance, Frijda and Sundararajan (2007) proposed the notion of *refined emotions*, which could be relevant in a musical context. This notion does not actually refer to a special subset of emotions (e.g. that anger is 'coarse' whereas love is 'refined'), but rather to a special *mode* of experiencing all the ordinary emotions—characterized by attitudes of detachment, restraint, self-reflexivity, and savouring. This mode of experiencing emotions may well occur in relation to music, yet it also occurs in connection with religion, gourmet food, and so forth. Does this mean that there is nothing unique about our musical experiences? Not necessarily. But the unique nature of musical experiences is perhaps not due to the emotions they involve. This leads us to the next question.

What is the role of emotion in musical experience?

The answer to this question depends on what musical experiences may entail. Gabrielsson's (2001) descriptive system indicates that they involve a number of features, such as physical, behavioural, perceptual, cognitive, existential, and developmental features. Emotion is only one of them. Hence, we should be careful not to equate 'musical experience' with 'emotion', because clearly there is much more to 'musical experience' than just emotion. Many musical experiences may not involve emotion at all. When emotions do occur, I think they contribute by a adding a more deeply *personal* significance to the music experience (e.g. by connecting it to our life history). But we should be more open to the possibility that much of what makes musical experiences unique are truly non-emotional aspects, such as the conscious perception of musical structure or form and its subtle dynamic changes over time; by avoiding to refer to such experiential *qualia* as 'emotion' or 'feeling', we can also avoid some of the controversy that has surrounded these concepts in musical contexts (Juslin & Västfjäll, 2008b).

On the other hand, if 'emotion' and 'feeling', as normally defined by emotion scholars, do not capture everything relevant in musical experiences, one might predict that, in the long term, the field of music and emotion may eventually be subsumed under the far broader field of 'music experience' to explain more comprehensively how music is experienced. This will, eventually, have to involve the thorny issue of how 'emotion' relates to 'aesthetic experience'. Common conceptions of aesthetic experience emphasize its focus on an art object's *aesthetic properties*—its form and content. And according to Levenson (2003), it is widely agreed that aesthetic properties are *perceptual* properties relevant to the *aesthetic value* of the object that possesses them (p. 6). What, exactly, should count as 'aesthetically valuable' is still debated. Is it beauty? Expressivity? Originality? It is similarly unclear whether an aesthetic response is necessarily emotional.

I have argued that, although an emotion may often co-occur with an aesthetic response, it is not a *required* feature for a listener's response to qualify as 'aesthetic'. Rather, 'emotion', 'preference', and 'aesthetic response' are partly independent phenomena that, however, tend to influence each other (e.g. Juslin *et al.*, 2010). A few examples may suffice to illustrate this point: First (as I should have made clear above), it is perfectly possible for a piece of music to evoke an emotion in a listener, without the listener experiencing anything like an 'aesthetic response'. For instance, a piece of music may subconsciously evoke sadness in a listener who does not even attend to the sounds, simply because the music has repeatedly been paired with sadness-evoking stimuli in the past (i.e. evaluative conditioning).

Second, it is possible to prefer a piece of music heard on the radio over a piece heard earlier, without the music arousing any emotion (with a synchronized response in experience, physiology, and expression).[7] In addition, this liking response need not involve an evaluation of the piece's quality as an 'art' object, because the music in question (say, a pop song) might not be regarded as 'art' and therefore does not invite an 'aesthetic attitude' in the listener.

Finally, despite the frequently occurring term 'aesthetic emotion', an aesthetic response may well occur without either emotion or liking. In fact, it has repeatedly been argued that an aesthetic response is—or should be—a 'detached' or 'distanced' consideration of an art object that does *not* let emotions 'come in the way'. Thus, we can evaluate an art object (including a piece of music), without *necessarily* experiencing any emotional response. Members of a jury in a piano performance contest repeatedly make evaluations of the aesthetic merit of different interpretations, but the circumstances may not be optimal for experiencing emotions.

With regard to music, emotions may *co-occur* with aesthetic evaluations (being aroused independently by the seven mechanisms), or they may follow partly *as a result* of an aesthetic evaluation. (If we do value an 'art' object very highly, chances are that we cannot avoid being 'moved' by the object!) But if emotions to music in everyday life were typically dependent on an aesthetic evaluation, then emotions such as *wonder* and *awe* should be frequent reactions to music. This is not the case—as we saw earlier in the chapter. This is presumably because emotions to music in everyday life are most commonly produced by mechanisms that are independent of the listener's aesthetic evaluation, if any. I acknowledge that there is plenty of disagreement on all of these issues. This leads me to the final question in this chapter.

Why can't we ever seem to agree on any of these issues?

There are probably many factors that contribute to current disagreements, such as conceptual confusion and a lack of relevant empirical data. And because the topic of musical emotions is so close to the heart of why most of us engage with music, one sometimes gets the impression that scholars are motivated by what they *want* emotional responses to music to be, rather than what they really *are* for most people. However, the most important source of disagreement, in my view, is that scholars are talking about different things: we need to recognize that *musical emotion is not a unitary phenomenon*. Take the issue of mechanisms, for instance. We can ask several questions, such as: Which emotions can music arouse? How early do musical emotions develop? Is the listener active or passive in the causal process? How much time does it take to arouse an emotion through music listening? Are musical emotions innate or learned reactions? For all these questions, the answer depends on the precise mechanism concerned (cf. Table 7.1). Thus, I would like to voice a plea for more precision in talking about musical emotions, so that we can separate genuine disagreement on substantial issues from mere miscommunication.

Coda: The social benefits of basic research

In this chapter, I have offered a broad description of the nature of musical emotions. The goal was to highlight the primary questions in this field, and what concrete answers the field has to offer. This relates to one of the themes in Sloboda's contribution to music psychology: that of asking the important questions (cf. Chapter 2).

In this final section, I will address another recurrent theme in Sloboda's contribution to the field, which is the 'applicability' of music-psychological research (see Part 7). Sloboda has emphasized the responsibility of scholars to consider the social benefits of their work. The question arises as to how best to assume this responsibility as a music researcher. Because I consider John my friend, I will respectfully and in the spirit of scholarly exchange take issue with his proposal, laid out for instance in Sloboda (2005), that the highest level of 'socially responsible engagement in research' is to focus *directly* on 'benefits'. I will submit that good basic research on theoretically relevant issues is of primary importance for applied research, and that the latter will in fact soon go astray without the foundation of the former. I will illustrate this in regard to music and emotion, the field I am most familiar with.

Current applications of research on musical emotions include music therapy, film music, marketing, health care, and the gaming industry (Juslin, 2009). Most of these applications are based on intuition, rather than systematic scientific knowledge. This does not mean, however, that there is no research aimed at these domains; for example, there is currently an abundance of studies on music therapy and other health applications. Rather, the problem is that research thus far has primarily adopted an approach to music that Sloboda (2005) has referred to as the 'pharmaceutical' (or 'vitamin') model of music, 'ascribing to the music a mandatory power of bringing about certain perceptual, cognitive or emotional responses in a listener' (p. 193). One example is the music provided by Muzak. Unwittingly, perhaps, studies with a focus on social benefits have tended to follow the same model: that is, applied research—with the best of intents—has tended to focus on superficial one-to-one relations between music and response, thus bypassing the theoretical understanding that is required to obtain some *control* over the phenomenon in question. That this approach does not work has been shown in many contexts, including music therapy: 'Musical selections that are relaxing and meditative to one client can be disruptive and annoying to another' (Guzzetta, 1991, p. 159).

An important implication of the multi-mechanism framework outlined above, which is a clear case of basic research (level 1 in Sloboda's scheme), is that a given piece of music might not be the 'same' stimulus for different listeners: how the listener will respond depends on the psychological mechanism activated in the event. Only a deep *theoretical* understanding of the underlying mechanisms will permit a practitioner to apply the music in a manner that actively manipulates particular mechanisms so as to achieve predictable effects on emotion and health. The theory required to do this is not likely to come from applied research (Sloboda's level 3),[8] whether due to time constraints or failure to understand its important role. Yet only by having this deeper understanding might social benefits be maximized. Sloboda (2005) admits that 'it is not always possible to make an accurate assessment of the applicability of research in advance of conducting the research' (p. 414). More importantly, in my view, *an applied approach may never discover the best solution to a practical problem.*

One possible reason for this counterintuitive fact is that basic research may afford to ask much broader questions than applied research can: the former can ask 'how does music evoke emotion?', whereas the latter may be forced to ask 'what music would calm this patient?' The irony is that approaches developed to answer the first question are also likely to offer more useful answers to the latter question, because they produce more flexible knowledge. This is an example of how basic research may lead to *greater* applicability and benefit (eventually) than applied research aimed *directly* at social benefits. I want to emphasize here that I do not wish to deny the central importance of considering social benefits in research, but rather that doing so to the *exclusion* of sound 'basic' research of theoretical relevance is likely to do more harm than good: there is no more applicable knowledge than that which derives from a theoretically sophisticated understanding of the phenomenon in question. Hence, conducting basic research may be just as valuable as research explicitly identified as 'applicable'. Sloboda's valorization of basic and applied approaches, in his hierarchy of 'levels of responsible social engagement', rests on an over-simplified view of the roles of 'basic' and 'applied' research and their relative benefits for society—clearly, we need both.

Sloboda's challenges to the field of music and emotion, his calls to come up with better answers, and his own landmark studies have themselves all served to 'sharpen' basic research approaches to exploring the music-emotional mind, by focusing on the crucial questions. This endeavour will, no doubt, continue to fascinate generations of music researchers—and will also hopefully lead to a range of social benefits.

Acknowledgements

This chapter is partly based on my opening address at the International Conference on Music and Emotion, 31 August 2009, Durham, UK. The research was supported by the Swedish Research Council. I am grateful to the reviewers for their helpful suggestions on an earlier version of this chapter. On a more personal note, I would like to thank John Sloboda for fruitful collaborations and friendship over the past 10 years.

Notes

[1] *Musical emotions* is used here simply as a short term for 'emotions that were aroused by music'.

[2] An additional type of evidence of emotions to music involves indirect measures such as writing speed, word association, and decision time (Juslin & Västfjäll, 2008a, Table 3).

[3] In the ESM, participants are provided with small palmtop computers that they carry with them at all waking hours during a week or so. During the week, the palmtop emits sound signals at certain predetermined or random intervals. Each time the participant hears the signal, he or she should respond to some questions administered by the palmtop about his or her latest musical experience (e.g. Juslin *et al.*, 2008).

[4] This may reflect the increasing use of portable music players (e.g. MP3 players, music cell phones), which tend to enhance the influences of choice (Sloboda *et al.*, 2001), familiarity (Bartel, 1992), and liking (Juslin *et al.*, 2008) of music—all of which may influence emotions.

[5] A simple form of unexpectedness (e.g. the sudden onset of a loud tone) would instead be an example of the mechanism termed *brain stem reflex*. Similarly, more general surprising features of a musical event (e.g. that a concert was better than a listener had expected) would instead be an example of the mechanism *cognitive appraisal*.

[6] The mechanisms described here do not address the lyrics of music. However, data from survey and ESM studies suggest that lyrics are rarely the cause of emotions to music (Juslin *et al.*, 2008, in press).

[7] *Preference* is generally regarded in the affective sciences as a long-lasting affective state of a low intensity (e.g. liking a particular artist or musical genre).

[8] It is slightly ironic that the 'social benefits perspective' that Sloboda (2005) has been advocating may itself contribute to the very 'vitamin model' of music that he clearly rejects.

References

Abeles, H. F., & Chung, J. W. (1996). Responses to music. In D. A. Hodges (Ed.), *Handbook of music psychology* (2nd ed.) (pp. 285–342). San Antonio, TX: IMR Press.

Bartel, L. R. (1992). The development of the cognitive-affective response test—music. *Psychomusicology, 11,* 15–26.

Becker, J. (2004). *Deep listeners: Music, emotion, and trancing.* Bloomington, IN: Indiana University Press.

Beedie, C. J., Terry, P. C., & Lane, A. M. (2005). Distinctions between emotion and mood. *Cognition & Emotion, 19,* 847–878.

Berlyne, D. E. (1971). *Aesthetics and psychobiology.* New York, NY: Appleton Century Crofts.

Blood, A. J., & Zatorre, R. J. (2001). Intensely pleasurable responses to music correlate with activity in brain regions implicated in reward and emotion. *Proceedings of National Academy of Sciences, 98,* 11818–11823.

Brown, S., Martinez, M. J., & Parsons, L. M. (2004). Passive music listening spontaneously engages limbic and paralimbic systems. *Neuroreport, 15,* 2033–2037.

DeNora, T. (2000). *Music in everyday life.* Cambridge, UK: Cambridge University Press.

Deutsch, D. (Ed.). (1999). *The psychology of music* (2nd ed.). New York, NY: Academic Press.

Dowling W. J., & Harwood, D. L. (1986). *Music cognition.* New York, NY: Academic Press.

Frey, W. H. (1985). *Crying: The mystery of tears.* Minneapolis, MN: Winston Press.

Fried, R., & Berkowitz, L. (1979). Music that charms. . .and can influence helpfulness. *Journal of Applied Social Psychology, 9,* 199–208.

Frijda, N. H., & Sundararajan, L. (2007). Emotion refinement: A theory inspired by Chinese poetics. *Perspectives on Psychological Science, 2,* 227–241.

Gabrielsson, A. (2001). Emotions in strong experiences with music. In P. N. Juslin, & J. A. Sloboda (Eds.), *Music and emotion: Theory and research* (pp. 431–449). Oxford: Oxford University Press.

Gabrielsson, A. (2002). Emotion perceived and emotion felt: Same or different? *Musicæ Scientiæ, Special Issue,* 123–147.

Griffiths, P. (1997). *What emotions really are.* Chicago, IL: University of Chicago Press.

Gutheil, E. A. (1952). Introduction. In A. Carpurso, V. R. Fisichelli, L. Gilman, E. A. Gutheil, J. T. Wright, & F. Paperte (Eds.), *Music and your emotions: A practical guide to music selections associated with desired emotional responses* (pp. 9–13). New York, NY: Liveright.

Guzzetta, C. E. (1991). Music therapy: Nursing the music of the soul. In D. Campbell (Ed.), *Music physician for times to come* (pp. 146–166). Wheaton, IL: Quest Books.

Hargreaves, D. J., & North, A. C. (Eds.) (1997). *The social psychology of music.* Oxford: Oxford University Press.

Harrer, G., & Harrer, H. (1977). Music, emotion, and autonomic function. In M. Critchley, & R. A. Henson (Eds.), *Music and the brain. Studies in the neurology of music* (pp. 202–216). London, UK: William Heinemann Medical Books.

Hodges, D. (2010). Psychophysiological measures. In P. N. Juslin, & J. A. Sloboda (Eds.), *Handbook of music and emotion: Theory, research, applications* (pp. 279–311). Oxford: Oxford University Press.

Huron, D. (2006). *Sweet anticipation: Music and the psychology of expectation.* Cambridge, MA: MIT Press.

Juslin, P. N. (2005). From mimesis to catharsis: expression, perception, and induction of emotion in music. In D. Miell, R. MacDonald, & D. J. Hargreaves (Eds.), *Musical communication* (pp. 85–115). Oxford: Oxford University Press.

Juslin, P. N. (2009). Emotional responses to music. In S. Hallam, I. Cross, & M. Thaut (Eds.), *Oxford handbook of music psychology* (pp. 131–140). Oxford: Oxford University Press.

Juslin, P. N., & Laukka, P. (2003). Communication of emotions in vocal expression and music performance: Different channels, same code? *Psychological Bulletin, 129*, 770–814.

Juslin, P. N., & Laukka, P. (2004). Expression, perception, and induction of musical emotions: A review and a questionnaire study of everyday listening. *Journal of New Music Research, 33*, 217–238.

Juslin, P. N., Liljeström, S., Laukka, P., Västfjäll, D., & Lundqvist, L.-O. (in press). A nationally representative survey study of emotional reactions to music: Prevalence and causal influences. *Musicae Scientiae, Special Issue.*

Juslin, P. N., Liljeström, S., Västfjäll, D., Barradas, G., & Silva, A. (2008). An experience sampling study of emotional reactions to music: Listener, music, and situation. *Emotion, 8*, 668–683.

Juslin, P. N., Liljeström, S., Västfjäll, D., & Lundqvist, L.-O. (2010). How does music evoke emotions? Exploring the underlying mechanisms. In P. N. Juslin, & J. A. Sloboda (Eds.), *Handbook of music and emotion: Theory, research, applications* (pp. 605–642). Oxford: Oxford University Press.

Juslin, P. N., & Sloboda, J. A. (Eds.). (2001). *Music and emotion: Theory and research.* Oxford: Oxford University Press.

Juslin, P. N., & Sloboda, J. A. (2010). The past, present, and future of music and emotion research. In P. N. Juslin, & J. A. Sloboda (Eds.), *Handbook of music and emotion: Theory, research, applications* (pp. 933–955). New York, NY: Oxford University Press.

Juslin, P. N., & Västfjäll, D. (2008a). Emotional responses to music: The need to consider underlying mechanisms. *Behavioral and Brain Sciences, 31*, 559–575.

Juslin, P. N., & Västfjäll, D. (2008b). All emotions are not created equal: Reaching beyond the traditional disputes. *Behavioral and Brain Sciences, 31*, 600–621.

Juslin, P. N., & Zentner, M. R. (2002). Current trends in the study of music and emotion: Overture. *Musicæ Scientiæ, Special Issue*, 3–21.

Kivy, P. (1990). *Music alone: Reflections on a purely musical experience.* Ithaca, NY: Cornell University Press.

Koelsch, S., Fritz, T., von Cramon, D. Y., Müller, K., & Friederici, A. D. (2006). Investigating emotion with music: An fMRI study. *Human Brain Mapping, 27*, 239–250.

Krumhansl, C. L. (1997). An exploratory study of musical emotions and psychophysiology. *Canadian Journal of Experimental Psychology, 51*, 336–352.

Levenson, J. (2003). Philosophical aesthetics: an overview. In J. Levenson (Ed.), *Oxford handbook of aesthetics* (pp. 3–24). Oxford: Oxford University Press.

Lundqvist, L.-O., Carlsson, F., Hilmersson, P., & Juslin, P. N. (2009). Emotional responses to music: Experience, expression, and physiology. *Psychology of Music, 37*, 61–90.

Mauss, I. B., Levenson, R. W., McCarter, L., Wilhelm, F. H., & Gross, J. J. (2005). The tie that binds? Coherence among emotion experience, behavior, and physiology. *Emotion, 5*, 175–190.

Meyer, L. B. (1956). *Emotion and meaning in music.* Chicago, IL: Chicago University Press.

Moors, A. (2009). Theories of emotion causation: A review. *Cognition & Emotion, 23,* 625–662.

Nielsen, L., & Kaszniak, A. W. (2007). Conceptual, theoretical, and methodological issues in inferring subjective emotion experience. In J. A. Coan, & J. J. B. Allen (Eds.), *Handbook of emotion elicitation and assessment* (pp. 361–375). Oxford: Oxford University Press.

North, A. C., & Hargreaves, D. J. (2010). Music and marketing. In P. N. Juslin, & J. A. Sloboda (Eds.), *Handbook of music and emotion: Theory, research, applications* (pp. 909–930). Oxford: Oxford University Press.

North, A. C., Hargreaves, D. J., & Hargreaves, J. J. (2004). Uses of music in everyday life. *Music Perception, 22,* 41–47.

Nyklíček, I., Thayer, J. F., & Van Doornen, L. J. P. (1997). Cardiorespiratory differentiation of musically-induced emotions. *Journal of Psychophysiology, 11,* 304–321.

Orne, M. T. (1962). On the social psychology of the psychological experiment with particular reference to demand characteristics and their implications. *American Psychologist, 17,* 776–783.

Panksepp, J. (1995). The emotional sources of 'chills' induced by music. *Music Perception, 13,* 171–208.

Patel, A. D. (2008). *Music, language, and brain.* Oxford: Oxford University Press.

Pike, A. (1972). A phenomenological analysis of emotional experience in music. *Journal of Research in Music Education, 20,* 262–267.

Rickard, N. S. (2004). Intense emotional responses to music: a test of the physiological arousal hypothesis. *Psychology of Music, 32,* 371–388.

Robinson, M. D., & Clore, G. L. (2002). Episodic and semantic knowledge in emotional self-report: Evidence for two judgment processes. *Journal of Personality and Social Psychology, 83,* 198–215.

Scherer, K. R. (1999). Appraisal theories. In T. Dalgleish, & M. Power (Eds.), *Handbook of cognition and emotion* (pp. 637–663). Chichester, UK: Wiley.

Scherer, K. R. (2003). Why music does not produce basic emotions: a plea for a new approach to measuring emotional effects of music. In R. Bresin (Ed.), *Proceedings of the Stockholm Music Acoustics Conference 2003* (pp. 25–28). Stockholm, Sweden: Royal Institute of Technology.

Scherer, K. R., & Zentner, M. R. (2001). Emotional effects of music: Production rules. In P. N. Juslin, & J. A. Sloboda (Eds.), *Music and emotion: Theory and research* (pp. 361–392). Oxford: Oxford University Press.

Scherer, K. R., Zentner, M. R., & Schacht, A. (2002). Emotional states generated by music: An exploratory study of music experts. *Musicæ Scientiæ, Special Issue,* 149–171.

Sloboda, J. A. (1985). *The musical mind: The cognitive psychology of music.* Oxford: Oxford University Press.

Sloboda, J. A. (1991). Music structure and emotional response: Some empirical findings. *Psychology of Music, 19,* 110–120.

Sloboda, J. A. (1992). Empirical studies of emotional response to music. In M. Riess-Jones, & S. Holleran (Eds.), *Cognitive bases of musical communication* (pp. 33–46). Washington, DC: American Psychological Association.

Sloboda, J. A. (2002). The 'sound of music' versus the 'essence of music': Dilemmas for music-emotion researchers. *Musicæ Scientiæ, Special Issue,* 235–253.

Sloboda, J. A. (2005). *Exploring the musical mind: Cognition, emotion, ability, function.* Oxford: Oxford University Press.

Sloboda, J. A., O'Neill, S. A., & Ivaldi, A. (2001). Functions of music in everyday life: an exploratory study using the experience sampling method. *Musicæ Scientiæ, 5,* 9–32.

Swanwick, K. (1985). *A basis for music education.* Windsor, UK: NFER-Nelson.

Thompson, W. F. (2009). *Music, thought, and feeling. Understanding the psychology of music.* Oxford: Oxford University Press.

Wells, A., & Hakanen, E. A. (1991). The emotional uses of popular music by adolescents. *Journalism Quarterly, 68,* 445–454.

Witvliet, C. V., & Vrana, S. R. (2007). Play it again Sam: Repeated exposure to emotionally evocative music polarises liking and smiling responses, and influences other affective reports, facial EMG, and heart rate. *Cognition & Emotion, 21,* 3–25.

Zentner, M. R., Grandjean, D., & Scherer, K. R. (2008). Emotions evoked by the sound of music: Characterization, classification, and measurement. *Emotion, 8,* 494–521.

Part 4

Sloboda's recall paradigm

Chapter 8

Salience of melodic tones in short-term memory: dependence on phrasing, metre, duration, register, and tonal hierarchy

Mario Baroni, Rossana Dalmonte, and Roberto Caterina

Abstract

The present research, developed in the field of studies on melody perception, aims to understand the features that contribute to making a single note salient during a test of short-term memory. A brief melodic fragment was presented to our subjects (musicians and non-musicians) together with a modified version with one single note varied. The subjects were invited to indicate which note had been changed. The analysis of the results revealed that the changed note was detected on the basis of its level of salience. Our first aim was to find out the features that make a note salient and hence its change detectable. Within this frame of reference we studied the salience of melodic tones in the short-term memory taking into account different aspects: location in the phrase, metre, duration, tonal hierarchy, register, and memory of previous experiences. A further aim was to test the relationships between the rules of a compositional grammar (Baroni, Dalmonte, & Jacoboni, 1999) and the actual perception of structures during the listening. The results showed that in some cases there is a convergence between composition rules and perception procedures, while in other cases important differences emerge.

John Sloboda and David Parker, in their seminal article on the immediate recall of melodies (1985), underline an aspect of melody perception that we consider particularly close to the topic of the present essay: 'memorizing single, well-formed tonal melodies involves building a mental model of the underlying structure'. Longuet-Higgins (1976) was thinking along the same lines when he stated that 'the listener builds a conceptual structure … which he commits to memory, and which subsequently enables him to recognise the tune'. However, in Sloboda and Parker's study the subjects were not only required to recognize a tune, but also to sing it. The authors noticed that the subjects found it hard to provide an exact reproduction of the melody. Often they memorized and sang a different melodic sequence after processing the retained material on the basis of frames of reference stored during their previous listening experience. In particular, they created new rhythmic sequences and new pitch patterns within previously internalized metric and harmonic schemata. The role of structural aspects such as these is also emphasized by Longuet-Higgins (1967, p. 647) when he observes that a listener has not only to perceive melodic intervals but also to interpret them within their tonal context: the same pitch or the same interval can have different syntactic meanings when inserted in two different keys, exactly like the words 'here' and 'hear' which, in a spoken sentence, must be differently interpreted depending on the context, even though they have the same sound.

Verbal language should not, of course, be seen as the only model for every form of communication. John Blacking (1984, p. 363), for example, claimed that the study of musical language 'will not progress unless we can consciously avoid methodologies and terminologies that were derived from the characteristics of speech and can think of music as itself a primary modelling system'. He referred to the system of rules underlying the organization of musical structures as 'musical grammar', a label that was widely shared by other authors. One of the problems discussed in the present chapter is precisely that of the relationships between the structural rules of musical language (grammar) and the frames of reference or musical schemata at work when listening to a melody. For example, a schema such as that proposed by Deutsch and Feroe (1981) regarding the internal hierarchical representation of pitch sequences in tonal music, has, in our opinion, similar functions in listening and in composing. In their concluding discussion the authors actually stress the link between their model and the representation of hierarchical structures proposed by music theorists, particularly by Schenker (whose analyses did much to shed light on composition models). It is worth quoting the final words of the article: 'It is unlikely that tonal music has evolved to accord with an arbitrary set of rules; rather it would be expected to reflect general principles of cognitive organization' (1981, pp. 520–521).

Among the various studies that have discussed aspects of melody perception and related them to analytical concepts, Sloboda and Parker's study appears particularly important. Over and above the already quoted aspects of metre and harmony they also studied segmentation (breath analysis) and similarities among phrases. On observing this set of features emerge from the results of their experiment, they hypothesized a connection with the musical grammar proposed by Sundberg and Lindblom (1976). This grammar is hierarchically organized from the point of view of phrasing, rhythm, and cadences, and symmetrically from the point of view of the melodic material, and of the tonal-harmonic structure. Its aim is to generate stylistic aspects of the folk repertory of Swedish nursery tunes. It may therefore be suitable for analysing the folk tune used by Sloboda and Parker in their experiment. In the present chapter too, a melodic grammar is considered, although of a substantially different nature: our aim is to relate the grammar to cognitive listening mechanisms.

For many years now, we have been studying the possibility of devising a system of rules able to explain the structure of European vocal melodies ranging from the Middle Ages to the twentieth century (Baroni *et al.*, 1999) and we have conceived these rules with a view to composition. In the present chapter we evaluate the hypothesis that particular melodic structures governed by grammatical rules can have a perceptive salience. In doing so we have also taken into account a suggestion by Fred Lerdahl (1988), who conceives listening as a system of cognitive constraints on compositional choices. In his article he discussed a famous work by Pierre Boulez (*Le Marteau Sans Maître*) in which compositional choices do not respect 'normal' listening rules based on cognitive constraints. However, as Deutsch and Feroe (1981) have observed, there have been epochs in European music in which listeners perceived structures and comprehended music in a way very similar to that followed by the composers when writing it. Epochs such as these covered a relatively short period of time, culminating at the end of the eighteenth century in central Europe where the Classical style flourished. In compositions written in this style it is more likely that the structures produced by given grammatical rules can also have perceptive salience and can be recognized by competent listeners. With this in mind, we chose to base our experiment on the two opening phrases of Don Ottavio's famous aria in *Don Giovanni* by Mozart: *Dalla Sua Pace la Mia Dipende*. This fragment—short as it is— shows two typical melodic profiles: the first is made up of leaps, the second of scalar degrees. Since the distinction between leaps and conjunct degrees is one of the most important aspects of our grammar, the extract seemed to be particularly suitable for our project.

We will now try to illustrate a selection of the grammatical rules proposed in our book, taking Mozart's melody as an example (see Example 8.1). According to our grammar of melody, the note on the first strong beat and that on the last strong beat of a melodic vocal phrase form an interval—named the *nuclear interval* or the *kernel*— which is the very pillar of the melodic phrase. Here, in the first phrase (*Dalla sua pace*) the kernel is the interval D-E (the third beat of a 4/4 is considered a strong beat), while in the second phrase the interval is G-D.

The notes directly connecting the two notes of the kernel by degrees— named the *nuclear scale* or the *kernel scale* of the phrase—are also very important from a structural and compositional point of view. In the first phrase the *nuclear interval* D-E

Example 8.1 Bars 1–2 from one of the arias of Don Ottavio in *Don Giovanni* by Mozart (simplified, without ornamentations).

coincides with the nuclear scale; in the second phrase the nuclear scale is G-F-E-D. The kernel and the kernel scale are a kind of deep structure of the melody: its surface features are obtained by the insertion of various types of *melodic figures*, whose notes are to be considered structurally less important. Differences can also be identified among the *melodic figures*. In brief, some figures add notes to the melodic profile proceeding by steps: for example the *neighbour-note figure* (here: D-C#-D in the second phrase). Others add notes by transposing a note of the nuclear scale to another note of the subjacent chord: *transposition figure* (here: D-B-G in the first phrase). We must also mention the *feminine cadences*, that is the notes on the last strong beats (E and D, respectively) followed by the note/notes on the following weak beats (here: C; C-B). Finally, our grammar assigns a higher *hierarchical role* to the main harmonic cycle, concluding on the first degree of the key (ending of second phrase in our example), while the conclusions of the phrases included in the main harmonic cycles are to be considered as belonging to a lower hierarchical level (in our example, the ending of the first phrase on the IV degree).

Our aim was to find out whether the structural roles of the kernels, of the kernel scale in the second phrase and of the notes added by the melodic figures, actually correspond to a concrete way of listening. In order to answer this question we prepared a test: the subjects were played recordings of pairs of short melodies (based on Don Ottavio's aria), the second melody of each pair differing from the first by just one note. The subjects had to identify the note that was different. The first of the two melodies of each pair was not exactly the same as Mozart's original, but very similar: the aria's basic harmonic and rhythmic structures were kept unchanged, but some of its pitches were modified. The test consisted of 20 pairs, that is, 20 models followed by their modified copies. On the basis of the responses given by the subjects, we hoped to identify the notes that were perceived the best and worst and, more generally, how the model and the copy were processed during listening. The 20 pairs are given in Appendix 8.1.

At the sixth conference on music analysis, held in Freiburg, Germany in October 2006, we presented a paper—'Melodic contour and perception of pitch' (based on the same melody by Mozart)—in which we tested the perceptual modalities of the melodic profile made up of jumps on the notes of the subjacent chord. At the 28th International Society of Music Education (ISME) Conference, Bologna, Italy, August 2008, we presented a paper—'Perception of emergent features in melody'—in which the same material was presented to the subjects in order to verify in which part of the melodic profile (in the first or in the second phrase) a change in the melody was better perceived.

Methodology

Aims

In the experiments presented in Freiburg and Bologna, we were particularly interested in the perceptibility of the notes added by the melodic figures, taking for granted that the 'pillar-notes' of the kernel would be perceived clearly. In the present work we aimed to search systematically for the perceptual emergence of each note in a larger number of subjects and also increased the number of the pairs to be tested. The objectives of the experiment were:

- To discover and explain how listeners (experienced and not experienced) perceive (or do not perceive) a changed note in a short melody first heard in its original version and then in its variant. In formulating the test and by examining its results, we aimed to answer the following questions:
  - Under what conditions does a melodic note become so salient that people are able to perceive its change?
  - What are the melodic conditions governing the various degrees of salience?
- To assess whether the melodic perception of salience has some similarity with the grammatical rules, in particular:
  - Are the two notes of the kernel perceived more clearly than the others?
  - Is the perception of the notes equally clear (or dull) in movement by leaps and by degrees?
  - How are the changed notes of a feminine cadence perceived?
  - Are the notes of the cadence of the second phrase better perceived than those of the first?

Subjects

A total of 64 musicians (students at the Bologna Conservatory, higher level) and 57 non-musicians (students of the Faculty of Psychology) were enrolled.[1]

Material

The 40 melodies are listed in Appendix 8.1. The true incipit of Don Ottavio's aria in *Don Giovanni* by Mozart (see Example 8.1) was never used as such, because the subjects might have already been familiar with it. As can be seen from Appendix 8.1, none of the 40 phrases actually reproduces Mozart's fragment. Each melody was submitted in two versions, the second being a variation by one note of the first ('model' and 'copy', respectively). The task was to discover which note was modified, obviously not in comparison with Mozart's aria, but compared with the first member of the pair. The melodies were submitted in monodic form—just the singer's voice without accompaniment—each version being modified through 'Melodine', a software able to modify pitches while keeping the timbre of the voice.[2]

---

[1] We thank maestro Carmine Carrisi (Director, Conservatoire of Bologna), Johannella Tafuri, Piero Mioli, Donata Bertoldi (professors at the Conservatoire) and professors Franca Emiliani, Stefania Stame, Vincenzo Natale, Pier Luigi Garotti (Department of Psychology) for their help in the experiment.
[2] We are grateful to Fabio Regazzi, a technician in the Department of Music, University of Bologna, for his general technical help, and particularly for his suggestion to use the software 'Melodine'.

Procedure

Since listening to 20 pairs of phrases could become tedious and this aspect could bias the results, we divided the subjects into two groups; each of them had to listen to 10 pairs of melodies. Pairs 1–10 were presented to 32 musicians and 32 non-musicians; pairs 11–20 were presented to 32 musicians and 25 non musicians.

Before the actual test, a pilot test was tried out on 13 subjects to verify whether a sequence of just 10 pairs could generate listening fatigue. We first presented 10 pairs, analysed the results, and classified them from a maximum to a minimum of difficulty for the subjects in finding the changed note. After a week we repeated the experiment after modifying the sequence: the three more 'difficult' pairs were played at the beginning and the three 'easier' pairs at the end. The results of the two tests were almost identical, thus confirming the absence of listening fatigue in processing of the 10 pairs of examples.

Instructions

Each subject was given two sheets of paper. On the first page they had to answer questions about their musical competence. On the basis of these answers we excluded from the scoring those university students (from the group of 'non-musicians') who said they had undergone some musical training (this was the reason for fewer subjects in the second group of non-musicians).

On the second page the syllables of the verbal text of the aria 'DA LA SUA PA-CE LA MIA DI-PEN-DE' were repeated 10 times. The subjects were told that in the second phrase of every pair of melodies, one syllable was sung on a different pitch in comparison with the first. They had to find this and mark it.

Results

Figure 8.1 illustrates the marked difference between the number of right answers given by musicians and non-musicians: the musicians performed much better than the non-musicians (the overall mean for musicians was 65.48%, and for non-musicians 27.22%). The differences between the musicians' and non-musicians' answers were statistically significant for most of the pairs according to the chi-square test (see Figure 8.1). It is also immediately evident that the changed note in some pairs was well recognized by both groups (pairs 17, 20, 11, 3), and for others the results were poor (pairs 16, 10, 7, 4). Our criterion for the interpretation of the answers was the actual number of right answers on single notes obtained from the sum of the mean scores of musicians and non-musicians. The maximum was 92% for pair 17, and the minimum was 9.15% for pair 16. The general mean was 46.35%.

However, we noticed that for some pairs (see, for example, pairs 1 and 6) the performance of non-musicians was considerably poorer than that of the musicians, and that this result raised doubt about the informativeness of the mean values on which we intended to base our analysis. But we also noted that, even at a lower level, the scores among the non-musicians showed a trend very similar to that of the musicians. To measure this 'trend' we calculated for each pair the distance of the score from the overall mean of their respective 'category' (musicians and non-musicians): 15 pairs

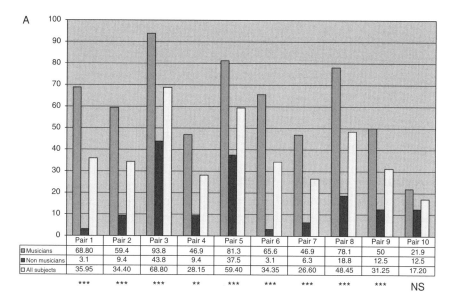

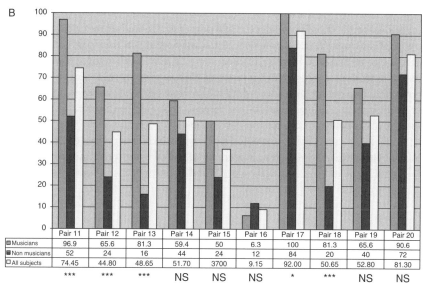

Fig. 8.1 Differences between musician and non-musicians with regard to correct recognition of the changed note in the 20 pairs of music phrases. 'All subjects' denotes the sum of the mean scores of musicians and non-musicians. Chi-square test: * $p < 0.05$; ** $p < 0.01$; *** $p < 0.001$; NS, not significant.

were congruent over or below the overall mean; the five non-congruent pairs (1, 6, 8, 13, and 18) reflect particular conditions which will be discussed further below.

Thus, having decided the nature of the data on which to base our analysis, the first problem we faced was how to interpret the considerable differences in perceiving the 20 changed notes. Our starting point was to place particular importance on the position of the note in the context of the phrase: it is well known, for example, that the first and last notes in a melody share particular salience properties (Boltz, 1991; Dowling & Harwood, 1986; Francès, 1954). In other words we noticed that the position itself could influence the salience of the note.

Location by zones and salience levels

On the basis of this criterion and of the rules of our grammar, we divided the notes of the two phrases into three segments (initial, central, final). This segmentation, however, is not merely the outcome of a mechanical procedure: the initial segment may (or may not) be preceded by an anacrusis, it may (or may not) include more than one note; similarly, the final segment may also include a weak beat and more than one note. Such problems of segmentation do not appear to have found a univocal solution in studies on melody; very often they are solved empirically, depending on the case and the particular nature of the melodic phrase. The nature of our melodic material suggested that we should consider the first note of each phrase as the 'initial part', and the segment from the last strong beat to the last note as the 'final part'. The 'central part' is located between these two segments (see Table 8.1). When there was more than one note we considered the mean result of correct answers regarding the changed notes. Ranging the six zones according to the results of the test (see Figure 8.1), we ordered them in six salience levels (see Table 8.2). Remember (see previous section) that the overall mean of correct answers was 46.35%.

The next task is to explain the reasons behind such different levels of salience. The most obvious explanation is that, in accordance with the previously quoted literature, the beginnings and the endings are perceived as particularly salient. However, we should not overlook the fact that our subjects were invited to listen to not just one

Table 8.1 Segmentation of the phrases into six zones and the mean values for the correct answers

Zone	Segment	Mean of correct answers (%)
First	1st note of the 1st phrase: pairs 10, 17	54.60
Second	1st note of the 2nd phrase: pairs 7, 20	53.95
Third	Central segment of the first phrase (two notes): pairs 1, 5, 6, 9, 11, 15, 16, 19	41.79
Fourth	Central segment of the second phrase (four notes): pairs 3, 8, 13, 18	54.14
Fifth	Ending of the first phrase (two notes): pairs 2, 4	31.27
Sixth	Ending of the second phrase (three notes): pairs 12, 14	48.25

Table 8.2 Six salience levels and mean of correct answers in each zone

Salience level	Mean of correct answers (%)
1	54.60 (first zone)
2	54.14 (fourth zone)
3	53.95 (second zone)
4	48.25 (sixth zone)
5	41.79 (third zone)
6	31.27 (fifth zone)

phrase, but to a melody consisting of two short phrases, which are possibly perceived as unity. This is common practice in the Classical style, where the structure of a melody is often made up of a non-conclusive phrase followed by another more conclusive one. Therefore, besides the three segments of each phrase, we must also consider a higher hierarchical level, in which the status of the three segments changes according to its presence in the first or in the second phrase. From this point of view, the ending of the first phrase and the beginning of the second are located in the middle of the whole melody, while the first note of the first phrase continues to be a starting point, and the ending of the second phrase is the conclusion of the whole melody.

The position of the note within the melody does not, however, exhaust all the conditions that may account for the mean salience scorings of the zones. We must remember, in fact, that each zone is not only characterized by its location in the melody, but also by the metric and rhythmic features of its notes, which remained the same in all the 20 pairs in the experiment. For example, the high mean score of the first zone (made up of a single note) is due not only to the location at the beginning of the melody but also to its metric position (strong beat) and to the duration of a quarter-note (the longest in the melody), both of these aspects being considered in the literature as producers of salience (Boltz, 1991, p. 241; Lerdahl, 1989, pp. 73–74; Schulkind, Posner, & Rubin, 2003, pp. 222, 241; Smith & Cuddy, 1989). The same features are also shared by the second zone, which obtained a slightly lower score (third salience level) probably because of its position at the beginning of the second phrase but in the middle of the whole melody. Also the ending of the first phrase (zone 5) is made up of two quarter notes, one of them on a strong beat. And yet it obtained the lowest average score (sixth salience level). In the case of zone 1 the interaction between location, duration, and metre increased the average salience of the zone because the three features were congruent with each other, while in zone 5 the weak location in the middle of the melody was not congruent with the duration and metric position of its notes.

The ending of the second phrase (zone 6), even though rhythmically less clear than the ending of the first phrase (zone 5), was much better perceived (fourth salience level), evidently because it was also the ending of the whole melody. In any case, our experiment brought to light a substantial perceptual difference between the beginnings and the endings both of the single phrases and of the whole melody: as far as our results might suggest, beginnings are better perceived than endings. The conflicting results reported regarding this point (Divenyi & Hirsch, 1978; Guilford & Nelson, 1936) may be due to differences in experimental conditions.

Finally, we compared the results of the two central fragments to try to answer the question why zone 4 (the central segment of the second phrase) received a much better score than zone 3. Since we could not assign to the central part of the phrase a quality of salience due to location, as we did for beginnings and endings, we were obliged to look for other motivations: the solution to this problem will be dealt with below, where a more detailed analysis is made of the whole system of features responsible for the salience of the single notes within the two zones (see below).

After ordering the different zones on the basis of their mean salience levels and stressing the particular influence of location as a perceptual quality for the beginnings and the endings, we now extended our analysis by examining in detail the scoring of the single notes. In the following section we report on our analysis of how many times the changed notes were present in each zone in the 20 pairs and how salient they were considered. For instance, zone 1 had two occurrences, whereas zone 3 had eight, and each of such occurrences received different scores that should have been taken into consideration.

Salience of single notes

In order to interpret the scoring of a single changed note, the first step is to compare it with the mean scoring of the zone to which it belongs. Even if two notes receive similar scores, their levels of salience are to be considered not as absolute values but as values relative to their context. For example, pair 2 and pair 6 received almost the same score (34.40 and 34.35, respectively), but while pair 2 was slightly above the mean score of its zone (31.27), pair 6 was considerably lower than the mean of its context (41.96) (see Figure 8.1 and Table 8.2). Even if their results are apparently the same, they did differ greatly in terms of salience.

Beginnings and endings

To examine the single notes present in the four beginning and ending zones we must take into consideration eight pairs (eight changed notes): two for each zone (see Table 8.3).

Table 8.3 Salience of single notes in beginnings and endings

Zone	Salience of the zone with its scoring	Pairs	Scoring of the changed notes
1 (one note) First note of the first phrase	54.6	10 17	17.2 92
2 (one note) First note of the second phrase	53.95	7 20	26.6 81.3
5 (two notes) Ending of the first phrase	31.27	2 4	34.4 28.15
6 (three notes) Ending of the second phrase	48.25	12 14	44.8 51.7

There is an evident difference between zones 1–2 and zones 5–6, since in zones 1–2 the perceptual level of the two notes is markedly different, while in zones 5–6 the results of the single notes are not too far from the mean of the zone. In the latter case we may hypothesize that the reason for a single note's score greatly depends on the features of salience of its zone.

A brief premise is necessary. In zones 1 and 2 we are obliged to connect the single notes of the zone with the notes that follow, since a single note is not enough to identify effective salience motivations: analysis needs a context. From this point of view the conditions of the first zone are as follows: in phrase 10 the model was B (followed by B-G) and the copy was D (followed by B-G). In phrase 17 the model was D (B-B) and the copy was G (B-B): see Examples 8.2 and 8.3.

In both cases we are dealing with notes with equal rhythmic patterns, and belonging to the same implicit subjacent G major chord. Beyond the obvious differences between the first notes also the intervals between the first and the following notes are different and influence the perception of the first note. We started our analysis from these aspects: in phrase 10 the difference is a repeated note versus a descending third; in phrase 17 it is a descending third versus ascending third, with inverted contour (for information on the perceptual relevance of inverted contours, see Dowling, 1978; Edworthy, 1985). The changes in the first notes produced different interval structures in the model and in the copy, which can apparently explain the different scores. But what we found difficult to explain was the huge difference in the scores between pair 10 and pair 17; this led us to think that mere observation of the intervals cannot give us a satisfactory explanation for the results. We return to this point later in the chapter.

The situation is similar in pairs 7 and 20 (first note of the second phrase). In pair 7 not only did the changed note modify the contour, but a striking difference also emerged if we compared the changed note with the last note of the preceding phrase: C-E in the model becomes C-G in the copy, with G being the peak note of the whole melody (see Example 8.4). (For more information about the relevance of the 'interval size accent', see Huron & Royal, 1996, p. 490.) However, this apparently favourable interval condition produced a very low score. In pair 20 we had the peak note G in the model and D in the copy: the changed note (a fourth lower) produced a leap of an ascending third and a reverse in the contour. If we also consider the interval with the final note of the previous phrase we note that in the model there is an ascending third and in the copy a descending second (see Example 8.5). In addition, the conditions

dal la sua pa ce la mi a di___ pen___ de   dal la sua pa ce la mia a di___ pen___ de

Example 8.2 Pair 10.

dal la sua pa ce la mi a di___ pen___ de   dal la sua pa ce la mi a di___ pen___ de

Example 8.3 Pair 17.

Da   la sua pa   ce   la   mia   di__ pen___ de   Da   la sua pa   ce   la   mia a di__ pen___ de

Example 8.4 Pair 7.

seem to be positive in this case: peak notes and contour difference are well recognized as important salience producers in comparative perceptions of melodies (Eitan, 1997; Watkins & Dyson, 1985). We were unsure, however, whether they could be considered so strongly positive as to explain the big difference in the evaluation results for pair 20. In conclusion, the reasons given so far to explain the results for the four pairs of zones 1 and 2 were not sufficient to satisfy our expectations from our analysis: other reasons needed to be looked for.

When we chose the material for our tests we were well aware that Mozart's melody could have been present in the memory of the subjects, thus greatly facilitating the recognition of the changed note. As mentioned above, we therefore did not propose using Mozart's melody in its original form. This, however, did not prevent models and copies from having one, or more than one, note in the same place several times, not only with the same rhythm, but also with the same pitch. For example, the note D which appears as the first note of the model and of the copy eight times at the beginning of the test may have resulted in an expectation of its reappearance in the same place. The general structure of our test possibly gave rise to several memory cues such as this, which may have influenced the recognition of the changed notes.

This same expectation effect has also been pointed out by Dowling and Harwood (1986, p. 162): 'the tension introduced by the departure of a specific note from the expectations invoked by invariants' introduces a perceptual conflict that may influence recognition processes. In our test we noted that an important cue of salience was produced by the discrepancy with the listener's constructed expectations: the more often one note appeared in the same place during the experiment (in the previously listened to pairs), the stronger was the expectation of its appearance in the pair under analysis. In pair 17, for instance, the changed note (G) conflicts with the expectation of the listeners, who had heard the pitch D in the same place not only in the model but also in nine other previously heard phrases (see Appendix 8.1). Our hypothesis is that the perception of G was a 'surprise' for the listeners. We defined the changed note that did not fulfil the expectation as an 'unfulfilled prediction'. On the contrary, the changed note that fulfilled the expectation was defined as 'verified prediction'. In this case, when listening to the changed note, the subjects expected precisely that note in that position and did not realize that it was different from the model; in other words, they did not compare the note under analysis with its model, but with the memory of phrases previously heard during the experiment.

Another example can be found in pair 10, where subjects expected D at the beginning because they had heard it 14 times before and they did not realize that the model

Da   la sua pa   ce   la   mia   di__ pen___ de   Da   la sua pa   ce   la   mia   di__ pen___ de

Example 8.5 Pair 20.

Example 8.6 Pair 9.

had B at the beginning. Similar effects might explain the different performances for pairs 7 and 20 (see Examples 8.4 and 8.5). Thanks to an 'unfulfilled prediction' the subjects performed very well in pairs 17 and 20, but they performed badly in pairs 7 and 10 due to the 'verified prediction'.

The psychological mechanism of the expectations—however—seems to work only with notes endowed with salient features, such as strong metric position and long duration at the beginning of a phrase. Notes not endowed with salient features went unrecognized even if they were heard several times in the previously heard phrases. Take, for example, pair 9 (see Example 8.6): the second note (G) received a low score (31.25) even if a B was heard in its place 10 times: it should have been recognized, albeit as a surprise, but it went unnoticed because of its short duration and weak metric position (see Appendix 8.1).

The above analyses show that salience is not a simple feature, but results from a complex convergence of multiple aspects of listening to music.

Central segments of the phrases

Having discussed the first and last zones of the two phrases we now turn our attention to the central parts. These two zones are located in a neutral position, considering the effects that beginnings and endings may have on the perception of the melody. Moreover, in our sample they are not only in weak positions within the phrases but are also made up of short notes (eighth and sixteenth notes), thus we may reasonably expect these conditions to result in low scores. But this was true only in one case: zone 3 (central segment of the first phrase) located at the fifth salience level (41.79%, see Table 8.2). On the contrary, zone 4 (central segment of the second phrase) obtained a score of 54.14% (second salience level).

Our results might have been due to the different registers of the two segments: Watkins and Dyson (1985, p. 105) and Lerdahl (1989, p. 74) have asserted that a relatively greater salience must be assigned to relatively higher pitches. But there could be another explanation: we have already noted the difference in the interval structure of the two segments (leaps versus scalar degrees). Studies on this matter have not yet been sufficiently developed, even though we believe this topic to be worthy of deeper investigation. Steve Larson (1997, pp. 104–105) described the perception of leaps to notes of the same subjacent chord by focusing on the two concepts 'auralizing' and 'trace': 'to auralize means to hear internally sounds that are not physically present; a trace is the internal representation of a note that is still melodically active: in a melodic leap the second note tends to support the trace of the first, leaving two traces in musical memory'. This may explain why, in our experiment, listeners more easily confused the changed note with another note of the subjacent chord. In a melodic fragment made up of scalar degrees this does not happen. Auralizing and trace perfectly fit the perceptual condition of two notes of the segment under analysis. Such a large number of features unfavourable for salience (weak metric position, short duration, low register, leap motion) suggested that we should pay particular attention to the central segment of the first phrase and submit to our subjects a relatively higher number of occurrences of this type: 8 of the 20 pairs had the changed note in this zone. Table 8.4 shows the results of the eight pairs.

At first glance it seems as if almost all pairs the first of the two eighth notes of the segment (see Appendix 8.1) received a better score. The second of the two notes achieved a low score even in pair 15 (see Example 8.7), where we had expected the significant interval change (from G^4 to B^3) to have been clearly perceived. This result persuaded us that in the case of leaps the weaker metric position prevails over all other features. Looking at the first of the two notes of the fragment the relatively stronger metric position was reinforced by another condition: in all four cases, in the model there was a B (the third degree of the scale, the least strong of the three most salient in the tonal hierarchy), which in the copy was changed to a G (tonic) or a D (dominant) (which never happened in the second notes of the fragment). Closer observation of the results revealed that the D (pairs 11 and 5) was better perceived than the G (pairs 9 and 19). Although this could appear to contradict the tonal hierarchy (Bartlett, 1993; Cuddy, 1993), it is nevertheless congruent with the perceptual importance of the higher register, which in these cases seemed to prevail over the tonal aspects.

Further evidence of the poor perceptibility of the two notes of this segment (fifth salience level, see Table 8.2) is provided by the fact that they can be easily confused with one another. Besides noting the correct answers, we also analysed the distribution of wrong answers among the 10 notes/syllables of the melody and we discovered that the wrong answers often regarded the notes immediately before or after the changed one, especially in this segment. As an example consider pairs 9 and 19 where the

Table 8.4 Salience of the two short notes in the central segment of the first phrase (zone 3)

Pairs	Changes	Score
1	In the second note	35.95
5	In the first note	59.40
6	In the second note	34.35
9	In the first note	31.25
11	In the first note	74.45
15	In the second note	37.00
16	In the second note	9.15
19	In the first note	52.8

Da la sua pa ce la mia di pen de Da la sua pa ce la mia di pen de

Example 8.7 Pair 15.

changed note was the first of the two. Even musicians confused the first with the second: 50% performed well, but 40.6% selected the second note (pair 9, see Figure 8.1 and Example 8.6). Similar results were obtained for pair 19: 65.6% performed well and 25% choose the second note instead of the first. In pairs 15 and 16 the changed note was the second one, but 12.5% of musicians selected the first versus 50% of right answers (pair 15). In pair 16 the results were even more striking: 6.3% chose the first note and only 9.4% the right one.

The extraordinary conditions of perceptibility of this fragment also explain the non-congruence observed early in our analysis between the answers of musicians and non-musicians. The task of recognizing the changed notes in this fragment was difficult for the musicians, and almost insurmountable for the non-musicians.

The last of the six zones of our sample—the central fragment of the second phrase (zone 4)—was particularly problematic, and we analysed it taking into consideration the changed notes of four pairs (see Table 8.5). The four changed notes had scores clearly above the general mean of the 20 pairs (46.35%). First let us discuss the changed note that was by far the best perceived (pair 3, see Example 8.8).

In the model, the subjects, for the first time (see Appendix 8.1), heard a scalar pattern, from G (initial note of the phrase) to C#. In the copy, a relatively large interval interrupted the scalar pattern and divided the first note from the second (G and D). The first note of the zone, even though very short and in a relatively weak position, was perceived as a salient pitch. When the strongly implicative scalar pattern of the model was not heard in the copy (Narmour, 1990) the listener reacted immediately and recognized the change. Also in pairs 8 and 18 the changed note broke the model's stepwise movement, and was well perceived by the subjects. The lower score was probably due to the smaller leap and the even weaker metric position. In pair 13 the interruption of the scalar pattern was not due to a jump but to a change in the contour, which according to Dowling (1978) is one of the most important cues in the perception of melody. The high mean result of this zone of the melody is due to the strongly implicative power of the scalar pattern.

Table 8.5 Salience of the notes in the central segment of the second phrase (zone 4, second level of salience, see also Tables 8.1 and 8.2)

Pairs	Changes	Score (%)
3	In the first note	68.80
8	In the fourth note	48.45
13	In the fourth note	48.65
18	In the third note	50.65

Da la sua pa ce la mia di___ pen___ de   Da la sua pa ce la mia di___ pen___ de

Example 8.8 Pair 3.

The good results in the recognition of the changed note in this zone—however—are essentially due to the performance of the musicians, since the non-musicians performed at a remarkably lower level. This did not happen in pair 3, due to the salience of the broken scalar pattern, but in pairs 8 (78.1 versus 18.8), 13 (81.3 versus 16) and 18 (81.3 versus 20) the good quality of the performance was largely due to the ability of the musicians. Non-musicians probably found it difficult to recognize the changed notes of short duration and in weak metric position. This observation is quite similar to the conclusions about zone 3. Results such as these clearly illustrate that the lack of salience in the notes of the central parts of the phrases requires a level of competence and concentration typical of people who are more familiar with expert listening (Peretz & Morais, 1987).

Discussion

The general framework of our research referred once again to the fundamental problem of memory for melody. In the study presented here, though, our focus was not the perception of *global* melodic shapes, as it was for example in Sloboda and Parker (1985), but rather the single notes of a melody: it was a study based on aspects of an *analytical* short-term memory. The comparison between a model and its copy allowed us to identify that some notes were better perceived and memorized than others and we interpreted this clearer recognition in terms of salience. On the basis of the results of our study, salience can be defined as a particular quality of a note that, for various reasons, is able to attract the listener's attention. Such quality, however, is definable only on the basis of a set of features: location in the phrase, metric position, tonal hierarchy, register, duration, and expectation from previous listening experience giving a particular salience quality to a note.

The changing landscape of musical language in the past century have gradually given rise to an increasing importance of elements of salience in listening to music. However, the tonal epoch listening flow is also strongly oriented by points of salience. However, a unanimously accepted theory on this topic has yet to be elaborated. According to Fred Lerdahl (1989, p. 73), for example, 'the more *stable* is the [event] that is more consonant or spatially closer to the (local) tonic, the more *salient* is the one that is in a strong metrical position, at a registral extreme … If one event turns out to be more stable and more salient, it unambiguously dominates the other, but if one event is more stable and the other is more salient there is a conflict in the rules. In tonal music stability almost always overrides salience'. Although this might be true in a large timespan analysis such as that proposed by Lerdahl, our experiment with single notes gave different results, for example when a higher register seemed to prevail over tonal conditions (see the analysis of pairs 5, 9, 11, 19).

The single features producing salience are well known in the literature, as already mentioned in our description of the results. As far as our experiment is concerned, we propose classifying such features within three main categories. Among the strongest 'salience producers' we include metric position, duration, high (versus lower) register, and tonal properties. These aspects characterize single notes independently of their position in the phrase. A second category concerns the initial and final locations of the notes in the melody. In these cases the location itself is a cue for salience: the more or less extended presence of silence that precedes the beginning and follows the ending of a musical phrase probably has the power to solicit the attention of the listener. Finally, implication and expectation phenomena, a third category of salience factors, are able to give importance to the notes of a melody because of the different mechanisms of memory. We are, in any case, dealing with phenomena that are partially linked to musical structures and partially to mental processes. The structural aspects prevail in the first group and the mental aspects in the third group.

The published literature includes important studies about the combined effects of different features in perceiving and memorizing melody. See, for example, the tradition of research on the relationships between tonal and metric accents (Boltz 1991; Jones, 1993; Jones, Summerell, & Marshburn, 1987; Monahan, 1993; Monahan, Kendall, & Carterette, 1987). In the present study we were especially interested in examining and evaluating not only these joint mechanisms but also the interactive strength of the different features present in each occurrence. For instance, the location of a note at the beginning or at the end of a phrase is not enough to define its salience. In our phrases the initial note was reinforced by its metric position, relatively long duration, and important level in the tonal hierarchy. It is only the concurrence of all these features and not the sole presence of one of them that makes the note well perceptible. In the final notes, on the contrary, the positive effect of the location was not supported by favourable conditions of metric position and tonal hierarchy. Despite the differences in the characteristics influencing the perceptual recognition of the notes of a melody, our experiment revealed that their effects are based on their combined action when they are congruent and on their mutual weakening when they conflict. An absolute evaluation of their individual strength, however, is not possible because of the overwhelmingly diverse contextual conditions in which they are active. Even if there have been attempts, such as that of Lerdahl (1989, p. 74), to assign relative strengths to each salience factor, in our opinion the matter has not yet attained credible consistency and requires further research.

The results of our experiment about the salience of every note of the melody raises the issue whether our opening questions about the relationships between grammatical rules and listening procedures have actually been answered satisfactorily. Regarding the two notes of the kernel (the notes on the first and the last strong beats of each phrase) the answer has not been univocal: the good mean scores obtained for the initial notes are in contrast with the poor mean scores for the notes on the final strong beats. Even among the four occurrences in the initial zones of the two phrases (see Table 8.3), the interacting/conflicting features produced different scores. The structurally eminent position of the kernel notes of the phrase are not sufficient to guarantee them a high level of salience. What is necessary for composition has ambiguous and complex relationships with what is salient in listening: the two aspects require a different approach. The rules of grammar govern every note: no note can be ungrammatical, but, on the contrary, not every note has to be salient.

More or less salient melodic features assure the melody a good balance of fluency, so that a few strong emergent points are connected by intermediate lower levels of salience. A grammar gives the composer a large range of possible rules within which they are free to choose what best corresponds to their expressive purposes (Baroni *et al.*, 1999). The composer knows how and when to attract the attention of the listener and intuitively applies the opportune grammatical rules. An example of balanced succession between low and high levels of salience can be found in the central segments of the first and the second phrases analysed here and whose different perceptual importance was accurately identified by the listeners. Such an effect was obtained by choosing particular melodic figures from those that could possibly connect the two notes of the kernel: in the first phrase leaps in low register, in the second phrase a movement by step in a high register. This can be considered a fairly positive finding in response to one of our initial questions ('Is the perception of the notes equally clear (or dull) in movement by leaps and by degrees?').

The so called 'feminine endings' of the two phrases, as already observed, were not picked up particularly well by our listeners, even if the silence after the last note of the second phrase attracted a greater interest than the conclusion of the first phrase. It is not arbitrary to speculate that a choice like this could be the fruit of the composer's broader design to move towards a stronger ending. Once again we are inclined to conclude that there is no strict correspondence between grammatical rules and the effects of salience, but without doubt there is a parallel between the level of perceptibility and the combinations of features that the grammar generates. Our sample could afford only a limited number of occurrences: in fact we analysed nothing more than a brief fragment of two bars. This limited experience has nevertheless offered some interesting starting points for a more detailed analysis.

References

Baroni, M., Dalmonte, R., & Jacoboni, C. (1999). *Le regole della musica. Indagine sui sui meccanismi della comunicazione*, EDT, Torino. (Engl. transl.: *A computer-aided inquiry on music communication. The rules of music*, Edwin Mellen Press, New York, 2003. French transl.: *Les règles de la musique. Étude sur les méchanismes de la communication*. Delatour, France 2007).

Bartlett J. C. (1993). Tonal structure of melodies. In T. J. Tighe, & W. J. Dowling (Eds.), *Psychology and music: The understanding of melody and rhythm* (pp. 39–61). Hillsdale, NJ: Lawrence Erlbaum.

Blacking, J. (1984). What languages do musical grammars describe? In M. Baroni, & L. Callegari (Eds.), *Musical grammars and computer analysis* (pp. 363–370). Firenze: Olschki.

Boltz, M. (1991). Some structural determinants of melody recall. *Memory & Cognition, 19*, 239–251.

Cuddy, L. L. (1993). Melody comprehension and tonal structure. In T. J. Tighe, & W. J. Dowling (Eds.), *Psychology and music: The understanding of melody and rhythm* (pp. 19–38). Hillsdale, NJ: Lawrence Erlbaum.

Deutsch, D., & Feroe, J. (1981). The internal representation of pitch sequences in tonal music. *Psychological Review, 88*, 503–522.

Divenyi, P. L., & Hirsch, I. J. (1978). Some figural properties of auditory patterns. *Journal of the Acoustic Society of America, 64*, 1369–1385.

Dowling, W. J. (1978). Scale and contour: Two components of a theory of memory for melodies. *Psychological Review, 85*, 341–354.

Dowling, W. J., & Harwood, D. L. (1986) *Music cognition*. New York, NY: Academic Press.

Edworthy, J. (1985). Interval and contour in melody processing. *Music Perception*, *2*, 375–388.

Eitan, Z. (1997). *Highpoints: A study of melodic peaks*. Philadelphia, PA: University of Pennsylvania Press.

Francès, R. (1954). Recherches expérimentales sur la perception de la mélodie. *Journal de Psychologie Normale et Pathologique*, *47–51*, 439–457.

Guilford, J. P., & Nelson, H. M. (1936). Changes in pitch of tones when melodies are repeated. *Journal of Experimental Psychology*, *19*, 193–202.

Huron, D., & Royal, M. (1996). What is melodic accent? Converging evidence from musical practice. *Music Perception*, *13*, 489–516.

Jones, M. R. (1993). Dynamics of musical patterns: How do melody and rhythm fit together? In T. J. Tighe, & W. J. Dowling (Eds.), *Psychology and music: The understanding of melody and rhythm* (pp. 76–92). Hillsdale, NJ: Lawrence Erlbaum.

Jones, M. R., Summerell, L., & Marshburn, E. (1987). Recognizing melodies: A dynamic interpretation. *Quarterly Journal of Experimental Psychology*, *39*, 89–121.

Larson, S. (1997). The problem of prolongation in tonal music: terminology, perception, and expressive meaning. *Journal of Music Theory*, *41*(1), 101–136.

Lerdahl, F. (1988). Cognitive constraints on compositional systems, In J. Sloboda (Ed.), *Generative processes in music: the psychology of performance, improvisation, and composition* (pp. 231–259). Oxford: Oxford University Press.

Lerdahl, F. (1989). Atonal prolongational structure. In S. Mc Adams, & I. Deliège (Eds.), *Music and the cognitive sciences*. Proceedings from the symposium on music and the cognitive sciences, 14–18 march 1988. Centre National d'Art et de Culture Georges Pompidou, Paris, France. *Contemporary Music Review*, *4*, 65–87.

Longuet-Higgins, H. C. (1976). Perception of melodies. *Nature*, *263*, 646–653.

Monahan, C. B. (1993). Parallels between pitch and time and how they go together. In T. J. Tighe, & W. J. Dowling (Eds.), *Psychology and music: The understanding of melody and rhythm* (pp. 121–154). Hillsdale NJ: Lawrence Erlbaum.

Monahan, C. B., Kendall, R. A., & Carterette, E. C. (1987). The effect of melodic and temporal contour on recognition of memory for pitch change. *Perception & Psychophysics*, *41*, 576–600.

Narmour, E. (1990). *The analysis and cognition of basic melodic structures: The implication realization model*. Chicago, IL: University of Chicago Press.

Peretz, I., & Morais, J. (1987). Analytic processing in the classification of melodies as same or different. *Neuropsychologia*, *25*, 645–652.

Schulkind, M. D., Posner, R. J., & Rubin, D. C. (2003). Musical features that facilitate melody identification: How do you know it's 'Your' song when they finally play it? *Music Perception*, *21*(2), 217–249.

Sloboda, J., & Parker, D. H. H. (1985). Immediate recall of melodies. In P. Howell, I. Cross, & R. West (Eds.), *Musical structure and cognition* (pp. 143–167). London: Academic Press.

Smith, K. C., & Cuddy, L. L. (1989). Effects of metric and harmonic rhythm on the detection of pitch alternations in melodic sequences. *Journal of Experimental Psychology: Human Perception and Performance*, *15*, 457–471.

Sundberg, J., & Lindblom, B. (1976). Generative theories in language and music descriptions. *Cognition*, *4*(1), 99–122.

Watkins, A. J., & Dyson, M. C. (1985). On the perceptual organisation of tone sequences. In P. Howell, I. Cross, & R. West (Eds.), *Musical structure and cognition* (pp. 71–119). London: Academic Press.

Appendix 8.1:

The 20 double versions of the musical phrase

Sloboda and Parker's recall paradigm for melodic memory: a new, computational perspective

Daniel Müllensiefen and Geraint A. Wiggins

Abstract

Sloboda and Parker (1985) proposed a new experimental paradigm for research on melodic memory in which participants are asked to listen to novel melodies and to sing back the parts they can recall from memory. In contrast to the many varieties of melodic recognition paradigms frequently used in memory research this sung recall paradigm can answer questions about how mental representations of a melody build up in memory over time, about the nature of memory errors, and about the interplay between different musical dimensions in memory. Although the paradigm has clear advantages with regard to ecological validity, Sloboda and Parker also note a number of difficulties inherent to the paradigm that mostly result from necessity to analyse 'dirty musical data' as sung by mostly untrained participants. This contribution reviews previous research done using the sung recall paradigm and proposes a computational approach for the analysis of dirty melodic data. This approach is applied to data from a new study using Sloboda and Parker's paradigm. This chapter discusses how this new approach not only enables researchers to handle large amounts of data but also make use of concepts from computational music analysis and music information retrieval that introduce a new level of analytic precision and conceptual clarity and thus provide a new interface which connects Sloboda's paradigm to rigorous quantitative data analysis.

The seminal study by John Sloboda and David Parker (1985) provided new insights into the construction of mental representations of melodic structures, and into mechanisms whereby learning of previously unknown melodies is accomplished over repeated attempts. In doing so, it introduced a new experimental paradigm for investigating melodic memory via sung recalls. The work is widely cited in subsequent literature on musical and melodic memory. However, despite the frequent citations and wide dissemination of the results of the study, the use of the recall paradigm has been limited to just a handful of subsequent studies. It has not achieved the level of usage and variation in the music cognition community achieved, for example, by paradigms based on recognition tasks.

In this chapter, we review the Sloboda and Parker paradigm from a methodological perspective, and hypothesize that one of the reasons why its uptake in the literature is at odds with the originality of results that it can produce is the relatively 'dirty' data it produces. A lack of standardized methods and the amount of manual work required to deal with these types of data seem to be major impediments to uptake of the paradigm. To ameliorate these drawbacks, we propose use of the computer as a tool for musical data analysis, and also as a means of model building and hypothesis generation. We demonstrate how it can help to make analysis procedures explicit and thus contribute to standardization. We reanalyse the original data from Sloboda and Parker's (1985) study, to demonstrate where computing technology can be applied and what additional value it can bring to the analysis of data from this very rich paradigm, whose full potential, we argue, has yet to be realized.

Paradigms for general memory research

In classic textbooks on experimental psychology (Anderson & Borkowski, 1978, 394–396; Kantowitz, Roediger, & Elmes, 1994, pp. 284–285; Kluwe, 1990), we find a well-developed canon of experimental paradigms that have been used to investigate verbal memory. The earliest go back to the very beginnings of psychology as a discipline and all of them have evolved and improved with time. For the purposes of the argument here a short description of each paradigm, in summary, will suffice.

Serial recall is the oldest experimental paradigm in the psychology of memory. It was first proposed by Hermann Ebbinghaus (1885) and has since been widely deployed in experimental studies, and considerably refined. Its basic task is to remember a list of items in order and recall them subsequently in the same order. Ebbinghaus and other well-known subsequent studies (e.g. Young, 1962) used meaningless syllables as experimental stimuli. Results generated by this paradigm inform us about the amount of repetition necessary to recall a list of items perfectly, the savings in effort and time when lists are relearned, and the decay of items in memory over time.

Paired-associate learning is another very early memory paradigm (Calkins, 1894) and can be directly linked to the stimulus–response concept of classical conditioning (Pavlov, 1927). Participants are given a list of pairs of items to memorize. They are then presented with a list containing one item of each pair, and asked to recall its match from the learned list before the match is shown. This process is repeated until the full list of pairs is memorized perfectly. Meaningless syllables and single words are used as items in verbal learning experiments using this paradigm. Central questions investigated concern item characteristics (e.g. the similarity between items, their imageability), the formation of association strengths, and the effects of cognitive mediators on recall performance.

Free recall, in contrast with serial recall, requires participants to learn a list of items, but leaves them free to recall the learned items in any order. If the study list is presented several times, then the position of the items is permuted, to avoid order associations. The most important observable in this paradigm is the effect of the position of an item in the study list on the probability of its recall. Regardless of the length of the study list, the initial items and the final items in the list are usually much better recalled than the items presented in middle positions (e.g. Murdock, 1962). These effects are known as *primacy* and *recency*; they can be reproduced very reliably with the *recency* effect usually being stronger than the *primacy* effect. One interpretation of these effects (Atkinson & Shiffrin, 1968) was that they suggest the existence of distinct memory stores where the first items of a list would have entered a long-term store and the last items would have still been present in a short-term store.

Recognition requires participants to study a list of items, but, in contrast to the recall paradigms described above, they are subsequently presented with a list containing items from the study list, and also new, previously unseen items. Participants are then asked to indicate which items were encountered previously, or one seen item can be presented along with several unseen items in a multiple-choice selection task. Recognition memory performance is generally much higher than recall memory performance (e.g. Shepard, 1967), though there are exceptions (Tulving, 1968). Not only can participants generally recognize high percentages (>80%) of long item lists (e.g. 500 items and more) but they are also able to maintain good recognition memories over long time intervals. This long-term performance is in clear contrast to the negative exponential forgetting curve that Ebbinghaus (1885) and others found with serial and other recall paradigms; it holds true for many different types of items (e.g. images, words).

Choosing a paradigm

There are good reasons for the existence and deployment of a wide range of experimental paradigms in memory research. First of all, different experimental procedures allow us to study different memory effects and to provide evidence for different types of hypothesis. For example, effects of list length and list position on correct recall from memory are typically studied using serial recall (Young, 1962), while ability to discriminate between stimuli has been investigated using the paired-associate learning paradigm (Underwood, Rundquist, & Schulz, 1959), and the effects of different rehearsal strategies can be revealed using the free recall procedure, for example with overt rehearsal (Rundus, 1974). Similarly, results from the various paradigms and their potential to falsify hypotheses of different nature have led to the proposal of correspondingly different memory models. For example, a specific class of memory trace model is primarily based on serial recall data (e.g. Nairne, 1990), while models using semantic hierarchies and clustering are often developed in connection with data from free recall studies (Tulving, 1968). Finally, data stemming from different experimental paradigms is often used to provide complementary evidence about the same model or hypothesis. This can help refute the claim that effects discovered with a certain paradigm are merely artefacts of that paradigm. Good examples are primacy and recency effects which reliably appear in both serial recall (Mueller, 1970) and free recall paradigms (Murdock, 1962). Complex, modern memory models that claim general applicability are usually based on data generated with diverse and very different paradigms. One such example is Baddeley's concept of working memory (1986, 2007) which is able to account for a large number of findings from recall studies using a variety of different tasks.

Paradigms in music memory research

Overview

Turning to research on memory for music, and specifically memory for *melodies*, we find a more limited range of basic experimental paradigms. If we naïvely suppose that the individual notes or pitch intervals of a melody are units comparable to words,[1] syllables, or digits in verbal memory research, then a free recall paradigm in a strict sense would be, by definition, melodically meaningless (though it might convey harmonic information): if notes are not recalled in a serial order, but freely, then it is hard to recognize the stimulus item and therefore to judge whether a participant has actually recalled it, and, if so, to what degree of accuracy. Some melodic recall studies include explicit instructions for the participants that the parts (sections, phrases, motives) of the melody items may be recalled in any order. Especially with longer melody items, this approach can make the experimental task much easier for the participants. Here, the paradigm comes closer to the verbal free recall paradigm, but it must still be considered a compromise variant of the basic melody recall procedure. We therefore conclude that there is essentially only one recall paradigm in music research, which is broadly comparable with verbal serial recall, *regardless of how the recall is actually performed in the experiment.* As we will see below, depending on the target group of participants, recall response modes can range from singing through playing on an instrument to using music notation or verbal labels for individual notes. In all instances though, the serial order of the recalled notes is of primary importance.

This said, it is possible, and not unreasonable, to define very abstract representations of melody which do not rely on strict note sequence—for example, by pitch class or interval counting. However, experience suggests that these are not good representations for musical memory: order does seem to be paramount, as one might expect. These representations can nevertheless be useful in applications such as music information retrieval (for example, harmonic interval statistics are used for this purpose by Pickens *et al.*, 2003).

---

[1] In fact, music is extremely context-sensitive, and, statistically, at least, there seems to be some comparison between sequences of three-or four-note chords and words (Mauch, Müllensiefen, Dixon, & Wiggins, 2008), though how deep this comparison runs is far from clear.

Nor is paired-associate learning often seen in music research. This may be again due to the sequential nature of music, and melodies in particular. It is hard to imagine a musically meaningful task where musical or melodic elements can be presented in pairs and to be encoded together. At least, one would have to consider passages of music that can be paired according to specific attributes (e.g. timbre, pitch range, tempo, specific rhythms). This paradigm would clearly make no musical sense at all if one took notes or intervals as the atomic elements to be remembered in pairs.

Recognition paradigms in music memory research

Recognition is the only other memory paradigm available for research on memory for melodies. Recognition has been used extensively over the past 40 years and has diversified into a few major subparadigms, the most important of which we now briefly describe.

Pitch comparison The **Deutsch paradigm** was first used by its eponymous designer in the early 1970s, in a tradition of many studies targeting short-term memory, its capacity, and the conditions for interference effects for verbal memory. Deutsch dedicated a series of studies to the limits of the auditory store holding pitch information and to the question of how memory representation for pitch could be eliminated by interference effects (Deutsch, 1970, 1972, 1974, 1975a, 1975b; Deutsch & Feroe, 1975). The paradigm used in these studies was later used by other researchers in follow-up studies. In its basic form, the Deutsch paradigm can be described thus. The participant is presented with a single target pitch which they are asked to keep in memory. Then, they listen to some intervening stimuli in an *interpolation* phase (called *retention* elsewhere): typically, the stimuli in the interpolation phase are varied as factors of the independent variable. These stimuli can be verbal auditory material or a varied number of pitches which can be more or less harmonically or melodically related to the target stimulus. Finally, a comparison pitch is played and the participant judges whether it is the same as the initial pitch or not.

The results generated by experiments using this paradigm seem to indicate that there may be a store for pitch information, separate from any verbal auditory store, and which is influenced only to a minor degree by other characteristics of a tone, such as loudness, timbre, or direction (i.e. the ear it is presented to). However, this pitch memory system, which has been hypothesized to be a separate subsystem in Baddeley's auditory working memory (Pechmann & Mohr, 1992), is fairly strongly influenced by pitches presented in the interpolation phase of the Deutsch paradigm. The interference with the memory representation of the target pitch is particularly strong if the interpolation pitches are close to the target in continuous pitch space, or if they are identical to the comparison pitch.

AB comparison is widely used in melodic memory research (e.g. DeWitt & Crowder, 1986; Dowling, 1972, 1978; Dowling & Fujitani, 1971; Idson & Massaro, 1978). It is similar to the Deutsch paradigm in that the participant is asked to compare two stimuli and indicate whether they are identical or not, and, sometimes, rate their confidence in their judgement. But with AB comparison, the target and comparison stimuli are longer melodic sequences, parts of real melodies, or excerpts from a polyphonic piece.

The retention phase between the presentation of the target stimulus, A, and the comparison stimulus, B, is less relevant than in the Deutsch paradigm: material presented in this phase often serves only as a distractor.

Variation in applications of AB comparison is often in the melodic attributes that are held the same or made different between A and B. The rationale is that, if two melodic sequences differ in a specific melodic attribute (e.g. contour) but participants nonetheless indicate that A and B are identical, then this particular attribute seems not to have been encoded in memory (Idson & Massaro, 1978, p. 554). Therefore, the paradigm is particularly well suited to uncovering which melodic attributes are encoded in memory, and how different melodic structures and contexts favour the encoding of particular attributes or combinations of attributes. The *scale and contour* theory of melodic memory (Dowling, 1978) is mostly based on data from AB comparison, and it has delivered much insight into how melodies of different lengths are encoded (Long, 1977), under which conditions interval versus contour information is encoded (Dowling & Bartlett, 1981; Dowling & Fujitani, 1971; Edworthy, 1983, 1985), and how the encoding process of melodic phrases proceeds during the course of a real listening experience (Dowling, Tillmann, & Ayers, 2002).

AB comparison is related to testing procedures from psychophysics, where two stimuli are to be compared with regard, for example, with difference in loudness or in pitch. Consequently, bias-free scoring procedures originally applied in psychophysical tests, such as d' (Green & Swets, 1966), are often employed in memory experiments of AB comparison to obtain values of the independent variable.

List-wise recognition is closer to the recognition procedure usually found in verbal memory experiments. In the study phase, short melodies are presented one after another forming a list. After a short retention interval, there is a test phase, in which another list of melodies is played to the participants. The test list contains melodies used in the study list as well as new melodies. Participants indicate whether each item on the test list was presented in the study phase, and rate their confidence in their judgement. In addition, or as an alternative, participants may be asked rate the pleasantness of the melodies. Pleasantness ratings haven been used as a measure of implicit memory (Halpern & Müllensiefen, 2008) on the basis that the previous exposure to the same melody increases its aesthetic appreciation (the mere exposure effect: Zajonc, 1968).

There are two major differences between list-wise recognition and AB comparison. First, in list-wise recognition, the significance of the retention phase is relatively very limited, and its length and the content are generally not part of the experimental design. Second, list-wise recognition admits greater distance in time and more intervening musical material between corresponding items on the study and test lists. If the lists are substantially long, then episodic memory representations of particular melody items are likely to be lost, due to interference or to decay of the original memory trace. This makes list-wise recognition well suited to implicit memory testing.

Dynamic recognition paradigm for familiar melodies was popularized by Matthew Schulkind and collaborators it in a series of publications (Schulkind, 2000, 2004; Schulkind, Posner, & Rubin, 2003) on the recognition of well-known tunes. In the first trial, participants listen to an incipit of a given length from a melody, and then are asked to indicate the title of the tune if they can recognize it. If a participant is unable to name the tune confidently, the incipit is played again, in repeated trials, with one more note from the melody included each time; there is a prompt for a recognition judgement after each trial. For each incipit length, the recognition rate across participants is recorded and is subsequently compared with melodic and rhythmic events happening or being completed at that point in the melody.

Recognition versus recall The greater diversification within the recognition paradigm corresponds with the far greater number of studies that have been published using recognition, rather than recall, as the participants' response. We will discuss some reasons for the dominance of the various forms of the recognition paradigm in research on melodic memory below. For now, we conclude by remarking that, in contrast to the few studies using a melodic recall paradigm, there is a plethora of melodic recognition studies in the literature and that recognition is significantly more prominent, more diversified and more developed in melodic memory research. Given the potential benefits of employing different memory paradigms in verbal research (finding different effects, coming up with different types of models, and corroborating the same effects/models from a different perspective, etc.), we suggest that there is a clear motivation to develop the recall paradigm for melodic memory. Furthermore, we will advocate the use of computers in the analysis and modelling of the melodic recalls generated from this paradigm.

Studies using recall paradigms for melodic memory

Studies using recall paradigms are much less common than those employing one of the variants of recognition surveyed above. The differences between recall studies lie mostly in whether novel or familiar melodies are used as experimental stimuli, in whether participants are musically trained or untrained (or perhaps the study compares performance between these two groups), and in the participants' response mode. It is worth briefly reviewing some recall studies here to provide a feel for the spectrum of existing methods, and to position the specific experimental paradigm of Sloboda and Parker (1985) therein.

Musical dictation was used by Deutsch (1980) to provide evidence for her hierarchical-generative system of mental representations (Deutsch & Feroe, 1981). Musically well-trained listeners listened to sequences of 12 sine tones, representing different degrees of structural difficulty. The tone sequences were produced from the Deutsch–Feroe model, applying different generative rules, to generate easier or more difficult sequences. Some sequences included leading tones, while others were mainly built around triads, and others were segmented on the basis of melodic versus temporal gaps. The participants' task was to write down, in staff notation, as much as they could remember from the stimuli. The notated responses were evaluated by calculating the relative number of correct pitches at the correct serial position. Deutsch found more correct recall for the easier melodies, that could be encoded more efficiently as predicted by the Deutsch–Feroe model. She therefore concluded that memorizing a melodic sequence consists of encoding the hierarchical structure of the sequence and its alphabet; a single chunk from the sequence (e.g. the incipit) would also have to be encoded, to allow for a subsequent reconstruction of the whole sequence from memory. The Deutsch–Feroe model is specified in a generative form, and producing sequences from it that can be used as experimental stimuli is straightforward. But it is not an analytic device capable of encoding an existing melody; to perform that more complex task, a fully functional parser would be needed. This memory model is therefore of limited use for experiments that use real, existing melodies as stimuli. The music dictation method employed in this experiment requires a good level of musical training among the participants and is therefore not suitable for exploring memory representation of untrained subjects.

To overcome this last limitation, Davies and Yelland (1977) asked their participants to draw from memory a representation of the contours of short, song-like, newly composed sequences, to which they had listened. Contour was represented as rising, falling, or horizontal lines between successive notes. The resulting drawings were scored according to the number of lines with correct inclination at the correct serial position. Davies and Yelland were not concerned with effects of melodic structure, but varied the number of repeated listenings and the type of training procedure used to familiarize participants with the contour drawing method as independent variables. As expected, participants drew increasingly more accurate contours over repeated listenings to the same melody. This corroborates the assumption that mental representations of melodies become more accurate with repeated exposure. With regard to the training procedure comparison, the best results came from participants who had practised contour drawing with well-known melodies from long-term memory in silence as opposed to another group that practised drawing novel melodies that were presented aurally and whose members received feedback on their drawings. Davies and Yelland interpret this group difference as pointing to the importance of comparing novel stimuli with settled internal representations. Also, it seems that contour information is not explicitly abstracted during listening, but that melodies are represented as tonal analogies from which abstractions such as contour can be derived in subsequent serial scans through the representation.

While Davies and Yelland's experimental procedure is suitable for participants with little or no musical training, it is limited to reflecting the accuracy of melodic contour encoding and it ignores other parameters such as interval size, harmonic implication or rhythmic duration. It also requires a transfer of 'up-and-down' information from the auditory domain into the visual domain, and so it is not possible to separately distinguish if participants with low scores had an inaccurate representation of the melody as an auditory object, or if they were less good at transferring information from the auditory domain to the visual response domain. The different training procedures could potentially have trained these two different processes to different degrees.

Contour label recall was used by Williamson, Baddeley, and Hitch (2006) (and similarly Keller, Cowen, & Saults, 1995) to test recall memory for short pitch sequences. It asks for recall of the contour of four-note isochronic pitch sequences from working memory. Each note of a sequence could be either 'high', 'medium', or 'low', in relation to the other notes. In each trial, after hearing the pitch sequence, participants were asked to fill out a matrix in a paper booklet indicating the contour category of each of the four notes. Since participants' responses are expressed in a written nota-tion requiring no musical knowledge, they need no musical training or any singing skills. The resulting data are very clean compared with sung recalls from the para-digms, described below, which require skilled transcription and expert analysis. In principle, the paradigm is not limited to the evaluation of memory representation of melodic contour (i.e. higher-than and lower-than judgements with respect to pitch height): judging duration or rhythmic categories as well as intervallic distance should, in theory, also be possible. However, it is limited in that, with musically untrained listeners, memory load issues can mean that it is possible test only a single musical dimension (contour or rhythm or intervals) at a time, so interactions between dimen-sions cannot be studied.

Also, experimental stimuli must be relatively simple and the number of different stimulus class labels is limited; Miller's (1956) rule of thumb of 7 ± 2 different magni-tude values or categories that are simultaneously manageable on the same perceptual dimension may possibly hold as an upper limit (for a more recent affirmation of Miller's original results, see Shiffrin & Nosofsky, 1994). However, many popular melodies make use of more than seven different pitches, and processing and memory constraints are aggravated by the requirement to report the category label of each note of a series in order. Determining the limits of the paradigm before floor effects are reached in terms of the number of different category classes, as well as with respect to number of musical dimensions that can be combined and in terms of the length of the note sequence would give valuable insight into to which degree this recall paradigm can be used with non-artificial melodic stimuli.

Vocal recall of known songs was used by Halpern (1989) and Levitin (1994) to determine the accuracy for the absolute pitch of melodies from well-known folk or pop songs. Here, the accuracy of the memory representation of the relative structure of the melodies was of less importance because only the first note (Halpern) or the first three notes (Levitin) sung by the participants were used for analysis; participants that failed to produce a stable pitch were excluded from the sample. The analysis of the sung recalls must have been quite laborious in both cases. In Halpern's study, the starting pitches of the folk songs were transcribed by an expert musician with refer-ence to a keyboard. Levitin used a computer program to estimate fundamental fre-quency using the Fast Fourier Transform. He determined the pitch of each of the three starting notes of the participants' recalls by selecting just the steady state portion of the sung notes with an audio editor and rounding the fundamental frequency to the near-est semitone. This paradigm is, in principle, quite similar to Sloboda and Parker's paradigm in that sung responses from memory are recorded and transcribed, and, in consequence, researchers using vocal recall face the same problems as Sloboda and Parker, which we outline below. A lot of expert work is required to transform the sung audio recordings into score notation and finally into a numerical representation of pitch. However, because Halpern (1989) and Levitin (1994) are only concerned with long-term memory for absolute pitch, and melodic structure, rhythmic, metric, phras-ing, and interval information in the sung recalls need not be transcribed, the complex-ity of the task is greatly reduced.

The Sloboda and Parker recall paradigm

The core component of the Sloboda and Parker's (1985) procedure is the request to participants to sing the stimulus melody item back from memory. The experimental procedure, as used in their original study, can be split into four stages:

1 A melody is played to the participant up to six times. After each repetition, the participant is asked to sing into a microphone and recording device those parts of the melody that they can remember.

2 The audio recordings are transcribed into music notation by a human expert.

3 From the notation, each recall is analysed with regard to different aspects such as metre, breathing breaks, melodic contour, and phrase structure.

4 The dependent variables are compared over the values of the independent variables of interest: trial number, participants' musical background, melody type, and presentation mode (e.g. with or without lyrics: Ginsborg & Sloboda, 2007).

To obtain accuracy scores for different types of errors, in step 3, and ultimately to enable quantitative analyses, Oura and Hatano (1988) developed a more formal scoring method which was subsequently used by Zielinska and Miklaszewski (1992), Drake, Dowling, and Palmer (1991) and Ogawa *et al.* (1995) with slight variations. In this scoring procedure, each phrase in the recall where a tonality can be identified is assigned to the best matching phrase in the original melody. Each phrase is then compared, in half-bar windows, to its counterpart in the original. If the half-bar window is identical to the original, it is labelled as *correct*. If it differs in either rhythm or contour, it is labelled as *modified* and if it differs in both parameters from the original it is declared *non-identified*. The windows are summed together by category (and error type) and their proportions with respect to the overall number of half-bars are taken as dependent variables for that particular trial.

While the method seems superficially straightforward, and the results that can be produced from it are of great interest, much cited, and truly complementary to what can be obtained from a recognition paradigm, it has been used only a few times in the 25 years since it was published. This disappointing uptake is due to some inherent difficulties with the method, most of which were discussed in the original article (Sloboda & Parker, 1985); we summarize them as follows.

1 The raw data recorded in these studies are extremely 'dirty', requiring expert interpretation. Participants are required to sing, and their singing may be inaccurate; in some places, it is necessary to infer which note(s) they *meant* to sing. The participants' singing is recorded, and it is possible that the recording may be imperfect; it is impossible to prevent this without breaking the paradigm, for obvious reasons.

2 There is 'no theory of melodic identity' (Sloboda & Parker, 1985, p. 159).Therefore, subjective judgements of the expert transcribers are crucial in doing the analysis. This subjectivity can clearly affect the results, and cannot be controlled.

3 It follows that there can be no standard, verified scoring method for these complex response data; that is, there is no theory of melodic *similarity* to give a

Table 9.1 Numbers of recalled fragments reported in studies applying Sloboda and Parker's recall paradigm

Study	Recalled fragments
Sloboda and Parker (1985)	48
Oura and Hatano (1988)	320
Zielinska and Miklaszewski (1992)	310
Ogawa *et al.* (1995)	80
Ginsborg and Sloboda (2007)	60
Müllensiefen and Wiggins (manuscript in preparation)	1900

measure of how close the attempts are to the original. Oura and Hatano (1988) aimed to address this with their procedure, which was described above.

4 A simple but very limiting issue is the amount of time it takes to transcribe the data and perform these analyses. No really large studies using the method have yet been published; those studies which have been carried out are listed, with their size, in Table 9.1. This last issue, superficially, is the kind of problem that one would like to solve by using a computer, on the grounds that computers can analyse data very quickly and very accurately. However, because music is fundamentally a perceptual and cognitive construct, any program used for these tasks needs to encode *human expert* levels of musical understanding. In the next section, we explore the extent to which this is currently possible, show what can be done, and examine prospects for the future.

Computational methods for researching melodic memory

Towards automatic support of Sloboda and Parker's paradigm

Our central idea in this paper is that the experimental paradigm proposed by Sloboda and Parker (1985) may be greatly facilitated by appropriate application of computational technology. Broadly, it should be possible to use computational methods to process, analyse, and compare recall data, thus allowing the method to be applied more widely.

We summarized the drawbacks with the method in the previous section, above; a computational approach can, at least in principle, help with most of them. Digital recording and post-hoc computational audio analysis can greatly help with problem number 1; this technology has been readily and cheaply available for more than a decade, though it is becoming established in music and music psychology research only recently (e.g. Cook, 2008). In particular, as noted above, the speed and repeatability of computer processing could help in principle with problem number 4; however, this is dependent on solutions to the more musical aspects in problems 2 and 3, which are very difficult. Sloboda and Parker's statement that there is 'no theory of melodic identity' (1985, p. 159) holds just as true 25 years on. However, there is now a substantial body of research leading towards computational theories of melodic similarity which are applicable in an analytical context. Progress towards a computational theory brings concomitant benefits beyond the immediate application: in particular, to build a program that embodies a theory, one must specify that theory to an extreme—indeed *absolute*—level of detail. Once such a specification is given and a program written, it can be tested to destruction against all the data available from studies involving humans, without problems of fatigue, priming, or even ethics. In this way, the computational approach not only facilitates the empirical work, but can make its analysis more rigorous and objective; new knowledge can be created in terms of novel hypotheses generated by the models.

Extant computational methods developed for various musical purposes can be applied in this context. Since musical memory, and hence musical similarity, de facto underpins the vast majority of musical behaviour (Wiggins, 2007), there is a rich seam of more general work to be mined and repurposed to help solve the current problem. There is not space here to review or even to list all the work that could contribute in this way, but some examples follow. Temperley (2001) and Huron (1995, 2006) have developed cognitively informed methods intended for computational music analysis; in particular, attempts to understand structural reference in this context help in our understanding of memory, for it is this which enables such reference to be understood. These essentially musicological approaches can be enhanced by models from mathematical music theory (e.g. RUBATO: Milmeister, Mazzola, & Thalmann, 2009), which generally aim to find mathematical systems underpinning perception and cognition, with a view to explaining why either the music or the perception is the way it is.

The study of music cognition in general (e.g. Eerola, Järvinen, Louhivuori, & Toiviainen, 2002; Krumhansl, 1990; Thomassen, 1982), from an empirical standpoint, allows different kinds of insight into what may be expected in perception of music, and can inform the construction of heuristics (see below) for helping with analysis of musical data, as well as supplying models of musical competence, such as memory.

In a practically motivated context, a significant amount of work in the field of music information retrieval is concerned with understanding of perceived similarity of various kinds, such as harmonic similarity, usually at the level of whole pieces, (e.g. Pickens *et al.*, 2003) and melodic similarity (e.g. Crawford, Iliopoulos, & Raman, 1998; Müllensiefen & Frieler, 2004a). Finally, since there seem to be shared effects and behaviours between music and language, it has proven useful to consider techniques from computational linguistics in the musical context (e.g. Downie, 2003).

Taken together, models and methods developed in these areas can already analyse many aspects of melodies that are of core interest in many psychological studies. These include: melodic identity and similarity (Müllensiefen & Pendzich, 2009); metrical structure, metre induction (Müllensiefen and Frieler, 2004b); (Eck, 2002; Volk, 2008); phrase structure (Pearce, Müllensiefen, & Wiggins, 2010; Temperley, 2001); rhythmic structure (Weyde, 2004); harmonic structure: tonality induction (Krumhansl, 1990; Longuet-Higgins & Steedman, 1971); accent strength (Müllensiefen, Pfleiderer, and Frieler, 2009), complexity (North & Hargreaves, 1995), expectedness (Pearce & Wiggins, 2006), high-level structure identification (Abdallah, Sandler, Rhodes, & Casey, 2006).

While computational methods are nowhere near the position of simulating a human listener as a whole, we suggest that the time is ripe to begin applying these methods to focused problems such as those provided by the Sloboda and Parker paradigm. Through feedback from such application, the methods will themselves be improved.

Computational modelling of perceived melodic similarity

A key issue in executing the Sloboda and Parker paradigm is the comparison of recalled melodies with the original stimulus. This is a hard task for human experts, not simply because it is a difficult task in any case, but in particular because the judgements required can sometimes be very subjective, based on the prior musical bias of the expert. One way one might increase objectivity would be to do the analysis automatically: this has the advantage of removing subjectivity based on purely human judgement. However, such judgements cannot, in the current state of the art, be made entirely reliably by computer. In this section, we briefly survey the state of that art, with a view to identifying what can be done and what needs further work. We also exemplify this concept with a short description of the *edit distance* (or *Levenshtein distance*), an algorithm that is very simple but which has proven to be effective for similarity computations in automatic text processing, computational biology (Gusfield, 1997), and also audio and music computing (e.g. Crawford *et al.*, 1998; Unal, Chew, Georgiou, & Narayanan, 2008).

We described the scoring procedure developed by Ogawa *et al.* (1995) in an earlier section. In this method, melodic similarity is measured by (manually) determining the identity of half-bar segments from the original melody and the sung recalls. This approach, while not computerized, is archetypal of computerized approaches. Because musical similarity is a multidimensional thing, it is necessary to be clear about which dimensions one is interested in (and, of course, this may be a parameter of one's study). It follows that, if we are interested in more than one dimension, but we need a linear scale for comparison, we also need a mathematical means of mapping vector distances in a multidimensional space on to scalar distances; fortunately, the mathematics required is undaunting to psychologists. Both the dimensions and mapping methods must correspond properly with perceived similarity; where there is ambiguity in human response, this should ideally be detectable in the measurement system (for example, two different multidimensional distances might map on to the same scalar distance). To produce a similarity measure which meets this specification in full is a very tall order, and much more research is required to do so.

However, we are in a position to begin. Assuming that we have transcriptions of all melodies in a symbolic format to start from, there are two essential steps in measuring melodic similarity: first, the melodies are transformed into one (or several) representation(s) which encode(s) all the dimensions of the music in which one is interested; second, the abstract representations are compared and a numerical value (usually normalized between 0 and 1) is derived to indicate the distance between them.

In the first step, the raw melodies (which might be represented, for example, only by a sequence of tuples of pitch and onset values) are transformed into one or more abstract representations that are cognitively more meaningful and of interest with regard to the similarity comparison. Melodic representations that can be usefully employed for similarity measurement include melodic intervals, melody contour, a sequence of durational or rhythmic values, and a sequence of tonality values that are implied by the melodic pitches. The important point about this step is that the raw melodic information is *abstracted* and melodies are represented as sequences of numerical or digit symbols. The transformation is in principal independent of the algorithm that is used to compare symbol sequences subsequently. The choice of transformation depends rather on whether the researcher deems it important with respect to the similarity measurement or whether it contains an optimal amount of information in an information-theoretical sense (Pearce & Wiggins, 2004). Of course, various different representations of the same melody (e.g. one containing pitch intervals and one containing rhythmic values) can be combined for subsequent similarity measurement.

In the second step, from the abstract representations of two melodies a similarity value from the interval [0, ..., 1] is computed where 1 indicates maximal similarity or identity and 0 indicates no similarity between the two melodies. In recent years, several different measures, and algorithms to implement them, have been proposed and tested in various applications needing to determine the similarity between melodies. These include geometric measures (Aloupis *et al.*, 2003; O Maidin, 1998), string matching techniques such as edit distance (Crawford *et al.*, 1998; Mongeau & Sankoff, 1990), n-gram measures (Downie, 2003; Uitdenbogerd, 2002), and hidden Markov models (Meek & Birmingham, 2002) from speech recognition, as well as the Earth Movers Distance algorithm (Typke, Wiering, & Veltkamp, 2007) from computer vision, and hybrid algorithms that combine the output of several different similarity measurement procedures (Müllensiefen & Frieler, 2004a). Here, by way of example, we briefly explain the edit distance measure, which, in recent years has proven to be a surprisingly effective comparison or benchmark algorithm that appears to be similar to informal and rather intuition-guided music-analytic applications of melodic similarity concepts (for a comparative discussion of quantitative and qualitative approaches to melodic similarity, see Müllensiefen & Pendzich, 2009).

The main idea behind the edit distance, or Levenshtein distance, is to treat the minimum number of operations ('edits') needed to transform one string into another as a measure of the distance between them. The permitted operations are insertion, deletion, and substitution. Since the operation of the algorithm is independent of the denotation of the symbols in the strings compared, we use letter strings to demonstrate the edit distance in our example. Consider the two letter strings SCHOENBERG and SCHUBERT. These strings can be aligned optimally by applying the series of operations applied to each letter that is recorded in the *edit transcript* shown. The symbol D denotes the deletion of a letter, I stands for insertion, S for a substitution, and M for a match of two letters, i.e. no operation is carried out.

String 1   S C C H O E N B E R G
String 2   S C H _ _ U B E R T
Edit Transcript M M M D D S M M M S

(9.1)

Since there are two deletions and two substitutions, the edit distance in this case is 4—if deletions and substitutions are given the same weight, though these amounts may be varied to achieve different matching behaviours. To arrive at a similarity value, rather than a distance metric, and to confine that value to the interval (0,1), we divide the distance value by the maximal distance (the length of the longer string) and subtract the result from one:

$$\sigma(s_1, s_2) = 1 - \frac{d_{edit}(s_1, s_2)}{\max(|s_1|, |s_2|)}$$

(9.2)

For our example, we thus obtain an edit distance similarity value of $1 - 4/10 = 0.6$. Of course, this same measure works with symbols representing pitch, intervals or rhythmic categories; all that we need is the ability to decide whether two symbols are the same, regardless of their meaning. What makes it attractive for music researchers is the fact that the quality of the operations (insertions, deletions, and substitutions) have parallels in musical composition, where it is common practice to produce variations or related pieces of music by, for example, inserting ornamental notes or by replacing certain structurally important notes by others that may serve a similar—or different—harmonic purpose. This neat simplicity is necessarily lost if we wish to consider more than one musical dimension at once, because of the intimate relationship between the dimensions of music, but Mongeau and Sankoff (1990) have adapted the measure to work better in these circumstances.

The description above, however, covers only the measure, and not the algorithm required to compute it. For edit distance to be useful, two strings must be aligned *optimally*—that is, with the smallest possible distance. This is often achieved, in $O(n^2)$ time and memory, using *dynamic programming* (Gusfield, 1997), whose implementation is straightforward. This, and the fact that the measure itself and its outputs are mostly easy to understand, have made edit distance a popular tool in computational music analysis in recent times.

Revisiting Sloboda's and Parker's results

Motivation

We now revisit the results of Sloboda's and Parker's paper as discussed in their nine conclusions (Sloboda & Parker, 1985, pp. 159–160). The primary purpose of reanalysing the musical data from the original study is not to refute or support the authors' findings, but rather to show how analytical algorithms can be usefully employed in cognitive studies, how they might help to cope with large amounts of difficult-to-analyse musical data, and how they might shed a different light on some analytical procedures that are commonly executed by human (as opposed to computational) effort.

As musical data, we used the 48 transcribed recalls that are given in appendix by Sloboda and Parker (1985). We applied similarity measurements and other algorithmic analysis methods to the research questions and results summarized at the beginning of their conclusion section. We limit ourselves to discussion of six out of the nine results, where the application of computational methods seem most straightforward and productive, and omit Sloboda and Parker's main findings 4, 5, and 7.

Main finding 1: 'No recall is perfect'

We measured the similarity between the target melody and each recall using the edit distance algorithm (see above). To have a 'second opinion' from a similarity algorithm that makes use of musical background information from a corpus, we also applied an asymmetric similarity algorithm proposed by Müllensiefen and Pendzich (2009), which is based on a conception of feature similarity proposed by Tversky (1977), the *Tversky.target.only* algorithm. We applied both algorithms only to the *pitch sequences* of the melodies. The maximal similarity values were 0.93, from edit distance, and 0.98, from the Tversky similarity algorithm. Both were measured for participant 5 on her sixth trial. Sloboda and Parker's assertion that, even for this simple folk tune and with some musically trained participants, there is no single 'note-for-note perfect' recall among the 48 attempts. The computational analysis corroborates this surprising limitation of human melody recall.

Main finding 2: 'Recalls are highly related to the original in many respects'

We measured the similarity between recalls and the target melody using our simple edit distance algorithm, but feeding it different types of musical information, viz., sequences of pitches, sequences of interpolated contour values, sequences of categorized rhythmic (duration) values, and sequences of implied tonalities at the bar level as derived from the Krumhansl–Schmuckler algorithm for tonality induction (Krumhansl, 1990). How these different types of musical information are obtained, through appropriate transformations from the raw melodic pitch and onset data, is documented by Müllensiefen and Frieler (2004a). We obtained mean similarity values, averaged over all 48 recalls, of 0.37 for pitch similarity, 0.21 for contour similarity, 0.56 rhythmic similarity, and 0.20 for similarity of implied tonalities. Taking into account that these values are averaged over all six trials and therefore include low similarity values from initial (and so mostly incomplete) trials, it seems fair to say that the recorded recalls were related to the target melody in many different respects. In particular, the similarity is found to some extent in all the dimensions tested. Thus, the original findings are supported.

Main finding 3: 'Metrical structure is preserved in almost all recalls'

We used the beat and metre extraction model of Frieler (2004) to induce the metre of the target melody and the recalls. The model uses temporal smoothing with Gaussian kernels, accent rules based on note durations and autocorrelation to determine the beat level, metre, and metrical phase from monophonic input. The model induced a 2/4 metre for the target melody, which is not unreasonable; the melody being actually notated in 4/4 may simply be because 4/4 metres are more common in Western musical styles. Eighty one per cent of the recalls were classified as having a 2/4 metre and 19% were classified as 4/4. So all trials had a simple duple metre, like the target melody. However, since 4/4 is the default for most (popular) Western music, this result is not so surprising; it would be interesting to apply the approach to recalls where the target was in triple and/or compound meter.

Main finding 6: 'Subjects vary significantly regarding their melodic and harmonic accuracy'

We compared the recalls of musical novices (participants 1–4) and musicians (participants 5–8) with regard to their melodic and harmonic accuracy (i.e. similarity to the target melody), as did Sloboda and Parker. We measured pitch edit distance to estimate pitch accuracy. Novices achieved a mean similarity of 0.30 over all trials and musicians reached a mean of 0.45, which proved to be a significant difference ($t(30.4) = 2.86$, p = 0.004). Similarly, mean harmonic similarity as measured by the edit distance over implied tonalities differed significantly between novices ($\bar{x}_{novices} = 0.09$) and musicians ($\bar{x}_{musicians} = 0.31$; $t(28.5) = 3.17$, p = 0.002). Although the difference between novices and musicians is significant for both measures, the it is much larger for the harmonic comparison. This supports Sloboda and Parker's conclusion that 'memory for harmonic structure seems to be related to musical expertise' (1985, p. 160).

We also compared rhythmic similarity values between the two groups. The resulting t-test shows no significant difference between the two groups of participants ($\bar{x}_{novices} = 0.59$; $\bar{x}_{musicians} = 0.54$; $t(45.5) = -0.75$, p = 0.77). Sloboda and Parker observed that while there are considerable differences between listeners regarding the memory retention of harmonic structure, metrical structure was abstracted well by all participants. This finding seems now to extend to rhythmic structure as well.

Main finding 8: 'Musicians and non-musicians differ in retention of harmony'

We looked at the development of the representation of harmonic structure in both groups of participants over the six trials, with main finding 6 (above) in mind. We averaged the harmonic similarity values, as measured by the edit distance on the implied tonalities, for each trial number over each participant group. The development is illustrated in Figure 9.1.

Figure 9.1 shows a clear increase in harmonic similarity between the musicians' recalls and the target melody from trial 4 on while the harmonic similarity between recalls of novices and the target melody stay at the same low level of similarity over all six trials. In contrast, no learning effect or improvement of accuracy in the mental representations seems to take place for the novices. Accordingly, a dependent sample t-test between novices' and musicians' mean recall similarity values indicated a significant difference ($\bar{x}_{differences} = 0.22$; $t(5) = 3.16$; p = 0.01). Therefore, it seems evident that the perceptual and cognitive abstraction and refinement of harmonic structure is achieved only by participants with some musical training.

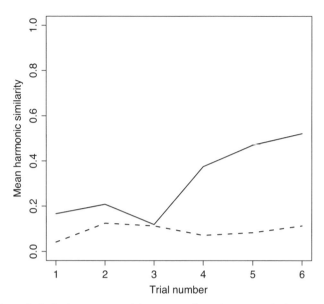

Fig. 9.1 Mean similarity between participants' recalls and target melody over trials. Solid line: musicians; dashed line: novices.

Main finding 9: 'Subjects do not show improvement on any measure over the six trials'

This is one of Sloboda and Parker's most interesting conclusions, since it seems to imply that human memory for melodies does not increase in accuracy with repeated exposure. To test whether there is actually no such learning effect, we averaged for each trial similarity for pitch, harmonic, rhythmic, and overall similarity (measure *opti2* combining duration weighted pitch values and a similarity measure on short pitch motives, see Müllensiefen & Frieler, 2004a, for details) over all participants and computed Pearson's correlation, *r*, between trials number and means similarity for each similarity measure. We found high and significant values of *r* for all similarity measures as given in Table 9.2. Figure 9.2 illustrates these correlations.

These correlations do suggest that a learning effect is taking place over repeated trials. The effect seems to be less strong for the rhythmic aspect of the memory representation than for the pitch and harmonic aspects. So, while Sloboda and Parker assert that recalls get longer over trials (starting at a mean of 16.5 notes for trial 1 and monotonically increasing to 26.625 notes for trial 6), we found that recalls also get more accurate and that participants also seem to refine their memory representations.

This is in line with results of Zielinska and Miklaszewski (1992), who found (using 10 instead of 6 trials) an increase in the number of correctly recalled half-measures.

Discussion

The translation of the six main analyses discussed in the previous section into computational methods proved to be very simple and straightforward. Translating main

Table 9.2 Values of Pearson's correlation coefficient r with corresponding p values for different similarity measures measuring the correlation between trial number and mean similarity with the target melody

Similarity measure	r	p Value
Edit distance, pitch	0.93	0.008
Edit distance, implied tonality	0.93	0.008
Edit distance, rhythmic category	0.77	0.08
opti2	0.91	0.01

findings 4, 5, and 7 into computational form requires some more detailed argumentation; they can probably be realized in more than one way.[2] Therefore, we defer these for future work, because the purpose of this chapter is merely to support our claim that analytical tasks in music cognition research can be solved computationally.

For main finding 4, 'subjects preserve phrase structure', one possible analysis would have been to compute, for each recall, the similarity between all possible pairs that can be created from the three phrases, A1, A2, and B. The overall similarity between pair (A1, A2) should then be higher than the similarity between pairs (A1, B) and (A2, B).

The translation of main finding 5, 'original rhythms are often replaced by metrical equivalents', would require the measurement of rhythmic similarity at the phrase

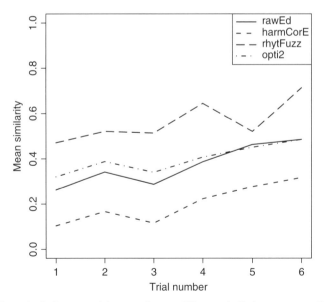

Fig. 9.2 Mean similarity over trials according to different similarity measures; Different line types represent the different similarity measures.

---

[2] Specifically, for main findings 4 and 5 the phrases all recalls need to be identified initially to enable the subsequent phrase-level analyses.

level, between original and recalled phrase, and a metre induction procedure giving both metre and phase information. The test would then be that, for most phrases, the induced metre and phase is identical to the original but rhythmic similarity to the original varies to a greater extent.

The claim from main finding 7, 'harmonic structure is preserved even when exact melodic structure is lost', is similar to main finding 5: Sloboda and Parker observe that while the recall of melodic details shows a greater variation, the more abstract harmonic structure, having fewer degrees of freedom, is less likely to vary and is often close to the original. This might be demonstrated by comparing the variation in harmonic with melodic similarity measurements, within a series of repeated measurement.

Conclusion and outlook

Several central questions motivated Sloboda and Parker's original study, including:

- How do memory representations build up over repeated exposure to the same novel melody?

- What melodic parameters or dimensions are easier to grasp and to encode and which ones or more difficult?

- How do people with and without musical training differ with respect to building up representations of melodies in memory?

In this chapter, we have demonstrated how a computational approach can help in answering these questions, and how the nature of the answers changes when a computer is involved as a tool for analysis and modelling. We have seen answers become necessarily very precise and quantitative; this we consider to be an advantage, especially if experiments are repeated with the same method but on different data or with different stimuli. However, one must take care not to confuse this necessary precision with greater validity—indeed, the converse can easily be the case. Therefore, in order to obtain valid results, the questions that the computer is supposed to answer must also be asked very precisely. This is no bad thing: the necessity to make explicit every tiny step from the formulation of the question (via the choice and implementation of a formal procedure) to the interpretation of the results can often win us additional insight into the phenomena under study. As can be seen from our discussion of melodic similarity algorithms, the use of computational models and algorithms offers the researcher a huge choice of analytic procedures—but, in consequence, that researcher must take responsibility for their decision and argue it. Though unavoidably painful at the beginning, this extra rigour in several aspects of methodology, can ultimately only be good for the field.

While we certainly do not suggest that the edit distance measure is necessarily the best measure of melodic similarity in the context of this experimental data, we chose it deliberately because it is easy to understand, and it is at least loosely connected to semi-formal procedures that musicologists use to determine similarity relations and derivative procedures between melodies. However, it would be interesting to reanalyse this experimental dataset with more complex similarity models that are claimed to have more cognitive validity (e.g. Müllensiefen and Frieler, 2004a; Müllensiefen and Pendzich, 2009). Then, employment of a computational procedure for determining melodic similarity would change status, from merely using an adequate tool, to modelling human behaviour with a cognitive-computational model—an epistemic transition for which we have argued in detail elsewhere (Pearce, Müllensiefen, & Wiggins, 2009; Wiggins, Pearce, & Müllensiefen, 2009).

Apart from answering Sloboda and Parker's questions in a computational way that is of a different quality, the use of computers to analyse and model data resulting from their experimental paradigm also enables us to ask some additional questions. Because these questions entail comparison across different melodic stimuli, we conducted a new experiment with Sloboda and Parker's design but using 14 different melodies and 30 subjects with acceptable singing abilities. As a result, we obtained about 1900 usable sung recalls which have been transcribed by a professional human transcriber. These data are about to be analysed using the computational approach proposed here. The additional questions that we hope to answer from the analysis of this new dataset concern mainly features of melodic structure, and they aim at being generalizable to the memory processing of Western popular melodies in general:

- How do musical features affect the recall of melodies?
- What makes a melody easy or difficult to recall?
- Which parts of a melody are represented first and most accurately?
- Does commonness or rarity of melodic features play a role?
- Are melodies in their song context and as audio excerpts recalled better than single-line melodies or is this vice versa?

To facilitate this type of feature analysis, we have developed an open source software toolbox, called FANTASTIC,[3] which computes summary and sequence-based features of monophonic melodies. FANTASTIC also enables researchers to model melody perception and cognitive processing in the context of a corpus of melodies and, therefore, it can take into account previous listening experience given a suitable corpus of music. The software has already proven useful in the analysis of experimental data from a recognition paradigm similar to the one used by Halpern and Müllensiefen (2008), and preliminary results suggest that objective measures of implicit and explicit memory performance, as well as subjective memory measures including false alarms and misses, can be explained to a certain degree by features of the melodic structure (Halpern, Müllensiefen, & Wiggins, 2008). Once our recognition dataset is fully analysed, we aim to model our recall data with the same feature approach, to see whether recall and recognition memory can be explained by the same structural features. This would supply strong evidence for the hypothesis that the performance of musical memory is indeed dependent on musical structure, and that we can explain and predict cognitive behaviour, at least partially, from the structure of the music itself.

---

[3] Feature ANalysis Technology Accessing STatistics (In a Corpus); download from our project website: http://www.doc.gold.ac.uk/isms/mmm/?page=Software\%20and\%20Documentation.

Acknowledgements

This research was supported by EPSRC project EP/D0388551, *Modelling Musical Memory and the Perception of Melodic Similarity*. It was inspired by the work of John Sloboda.

References

Abdallah, S., Sandler, M., Rhodes, C., & Casey, M. (2006). Using duration models to reduce fragmentation in audio segmentation. *Machine Learning, Special Issue on Machine Learning for Music*, 65(2–3), 485–515.

Aloupis, G., Fevens, T., Langerman, S., Matsui, T., Mesa, A., Rappaport, D., & Toussaint, G. (2003). Computing the similarity of two melodies. In *Proceedings of the 15th Canadian Conference on Computational Geometry*. Halifax, Canada: Dalhousie University.

Anderson, C., & Borkowski, J. G. (1978). *Experimental psychology*. Glenview, IL: Scott, Foresman and Company.

Atkinson, R., & Shiffrin, R. (1968). Human memory: a proposed system and its control processes. In K. Spence, & J. Spence (Eds.), *The psychology of learning and motivation*. New York, NY: Academic Press.

Baddeley, A. (1986). *Working memory*. Oxford: Oxford University Press.

Baddeley, A. (2007). *Working memory, thought and action*. Oxford: Oxford University Press.

Calkins, M. (1894). Association. *Psychological Review*, 1, 476–483.

Cook, N. (2008). Techniques for analysing recordings. In N. Cook, E. F. Clarke, D. Leech-Wilkinson, & J. Rink (Eds.), *The Cambridge companion to recorded music*. Cambridge, UK: Cambridge University Press.

Crawford, T., Iliopoulos, C., & Raman, R. (1998). String-matching techniques for musical similarity and melodic recognition. *Computing in Musicology*, 11, 73–100.

Davies, J., & Yelland, A. (1977). Effects of two training procedures on the production of melodic contour, in short-term memory for tonal sequences. *Psychology of Music*, 5(2), 3–9.

Deutsch, D. (1970). Tones and numbers: Specificity of interference in immediate memory. *Science*, 168, 1604–1605.

Deutsch, D. (1972). Octave generalization and tune recognition. *Perception & Psychophysics*, 11(6), 411–412.

Deutsch, D. (1974). Generality of inference by tonal stimuli in recognition memory for pitch. *Quarterly Journal of Experimental Psychology*, 26, 229–234.

Deutsch, D. (1975a). The organization of short-term memory for a single acoustic attribute. In D. Deutsch, & J. Deutsch (Eds.), *Short term memory*. New York, NY: Academic Press.

Deutsch, D. (1975b). Two-channel listening to musical scales. *Journal of the Acoustical Society of America*, 57, 1156–1160.

Deutsch, D. (1980). The processing of structured and unstructured tonal sequences. *Perception & Psychophysics*, 28(5), 381–389.

Deutsch, D., & Feroe, J. (1975). Disinhibition in pitch memory. *Perception & Psychophysics*, 17, 40–51.

Deutsch, D., & Feroe, J. (1981). The internal representation of pitch sequences in tonal music. *Psychological Review*, 88, 503–522.

DeWitt, L., & Crowder, R. (1986). Recognition of novel melodies after brief delays. *Music Perception*, *3*(3), 259–274.

Dowling, W., Tillmann, B., & Ayers, D. (2002). Memory and the experience of hearing music. *Music Perception*, *19*(2), 136–149.

Dowling, W. J. (1972). Recognition of melodic transformations: Inversion, retrograde, and retrograde inversion. *Perception & Psychophysics*, *12*(5), 417–421.

Dowling, W. J. (1978). Scale and contour: Two components of a theory of memory for melodies. *Psychological Review*, *85*(4), 341–354.

Dowling, W. J., & Bartlett, J. C. (1981). The importance of interval information in long-term memory for melodies. *Psychomusicology*, *1*, 30–49.

Dowling, W. J., & Fujitani, D. S. (1971). Contour, interval, and pitch recognition in memory for melodies. *Journal of the Acoustical Society of America*, *49*(2, Part 2), 524–531.

Downie, J. S. (2003). *Evaluating a simple approach to music information retrieval. Evaluating a simple approach to music information retrieval. Conceiving melodic n-grams as text.* Ph.D. thesis. London (Ontario), Canada: Faculty of Information and Media Studies, University of Western Ontario.

Drake, C., Dowling, W., & Palmer, C. (1991). Accent structures in the reproduction of simple tunes by children and adult pianists. *Music Perception*, *8*(3), 315–334.

Ebbinghaus, H. (1885). *U das Ged¨achnis. Untersuchungen zur experimentellen Psychologie.* Amsterdam: Bonset.

Eck, D. (2002). Finding downbeats with a relaxation oscillator. *Psychological Research*, *66*(1), 18–25.

Edworthy, J. (1983). Towards a contour-pitch continuum theory of memory for melodie. In D. Rogers, & J. Sloboda (Eds.), *The acquisition of symbolic skills* (pp. 263–271). New York, NY: Plenum.

Edworthy, J. (1985). Interval and contour in melody processing. *Music Perception*, *2*(3), 375–388.

Eerola, T., Järvinen, T., Louhivuori, J., & Toiviainen, P. (2002). Statistical features and perceived similarity of folk melodies. *Music Perception*, *18*(3), 275–296.

Frieler, K. (2004). Beat and meter extraction using gaussified onsets. In C. Lomeli Buyoli, & R. Loureiro (Eds.), *Proceedings of the 5th International Conference on Music Information Retrieval* (pp. 178–183). Barcelona: Universitat Pompeu Fabra.

Ginsborg, J., & Sloboda, J. A. (2007). Singers' recall for the words and melody of a new, unaccompanied song. *Psychology of Music*, *35*(3), 421–440.

Green, D., & Swets, J. (1966). *Signal detection theory and psychophysics*. New York, NY: Wiley.

Gusfield, D. (1997). *Algorithms on strings, trees, and sequences: Computer science and computational biology*. Cambridge: Cambridge University Press.

Halpern, A. (1989). Memory for the absolute pitch of familiar songs. *Memory & Cognition*, *17*(5), 572–581.

Halpern, A., & Müllensiefen, D. (2008). Effects of timbre and tempo change on memory for music. *Quarterly Journal of Experimental Psychology*, *61* (9), 1371–1384.

Halpern, A., Müllensiefen, D., & Wiggins, G. (2008). *Modelling memory responses in a memory recognition task.* Talk at the 10th International Conference for Music Perception and Cognition (ICMPC10), Sapporo (Japan).

Huron, D. (1995). *The humdrum toolkit: Reference manual.* Menlo Park, CA: Center for Computer Assisted Research in the Humanities.

Huron, D. (2006). *Sweet anticipation: Music and the psychology of expectation.* Cambridge, MA: MIT Press.

Idson, W., & Massaro, D. (1978). A bidimensional model of pitch in the recognition of melodies. *Perception & Psychophysics, 24*(6), 551–565.

Kantowitz, B. H., Roediger, H. L. I., & Elmes, D. G. (1994). *Experimental psychology: understanding psychological research.* Minneapolis: West.

Keller, T., Cowen, N., & Saults, J. (1995). Can auditory memory for tone pitch be rehearsed? *Journal of Experimental Psychology: Learning, Memory and Cognition, 21*(3), 635–645.

Kluwe, R. (1990). Gedächtnis und Wissen. In H. Spada (Ed.), *Allgemeine psychologie* (pp. 115–187). Stuttgart: Hans Huber.

Krumhansl, C. L. (1990). *Cognitive foundations of musical pitch.* Oxford Psychology Series 17. Oxford: Oxford University Press.

Levitin, D. J. (1994). Absolute memory for musical pitch: Evidence from the production of learned melodies. *Perception & Psychophysics, 56*(4), 414–423.

Long, P. (1977). Relationships between pitch memory in short melodies and selected factors. *Journal of Research in Music Education, 25*(4), 272–282.

Longuet-Higgins, C., & Steedman, M. (1971). On interpreting Bach. *Machine Intelligence, 6,* 221–242.

Mauch, M., Müllensiefen, D., Dixon, S., & Wiggins, G. (2008). What's a work in harmony? In: K. Miyazaki, Y. Hiraga, M. Adachi, Y. Nakajima, and M. Tsuzaki (Eds.), *Proceedings of the 10th International Conference for Music Perception and Cognition* (pp. 683–689), 25–29 August 2008, Sapporo, Japan (CD). Adelaide: Causal Productions.

Meek, C., & Birmingham, W. (2002). Johnny can't sing. a comprehensive error model for sung music queries. In M. Fingerhut (Ed.), *Proceedings of the Third International Conference on Music Information Retrieval* (pp. 124–132). Paris: IRCAM.

Miller, G. (1956). The magical number seven plus or minus two: some limits on our capacity for processing information. *Psychological Review, 63,* 81–97.

Milmeister, G., Mazzola, G. B., & Thalmann, F. (2009). *The Rubato composer musicsoftware.* Berlin: Springer.

Mongeau, M., & Sankoff, D. (1990). Comparison of musical sequences. *Computers and the Humanities, 24,* 161–175.

Mueller, J. (1970). Response properties of the position indicant in serial learning. *Journal of Experimental Psychology, 84,* 35–39.

Müllensiefen, D., & Frieler, K. (2004a). Cognitive adequacy in the measurement of melodic similarity: Algorithmic vs. human judgments. *Computing in Musicology, 13,* 147–176.

Müllensiefen, D., & Frieler, K. (2004b). Optimizing measures of melodic similarity for the exploration of a large folk-song database. In *Proceedings of the 5th International Conference on Music Information Retrieval* (pp. 274–280). Barcelona: Universitat Pompeu Fabra.

Müllensiefen, D., & Pendzich, M. (2009). Court decisions on music plagiarism and the predictive value of similarity algorithms. *Musicæ Scientiæ, Discussion Forum 4B,* 257–295.

Müllensiefen, D., Pfleiderer, M., & Frieler, K. (2009). The perception of accents in pop music melodies. *Journal of New Music Research, 38*(1), 19–44.

Murdock, B. (1962). The serial position effect of free recall. *Journal of Experimental Psychology, 64,* 482–488.

Nairne, J. S. (1990). A feature model of immediate memory. *Memory & Cognition, 18,* 251–269.

North, A. C., & Hargreaves, D. J. (1995). Subjective complexity, familiarity, and liking for popular music. *Psychomusicology, 14*, 77–93.

O Maidin, D. (1998). A geometrical algorithm for melodic difference in melodic similarity. *Computing in Musicology, 11*, 65–72.

Ogawa, Y. T. K., & Mito, H. (1995). Modification of musical schema for Japanese melody: A study of comprehensible and memorable melody. *Bulletin of the Council for Research in Music Education, 127*, 136–141.

Oura, Y., & Hatano, G. (1988). Memory for melodies among subjects differing in age and experience in music. *Psychology of Music, 16*, 91–109.

Pavlov, I. P. (1927). *Conditioned reflexes: An investigation of the physiological activity of the cerebral cortex* (G. V. Anrep, Trans.). London: Oxford University Press.

Pearce, M. T., Müllensiefen, D., & Wiggins, G. (2009). ¨Melodic grouping in music information retrieval: New methods and applications. In R. Zbigniew, & A. Wieczorkowska (Eds.), *Advances in music information retrieval*, Studies in Computational Intelligence. Berlin: Springer.

Pearce, M. T., Müllensiefen, D., & Wiggins, G. A. (2010). Melodic grouping in music information retrieval: new methods and applications. In: R. Zbigniew & A. Wieczorkowska (Eds.), *Advances in music information retrieval. studies in computational intelligence*, vol. 274 (pp. 365–390). Berlin: Springer.

Pearce, M. T., & Wiggins, G. A. (2004). Improved methods for statistical modelling of monophonic music. *Journal of New Music Research, 33*(4), 367–385.

Pearce, M. T., & Wiggins, G. A. (2006). Expectation in melody: The influence of context and learning. *Music Perception, 23*(5), 377–406.

Pechmann, T., & Mohr, G. (1992). Interference in memory for tonal pitch: Implications for a working-memory model. *Memory & Cognition, 20*(3), 314–320.

Pickens, J., Bello, J. P., Monti, G., Sandler, M. B., Crawford, T., Dovey, M., & Byrd, D. (2003). Polyphonic score retrieval using polyphonic audio queries: A harmonic modeling approach. *Journal of New Music Research, 32*(2), 223–236.

Rundus, D. (1974). Output order and rehearsal in multi-trial free recall. *Journal of Verbal Learning and Verbal Behaviour, 13*, 656–663.

Schulkind, M. D. (2000). Perceptual interference decays over short unfilled intervals. *Memory & Cognition, 28*(6), 949–956.

Schulkind, M. D. (2004). Serial processing in melody identification and the organization of musical semantic memory. *Perception & Psychophysics, 66*(8), 1351–1362.

Schulkind, M. D., Posner, R. J., & Rubin, D. C. (2003). Musical features that facilitate melody identification: How do you know it's 'your' song when they finally play it? *Music Perception, 21*(2), 217–249.

Shepard, R. (1967). Recognition memory for words, sentences, and pictures. *Journal of Verbal Learning and Verbal Behaviour, 6*, 156–163.

Shiffrin, R., & Nosofsky, R. (1994). Seven plus or minus two: A commentary on capacity limitations. *Psychological Review, 101*(2), 357–361.

Sloboda, J. A., & Parker, D. H. (1985). Immediate recall of melodies. In P. I. C. Howell, & R. West (Eds.), *Musical structure and cognition* (pp. 143–167). London: Academic Press.

Temperley, D. (2001). *The cognition of basic musical structures*. Cambridge, MA: MIT Press.

Thomassen, J. (1982). Melodic accent: Experiments and a tentative model. *Journal of the Acoustical Society of America, 71*, 1596–1605.

Tulving, E. (1968). When is recall higher than recognition? *Psychonimic Science*, *10*, 53–54.

Tversky, A. (1977). Features of similarity. *Psychological Review*, *84*(4), 327–352.

Typke, R., Wiering, F., & Veltkamp, R. (2007). Transportation distances in human perception of melodic similarity. *Musicæ Scientiæ, Discussion Forum 4A*, 153–181.

Uitdenbogerd, A. L. (2002). *Music information retrieval rechnology*. Ph.D. thesis, RMIT University of Melbourne, Australia.

Unal, E., Chew, E., Georgiou, P., & Narayanan, S. (2008). Challenging uncertainty in query by humming systems: A fingerprinting approachenging. *IEEE Transactions on Audio, Speech, and Language Processing*, *16*(2), 359–371.

Underwood, B., Rundquist, W., & Schulz, R. (1959). Response learning in paired-associate lists as a function of intralist similarity. *Journal of Experimental Psychology*, *58*, 70–78.

Volk, A. (2008). Persistence and change: Local and global components of metre induction using inner metric analysis. *Journal of Mathematics and Computation in Music*, *2*(2), 99–115.

Weyde, T. (2004). Modeling rhythmic motif structure with fuzzy logic and machine learning in music query: Methods, models, and user studies. *Computing in Musicology*, *13*, 35–50.

Wiggins, G., Pearce, M., & Müllensiefen, D. (2009). Computational modelling of music cognition and musical creativity. In R. Dean (Ed.), *The Oxford handbook of computer music and digital sound culture*. Oxford: Oxford University Press.

Wiggins, G. A. (2007). Models of musical similarity. *Musicæ Scientiæ, Discussion Forum 4A*, 315–337.

Williamson, V. J., Baddeley, A. D., & Hitch, G. J. (2006). Music in working memory? examining the effect of pitch proximity an the recall performance of nonmusicians. In M. Baroni, R. C. Addessi, & M. Costa (Eds.), *Proceedings of the 9th International Conference of Music Perception and Cognition (ICMPC9)* (pp. 1581–1589). Bologna: Society of Music Perception and Cognition (SMPC) AND European Society for the Cognitive Sciences of Music (ESCOM).

Young, R. (1962). Tests of three hypotheses of the effective stimulus in serial learning. *Journal of Experimental Psychology*, *63*, 307–313.

Zajonc, R. (1968). Attitudinal effects of mere exposure. *Journal of Personality and Social Psychology Monograph Supplement*, *9*, 1–27.

Zielinska, H., & Miklaszewski, K. (1992). Memorising two melodies of different style. *Psychology of Music*, *20*, 95–111.

Part 5

Musical achievement and expertise

Chapter 10

Musical encounters
of the temporary kind

Frederick A. Seddon

Abstract

As music educators in the current financial climate we are often required to 'justify' our subject within the curriculum. This has resulted in many music educators emphasizing the benefits of learning music in relation to how it can enhance learning in other areas of the curriculum instead of emphasizing the intrinsic benefits of music making. This chapter explores the possibility of encouraging wider engagement with music making by offering opportunities for people to have an 'encounter' with music over brief periods of time. People's perception of music making can often be based on a widely held societal view that it is a 'specialist' activity requiring innate talent, musical literacy, and dedication to regular long-term practice. This view can result in a reluctance by many people to become involved in music making because they consider they either do not have the necessary talent or do not wish to make a long-term commitment to musical practice. A research study that enabled complete beginners to learn to play an improvised 12-bar blues on an electronic keyboard in an e-learning environment, after a total of nine hours engagement with the learning material, is presented in order to exemplify one possibility of providing such a temporary 'encounter'.

This chapter examines the relationship between past and current music educational practices and the societal perception of music as a 'specialist' activity. People's perception of music making is often based on a widely held societal view that it is a 'specialist' activity requiring innate talent, musical literacy, and dedication to regular long-term practice. This view can result in a reluctance by many people to become involved in music making because they consider they either do not have the necessary talent or do not wish to make a long-term commitment to musical practice. This chapter also explores the possibility of encouraging wider engagement with music making by offering opportunities for people to have an 'encounter' with music over brief periods of time. A research study that enabled 'adult beginners' to learn to play an improvised 12-bar blues on an electronic keyboard in an e-learning environment, after a total of nine hours engagement with the learning material, is presented in order to exemplify one possibility of providing such a temporary 'encounter'.

John Sloboda gave a keynote presentation at the Second International Conference for Research in Music Education (RIME), University of Exeter, 3–7 April 2001, which was subsequently published as an article 'Emotion, functionality and the everyday experience of music: where does music education fit?' in the international peer-reviewed journal *Music Education Research* (Sloboda, 2001). In his keynote presentation and the subsequent article, Sloboda raised some very pertinent questions related to the 'meaning of music', which he argued coalesced around a 'dominant ideology' that gained sufficient inter-group consensus among stakeholders in music education (e.g. teachers, students, parents, government, etc.) to generate a 'stable educational agenda'. Sloboda argued that this consensus between stakeholders was disintegrating because recent research had shown that (2001, p. 243):

> (i) many school music educators have little respect for or understanding of the musical lives of those they teach; (ii) that the musical enthusiasms and inspirations of many young people are not addressed by the current curriculum; (iii) that the transition from primary to secondary school is a key 'parting-of-the-ways' between young people and their music teachers; (iv) that music retains a key and central role in the lives of most people who see themselves as 'not musical', and that emotional self-management is at the heart of this role.

Sloboda further argued that classroom music, as it was conceptualized during this period, was not an appropriate vehicle for mass music education in the twenty-first century and that much could be learned from examining out-of-school music provision (Sloboda, 2001). This chapter will argue that Sloboda was correct in his argument then and, in spite of the many changes to music education that have taken place in the intervening years, little has changed that addresses the fundamental philosophical, economic, and ethical arguments surrounding the focus on music performance and literacy skills in the Western classical tradition that still permeate music education. The chapter reviews research reporting on current music education practice and offers one practical example for an alternative approach to music education by reporting research conducted with trainee primary school teachers, engaging with a project specifically designed to affect their concept of music performance and confidence in their individual musical abilities.

Review of the literature

One of the reasons many pupils drop out of engagement with formal music in secondary schools is the miss-match between their musical environment and that of their music teachers (York, 2001). Most music teachers have university degrees based in classical music performance and are trained as classical pianists, organists, or singers (York, 2001). These music specialist teachers are steeped in their own musical environment, listen to Radio 3 and Classic FM, read *BBC Music Magazine*, and know very little about other genres of music. When music teachers do employ music from their pupils' genres, there is a tendency for them to employ this music as a vehicle to entice pupils towards generating interest in other genres of music that teachers feel are more appropriate to study in school (York, 2001). This exemplifies Sloboda's assertion that some music teachers lack respect or understanding of the musical lives of their pupils. Sloboda suggested there was a shift in the 'stable music education agenda', based on an implicit agreement between stakeholders, which took place around the mid twentieth century and was based on major cultural shifts during the 1960s. Prior to this shift, the dominant music education curriculum could be described as promoting the understanding and appreciation of music from the Western classical tradition, which was best achieved by learning to play an instrument, preferably a traditional, acoustic orchestral instrument and focusing on learning to play works from the classical 'canon'. Furthermore, composing music was considered the ultimate result of a musical education, engaged in only by the gifted few who have the talent to produce masterworks. This type of music curriculum meant that music could only be taught by music specialists. Post 1960s, concessions were made and other genres of music were considered to be appropriate 'stopping points' for people as they progressed towards the ultimate goal of classical performance and/or composition. This meant that music education still had to be controlled by people who had received a 'classical' training in music in the Western tradition (Sloboda, 2001).

Sloboda suggested that because of cultural changes such as multiculturalism, youth culture, electronic communication, feminism, secularism, niche cultures, and postmodernism there was no longer a consensus between stakeholders in music education based on the prioritization of educational enterprises around the classical canon. He proposed a greater variety in music provision and drew on what he described as 'the somewhat anarchic mixed economy of out-of-school music provision' (2001, p. 252) to exemplify his proposition. He proposed the following changes: (1) varied providers at national, regional, and local levels; (2) varied funding to include state, voluntary, and commercial funding by legitimate stakeholders; (3) varied locations with programmes being delivered in the community, schools, music centres, shops, homes, and cultural centres; (4) varied roles for educators to reflect the wide range of musical cultures and activities young people engage in; (5) greater flexibility of 'entry and exit' points for engagement with music with long-term syllabi for those requiring them and short-term syllabi for others; (6) varied activities to reflect young people's musical interests; (7) varied accreditation of achievement by broadening the range of qualifications on offer; and (8) varied routes to training competence by broadening the type of training for music educators (Sloboda, 2001).

It is interesting to note Sloboda's perception of music education at the turn of the millennium and to examine the results of more recent research in this field. Since 2001, research has examined the effects of the introduction of more informal music learning into the school environment (Green, 2006; Söderman & Folkestad, 2004; Westerlund, 2006). Other research has examined young people's perspectives of music both inside and outside the school environment (Lamont, Hargreaves, Marshall, & Tarrant, 2003), identities, and attitudes of music specialist secondary school classroom teachers (Hargreaves, Purves, Welch, & Marshall, 2007), music specialist teachers' beliefs on instrumental teaching (Baker, 2005, 2006; Mills, 2003, 2006) and also trainee and practising non-music specialist teachers' confidence in teaching music in the primary school classroom (Hennessy, 2000; Holden & Button, 2006; Rogers, Hallam, Creech, & Preti, 2008; Seddon & Biasutti, 2008). Taken collectively, this prior research undertaken post 2001 gives an overview of developments across music education in relation to the issues raised by Sloboda in 2001.

Söderman and Folkestad (2004) studied music creation within two 'hip-hop' groups in Sweden and reported the importance of the lyrics and cultural knowledge among hip-hoppers in the creation of their music, the potential for global interaction via the internet, and the relationship to life-long learning with the changeable elements of hip-hop. Green (2008) demonstrated the beneficial effects on adolescent motivation during secondary school music lessons when conducted through peer-directed learning techniques similar to those employed by popular musicians. Green's findings confirmed those of Westerlund (2006), who argued informal music learning can develop knowledge-building communities and musical expertise in formal music education. Lamont *et al.* (2003) reported that listening to music formed an important part of pupils' lives and that music making was also more prominent than suggested by prior research. However, they also found that there was a greater commitment to music outside school and that this involvement was transitory for some of their participants. Pertinent to the outcomes of this research are the identities and attitudes of the individuals who become music teachers in the secondary school classroom. Hargreaves *et al.* (2007) describe some positive changes in music education in the new millennium, for example, a narrowing of the division between informal and formal provision, increase in pupil enjoyment of school music, and an improvement in the quality of school music teaching. This finding was supported by a reported increase in the quality of primary and secondary school music teaching by the UK government's Office for Standards in Education (OfSTED) during this period. An interesting question is what had changed to bring about these reported improvements in music education?

Certain campaigns were implemented at the turn of the millennium, for example 'Music for the Millennium' initiated by the *Times Educational Supplement* and supported by prominent figures from the world of classical music, Sir Peter Maxwell Davies and Sir Simon Rattle. This campaign produced a response from the then Labour Government. Funding was made available to increase the availability of instrumental tuition in schools, and lottery funds were made available to support extracurricular music making by under-18s. In 2004, the Labour Government's 'Music Manifesto' was launched, which addressed some of the issues raised by Sloboda in 2001, for example, broadening the scope of music and encouraging greater integration between schools and other stakeholders. The Music Manifesto promoted the idea that music should not be dominated by a small number of experts with highly cultivated skills in the Western classical tradition. The manifesto stated that music should be more widely accessible with less distinction between 'vocational' and 'recreational' music making embracing both in-school and out-of-school activities. Other schemes initiated in the early part of the twenty-first century were designed to broaden the appeal of music education to young people inside and outside schools. These included a £10 million government sponsored national campaign, led by the composer Howard Goodall, to improve the teaching of singing in the primary school classroom and a four-year project, funded by the Paul Hamlyn Foundation, called 'Musical Futures' designed to foster a range of new initiatives in music education.

Nevertheless, even following on from the above campaigns and the reported improvements in music education provision, only 7–9% of school pupils opt to continue to study music at GCSE examination level, only between 10% and 15% of that original 7–9% continue to study music at A level and an even smaller proportion go on to study music in higher education (Saunders, 2008). Those students who do continue studying music in higher education have usually followed a traditional academic route of GCSE and A level qualifications prior to embarking on an undergraduate music degree at a university or a music college, where they are trained in a 'classical' tradition. Very few of these music graduates have had any experience in jazz, popular, or non-Western music (Hargreaves, Purves, Welch, & Marshall, 2007), also few of them primarily aspire to be music teachers in secondary schools and even fewer aspire to teach in primary schools (Mills, 2005). This situation led to researchers proposing that music teacher recruitment requires change in order to reflect the broader range of skills required by music teachers in the twenty-first century (Hargreaves et al., 2007; Westerlund, 2006).

There has also been much discussion about the advantages and disadvantages of employing music specialist teachers to teach music in primary schools (Hennessy, 2000; Holden & Button, 2006; Jeanneret, 1997; Mills, 1989, 1996). Prior research in the UK has established that non-music specialist trainee primary school teachers report low levels of confidence in their ability to teach music in the classroom (Holden & Button, 2006; Hennessy, 2000). Researchers attributed this lack of confidence to non-music specialist trainee primary school teachers' perceptions of musical skills and their acquisition. Many trainee primary school teachers begin their training with a deeply rooted view that teaching music requires 'gifts' grounded in instrumental performance skills and the reading of musical notation (Hennessy, 2000). Furthermore, there is also evidence that secondary school pupils perceive musical skills as fixed (Austin & Vispoel, 1998). This indicates that by the time trainee primary school teachers begin their university courses, they believe their musical abilities cannot be fundamentally changed (Bouffard, Boisvert, & Markovits, 1998). This belief can lead them to have low expectations of their future 'non-gifted' pupils, which initiates 'a cycle of low expectation' in the development of musical skills for the majority of individuals within the education system (Hennessy, 2000). Other researchers argued that it was not the level of musical skill itself but the relationship between that skill and the confidence to teach music that was important (Bresler, 1993; Brown, 1993; Gifford, 1991, 1993; Russell-Bowie, 1993). Also, Glover and Ward (1993) make the important distinction that it is more likely a lack of confidence in their own informally acquired musical skills rather than a lack of formal musical tuition that inhibits the non-music specialist's confidence in teaching music in the primary classroom. Other research has recommended an exploration of the student's own musicality through 'encountering' music to address issues of confidence (Bennett, 1992; D'Ombrain, 1974; Gerber, 1992; Gifford, 1991).

Researchers also investigated the concept of 'musicality' in general as many individuals in society consider themselves to be 'unmusical' (Shuter-Dyson, 1999). Ruddock and Leong (2005) investigated relationships between non-musicians' concepts of 'musical' and their judgements of their own musicality. Ruddock and Leong (2005) asked: (1) what did participants understand by the term 'musical'? (2) What factors contributed to this perception? and (3) How does their perception impact on their involvement with music? They concluded that participants' negative judgements of their own musicality were related to (1) 'thwarted desire to make music at some period in their life' and (2) 'lack of analytical understanding of music and an inability to play an instrument'. Their participants also reported being adversely affected by a particular formal music learning situation in their past.

Based on the evidence of the research reviewed above it is argued that Sloboda's perception of the problems facing music education at the turn of the millennium were basically correct. Also, in spite of the progress made over the past eight years towards addressing these problems by various government and private initiatives, the overall situation remains largely unchanged. It could be argued that music in schools is still regarded by the majority of stakeholders in music education and society at large as a 'specialist' subject only to be engaged in by those with the 'talent' to succeed in learning to perform at an advanced level, standard works from the classical canon. This 'specialist' perception gives rise to the belief that achieving this goal requires dedication to intensive study and practice over a number of years under the tutelage of a recognized expert.

If current music education practices foster the above perception of music as 'specialist' and this perception is widespread in society, it is hardly surprising that the majority of people regard themselves as 'unmusical' if they directly compare themselves to this 'expert' standard. If people are to have any confidence in their potential musical abilities then they need to experience a degree of success in their engagement with music. Given the time available to most individuals who have not made a commitment to music as a potential career, success at this musical engagement must be achieved in a relatively short period of time. Furthermore, it should also be acknowledged that at the end of the brief period of engagement with music, the person may choose another musical activity to engage with or decide that this 'musical encounter of a temporary kind' may be the only one they wish to have. The temporary musical experience should be sufficiently rigorous enough to reward and give satisfaction to the learner, while at the same time dispelling the notion that anyone who can play an instrument is in some way 'magical' or 'gifted'. The learner should be left feeling that playing a musical instrument is something anyone can achieve, all it requires is time and effort on behalf of the learner, while at the same time understanding that playing an instrument to a very high professional level does require dedication and tuition (Sloboda, Davidson, Howe, & Moore, 1996). One such 'musical encounter of a temporary kind' was adopted as the research task in a study investigating musical confidence (Seddon & Biasutti, 2008).

The research study

Seddon and Biasutti (2008) is a pilot exploratory study conducted with three participants who were all non-music specialist trainee primary school teachers. The participants

Table 10.1 Summary of 'blues activities'

Number	'Blues activities' content
1	Memorize and play three two-fingered blues chords, left hand only, over a 12-bar chord sequence in time with metronome beat
2	Play 12-bar chord sequence, left hand only, extended over 48 bars in time with bass and drum backing tracks
3	Memorize and play blues scale of A, right hand only, in time with metronome beat
4	Copy four example riffs, right hand only, in time with bass and drum backing tracks
5	Improvise blues riffs, right hand only, in time with bass and drum backing tracks
6	Play 12-bar chord sequence and improvise, with both hands together, over 48 bars, in time with bass and drum backing tracks

were interviewed prior to and after engaging with six 'blues activities' (see Table 10.1), presented as illustrated text with supporting audio files in an e-learning environment. Participant engagement with the 'blues activities' on keyboard was videotaped. Qualitative analysis of the interview text at time 1 and time 2 and the videotaped learning process was triangulated to support researcher interpretations of changes in participants' perception of their own musicality and confidence in being able to teach music in the primary school classroom. The results were presented as three case studies and revealed an increase in the participants' levels of confidence in their own musicality and ability to teach music in the primary school classroom. During the study, the participants learned to play an improvised 12-bar blues on an electronic keyboard during six 'blues activities'.[1] Blues music was employed for the learning sessions because blues is a genre that underpins much of the popular music people listen to. In addition, blues music has a relatively simple and repetitive construction that facilitates learning to play by ear. It also provided an opportunity for creative music making through improvisation on a blues scale. The keyboard was chosen as the vehicle for music making as it is reasonably familiar to most people and at this initial stage in learning, does not require specific skills such as having to hold an instrument (e.g. guitar or trumpet) or learning how to produce an embouchure (e.g. flute or saxophone).

After the 'blues activities' intervention, all three participants were able to play a 12-bar blues improvisation on the keyboard with both hands together. The qualitative analysis of the interviews revealed the following emergent concepts: at time 1, 'personal musical ability', 'perception of a musician', 'prior music learning experiences'; and at time 2, 'personal musical ability'. Comparison between the concepts 'personal musical ability' at time 1 and time 2 revealed changes in participant attitudes to their own musical ability after the 'blues activities' intervention. Examples of participant statements from Seddon and Biasutti (2008) are restricted to those directly relevant to the argument presented in this chapter (i.e. those related to the participants' perception of changes in their personal musicality). Examples of the emergent concepts at time 1 and time 2 and researcher interpretations of those concepts are reported separately for

[1] © Dr Frederick A. Seddon, 2005.

each of the three case studies. The participants' names have been changed to protect their anonymity.

Case 1

Laura was a 21-year-old student in the third year of a four-year bachelor's degree course, training to be a primary school teacher. Her main subject was Foreign Languages. She has no prior experience of formal instrumental music tuition. The following quotation illustrates the perception of her personal musical ability at time 1 prior to engaging with the 'blues activities':

> I haven't tried to play [music] a lot. I feel rhythm in different situations for example, in dancing I feel the rhythm, and I am able to enter into the rhythm of a song and to repeat it. I like very much repeating what I hear. In order to be able to repeat and re-interpret, I need to make the music mine! First, I must appropriate it and then maybe I become able to repeat.

In spite of declaring earlier in the interview that she had no musical skills, Laura believed she has well-developed aural musical skills. It is evident that she did not regard these aural skills as important possibly because she has not been taught them in a formal situation. The following quotation illustrates her perception of a 'musician':

> A musician is someone who is able to transmit what he would like to say. To 'transmit' is for me the best expression because actually you use another language, you leave the classical [verbal] mode of communication to express through other signs, with other means.

This statement can be interpreted to indicate that Laura's concept of a musician implies a level of performance skill because she focuses on the performer's ability to express and communicate to the audience through their performance. The following quotation gives some insight into her prior music learning experiences:

> There were some fellow pupils who studied music individually outside school and comparing me to them I felt a little bit unprepared … You learned through exercises but you did not really understand what you were doing. There was something missing.

Laura's experience of learning music at school left her with feelings of inadequacy when she compared herself to her formally trained peers. Engaging with 'musical exercises' left her confused and the 'something missing', possibly a more practical music making element, she felt created a barrier to her learning. The following quotation reveals her perception of her personal musicality at time 2, after her engagement with the 'blues activities':

> I think I have more understanding of rhythm, I am aware of the cadence when an instrument starts to play, when another one starts. Also, the spaces at the beginning and at the end, the introduction … I imagined that if I had heard what I have played … I would have told myself 'good result'.

This statement revealed that Laura now had more confidence in her own musical ability. She has been able to apply her informally learned aural skills and extend them in the practical learning environment through music making. She made a very positive self-evaluation of her new musical skills, which can be regarded as performance, improvisation, and an awareness of musical analysis.

Case 2

Lisa was a 22-year-old student in the final year of a four-year bachelor's degree course, training to be a primary school teacher. Her main subject was Science. She took a 'traditional' course of piano lessons for approximately one year, 10 years previously. The following quotation illustrates her perception of her personal musical ability at time 1 prior to engaging with the 'blues activities':

> Well, I like music very much … to sing since I was a child. I have always had a very big passion [for singing] and in fact I am part of a little church choir, which is a very relaxed one and I am fond of it. I like it.

Lisa had a fondness and liking for music making and she recognized that she has some musical skills, which she had mostly acquired in informal learning situations such as her church choir. As these skills were 'learned' in a 'relaxed' situation rather than 'taught' in a more formal situation she probably did not consider them 'professional'. The following quotation illustrates her perception of a 'musician':

> Fundamentally, someone who can play an instrument … You need to have an ear, it is also an innate talent but you can develop it.

Lisa associates being musical with the ability to play an instrument and having a 'musical ear'. She not only believes there is an 'innate talent' involved in becoming a musician but also believes anyone can develop their amateur musical skills. She is perhaps distinguishing here between a trained professional musician and a 'gifted' amateur. The following quotation gives some insight into her prior music learning experience:

> At middle school we played a lot the recorder and the teacher let us play a lot … I did more listening at secondary school.

Lisa's 'traditional' music education involving recorder playing and listening to music and possibly her one year's 'traditional' piano course had formed and reinforced her somewhat restricted view of what a musician is. The following quotations reveals Lisa's perception of her personal musicality at time 2, after her engagement with the 'blues activities':

> Yes … this idea [that anyone can become a musician] remains, in the sense that approaching and trying hard are important. Trying is fundamental.
>
> Yes, I mean that you need to 'put yourself in the game' so, you don't just need to listen to a bit of music
>
> The exercises [in the blues activities] in particular were structured so that you had to follow the rhythm to change the notes and the chords to be able then to coordinate both hands together. To do that you need practice.

Engaging with the blues activities seems to reinforce Lisa's idea that acquiring ability in making music is about trying hard and practice, she no longer talks about music being an 'innate ability'. For her, focusing exclusively on listening to music is not enough, music making is also necessary.

Case 3

John was a 21-year-old student in the final year of a four-year bachelor's degree course, training to be a primary school teacher. His main subject was Art. He had no prior experience of formal instrumental music tuition. John was a member of a theatre company and in this situation has performed as a singer. He learnt his vocal parts by ear through listening and copying. The following quotation illustrates John's perception of his personal musical ability at time 1 prior to engaging with the 'blues activities':

> I don't have any musical experience but I am part of a theatre … Yes, I do the vocal accompaniments in the sense that I adapt myself to the notes, I can reproduce them if someone makes me hear them and I tune with them at the same time … I can play the flute [recorder] but I cannot read the notes.

John began by saying that he did not have musical experience and then went on to describe his musical experience. Probably, he equated musical experience with playing an instrument. He had quite well-developed aural musical abilities but he did not read music, and like many students did not regard the recorder as a 'proper' musical instrument. This statement reveals his belief that musicians play instruments and are able to read music. The following quotation illustrates John's perception of a 'musician':

> musicians are artists. In my company there is a man … he can play any kind of instrument … and you can really see the passion he puts in … I think that a musician is like that even if he is not at a high level, it is sufficient that he can play.

This statement confirms that John relates being a musician to performance on an instrument. It is interesting to note that he regarded musicians as 'artists' and that this artistry is linked to versatility and passion more so than technical expertise. The following quotation gives some insight into his personal music learning experience:

> Oh God, I've had a bad experience. Well, it has happened to me I sang a note out of tune and this was a very negative experience.

Negative music learning experiences in the past have probably contributed to John's lack of confidence in his own musical abilities. The following quotation reveals John's perception of his personal musicality at time 2, after his engagement with the 'blues activities':

> Actually before having this experience I thought I was a little musical and now I think I am … a little more musical … I think I have improved my ear a bit. Listening to the backing tracks I was able to listen well … In addition, improvisation, I liked doing it very much! I did what I wanted on my own! And now in this thing I feel a bit more musical, most of all in being able to adapt what I am playing to the backing track … the course made me feel more aware of what I can do as a musician and in life.

This statement reveals that John felt more musical having had success at learning to play a blues improvisation. John recognizes an improvement in his musical ear and his ability to improvise. The statement also reveals his enjoyment during music making and the feeling of autonomy while learning. The final part of the statement is particularly interesting as John seemed to have gained some overall confidence as a 'musician' and felt this could transfer to other areas in his life.

Some general observations from participant interviews

Results from the analysis of the interview sessions at Time 1 revealed that all three participants had some musical abilities prior to engaging with the 'blues activities'. In spite of this, they all lacked confidence in their personal musical abilities, because their abilities did not match what they believed a 'musician's' abilities should be. This finding supported results of research by Ruddock and Leong (2005) who reported participants' negative judgements of their own musicality in relation to what they considered being 'musical'. In other words, participants lacked confidence in their own informally acquired musical skills. All three participants in the current study related being a musician to playing an instrument, reading music, and having a 'musical ear'. They also gave importance to 'innate talent' and 'starting to learn at an early age' supporting the findings of Hennessy (2000) who reported links between participants' perceptions of musicality and special 'gifts'. However, in spite of this perceived 'talent' requirement, all participants believed anyone could become a musician if they tried hard enough. This apparent contradiction probably reflected diverse notions of what it means to be a 'musician'.

Based on the examples cited above it is proposed that engaging with the 'blues activities' allowed the participants to 'encounter' music. This 'encounter' fostered improvements in participants' aural skills while simultaneously making them aware of and broadening, their informally acquired knowledge of harmony and structure. Statements made in the Time 2 interviews revealed the learning strategies they adopted to be similar to those employed by pop musicians, for example, listening, copying, practising individually, with other musicians and improvising (Green, 2001). For example:

> Well, I listened a lot to the tracks that were already there to take them as a model and most of all in the last lesson. Because you had to play it directly without the support of the tracks, I opened the previous lesson to listen again to it. Then, I also opened my version to listen to the difference. For me, someone even if he is not particularly expert, has the ability to hear where the tracks are different when you arrive a little bit late and to confront … I understood many things in this way. First, I experimented and I made many mistakes … then I listened again many times and I understood where the error was because you really hear it! For example, at the beginning I made mistakes playing the notes of the chord singularly instead of playing them both together! Then listening repeatedly, I got enlightened! *Laura (Time 2)*.

All participants reported enjoying engaging with the 'blues activities' and for them success was achieved in a relatively short period of time (a total of nine hours maximum per participant, undertaken over a period of six weeks). All participants also reported that they enjoyed the autonomy of working without a teacher being present.

It is argued that the musical 'encounter' described above improved the participants' confidence in their own musicality. This 'encounter' is a single example of the kind of confidence building activity that might convince people that playing music is an achievable goal for everyone. On its own, learning to play a 12-bar improvised blues is insignificant, but as part of a radical change in the provision of music education, from primary school through to higher education, it could help to break the 'cycle of low expectation' in the acquisition of musical abilities held by the general population.

Over the past few years, much has been achieved towards introducing and encouraging broader based music education for all, through excellent initiatives such as the 'Musical Futures' scheme and private and government initiatives discussed in the literature review of this chapter. However, initiatives that provide increased access to formal instrumental lessons and singing programmes, headed up by famous musicians from the 'classical' world, can give the impression that they are more focused on reviving the ailing 'classical' system rather than creating a new broader based music education for all. If music education is to provide a comprehensive musical experience for all it will require a new inter-group consensus among stakeholders and a commitment to raising the importance of music in the curriculum accompanied by the funding to implement the new consensus. Change in practice is required across the full range of music education from primary through to higher education to create a system based on inclusion at all levels rather than exclusion based on high levels of performance skills in the 'classical' genre (Hargreaves *et al.*, 2007; Sloboda, 2001; Westerlund, 2006).

Returning to Sloboda (2001), the reasons proposed for the disintegrating consensus between stakeholders in music education and the seven points proposed to provide greater variety in music provision offer a blueprint to assist the overall planning of long overdue radical changes in music education. If music educators are to have respect and understanding for the musical lives of those they teach, recruitment of music teachers should include a wider range of musicians including those without formal performance qualifications but who have demonstrable musical skills in a wider range of musical genres (e.g. rock, pop, blues, folk, hip-hop, rap). With such musicians directly involved in music education it is much more likely that the musical enthusiasms and aspirations of all young people will be addressed. There should be no 'parting of ways' between young people and their music teachers in the transition from primary to secondary school. This means there should be no enforced 'specialization' based on performance excellence, literacy in traditional notation and specific musical genre at any stage in the secondary school. No pupil should leave secondary education considering themselves 'not musical'; they should be offered opportunities to engage with musical activities at which they can achieve feelings of success. Providing this inclusive music education would have many practical difficulties in the current system. Changes in provision, based on the seven points of variety proposed in Sloboda (2001), could assist in delivering modular courses designed to build confidence in personal musicality based on the concept of 'musical encounters of a temporary kind'.

Providers at a national, regional, and local level can be involved in offering modular courses that respond to the learner's needs and availability of teacher skill at all three levels. Regional and local levels should be flexible enough to respond to particular

OBSERVATIONS FROM PARTICIPANT INTERVIEWS | 201

regional and local interests. For example, in a local area there may be a particular interest in a specific genre or style not reflected regionally or nationally. It is quite likely that the local interest is rooted in the local musicians' activities. These local musicians could be recruited to engage with pupils in a peer-learning situation under the supervision of a professional 'facilitator'. There would of course be financial implications in such a system but funding for this kind of system could come through a combination of state, voluntary, and commercial funding. The music business is currently going through fundamental changes in the way it markets its products and this situation provides the opportunity for legitimate stakeholders to seek alternative ways of funding this kind of music education. As Sloboda suggested, music education can take place in a variety of situations, for example, schools, music centres, shops, homes, and cultural centres. Probably the most flexible location currently available is the e-learning environment, as exemplified in the 'blues activities' in the research presented in this chapter. Also, the internet can provide a huge range of possibilities in music learning. For example, a search for music lessons on YouTube reveals some excellent content for engaging with music in many different ways, in a wide variety of styles and genres, in a variety of presentation formats. The main problem with this material is that most of the content is provided by musicians, not educators, and lacks the sequential structure and support systems learners need to achieve success at learning. Future music teachers could be educated as facilitators experienced in compiling this content into meaningful courses that can be accessed in virtual learning environments by learners at all stages. A music teacher should be someone with a broad range of musical experience who is educated to facilitate others to create a lively virtual or face-to-face learning environment. It is impossible for one individual to have the all the necessary experience in all forms of musical activities and technologies that reflect young peoples' varied and volatile musical interests, but it is possible to educate individuals to identify others with the required skills and to recruit, facilitate, and support learning activities. Good teachers will only result from good teacher education that focuses on educational skills and not specific performance skills. It is long past the time we moved away from the notion 'those who can do, those who can't teach' towards one of 'those who can do but can't necessarily assume they can teach'. Flexibility and variety are the keywords and should be applied not only to the kind of music education offered but also to 'entry and exit' points of access to music education and syllabus lengths that follow principles of life-long learning. For example, adults who have engaged in professional musical activities that resonate with young people's musical interests could be recruited to be involved with music education courses that provide the content for developing this style or genre of music. Obviously, a broad range of accreditation would be required to validate the multiplicity of activities learners would be able to engage with. For practical and motivational reasons, this accreditation would probably need to rely heavily on peer- and self-evaluation. It would still be possible to employ accreditation in the selection of trainee music teachers entering higher education but this accreditation should be employed flexibly to ensure recruitment of people with existing, emerging, or developing non-mainstream skills.

If the proposed changes to music education are to be implemented, it is of paramount importance that the existing 'specialist' system is securely maintained and developed. Opportunities for individuals who want to follow the established pathway to performance excellence in traditional institutions must be sustained. However, this raises financial and ethical issues for society in general. For example, should public funding be allocated to provide broadly based music education for everyone in society, while at the same time educating future music teachers who have come through the proposed revised system and seek to return to that system to sustain and develop music education for all? Or, should public funding sustain a music education system that promotes the training of musical performers, capable of performing specific musical genres to a world-class standard, even when a very small percentage of those trained in this way are subsequently able to sustain themselves in performance careers and find it necessary to turn to teaching music, which they do not aspire to nor have they been adequately educated to do? This is the current ethical, political, and financial dilemma of music education.

References

Austin, J. R., & Vispoel, W. P. (1998). How American adolescents interpret success and failure in classroom music: Relationships among attributional beliefs, self-concept and achievement. *Psychology of Music, 26*(1), 26–46.

Baker, D. (2005). Peripatetic music teachers approaching mid-career: a cause for concern? *British Journal of Music Education, 22*(2), 141–153.

Baker, D. (2006). Life histories of music service teachers: The past in inductees' present'. *British Journal of Music Education, 23*(1), 39–50.

Bennett, P. D. (1992). Rethinking expectations. *Journal of Music Teacher Education, 1*(2), 22–27.

Bouffard, T., Boisvert, M., & Markovits, H. (1998). Self-perception and cognitive development. *British Journal of Educational Psychology, 68*(3), 321–331.

Bresler, L. (1993). Music in a double-bind: Instruction by non-specialists in elementary schools. *Bulletin of the Council for Research in Music Education, 115*, 1–13.

Brown, E. A. (1993). Elementary music education curricula in the public schools of Canada. *Dissertation Abstracts International, 54*(5), 1716A.

DfES. (2004). *The music manifesto*. Available at: www.musicmanifesto.co.uk/ (accessed 30 August 2010).

D'Ombrain, G. (1974). Music in Australian education institutions: teacher training. *Australian Journal of Music Education, 15*, 23–25.

Gerber, L. (1992). The second door. *Journal of Music Teacher Education, 1*(2), 22–27.

Gifford, E. (1991). *An investigation into factors affecting the quality of music education in pre-service teacher training*. Doctoral dissertation, University of London, London.

Gifford, E. (1993). The musical training of primary teachers: old problems, new insights and possible solutions. *British Journal of Music Education, 10*(1), 33–46.

Glover, J., & Ward, S. (1993). *Teaching music in the primary school*. London: Cassell.

Green, L. (2001). *How popular musicians learn: A way ahead for music education*. Aldershot: Ashgate.

Green, L. (2006). Popular music education in and for itself, and for 'other' music: Current research in the classroom. *International Journal of Music Education, 24*(2), 101–118.

Green, L. (2008). *Music, informal learning and the school: a new classroom pedagogy*. Aldershot: Ashgate.

Hargreaves, D. J., Purves, R. M., Welch, G. F., & Marshall, N. A. (2007). Developing identities and attitudes in musicians and classroom music teachers. *British Journal of Educational Psychology*, *77*, 665–682.

Hennessy, S. (2000). Overcoming the red-feeling: The development of confidence to teach music in primary school amongst student teachers. *British Journal of Music Education*, *17*(2), 183–196.

Holden, H., & Button, S. (2006). The teaching of music in the primary school by the non-music specialist. *British Journal of Music Education*, *23*(1), 23–38.

Jeanneret, N. (1997). Model for developing pre-service primary teachers' confidence to teach music. *Bulletin of the Council for Research in Music Education*, *133*, 37–44.

Lamont, A., Hargreaves, D. J., Marshall, N. A., & Tarrant, M. (2003). Young people's music in and out of school. *British Journal of Music Education*, *20*(3), 229–241.

Mills, J. (1989). The generalist primary teacher of music: A problem of confidence. *British Journal of Music Education*, 6(2), 125–138.

Mills, J. (1996). Primary student teachers as musicians. *Bulletin of the Council for Research in Music Education*, *127*, 122–126.

Mills, J. (2003). Teachers' beliefs about effective instrumental teaching in schools and higher education. *British Journal of Music Education*, *20*(1), 5–27.

Mills, J. (2005) *Music in the school*. Oxford: Oxford University Press.

Mills, J. (2006). Performing and teaching: the beliefs and experience of music students as instrumental teachers. *Psychology of Music*, *34*(3), 372–390.

Rogers, L., Hallam, S., Creech, A., & Preti, C. (2008). Learning about what constitutes effective training from a pilot programme to improve music education in primary schools. *Music Education Research*, *10*(4), 485–497.

Ruddock, E., & Leong, S. (2005). I am unmusical! The verdict of self-judgement. *International Journal of Music Education*, *23*(9), 9–22.

Russell-Bowie, D. (1993). Where is music education in our primary schools? *Research Studies in Music Education*, *1*, 52–58.

Saunders, J. (2008). *Pupils and their engagement in secondary school music*. Unpublished PhD thesis. London: Institute of Education, University of London.

Seddon, F. A., & Biasutti, M. (2008). Non-music specialist trainee primary school teachers' confidence in teaching music in the classroom. *Music Education Research*, *10*(3), 403–421.

Shuter-Dyson, R. (1999). Musical ability. In D. Deutsch (Ed.), *The psychology of music* (2nd ed.) (pp. 627–651). San Diego, CA: Academic Press.

Sloboda, J. A. (2001). Emotion, functionality and the everyday experience of music: where does music education fit? *Music Education Research*, *3*(2), 243–253.

Sloboda, J. A., Davidson, J. W., Howe, M. J. A., & Moore, D. G. (1996). The role of practice in the development of performing musicians. *British Journal of Psychology*, *87*, 287–309.

Söderman, J., & Folkestad, G. (2004). How hip-hop musicians learn: strategies in informal creative music making. *Music Education Research*, *6*(3), 313–326.

Westerlund, H. (2006). Garage rock bands: a future model for developing musical expertise? *International Journal of Music Education*, *24*(2), 119–125.

York, N. (2001). *Valuing school music: A report on school music*. London: University of Westminster and Rockschool Ltd.

Chapter 11

Routes to adolescent musical expertise

Antonia Ivaldi

Abstract

Research on the development of musical talent has documented quite substantially the role of the teacher, family, and practice. The two key studies conducted by Sloboda and Howe (Howe & Sloboda, 1991a, 1991b, 1991c; Sloboda & Howe, 1991, 1992) and Davidson, Howe, Moore, and Sloboda (Davidson, Howe, Moore, & Sloboda, 1996; Davidson, Moore, Sloboda, & Howe, 1998; Howe, Davidson, Moore, & Sloboda, 1995; Sloboda, Davidson, Howe, & Moore, 1996) have made significant contributions to the field by looking closely at these three factors. Earlier and later research has also placed similar emphasis on the role of the teacher, family and practice (see, for instance, Moore, Burland, & Davidson, 2003; Sosniak, 1985). While this research has included the talented musician's involvement in activities outside the instrumental lesson, and key influential events, it has not been conducted and reported in the same level of detail. Nor has it identified and explored young, talented musicians' own views as to what they have considered to be important in their own musical development, alongside their own musical beliefs and values associated with each route. The pilot study reported in this chapter aims to build on the seminal work by Sloboda *et al.* by focusing on the musical activities and key influences beyond that of the music lesson, practice, teacher, and family, with the aim of documenting the additional routes undertaken by adolescents, and by exploring further the role that these play in the development of adolescent musical excellence.

This chapter revisits the original studies on young musicians' expertise published by Sloboda and colleagues in the 1990s. Their work made a substantial contribution to our understanding of the roles of the family, teacher, and practice in the development of the young musician. Here, I report the findings of a study that aimed to build on this seminal work in three ways. First, I collected data from two contrasting music educational settings—the junior conservatoire and county music service—to complement the original data that came predominantly from a specialist music school; second, I return to Howe and Sloboda's (1991a) notion of 'routes' towards musical excellence by providing more detailed evidence of the musical activities in which accomplished young musicians are engaged; and third, I draw on aspects of another large-scale project conducted at Keele University—the Young People and Music Participation Project (O'Neill, Ryan, Boulton, & Sloboda, 2000; Sloboda, 2005) in order to explore young musicians' ability self-perceptions and values for musical activities, and the factors they perceive to be the most important in their musical development. By placing emphasis on what young musicians find important, it is hoped that we can gain a deeper understanding of what motivates them to become better musicians.

Throughout the chapter I have used the term 'musical expertise' rather than 'talent'. The literature on 'talent' suggests innate potential or giftedness, which is not the focus of this chapter. 'Expertise', in contrast, emphasizes the importance of engagement and practice for optimal musical development. (For a full discussion of these terms see Howe, Davidson, & Sloboda, 1998.)

Biographical precursors of musical excellence

One of the earliest studies on musical excellence documented three periods of musical development. Sosniak (1985) interviewed 21 American concert pianists under the age of 40, who were asked to provide retrospective accounts of their musical development. Information was given regarding music lessons, the practice they undertook, involvement in recitals, competitions and performances, and the role of the family and specialized teacher across early, middle, and advanced years as a musician. In the early years, Sosniak found that music played a significant part in the pianists upbringing, whereby the pianists were expected, by their family, to learn to play the piano; practice and lessons were the priority over all other activities and school work. By the middle years the pianists had made a full commitment to being a musician; they had specialist teachers, their general education became less significant, and families made significant commitments when it came to time, money, and lifestyle. As the pianists reached the advanced years, they had received tuition from expert musicians, taken part in different types of national and international competitions, and become responsible for their own professional development. Sosniak posited that categorizing musical development using these time periods was more meaningful than using categories defined by age, as this was a more accurate reflection of the experience gained.

In a similar study, Manturzewska (1990) interviewed 165 professional musicians between the ages of 21 and 89 about their early musical experiences, musical training, career development, leisure activities, self-beliefs and values for music, and socioeconomic status. Manturzewska found that the most important factors for enhancing musical development were the familiar environment and intrinsic motivation for music. Six stages of development were also proposed from guided music development, acquiring a technical performing ability, developing an artistic identity, attending a specialized music college to entering the music profession—where individuals become established teachers and performers.

In the 1990s, two key studies were conducted by Sloboda and Howe, and Sloboda and colleagues that examined the precursors of musical excellence with young people aged 8–18. This research concentrated on the roles of the family, teacher, and practice. In the first of the two studies, Sloboda and Howe (1991, 1992) and Howe and Sloboda (1991a, 1991b) aimed to improve on previous biographical research (e.g. Manturzewska, 1990; Sosniak, 1985) by interviewing exceptionally able children whose reports would thus be of much more recent experiences. Forty-two pupils aged between 10 and 18, balanced for age, sex, first-study instrument, and ability, were recruited from Chetham's School of Music, a specialist music school in the north-west of England. Staff at the school categorized the children as having outstanding or exceptional ability, and average or unexceptional ability. In the course of individual interviews each student was asked to talk about their early experiences of learning music, and to identify key events and experiences that they considered to be influential. The parents of the children were also interviewed in order to confirm the accuracy of the children's accounts, and to provide any other missing information.

Sloboda and Howe (1991, 1992), and Howe and Sloboda (1991a, 1991b) found that most pupils did not show any specific early signs of musical potential. The more highly accomplished pupils came from less musically active families, having had fewer lessons before they came to the school. Parents were actively engaged in the child's musical development, either through supervision or encouragement, and siblings who played instruments were influential, particularly older siblings who tended to act as role models. These pupils did not do more practice than others, but their practice time was more evenly shared between a number of instruments. All the pupils were involved in musical activities besides their instrumental lessons (although it should be noted that these extra musical activities are part of the school's curriculum). They recognized the influence and limitations of particular teachers, highlighting the personal characteristics of their first teacher, which had determined their development. They reported enjoyment in listening to music and performing music. Finally, it was apparent that their own musical experiences were influenced by beliefs about musical talent in that they were more confident in their own ability. On the basis of these findings, Howe and Sloboda (1991a) concluded that musical achievement depends on more than one factor alone: the family, teacher, and practice all play important roles.

The second key study, conducted by Sloboda *et al.* (published in a series of papers, see Davidson *et al.*, 1996, 1998; Howe *et al.*, 1995; Sloboda & Davidson, 1996; Sloboda *et al.*, 1996), built on the Chetham's project by extending the sample to 257 children aged 8–18. The sample consisted of a target group—pupils from Chetham's School of Music—and four comparison groups: those who had applied to Chetham's but were not awarded a place; those whose parents made enquiries about their child attending Chetham's but who did not follow it up; those learning instruments at a non-specialist state school; and those attending a non-specialist state school and who had given up playing a musical instrument. Examination grades were also used to confirm the categorization of pupils into each group. As in the Chetham's project, all participants were interviewed, and some kept a diary of their musical activity for 42 weeks. In summary, it was found that the only reliable indicator of future musical ability was the age at which the child first sang: 40% of those in the target group had started to sing in the first 2 years of life compared to only 25% of those in the comparison groups. Furthermore, the highest-achieving pupils (those in the target group, and to a lesser degree, those in the first comparison group) had parents who were actively involved in their music making during the earliest stages of learning. Those children who gave up tended to have parents showing the least interest in music. The highest-achieving pupils rated their first teacher's personal characteristics, such as friendliness, higher than the comparison groups. This group also tended to have studied with more teachers, receiving more individual instruction. Finally, there was a strong relationship between formal practice and achievement: high achievers were more regular in their practice habits and spent more time practising each week.

Social-environmental factors of musical expertise

Subsequent research that has built on the findings of these two key studies has explored the role of social-environmental factors during the child's musical development. Moore *et al.* (2003) argue that factors such as the family, teachers, and practice alone are not enough to identify those who are most likely to become successful musicians. In order to explore this further, they contacted 20 participants from the original studies by Sloboda and colleagues (see Burland & Davidson, 2002) eight years after the study. The results indicated that those who were pursuing professional careers as musicians had participated in more performances, improvised more during their practice sessions, and had mothers present at home during their early years, in comparison with those who were pursuing alternative careers but were still involved in music as a hobby.

Motivation for playing an instrument

In addition to key factors such as the family, teacher, and practice, Howe and Sloboda (1991a, 1991b) found that the child's musical experiences, including the extent to which they enjoyed performing, were influenced by their own beliefs regarding musical ability and whether or not they perceived themselves to have musical talent. There is now a growing body of research on achievement motivation and music, the findings of which suggest that it is not enough to just look at the role of practice or additional music making activities in musical development; rather, we should be looking at these factors in relation to motivational variables, such as ability beliefs and values for music.

Ability beliefs and values, which have been shown to underlie the motivation to achieve, predict individual differences in achievement (Eccles, O'Neill, & Wigfield, 2005). Ability beliefs can be conceptualized as self-perceptions surrounding self-concept of ability and expectancies for success; in other words, how good an individual feels he or she is at a particular activity. In contrast, subjective task values are associated with perceived attainment value (the level of importance an individual places on doing well at a given activity), intrinsic motivation (how much an individual enjoys the activity), and extrinsic utility value (an individual's perception as to how useful the activity is going to be in relation to their future goals) (Eccles & Wigfield, 1995; Eccles-Parsons, Adler, Futterman, *et al.*, 1983; Wigfield, Eccles, Yoon, *et al.*, 1997). Eccles and colleagues developed scales to measure these two indicators of achievement; for a detailed discussion of their reliability and validity see Eccles *et al.* (2005). These scales were used to explore the roles of ability self-perceptions and values in the context of playing a musical instrument. In the Young People and Music Participation Project, a longitudinal study of 1500 children in the UK, O'Neill *et al.* (2000) and Sloboda (2005) found that those who played instruments had higher ability self-perceptions and values than those who did not, and that overall, the children had higher values than ability self-perceptions for instrumental music. Similar results were obtained from a study of adolescents (see Ivaldi & O'Neill, 2010): those who played an instrument had higher ability self-perceptions and values for music than those who did not. These findings have important implications for engagement, suggesting that young people are more likely to engage in musical activities when they believe in their ability and value the activity (O'Neill, 1999).

The scales developed by Eccles *et al.* (2005) have been shown to be reliable and valid measures of ability self-perceptions and values in a range of different domains. For the purposes of this chapter I have used them to extend research on playing a musical instrument by investigating their roles in a variety of musical activities undertaken by accomplished young musicians.

The current study

In this section, I adopt Howe and Sloboda's (1991a) notion of routes to adolescent musical expertise to provide a context for the present study conducted with young people in two musical educational settings. Sloboda and colleagues had recruited accomplished young musicians from one specialist music school (full-time, day or boarding) only. In contrast, I explore the experiences of young people at a junior conservatoire and two county youth ensembles in order to demonstrate musical engagement in two alternative settings.

Howe and Sloboda (1991a) concluded that there is more than one route to musical excellence, and while each is unique to the individual, the family, teacher, and practice all have important roles. The term 'routes' is used in this chapter to highlight factors other than the family, teacher, and practice such as the variety of music making activities and key influences that may contribute to the overall development of music competence. They also include motivational constructs such as ability self-perceptions and values for music and adolescent musicians' views as to what they consider to have been important in their own musical development.

In summary, I will address the following: (1) What musical activities are adolescent musicians taking part in, or have been involved in? (2) What are their ability self-perceptions and values for these activities? (3) What factors do adolescent musicians perceive to be important in their musical development?

Alternative music educational setting

The literature on motivation focusing on ability self-perceptions and values has demonstrated clear differences between musicians and non-musicians (e.g. Ivaldi & O'Neill, 2010; O'Neill *et al.*, 2000; Sloboda, 2005). However, the question has not been addressed as to whether similar differences exist between adolescent musicians of different ability levels in different musical contexts. I compared two such groups. A total of 107 adolescents were recruited: 59 from a junior conservatoire ('junior conservatoire pupils') and 48 from two local music services ('county-level pupils') in the northwest of England. The two music services were recruited as they were in the same geographical areas as the junior conservatoire. All pupils came from the same county as the pupils in the original Sloboda studies.

The two groups were selected for comparison because they were similar in many respects, but also demonstrated important differences. First, both groups contained pupils who were committed to music (beyond, for example, studying music only as part of the National Curriculum), but the junior conservatoire pupils had been required to demonstrate a higher level of musicianship than the county-level pupils both when they auditioned, and to retain their places, at the conservatoire each year. Second, while both groups were involved in similar music making activities, the junior conservatoire pupils received more tuition on their instruments, and also attended compulsory lessons in theory, harmony, aural training, and composition. These differences might well have implications for the ability self-perceptions and values of the pupils and the factors they perceived to have contributed to their musical development.

Pupils recruited from the two music services were combined to create the county-level group because they were similar in ability and were involved in similar activities. Pupils recruited from the first music service were selected from the county youth ensembles that were organized by the music service. Membership for each ensemble was by audition, and for advanced players only (grade 7 of the Associated Board of the Royal Schools of Music, and above). While the standard entry requirement was (arguably) considered lower compared with the junior conservatoire, music services recruit young people who nevertheless have the potential to be accepted by a specialist music school or a junior conservatoire.

The county-level pupils met every other week for a day and were either involved in the jazz orchestra, symphony orchestra, concert band, or brass band. Ensemble membership also included participation in courses, concerts, and overseas tours. Besides these activities, individual and group instrumental lessons were available at an additional cost. Pupils recruited from the second music service came from one music centre which offered a wide range of musical ensembles including flute and clarinet choirs, percussion, concert band, jazz orchestra, guitar, choir, string, and orchestral, all at different levels. Entrance to the senior ensembles (advanced level—grades 5–8) was by audition. Pupils met for weekly rehearsals in the evenings, and many were involved in more than one ensemble. Ensemble membership included giving concerts and going on tour. Individual and group instrumental tuition was offered at the pupils' schools, during the school day, by peripatetic teachers employed by the music service.

Entry to the junior conservatoire, which advertises itself as providing specialist training for young people aged 8–18 with exceptional ability, was by audition. The standard entry requirements to the junior department could be considered to be equivalent to those of the specialist music school used in the Sloboda studies. Each Saturday during term-time pupils received one-to-one instrumental tuition in their first and second study instruments, attended classes in aural training, theory, harmony, and composition, received ensemble coaching, and played in a variety of ensembles (including orchestral, vocal, percussion, and jazz). Many junior conservatoire pupils also played in county-level and national ensembles such as their local youth orchestras, the National Children's Orchestra, and the National Youth Orchestra.

In summary, the basis for the comparison between the two groups was that the pupils at county level and at the junior conservatoire shared similar levels of interest in and commitment to music, and were involved in a number of similar activities. They had different levels of musical expertise, however, and received different kinds of teaching, both in nature and quantity. In order to obtain information from respondents with a wide range of musical experience pupils were recruited from both educational settings in two age groups: 13–15 and 17–19 years. Information regarding their experience was acquired by asking respondents if they had achieved grade 8 standard (according to music examination boards such as the Associated Board of the Royal Schools of Music) or equivalent on at least one instrument. Data regarding age and experience are presented in Table 11.1.

Pupils in both age groups, in both settings, reported playing or having played up to seven different instruments (including voice), although they did not necessarily receive formal lessons on these instruments. While 47 junior conservatoire pupils played three instruments (80%), only 29 county-level pupils did so (60%); 31 junior conservatoire pupils played four or five instruments (53%) in comparison with 22 county-level pupils (46%); and four junior conservatoire pupils (7%) and five county-level pupils (10%) played six or seven instruments. These figures did not include instruments that pupils had learned to play as a whole class at school.

For junior conservatoire pupils the modal age for starting the first instrument was 6 years, while for county-level pupils the modal age for starting the first instrument was 7 years. For 40 of the 107 respondents (38%), their main instrument was the same as the first instrument they started on. There were only four respondents who reported singing as their main instrument. However, it should be noted that for 20 respondents (19%) it was unclear what their main instrument was.

Measuring activities and motivation

All respondents completed a questionnaire in five sections: (1) information regarding the first instrument they had started learning and the one(s) they now considered their main instrument(s), including voice, (2) the different musical activities they were involved in, (3) their ability self-perceptions and values relating to these activities (adapted from Eccles et al., 2005; O'Neill et al., 2000), (4) other influences, such as role models (from Ivaldi & O'Neill, 2008), and (5) the factors they perceived to have been the most important in their musical development so far, and their aspirations for

Table 11.1 Age and experience of respondents, broken down by group

Age	Junior conservatoire			Age	County level		
	Males	Females	Achieved grade 8 or equivalent on at least one instrument		Males	Females	Achieved grade 8 or equivalent on at least one instrument
13–15	14	18	10 (17%)	13–15	14	16	1 (2%)
17–19	16	11	31 (53%)	17–19	7	11	15 (31%)
Total	30	29	41 (70%)	Total	21	27	16 (33%)

the future. For example, in section 2 activities included composing, improvising, musicianship, playing with others etc. In section 3, in order to measure ability self-perceptions, respondents were asked how good they thought they were at playing an instrument, how good they would be at playing a new instrument, how good they thought they were compared with other teenagers, how good they were at playing an instrument compared to other activities they did, how good they thought they were compared to others in their music class, and how good they would be in a job playing an instrument. In order to measure values, respondents rated items on usefulness (e.g. how useful is being able to play an instrument, how useful is being able to play an instrument when you are older), importance (e.g. how important is it to be good at playing an instrument, how important is playing an instrument compared with other activities you do, how important is it to put a lot of effort into playing an instrument, how important is it to be given the chance to play an instrument), and interest (e.g. how much do you like playing an instrument, how much fun is playing an instrument, how interesting is playing an instrument). These questions were then applied to each of the different activities. In section 5 the factors were made up the activities the pupils had talked about in the questionnaire. Demographic information including age, sex, and ethnicity was also obtained. The questionnaire took around 45 minutes to complete with the majority being completed when respondents attended the junior conservatoire or an ensemble rehearsal at their music centre. The research was conducted in accordance with the British Psychological Society's ethical code; consent was obtained prior to the completion of the questionnaire, including parental consent for the 13–15-year age group.

What musical activities are adolescent musicians taking part in, or have been involved in?

Each respondent was asked to list all the musical activities they were or had been engaged in for six months or more, excluding school music lessons such as preparation for GCSE or A level, for each of the following categories: musicianship, composition, improvisation, small chamber ensemble, orchestras, solo performance, summer schools, competitions, other musical activities, and concert attendance. For each category they were asked to select the activity (if they took part in more than one) that they considered the most important for their own musical development. Associations were found between group (junior conservatoire and county level) and each of the activities described below, with more junior conservatoire than county-level pupils taking part in each activity (see Table 11.2 for percentages of respondents in each group and the total percentage of the sample who (had) engaged in each activity).

Musicianship. Both groups reported taking theory and aural training classes but the junior conservatoire pupils also learned Dalcroze. Of this group 22.7% nominated either theory or aural training as most important for their musical development; 36.4% of the county-level pupils nominated theory as the most important.

Chamber groups. All respondents reported being involved in duets, quartets, and quintets, but the junior conservatoire pupils were also involved in trios. Of this group 25.5% nominated playing in quartets to be the most important chamber group activity in their musical development; 7.8% of county-level pupils nominated playing in a clarinet choir as the most important. (It should be noted that clarinet choirs differ from most chamber groups in that they are usually directed by a conductor.)

Composition lessons. Both groups had individual and group composition lessons at school; junior conservatoire pupils also had group and individual lessons at the conservatoire. Of this group 67.3% of pupils nominated taking part in group composition lessons at the conservatoire to be the most important for their musical development; 8.2% of the county-level pupils nominated group composition lessons at school to be the most important.

Table 11.2 Percentages of junior conservatoire and county-level pupils engaging (engaged) in musical activities for six months or more*

Activity	Junior conservatoire (%)	County level (%)	Total percentage of sample
Orchestras (non-sig.)	50.0	44.2	94.2
Concerts/musical events	54.3	39.0	93.3
Solo performance	55.1	29.2	84.3
Musicianship lessons	46.2	26.0	72.2
Chamber groups	49.0	20.2	69.2
Competitions	45.2	23.1	68.3
Other ensembles	41.0	22.0	63.0
Composition lessons	46.2	8.5	54.7
Summer schools	39.8	14.6	54.4
Improvisation lessons (non-sig.)	3.8	3.8	7.6

*Note, while both groups had engaged in each activity, percentages are calculated from the total number of activities pupils were involved in from each group, within each category.

Solo performance. All respondents had performed at least one piece solo in a concert, at school, locally or as part of a county-level event. Some had played concertos at school or locally. Some of the junior conservatoire pupils had given solo performances at the conservatoire, and had also played concertos at the conservatoire and with county and national youth orchestras. Of this group 13.6% considered solo performance at school and at the conservatoire to be the most important factor in their musical development. Of the county-level pupils, 15.2% considered taking part in solo performance at school to be the most important factor.

Competitions. Respondents in both groups had taken part in competitions open to their school year and their whole school, at a music centre, and at local, national and international levels, and 49% of junior conservatoire and 11.3% of county-level pupils nominated taking part in competitions at county level to be the most important factor in their musical development.

Summer schools. Both groups had attended summer schools. Respondents' attendance at specific types of summer school are not reported here because they were too varied to code into meaningful categories.

Other ensembles not relating to main instrument. Both groups were involved in choirs, duets, trios, quartets, chamber ensembles, orchestras and musical theatre, and 31.3% of junior conservatoire pupils nominated singing in a choir to be the most important factor in their musical development, while 12.5% of county-level pupils nominated playing in an orchestra as the most important factor.

Concerts/musical events. Both groups had attended orchestral and chamber concerts, opera, ballet, pop and rock concerts, jazz and folk concerts, and musicals. Junior conservatoire pupils had also attended solo recitals; 31.3% of junior conservatoire and 17.9% of county-level pupils considered attending orchestral concerts to be the most important type of concert/musical event in their musical development.

No association was found between the two groups and their engagement in orchestras and improvisation. Respondents in both groups played in orchestras at school, local and county level, but junior conservatoire pupils also played in national youth orchestras. Few pupils in either group reported taking improvisation lessons. Overall, the musical activity in which the most junior conservatoire pupils engaged (55.1%) was giving solo performances, while that in which the most county-level pupils engaged (44.2%) was playing in an orchestra.

What are adolescents' ability self-perceptions and values for these activities?

Each respondent was asked a series of questions, deriving from those used in the scales outlined by Eccles *et al.* (2005), relating to their ability self-perceptions and values for the activities presented above. The ability self-perceptions items included questions as to how good they thought they were at a particular activity and how good they thought they would be at that activity compared to other activities they do. These items were rated using a Likert scale of 1 (not at all) to 7 (a lot) and were subsequently summed to make a composite score for 'ability self-perceptions'. The subjective task value items included questions as to the perceived importance, usefulness, and enjoyment of the activity, and were rated using the same Likert scale. These items were summed to make a composite score for 'values'. It was these composite scores for ability self-perceptions and values that were used in the analyses reported below.

Differences were found between group (junior conservatoire and county-level pupils) and age (13–15 and 17–19), for ability self-perceptions for each of the activities, and values for each of the activities. Significant results were found for the following ability self-perceptions and/or values relating to the following activities: *playing a musical instrument, playing in chamber groups, composing, competitions, summer schools, solo performance,* and *performing with others.* (Full details, including means and standard deviations, are reported in Tables 11.3 and 11.4.)

A main effect was found for age and ability self-perceptions for four of the activities only. Further analyses indicated effects on age and ability self-perceptions for the activities *playing in a chamber group, taking part in competitions and summer courses,* and *performing with others,* with those in the 17–19 age group having higher ability self-perceptions than those in the 13–15 age group. Effects on group and ability self-perceptions for the activities *playing* an *instrument* and *solo performance* were also found, such that the junior conservatoire pupils had higher beliefs for these activities than county-level pupils. An interaction was found between group and age for the activity competitions/festivals with 17–19 year olds and 13–15 year olds in the county-level group having the highest and lowest ability self-perceptions for competitions, respectively.

A main effect was found for age and values for three of the activities, and group and values for four of the activities only. Further analyses indicated effects on age and values for the activities *playing an instrument, playing in a chamber group,* and *performing with others,* such that those in the 17–19 age group had higher values for these activities than those in the 13–15 age group.

Effects were also found on group and values for the activities *playing an instrument, composing, summer courses,* and *solo performances* where the junior conservatoire pupils had higher values for these activities than the county-level pupils.

What factors do adolescent musicians perceive to be important in their musical development?

There were significant differences between the two groups' ratings of importance of 11 of the 20 activities perceived as contributing to respondents' own musical development. As shown in Figure 11.1 and Table 11.5, junior conservatoire pupils gave higher ratings than the county-level pupils to all activities except *attending a music centre.* The largest differences between the ratings of the junior conservatoire pupils and county-level pupils were for *solo performance* and *attending a junior conservatoire,* both rated more important by junior conservatoire pupils. Junior conservatoire pupils rated *individual lessons* and *enjoying music* as the most important contributors to their musical development, while county-level pupils rated *individual lessons* most important.

Finally, when pupils were asked to rank the top three activities in order of importance, 18.5% of junior conservatoire pupils ranked *enjoying music* highest, while 11.1%

Table 11.3 Mean scores for ability self-perceptions and values relating to musical activities, according to group and age*

	Age	Playing		Chamber group		Composing		Competitions		Summer course		Solo performance		Performing	
		Mean	SD	Mean	SD	Mean	SD	Mean	SD	Mean	SD	Mean	SD	Mean	SD
Ability beliefs Junior conservatoire	13–15	5.5	1.4	5.1	1.4	–	–	5.2	1.6	5.3	1.6	5.5	1.6	5.7	1.5
	17–19	5.9	1.4	5.8	1.5	–	–	5.2	1.5	5.9	1.7	5.9	1.7	6.0	1.6
County level	13–15	5.1	1.4	4.5	1.4	–	–	3.9	1.4	3.9	1.6	4.0	1.6	5.1	1.6
	17–19	5.3	1.5	5.8	1.6	–	–	5.6	1.7	5.5	2.0	5.3	1.9	6.1	1.6
Values Junior conservatoire	13–15	6.3	1.4	5.6	1.6	3.1	1.5	–	–	5.8	1.7	6.3	1.7	6.3	1.5
	17–19	6.5	1.4	6.2	1.6	4.1	1.8	–	–	6.2	1.8	6.4	1.6	6.5	1.5
County level	13–15	5.6	1.5	5.6	1.6	5.1	1.9	–	–	4.1	1.7	4.8	1.7	5.2	1.7
	17–19	6.3	1.7	6.3	2.0	4.9	2.1	–	–	5.4	2.1	5.6	2.0	6.5	1.6

*Raw data were screened for outliers, skewness, and kurtosis and were transformed accordingly. In order to compensate for violations of test assumptions, results are reported with a significance level of $p < 0.01$, rather than $p < 0.05$.

Table 11.4 Summary of MANOVAs for ability self-perceptions and values relating to musical activities, according to group and age*

		Univariate							
		Multivariate	Playing	Chamber Group	Composing	Competitions	Summer course	Solo Performance	Performing
Ability beliefs	Group		$p < 0.01$					$p < 0.01$	
	Age	$p < 0.001$		$p < 0.001$		$p < 0.01$	$p < 0.01$		$p < 0.01$
	Group × age					$p < 0.01$			
Values	Group	$p < 0.001$	$p < 0.01$		$p < 0.01$		$p < 0.01$	$p < 0.001$	
	Age	$p < 0.01$	$p < 0.01$	$p < 0.01$					$p < 0.001$
	Group × age								

*Raw data were screened for outliers, skewness, and kurtosis and were transformed accordingly. In order to compensate for violations of test assumptions, results are reported with a significance level of $p < 0.01$, rather than $p < 0.05$.

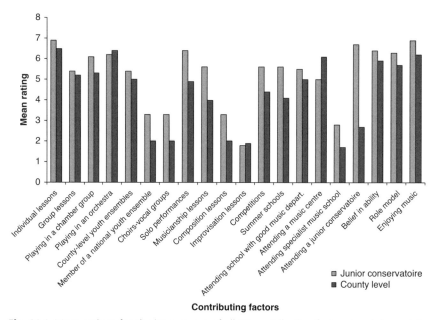

Fig. 11.1 Mean ratings for the importance of all 20 contributing factors in adolescents' musical development.

of county-level pupils ranked *individual lessons* highest. (See Table 11.5 for full details.)

Discussion and conclusion

Howe and Sloboda (1991a, 1991b) concluded from their studies that children are involved in musical activities besides their instrumental lessons, and that there is more than one route to musical excellence. My aim in this chapter was to explore two possible alternative routes. This was achieved by highlighting the different activities undertaken by adolescents from educational settings other than specialist music schools, and by investigating the adolescents' associated beliefs and values for these activities. By combining expectancy-value theory with previous research on musical expertise, this study has offered new insights into how adolescents may become accomplished musicians.

What musical activities are adolescent musicians taking part in, or have been involved in?

Adolescents take part in a number of different musical activities besides their instrumental lessons. These include musicianship lessons, playing in chamber groups, playing in orchestras, solo performance, composition and improvisation lessons, competitions, summer schools, other activities not relating to their main instrument, and attending musical events/concerts. Junior conservatoire pupils reported taking part in significantly more activities than did county-level pupils except playing in

Table 11.5 Mean scores of significant results for 'contributing factors'

	Junior conservatoire		County level	
	Mean	SD	Mean	SD
Individual lessons**	6.9	1.3	6.5	1.8
Singing in choirs/vocal groups*	3.3	2.1	2.0	2.3
Composition lessons*	3.3	2.1	2.0	2.1
Summer schools*	5.6	2.2	4.1	2.1
Competitions*	5.6	2.0	4.4	2.0
Solo performances**	6.4	1.8	4.9	2.0
Attending specialist music school*	2.8	2.5	1.7	2.1
Attending a junior conservatoire**	6.7	1.7	2.7	1.7
Attending a music centre*	5.0	2.2	6.1	1.9
Member of a national youth ensemble*	3.3	2.3	2.0	2.3
Enjoying music**	6.9	1.5	6.2	1.9

*$p < 0.01$; **$p < 0.001$.

orchestras and having improvisation lessons. The activity reported by the largest proportion of junior conservatoire pupils was solo performance, while that reported by the largest proportion of county-level pupils was playing in orchestras. This finding is to be expected, however, given that county-level students attend a music centre specifically to play in a music ensemble. The activity reported by the fewest pupils in each group was improvisation. While only eight respondents (four from each group) reported having improvisation lessons, the values ratings for all respondents in the sample (a mean of 4.6 for junior conservatoire and 4.1 for county-level pupils) clearly demonstrate an awareness of its potential for their musical development. Given existing evidence for the role of improvising in learning to perform (see, for instance, Lehmann, Sloboda, & Woody, 2007; Moore et al., 2003), music services and junior conservatoires should include opportunities for improvisation in their curricula.

Respondents listed a range of different types of activities (e.g. chamber ensembles: duets, trios, quartets, quintets) at different levels (e.g. school, county, national), within the categories provided. Activities not relating specifically to their main instrument were also detailed, including musical events they had attended. The finding that almost all the respondents reported going to orchestral concerts, with half claiming they were the most important influence on their musical development, suggests a possible link with role model literature (e.g. Ivaldi & O'Neill, 2008), particularly as role models were also perceived to be an important factor in the adolescents' musical development (see Figure 11.1). It is possible that these orchestral concerts provided inspiration, perhaps in the form of potential role models for the adolescents. Indeed, Sloboda and Howe (1991) found that 24% of their Chetham's sample identified live professional performances as having some motivational influence.

In summary, the findings illustrate a high level of musical activity for both junior conservatoire and county-level pupils. While there were differences in the extent to which pupils from each group were engaged in each activity, there were very few differences between the groups in the range of activities in which they took part.

What are adolescents' ability self-perceptions and values for these activities?

O'Neill *et al.*'s (2000) and Ivaldi and O'Neill's (2010) research has clearly demonstrated that musicians have higher ability self-perceptions and values for music than non-musicians. The present study, however, compared the ability self-perceptions and values for music of two groups of musicians who engaged in similar activities. For all activities the junior conservatoire pupils had higher ability self-perceptions than county-level pupils, although the difference between the two groups was significant only for *playing an instrument* and *solo performance.* Similar results were found for values for each of the activities, but significant differences were only found for the activities *playing an instrument, composing, summer courses,* and *solo performances.* When it came to ability self-perceptions for each activity by age, the 17–19 age group had higher beliefs for each activity than the 13–15 age group, except for composing. Significant differences were only found for the activities *playing in a chamber group, taking part in competitions* and *summer courses,* and *performing with others.* Similar results were found for values for each of the activities, except for composing and improvising, such that those in the 17–19 age group had higher values than those in the 13–15 age group. Significant values were found for the activities *playing an instrument, playing in a chamber group,* and *performing with others.*

The non-significance of the differences could be attributed to the similarity of the two groups. More detailed analyses of each activity, such as how frequently it occurred, where, with whom, and in particular, in relation to their aspiration beliefs, might give rise to alternative explanations.

In general, the finding that older respondents had higher ability self-perceptions and values for the activities than the younger respondents may be due to the latter not yet having had the opportunity to engage in some of the activities identified, so the results could be attributed to the older respondents' confidence, acquired over time. These results contradict those of Eccles, Wigfield, Harold, and Blumenfeld (1993), who suggested, on the basis of research with school children asked to rate musical ability in relation to their other school subjects, that ability self-perceptions and values for instrumental music decline with age, possibly as a result of perceptions becoming more accurate. For children identified as 'talented' and engaging in specialist training in music, sport, art, etc., it is likely that ability self-perceptions and values will increase with age. Research has yet to determine the extent to which, however, these ability self-perceptions and values continue to increase as individuals develop as musicians.

Overall, all groups had the highest ability self-perceptions for the activity performing with others, while the junior conservatoire pupils and county-level pupils, and those in the 13–15 age group had the lowest ability self-perceptions for singing in a choir, while those in the 17–19 age group had the lowest ability self-perceptions for composing. Overall, junior conservatoire pupils and those in the 17–19 age group valued performing with others the most, while county-level pupils and those in the

13–15 age group valued playing an instrument the most. For junior conservatoire and county-level pupils, and those in the 13–15 age group, participating in a choir was the least valued activity, while for those in the 17–19 age group, composing was the least valued activity.

While it is likely that more accomplished musicians will have higher ability self-perceptions and values for music, researchers should always measure these motivational indicators, regardless of whether the musician is engaged in the activity or not. Armed with the appropriate evidence, educators are in a position to encourage the young musician who holds low self-confidence beliefs for an activity they are already engaged in, or provide opportunities for those wanting to participate in new activities that they value highly and consider to be important to their overall musical development. Adolescents are able to distinguish their ability self-perceptions and values for activities, regardless of the extent to which they are engaged in them.

What factors do adolescent musicians perceive to be important in their musical development?

Having individual lessons was perceived as the most important factor in respondents' musical development, irrespective of group; junior conservatoire pupils rated enjoying music as equally important. Enjoying performing (as opposed to listening to music) has been found to be an important factor in musical development. For example, Howe and Sloboda (1991b) report evidence from interviews with pupils at Chetham's that performing brought them 'real joy' (p. 59). This may have important implications for motivation, where enjoyment has been found to be a contributing factor towards musical success (see, further, O'Neill, 2002). However, more information needs to be obtained as to what it actually is in music that the pupils enjoy, in order to be able to discuss the implications for motivation in a more meaningful way.

The wider context

In this chapter, I have shown that young musicians follow similar routes to musical expertise, but the degree to which they are engaged in musical activities, and their ability self-perceptions and values for these activities, are different. Similarly to the Chetham's pupils in the original Sloboda studies, it could be argued that those in the junior conservatoire group are well on their way to becoming expert musicians; pupils are involved in a wide variety of musical activities, and their ability self-perceptions and values for these are high. County-level pupils show similar patterns but to a lesser extent. Nevertheless, a number of them have the potential to develop into talented musicians.

These findings have important implications for music learning in general. There is a growing literature on the engagement of children in state schools with music (e.g. Lamont, Hargreaves, Marshall, & Tarrant, 2003; O'Neill et al., 2000). Future research in this area may benefit from looking at the variety of routes undertaken by adolescents who define themselves as musicians, particularly when it comes to their perceptions of what have been the most important factors in their musical development, in order for educators to become more aware of the activities valued by young musicians. Ultimately, if adolescents value an activity, they are more likely to want to engage in it and develop in their chosen area. By identifying the factors important to them, it is hoped that more young people will excel in music, and fewer musicians will give up.

In addition, the socio-economic status of the pupils taking part in the study should be considered when interpreting the results. Ivaldi and O'Neill (2009) found that adolescents in their study constructed a category of privilege when talking about a professional musician who was a former pupil of a specialist music school. For these adolescents, not having a private education—or not being posh—was viewed as a barrier to high musical attainment. It is possible that in the present study, the musicians who did not pay to attend a specialist music environment held similar beliefs.

In conclusion, it is important to consider the role that the factors explored here have in the wider context—in addition to the role of the teacher, practice, and music lessons. I believe that the work of Sloboda and his colleagues has provided an important platform from which to explore further the young musician's journey towards musical expertise. By obtaining a more detailed picture of young people's specialist musical activities, and their perceptions as to what has contributed to their success, we can continue to develop a greater understanding of the factors that enable adolescents to become expert musicians.

Acknowledgements

I would like to thank the staff and pupils at Lancashire Music Service, Bolton Music Service, and the Junior Royal Northern College of Music for making this research possible. In particular, I would like to thank Geoffrey Reed and Karen Humphreys, at the Royal Northern College of Music, for their significant contribution to the development of this project. Special thanks also go to Jane Ginsborg for her detailed comments on earlier drafts, and to John Sloboda for the valuable discussions we had at the start of the project, upon which this research is based.

References

Burland, K., & Davidson, J. W. (2002). Training the talented. *Music Education Research*, 4(1), 121–140.

Davidson, J. W., Howe, M. J. A., Moore, D. G., & Sloboda, J. A. (1996). The role of parental influences in the development of musical performance. *British Journal of Developmental Psychology*, 14(4), 399–412.

Davidson, J. W., Moore, D. G., Sloboda, J. A., & Howe, M. J. A. (1998). Characteristics of music teachers and the progress of young instrumentalists. *Journal of Research in Music Education*, 46(1), 141–160.

Eccles, J. S., O'Neill, S. A., & Wigfield, A. (2005). Ability self-perceptions and subjective task values in adolescents and children. In K. Anderson Moore, & L. H. Lippman (Eds.), *What do children need to flourish?* (pp. 237–249). New York, NY: Springer.

Eccles, J. S., & Wigfield, A. (1995). In the mind of the actor: The structure of adolescents' achievement values and expectancy related beliefs. *Personality and Social Psychology Bulletin*, 21, 215–225.

Eccles, J. S., Wigfield, A., Harold, R. D., & Blumenfeld, P. C. (1993). Age and gender differences in children's self-and task perceptions during elementary school. *Child Development, 64*, 830–847.

Eccles-Parsons, J. S., Adler, T. F., Futterman, R., Goff, S. B., Kaczala, C. M., Meece, J. L., *et al.* (1983). Expectancies, values and academic behaviors. In J. T. Spence (Ed.), *Achievement and achievement motives* (pp. 75–146). San Francisco, CA: W. H. Freeman.

Howe, M. J. A., Davidson, J. W., Moore, D. G., & Sloboda, J. A. (1995). Are there early childhood signs of musical ability? *Psychology of Music, 23*(2), 162–176.

Howe, M. J. A., Davidson, J. W., & Sloboda, J. A. (1998). Innate talents: Reality or myth? *Behavioral and Brain Sciences, 21*, 399–442.

Howe, M. J. A., & Sloboda, J. A. (1991a). Young musicians' accounts of significant influences in their early lives.1. The family and the musical background. *British Journal of Music Education, 8*(1), 39–52.

Howe, M. J. A., & Sloboda, J. A. (1991b). Young musicians' accounts of significant influences in their early lives.2. Teachers, practicing and performing. *British Journal of Music Education, 8*(1), 53–63.

Howe, M. J. A., & J. A. Sloboda (1991c). Early signs of talents and special interest in the lives of young musicians. *European Journal for High Ability, 2*, 102–111.

Ivaldi, A., & O'Neill, S. A. (2008). Adolescents' musical role models: Whom do they admire and why? *Psychology of Music, 36*(4), 395–415.

Ivaldi, A., & O'Neill, S. A. (2009). Talking 'privilege': Barriers to musical attainment in adolescents' talk of musical role models. *British Journal of Music Education, 26*(1), 43–56.

Ivaldi, A., & O'Neill, S. A. (2010). Adolescents' attainability and aspiration beliefs for famous musician role models. *Music Education Research, 12*(2), 179–197.

Lamont, A., Hargreaves, D. J., Marshall, N. A., & Tarrant, M. (2003). Young people's music in and out of school. *British Journal of Music Education, 20*(3), 229–241.

Lehmann, A. C., Sloboda, J. A., & Woody, R. H. (2007). *Psychology for musicians.* Oxford: Oxford University Press.

Manturzewska, M. (1990). A biographical study of the life-span development of professional musicians. *Psychology of music, 18*, 112–139.

Moore, D. G., Burland, K., & Davidson, J. W. (2003). The social context of musical success: A developmental account. *British Journal of Psychology, 94*(4), 529–549.

O'Neill, S. A. (1999). The role of achievement motivation in the practice and achievement of young musicians, In S. Won Yi (Ed.), *Music, mind, and science* (pp. 420–433). Seoul: Seoul National University Press.

O'Neill, S. A. (2002). *Motivation and children's in-school and out-school engagement in instrumental music: a longitudinal analysis.* Paper presented at the 7th International Conference on Music Perception and Cognition, Sydney, Australia.

O'Neill, S. A., Ryan, K. J., Boulton, M. J., & Sloboda, J. A. (2000). *Children's subjective task values and engagement in music.* Paper presented at the British Psychological Society Annual Conference, Winchester, UK.

Sloboda, J. A. (2005). *Exploring the musical mind.* Oxford: Oxford University Press.

Sloboda, J. A., & Davidson, J. W. (1996). The young performing musician, In I. Deliège, & J. A. Sloboda (Eds.), *Musical beginnings* (pp. 171–190). Oxford: Oxford University Press.

Sloboda, J. A., Davidson, J. W., Howe, M. J. A., & Moore, D. G. (1996). The role of practice in the development of performing musicians. *British Journal of Psychology, 87*, 287–309.

Sloboda, J. A., & Howe, M. J. A. (1991). Biographical precursors of musical excellence: An interview study. *Psychology of Music, 19*, 3–21.

Sloboda, J. A., & Howe, M. J. A. (1992). Transitions in the early musical careers of able young musicians: Choosing instruments and teachers. *Journal of Research in Music Education, 40*(4), 283–294.

Sosniak, L. (1985). Learning to be a concert pianist. In B. S. Bloom (Ed.), *Developing talent in young people* (pp. 19–67). New York, NY: Ballantine.

Wigfield, A., Eccles, J. S., Yoon, K. S., Harold, R. D., Arbreton, A. J. A., Freedman-Doan, C., *et al.,* (1997). Change in children's competence beliefs and subjective task values across the elementary school years: a 3-year study. *Journal of Educational Psychology, 89*, 451–469.

Chapter 12

The musical child prodigy (wunderkind) in music history: a historiometric analysis

Reinhard Kopiez

Abstract

This historiometric study on the musical child prodigy (wunderkind) is based on a sample of 213 European-wide reports in *Allgemeine Musikalische Zeitung* (the most important music journal in the first half of the nineteenth century) between 1798 and 1848. A quantitative analysis of biographical data revealed a mean age of 10.73 years at the first public performance (time of report). Over a period of 50 years no differences in the prodigies' ages at the performance debut could be observed between groups of instruments (pianists, string players, singers). Data analysis revealed an increase in wunderkind reports, which reached a peak between 1821 and 1825—the historical beginning of the virtuosic era. Female prodigies performed on the piano or as singers ('feminine' instruments), while male prodigies played the flute, clarinet, and violin, the 'masculine' instruments. The association between gender and instrument choice in the nineteenth century was different compared with that today. Finally, it is argued that in every era people seem to be enthralled to the remarkable musical achievements of very young children. However, nowadays this public passion is fulfilled through viewing of television talent contests and video-sharing websites.

Throughout John Sloboda's research, aspects of musical development and outstanding musical achievement were the focus of his work. Two shining illustrations are his investigation into the nature of a young savant's musical memory (Sloboda, Hermelin, & O'Connor, 1985) and his analysis of expertise development in jazz using Louis Armstrong as an example (Sloboda, 1991). He was interested in 'children who showed exceptional precocity at various musical skills' (Sloboda, 2005, p. 249) and was involved in a study to determine early predictors of outstanding musical achievement (Howe, Davidson, Moore, & Sloboda, 1995). My contribution to this volume is dedicated to John's work (for an overview see Sloboda, 2005) as it explores some historical prerequisites of the wunderkind (child prodigy) phenomenon.

Children with early signs of extraordinary achievement, so-called prodigies or 'wunderkinder', have always captivated the scientific community and the interest of the general public. Today, a prodigy is defined as 'a person who achieves great success when relatively young' (Pearsall, 1999, p. 1653). In his dissertation on the history of musical child prodigies, Stevens (1982) gives an account of such prodigies from the ancient world (pp. 8–10.). For example, the ancient Greek god Apollo was said to have felt longing for the sound of the *lyra* and *kithara* shortly after birth. The most well-known example of a musical child prodigy from the Middle Ages is Hildegard von Bingen (1098–1179). At the age of 8 years, she received tuition in psalm singing in a Benedictine monastery and later became one of the most famous female composers in music history. However, the reason for the rare number of reports on early outstanding achievement is due not only to a lack of documentation, but also to the historically late development of the concept of childhood.

Thus, to understand the fascination with early accomplishment, we have to consider a larger historical framework. An early framework was given by Ariès (1962) in his comprehensive history of childhood: as the author reveals, there had been no consciousness in society with regard to an autonomous 'childhood' prior to the seventeenth century. But changes in attitude towards childhood and individual accomplishment made people take more notice of early achievement. Thus, anecdotal reports of child prodigies were replaced by systematic descriptions of young individuals. The next historical framework to consider is the development of individualistic concepts in humans, which emerged in the Western world between the fifteenth and sixteenth centuries. Based on examples from art, philosophy, and religion, Jansz (2004) argues that there was a 'shift from the collective to the individual from the fifteenth century onward' (p. 17). In the continuing historical process of the eighteenth century, group membership and birth status lost their determining power. Once demographic and economic background was no longer sufficient to explain an individual's outstanding achievement, alternative explanations were needed. For example, anatomical differences (as given, for example, by disciplines such as phrenology) became of interest to explain mental differences among people. In other words, in the eighteenth and nineteenth centuries, the new 'psychological perspective was the outcome of individualization' (Jansz, 2004, p. 40). These two historical frameworks may explain the increasing public interest in musical child prodigies and a cumulative number of reports in contemporary sources.

The first extensively documented (non-musical) prodigy baby was Christian Heineken, born on 6 February 1721 in Lübeck, Germany (see Hennig, 1999). By the age of 14 months he could read and knew parts of the Old Testament by heart; a couple of weeks later he could also recite selections of the New Testament and was able to remember 200 church songs. He showed an extraordinary memory, could give extensive reports on historical facts, and gained fame after he was presented to the Danish court in 1724, where he was examined thoroughly. Christian Heineken was the first child to labelled as a 'wunderkind' (Stevens, 1982, p. 4). However, due to serious health problems, he died on 27 June 1725 at the very young age of 4 years. Although this early report on a child prodigy is of historical interest, when considering it from a modern scientific approach, we need to be careful about its reliability.

In the musical domain, early psychological reports on extraordinary achievements of young children began to appear at the start of the twentieth century. As Révész (1916, p. 63) reported, around 1910 Erich Moritz von Hornbostel tested the musical hearing skills of the 13-year-old composer prodigy, Erich Wolfgang Korngold (1897–1957) in Vienna. Between 1910 and 1914 Révész conducted a long-term case study on the young pianist and composer, Erwin Nyiregyházi (1903–1987). Révész was so enthusiastic about this child that he wrote, 'he has the capability of the young Mozart' (Révész, 1916, p. 3, transl. R. Kopiez). However, after brief success as a pianist and film composer, this prodigy experienced one disaster after another, characterized by numerous divorces and social decline (see Bazzana, 2007).

In the late twentieth and early twenty-first century, researchers have continued to be fascinated with young children with exceptional skills. For example, publications on this topic can be found with regard to musical prodigies in general (Fisher, 1973; Kenneson, 1998), and also musical savants (Miller, 1989), gifted artistic and musical children (McPherson & Williamon, 2006; Winner, 1996), and disabled musicians (Ockelford, 2008). Howe et al. (1995) interviewed 257 parents of music students who differed in the extent of their mastery. However, only one early predictor could be found for the most successful musicians: singing at an early age.

From the perspective of music psychology, the explanation of extraordinary musical achievement in children with reference to inexplicable and wondrous abilities is to be considered critically. First, there is no objective definition of achievement and age that could serve as a criterion for the classification of a wunderkind; second, based on expertise theory, alternative explanations can be given for outstanding achievements. As reported by Sloboda (2005, p. 251), children classified as prodigies show a 'high degree of intrinsic motivation for engagement with a single activity sustained over many years'; they live in a supportive environment with access to instruments and training; and they spend a significant amount of time engaged with the materials relevant to skill acquisition. Controlled investigations under laboratory conditions showed a different picture, which disproved the common idea of innate talent. In a case study of the musical savant NP, Sloboda et al. (1985) demonstrated that the 'verbatim' metaphor for an extraordinary musical memory was erroneous. In addition, the role of extensive practice remains unreported in other publications of child prodigies (Sloboda, Davidson, Howe, & Moore, 1996). As an extreme example, the neuroscientist Lutz Jäncke claimed that not even Mozart was a wunderkind, and his achievement could be explained by his early initiation into music and extensive, deliberate practice (see Wolff, 2006). Finally, musical prodigies can only be understood in their respective social and historical contexts. Stevens' (1982) comprehensive list of musical child prodigies in music history, although the first to be published, comprised a highly heterogeneous sample. The author did not indicate the use of an objective criterion for the inclusion of children in his list of child prodigies. He also used an a posteriori approach from an historical perspective rather than an a priori and contemporaneous report such as the historiometric study published in the *Allgemeine Musikalische Zeitung* (AMZ). Thus Stevens' list of persons considered as wunderkinder may be biased. Our sample, based on the AMZ reports, is much more homogeneous and considers only those children who were designated as child prodigies in early childhood irrespective of their later careers. In contrast, Stevens considered only those children who continued successfully as musicians into adulthood. Although the diagnostic criteria for a wunderkind may be different from those that may be selected today, the AMZ sample is more objective and considers only those children who received a certain amount of public attention for their musical productions. It also steers clear of a 'romantic determinism' of prodigies and their later careers.

Rationale of the study

Based on an explorative historiometric approach, this study intended to contribute to a better understanding of the historical changes in the phenomenon of musical prodigy in the first half of the nineteenth century. The historiometric approach was introduced by Simonton (1990) to apply 'quantitative analyses on data concerning historical individuals' (p. 3) or multiple cases. Recently, this promising approach has been used to provide an explanation of the musical development of famous musicians (Lehmann, 2006) and the lifespan development of Clara Schumann (Kopiez, Lehmann, & Klassen, 2009). Here I will try to answer three questions: First, how has the frequency of reports on musical prodigies changed over decades? Second, what are the preferred instruments played by prodigies? Third, what was the average age at the moment of the reported first public performance?

Method

The data used for this study was collected from all 50 volumes of the German music journal AMZ, published in Leipzig (Germany) from 1798 to 1848. The AMZ was the 'authoritative music journal of its time' (Krause, 1996, p. 1064) and received reports on musical events from its foreign correspondents all over Europe. Thus, it is fair to assume that this data collection is representative of the majority of wunderkind reports in the first half of the nineteenth century. The extracted reports were compiled by Fuchs (2003) and resulted in an extensive list of 213 musical child prodigies. However, although the author gave the relevant data she did not provide any analysis. The data comprised the name of the prodigy (e.g. Franz Liszt), the location of the first performance (e.g. Vienna), the instrument (e.g. violin), the age at the time of first performance and the year of performance. As a test of the sample's validity, the names of the reported children were compared with Stevens' extensive data collection on musical prodigies (1982). Only 24 of the 213 names in Fuchs' collection were congruent with Stevens' list.

Results

Changes in frequencies of reported public performances

The distribution of the number of reports on wunderkinder (see Figure 12.1) in the AMZ shows a clear deviance from equal distribution ($[\chi^2(47, N = 213) = 76.57, p = 0.004]$)

with an expected mean number of 4.4 concerts per year. This can best be described as a bimodal distribution: starting in 1798, the frequency of reports increased over a period of about 25 years, reaching its maximum between 1821 and 1825. After a first decline between 1829 and 1833, a second peak was reached between 1839 and 1842. This bimodal distribution of reports can be interpreted in terms of two cohorts, separated by a time distance of about 20 years.

Distribution of instruments

The distribution of preferred instruments for performing (see Table 12.1) reveals a clear picture: the list is dominated by four instruments, piano, violin, voice, and flute, which account for 87.9% of all reported performances. One child played an exotic instrument, the *csakan* (a so-called duct flute in the shape of a walking stick), which was popular in Austria between 1807 and 1840. Although I cannot exclude that in some cases (e.g. Franz Liszt) the programmes performed also contained creative contributions such as improvisations, most of the performances were characterized by reproductive activities (for examples of reprinted concert programmes see Bodsch, Biba, & Fuchs, 2003) and the performance of standard repertoire. However, the list also has a minority of child composers (Erasmus Kessler, 14 years old, Vienna, 1821; Renaud de Vielbach, 13 years old, Paris, 1841; Geiger [no first name indicated], 9 years old, Vienna, 1844).

Another interesting aspect of Table 12.1 is the difference in instrument frequencies between the sexes. The piano was performed in equal measure by boys and girls [$\chi^2(1, N = 106) = 0.36, p = 0.54$]). However, 65.7% of the girl prodigies were pianists

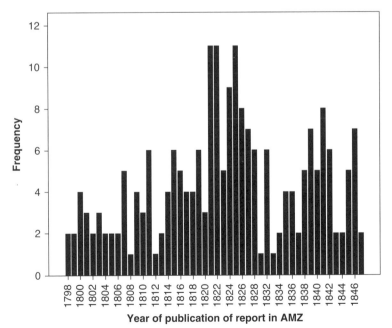

Fig. 12.1 Distribution of the number of published reports on child prodigies in the *Allgemeine Musikalische Zeitung* over a period of 50 years (1798–1848).

Table 12.1 Distribution of choice of instruments of all 213 musical child prodigies reported in the *Allgemeine Musikalische Zeitung* between 1798 and 1848. Percentages are indicated in parentheses.

Instrument	Number (%)		
	Boys	Girls	Total (%)
Piano	52 (39.7)	46 (65.7)	106 (51.5)
Violin	43 (32.8)	5 (7.1)	51 (24.8)*
Singing	2 (1.5)	11 (15.7)	13 (6.3)*
Flute	11 (8.4)	–	11 (5.3)
Violoncello	5 (3.8)	1 (1.4)	6 (2.9)
Guitar	3 (2.3)	1 (1.4)	4 (1.9)
Harp	–	4 (5.7)	4 (1.9)
Clarinet	3 (2.3)	–	3 (1.5)
French horn	3 (2.3)	–	3 (1.5)
Composition	2 (1.5)	–	3 (1.5)
Organ	1 (.8)	–	1 (.5)
Csakan (duct flute)	1 (.8)	–	1 (.5)
Valid	126	68	206
Missing	5	2	7
Total	131	70	213

Note: Differences between the frequencies for the two sexes and the sums of frequencies is because of some missing first names. In seven cases no instrument was indicated.

*χ^2 test on equal distribution of sex of performer in the respective instrument, significant at the $p < 0.01$ level; in case of frequencies of n <5, statistics could not be computed.

compared with 39.7% of the boys. For the violin the picture was different: 43 (32.8%) boys but only 5 (7.1%) girls played it ($[\chi^2(1, N = 51) = 30.08, p = 0.00]$). While singing prodigies were predominately girls (15.7% $[\chi^2(1, N = 13) = 6.23, p = 0.01]$), flute players tended to be boys (8.4%). Against a background of current studies on gender associations with musical instruments (for an overview see McPherson & Davidson, 2006, p. 334), there are noticeable differences between the nineteenth century and today. For example, the flute and the clarinet have undergone a change of their 'masculine' character and are nowadays associated with 'feminine' qualities and preferably played by female instrumental beginners.

Age at the time of performance

The distribution of the children's ages at the time of their first public performance as reported in the AMZ is shown in Figure 12.2. Prodigies performed at a mean age of 10.73 years (SD 2.47 years). The youngest children (performing the violin and the harp) were only 4 years old; the oldest children (performing the piano and the violin) were 16 years old. There were no statistically significant differences in the age of

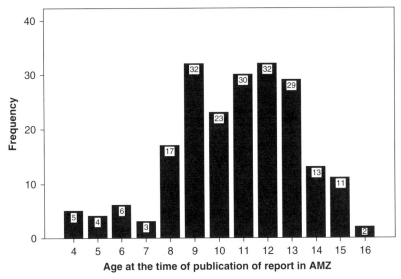

Fig. 12.2 Distribution of musical prodigies by age denoted in the reports published in the *Allgemeine Musikalische Zeitung* over a period of 50 years (1798–1848).

performance between the sexes [$F(1, 161) = 0.11$, $p > 0.67$], instrument groups recoded into the three major groups of pianists, string players, and singers [$F(2, 161) = 0.88$, $p > 0.41$], or for the relation between gender and instrument group [$F(2, 161) = 0.07$, $p > 0.93$]. In other words, regardless of the instruments played by the prodigies, there is no evidence for differences in the average age levels at the first performance with regard to sex or instrument. The finding of an approximately constant age at first performance over a reported period of 50 years was confirmed by a correlation analysis between age of first performance and the year of publication in the AMZ [$r(207) = 0.025$, $p < 0.72$]. However, we have to bear in mind that the reported age is not always identical with the biological age, and prodigies were sometimes reported as being one to two years younger than they were (e.g. in the case of Franz Liszt, his age was sometimes reduced by 1 year, see Walker, Eckart, & Mueller, 2008).

Distribution of places of performance

The distribution of the cities where the performance occurred in the reports showed an interesting pattern. First, in about 45% of all reports, a concentration of wunderkind activities in five major European cities was observed (Vienna: n = 34, Berlin: n = 23, Prague: n = 16, Frankfurt/M.: n = 11, Paris, n = 11). Second, several children (17.3%) performed in only one city. In the case of Vienna, this concentration of activities is consistent with the city's significance as one of the major music hubs of the first half of the nineteenth century. During the early years of the nineteenth century, Vienna had an 'international standing as a centre of musical culture' (Antonicek, Beales, Botstein, Klein, & Goertz, 2009) that benefited from the activities of Haydn and Beethoven. Moreover, there was a growing population of music-loving people living in the city, for example, by the 'Gesellschaft für Musikfreunde,' which was founded as a civic concert organizer in 1814, or by the Vienna Philharmonic, founded in 1842. The same was true for Berlin: 'From the early 19th century Berlin has been visited by almost every notable virtuoso and important soloist' (Becker, Green, Canning, Fábián, & Roesler, 2009), such as Paganini in 1829, Clara Schumann in 1835, or Liszt in 1841. The importance of Vienna as Europe's main 'music city' is also reflected in Clara Schumann's concert activities, 16.0% of which occurred in Vienna between 1828 and 1840 (see Kopiez *et al.*, 2009).

Discussion

The quantitative analysis of first public wunderkind concerts considered 213 reports from the AMZ over a period of 50 years, as listed by Fuchs (2003). Based on these data, on average about four performances of prodigies were reported per year. The number of reports differed significantly between the years with a maximum of 11 reports per year between 1821 and 1825. Although the AMZ was the most important music journal of its time, it is unrealistic to assume that every wunderkind concert was visited and reported by the journal's correspondents. Thus, it is likely that the true number of wunderkind performances might be underestimated and will remain unknown.

Concerning the distribution of instruments, the piano was identified as the main instrument in wunderkind concerts, followed by the violin, voice, and the flute. However, a clear gender effect on instrumental preference was observed: the piano and voice were considered 'feminine' instruments, while the violin and the flute were more 'masculine' instruments. Although there are no data on historical changes in preferences for musical instruments as a function of gender, the results can be interpreted against the background of the current discussion about 'music and gender' (see O'Neill, 1997). Although we cannot be sure that instrumental choices in the nineteenth century were made by the children's' parents, we find a different picture of 'masculine' and 'feminine' stereotypes in parents' instrumental choices today. When asked to select a musical instrument for their child, today's parents usually choose the clarinet, flute, or violin for a girl, and drums, trombone, and trumpet for a boy. However, this gender stereotyping seems to be acquired as it was not found in the instrument choices for young children (O'Neill, 1997). These gender-stereotyped preferences seem to change only very slowly over time. Based on data from 165 boys and 338 girls (age range 12–17 years), Scheuer (1988, p. 89) found the following ranking of 'masculine' instruments played by boys: guitar (32%), piano (18%), and recorder (14%). The 'feminine' instruments played by girls were recorder (53%), guitar (32%), and piano (26%). In two additional preference tests (sounding questionnaire and visual preference test), girls showed a clear preference for smooth sounds and 'middle-class' instruments (e.g. piano and violin), while boys preferred powerful sounds and electrified instruments (e.g. brass instruments, organ, guitar, see Scheuer, 1988, p. 121). Data from the 1990s provide evidence for a slight tendency towards a limited increase 'in the proportion of girls playing masculine instruments' (O'Neill, 1997, p. 56).

Although the average age of a wunderkind in this study (10.73 years) at his or her first public performance is just pre-pubertal (which is characterized by maximizing skills while still presenting a childish appearance), it is much harder to determine the performance level of the children. Of course, performance criteria for the designation of a child as a wunderkind in the past might have been different from the criteria of today. This uncertainty could only be resolved by considering the performed repertoire of each reported case. However, two factors give evidence for the assumption of a lower level of performance skills compared with the technical capabilities of young performers today: First, we have to bear in mind that a wunderkind recital was a heterogeneous mixture of pieces comprising different collaborators, and the wunderkind played in only part of the concert. For example, at Clara Wieck's first public concert on 8 November 1830 (at the age of 11), the first part of the concert started with an orchestra overture by Auber, followed by variations performed by a singer. In this first part, Clara presented the more demanding *Variations Brillantes*, op. 23, for a piano solo by Herz. In the second part of the concert, Clara Wieck started with the less demanding, but audience-captivating, *Quatuor Concertant* by Czerny (for four pianos and orchestra), followed by her own (less demanding) *Romance* for physharmonica and piano. The concert ended with a song by Rossini (performed by an invited singer) and variations for piano solo composed by Clara herself (for details see Kopiez, 1997). In other words, the audience was supposed to be attracted more by a wide range of pleasing pieces than only by Clara's overwhelming technical superiority.

The assumption of a lower level of early mastery in the nineteenth century is supported by quantitative analyses of the historical development of expert performance (Lehmann & Ericsson, 1998). Briefly, the authors showed that 'more recent prodigies have been more advanced in their performance skills than prodigies from earlier times' in performing more difficult works at an earlier date (p. 85, see also Lehmann, 2006).

Finally, the question remains whether the musical wunderkind is a phenomenon of historical interest only. On the contrary, it seems that every time period has its own perspective on musical child prodigies. Since the late twentieth century mass media has played a crucial role in the generation of publicity for high achievement in young children, and public fascination for it seems to be undiminished. However, the wunderkind concerts in Vienna and Berlin of the past have been partially replaced today by the opportunities afforded by television and the internet (e.g. YouTube). Some current examples include the classical pianists Marc Yu and George Li (10 and 13 years old at the time of writing), Connie Talbot (6 years old, singer and finalist of the 2007 television contest *Britain's Got Talent*), Bianca Ryan (11 years old, singer and winner of the 2006 television contest *America's Got Talent*), and, of course, Michael Jackson. Even at the age of about 8 years he had showed extraordinary talent in his dance moves and singing ability and started his solo career at the age of 13 in 1971 with the solo hit 'Got to be There', after years of extensive skill acquisition and optimization in the band The Jackson 5. The extraordinary public interest in musical prodigies is also reflected by the degree of media distribution: the video of Bianca Ryan's live performance of the very demanding song, 'And I am Telling You' was viewed over 2 000 000 times on the video-sharing websites YouTube and Metacafe between January 2007 and 2008. These examples not only give support for the 'acceleration hypothesis of musical expert performance' (Lehmann & Ericsson, 1998), but they also show that the wunderkind phenomenon has also gained ground in popular music.

Summary and conclusions

I have tried to add a new perspective to the phenomenon of musical child prodigies by considering its historical development. Based on historiometric analyses I have shown that the rising interest in outstanding achievement at a very young age began in the first half of the nineteenth century. This increasing interest in early achievements was accompanied by an increasing general interest in childhood as an autonomous period of life. Although in some cases a public performance was reported at the very early age of 4 years, the majority of musical child prodigies usually appeared on stage at 8 years and older. If we compare our findings with the development of outstanding skills in other artistic domains, there is evidence that instrumental performance seems to have a special position. For example, there are almost no reports on outstanding accomplishments in painting before the age of 8: Picasso finished his first painting (*Le Picador*) in 1890 at the age of 9. I suggest that the domain of music performance benefits from the early development of the sensorimotor system, whereas other domains may depend more on cognitive maturation as a prerequisite for development of creative processes. Finally, one can assume that the allure of musical child prodigies will continue to flourish and will also offer us insight into the very early stages of human development.

Acknowledgements

The database for this historiometric analysis can be downloaded from the website http://musicweb.hmtm-hannover.de/prodigies. I am indebted to Roger Chaffin, Marco Lehmann, Andreas C. Lehmann, and an anonymous reviewer for helpful comments on an earlier version of this essay.

References

Antonicek, T., Beales, D., Botstein, L., Klein, R., & Goertz, H. (2009). *Vienna.* Grove music. Available at: www.oxfordmusiconline.com (accessed 9 January 2009).

Ariès, P. (1962). *Centuries of childhood: A social history of family life* (R. Baldick, Trans.). New York, NY: Vintage Books.

Bazzana, K. (2007). *Lost genius. The story of a forgotten musical maverick.* Toronto: McClelland & Stewart.

Becker, H., Green, R. D., Canning, H., Fábián, I., & Roesler, C. A. (2009). *Berlin.* Grove Music. Available at: www.oxfordmusiconline.com (accessed 2 January 2009).

Bodsch, I., Biba, O., & Fuchs, I. (Eds.). (2003). *Beethoven und andere Wunderkinder [Beethoven and other child prodigies].* Bonn: StadtMuseum.

Fisher, R. B. (1973). *Musical prodigies: Masters at an early age.* New York, NY: Association Press.

Fuchs, I. (2003). Wunderkinder in der Leipziger 'Allgemeinen musikalischen Zeitung' 1798–1848 [Child prodigies in Leipzig's General Musical Newspaper (AMZ)]. In I. Bodsch, O. Biba, & I. Fuchs (Eds.), *Beethoven und andere Wunderkinder* (pp. 59–76). Bonn: StadtMuseum.

Hennig, K. J. (1999). Ein Kind zum Anbeten [A child to adore]. *Die Zeit, 52,* 76.

Howe, M. J. A., Davidson, J. W., Moore, D. G., & Sloboda, J. A. (1995). Are there early childhood signs of musical ability? *Psychology of Music, 23*(2), 162–176.

Jansz, J. (2004). Psychology and society: An overview. In J. Jansz, & P. van Drunen (Eds.), *A social history of psychology* (pp. 12–44). Oxford: Blackwell.

Kenneson, C. (1998). *Musical prodigies: Perilous journeys, remarkable lives.* Portland, OR: Amadeus Press.

Kopiez, R. (1997). 'Singers are late beginners': Sängerbiographien aus Sicht der Expertiseforschung. Eine Schwachstellenanalyse sängerischer Ausbildungsverläufe ['Singers are late beginners': Singer biographies from the perspective of expertise theory. An analysis of weak points in singers' training histories]. In H. Gembris, R.-D. Kraemer, & G. Maas (Eds.), *Musikpädagogische Forschungsberichte 1996* (pp. 37–56). Augsburg: Wissner.

Kopiez, R., Lehmann, A. C., & Klassen, J. (2009). Clara Schumann's collection of playbills: A historiometric analysis of life-span development, mobility, and repertoire canonization. *Poetics, 37*(1), 50–73.

Krause, P. (1996). Leipzig/7. Musikverlage und Musikzeitschriften. In L. Finscher (Ed.), *Die Musik in Geschichte und Gegenwart [Music in history and present]* (2nd ed.), Vol. 5, Sachteil (pp. 1063–1064). Kassel: Bärenreiter.

Lehmann, A. C. (2006). Historical increases in expert music performance skills: Optimizing instruments, playing techniques, and training. In E. Altenmüller, M. Wiesendanger, & J. Kesselring (Eds.), *Music, motor control and the brain* (pp. 3–24). Oxford: Oxford University Press.

Lehmann, A., & Ericsson, K. A. (1998). Historical developments of expert performance: Public performance of music. In A. Steptoe (Ed.), *Genius and the mind. Studies of creativity and temperament* (pp. 67–96). Oxford: Oxford University Press.

McPherson, G. E., & Davidson, J. W. (2006). Playing an instrument. In G. E. McPherson (Ed.), *The child as musician: A handbook of musical development* (pp. 331–351). New York, NY: Oxford University Press.

McPherson, G E., & Williamon, A. (2006). Giftedness and talent. In G. E. McPherson (Ed.), *The child as musician: A handbook of musical development* (pp. 239–256). New York, NY: Oxford University Press.

Miller, L. K. (1989). *Musical savants. Exceptional skill in the mentally retarded.* Hillsdale, NJ: Lawrence Erlbaum.

O'Neill, S. A. (1997). Gender and music. In D. J. Hargreaves, & A. North, C. (Eds.), *The social psychology of music* (pp. 46–63). Oxford: Oxford University Press.

Ockelford, A. (2008). *In the key of genius. The extraordinary life of Derek Paravicini.* London: Hutchinson.

Pearsall, J. (1999). *Concise Oxford dictionary* (10th ed.). New York, NY: Oxford University Press.

Révész, G. (1916). *Erwin Nyiregyházi: Psychologische Analyse eines musikalische hervorragenden Kindes [The psychology of a musical child prodigy].* Leipzig: von Veit.

Scheuer, W. (1988). *Zwischen Tradition und Trend. Die Einstellung Jugendlicher zum Instrumentalspiel. Eine empirische Untersuchung [Between tradition and trend. Attitudes of adolescents towards playing an instrument. An empirical investigation].* Mainz: Schott.

Simonton, D. K. (1990). *Psychology, science, and history: An introduction to historiometry.* New Haven, CT: Yale University Press.

Sloboda, J. A. (1991). Musical expertise. In K. A. Ericsson, & J. Smith (Eds.), *Toward a general theory of expertise. Prospects and limits* (pp. 153–171). Cambridge: Cambridge University Press.

Sloboda, J. A. (2005). *Exploring the musical mind*. New York, NY: Oxford University Press.

Sloboda, J. A., Davidson, J. W., Howe, M. J. A., & Moore, D. G. (1996). The role of practice in the development of performing musicians. *British Journal of Psychology, 87*(2), 287–309.

Sloboda, J. A., Hermelin, N., & O'Connor, N. (1985). An exceptional musical memory. *Music Perception,* 3(2), 155–169.

Stevens, G.-H. (1982). *Das Wunderkind in der Musikgeschichte [The Wunderkind in the history of music]*. Doctoral dissertation, University of Münster, Germany.

Walker, A., Eckart, M., & Mueller, R. C. (2008). *Liszt, Franz*. Grove Music. Available at: www.oxfordmusiconline.com (accessed 29 December 2008).

Winner, E. (1996). *Gifted children*. New York, NY: Basic Books.

Wolff, P. (2006). Kein Wunder! [No miracle!]. *Süddeutsche Zeitung Magazin – SZ Wissen, 9,* 57–59.

Chapter 13

Another exceptional musical memory: evidence from a savant of how atonal music is processed in cognition

Adam Ockelford

Abstract

This chapter builds on the empirical work reported by Sloboda, Hermelin, and O'Connor in 1985, in which a musical savant ('NP') attempted to learn a tonal piece by Grieg and a whole-tone composition by Bartôk. NP's error rate was 8% in the former and 63% in the latter, suggesting his ability to reproduce music (at least in the short term) was confined to tonal music and was structurally based. In the current study, a second savant ('DP'), publicly renowned for his capacity for reproducing many thousands of pieces from memory, attempted to learn an atonal piece by Schoenberg and a specially composed tonal 'equivalent', which as far as possible matched the original in terms of global structure, number of notes, frequency of occurrence of melodic intervals, density, and rhythmic complexity. The results showed that DP too, despite having absolute pitch and the ability to disaggregate simultaneous clusters of four pitches with 100% accuracy, found the atonal music more difficult to memorize than the tonal. Indeed, he imposed conventional structures on the Schoenberg piece, altering pitches so they fitted within a quasi-tonal framework. The implications for DP's creativity are discussed, and the potential contribution of the findings to the ongoing debate on the place of 'compositional' and 'listening' grammars in the musical experience.

I first met John Sloboda in 1988 at a conference in Reading organized by the then Society for Research in Psychology of Music and Music Education (now known rather more succinctly as SEMPRE[1]). I was presenting a paper concerning the music education of blind children, including those with intellectual impairments, an enterprise in which I was joined by my pupil, Derek Paravicini, a prodigious musical savant. Today, Derek's exceptional pianistic talents in the context of his severe learning difficulties are internationally recognized, but at the time he was just 9 years old and attended a special school in London where I was the music teacher (see Ockelford, 2007a).

One of the most important frames of reference for my presentation was John's seminal paper, 'An exceptional musical memory', written with Beate Hermelin and Neil O'Connor, which had recently appeared in *Music Perception* (Sloboda, Hermelin, & O'Connor, 1985). This gave an account of research in which a musical savant ('NP') attempted to learn a 'tonal' piece by Grieg (the *Melodie*, from his collection of *Lyric Pieces*, op. 47, no. 3, for piano) and a so-called 'atonal' composition by Bartók (the *Whole-Tone Scale* from *Mikrokosmos*, Book 5). Overall, NP's error rate was 8% in the former and 63% in the latter, which was taken to suggest that his ability to reproduce music (at least in the short term) was confined to 'tonal' pieces and was therefore 'structurally based' (1985, p. 166).

Replications of the experiment with other savants subsequently produced rather different results, however. For example, Leon Miller's study of Eddie, a young, visually impaired, learning disabled pianist, revealed an accuracy in reproduction over five trials of 72% for the Grieg and 37% for the Bartók.[2] Miller observes that, for Eddie, 'the whole-tone piece clearly was a novel and interesting challenge. At the first trial he began experimenting with the pattern of intervals it contained. In later sessions with his teacher the complete piece was taught to him and it became part of his active repertoire' (1989, pp. 145–6). Miller concluded that 'the present results suggest savant skill or interest is by no means restricted to the traditional diatonic scale' (1989, pp. 145–6).

The difference in the fidelity with which the two pieces were reproduced was even less marked in the case of a high functioning autistic savant ('TR'), who was studied by Robyn Young and Ted Nettelbeck. TR is said to have replicated the Grieg almost perfectly, with the preservation of melody and harmony, although on occasion melodic embellishments were omitted and different inversions of chords were substituted (Young and Nettelbeck, 1995, p. 242). TR's exceptional abilities were similarly in evidence in his reproduction of the Bartók: although, like NP and Eddie, he is reported to have found the piece more difficult than Grieg's *Melodie*, he made relatively few errors, and these were 'predominantly due to the interpolation of material consistent with the whole-tone scale' (1995, p. 242).

Theoretical assumptions

To interpret and understand these differing results we need to unpack some of the key assumptions underlying Sloboda and colleagues' original research. We begin with the belief that expertise (exemplified in this case by successful learning and recall) requires 'structural knowledge' (1985, p. 158). But what *is* musical structure, what form does 'music-structural knowledge' take, and why should it aid memory?

It has long been acknowledged in a wide range of musicological literatures—from the celebrated early twentieth-century *Harmonielehre* of Heinrich Schenker (1906) and Arnold Schoenberg (1911), for example, to the influential texts on music and meaning formulated by Leonard Meyer (1956, 1967, 1973) and the innovative, mathematically inspired thinking of David Lewin (1987)—that structure equates to *patterns* in sound, to *regularities* in the perceived sonic fabric. From a psychological standpoint, these are thought to facilitate the processing of perceptual information by enabling it to be encoded parsimoniously, thereby making fewer demands on data storage and retrieval: see, for example, Simon and Sumner (1968), Deutsch (1980), Deutsch and Feroe (1981), and Lerdahl and Jackendoff (1983, p. 52).

My own position, developed over the past two decades or so and conceptualized as 'zygonic' theory (for instance, Ockelford, 1991, 1999, 2002, 2004, 2005a, 2005b, 2006a, 2009, 2010a), is that all the diverse guises in which musical structure appears, whether melodic or harmonic, rhythmic or metric, motivic or thematic, tonal or textural, formal or processive, hierarchic or architectonic … stem from one common principle: *imitation*. This in turn implies the potential repetition (exact or approximate) of all the perceived aspects of musical sound: notes, intervals, chords, and keys; durations, interonset intervals, accents, and metres; and timbres, dynamics, modes of articulation, and textures. Analysis shows that, in Western classical music, at least, over 40 forms of repetition may be in operation at any one time, functioning in an integrated way, variously reinforcing or complementing one another, or even jockeying with each other for perceptual supremacy (Ockelford, 1999, pp. 704–761; 2010a, pp. 106–129).

As far as their impact on memory is concerned, I believe it is helpful to think of these manifestations of structure as being at the level of *events*, *groups*, or *frameworks* (cf. Ockelford, 2008a, pp. 99–102). In relation to Bartôk's *Whole-Tone Scale*, an example of structure pertaining to events is to be found at bar 3, where successive notes that constitute the top line are separated in terms of pitch by a common interval (the major 2nd, or 'whole-tone') and in the context of perceived time by an interonset interval of a quaver (equating to a little over a quarter of a second at the tempo marked). This arrangement can be interpreted zygonically and represented visually as shown in Figure 13.1. The three 'primary interperspective relationships' of *pitch* ('primary' since they are at the level adjacent to the perceptual surface and 'interperspective' since they exist between *perceived aspects* of sound) are shown linking successive notes (D, E, F$^\sharp$, and G$^\sharp$). Zygonic theory hypothesises that the cognitive acknowledgement of this pitch structure occurs through the (typically non-conscious) mental formulation of 'secondary zygonic relationships', which reflect the fact that the second primary relationship is a repetition of the first, and that the third repeats the second. A corresponding series of relationships is assumed to unfold in relation to the *onsets* of the notes. Analysis suggests that recognition of this coordinated pitch-time structure offers an advantage to memory over the 'raw' data of 25%, since in each domain, four perceptual values can be encoded as a single primary relationship and two secondaries.

An example of structure relating to groups, which can be interpreted as zygonic relationships of rhythm and 'profile'[3] operating in parallel, is to be found in bars 1 and 5 of *Whole-Tone Scale* (see Figure 13.2). Here the implied advantage to memory is 50%.

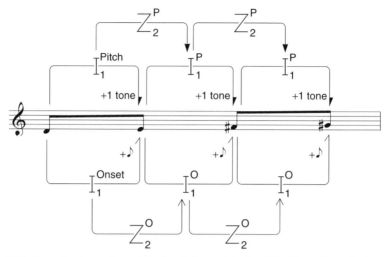

Fig. 13.1 Example of structure at the level of *events* in Bartók's *Whole-Tone Scale*.

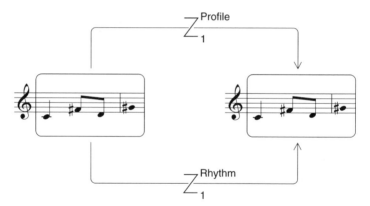

Fig. 13.2 Example of structure at the level of *groups*.

Finally, an example of structure pertaining to a framework is to be found in bars 13 and 14 of *Whole-Tone Scale*. The equidistant pentatonic substructure that is established in the opening six bars and reaffirmed in bars 7–12 appears again in bar 13, simultaneously at two new pitch levels (see Figure 13.3). Frameworks such as this enable pitches not only to be encoded as qualia in their own right and as the intervals between them, but also in a more abstract way—metaphorically, as rungs on a ladder. These may either be gauged successively in relative terms (whereby the contour in the right hand (RH) of bars 13 and 14 would be represented as +1, +1, +1, −1, −1, −1, for instance) or in relation to a perceptually predominant 'rung', which, in the passage in question, is likely to be the G$^\flat$ (as it is emphasized through being sustained), yielding the following series of values: 0, +1, +2, +3, +2, +1, 0.

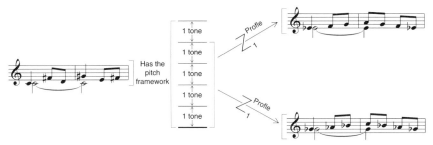

Fig. 13.3 Example of structure at the level of *frameworks*.

Although the symmetry of the whole-tone scale means that neither of these representations confers a processing advantage over those that deal more directly in the pitches and the intervals between them (see Figure 13.1), they nonetheless offer another perceptual dimension to the stimuli and offer distinct routes to codifying their underlying structure. And it seems likely that what may be termed music's 'structural multidimensionality' is an asset to the would-be memorizer: research reaching right back to Pollack and Ficks (1954) (discussed in Miller, 1956) suggests that multidimensional auditory percepts, which are richer in information than those that vary in one dimension, offer more for the mind to seize on. One can hypothesize that independent qualities pertaining to a single event mutually reinforce each other in recall and enable cross-domain assumptions to be made to fill the lacunae that may occur as traces decay.

Turning to Grieg's *Melodie*, for example, the structure underlying the three-note descent—fifth-octave F, E, D—that occurs in the RH at bar 10, can be heard at the level of events as a semi-regular descending pattern (a minor 2nd followed by a major 2nd); at the level of groups as an exact transposition of the figure comprising the melody in the second half of bar 2 (and a tonal reproduction of the comparable motives found in bars 4 and 6); and at the level of frameworks as a repeated stepwise descent, functioning as the mediant, supertonic, and tonic scale-steps in D minor,[4] as well as fulfilling the harmonic roles of the third, ninth, and root with respect to the accompanying chord (a replication of the functions and roles found in the second half of bar 2). Zygonically, these parallel structures may be represented as shown in Figure 13.4. As we shall see, evidence of just which structures are cognitively acknowledged and remembered may be provided by the nature and pattern of errors made in recall: some structures may be preserved, whereas others may be transformed, disregarded, or even replaced by forms of organization that were not originally present.

Another important factor in musical memory that was implicated in the design of Sloboda and colleagues' (1985) experiment was that current perceptual input has the capacity to reactivate similar materials that are held in a long-term store: one of their aims was to ascertain whether NP would be able to remember music utilizing *familiar* structures better than a piece that used forms of organization that were *less familiar* (1985, p. 158)—in particular the 'tonal' construction of the Grieg as opposed to the whole-tone make-up of the Bartók (1985, p. 165). That is to say, there was an underlying assumption that NP may have the ability to abstract the pitch framework of a passage by listening to it, and that this may revive memories of other, similar

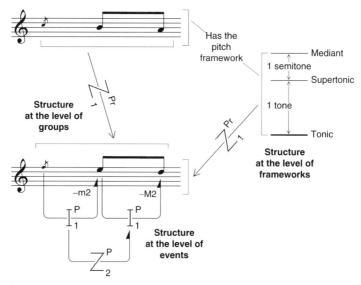

Fig. 13.4 Example of structures at the level of *events*, *groups*, and *frameworks* operating together in a fragment of Grieg's *Melodie*.

(or even identical) frameworks that had been abstracted from pieces in the past. In the case of 'tonal' frameworks, it is worth noting that these would comprise more than a neutral intervallic schema, also capturing their idiosyncratic patterns of use, yielding a context-sensitive matrix of probabilities that are realized in cognition as the distinct tendencies associated with different members of the diatonic scale (Huron, 2006). Bharucha (1987) contrasts these so-called 'schematic' memories with 'veridical' traces: long-term representations of particular groups of sounds.

Hence it is possible to model the interaction of short-term and long-term memory with the three forms of structure identified above (pertaining to events, groups, and frameworks) as shown in Figure 13.5. Note that this bears a close resemblance to the routes through which I hypothesize that expectation in music can occur (Ockelford, 2006a, p. 127).

Finally, in this introductory presentation of theories and concepts that potentially have a bearing on our understanding of musical memory, it is beneficial to consider the three forms of structure in relation to the *creation* and *cognition* of music; comparable with what Fred Lerdahl refers to as 'compositional' and 'listening' grammars (1988). It is quite possible that some of the structures employed by composers will not be recognized by listeners (Figure 13.6). Conversely, it is conceivable that listeners (attending with an music-analytical mindset) may identify structures that composers did not intentionally use. And there may be what Lerdahl (1988) refers to as 'natural' grammars at work, of which neither listeners nor composers are consciously aware. Because, as we have seen, music is structurally multidimensional, the experiences of composers and listeners that differ with respect to the forms of organization that are detected may both still be coherent (and, we may surmise, aesthetically fulfilling)—see

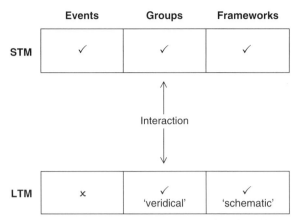

Fig. 13.5 Model of the interaction of short-term memory (STM) and long-term memory (LTM) taking into account structures at the level of *events*, *groups*, and *frameworks*.

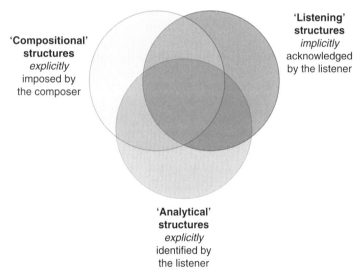

Fig. 13.6 Representation of the relationship between the cognition of 'listening', 'compositional' and 'analytical' structures.

Ockelford, 2009, p. 86–88. Occasionally, as we shall see, a compositional grammar and a listener's perception of it may conflict, and, through a failure of accommodation, may be misremembered and, consequently, produce systematic errors in recall.

To summarize, musical structure facilitates memory by enabling information to be encoded parsimoniously. It can occur at the level of events, groups, and frameworks. This may be captured in *short-term* or *long-term* memory, which interact in the dynamic process of remembering. Music is typically *structurally multidimensional*, which means that pieces can validly be heard and remembered in different ways. However, errors in recall may be an indication of a listener's constraints (or preferences) in music-structural cognition.

Revisiting the findings of Sloboda, Hermelin, and O'Connor (1985)

The theoretical assumptions made in the previous sections can be used to interrogate the results that Sloboda and colleagues obtained with NP, and to re-evaluate the conclusions they drew. First, in relation to *Whole-Tone Scale*, NP's relatively poor recall led the authors to contend that he 'needs to code material in terms of tonal structures and relations', and that his 'exceptional ability cannot at present survive outside that framework' (1985, p. 165). But is this view compatible with the hypotheses set out above? Consider NP's pattern of errors in his production of the Bartók. It appears that his grasp of the whole-tone pitch framework on which the piece is based was not actually an issue, since he adhered to it for the great majority of the time, only occasionally straying into quasi-diatonic territory (according to Miller, who re-analysed Sloboda *et al's.*, 1985 data).[5] Nor, apparently, did NP find encoding structure at the level of groups problematic, since the same melodic error was repeated 'frequently' (Sloboda *et al.*, 1985, p. 164), implying the preservation of form over content. In fact, it was at the level of events that NP evidently had difficulties: for example, 19 of the 34 mistakes that he made (56%) were due to melody notes being interchanged, with the commonest error being as shown in Figure 13.7.

What are we to make of this? Was the (oft repeated) mistake the product of more or less unpredictable 'noise' in cognition brought about by short-term memory overload, or was there perhaps something more systematic going on? Zygonic analysis of the opening of the melody of *Whole-Tone Scale* shows how deceptively complex the structure is. Despite the symmetry of the underlying intervallic framework, there is surprisingly little surface regularity in the domain of pitch as the music unfolds, with the potential presence of only two primary zygons out of a latent 21 relationships between the first seven notes (yielding a 'zygonicity' in this respect of only 0.095)[6]—see Figure 13.8. Moreover, these primary zygonic relationships of pitch function neither

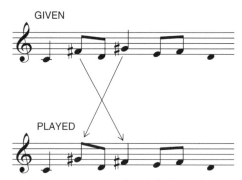

Fig. 13.7 NP's common 'interchange' error (after Sloboda *et al.*, 1985, p. 164). © 1985 by the Regents of the University of California. Published by the University of California Press.

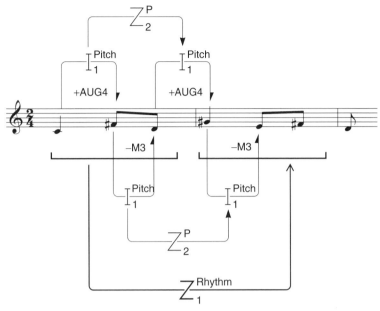

Fig. 13.8 Structures in the opening segment of *Whole-Tone Scale* in the domains of pitch and perceived time functioning out of step.

between successive nor metrically equivalent notes, reducing their likely structural impact. And while four of the six intervals between sequentially adjacent pitches can be considered to be linked through secondary zygonic relationships, again, these are not paralleled in the domain of perceived time. In fact, the initial rhythmic structure (in which the pattern of durations and interonset intervals in bar 1 is repeated in bar 2) runs *counter* to the organization of pitch. It seems probable that this asynchrony, which produces cross-domain structural conflict, may hinder processing and recall.

NP's rearrangement, incurred through the interchange of notes 2 and 4, creates a regular pitch descent and aligns it with the underlying crotchet beat, simplifying the structure in perceptual terms (see Figure 13.9). We can only speculate whether this modification was purely fortuitous or was brought about through an intuitive process of regularization (whereby qualia were transformed in cognition to form a more parsimoniously encodable pattern). The fact that NP repeated his 'error' suggests that his version was indeed more readily memorable than the original, though, as we have observed, recapitulating his mistake arguably enabled him to maintain structure at the thematic level.[7]

To reiterate, neither group- nor framework-level structures were significantly compromised in NP's recall. Hence, it appears *not* to be the case that NP needed to code music in terms of familiar 'tonal' structures. We will return to the issue of precisely what constitutes a 'tonal' structure shortly, since Sloboda *et al.*'s assertion that the Bartôk was 'atonal'—a core assumption in the design of their experiment—is problematic.

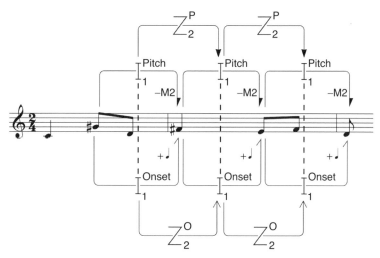

Fig. 13.9 In NP's version, structures in the domains of pitch and perceived time run in parallel.

But first, we need to answer the question of *why* NP's performance in relation to Grieg's *Melodie* (and, indeed, those of the other savants) was better than their efforts to recall Bartók's *Whole-Tone Scale*, if comprehension of its pitch framework was not an issue.

Again, we will approach this problem by examining the structure of the *Melodie* in some detail: once more, in relation to the first seven melodic events, since these set the scene for what follows, introducing the material from which the remainder of the work grows. Here there are three potential primary zygons of pitch (see Figure 13.10) (yielding a zygonicity of 0.143), but, unlike the *Whole-Tone Scale*, their structural significance is underlined by sequential adjacency (in the case of the opening three Cs) or perceptual affinity (in the case of the two Bs, since the A interpolated between them, although consonant with the underlying harmony, has the effect of prolonging[8] the first B). With regard to melodic intervals, five can be considered to be subject to secondary zygonic influence, on each occasion between *successive* notes. Hence we may surmise that they are likely to be aurally prominent, despite the fact that only one of the secondary pitch zygons functions in parallel with comparable repetition in the domain of perceived time (in the second half of bar 2, involving the three quavers, B, A, B). Finally, it is important to note that this melodic structure, tightly integrated across the dimensions of pitch and perceived time, unfolds atop a highly repetitive harmonic background (zygonicity 0.75).

Given this level of structural coherence, which, through motivic and thematic repetition and development subsequently pervades the entire piece, it is, perhaps, little wonder that NP appeared to have few problems in reproducing Grieg's *Melodie* with a high degree of accuracy:[9] by trial 7, we are told, after about 12 minutes, and having heard no section of the piece more than four times, he 'provided an almost note-perfect performance' (Sloboda *et al.*, 1985, p. 160). Similarly, extrapolating from the data

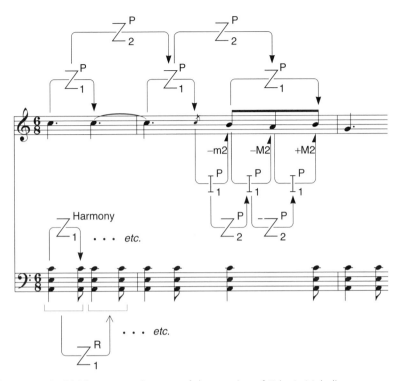

Fig. 13.10 The highly structured nature of the opening of Grieg's *Melodie*.

pertaining to Eddie's final attempts at each segment shows him achieving an accuracy (gauged through a note-matching paradigm) of 75% (Miller, 1989, p. 140). TR's recall was apparently even better.

> [He] was able to play the initial 7 bars of the Grieg after one hearing with only one incorrect note. This error (substituting a D for a B in bar 6) was, however, harmonically consistent. Three embellishments in bars 2, 4, and 6 were also omitted. He heard these seven bars 10 times in total because they repeated in bars 41–48 and, with the exception of one missed embellishment in the fourth reproduction of the second bar, his performance was perfect. In addition, rhythm was preserved and the melody was correctly reproduced throughout the performance, except that on one occasion he played different inversions of the written chord (i.e. he retained harmonic identity but not a literal rendition). (Young and Nettelbeck, 1995, p. 242.)

This detailed account of TR's very few errors enables us to infer that, in addition to encoding structure at the level of events, he was also parsing the music as groups (suggested by the consistent omission of embellishments in his first attempt at the opening 8 bars, since these all fulfil an equivalent function in transformations of a two-bar phrase) and frameworks (shown by his initial displacement of a note in the left hand (LH) of bar 6 by another that conformed to the harmony, and elsewhere by the use of different inversions of chords). Similarly, NP's errors were said to be 'overwhelmingly structure preserving' (Sloboda *et al.*, 1985, p. 165).

To conclude this review, we return to the notion of 'atonality', since although it is central to the design of the empirical work under investigation, there are apparent contradictions in what is reported. For example, Sloboda *et al.*, while designating the Bartók as 'atonal', assert that NP's interchange error (see Figure 13.9) shows that he 'coded these notes [the F♯ and the G♯] not with respect to their immediate neighbors but with respect to the initial C' (1985, p. 164). Yet hearing pitches in relation to a reference point in this way is a core characteristic of 'tonality', which, as we have observed, entails members of a pitch framework being assigned different functions that derive from a listener's (typically non-conscious) perception of idiosyncratic patterns of usage. In his *Whole-Tone Scale*, in which such assignation is potentially difficult because each step of the underlying framework is equal in size, Bartók starts by unambiguously 'tonicizing'[10] key notes in each phrase by sustaining them against the melody, whereby they act as perceptual 'anchors', from which the pentatonic runs do not stray. Moreover, these same anchor notes are initially used to begin and end melodies, reinforcing their prominence, and imbuing them with potentially cadential authority—the power at the end of phrases to make listeners sense closure, a key feature of pitches that act as tonics. It is important to acknowledge too that Bartók, despite some of his music subsequently being analysed in atonal terms, was opposed to the use of 'atonality', and regarded all his music as having a tonal foundation (Bartók, 1928/1976, p. 338). It is possible that the practice of thinking about his music in this way arose because of some theorists' *unfamiliarity* with the folk sources of many of Bartók's mature compositions, coupled with their failure to acknowledge that pitch frameworks from outside the 'mainstream' major/minor Western tradition could function tonally too.

To summarize, the *Whole-Tone Scale* is not atonal. Admittedly, it uses a pitch framework that is encountered less frequently in the West than the major and minor diatonic scale systems, and it is based on equally spaced intervals, but Bartók counters both of these potential obstacles to hearing the music tonally by tonicizing notes as the piece unfolds. It is worth reiterating that none of the three savants had problems in recalling this aspect of structure. Therefore, the premise that NP performed relatively poorly because the music was 'atonal' must be discounted. That does beg two questions, however:

♦ How would a savant perform if he or she did *not* pick up on the tonal pitch framework of a piece—if this feature of compositional grammar were not recognized?

♦ How would a savant perform in seeking to recall a piece that did *not* use a tonal pitch framework?

The theoretical thinking set out above suggests two possible outcomes:

♦ The lack of a tonal framework (or the failure to recognize one) will have a negative impact on memory since an important source of information about musical events—their perceived functionality in relation to one another—will be missing, making the perceptual input more impoverished and less easy to encode parsimoniously. This is likely to lead to short-term memory overload, with asystematic patterns of error at the level of events and groups.

◆ A tonal framework (or frameworks) will be *imposed*, more or less consistently, in order to 'make sense' of the music: that is, new material will be modified to facilitate assimilation. This is likely to be shown by the omission of values, or by their 'migration' at the level of events to conform to familiar structures, and through these errors being made consistently, at the level of groups.

Experiment 1

This set out to address the first question: namely, how would a savant perform if he or she did *not* pick up on the tonal pitch framework of a piece?

Subject

Derek Paravicini[11] agreed to participate in the research. For a number of reasons, Derek made a particularly suitable subject. He has an acute sense of absolute pitch (AP), which enables him to reproduce on the keyboard not only individual notes, but clusters of four pitches with 100% accuracy[12] (Ockelford, 2008a, pp. 218–225; Pring, 2008). Derek is a fluent pianist, so in music of moderate difficulty, considerations of technique do not typically corrupt or constrain his efforts to reproduce what he hears. He is thoroughly conversant with the natural grammars of what may be termed the Western musical 'vernacular', particularly the diatonic major and minor scale systems. Before the current research project, he had been exposed to little twentieth-century music that moves beyond these conventions, though, and he was not known to have attempted to play atonal music. Finally, Derek had taken part in memory trials before (see, for example, the reports in Ockelford, 2007b, 2008a; Ockelford & Pring, 2005), and was familiar with the 'listen and play' protocol. Here, he had shown himself to be patient, reliable, and motivated in research situations, applying himself diligently to the task in hand, and appearing to give of his best, even when tasks were repeated several times. However, then as now, Derek has a very low level of metacognitive ability, even in relation to music: for such an advanced performer, it is extraordinary how little his efforts appear to be informed by explicit knowledge. While this lack of conscious understanding can be regarded as an advantage in tasks intended to be undertaken intuitively (since they will not be contaminated by conceptual bias or volitional strategies), it means that virtually the *only* data that are available exist in the form of music, and that the primary form of analysis must be musicological. The extent to which information such as this can validly be used to infer features of music cognition is an important epistemological issue that is taken up elsewhere (Ockelford, 2008b) and below.

Material

Bartók's *Whole Tone Scale* was used as the source of material for this experiment since (1) it was highly unlikely that Derek would have encountered it through incidental exposure (and had he been familiar with the piece, this would quickly have become apparent), (2) it enabled comparisons with the studies by Sloboda *et al.*, Miller, and Young and Nettelbeck mentioned above, and (3) it was well-suited to test the first research question (which asked what would happen if the subject did *not* pick up on the tonal pitch framework of a piece). The reason for this is set out below.

Whole-Tone Scale was modified somewhat to bring it structurally into line at the level of groups with the pieces used in Experiment 2, so that comparisons could be made in relation to Derek's recall of each. This yielded five segments, disposed as follows. The opening 'A₁' (a shortened version of the original) was followed by the LH of bars 13–16 (B₁), after which came the RH of the same passage ('B₂'), then both these lines together, moving in parallel minor thirds ('B₃'). Finally, there followed a variant of the opening (also in thirds) derived from bars 10–12. This yielded the stimulus material showed in Figure 13.11.

The revised design of the middle segments (B₁, B₂, and B₃) was also intended to test Derek's strategies for dealing with unfamiliar pitch frameworks, for while B₁ and B₂ use pentatonic whole-tone scale systems in a readily identifiable way, the effect of their combination in B₃ is by no means perceptually straightforward. The frameworks are three semitones apart, giving the segment a 'sweet and sour' character: while the consonant sound of whole tones pervades the texture and there are no direct discords (i.e. dissonant pairs of notes that are struck at the same time), there are a number of

Fig. 13.11 The materials used in Experiment 1, adapted from Bartôk's *Whole-Tone Scale*.

implied semitonal clashes (for example, between G and G$^\flat$, and A and A$^\flat$). The simplest way of 'making sense' of this passage structurally as it unfolds is to allow the two melodic lines (and the frameworks that underpin them) to continue to exist as discrete entities in one's mind, as they did in B$_1$ and B$_2$. This appears to be what TR did: he is reported to have recognized the whole-tone scale system that lies at the heart of the Bartók as a *conceptual* entity (Young & Nettelbeck, 1995, p. 243), which, the authors hypothesize, helped him keep both parts in simultaneous passages intact even though their underlying pitch frameworks were at an interval of transposition (three semitones) that made them mutually incompatible (1995, p. 242).[13] However, there is something intoxicating about their combined effect, and informal discussion with a range of listeners suggests that the ear can easily be drawn into hearing the two parallel strands as one sonority, with a complex and unconventional pitch framework comprising (in ascending order) a tone, five semitones, and a further tone. As far as Derek was concerned, there seemed to be a strong possibility that this 'vertically integrated' style of listening would be the one that he would adopt, particularly given his tendency to hear contrapuntal music (made up of separate 'horizontal' strands) largely homophonically (as a series of harmonies)—shown through his previous reproductions of Bach fugues, for example, which preserve chordal sequences though not necessarily individual lines.

So, according to the two outcomes predicted above, since segment B$_3$ comprises 13 events (which previous observation had suggested would be beyond the span of Derek's short-term memory), and has semitonal conflicts to one adopting a homophonic listening style (which may interfere with efforts to code events at the primary zygonic level), it was likely that he would *either* make asystematic errors *or* impose a background structure to bring the material within a familiar diatonic framework. In the second of these scenarios, the most likely contender would seem to be E$^\flat$ minor, given the tonicizing effect of the sustained E$^\flat$ at the bottom the texture, the sustained G$^\flat$ above it, and the conformance of six of the eight pitches in the segment (75%) to this key (E$^\flat$, F, G$^\flat$, A$^\flat$, and B$^\flat$ and C). E$^\flat$ major would appear to be a second option, also bearing 75% conformance (E$^\flat$, F, G, A$^\flat$, and B$^\flat$ and C) and with possibility of the G$^\flat$ and A$^\flat$ treated as chromatic auxiliaries (or errors)—see Figure 13.12.

Procedure

The task of attempting to memorize the revised Bartók was undertaken by Derek as part of a day's other musical activities, including recording familiar repertoire and performing with a singer (a broadly typical schedule for him). I had previously recorded the materials using a Yamaha digital stage piano, feeding MIDI data through an RME Fireface to an Apple MacBook Pro running Cakewalk's SONAR 6 (Producer Edition). Verification was achieved by subsequently notating the data via Sibelius 5.

The session was organized as shown in Table 13.1.

Derek's responses were recorded on video and back through the same MIDI system (in unquantized form), which meant that the rhythms needed 'tidying up' to accord with conventional notation. Generally, Derek's efforts were unambiguous in this respect. Occasionally, though, there were hesitations (uncharacteristic of his playing) and wherever these occurred, they are marked on the transcriptions that follow, and their potential significance is discussed below.

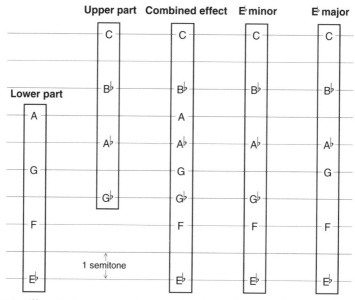

Fig. 13.12 Different whole-tone scales operating in parallel approximate to fragments of major and minor scales.

Table 13.1 Experiment 1: session organization

Listen to the whole 'piece' through	(2×)
Listen to first segment and then play	(4×)
Listen to second segment and then play	(4×)
Listen to third segment and then play	(4×)
Listen to fourth segment and then play	(4×)
Listen to fifth segment and then play	(4×)
Listen to whole 'piece' and then play	(2×)

The chunks were designed to be of such length and complexity as to lie just beyond Derek's observed short-term memory capacity (see above), so that he would be likely to make some errors (that would give a fair indication of his coding strategies and their limitations), but not so many as to preclude meaningful analysis. (Attempting to recall the whole 'piece' would occur only after it had been heard all through three times and each of its five segments had been played four times.) The replications within the experiment meant it would be possible to observe how Derek's recall evolved in the short term with repeated stimuli. Previous work (in which Derek had learnt a specially composed piece called the *Chromatic Blues*—see Ockelford, 2007b, 2008a, pp. 225–244; Ockelford & Pring, 2005) had shown that Derek's initial attempt to reproduce a passage became for him the most potent trace, even when the original was played again, and that the most substantial improvements occurred through the recruitment of long-term memory.

Results

The results are transcribed in Figure 13.13.

Analysis and discussion

The extent to which Derek's efforts at recall were derived from the original material and the influence of his errors on subsequent trials are charted quantitatively below (see the analysis pertaining to Experiment 2). However, the key findings in relation to

Fig. 13.13 Transcription of Derek's responses to the *Whole-Tone Scale* materials.

Fig. 13.13 (*Continued*) Transcription of Derek's responses to the *Whole-Tone Scale* materials.

the current question of the consequences of Derek recognizing, or failing to recognize, the tonal pitch framework of a piece are as follows:

◆ Without exception, Derek's recall of segments 1–3 conformed to the whole-tone pentatonic scale utilized in each (although pitch structure at the level of events had an average error rate of 30%). Moreover, the sense of a tonic was consistently maintained, with responses invariably beginning and ending on the same note, in the manner of the original segments. Indeed, on two occasions these tonics were doubled at the lower octave, perceptually reinforcing their anchoring effect. Clearly, then, in these excerpts, Derek had no problem in encoding structure at the level of frameworks, despite surface detail being misremembered.[14]

◆ In the fourth segment, however, which, as we have seen, is founded on two different whole-tone scale systems functioning simultaneously (implying a form of bitonality), Derek's responses were materially different. On only one occasion, in the lower melodic strand of Trial 2, did he adhere to the original pitch framework

Fig. 13.13 Cont'd

of a line (and even here, the top part was changed). In every other case, events were selectively modified, in accordance with Prediction 2, to conform to the scale systems of either E♭ major or E♭ minor, as Derek struggled to reconcile the novel material that he was hearing with pitch frameworks whose principles of operation were familiar to him and that he found comprehensible. His indecision becomes audible—discomforting, even—in Trial 3, as he vacillates between the major and minor modes, with no convincing resolution. Subsequent comments (unusual for him—see note 19) indicate that he was aware that what he had produced had significant errors, but (unlike TR) he lacked the conceptual understanding that would have enabled him to divide the perceptual surface into two transpositionally equivalent halves, so facilitating the cognition of the underlying pitch structure. In the absence of such a strategy, the capacity of his short-term memory was evidently exceeded, and his efforts at recall represent the uncomfortable compromise that he had to make between the forces of assimilation and accommodation.

◆ Segment 5 also adopts a bitonal approach, but here, because each line uses five successive pitches from the whole-tone scale (rather than the four found in the previous segment), reconciliation with the conventional major and minor modes is more problematic, and Derek did not attempt it. Rather, he regularized structure at the level of events by recalling the whole-tone quaver pairs from Trials 2, 3, and 4 of Segment 1 and allowing the pentatonic scale in the top part to predominate, which was reproduced with an average 29% errors, and only once straying from the given pitch framework (see the hesitation in Trial 4). The lower part was remembered far less consistently, though, with an average error rate of 62%, and frequent departures from the original pentatonic scale system. Furthermore, there was an average 40% difference in the domain of pitch between the lower part of each of Derek's reproductions of Segment 5. This outcome accords with Prediction 1, which hypothesized that, where pitch frameworks failed to be recognized, a likely consequence would be the overload of short-term memory, with asystematic patterns of error at the level of events and groups.

In summary, then, these findings indicate that when a compositional grammar is employed that Derek cannot detect, he either imposes a familiar framework upon the material, employing systematic migration at the level of events, or struggles to manage the perceptual load, resulting in erratic errors at all structural levels. What happens to such data in longer-term recall was one of the issues explored in Experiment 2.

Experiment 2

This set out to address the second research question: namely, how would a savant perform in seeking to recall a piece that did *not* use a tonal pitch framework?

Subject

Derek Paravicini again agreed to participate.

Material

A musically self-contained section of an authentic piece of 'atonal' music was selected—the opening 11 bars of Schoenberg's *Klavierstück*, op. 11, no. 1 (see Figure 13.14)—which were deemed to be of sufficient length and complexity to demonstrate the principles involved and yet be of a level of difficulty that would not impair Derek's capacity to play back immediately what he had heard (so that issues of performability would not interfere with the results). The Yale music theorist Allen Forte once described op. 11, no. 1 as 'Schoenberg's first atonal masterpiece'[15] and dubbed it the *Magical Kaleidoscope* on account of what he believed to be its cellular (rather than tonal) pitch structure (1981).[16] This was the title given to the piece (which necessarily had to be distinct and memorable) in working with Derek. As well as having no sense of being rooted in a particular key, a consistent sense of metre is elusive in op. 11, no. 1 too (the written time signature of 3/4 notwithstanding): informal evidence suggests that listeners attending without the benefit of a score find it difficult to identify a regular hierarchy of pulses. This can be attributed in part to the frequent absence of material on the first

Fig. 13.14 Opening of Schoenberg's *Klavierstück*, op. 11, no. 1, known as the *Magical Kaleidoscope*.

beat of the bar (four out of the 11 downbeats are silent) and partly to the way in which similar sonorities shift subtly in relation to the beat in bars 4–8. Hence the ear is left 'floating' in the domains of pitch *and* perceived time, and one has the feeling that Schoenberg was seeking to free himself from traditional constraints in *both* dimensions (cf. Rochberg, 2004, p. 95). In relation to the current empirical work, the ametrical nature of op. 11 meant that there was a possibility that the predictions made in relation to Derek's recall of pitch may apply in the domain of perceived time too, and, although this issue is not central to the research questions addressed here, the nature of Derek's *rhythmic* errors are of interest, and will also be reported, with the hope of stimulating future lines of enquiry.

A further, tonal and unambiguously metrical, passage was required for the purposes of comparison. However, given the possible confusion of results pertaining to a subject's recollection of the pitch and metrical frameworks of a piece with other aspects of its structure operating at the level of events and groups (as observed in NP's recall of Bartók's *Whole-Tone Scale*), it was necessary to create stimulus material that differed structurally from op. 11, no. 1 only with respect to offering a sense of tonality and a clear impression of metre. This was achieved through using a zygonic music-theoretical approach to inform the creation of the new piece, with the results described below. There were other constraints, of a more practical nature, too: it was essential that the music should bear no thematic resemblance to existing works, for example, and technically it needed to be well within Derek's grasp. And it had to have a memorable title, distinct from the *Magical Kaleidoscope* (*MK*); the name chosen was *Kooky Minuet* (*KM*)—see Figure 13.15.[17]

Comparative analyses of the *MK* and *KM* show just how similar they are in many structural dimensions, despite the considerable perceptual difference engendered by the presence of consistent tonal relationships in *KM*. At the level of groups, for example, both pieces are couched in the same variety of ternary form with five segments (A_1 B_1 B_2 B_3 A_2), in which the middle ('B') section has three iterations (produced largely through rhythmic variation) and the initial ('A') section is modified somewhat on its reprise at the end of the passage. Both *MK* and *KM* have the same number of notes per segment, respectively 13, 11, 11, 13, and 13, a total of 61. These events extend over 45 seconds in the performance of *MK* that Derek heard and 40 seconds in the case *KM*.

Fig. 13.15 Specially composed tonal equivalent of Schoenberg's op. 11, no.1, known as the *Kooky Minuet*.

At the level of events, the moment-to-moment structure of *KM* necessarily differed somewhat from that of *MK*, since it is the nature of transitions between successive pitches, the disposition of simultaneities and, more broadly, the context-sensitive frequencies of occurrence of relative values, upon which a sense of tonality is founded. However, given the aim of trying to ensure that both passages would be equally memorable at the level of events, it was important that the overall *degree of structure* present should be maintained, segment by segment. That is to say, the set of relative pitches used in comparable segments of *MK* and *KM* should have equal zygonicity. This is achieved as shown by the data presented in Figure 13.16.

Even in terms of the more exacting mode of comparison that assesses the distribution of melodic intervals between *successive* notes, the similarity between *KM* and *MK*

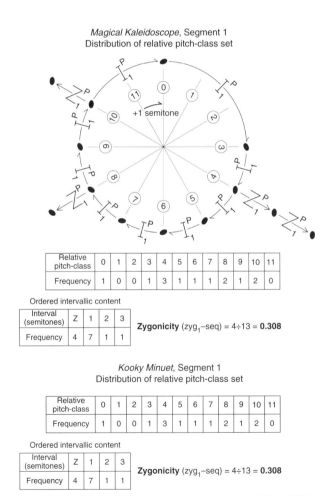

Magical Kaleidoscope, Segment 1
Distribution of relative pitch-class set

Relative pitch-class	0	1	2	3	4	5	6	7	8	9	10	11
Frequency	1	0	0	1	3	1	1	1	2	1	2	0

Ordered intervallic content

Interval (semitones)	Z	1	2	3
Frequency	4	7	1	1

Zygonicity $(\mathrm{zyg}_1\text{-seq}) = 4 \div 13 = \mathbf{0.308}$

Kooky Minuet, Segment 1
Distribution of relative pitch-class set

Relative pitch-class	0	1	2	3	4	5	6	7	8	9	10	11
Frequency	1	0	0	1	3	1	1	1	2	1	2	0

Ordered intervallic content

Interval (semitones)	Z	1	2	3
Frequency	4	7	1	1

Zygonicity $(\mathrm{zyg}_1\text{-seq}) = 4 \div 13 = \mathbf{0.308}$

Fig. 13.16 Comparisons of the relative pitch-class sets used in *MK* and *KM*, segment by segment.

Magical Kaleidoscope, Segments 2 and 3
Kooky Minuet, Segments 2 and 3

Distributions of relative pitch-class sets

Relative pitch-class	0	1	2	3	4	5	6	7	8	9	10	11
Frequency	1	0	1	0	0	1	1	1	2	1	2	1

Ordered intervallic content

Interval (semitones)	Z	1	2	3
Frequency	2	6	3	0

Zygonicity (zyg$_1$–seq) = 2÷11 = **0.154**

Magical Kaleidoscope, Segment 4
Kooky Minuet, Segment 4

Distributions of relative pitch-class sets

Relative pitch-class	0	1	2	3	4	5	6	7	8	9	10	11
Frequency	1	0	1	0	1	1	1	1	2	2	2	1

Ordered intervallic content

Interval (semitones)	Z	1	2	3
Frequency	3	8	2	0

Zygonicity (zyg$_1$–seq) = 3÷13 = **0.231**

Magical Kaleidoscope, Segment 5
Kooky Minuet, Segment 5

Distributions of relative pitch-class sets

Relative pitch-class	0	1	2	3	4	5	6	7	8	9	10	11
Frequency	1	0	1	0	1	1	2	1	2	1	2	1

Ordered intervallic content

Interval (semitones)	Z	1	2	3
Frequency	3	8	2	0

Zygonicity (zyg$_1$–seq) = 3÷13 = **0.231**

Fig. 13.16 (*Continued*) Comparisons of the relative pitch-class sets used in *MK* and *KM*, segment by segment.

is still high, at 78%,[18] with the majority of intervals being four semitones or smaller: over 90% in each case. Moreover, the *range* of both pieces is identical—two octaves and five semitones—and sets of the pitch-classes (pcs) are virtually identical (*KM* uses all 12 pcs, whereas *MK* omits E^b; see Ockelford, 2005a, p. 115). It is in the domain of *harmonic* intervals that the main difference in the domain of pitch is to be found (unsurprisingly, as certain intervals and combinations thereof evoke percepts that are strongly associated with conventional Western tonality). Here the distributions are only 56% similar. Observe, in particular, the variation in the numbers of intervals comprising three semitones (equivalent to a minor 3rd), four semitones (a major 3rd) and seven semitones (a perfect 5th)—constituents of diatonic triads, and one semitone (a minor 2nd) and 11 semitones (a major 7th)—astringent discords in Figure 13.17.

In the domain of perceived time, there are important similarities too—as well as some key differences. The distributions of relative durations used are 72% similar (Figure 13.18). More significant, perhaps, in perceptual terms, are the distributions of interonset intervals (expressed as ratios) between successive notes, which have a similarity of 78%. Observe also that the average *density* of each stimulus (in terms of the number of simultaneous notes per event) is very similar.

However, a crucial aspect of rhythm is the 'relative metrical location' ('RML') of events (that is, their position in relation to the prevailing metre; see Ockelford, 2006a, p. 133), and here, there are notable differences between *MK* and *KM*. For example, only 64% of the first beat 'slots' in *MK* are filled with the onsets of notes, as opposed to 100% in *KM*, and the RMLs of the first notes of the 'B' segments in *MK* are different in each case, whereas in *KM* they are the same (see comments above). Hence there is a far stronger sense of metre functioning in *KM* than *MK*. (See Figure 13.19.)

In summary, then, the substantive difference between the passages is that the structure pertaining to the pitch and perceived temporal frameworks that are used engender in one case (*KM*) a clear sense of tonality and a strong impression of metre, and in the other (*MK*) do not. That is, in *KM*, it was hypothesized that Derek would be able to gauge events *functionally* in relation to others, whereas in *MK*, he would not. It was anticipated that this would lead him either to experience overload in short-term memory, resulting in frequent and asystematic errors, or to *impose* frameworks on what he heard, leading to systematic inaccuracies in recall.

		Interval (semitones)	Z	1	2	3	4	5	6	7	8	9	10	11	12
Melodic	MK	Frequency	2	14	7	8	7	1	0	0	1	0	0	1	0
		Relative frequency	5%	44.5%	17.5%	20%	17%	2%	0%	0%	2%	0%	0%	2%	0%
	KM	Frequency	1	24	7	3	5	0	1	1	2	0	0	0	0
		Relative frequency	2%	55%	16%	7%	11.5%	0%	2.5%	2.5%	4.5%	0%	0%	0%	0%
Harmonic	MK	Frequency	0	5	3	4	9	4	7	0	3	5	6	4	1
		Relative frequency	0%	10%	6%	7.5%	17.5%	7.5%	14%	0%	6%	10%	12%	7.5%	2%
	KM	Frequency	0	1	15	1	4	7	6	2	6	3	0	1	0
		Relative frequency	0%	2%	33%	2%	9%	15%	13%	4.5%	13%	6.5%	0%	2%	0%

$$\text{Similarity (\%) } MK \text{ and } KM \text{ (melodic intervals)} = 100 - \Sigma \left(\frac{\Sigma \left| x_i - \left(\frac{\Sigma x_i}{x} \right) \right|}{x} \right) \%$$

$$= 78\%$$

$$\text{Similarity (\%) } MK \text{ and } KM \text{ (harmonic intervals)}$$
$$= 56\%$$

Fig. 13.17 Comparisons of the melodic and harmonic intervals used in *MK* and *KM*.

Interonset interval distribution matrices

Magical Kaleidoscope

	♪	♩	♩.	𝅗𝅥	𝅗𝅥𝅗𝅥.
♪	14	2	2	0	0
♩	0	2	4	2	0
♩.	2	1	2	0	0
𝅗𝅥	0	2	0	0	0
𝅗𝅥𝅗𝅥.	0	0	0	0	0

Kooky Minuet

	♪	♩	♩.	𝅗𝅥	𝅗𝅥𝅗𝅥.
♪	16	3	1	3	0
♩	4	7	2	4	0
♩.	2	1	0	0	0
𝅗𝅥	0	3	1	0	0
𝅗𝅥𝅗𝅥.	0	0	0	0	0

Interonset ratio distributions

	Interval (ratio)	1:1	1:2	1:3	1:4	2:1	2:3	3:1	3:2	4:3
MK	Frequency	28	4	2	0	2	4	2	1	0
MK	Relative frequency	65%	9.5%	4.5%	0%	4.5%	9.5%	4.5%	2.5%	0%
KM	Frequency	23	7	1	3	7	2	2	1	1
KM	Relative frequency	49%	15%	2%	6%	15%	4.5%	4.5%	2%	2%

Similarity (%) MK and KM (intervallic ratio)

= **78%**

Simultaneous notes per event

Density	1	2	3	4	
MK	18	15	5	21	Average density = 2.51
KM	14	4	23	6	Average density = 2.49

Fig. 13.18 Comparisons of the distributions of interonset intervals in *MK* and *KM*, and of chordal densities.

	RML	0.5	1	1.5	2	2.5	3	3.5
MK	Frequency	0	7	5	11	6	11	6
MK	Proportion of slots filled	0%	64%	45%	100%	55%	100%	45%
KM	Frequency	0	8	3	8	5	8	5
KM	Proportion of slots filled	0%	100%	38%	100%	63%	100%	63%

Fig. 13.19 Comparison of the distribution of events within metrical structures in *MK* and *KM*.

Procedure

As before, the memory tasks were undertaken by Derek as part of his usual schedule of learning, performing and recording. Although the *MK* and *MK* tests occurred on the same day, the work was undertaken in different sessions, and no interference was evident at the time or revealed in subsequent analysis (see below). I had previously recorded the materials and Derek reproduced them using the same equipment as in Experiment 1. Again, Derek's efforts were 'tidied up' rhythmically so as to make sense in notational terms; where rhythmic uncertainties occurred (such as hesitations) these were marked on the score; and the transcriptions were verified by a musician with no prior knowledge of the project.

Results

The results are transcribed in Figures 13.20 and 13.21.

Analysis and discussion

In the research undertaken previously by Sloboda *et al.*, Miller, and Nettelbeck and Young, different protocols were employed for measuring the fidelity of reproduction. Here, the notion of 'derivation', central to zygonic theory, is used to underpin the analyses that follow, since it arguably offers a more valid means of gauging how the

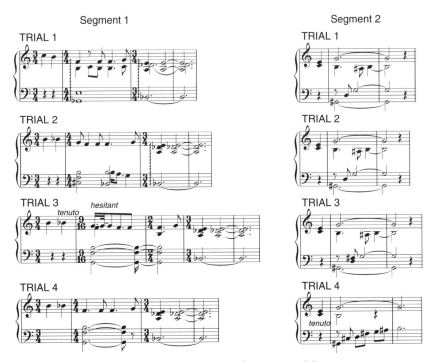

Fig. 13.20 Transcription of Derek's responses to the *MK* materials.

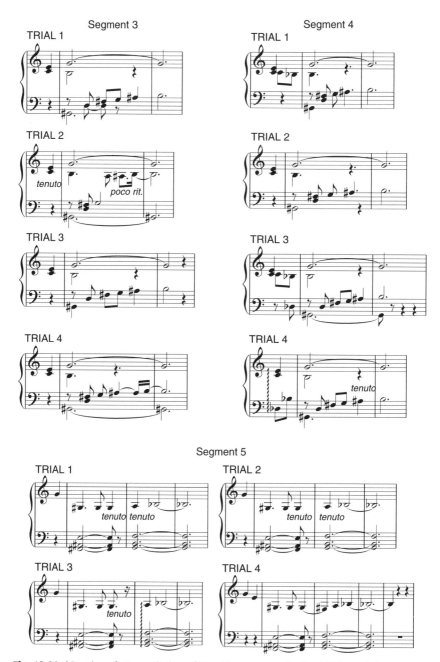

Fig. 13.20 (*Continued*) Transcription of Derek's responses to the *MK* Materials.

material that Derek reproduced was related to what he had heard than simple note-matching. This is because measures of similarity alone, particularly in cases where the error rate is high, run the risk both of 'false positives', since the constraints on music imposed by the use of frameworks in the domains of pitch and perceived time mean that there is a strong likelihood that some events or transitions will be the same by chance, and of 'false negatives', as even perceptually straightforward transformations, through which one group of notes may be regarded intuitively as deriving from another, may involve high levels of surface variety. Most importantly, though, it is the question of musical *derivation* rather than *similarity* that is the appropriate proxy through which we can interrogate and seek to understand matters of recall. Of course, similarity is an important element in the notion of derivation, but, as the potential for false positives and negatives shows, it does not make up the whole picture: as I argue elsewhere (Ockelford, 2004) *context*—and in particular, *salience*—is also crucial in gauging whether one musical object can reasonably be deemed to derive from another.

The algorithm set out below, which was developed to determine the zygonicity of relationships *between* groups of notes (that is, the strength with which one group of

Fig. 13.21 Transcription of Derek's responses to *KM*.

Fig. 13.21 (*Continued*) Transcription of Derek's responses to *KM*.

notes is deemed to derive from the other), seeks to take into account both similarity *and* salience (Ockelford, 2005a, 2006a, 2007b). The result is termed the 'derivation index' (Ockelford, 2008a). The two chief conveyors of musical structure, pitch and perceived time (Boulez, 1963/1971, p. 37), are scrutinized separately. The former includes considerations of pitch, pitch-class, and melodic and harmonic intervals.

The latter has regard to interonset intervals, durations and relative metrical location. Data are 'streamed' according to their position in the texture ('top', 'middle', or 'bottom', where 'middle' may include a number of simultaneous sounds), since there is evidence that the salience of events may vary according to their relative textural location (Ockelford, 2008a, p. 224). The procedure is as given below.

Algorithm for calculating the derivation index of one group of notes from another

Zygonicity in the domain of perceived time

- Align the two series of events to ensure maximal congruence (in order of priority) of interonset interval, duration and RML.
- Events may be omitted from either series provided that sequentiality is not compromised.
- For each match count 1.
- For correct onset but incorrect duration, count 0.5.
- The raw score is the number of zygonic relationships of rhythm = #Z(R)
- Let the total number of actual and potential sequential relationships between events in the domain of perceived time = #Rel
- The strength of derivation of rhythm is ZYG(R) ('zygonicity' of rhythm), where **ZYG(R) = #Z(R)/#Rel**

Zygonicity in the domain of pitch

- Align the two series of events to ensure maximal congruence in the domain of pitch (taking into account individual notes and intervals).
- Events may be omitted from either series, provided sequentiality is not compromised.
- For each match count 1.
- For correct pitch-class but incorrect octave, count 0.5.
- Discounting exact or partial matches involving pitch-class, identify among any remaining pitch events intervallic matches between sequentially adjacent events (the minimum number of events involved in any intervallic match is two).
- For each event involved in an intervallic match, count 0.5.
- The raw score is the number of zygonic relationships of pitch = #Z(P)
- Let the total number of actual and potential sequential relationships between events in the domain of pitch = #Rel
- The strength of derivation of pitch is ZYG(P) ('zygonicity' of pitch), where **ZYG(P) = #Z(P)/#Rel**

Global zygonicity

- Zygonicity in the domains of pitch and perceived time can be expressed as: **ZYG(P+R) = (#Z(P)+#Z(R))/(#Rel·2)**.

It could be argued that this process is more subjective (and therefore less reliable) than a protocol that entailed same/different note-for-note matching, whose results would be unequivocal. But work to date (see, for example, Ockelford, 2006b, 2007c, 2010b) suggests that the 'zygonicity' measure does appear to give intuitively more satisfying results, and although using musical *meta*cognition to interrogate music-cognitive processing is not unproblematic, it is probably less perilous than relying on an apparently more rigorous, but less ecologically sensitive, mathematical approach. Of course, there are ways of addressing the subjectivity problem, including using two raters or more, and in the current project, the scores were verified by another musician who was not otherwise involved in the research.

To give an example of the algorithm in action, see Figure 13.22, which shows Segment 1 of *KM*, and Derek's initial response to it. Taking first the top line, there are

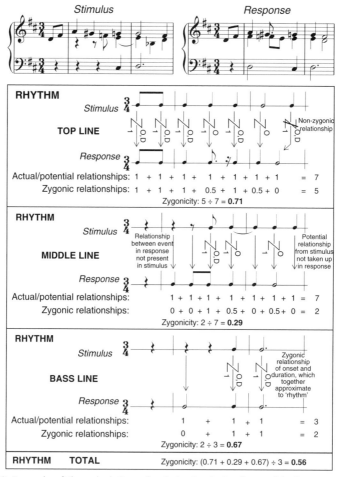

Fig. 13.22 Example of the calculation of a derivation index ('zygonicity').

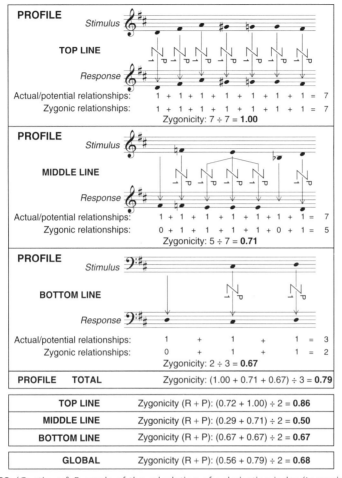

Fig. 13.22 (*Continued*) Example of the calculation of a derivation index ('zygonicity').

seven events in both the stimulus and the response. In the domain of pitch, Derek's recall is entirely accurate ($7 \div 7$ events correct, zygonicity = 1). With regard to rhythm, the first three events are identical, but the fourth has a different duration, and therefore scores 0.5. The fifth event is accurately reproduced, while the sixth has the correct onset relative to the proceeding note but the wrong duration, giving a further score of 0.5. The seventh event scores 0. Hence the zygonicity of rhythm in the top part is $5 \div 7 = 0.71$. Although the middle part comprises only four events in the original, Derek's effort at reproduction yields six notes (with a total number of actual or potential relationships of seven), of which five are correct in the domain of pitch (zygonicity = 0.71), and $1 + 0.5 + 0.5 = 2$ in the domain of perceived time (zygonicity = 0.29). In the bottom part, two of the three notes that Derek plays are correct with respect to pitch and rhythm (zygonicity = 0.67 in each case). Hence the zygonicity for pitch in the segment as a whole is $(1 + 0.71 + 0.67) \div 3 = 0.79$, and for rhythm is $(0.71 + 0.29 + 0.67) \div 3 = 0.56$. Global zygonicity = $(0.79 + 0.56) \div 2 = 0.68$. The potential significance of these differences becomes apparent in the context of the other scores obtained for each trial in relation to *MK* and *KM*, which form the basis of the discussion that follows.

Magical Kaleidoscope, Segment 1 (bars 1–3)

Derek's first attempt to recall this segment was extraordinary to witness. Here was someone who had shown that he could consistently disembed highly dissonant nine-note clusters with a striking immediacy and over 93% accuracy (Ockelford, 2008a, p. 222; Pring, 2008, pp. 219–222), and whose public piano performances were characterized by precision. Yet here, in an excerpt of textural and technical simplicity, Derek played the very first note incorrectly, substituting a fifth octave C for the original fourth octave B. I was listening to Derek's efforts at the time (rather than watching him play), and what I heard seemed so unlikely that I felt obliged to check that the keyboard had not somehow slipped into transposing mode. But he really had made a mistake, and the errors continued, with a derivation index in the domain of pitch for the segment as a whole of only 0.34. This low figure suggests that the lack of a tonal framework had engendered a high level of confusion in Derek's mind (in accordance with Prediction 1), sufficient even to overwhelm his acute sense of AP: neither the individual percepts nor the relationships between them were spared. Admittedly, Derek's response does afford a sense of 'atonality', though it is rather different from the one Schoenberg originally intended. Rhythm too is poorly reproduced (also with a derivation index of 0.34), despite being seemingly straightforward at this early stage in the piece. Given that Derek's previous results in this domain were considerably more successful (Ockelford & Pring, 2005), one can only suppose that there was a cross-over effect, whereby difficulties in relation to pitch had a negative impact on the recall of rhythm.

Derek's confusion was confirmed as, in the course of the next two attempts, he tried different pitch combinations, apparently trying to square the circle of satisfying both the need for accurate reproduction of individual notes and conforming to tonal syntax.[19] His indecision is reflected in uncharacteristic hesitations and slips. These are particularly evident in his approach to the first chord (at the beginning of the second bar): in Trials 2 and 3 the preceding note is sustained, giving the impression that Derek was taking time to think what to do next. The chord itself evolves over the course of the first three trials, with changes particularly evident in the bass, where the $G^{\flat}$ migrates via $C^{\sharp}$ to a G, allowing the harmony to 'resolve' to G^7 (the nearest available 'tonal' option to Schoenberg's original sonority). Here, then, is evidence of Prediction 2, whereby atonal material is modified to conform to a familiar tonal framework. We now consider how this compares with Derek's recall of the opening of *KM*.

Kooky Minuet, Segment 1 (bars 1 and 2)

One's immediate impression that Derek's first attempt at recalling this tonal excerpt is more successful than his efforts in relation to the opening of *MK* is borne out by the passage's derivation index of 0.70, indicating a superiority over the latter of a little over 100%. Nonetheless, several errors do occur (which grow in number through Trials 2, 3, and 4). These inaccuracies are largely due to the increasing *addition* of material, whereby Derek 'fills in' the implied harmonic gaps left by the open texture (such as the D and F$^\#$ that he introduces beneath the melodic A), although there are *omissions* too (the B$^\flat$ in bar 2) and some material is *altered* (the rhythm of the cadential appoggiatura). Hence, all three logical mechanisms for the non-isometric transformation of musical material are utilized in the space of a few seconds, as Derek compensates for the limitations of his short-term recall (cf. Ockelford, 2009; Repp, 1997). Given that errors could be made at the level of events, groups or frameworks, it is of interest to note that, if something has to 'give', it is invariably the former rather than the latter—the tonal system constituting an accurately remembered backdrop upon which surface detail is reproduced with more or less fidelity.

Given the structural equivalence of the two opening segments from *MK* and *KM* in all respects apart from the presence or absence of a pitch framework deployed according to the 'common practice' conventions of Western major tonality, it is reasonable to assume that it was Derek's recognition of this feature that accounted for his greater success in recalling the material from *KM*. Unpacking this assumption further, we can surmise that his superior performance in the 'tonal' condition arose because: (a) it permitted him to remember more of the stimulus by enabling him to encode the 13 events more efficiently, or (b) it allowed him to make coherent assumptions where his short-term memory capacity was exceeded, or (c) both.

Segments 2, 3, and 4

Similar observations apply to the three segments that make up the 'B' sections of each piece. In Segments 2 and 3 of *MK*, four events in particular contribute to the sense of atonality: the B$^\flat$ in the context of what is otherwise an initial C major harmony, and the G$^\#$, F$^\#$ and A framed within the G major triad that follows. Note that the non-harmonic A$^\#$ can be heard tonally as ornamenting the succeeding B. Derek's approach is consistently to omit the B$^\flat$ and to transpose the A down to a G, despite hearing each eight times in the course of the trials pertaining to Segments 2 and 3. By replacing the A with a G, Derek also resolves the issue of the preceding F$^\#$, enabling it to function like the following A$^\#$—as a chromatic ornament—something which he consistently maintains. This way of hearing the ascending run of quavers in the middle of the texture, as chromatic-diatonic pairs, is reinforced in Trial 4 of Segment 2, when Derek completes the pattern by adding a C$^\#$ before the D. Rhythmically, Derek's recall is poor across Segments 2 and 3, with an average derivation index of only 0.39 (as opposed to 0.71 in the domain of pitch). This is largely due to his habit of sustaining the 'harmony notes' to which their chromatic neighbours 'resolve', bolstering his imposed sense of tonality. These changes all conform to Prediction 2; the one concession to atonality that remains is the G$^\#$ in the bass, although to this listener, at least, the effect is of a residual 'error' within an otherwise tonal passage.

In relation to the eight trials pertaining to Segments 2 and 3, it is evident that, having once regularized what he had heard, the cognitive urge to maintain the structures he had imposed was strong enough to overwhelm Derek's perception at the level of events, despite the reinforcement offered by the multiple presentations of the original stimuli. This is reflected in the difference between the strength of derivation of Derek's responses from the source materials and the strength with which each of his attempts derives from the one that precedes: the average derivation index of the former is 0.55, whereas that of the latter is 0.77. That is to say, Derek was far more influenced by his own versions of events than the stimuli from which they are drawn, despite the fact that these were repeatedly interpolated between his own reproductions. Again, this conforms to Prediction 2, with errors being repeated consistently.

Segment 4 of *MK* has two additional notes, D$^\flat$ and C, which appear at the outset in the bass. These are set against a more fragmented RH rhythm than used hitherto, in which the two parts move out of step. Interestingly, this change stimulates Derek to reproduce the B$^\flat$ for the first time in Trial 1, though this disappears again in Trial 2, only to reappear with the D$^\flat$ in different configurations in Trials 3 and 4. That is to say, each version of the opening bar is different, and all are incorrect—suggestive of the cognitive confusion envisaged in Prediction 1.

The net result of asystematic errors like these and the imposition on other occasions of a tonal framework is average global derivation indices across each set of four trials of Segments 2, 3, and 4 of *MK* of 0.48, 0.62, and 0.55. In contrast, Derek's recall of Segments 2, 3, and 4 of *KM* yields indices of 0.86, 0.75, and 0.61 (an average 19% higher). Here, the given tonal framework is respected without exception, although there are *systematic* errors in the domains of pitch and perceived time. For example, the stylistically unusual (though syntactically plausible) F$^\sharp$ with which the inner part kicks off is consistently replaced with a C$^\sharp$ (forming a standard dominant harmony in root position rather than the submediant in first inversion implied by the F$^\sharp$). And, as the rhythmic complexity of the segments grows through the use of a progressively more contrapuntal texture, so Derek increasingly 'homophonizes' what he hears, chunking the 'horizontal' lines into 'vertical' sonorities. This tendency is almost entirely responsible for the decline in fidelity of reproduction across the three segments.

Segment 5

In *MK*, Segment 5 replicates the rhythm (though not the profile) of Segment 1, and Derek appears to recognize this, since the first three trials end with the same rhythmic error that characterized his renditions of the opening phrase. There are a number of other inaccuracies too, including, for example, his systematic strengthening of the downbeats by shifting the LH chords forward by a crotchet—suggestive of Prediction 2 operating in the domain of perceived time.

In the domain of pitch, as before, Derek makes both erratic and structure-seeking errors. In Trial 1, for example, the opening F$^\sharp$ and D are replaced with a G for no discernable music-structural reason, in accordance with Prediction 1. As the error is repeated in subsequent trials, however, it acquires a musical logic of its own (thereby supporting Prediction 2). The first chord, which does not conform to Western tonal conventions, is also subtly modified to become what is effectively a 'dominant major 9th' chord, by omitting the C and subsequently the A (that are not compatible with this harmony) and adding an A$^{\sharp}$ (that is)—further corroborating Prediction 2. Derek ends the phrase in the same way as Schoenberg, on a G^7 chord with an added minor 3rd, which, in its original context supports the atonal feel, but in Derek's re-creation, has a tonal, 'Blues' effect.

Segment 5 of *KM* is, once more, reproduced considerably more accurately (with an average derivation index of 0.70, as opposed to 0.45 for Segment 5 of *MK*), and the errors that Derek does make are entirely structure-preserving in the realm of perceived time and, in the domain of pitch, serve to *simplify* things by reducing the level of chromaticism. For example, the initial D$^{\sharp}$ becomes a more orthodox D$^{\flat}$, and the chromatic G$^{\sharp}$ is omitted altogether. Through these means, the underlying harmonic progression of B, E, A, D is simplified to D, A, D.

Segments 1–5: quantitative comparison

The foregoing descriptions suggest qualitative differences in the way that Derek processes tonal and atonal (and metrical and ametrical) music. In relation to atonal or ametrical music, when (we can assume) the capacity of his short-term memory is exceeded, he makes two types of error: asystematic, as in Prediction 1, and structure enhancing, as in Prediction 2. With tonal and metrical music, in contrast, Derek's errors are purely systematic, *reinforcing* the prevailing tonality and metre through the addition of notes that accord with the frameworks provided, *simplifying* what is presented through the omission or material, or *making it more conventional* by replacing stylistically less usual relative values and transitions with ones that are encountered more frequently. These forms of assimilation are similar to those set out in Prediction 2 and may therefore be underpinned by the same types of cognitive manipulation.

Derek's ability to infer tonal and metrical 'grammars' from what is presented, with its concomitant absence of asystematic errors in memory, has a significant impact on his accuracy of recall. This is reflected in the different derivation indices pertaining to each of the pieces that Derek reproduced (Figure 13.23). Taking his recall in the domains of pitch and rhythm together, Derek's versions of the five segments of *KM* (M = 0.70, SD = 0.10) were significantly more strongly derived from the originals than were those of *MK* (M = 0.47, SD = 0.11), t(19) = 7.39, p <0.0001. Similarly, the *Whole-Tone Scale* segments (M = 0.62, SD = 0.10) were significantly more accurately recalled than those of *MK* t(19) = 5.37, p <0.0001. Note, however, that the difference between *Whole-Tone Scale* and *KM* was far less marked t(19) = 2.22, p =0.04.

Separate analyses of Derek's recall of the pitch and perceived temporal components of each piece provide insights into the nature of his cognitive processing that pertains to different perceptual domains. With regard to *profile* (i.e. melodic and harmonic intervals), the average derivation indices are as follows: *Whole-Tone Scale* (M = 0.64, SD = 0.13), *MK* (M = 0.61, SD = 0.17), and *KM* (M = 0.83, SD = 0.10). The difference between *Whole-Tone Scale* and *MK* is not significant, whereas the differences between *MK* and *KM*, t(19) = 6.51, p <0.0001 and *Whole-Tone Scale* and *KM*, t(19) = 8.80, p <0.0001, are—the implication being that, whether a tonal pitch framework is not recognized (as in the 'bitonal' sections of *Whole-Tone Scale*) or non-existent (as in *MK*),

Derivation indices for Derek's recall of *Whole-Tone Scale*,
trial by trial and segment by segment

		Segment 1			Segment 2			Segment 3			Segment 4			Segment 5		
		Rhythm	Profile	Global	Rhythm	Profile	Global	Rhythm	Profile	Global	Rhythm	Profile	Global	Rhythm	Profile	Global
Trial 1	Top	0.71	0.64	0.68	0.45	0.73	0.59	0.50	0.75	0.63	0.75	0.63	0.69	0.79	0.71	0.75
	Middle	–	–	–	–	–	–	–	–	–	–	–	–	–	–	–
	Bottom	–	–	–	–	–	–	–	–	–	–	–	–	0.69	0.38	0.53
	Total	**0.71**	**0.64**	**0.68**	**0.45**	**0.73**	**0.59**	**0.50**	**0.75**	**0.63**	**0.72**	**0.63**	**0.67**	**0.73**	**0.53**	**0.63**
Trial 2	Top	0.53	0.59	0.56	0.46	0.69	0.58	0.46	0.83	0.65	0.86	0.71	0.79	0.92	0.67	0.79
	Middle	–	–	–	–	–	–	–	–	–	–	–	–	–	–	–
	Bottom	–	–	–	–	–	–	–	–	–	1.00	0.83	0.92	0.86	0.57	0.71
	Total	**0.53**	**0.59**	**0.56**	**0.46**	**0.69**	**0.58**	**0.46**	**0.83**	**0.65**	**0.92**	**0.77**	**0.85**	**0.88**	**0.62**	**0.75**
Trial 3	Top	0.35	0.42	0.38	0.42	0.69	0.56	0.58	0.83	0.71	0.65	0.60	0.63	0.93	0.71	0.82
	Middle	–	–	–	–	–	–	–	–	–	–	–	–	–	–	–
	Bottom	–	–	–	–	–	–	–	–	–	0.67	0.44	0.56	0.92	0.17	0.54
	Total	**0.35**	**0.42**	**0.38**	**0.42**	**0.69**	**0.56**	**0.58**	**0.83**	**0.71**	**0.66**	**0.53**	**0.59**	**0.92**	**0.46**	**0.69**
Trial 4	Top	0.53	0.50	0.52	0.38	0.83	0.60	0.50	0.83	0.67	0.79	0.86	0.82	0.75	0.75	0.75
	Middle	–	–	–	–	–	–	–	–	–	–	–	–	–	–	–
	Bottom	–	–	–	–	–	–	–	–	–	0.93	0.57	0.75	0.70	0.40	0.55
	Total	**0.53**	**0.50**	**0.52**	**0.38**	**0.83**	**0.60**	**0.50**	**0.83**	**0.67**	**0.86**	**0.71**	**0.79**	**0.73**	**0.62**	**0.67**

Means across all segments and trials

	Rhythm	Profile	Global
Melody	0.56	0.67	0.62
Inner	–	–	–
Bass	0.79	0.50	0.65
Total	**0.61**	**0.66**	**0.64**

Fig. 13.23 Derivation indices for Derek's recall of (a) *Whole-Tone Scale*, (b) *MK*, and (c) *KM*.

Derivation indices for Derek's recall of *MK*, trial by trial and segment by segment

		Segment 1			Segment 2			Segment 3			Segment 4			Segment 5		
		Rhythm	Profile	Global	Rhythm	Profile	Global	Rhythm	Profile	Global	Rhythm	Profile	Global	Rhythm	Profile	Global
Trial 1	Top	0.56	0.25	0.41	0.75	1.00	0.88	0.50	1.00	0.75	0.00	1.00	0.50	0.64	0.29	0.46
	Middle	0.22	0.28	0.25	0.15	0.40	0.28	0.33	0.67	0.50	0.44	0.88	0.66	0.00	0.75	0.38
	Bottom	0.00	1.00	0.50	0.50	1.00	0.75	0.50	1.00	0.75	0.00	0.33	0.17	0.00	1.00	0.50
	Total	**0.34**	**0.34**	**0.34**	**0.27**	**0.54**	**0.40**	**0.38**	**0.75**	**0.56**	**0.27**	**0.77**	**0.52**	**0.35**	**0.54**	**0.44**
Trial 2	Top	0.50	0.44	0.47	0.75	1.00	0.88	0.50	1.00	0.75	0.00	1.00	0.50	0.64	0.29	0.46
	Middle	0.22	0.33	0.28	0.15	0.40	0.28	0.50	0.78	0.64	0.31	0.75	0.53	0.00	0.75	0.38
	Bottom	0.00	0.33	0.17	0.50	1.00	0.75	0.50	1.00	0.75	0.17	0.33	0.25	0.00	1.00	0.50
	Total	**0.31**	**0.38**	**0.35**	**0.27**	**0.54**	**0.40**	**0.50**	**0.83**	**0.67**	**0.23**	**0.69**	**0.46**	**0.35**	**0.54**	**0.44**
Trial 3	Top	0.35	0.40	0.38	0.75	1.00	0.88	0.50	1.00	0.75	0.00	1.00	0.50	0.64	0.29	0.46
	Middle	0.13	0.38	0.25	0.15	0.50	0.33	0.38	0.75	0.56	0.56	0.88	0.72	0.00	0.75	0.38
	Bottom	0.00	0.50	0.25	0.50	1.00	0.75	0.50	1.00	0.75	0.17	0.67	0.42	0.00	1.00	0.50
	Total	**0.23**	**0.40**	**0.31**	**0.27**	**0.62**	**0.44**	**0.41**	**0.82**	**0.61**	**0.38**	**0.85**	**0.62**	**0.35**	**0.54**	**0.44**
Trial 4	Top	0.69	0.38	0.53	0.75	1.00	0.88	0.50	1.00	0.75	0.00	1.00	0.50	0.64	0.36	0.50
	Middle	0.17	0.67	0.42	0.56	0.67	0.61	0.44	0.75	0.59	0.50	0.88	0.69	0.00	0.75	0.38
	Bottom	0.00	0.50	0.25	0.50	1.00	0.75	0.50	1.00	0.75	0.00	0.67	0.33	0.00	1.00	0.50
	Total	**0.41**	**0.50**	**0.45**	**0.58**	**0.75**	**0.67**	**0.45**	**0.82**	**0.64**	**0.31**	**0.85**	**0.58**	**0.35**	**0.58**	**0.46**

Means across all segments and trials

	Rhythm	Profile	Global
Melody	0.53	0.52	0.53
Inner	0.29	0.62	0.46
Bass	0.14	0.73	0.43
Total	**0.34**	**0.61**	**0.47**

Fig. 13.23 (*Continued*)

Derivation indices for Derek's recall of KM, trial by trial and segment by segment

		Segment 1			Segment 2			Segment 3			Segment 4			Segment 5		
		Rhythm	Profile	Global	Rhythm	Profile	Global	Rhythm	Profile	Global	Rhythm	Profile	Global	Rhythm	Profile	Global
Trial 1	Top	0.71	1.00	0.86	0.83	1.00	0.92	0.33	1.00	0.67	0.40	0.80	0.60	0.79	0.71	0.75
	Middle	0.29	0.71	0.50	0.88	0.75	0.81	0.50	0.75	0.63	0.00	0.75	0.38	0.60	0.80	0.70
	Bottom	0.67	0.67	0.67	0.88	1.00	0.94	0.63	1.00	0.81	0.38	1.00	0.75	0.50	0.50	0.50
	Total	**0.56**	**0.79**	**0.68**	**0.86**	**0.91**	**0.89**	**0.50**	**0.91**	**0.70**	**0.38**	**0.85**	**0.62**	**0.68**	**0.71**	**0.70**
Trial 2	Top	0.71	1.00	0.86	0.83	1.00	0.92	0.83	1.00	0.92	0.30	0.80	0.55	0.79	0.71	0.75
	Middle	0.29	0.43	0.36	0.63	0.50	0.56	0.50	0.75	0.63	0.38	0.75	0.56	0.60	0.80	0.70
	Bottom	0.67	0.67	0.67	0.63	0.75	0.69	0.63	1.00	0.81	0.50	1.00	0.75	0.50	1.00	0.75
	Total	**0.53**	**0.71**	**0.62**	**0.68**	**0.73**	**0.70**	**0.64**	**0.91**	**0.77**	**0.38**	**0.85**	**0.62**	**0.68**	**0.79**	**0.73**
Trial 3	Top	0.71	1.00	0.86	0.83	1.00	0.92	0.83	1.00	0.92	0.20	0.80	0.50	0.79	0.79	0.79
	Middle	0.29	0.43	0.36	0.88	1.00	0.94	0.50	0.75	0.63	0.38	0.75	0.56	0.60	0.60	0.60
	Bottom	0.67	0.67	0.67	0.88	1.00	0.94	0.63	1.00	0.81	0.63	1.00	0.81	0.50	0.50	0.50
	Total	**0.53**	**0.71**	**0.62**	**0.86**	**1.00**	**0.93**	**0.64**	**0.91**	**0.77**	**0.38**	**0.85**	**0.62**	**0.68**	**0.68**	**0.68**
Trial 4	Top	0.71	1.00	0.86	0.83	1.00	0.92	0.83	1.00	0.92	0.20	0.80	0.50	0.79	0.79	0.79
	Middle	0.25	0.38	0.31	0.88	1.00	0.94	0.50	0.75	0.63	0.38	0.75	0.56	0.60	0.60	0.60
	Bottom	0.67	0.67	0.67	0.88	1.00	0.94	0.63	1.00	0.81	0.63	1.00	0.81	0.50	0.50	0.50
	Total	**0.50**	**0.67**	**0.58**	**0.86**	**1.00**	**0.93**	**0.64**	**0.91**	**0.77**	**0.38**	**0.85**	**0.62**	**0.68**	**0.68**	**0.68**

Means across all segments and trials

	Rhythm	Profile	Global
Melody	0.66	0.89	0.78
Inner	0.47	0.66	0.57
Bass	0.64	0.88	0.76
Total	**0.60**	**0.83**	**0.70**

Fig. 13.23 (Continued) Derivation indices for Dereks recall of (a) *Whole-Tone Scale*, (b) *MK*, and (c) *KM*.

the effect on Derek's accuracy of recall is much the same in that, as we have seen, he will either make asystematic errors or impose a structure where none exists, or both.

The position with regard to rhythm is quite different, with the following average derivation indices pertaining to each series of 20 trials: *Whole-Tone Scale* (M = 0.61, SD = 0.18), *MK* (M = 0.34, SD = 0.09) and *KM* (M = 0.60, SD = 0.16). The differences between *Whole-Tone Scale* and *MK*, $t(19) = 5.27$, $p < 0.0001$, and *MK* and *KM*, $t(19) = 6.90$, $p < 0.0001$, are both highly significant, while, in contrast, the average derivation indices of *Whole-Tone Scale* and *KM* are virtually identical. The implication here is that Derek was able to recognize and utilize the regularity of the metrical frameworks expressed by *Whole-Tone Scale* and *KM* to facilitate recall, but where he failed to recognize the presence of a consistent metre (in *MK*), the result was a litany of asystematic and structure-seeking errors, significantly greater in number even than those pertaining to pitch in the same piece $t(19) = 8.34$, $p < 0.0001$. This suggests that, in Derek's case at least, perceived ametricality may be even more cognitively challenging than atonality.

Derek's recall of *MK* and *KM* as a whole

In each case, having completed the trials pertaining to individual segments, Derek attempted to play *MK* and *KM* as a whole, having heard the piece or section in question right through. This procedure was repeated immediately. The results are shown in Figures 13.24 and 13.25.

It is evident that Derek was overwhelmed by the task of trying to remember *MK*. As the transcription shows, his first attempt was remarkably brief, and was virtually identical to his response to Segment 5, repeated. As a result, the level of derivation from *MK* as a whole is almost immeasurably low—estimated at 0.08 (with the derivation index of rhythm being 0.05 and profile, 0.11). At his second attempt, Derek started in the same way (with his version of Segment 5, repeated), before moving on, in bars 5 and 6, to material that most closely resembles features of the Segment 1. This was followed, in bars 7 and 8, by a further rendition of Segment 5, then, in conclusion, elements from the end of Segment 1. Hence, his account of *MK* was in the form $A_1 A_2 B_1 A_3 B_2$. So, again, there is little resemblance to the original in terms of global structure—or detail, with an estimated derivation index of 0.17 (with rhythm, 0.11 and profile, 0.23). It appears that the effect of atonality and, to an even greater extent, perceived ametricality, over time appears to have a cumulatively negative impact on cognitive processing, with a catastrophic effect on memory.

Derek fared considerably better in relation to *KM*, which has a global derivation index of 0.44 at the first attempt (0.39 for rhythm and 0.49 for profile) and 0.42 at the second (0.36 for rhythm and 0.48 for profile). As these figures suggest, Derek's responses shared many similarities, with a derivation index of the second from the first of 0.88 (0.84 for rhythm and 0.92 for profile). In both cases, the reproductions of Segments 1 and 5 were similar to those in the previous, individual trials, and Derek's main error was in conflating the three central segments (2, 3, and 4), which, in the stimulus, resemble each other closely. Hence, structurally, his account of *KM* can be represented as $A_1 B_1 A_2$. Note that if his single response to Segments 2, 3, and 4 is

TRIAL 1

TRIAL 2

Fig. 13.24 Derek's recall of *MK*, complete.

TRIAL 1

TRIAL 2

Fig. 13.25 Derek's recall of *KM*, complete.

considered as a valid rendition of each, then the global derivation indices of his two attempts at *KM* rise to 0.68 on Trial 1 and 0.66 on Trial 2. These 'structurally adjusted' figures show Derek achieving a relative accuracy of recall between four and eight times better than he attained in relation to *MK*. Given the controlled nature of the stimuli, which, as we have seen, were designed so that the tonal and metrical frameworks were the only aspects of structure that varied significantly—and given that, with one exception,[20] Derek's attempts respected the tonal and metrical frameworks—we can surmise that it was these that played a key role in facilitating his cognitive processing, memory and recall.

Long-term recall—one week and one year later

In order to ascertain what the long-term effects of the presence or absence of tonal and metrical frameworks (or the failure to recognize them) may have on memory, Derek agreed to take part in two further tests, respectively a week and a year after the learning phase. In the course of other recording sessions, and using the same equipment as previously, he was asked to reproduce whatever he could recall of *MK* and *KM*. Derek had not heard either stimulus in the intervening periods, nor, as far as the researchers could ascertain, had attempted to play them.[21] The results after one week are shown in Figure 13.26.

Derek's version of *MK* after the seven-day break is startling. There is very little of the original material left (with an estimated global derivation index of 0.06). In music-analytical terms, it appears that Derek takes a tonalized and re-metricized version of the opening figure, which retains the notion of an unharmonized anacrusis moving to a discord in the next bar, and improvises on it. In his version, the first phrase is cast as a series of 'dominant 7th' chords, which resolve onto one another in various ways in a manner reminiscent of Western late-Romantic harmonic sequences—the style from which Schoenberg's atonality evolved. It is as though Derek takes a stylistic step back to regain his tonal footing. In the course of his extemporisation, two prominent atonal harmonies remain from Schoenberg's *MK*: the chord of B$^\flat$ minor with an added A that is originally heard at the conclusion of the first phrase in bar 3, and the final chord of G^7 with an added B$^\flat$. Derek resolves both these atonal aggregations, enabling them to function as chromatic harmonies: the A in the B$^\flat$ minor chord moves down to a G, and forms part of an E$^{\flat 7}$ harmony in second inversion (see bar 5 of Derek's rendition), and the B$^\flat$ in the G^7 chord moves up to is neighbouring B$^\natural$ to form a 'dominant 7th' chord (upon which Derek's version concludes). The derivation of this version from his previous attempt (index 0.22) is stronger than from the original stimulus, although a considerable degree of change has occurred nonetheless. It appears that the process of assimilation to tonal and metrical regularity has taken another step in the course of storage in and retrieval from long-term memory. That is to say, there is evidence that Prediction 2 pertains not only to material being processed in the short term, but in long-term memory too.

In contrast, Derek's version of *KM* one week on strongly resembles the original, though his recollection of the global structure is eccentric. He plays his versions of the first two segments four times (A_1 B_1 A_1 B_1 A_1 B_1 A_1 B_1), followed by a period of silence, at which point he was prompted verbally with 'Anything else, Derek?', whereupon he played his rendition of the final segment twice. In terms of determining the derivation index, matching segment for segment yields a figure of 0.69 (rhythm 0.56 and profile 0.83). The strength of derivation from his previous attempt is 0.82 (rhythm 0.73 and profile 0.87). Once, more the tonal and metrical frameworks of the original are broadly preserved (with the perseveration of the single metrical error noted above). When put alongside the *MK* data, these findings reinforce the hypothesis that the recognition of frameworks in pitch and perceived time, together with their probabilistic patterns of utilisation, greatly facilitate the operation of Derek's long-term musical memory.

Fig. 13.26 Derek's recall of *MK* and *KM* after one week.

Finally, Derek was asked, one year later, to play whatever he could remember of the two pieces. The results are shown in Figure 13.27. When asked to play *MK*, it is interesting to note that Derek paused and asked to hear the recording first—an unusually explicit indication from him that he did not feel he could recall the piece. Indeed, he articulated his uncertainty again during the course of the attempt, saying 'Can't remember' after the first two phrases (although he did subsequently add two more). The transcription shows that, at this stage, the trace of *MK* has almost entirely decayed. All that remains is the opening pattern of a melodic anacrusis moving to a discord on a downbeat (in which the melody note functions as an appoggiatura). As before, Derek improvises on this, producing three versions of the same phrase, though with only a passing resemblance to *MK* proper (derivation index estimated at 0.08).

Fig. 13.27 Derek's recall of *MK* and *KM* after one year.

The two atonal chords that were present after a week have now gone, and the only remaining suggestion of atonality is in the opening two notes (which appear to be taken from Derek's original responses in Trials 2, 3, and 4 to Segment 1)—although these are resolved with reference to the higher discord that follows (D^{b7} with an added 9th and raised 11th)—and the F$^\sharp$ that follows after a hesitation (in bar 3). This is left hanging awkwardly, out of line with an otherwise tonal framework. Metrically, Derek's hesitations make it difficult to discern any underlying regularity, and the overall effect is of temporal fragmentation. So there is evidence here of Predictions 1 and 2 working in the context of long-term memory: Derek seeks to impose tonal order on the fragment of *MK* that he can recall, but, seemingly aware that this is not the 'right answer', he introduces a pitch (F$^\sharp$) that he is aware lies outside the tonal system, in order to re-create something of the original effect of the Schoenberg. Meanwhile, and partly, it appears, as a consequence of his doubts pertaining to pitch, there are asystematic patterns of error in the domain of perceived time.

KM produces a very different result, however, which is now in the form $A_1 B_1 A_2 A_1 B_1 A_2$. This has a structurally corrected strength of derivation index of 0.66 from the original, and 0.80 from his last attempt. That is to say, Derek's memory of *KM* seems hardly to have shifted in the course of 12 months. Again, given the structural equivalence of *KM* and *MK*, this provides further evidence that the presence of recognizable tonal and metrical frameworks is important to the successful functioning of Derek's musical memory.

Conclusion

In summary, it was found that the memory performance of one savant (Derek Paravicini) was adversely affected when either he did not *recognize* the tonal pitch framework of a piece, or where one *did not exist*: the effect was the same in either case, and resulted in two types of error: 'asystematic', in which mistakes at all structural levels were unpredictable and were not repeated; and 'systematic', in which material was assimilated into familiar patterns of organization through the modification or omission of values, constituting changes which were likely to re-occur. That is to say, the empirical work reported here supports the earlier anecdotal observation that, if the *probabilistic* way in which pitch frameworks are used to create a sense of 'tonality' is destroyed, then Derek's ability to process musical content and structure at the level of events and groups is seriously impaired too. We can further hypothesize that, for him, the probabilistic utilization of pitch frameworks facilitates cognitive encoding that is both rich yet parsimonious. The data presented here suggest, moreover, that comparable phenomena are at work in the domain of perceived time—in relation to *metrical* frameworks. And Derek's efforts at recalling music immediately, after a week and then a year point to similar principles operating with respect to both short- and long-term memory.

Of course, while these findings have intrinsic value—not least to those supporting Derek in learning new repertoire—of more general interest is the extent to which they may be more broadly applicable. That is: what do the results suggest, if anything, about how 'typical' listeners process atonal or ametrical pieces (or those using unfamiliar frameworks, or familiar frameworks in novel ways)? It could be argued that to seek to generalize from Derek's research data would be inappropriate, since, as a savant, he is by definition an 'atypical' musician; his acute sense of absolute pitch alone, for example, sets him apart from the great majority of other listeners. There is, however, evidence that militates against this view, one source of which is to be found in the precedents of other researchers having previously used savant data to consider the nature of 'neurotypical' human abilities—to test issues of modularity in intelligence, for instance (see, for example, Smith & Tsimpli, 1995). Indeed, in their 1985 article, Sloboda *et al.* claim that NP's cognitive architecture resembles that of a 'typical' expert memorizer, and infer that even a moderate level of general intelligence is not necessary for the advanced development of certain musical skills (p. 166). That is to say, their findings both *contextualize* the specific in the general, but also use the specific to *inform our understanding* of the general. A second source of evidence for the validity of generalising from Derek's data lies in the fact that other musicians frequently learn and practise pieces alongside him, and engage with him in sophisticated improvisations, implying a commonality in the way that they and he are processing music. Arguably, then, Derek functions like most other people as a *listener* (a 'super listener', perhaps, given his ability to recognize pitches and disaggregate chords) in that his musical understanding is implicit rather than explicit, perceptual rather than conceptual, intuitive rather than intellectual. However, where he differs from the vast majority is in his capacity to *reproduce what he hears* on the keyboard—entire, complex musical textures that amount to far more than the short vocal fragments that are all most people can manage to replicate (though even this capacity is far more limited than one may imagine—see Sloboda, 1985/2004). Inevitably then, most empirical work in the musical domain relies on indirect evidence obtained through verbal or other responses, whereas Derek offers us a privileged window direct into his musical mind and, perhaps, into 'the musical mind' more generally.

So let us consider how the findings pertaining to Derek's efforts at recall potentially illuminate the cognitive processing that may occur in most people in relation to atonal music. Anecdotally, listeners complain that atonal pieces sound 'discordant' or 'wrong' and that they are difficult to remember (cf. Bernstein, 1976, p. 273; Rochberg, 2004, p. 95). Both these observations accord with Derek's attempts to reproduce *MK*, in that he 'corrected' notes that were outside traditional diatonic and metrical frameworks and found it difficult to remember the music in the short term—and impossible over extended periods of time. Does this mean that 'typical' listeners are adopting strategies in line with Prediction 2: attempting to make sense of the music by imposing familiar frameworks (and hearing values outside these are 'errors')? And does Prediction 1 hold true for them: that through failing to encode material parsimoniously they are unable to store or retrieve it? Both possibilities seem likely, although empirical verification would be difficult: limited evidence could be gained through vocal reproduction tasks or through using recognition paradigms—both areas of potential future research.

Finally, what, if anything, could composers glean from Derek's results? Is atonal music (or music whose tonality is difficult to perceive) ever likely to succeed in attracting broadly based, non-specialist audiences, who are not prepared or able to listen to music in other than in a non-conceptual (non-musicological) way? The answer must surely lie in providing alternative or supplementary structures that can be grasped quickly and intuitively: in Lerdahl's (1988) terms, to provide them with an accessible listening grammar. As Bartók (1920/1976, p. 458) writes: 'atonal music does not exclude certain exterior means of arrangement, certain repetitions (in a different position, with changes, and so forth), … refrain-like appearances of certain ideas, or the return to the starting point at the end.' In terms of present nomenclature, this equates to structure at the level of events and groups. That is to say, if structure at the level of frameworks is absent or unperceived, then other forms of organization will be required to make the music generally comprehensible, memorable and, ultimately, enjoyable.

Acknowledgements

With thanks to Derek Paravicini, for his willing and good-humoured participation in this study, to Graham Welch, Professor of Music Education at the Institute of Education (IoE), University of London, and to Evangelos Himonides, Lecturer in IT and Music Technology Education at the IoE, for their support in conceptualizing the project and assistance in gathering the data.

Notes

[1] The Society for Education, Music and Psychology REsearch.

[2] Using a note-matching procedure to gauge accuracy, which differed somewhat from Sloboda and colleagues' error-counting protocol.

[3] A series of melodic or harmonic intervals—the equivalent of rhythm in the domain of pitch; see Ockelford, 2006a, p. 99.

[4] Potentially conferring a processing advantage over encoding as successive intervals, since, in the Western diatonic system, successive steps in pitch frameworks may be separated by *different* intervals.

[5] Similar results were obtained for Eddie, the young savant with whom Miller worked. In TR's case, Young and Nettelbeck report that there was no 'deviation into the diatonic system', implying that he was 'clearly aware of how the whole tone scale operates' (1995, p. 242).

[6] 'Zygonicity' is a measure of the 'orderliness' of a passage or feature thereof, whereby the number of *zygonic* relationships between events is expressed as a proportion of the total number of *potential* relationships, where the maximum is 1 and the minimum is 0. For further information see Ockelford (2005a, pp. 73–4).

[7] There is also evidence from memory studies with Derek Paravicini (for example, Ockelford & Pring, 2005, p. 906), that *production* of material has a significant interference effect, even when the original is repeated between attempts. Zygonic analysis shows that the most powerful influence on Derek was not rehearing the original, but his latest or even penultimate performance of it—even though these occurred *before* rehearing the original stimulus.

[8] A Schenkerian concept, whereby a note or notes, or harmony or harmonies, is deemed to have the effect of extending another in time. For recent work that demonstrates the perceptual reality of prolongation near the musical surface, see Martinez (2007).

[9] Note that the central chromatic passages would present no particular difficulties to people (such as NP) who had absolute pitch.

[10] Another concept borrowed from Heinrich Schenker (1906).

[11] With his consent, Derek is named in this research, as he is in any case a public figure and since, despite the realistic accounts of his abilities in his biography (Ockelford, 2007a) and on his website, misinformation about him continues to be circulated—his supposed powers of 'instant and perfect recall' for example—whereas the way his memory works is much more subtle (through no less remarkable) than that. It is hoped that research such as that reported here will gradually inform popular perceptions of Derek's musical capabilities.

[12] Even 10-note chords are reproduced with over 90% accuracy (Ockelford, 2008a).

[13] It seems that NP was not able to adopt this strategy, and he evidently found the passage bewildering, since he played nothing at all after hearing it for the first time. The second time, extrapolation from Miller's re-analysis of Sloboda *et al.*'s data using the note-for-note matching paradigm (mentioned above), suggests an accuracy of 58% (that is, a little over half the notes were right). Eddie (using the same protocol) apparently only managed 45%. In neither case is it clear what the precise nature of the errors was.

[14] Derek's recall of Segment 1 evolved over Trials 1 and 2, such that pairs of quavers a tone (one scale-step) apart came to dominate. Rather as NP's efforts had done previously (though he used a subtly different mechanism—see Figure 13.9), this imbued the surface of the music with greater moment-to-moment regularity, leading to a simplification of structure at the level of events, and so making it easier to remember (evidence for which is shown by Derek's responses being more similar to each other than to the original): an intuitive strategy,

perhaps, when short-term memory was overloaded, to enable him to preserve deeper structures. In Segments 2 and 3, Derek continued to rely almost exclusively on pairs of quavers (or longer durations whose onsets were a quaver apart) delineating whole tones, suggesting systematic interference between segments.

[15] The term 'atonality' was not one that Schoenberg himself used, though he does refer to 'renouncing a tonal centre' in works of his 'second period' (which includes his op. 11 piano pieces) (1949/1975, p. 86). He writes: 'the overwhelming multitude of dissonances cannot be counterbalanced any longer by occasional returns to tonic triads as represent a key. It seemed inadequate to force a movement into the Procrustean bed of tonality without supporting it by harmonic progressions that pertain to it. This dilemma was my concern ... That I was the first to venture the decisive step will not be considered universally a merit—a fact I regret but have to ignore.'

[16] Forte has specialized in studying the music of the so-called 'Second Viennese School', embracing works by Schoenberg, Berg, and Webern, whose use of pitch frameworks consciously moved away from the patterns of idiosyncratic usage that created the effect of 'tonality'—a radical approach which was eventually codified in Schoenberg's 'serial' procedures. Here, notionally, at least, each pitch has equal structural weight. Forte's approach to explaining the structure of atonal music is termed 'set-theoretical analysis', which holds that one group or 'set' of pitches can be regarded as *equivalent* to another, irrespective of transposition or inversion, the octave in which values are realized, whether or not they are repeated, and, additionally (quite unlike serialism), the order in which they occur (Forte, 1973). The result is that musical textures are parsed as a series of contiguous or overlapping pitch-cells, which may be regarded as more or less closely related through mathematically calculated indices of similarity (see, for example, Isaacson, 1990; Ockelford, 2005a, pp. 67–119). The lack of any evidence that such pitch sets and the relationships between them played any part in the process of composition of op. 11, no. 1 and pieces like it, or are part of the 'typical' listening experience of this and similar works, and are therefore of any significance beyond a small community of expert music analysts, has been a matter of some contention (see, for instance, Mailman, 2007) although the possibility of acknowledging that 'analytical' grammars may work alongside those identified by Lerdahl as pertaining to composition and listening (see above) does seem to offer one way out of the epistemological impasse (Ockelford, 2009). In this regard, it is interesting to note that Derek's efforts at reproducing op. 11, no.1 bore no relationship to the structure or content of the pitch-sets identified by Forte in his analysis, nor, indeed, to the author's supposedly more 'perceptible' account (see Ockelford, 2005a, p. 110). The extent to which Derek's reproductions (1) can be taken to illustrate his cognitive representation of atonal music and, more controversially, (2) can be considered to be broadly representative of how 'typical' (i.e. 'intuitive') listeners reconstruct such music in memory is considered in later sections of this chapter.

[17] The reverse approach to that adopted by Lalitte, Bigand, Kantor-Martynuska, & Delbé (2009), who used specially constructed atonal versions of Beethoven piano sonatas to investigate the contribution of tonal relationships to the perception of musical ideas. Here, however, it seems that structure at the level of events and groups was not controlled with the same rigour as in the current work.

[18] Using the following similarity measure (Ockelford, 2005a, p. 41):

$$\text{Similarity of two sets of values } (\%) = 100 - \Sigma \left(\frac{\Sigma \left| X_i - \left(\frac{\Sigma X_i}{X} \right) \right|}{X} \right) \%$$

[19] The difficulties that Derek was having with the task at this point raised ethical concerns as to whether it was appropriate to expect him to continue, and he was asked whether he was comfortable to carry on (to which he replied in the affirmative). It is interesting to note that, when asked afterwards how similar his version of *MK* was to the original, he replied 'not at all like it', a level of metacognition and verbal expression quite exceptional for him. Interestingly, John Sloboda has reported having similar concerns about NP, who showed signs of distress at being asked to reproduce the Bartók.

[20] The two quavers that open bar 3, which Derek evidently hears as an anacrusis—implying a more conventional 'harmonic rhythm', in which the dominant on the weak beat is resolved to the tonic on the strong.

[21] Derek tends to connect particular pieces with certain people or occasions, and very rarely offers to play music that is outside the context or contexts with which he associates it.

References

Bartók, B. (1920/1976). The problem of new music. In: B. Suchoff (Ed.), *Béla Bártok essays* (pp. 455–459). London: Faber and Faber.

Bartók, B. (1928/1976). The folk songs of Hungary. In: B. Suchoff (Ed.) *Béla Bártok essays* (pp. 331–339). London: Faber and Faber.

Bernstein, L. (1976). *The unanswered question*. Cambridge, MA: Harvard University Press.

Bharucha, J. (1987). Music cognition and perceptual facilitation: a connectionist framework. *Music Perception, 5*(1), 1–30.

Boulez, P. (1963/1971). *Boulez on music today* (S. Bradshaw and R.R. Bennett, Trans), London: Faber and Faber.

Deutsch, D. (1980). The processing of structured and unstructured tonal sequences. *Perception and Psychophysics, 28*(5), 381–389.

Deutsch, D., & Feroe, J. (1981). The internal representation of pitch sequences in tonal music. *Psychological Review, 88*(6), 503–522.

Forte, A. (1973). *The structure of atonal music*. New Haven, CT: Yale University Press.

Forte, A. (1981). The magical kaleidoscope: Schoenberg's first atonal masterwork, op. 11, no. 1. *Journal of the Arnold Schoenberg Institute, 5*, 127–168

Huron, D. (2006). *Sweet anticipation: Music and the psychology of expectation*. Cambridge, MA: MIT Press.

Isaacson, E. (1990). Similarity of interval-class content between pitch-class sets: the IcVSIM relation. *Journal of Music Theory, 34*(1), 1–27.

Lalitte, P., Bigand, E., Kantor-Martynuska, J., & Delbé, C. (2009). On listening to atonal variants of two piano sonatas by Beethoven. *Music Perception, 26*(3), 223–234.

Lerdahl, F. (1988). Cognitive constraints on compositional systems. In: J. Sloboda (Ed.), *Generative processes in music: The psychology of performance, improvisation and composition* (pp. 231–259). Oxford: Clarendon Press.

Lerdahl, F., & Jackendoff, R. (1983). *A generative theory of tonal music*. Cambridge, MA: MIT Press.

Lewin, D. (1987). *Generalized musical intervals and transformations*. New Haven, CT: Yale University Press.

Mailman, J. (2007). Review article: Repetition in music: Theoretical and metatheoretical perspectives. *Psychology of Music, 35*(2), 363–375.

Martinez, I. (2007). *The cognitive reality of prolongation*. Unpublished Ph.D. thesis, Roehampton University, London.

Meyer, L. (1956). *Emotion and meaning in music*. Chicago, IL: University of Chicago Press.

Meyer, L. (1967). *Music, the arts, and ideas*. Chicago, IL: University of Chicago Press.

Meyer, L. (1973). *Explaining music*. Chicago, IL: University of Chicago Press.

Miller, G. (1956). The magical number seven, plus or minus two: some limits on our capacity for processing information. *Psychological Review, 63*(2), 81–97.

Miller, L. (1989). *Musical savants: Exceptional skill in the mentally retarded*. Hillsdale, NJ: Lawrence Erlbaum.

Ockelford, A. (1991). The role of repetition in perceived musical structures. In: P. Howell, R. West, & I. Cross (Eds.), *Representing musical structure* (pp. 129–160). London: Academic Press.

Ockelford, A. (1999). *The cognition of order in music: A metacognitive study*. London: Roehampton Institute.

Ockelford, A. (2002). The magical number two, plus or minus one: some limits on our capacity for processing musical information. *Musicæ Scientiæ, 6*(2), 177–215.

Ockelford, A. (2004). On similarity, derivation and the cognition of musical structure. *Psychology of Music, 32*(1), 23–74.

Ockelford, A. (2005a). *Repetition in music: Theoretical and metatheoretical perspectives*. Aldershot: Ashgate.

Ockelford, A. (2005b). Relating musical structure and content to aesthetic response: A model and analysis of Beethoven's Piano Sonata op. 110. *Journal of the Royal Musical Association, 130*(1), 74–118.

Ockelford, A. (2006a). Implication and expectation in music: a zygonic model. *Psychology of Music, 34*(1), 81–142.

Ockelford, A. (2006b). Using a music-theoretical approach to interrogate musical development and social interaction. In: N. Lerner, & J. Straus (Eds.), *Sounding off: Theorizing disability in music* (pp. 137–155). New York, NY: Routledge.

Ockelford, A. (2007a). *In the key of genius: The extraordinary life of Derek Paravicini*. London: Hutchinson.

Ockelford, A. (2007b). A music module in working memory? Evidence from the performance of a prodigious musical savant. *Musicæ Scientiæ, Special Issue*, 5–36.

Ockelford, A. (2007c). Exploring musical interaction between a teacher and pupil, and her evolving musicality, using a music-theoretical approach. *Research Studies in Music Education, 28*(1), 3–23.

Ockelford, A. (2008a). *Music for children and young people with complex needs*. Oxford: Oxford University Press.

Ockelford, A. (2008b). Beyond music psychology. In: S. Hallam, I. Cross., & M. Thaut (Eds.), *Oxford handbook of music psychology* (pp. 539–551). Oxford: Oxford University Press.

Ockelford, A. (2009). Similarity relations between groups of notes: music-theoretical and music-psychology perspectives. *Musicæ Scientiæ, Discussion Forum 4B*, 47–93.

Ockelford, A. (2010a). Zygonic theory: Introduction, scope, prospects. *Zeitschrift der Gesellschaft für Musiktheorie, 6*(1), 91–172.

Ockelford, A. (2010b). Imagination feeds memory: exploring evidence from a musical savant using zygonic theory. In: D. Hargreaves, D. Miell, & R. MacDonald (Eds.), *Musical*

imaginations: Multidisciplinary perspectives on creativity, performance and perception.
Oxford: Oxford University Press.

Ockelford, A., & Pring, L. (2005). Learning and creativity in a prodigious musical savant. *International Congress Series, 1282,* 903–907.

Pollack, I., & Ficks, L. (1954). Information of elementary multidimensional auditory displays. *Journal of the Acoustical Society of America, 26,* 155–158.

Pring, L. (2008). Memory characteristics in individuals with savant skills. In: J. Boucher, & D. Bowler (Eds.), *Memory in Autism: Theory and evidence* (pp. 210–230). Cambridge: Cambridge University Press.

Rochberg, G. (2004) *The aesthetics of survival: a composer's view of twentieth-century music,* Ann Arbor, MI: University of Michigan Press.

Schenker, H. (1906). *Harmonielehre.* Vienna: Universal Edition.

Schoenberg, A. (1911). *Harmonielehre.* Vienna: Universal Edition.

Schoenberg, A. (1949/1975). My evolution. In: L. Stein (Ed.), *Style and idea: Selected writings of Arnold Schoenberg* (pp. 79–92). Berkeley, CA: University of California Press.

Simon, H., & Sumner, R. (1968). Pattern in music. In: B. Kleinmuntz (Ed.), *Formal representation of human judgement* (pp. 219–250). New York, NY: John Wiley and Sons.

Sloboda, J. (1985). Immediate recall of melodies. In: J. Sloboda (Ed.), *Exploring the musical mind: Cognition, emotion, ability, function* (pp. 71–96). Oxford: Oxford University Press.

Sloboda, J., Hermelin, H., & O'Connor, N. (1985). An exceptional musical memory. *Music Perception, 3*(2), 15–170.

Smith, N., & Tsimpli, I.-M. (1995). *The mind of a savant: language, learning and modularity.* Oxford: Blackwell.

Repp, B. (1997). The aesthetic quality of a quantitatively average music performance: two preliminary experiments. *Music Perception, 14*(4), 419–444.

Young, R., & Nettelbeck, T. (1995). The abilities of a musical savant and his family. *Journal of Autism and Developmental Disorders, 25*(3), 231–248.

Part 6

Examining musical performance

Chapter 14

Off the record: performance, history, and musical logic

Nicholas Cook

Abstract

Empirical approaches to the study of recorded performance, originally developed by psychologists and subsequently adopted by music theorists, are opening up new areas of historical study. Both psychology and music theory, however, are oriented towards general principles rather than historical contingencies; an example is Schenkerian performance pedagogy, which applies insights drawn from the work of Heinrich Schenker (1868-1935) to present-day performance. But today's performance style is quite different from that with which Schenker was familiar. Comparison of Schenker's 1925 article on Schubert's Impromptu Op. 90 No. 3 (which includes prescriptions for performance as well as a structural analysis) with a 1905 piano roll by Eugen d'Albert, a pianist Schenker particularly admired, suggests a 'rhetorical' approach fundamentally opposed to the structurally oriented approaches advocated by Schenkerian pedagogy today. It also evidences a striking disconnect between the modernist theoretical approach set out in Schenker's 1925 article and his decidedly pre-modern sense of how music should go in performance.

Style and history

There is always a tension between the veridical description of individual phenomena and explanation of them in terms of general principles. In the human sciences at least, data never come in such a clean and tidy form as to fit theories without a degree of approximation, making it necessary to dig under the details of surface appearances to discover the underlying phenomena (which is close to saying that people select facts to fit theories). There is in short a permanent tension between the urge to describe and the urge to explain.

In the study of music, one of the main forms of this tension revolves around history. At one extreme there is historical musicology and criticism, the aim of which is to do justice to the particularity of musical practices and experiences. At the opposite extreme lies music theory, or at least those branches of music theory that concern themselves with general principles of well-formed structure, what is sometimes referred to as musical 'grammar' or 'syntax'. In his seminal book *The Musical Mind*, John Sloboda was one of the first to explore seriously the analogy between Schenkerian theory (then as now the dominant theoretical model for the tonal practices of Western 'art' music) and structural linguistics: while languages change, of course, seeing music theory from this perspective necessarily emphasizes the synchronic dimension of musical sense-making, and more generally one might say that the extremely fruitful convergence which took place in the 1980s between music theory and psychology (and in which Sloboda played a pioneering role) tended to sideline the historical dimension of musical understanding. And nowhere, arguably, was this more the case than in the study of performance, in which the generative approach to performance expression strikingly demonstrated the value of working on the borderlines between music theory and psychology.

An example of psychologically based performance theory that illustrates my point, and that is particularly relevant to my subject matter, is Neil Todd's model of phrase arching, the easily observable tendency of pianists playing common-practice repertory to get faster and louder as they play into a phrase, and slower and softer as they come out of it. Todd developed a mathematical model that involved fitting curves to composed phrase structures at multiple levels (such as 2, 4, 8, or 16 bars), and comparing the summed profiles to the timing and dynamics of actual performances; he also used the curves to create synthesized performances, and his realization of Schubert's G♭ Impromptu op. 90, no. 3 (D. 899) proved to be quite a convincing imitation of the recordings of present-day performers such as Murray Perahia and Benjamin Frith. For Todd, phrase arching lies at the heart of expressive performance, and he explained its effect in terms of the mechanisms underlying the sense of self-motion: this, he said, is why phrase arching sounds so 'natural' (Todd, 1992, p. 3549). The explanatory success of the model, then, is measured by the extent to which the theory fits the observable phenomena, which is to say by the lack of space it allows for such contingent factors as particular pianists' tastes or intentions, the particular nature of the repertory being performed, the specific circumstances of the performance—and most of all, historical change in performance style.

Although I characterized music theory in the abstract as unhistorical—the disciplinary identity of music theory lies in its synchronic approach, in its reduction of observable phenomena to more general principles—in practice most music theorists attempt to temper their structuralism with a degree of historical awareness. The resulting tension is an almost ubiquitous feature of the music-theoretical literature. In his small book *Musical Form and Musical Performance*, one of the key early texts in musical performance theory, Edward T. Cone carefully distinguished between the phrase organization of baroque, classical, and romantic music: in these three styles, he said, the controlling unit is respectively the beat, the bar, and the four-bar phrase (Cone, 1968, Chapter 3). But at the same time Cone spoke without historical qualification when he described the phrase as 'a microcosm of the composition' (1968, p. 26), and made it the basis of his well-known ball-throwing model of rhythmic structure in music: according to

this, phrases, sections, and even whole compositions can be analysed in terms of combinations of an initial downbeat (/, equivalent to the throwing of a ball), a period of
motion (∪, or when accented –), and a cadential downbeat (\, as the ball is caught).
Cone offered this as no more than a metaphor, in which the symbols refer to musical
functions rather than, as with Todd, directly specifying performance parameters.[1]
Yet—again as with Todd—it is based on general physical principles (gravity and
momentum), and in this way implies a claim of naturalness that is none the less pervasive for being more discreetly expressed.

Despite its more humanistic formulation, Cone's model carries similar implications
to Todd's in terms of agency and historical contingency. In essence the claim that lies
behind Cone's model is that articulate performance 'expresses' formal structure
(a telling formulation, in that it appropriates for music theory a term that most people
might associate with emotional meaning). Figure 14.1a, for example, analyses Chopin's
A major Prelude into two large phrases, each made up of four 6/4 'hypermeasures'
(these consist of pairs of notated 3/4 bars): each large phrase is interpreted as a
single ball-playing motion (/∪ ∪\). But by itself, Cone continues, this interpretation
would result in a sense of premature closure half way through the piece: there is
another level at which the performer should project the whole piece as a single ball-
throwing gesture, as shown in Figure 14.1b. At the same time Figure 14.1b shows
how this higher-level motion leads to a reinterpretation of the lower-level pattern:
at the points marked 4 and 5 (the figures now represent hypermeasures), the \ and /
have been replaced by accents (–), the result being that the downbeats and accents
at hypermeasures 1, 4, 5, and 8 now spell out the music's underlying melodic
motion, B-C♯-B-A.

In his account of this music, Cone is not analysing a specific performance (unless,
of course, he is by implication analysing his own). He is rather saying how the music
is, as theorists do, and hinting at how this might be expressed in articulate performance: 'the arrival of a strong measure', he says by way of example, 'must be heralded by
careful temporal adjustment rather than by simple accentuation' (Cone, 1968, p. 42).

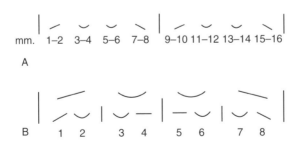

Fig. 14.1 Cone's analyses of Chopin, A major Prelude. From *Musical Form and Musical
Performance*, by Edward T. Cone © 1968 by W.W. Norton and Company Inc. Used by
permission of W.W. Norton amd Company Inc.

This is classic music theorist's discourse, in which no quarter is given to the exercise of personal taste or subjectivity. Conclusions for how the music is to be played are drawn directly from analysis of the music itself: it follows that agency is limited to the choice of one analytical interpretation over another (not that Cone gives much indication that there might be equally valid ways to think about *that*). An approach like this, which goes from structure to performance—which maps score-based, structural analysis onto the practice of performance—allows no space for performers' creativity. Ultimately, it would seem, the job of a performer is to convey to the audience the structure embodied in the score. That Cone should have adopted such a position, and bequeathed it to the music-theoretical subdiscipline of performance analysis, is not so surprising when one remembers that he was himself an active and accomplished composer.

It is not hard to recognize Cone's B-C#-B-A motion as Schenkerian analysis in plain clothes (the uniform version might be $\hat{2}$ -N- $\hat{2}$ - $\hat{1}$, or for the ultra-orthodox, [$\hat{3}$ -] $\hat{2}$ -N- $\hat{2}$ - $\hat{1}$). And it is in its Schenkerian form that the structure-to-performance approach is most influential today. Top-down analysis—that is, analysis that proceeds from a synoptic representation of the whole towards the differentiation of its parts at successively detailed levels—gives rise to an image of music as a complex structure of entailments, which is then mapped onto performance practice, largely by reference to principles described in an unfinished book, *The Art of Performance,* on which Schenker worked intensively around 1911 (more about this later). As with Cone, the process does not acknowledge agency: one of Schenker's slogans was 'no interpretation!' (Rothstein, 1984, p. 10), by which he meant that there could be only one correct analytical understanding of a piece of music—although he admitted that there is a variety of technical devices by which that understanding might be legitimately translated into performance, and therein lies the performer's freedom. (Seen this way, performance can involve artistry, but hardly creativity.) Nor did Schenker's approach allow much room for historical contingency: he insisted in Leibnizian manner on the permanence of musical ideas, criticising the piano virtuoso and editor Hans von Bülow for his attempts to adapt for the modern grand piano eighteenth-century music originally written for the clavichord (such adaptations reflect 'an historical point of view that is tempered with feelings of goodwill and pity, etc', Schenker, 1976, p. 21, sniffed).

This is music theory supported by the full panoply of German idealism, and its installation as a major stream in performance pedagogy today is paradoxical testimony to the unpredictability of historical contingency. (It might perhaps be argued that in the conservatory context relativism, historical or otherwise, is simply out of place.) But it is with the issue of musical style that I am concerned here. Schenkerian performance pedagogy interprets principles derived from Schenker's writings in terms of the performance style of post-1945 modernism, a style that remains broadly current today. And here there is another and sharper paradox, for this style is utterly unlike that of Schenker's day, and in particular unlike that of 1890s Vienna, where Schenker seems to have formed the basic musical sensibilities that he retained through his life (Cook, 2007). In this chapter, taking Schubert's op. 90, no. 3 as a case study, I stage an

encounter between an example of Schenker's writing on performance and two recordings from his own time, one of them by a performer whom Schenker particularly
admired. My purpose in doing this is to place the structure-to-performance approach
within its historical context, and to suggest that what are commonly seen as permanent music-theoretical or psychological principles governing articulate performance
are in fact expressions of a particular stylistic preference, and as such historically contingent. Another way of saying this is that, in performance analysis, the urge to explain
has overwhelmed the urge to describe.

D'Albert and Schubert's G♭ Impromptu

It was in the mid 1890s, when he was a prolific critic as well as a minor composer and
performer, that Schenker was most directly engaged with Viennese concert life, and
one of the performers whom he most admired at that time was Eugen d'Albert (1864–
1932), the Glasgow-born pianist and composer who went to study in Vienna in 1881
and came to regard himself as a German musician by adoption. Schenker published a
laudatory article on him in 1894, and included d'Albert in the lists of outstanding
musicians he compiled in 1895 and 1896 (Schenker, 1990, pp. 117–121, 130, 326),
although his praise subsequently became distinctly fainter (but that was a standard
pattern with Schenker). D'Albert made a modest number of recordings, both piano
rolls and audio discs, and among them was a piano roll of Schubert's op. 90, no. 3; we
know from Paul Roës[2] that this was one of d'Albert's encore pieces (it is perhaps
unfortunate that most early piano recordings are of encore pieces), and d'Albert
played it in Liszt's edition, transposed to G major and with the tune in doubled octaves
for the final section.[3] The roll was cut on 19 May 1905, using the then very new Welte
Mignon reproducing system, and issued as Welte 422.

   This is one of the few reproducing piano systems that provides accurate timing
information; dynamic information by contrast is only approximate, since there was
just one pump for the upper half of the keyboard and another for the lower. (Given
that, the dynamics are surprisingly convincing, though they do seem to vary between
one transfer and another.) Though later Welte rolls were plainly edited, with mistakes
being manually corrected, this does not seem to apply to early examples, in which
mistakes are allowed to stand.[4] It is reasonable, then, to think that this roll, which has
been issued in two commercial transfers,[5] affords a reasonably dependable insight into
how d'Albert played in the first years of the twentieth century. And what makes it particularly valuable in the present context is that op. 90, no. 3 is one of relatively few
pieces about which Schenker published detailed directions for performance, although
he did not do this until two decades later: his article on op. 90, no. 3 appeared in 1925,[6]
in the final issue of his one-man journal, *Der Tonwille*. (Schenker based his article
on the editions of op. 90, no. 3 commonly available at this time, again in G major
and barred in 2/2 rather than 4/2, though he deplored the deviations from Schubert's
original.) In addition to the performance directions, the article includes an analysis
using Schenker's then newly developed graphic technique, and in this way op. 90, no. 3
provides an opportunity to triangulate three separate sources: Schenker's analysis,

his detailed account of how the music should go in performance, and the record of how it was played by a pianist who—at least at one time—ranked among Schenker's favourites.

How then might d'Albert's performance of op. 90, no. 3 be described? Tempo modification is a highly salient characteristic not only of d'Albert's playing but also of op. 90, no. 3, because it is directly expressed in the constant quaver figuration, and as a result the conventional tempo graph is more informative about d'Albert's style than is often the case. In Figure 14.2 slower tempi (that is, longer beat durations) appear at the top of the chart, because this invokes the same gravitational metaphor as does Cone's thrown ball. The principal means by which d'Albert shapes his performance is the use of slow rallentandi that target particular expressive points. From bar 5 (first half of bar 3 in modern editions), for example, it is as if d'Albert trudges uphill, slowing down to the melodic crotchets in bar 6, then regaining a little speed, only to slow down again through bar 7: the result is to throw an accentual weight onto the melodic A (I shall refer to the piece as in G major) that marks the crest of this gesture, at bar 8. Though my description may be followed by reference to the graph in Figure 14.2, the metaphor is far more vivid when the graph is incorporated within a playback and visualization environment, such as Sonic Visualiser.[7]

Because of the shared gravitational metaphor, it is possible to convey some aspects of the effect by adopting and adapting the analytical symbols Cone used to elaborate his thrown ball model. In Figure 14.3, / denotes the process that generates accentuation (generally rallentando, though in principle the symbol references a function rather than a parameter), while \ denotes the point at which the accent falls and is released. At bar 8, it is as if a switch is tripped: the tension accumulated through the preceding

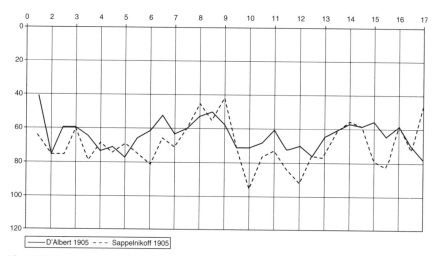

Fig. 14.2 Tempo graph of d'Albert's and Sapellnikoff's 1905 piano rolls of Schubert's op. 90, no. 3, bars 1–16 (based on barring in 2/2). Values are shown at the end of beats.

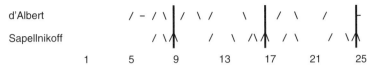

Fig. 14.3 Analysis of d'Albert's and Sapellnikoff's 1905 piano rolls of Schubert's op. 90, no. 3, bars 1–25.

rallentando is discharged, and d'Albert so to speak freewheels through the beginning of the next phrase, with the process of accumulating tension not beginning again until bar 10. The accent at bar 8 has no duration—the release is instantaneous— but there are cases where the accent falls on a group of notes and consequently has duration: this applies to the crotchets at bar 6, where the accentuation takes the form of prolongation rather than a momentary discharge of tension, and this is marked in Figure 14.3 by a different symbol (–). D'Albert's way of playing these crotchets, as it were creating extra time in order to accommodate the denser note values, was sufficiently idiosyncratic to be commented on by his commentaries: according to Roës, 'he played the eighth notes of the melody relatively slower than the quarter notes, thus giving to that long melodic line a superhuman tranquility'.[8]

Performance qualities are always thrown into relief by comparison, and there is a second Welte roll of op. 90, no. 3 from 1905, by the Russian pianist and confidant of Tchaikowsky, Vassili Sapellnikoff (1868–1941):[9] it was cut on 1 December, just over six months after d'Albert's. (This is not simple coincidence: following the perfection of the Welte Mignon mechanism in 1904, the company embarked on an ambitious recording programme encompassing major pianists from all over Europe.) As can be seen in Figure 14.2, Sapellnikoff makes as much use of rubato as d'Albert,[10] and he too creates accentuation through rallentando. But he deploys it in a rather different manner. For example, Sapellnikoff accentuates the cadential A at bar 8 and G at bar 16, so concluding each phrase in a parallel manner. D'Albert's approach is more roundabout: as we have seen, he too emphasizes the A at bar 8, but at the end of the second phrase it is not the G but the A at bar 15 that he emphasizes—not the cadential note but the appoggiatura to it. His nuance can still be seen as expressing the conclusion of the phrase, but indirectly, with the agogic accent on the A triggering a melodic and harmonic process of resolution, and the result is that his shaping of the two phrase ends is not parallel. Or as another example, Sapellnikoff articulates not only the conclusion of each phrase, but also the initiation of the following one, resulting in the characteristic double peaks at bars 8–9 and 16–17. By contrast, d'Albert repeatedly de-emphasizes the beginnings of phrases, playing through or swallowing them, as we saw at bar 9: at bar 17, to the extent that the phrase beginning is marked at all, it is by hand breaking (the anticipation of the right hand by the left) and by dynamic emphasis.

Although d'Albert and Sapellnikoff create accentuation by similar means, then, they appear to think of the music differently: Sapellnikoff responds in a relatively straightforward manner to such design features as the beginning and ends of phrases, whereas in the case of d'Albert the relationship of structure and performance is less direct.

In general the same picture emerges from the following section. Here, admittedly, both d'Albert and Sapellnikoff mark the cadential Gs at bars 31 and 47, and at bar 33 d'Albert actually marks the phrase beginning more clearly than Sapellnikoff. But elsewhere it is Sapellnikoff who responds more directly to design features. A convenient way of comparing tempo profiles is in terms of vectors, classifying them according to whether the profile rises or falls between any two points; analysed this way, d'Albert and Sapellnikoff share a common profile throughout bars 18:2 to 24:2, reflecting the extent to which easily distinguishable performers can share a common stylistic 'language'. But as Figure 14.4 indicates, the differences are more telling.

Sapellnikoff's performance reflects the melodic and harmonic sequence between bars 17–20 and 21–4: the vector is in each case identical (though the quantities differ significantly), except that he adds an accent to reflect the downbeat at bar 25, so creating yet another double peak. By contrast d'Albert plays bars 21–4 quite differently from 17–20, and in particular he de-emphasizes the appoggiatura at bar 23, breaking the parallel with 19. The anticipated accent is postponed, with the resulting growth in intensity culminating in a prolongation (accent with duration) at bar 25, as shown in Figure 14.3. In this way d'Albert creates a particularly magical effect, or perhaps it would be more accurate to say that he realizes with special effect an expressive potential inherent in Schubert's score. In terms of phrase structure, bar 25 is a major downbeat, yet Schubert has chosen to maintain not only the same harmony across the phrase break, in contravention to any reputable student's harmony manual, but also the same inversion and register. In fact bar 25 is an almost exact repeat of bar 24, and the result is the creation of an auditory oxymoron, an effect of pregnant emptiness. By using tempo modification to throw additional weight onto this point d'Albert adds decisively to the effect, and as his quaver figuration audibly falters, it is as if for a moment time stood still. This is an effect highly characteristic of d'Albert's pianism, and none the less poetic because one cannot put into words exactly what it means. What one can however say with confidence is that it is an effect very much at odds with the ideal of articulate performance adumbrated by post-1945 modernism.

It would be quite incorrect to pass off Sapellnikoff as some kind of proto-modernist: his tendency to mark the design features of the music is expressed through a 'language' of rubato that barely survived the First World War, let alone the second. But the contrast between these two early twentieth-century pianists does highlight the extent in which d'Albert underplays or simply ignores structure as an analyst might see it. A comparison of Figures 14.1 and 14.3 makes the point. For Cone, structure is the principal locus of musical coherence, and so Figure 14.1 is self-explanatory; it is an embodiment of musical logic, and might be expected to underlie any given performance interpretation. Figure 14.3, by contrast, makes no sense in itself: it is purely descriptive, an epiphenomenon of factors or decisions made elsewhere, or of pure contingency. In other words, Cone's structure-to-performance model, with its regular pattern of phrase-based impulses, does not correspond at all closely to d'Albert's performance style. The way in which d'Albert hurries through section breaks might almost suggest a use of inverse phrase arching, but that too would be misleading: the point is that phrase structure is simply not a strong predictor of his playing of op. 90, no. 3, in the way that is of Perahia's or Frith's. The basis of d'Albert's interpretation

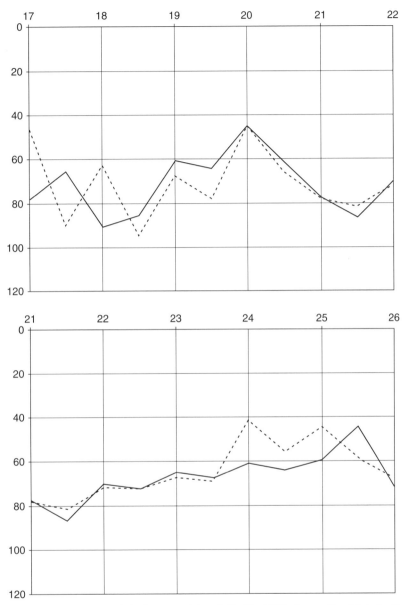

Fig. 14.4 Tempo graphs of d'Albert's and Sapellnikoff's 1905 piano rolls of Schubert's op. 90, no. 3, bars 17–21 and 21–5. Values are shown at the end of beats.

lies rather in the identification of certain moments for expressive emphasis, points which may or may not (but more often do not) coincide with those treated as significant by traditional analysis. In short, d'Albert's playing, which Schenker so admired, embodies a sense of how music goes that is basically different from that embodied in Todd's model of phrase arching, in the model of rhythmic structure expressed through

Cone's ball-throwing metaphor, or in modern performance pedagogy based on Schenker's analytical method.

The problem might of course be that theorists working in the tradition of reductive analysis exemplified by Schenker's method have formulated their idea of structure too narrowly. The psychologist Richard Parncutt has proposed a general model of performance accentuation, the basic principle of which is that 'performed accents reinforce immanent accents' (Parncutt 2003, p. 175). By 'immanent' accents Parncutt means any points of emphasis that are inherent in the composition. These may be determined by aspects of linear-harmonic structure, as understood by Schenkerian analysts, but they may equally result from the kinds of features that such analysts see as 'design' rather than structure, such as melodic contours, harmonic consonance, and dissonance, or aspects of texture. Through this more generous interpretation, Parncutt's hypothesis might seem to hold out the possibility of generalizing the structure-to-performance approach beyond the structuralist—that is, modernist—playing styles with which it is today associated. But the very generosity of the model means that its cash value is severely limited. Parncutt (2003, p. 175) writes that his model allows for

> a wide variety of interpretations of a given piece of piano music. Musical scores typically include many different kinds of immanent accents, of varying strengths. The performer is thus presented with a wide variety of accents, occurring both individually and in various combinations. It would appear to be a matter of artistry to decide which of these accents should be emphasized in performance, and which of the various possible means of expression should be used for this purpose.

Another way of putting this is that music is so rich in potentially expressive moments that to simply identify them explains very little; what matters, then, is the performer's selection. But as d'Albert frequently plays repeated passages quite differently from how he played them first time round, it is hard to see that the selection could be explained by any structural criteria, however generously the concept of structure is defined. In short, Parncutt's model does not so much solve the original problem as repackage it as 'artistry'.

Parncutt does not set his argument into a historical context. There is however a long tradition of theoretical and pedagogical commentary into which it falls, and which suggests a possible way of resolving the problem. I shall cite just two examples from this tradition. The first is C. P. E. Bach, whose *Essay on the True Art of Playing Keyboard Instruments*, some of which goes back to 1753, is perhaps—when its longevity is taken into account—the single most influential text in the history of Western 'art' music performance. Bach (1974, p. 163) writes that 'dissonances are played loudly and consonances softly, since the former rouse our emotions and the latter quiet them', an unexceptionable statement which precisely describes what d'Albert does (for instance in bars 15–16 of op. 90, no. 3). But Bach throws his net more widely. He prescribes the same emphasis for 'all tones of a melody which lie outside the key', and again for 'an exceptional turn of melody which is designed to create a violent affect'. And the same association of points of emphasis with affective expression recurs much closer to d'Albert's (and Schenker's) own time in the writings of the Swiss theorist and pedagogue Matthis Lussy, whose *Traité de l'expression musicale* was published in 1874.

Central to Lussy's theory of performance is the *accent pathétique*, which he sees as prompted by 12 kinds of musical event: among these are dissonances and foreign tones, while others include upper neighbour notes, particularly long notes, and notes approached by leap. (Most of the notes that d'Albert chooses to emphasize fall under one or other of Lussy's headings.) But again the affective dimension is crucial: as if carrying on from where Bach left off, Lussy writes that 'it is precisely these unexpected, irregular, exceptional notes, without musical logic, which most particularly have the ability to affect the sentiment'.[11]

Parncutt (2003, p. 175) observes that 'an immediate problem with the hypothesis that performed accents reinforce immanent accents is that it is difficult to falsify', since 'just about any performance might be related to a pattern of accents that have been selected *post hoc* to account for the performer's expressive profile'. Actually the same might be said of the performance-to-structure approach as a whole: if a performer articulates structure that will be taken as confirmation of the structure-to-performance approach, but if he or she doesn't, it can be argued that the performance can be understood only in terms of its deviation from structure, thereby once again confirming the approach. And the same slackness of fit between evidence and interpretation also pervades the reading of period treatises. The theorist Michael Green (1994, p. 216) concludes his study of Lussy's *Traité* as follows: 'there is more to a good performance than simply knowing which surface events to respond to … It is essential that the common response to individual events be carefully controlled so that the structure is clearly articulated'. In effect he is invoking Lussy as a period proponent of the structure-to-performance approach, so strengthening the assumption that it embodies permanent principles of articulate performance. But on a more straightforward (that is, less ideologically loaded) reading Lussy is saying just the opposite. He is saying that it is precisely the notes which *lack* musical logic that are essential to the music's expressive meaning, and as such represent the basic cues around which effective performance must be organized.

If we see d'Albert's playing in these terms, then its basis is not the expression of pre-established structure, whether defined in Todd's, Cone's, Schenker's, or even Parncutt's terms. It is, rather, structure's other: the unexpected, the irregular, the exceptional notes, the *accents pathétiques*, that constitute the central pillars of d'Albert's performance, from which are subtended the spans of accelerando and rallentando through which the performance is shaped from moment to moment. Time in d'Albert's performance, then, does not arise through progressive subdivision, in the manner of an analysis that proceeds by stages from a synoptic view of the whole to the interpretation of individual moments. Nor is it a neutral medium within which evenly graduated musical objects are placed. Instead time is shaped on the fly around the moments that d'Albert picks out for expressive treatment, and the result is a constant ebb and flow of tempo, an effect of continuous inhalation and exhalation, a necessary aspect of which is the characteristic way that d'Albert rushes or snatches at short passages, such as at the transitions between sections. That is a way of playing that has long been out of favour, possibly as a result of the impact of recordings, and it is the source of d'Albert's present-day reputation for uncertain rhythmic control: even the unnamed author of the liner notes on the Dal Segno transfer of op. 90, no. 3, whom one might have expected to be on d'Albert's side, refers to his 'strange rhythmic lapses'. I would rather see it as an integral component of d'Albert's pianistic style: a style that is predicated on the communication of moment-to-moment expressiveness, which is why—in contrast to the 'structuralist' style of late twentieth-century common practice—I shall refer to it as 'rhetorical'.

Schenker and d'Albert

D'Albert may have been one of Schenker's most admired pianists around the turn of the century, but as I said, Schenker's *Tonwille* article dates from 20 years later, following the development in all its basics of the graphic analytical technique for which Schenker is known today. The analysis round which the essay is built is an early but well formed example the of $\hat{3}$ - $\hat{2}$ - $\hat{1}$ *Urlinie*: the first of the analytical charts contains five structural layers, and these supply the organization for the analytical commentary that takes up about two-thirds of the article. The last third (Schenker, 2005, pp. 141–142) consists of the detailed performance prescriptions to which I referred, prefaced by a few general comments. Given the momentous developments in Schenker's thinking about music during this period, one might expect that, whatever Schenker thought of d'Albert's playing in 1905, by 1925 his sense of how music should go would have changed out of all recognition. But is this in fact the case?

At the most general level, Schenker directs that 'The melodic line must be prominent, penetrating in tone, floating clearly above the dark accompaniment of the right and left hands', and that accented passing notes should be played more strongly than their resolutions, in the manner of 'the best singing artists'. Even allowing for the inaccuracy of the Welte recording process, it seems clear that this is an accurate description of what d'Albert does. But then, so do any number of other pianists, while Schenker's directions for the playing of accented passing notes can be matched from any number of other performance treatises (such as Bach's, 1974, p. 151, which also includes the comparison with singers). There are also some quite specific points of coincidence. For instance, Schenker writes of bar 154 that 'there should be a hesitation in the first quarter, and a resumption of motion in the remaining quarter notes', and that, too, is exactly what d'Albert does. Again, Schenker specifies that

> In bar 66, the first quarter note hesitates, the remaining ones move forward more rapidly. The same holds true in bar 68, despite the closing off of the section, so that the last quarter note, d^1, moves without pause towards c^1 in bar 69. The sectional division is not to be expressed by the usual *ritardando* at the closing cadence.

D'Albert does all this; he even makes the left-hand semiquavers at bar 71 sound like a glissando, as Schenker prescribes. And as for the linking of sections without *ritardando*, that is what d'Albert does throughout most of this performance, apart from an exaggeratedly rhetorical fermata before the transfigured return of the opening theme at bar 109—transfigured because of the Lisztian octaves and spread chords.

But it would beggar belief if Schenker's prescriptions and d'Albert's playing corresponded throughout, and they don't. One obvious difference comes right at the beginning. Schenker writes, very characteristically, that

> the law of performance governing note repetitions in general demands that the two half notes of bar 2 be directed towards the whole note of bar 3, with the sort of acceleration that the accentuation in bar 3 makes obvious. The changes of pulse in bars 1–3 in this way hold

the key to performance of the entire piece. All is lost if b^1 in bar 1 is more strongly emphasized than b^1 in bar 2, and if bar 2 is not directed towards bar 3 in the manner of an upbeat
… Schubert's marking < > in bar 7 demands a movement in bars 5 and 6 whose goal is b^1
in bar 7—thus one should not get lost in the quarters of bar 6.

This is not at all how d'Albert plays the opening: he emphasizes the B at bar 2 rather than 3, accelerates through bars 3–4, puts a dynamic accent on the A at bar 5,
luxuriates ('gets lost') in the crotchets, and then slows down to the A in bar 8, to which
(as we have seen) he gives an agogic emphasis. So on a literal reading all is indeed lost
(although curiously, d'Albert—who as I said often plays repeats differently—gets it
right at bar 11, while Sapellnikoff gets it right from the start). But we should not be
looking for so literal a reading. Both Schenker's prescription and d'Albert's performance are structured by means of a hierarchy of tones, with relative salience being
expressed through what Schenker terms 'changes of pulse'. The difference is not in
what I termed the 'language' of rubato: it is rather in the underlying interpretation, for
in essence d'Albert stresses B in bars 1–4 and A in bars 5–8, in the manner of a traditional harmonic reduction, whereas both of Schenker's analytical charts show that he
sees the B as an *Urlinie* note ($\hat{3}$) that falls to A ($\hat{2}$) only at bar 8.

Again, Schenker speaks in this passage of accelerating to the point of accentuation,
whereas d'Albert characteristically creates accentuation through slowing down. But
then, the psychological principle is in each case the same: if an accent is a point in the
music that is 'marked for consciousness', as Cooper and Meyer (1960, p. 4) put it, then
this marking can be accomplished by any kind of deviation from an established norm,
so that accelerando will do as well as rallentando. And what is striking is that Schenker's
prescriptions for performance convey the same mobile tempo that is audible on
d'Albert's roll. At the beginning of bar 19, for instance, Schenker says it is 'important
that … the first two accompanying eighth notes, d^1 and e^1, should be played with
slight hesitation; the difference should be made up by acceleration in the third quarter'.
At that particular point d'Albert does the exact opposite, but it is a perfect description
of what I described as the effect of faltering at the beginning of bar 25. Nor is this an
isolated reference on Schenker's part. I count 12 specific mentions in Schenker's two-
page text of hesitating, delaying, lingering, and pausing on the one hand, and of
resuming motion, hurrying forward, pushing forward, and accelerating on the other.
All this evokes the same continuous process of inhalation and exhalation that
I described in d'Albert's playing. And indeed the second and third sentences of
Schenker's section on performance provide a succinct summary of d'Albert's style:

> One should not simply announce one note after the other: rather, one should lead toward
> and retreat from significant notes. This results in spoken melody, or sung speech.

Such a description is of course peculiarly appropriate to the G$^\flat$ Impromptu, in effect
a *Lied ohne Worte* a few years *avant la lettre*: perhaps it is not too fanciful to suggest
that the sometimes unpredictable accents of d'Albert's performance create an impression that the music is full of words, even though they remain unspoken. But it is also
an accurate characterization of d'Albert's way of playing. In short, Schenker's prescriptions, even though they date from as late as the mid 1920s, reflect a rhetorical
performance style (and Schenker's reference to sung speech licenses my use of

that term), the foundation of which is the expressive shaping of individual moments through a constantly mobile tempo.

And how far do either Schenker's prescriptions or d'Albert's performance correspond to the structural analysis which makes up the main part of Schenker's article? The most direct connection I have already mentioned: the interpretation of the opening B as falling to A at bar 8, not 5, as indicated in both Schenker's analytical charts and his performance directions (though not as performed by d'Albert). Perhaps a similar connection might be made with Schenker's (2005, p. 137) observation that the opening section 'concludes not with the cadence in bar 16, but with the one in bar 48', on the grounds that bars 1–48 are unified by a $\hat{3}$ - $\hat{2}$ - $\hat{1}$ succession: that would fit with the way d'Albert plays through bars 16–17, although Schenker does not comment on this in his performance prescriptions. But it is hard to find anything beyond these rather insubstantial connections. While many of the performance prescriptions are concerned with the nuancing of specific notes or points in the music, usually in terms of tempo though sometimes of dynamics, articulation, or pedalling, there is no general correlation between these points and the prolongations shown in Schenker's graphic analysis. And Schenker's analytical commentary focuses principally around issues that are generated by the theory rather than by the music, such as the organization of the middle section round B and its neighbour note C, compensating for the lack of neighbour-note elaboration in the initial section; the means by which premature closure is avoided within the music's outer sections (by retaining the emphasis on $\hat{3}$ until the final descent); the means by which E minor and C major are established as autonomous middle ground keys rather than mere scale degrees of G; and the need to understand the occasionally extreme chromatic modulation 'against the norms of the diatonic system' (Schenker, 2005, p. 141). None of these are really suitable candidates for performance intervention.

In short, there is a striking lack of connection between Schenker's analysis on the one hand, and what he has to say about performance (or what d'Albert plays) on the other, and the question arises: why might this be? I have two alternative explanations to propose, the first more modest in its implications, the second more sweeping. The modest explanation arises out of the specific nature of op. 90, no. 3. Bars 1–48, with which I have been primarily concerned in this chapter, consist of unambiguous four-bar phrases organized into regular powers-of-two groups. Even in the middle section, with its three-bar phrases and elisions, structure is more or less unambiguously specified by means of melodic contour and harmony. So, if d'Albert de-emphasizes phrase and section structure by playing through the cadences rather than observing 'the usual *ritardando*', as Schenker put it, that is perhaps because the structure is already sufficiently self-evident: as Cone (1968, p. 31) comments, 'of course, the more explicitly the rhythmic form has been written into the music, the less the performance is required to add'. Similarly, if it is argued that Lussy's unexpected, irregular, and exceptional *accents pathétiques* emerge only in the context of the expected, the regular, and the normal—in other words out of structure as conventionally defined—then it might be claimed that the latter has been so firmly hard-wired by Schubert that d'Albert can afford to direct virtually all his efforts towards the former. The question then is what d'Albert does with more 'discursive' music, to use Julian Johnson's (2002) convenient term, such as Beethoven's Sonata Op 101, which d'Albert recorded twice on piano rolls,[12] and about the performance of which Schenker of course had a great deal to say. (That will be the next phase of this project.) But this more modest explanation still goes only part of the way. Recall that it was this very piece that Todd chose to illustrate his model of expressive performance, which is exclusively based on phrase structure, and that modern pianists such as Perahia and Frith employ phrase arching very much as described by Todd. Even if the disconnect between structure and performance as represented by Schenker's prescriptions or d'Albert's roll reflects the specific nature of this piece, it still evidences an approach very different from that of modern pianists.

The more sweeping explanation, of course, would be that, for Schenker, analysis and performance were more distinct than his disciples and commentators have supposed—in fact probably more so than Schenker himself would have wished. In the end, reading Schenker's performance prescriptions in light of d'Albert's recording cannot give us certainty about just how Schenker thought op. 90, no. 3 should go, let alone how he played it himself: the fact that Schenker speaks in his commentary of creating accentuation through accelerando, whereas on this piano roll d'Albert creates it through slowing down, is sufficient evidence of this. But it is plain that, in 1925, he was still thinking of it in terms of the mobility of tempo, the 'language' of rubato, the 'speaking' style of playing that I have called 'rhetorical' performance. And that suggests that his basic sense of how music goes remained untouched by the development of his analytical method, which in effect shaves off the filigree details of classical music to reveal the streamlined, directional lines that lie beneath. In Peter Gay's (1978, p. 2) words, 'modernist hated modernity', and the cap fits Schenker: the directions for performance that accompany his modernising analyses, for the most part dogmatically asserted with an air of self-evidence, provide an insider's access to performance of the old school as practised at the Viennese *fin de siècle*. By 1925, when the *Tonwille* essay was published, that world must have come to seem almost as irrecoverable as it does today, and Schenker's writings on performance are saturated with nostalgia: it was in the same year, though in another context, that Schenker (1994, p. 111) wrote, 'Anyone who has heard performances of masterworks twenty years ago can scarcely believe how performance could become already so much worse today'.

Such a disconnect between analysis and performance, of course, flies in the face not only of present-day performance pedagogy in the Schenkerian tradition, but also of the basic principles that lie behind his unfinished book of 1911, *The Art of Performance*— the basic principles of what I have termed the structure-to-performance approach. But the contradictions are already there in Schenker's writings. The starting point for *The Art of Performance* is that a composer's notation 'does not indicate his directions for the performance but, in a far more profound sense, represents the effect he wishes to attain'; elsewhere he writes that 'this effect then serves to justify any means [the performer] might use to produce it' (Schenker, 2000, pp. 5, 78). (A few years earlier Schenker, 1984, p. 69, had expressed the point more graphically: 'even the nose may assist, as long as the proper meaning is conveyed'.) But this is wholly incompatible with the performance directions in Schenker's essay on op. 90, no. 3, which extend to the stipulation of gestural minutiae: in bar 36 'the hand should remain steeply angled over the keys', on the upbeat to bar 65 'the hand is lifted, it strokes the air in an arc', while at bar 85 'the left hand should be held erect on the first eighth, and the figure … should be played lightly, almost as if one did not intend to produce actual sounds' (Schenker, 2005, p. 142). And more generally it is hard to reconcile the modernizing thrust of the structure-to-performance approach erected on the foundation of Schenker's 1911 text, the core paradigm of which is the clarification of structure, with the values expressed in Schenker's monograph on Beethoven's Ninth Symphony, published the very next year: there Schenker launched[13] a vitriolic attack on Wagner's reorchestration of the symphony, condemning Wagner's 'clarification-mania', the manner in which he stripped off the 'gentle, artificial camouflaging' with which Beethoven clothed his music in order to give it 'variety and contrast' (Schenker, 1992, pp. 71, 84, 87). It is an example of the difference between modernism as it is generally understood today—Bauhaus or international modernism, based on an aesthetic of disclosure—and the modernism of the Viennese *fin de siècle*, with its emphasis on depth, concealment, and illusion. But it is also the difference between Schenker's modernist music theory and a decidedly premodern sense of how music should go in performance.

What Schenkerians forget is that there is no such book as *The Art of Performance*. What is published under that name is an assemblage of fragments, many but not all of them substantial, and many but not all of them written in 1911. Schenker returned to the project from time to time throughout his life, even into the 1930s. But the fact is that he did not complete it, and the case of Schubert's G♭ Impromptu suggests why not. The mapping of analysis onto performance, of theory onto practice, was possible only on the basis of a modernist style of performance, what I have called 'structuralist' performance—a style of which the first signs appeared in the interwar period, but to which Schenker never reconciled himself. That, however, is another story.

This chapter has presented no more than a pilot study, an initial scoping of the field. On the one hand d'Albert's roll could be placed in the context of other recordings of op. 90, no. 3 (including that of another pianist Schenker admired, Emil von Sauer, though it was not made until 1940), as well as that of d'Albert's performances of other repertory. On the other hand there is material for much more intensive study of Schenker's views on performers and performance, ranging from his published articles and analyses to his voluminous diary entries and annotated scores. But this initial foray has already suggested a number of conclusions. The history of Schenkerian theory as a whole is one of appropriation: an approach deeply rooted in the values and ideologies of *fin-de-siècle* Vienna was fundamentally re-engineered for the utterly different circumstances of post-war America (Cook, 2007; Rothstein, 1986), and it becomes obvious that this applies as much to Schenker's thinking on performance as to other aspects of his theory. The structure-to-performance approach espoused today by both music theorists and psychologists, then, presents itself as dealing with general principles, but does so by virtue of treating as a paradigm what is in reality simply a historical performance style: what I have called the 'structuralist' style of the second half of the twentieth century, which represents an extraordinarily enduring expression of the values of international modernism. (Modernism has remained entrenched in the discourses and practices of classic music performance to an extent that is hardly paralleled in other arts.) In saying this I do not mean to imply that musical performance is an exclusively social construction: the creation of accent through deviation from an established norm, for instance, may well represent a general principle comparable to those of gestalt psychology. But the point is the extent to which performance style involves the culturally contingent elaboration of such general principles. Under such circumstances description may turn out to be more useful than explanation, and we should probably be suspicious of any theoretical approach to performance that claims to explain too much, especially when it comes at the expense of agency. While my purpose in this article has been to contextualize and in that sense delimit the scope of the psychological approaches to musical performance which Sloboda pioneered, I hope in so doing to have created space for the concern with particularity, with the actions and experiences of real people, which has at the same time so strongly informed his work.

The striking paradox that emerges from this study is that Schenker's theory has in this way been invoked to support a style of performance quite different from, even opposed to, the 'rhetorical' style to which Schenker subscribed. This could only come about because of what I described as the disconnect between Schenker's theoretical conceptualization of music on the one hand, and his basic sense of how music goes on the other. And this suggests a final reflection. Performance style represents a largely unconscious level of musical culture: like Bourdieu's habitus, it is a socially acquired, embodied sense of the reality of things that lies largely below the radar of critical observation. It feeds into theoretical and historiographical conceptualization, yet is peculiarly disconnected from them. It suffuses the documents on which the history of music is based, and yet cannot be fully reconstructed from them. Performance style, in short, is the elephant in the musicological room.

Notes

[1] 'It is probably unnecessary to insist here that there is no necessary correlation between strong measures and dynamic accents … Dynamic variation is only one of the means a good performer will use to indicate … the shape of a phrase. Subtle temporal adjustments (e.g. agogic accent and rubato) are equally at his disposal' (Cone, 1968, p. 31).

[2] Quoted from Roës (1978). Available at: www.arbiterrecords.com/notes/147notes.html (accessed 25 September 2010).

[3] At the time of writing, this edition is freely available on the web: Available at: http://imslp.info/files/imglnks/usimg/7/76/IMSLP05860-Schubert_-_impromtus_op90_cotta_edition.pdf (accessed 25 September 2010).

[4] Details of the Welte Mignon recording process are available at: www.pianola.org/reproducing/reproducing_welte.cfm (accessed 25 September 2010). I have benefitted from discussion of these matters with Denis Hall.

[5] *The great pianists.* Volume 6. *Eugène d'Albert*, Dal Segno 022 (2008); *Berühmte Pianisten der Jahrhundertwende spielen Beethoven und Schubert*, Teldec 8.43929 (1988).

[6] Not 1924, the printed publication date (Schenker, 2005, p. v).

[7] Available at: www.sonicvisualiser.org/ (accessed 25 September 2010).

[8] There are no eighth notes in the melody of op. 90, no. 3, so I assume the reference is to quarter and half notes.

[9] Welte 950. My thanks to Denis Hall for supplying me with a transfer of this roll.

[10] When normalized for average tempo, the beat data for Sappelnikoff's performance yields a standard deviation (which can be regarded as a rough measure of rubato) 6% higher than d'Albert's.

[11] Lussy (1874, p. 7, Green, Trans., 1994, p. 197).

[12] Complete on 2 June 1914 (Welte 2972–3), and the second and third movement only around 1927 (Welte 0274–5).

[13] Or rather renewed: Schenker was recycling his article 'Beethoven—"Retouche"', originally published in 1901 (reprinted in Schenker, 1990, pp. 259–268).

References

Bach, C. P. E. (1974 [1753/1762]). *Essay on the true art of playing keyboard instruments* (W. J. Mitchell, Trans.). London: Eulenberg Books.

Cone, E. T. (1968). *Musical form and musical performance.* New York, NY: Norton.

Cook, N. (2007). *The Schenker project: Culture, race, and music theory in* fin-de-siècle *Vienna.* New York, NY: Oxford University Press.

Cooper, G., & Meyer, L. B. (1960). *The rhythmic structure of music.* Chicago, IL: University of Chicago Press.

Gay, P. (1978). *Freud, Jews, and other Germans: Masters and victims in modernist culture.* New York, NY: Oxford University Press.

Green, M. (1994). Matthis Lussy's *Traitè de l'expression muscale* as a window into performance practice. *Music Theory Spectrum, 16,* 196–216.

Johnson, J. (2002). *Who needs classical music? Cultural choice and musical value.* Oxford: Oxford University Press.

Lussy, M. (1874). *Traité de l'expression musicale—accents, nuances, et movements dans la musique vocale et instrumentale.* Paris: Berger-Levrault & Heugel.

Parncutt, R. (2003). Accents and expression in piano performance. In K. W. Niemöller (Ed.), *Perspektiven und Methoden einer Systemischen Musikwissenschaft (Festschrift Fricke* (pp. 163–85). Frankfurt am Mein: Peter Lang.

Roës, P. (1978). *Music, the mystery and the reality* (E. McGray, Trans.). Chevy Chase, MD: E. and M. Publishing.

Rothstein, W. (1984). Heinrich Schenker as an interpreter of Beethoven's piano sonatas. *19th-Century Music, 8,* 3–28.

Rothstein, W. (1986). The Americanization of Henrich Schenker. *Theory Only, 9*(1), 5–17.

Schenker, H. (1976). A contribution to the study of ornamentation (H. Siegel, Trans.). *Music Forum, 2,* 1–139.

Schenker, H. (1984). *J. S. Bach's Chromatic Fantasy and Fugue* (H. Siegel, Trans.). New York: Longman.

Schenker, H. (1990). Heinrich Schenker als essayist und kritiker. In Federhofer H (Ed.), *Gesammelte Aufsätze, rezensionen und kleinere berichte aus den jahren 189101901.* Hildesheim: Georg Ohlms Verlag.

Schenker, H. (1992). Beethoven's *Ninth Symphony: A portrayal of its musical content, with running commentary on performance and literature as well.* J. Rothgeb, Trans.) (Ed.). New Haven, CT: Yale University Press.

Schenker, H. (1994). *The masterwork in music: A yearbook.* Volume 1 (1925). W. Drabkin (Ed.), (I. Bent, *et al.*, Trans). Cambridge: Cambridge University Press.

Schenker, H. (2000). *The art of performance.* H. Esser (Ed.), (I. Schreier Scott, Trans.). New York, NY: Oxford University Press.

Schenker, H. (2005 [1923–1924]). *Der Tonwille: Pamphlets/quarterly publication in witness of the immutable laws of music: Issues 6–10 (1923–1924).* W. Drabkin (Ed.), (I. Bent *et al.*, Trans.). New York, NY: Oxford University Press.

Todd, N. (1992). The dynamics of dynamics: a model of musical expression. *Journal of the Acoustical Society of America, 91,* 3540–3550.

Chapter 15

Expressive variants in the opening of Robert Schumann's *Arlequin* (from *Carnaval*, op. 9): 54 pianists' interpretations of a metrical ambiguity

Andreas C. Lehmann

Abstract

This chapter presents an analysis of 54 recorded interpretations by famous pianists of the opening of Robert Schumann's *Arlequin* (from his *Carnaval*, 1834/1835). Some recordings suggest an unexpected four-beat measure clashing with the 3/4 time signature. In the analysis I describe the expressive variants in detail and try to relate them to schools of playing, gender, and age of performer, year of recording, and tempo of the recording. The results reveal gender and effects of tempo, and the source of the delay responsible for the audible result was the first beat of every uneven measure; pupil–teacher traditions could not be found. Expressive variants due to notational ambiguity may go unnoticed by performers and create aesthetic results that show both systematic application of certain rules and idiosyncratic variability.

Interpretation of a piece of music requires a performer to creatively make sense of the printed score. Interpretation is in essence an attempt at re-creating the composer's mental representation of the acoustical image. The result is a rendition that deviates from the deadpan, mathematically calculated one in systematic ways. 'It should be noted that terms such as *expressive deviations* or simply *expression* … refer to physical phenomena, that is, deviations in timing, articulation, intonation, and so on in relation to a literal interpretation of the score' (Gabrielsson, 1999, p. 522 [original emphasis]).

Gabrielsson emphasizes that those deviations are the physical correlates of expression, since 'expression's domain is the mind of the listener' (Kendall & Carterette, 1990, p. 131, cited in Gabrielsson, 1999, p. 522). Since the nineteenth century when musicians started to perpetuate a canon of classical masterpieces, the hermeneutic process necessary to actualize a particular piece has been initiated again and again. Only since the advent of mechanical recording devices have we been privy to the resulting artistic products by outstanding musicians. The accumulation of such artefacts forms the basis for a discourse about interpretations that was hitherto impossible. It also changes the focus of musicology away from the printed score to the performer and listener. 'Musical performance studies can ... be seen an expression of interest in the social usage of music, and in the meaning that is created in the act of performance' (Cook, 2007, p. 184; see also Clarke, 2004). This chapter begins with an outline of a three-level model of thinking about interpretation (see Lehmann, Sloboda, & Woody, 2007, p. 89) which starts with the individual artistic decisions at the highest level, followed by subordinate levels of rule-generated interpretation and unintended variability. Using data from performances of a piece by Robert Schumann, I explore the relation of notation and expression (always an important part of John Sloboda's work), here understood as interpretational freedom.

The first and most basic reasons for deviating from the written text are largely unintended ones, such as variability in the motor execution or irregularities caused by the instrument. For example, unwanted timing variability increases with larger interonset intervals (Wing & Kristofferson, 1973). Also unintended is the temporal lead that pianists show for melodic notes of chords within one hand or between hands. Goebl (2001) found that this melody lead resulted from a confounding of onset with loudness (measured as key velocity); given that melody notes are deliberately emphasized by the performer, the hammer velocity is faster despite only minimal anticipation of the note at the finger-key level.

A second and more interesting kind of deviation between the notation prescribed and an actualized performance (cf. Meyer, 1973, cited in Gabrielsson, 1987, p. 85) is due to the rule-based generation of musical expression. It appears to be guided by expectations and embodied cognitions that emerge from performance practices to which a musician has become accustomed during training. Although the research on systematic variations goes back to the work of Bengtsson in the 1960s, more recent work is widely known as the 'analysis-by-synthesis' approach (Friberg, Bresin, & Sundberg, 2006; see Kopiez, 2005, for a historical review of performance research). A typical finding is that a classical music performance includes typical phrase arch structures with final lengthenings (retards). Easily observable rules also pertain to the expressive shades of sequences and repetitions (cf. Sloboda, 1985, p. 83). In fact, some of those 'deviations from the exact' even follow mathematical models, and, in a study using 24 performances of Schumann's *Träumerei*, Repp (1992a, 1992b) found that the timing shapes could best be described as quadratic functions (parabolas) and that such shapes were preferred by listeners. Expressive features of the systematic kind seem to be so entrenched that it is impossible for performers to even willingly suppress them completely. Asking them to adhere strictly to the score simply produces renditions with markedly reduced expressiveness (e.g. Palmer, 1988).

John Sloboda, who used to be a fairly accomplished pianist himself (ATCL degree in 1968 from Trinity College of Music) but chose to forego a career in music in favour of one in psychology, investigated issues related to music notation in the early part of his career. Among those issues were the relations between musical structure and performance, specifically how the visual structure of the input might influence a resulting performance. His personal experience with Bach's piano concerto in D minor prompted him to conclude that sometimes the 'patterning of the notes will not suggest a single interpretation, or may even be misleading' (Sloboda, 1985, p. 83). He followed up his observation with an experiment in which he presented a metrically ambiguous melody under different notational conditions (Sloboda, 1983). The pianists who took part in the experiment reacted in predictable ways to the changes at first sight by creating upbeats and stressing the strong beats relative to the barlines. However, Sloboda noted that the choices among the available expressive devices were subject to substantial individual differences (p. 84). In the present study, the metrical properties were not experimentally manipulated but investigated using naturally occurring data with a notational ambiguity.

The third and last level of deviations from the notated score concerns idiosyncratic habits and deliberate decisions. Traditionally, musicologists and music critics have been the ones in charge of comparing and adjudicating individual performances with regard to expressive features. However, while they tacitly assume that all interpretive devices are the outcome of artistic choices, the discussion of musical expression suggests a more differentiated view of the facts. In the light of the apparent mystery surrounding the multitude of commercially available interpretations, it is not surprising that musically trained researchers have been trying to discover methods to describe and explain individual differences (see Clarke, 2004, for a methodological review). Bruno Repp has published a number of studies in which he groups several interpretations of the same piece using factor analytic procedures. An important conclusion from those studies is that despite all freedom of interpretation, the musical structure suggests a limited amount of plausible readings. For example, after analysing 10 recordings of a prelude by Debussy (Repp, 1997), the author stated that professional pianists' artistic products showed stronger individuality than those of the students, who were more similar to each other. Despite some constraints on how to read a certain score, there are always performers who will not fit any mould—the same is true in our study with a recording by Horowitz.

Sloboda and Lehmann (2001) investigated listeners' perceptual reality, or salience, of pianists' deliberate interpretive choices. Ten performances of Chopin's E minor prelude were recorded by accomplished piano players who also gave interviews regarding their interpretations. Next, participants in an experiment were asked to continuously track perceived expressivity while listening to the recorded excerpts. Finally, the recorded trajectories for individual performances were compared with the piece's average trajectory (profiles were aggregated across listeners). Detected deviations were tested for statistical reliability and related to probable causes in the MIDI performance data. One important finding was that listeners were indeed able to react to particular places in the performance that distinguished a specific performance from others. Furthermore, almost all such spots could be linked to decisions that the performers had explicitly mentioned

Fig. 15.1 The first eight measures of Robert Schumann's *Arlequin* (no. 3, from *Carnaval* op. 9; Rönnau, 1979, p. 89) with all measured note durations numbered consecutively.

in the interviews. Thus, distinguishable interpretive features were rooted in deliberate artistic decisions—not in incidental and arbitrary readings of the musical score.

The main goal of the present study was to document in some detail a peculiar perceptual-notational phenomenon in the opening phrase of Robert Schumann's *Arlequin* from the series of pieces entitled *Carnaval* (op. 9; see Figure 15.1), composed between 1834 and 1835 (Appel, 2005). The Arlequin or Harlequin (Italian *arlecchino*; German *Harlekin*) is a figure from the Italian Commedia del Arte, a Renaissance comedy genre; his main traits are childlike ignorance, wit, grace, and his always being in trouble (and in love), but there is also a demonic side to him (Harvey, 1932). He clearly matches a Florestan-type of character in Schumann's dualistic virtual personality. Analytically, the first four notes contain a programmatic motif (in German: A-Es-C-H = ASCH), alluding to the location of Robert's fiancé at the time or the tone-letter correspondences in the name 'S̲c̲h̲um̲a̲nn̲' (Appel, 2005). There are several possible ways of describing the acoustic impression the opening bars evoke on the listener, but all are likely to represent the performer's intention to depict the above-mentioned arlequinesque character.[1]

We started from the casual observation that the emerging auditory *Gestalts* gave hardly any cues as to the possible notation of the music. It was only when consulting the score that we found a 3/4 beat time signature throughout. Such effects, which Krebs (1999, p. vii) calls 'pathological metrical states', are common in Schumann's music, and also found in music by Berlioz, Brahms, and Schoenberg, in which notation and actualized performance diverge because structural physical markers (bar lines) do not necessarily follow the perceptually salient entities. While the *Träumerei* has been used many times in music psychology experiments, it might be worthwhile looking at a different piece that, due to its notational ambiguity, offers a great amount of freedom for interpretation. The extent of this creative freedom is at the heart of this descriptive study.

Method

Data from recordings of R. Schumann's *Arlequin*

The groundwork for this collection of 54 recordings of Robert Schumann's *Arlequin* was laid by pianist Peter Manzi in his thesis (Manzi, 1996), for which the author (who was a pianist) had assembled 58 mostly commercially available recordings and

---

[1] Some musical examples are available at: www.hfm-wuerzburg.de/en/professors-teachers/
lehmann/research/projects.html (accessed 2 Nov, 2010).

measured the interonset intervals of the opening 28 notes using a computer program (wave editor). Onsets were detected by looking at the amplitude curve and identifying the earliest upswing for the start of a note, that is, the physical onset (e.g. Gabrielsson, 1987, for a similar method). The oldest recording dated from 1923, the most recent one from 1994. Fifty per cent of the recordings originated from the years 1958 to 1982. Manzi had included his measurements in the appendix to his thesis and provided all recordings on an accompanying cassette tape.[2] In this study we analysed the first 28 interonset intervals resulting from the first 29 notes of the opening 8 measures in *Arlequin* (see Figure 15.1). For this reanalysis, the timing data were entered into statistical software, and all recordings from the cassette tape were digitized onto CD. We omitted four remastered versions from the original set (no. 2, 25, 41, and 48 on the 1996 tape) and used only the original recordings.[3]

To assess the reliability of Manzi's data, we randomly selected five recordings and imported them into a wave editor to compare our readings with those provided by Manzi. We ascertained the overall length and several salient tones. All readings agreed with a tolerance of several milliseconds (length between 0 and 15 ms, onsets between 0 and 9 ms). Considering that the interonset intervals varied between an average of 80 ms for the shortest and 386 ms for the longest interval, we judged the measurement error to be negligible. Also, by comparing several recorded notes in six randomly selected tracks with an electronic tuning device, we made sure that the original tempo had not been distorted through recording or mastering.[4] The largest deviation amounted to about 15 Hz. Thus, the measurements of the 27 interonset intervals were accepted as reliable, and the recordings were subjected to further timing analyses.

To the timing information extracted from the recordings we added data on the recording date and age of the performer at the time of recording. We also verified and used information on teacher–pupil relationships that were given as genealogies in Manzi's thesis. Moreover, we assembled information about nationality, gender, and birth dates for the performers from various standard sources (Dubal, 1990; Grove Online, 2008; Range, 1964).

Performers of the 54 recordings

The sample was one of convenience. Ten of the performers were female. The year of birth of the oldest performer (Emil v. Sauer) was 1862, the youngest was born in 1961 (Cecile Licad). Fifty per cent of the pianists were born between 1896 and 1930. This range, along with a fair spread of nationalities from all over the world assured a heterogeneous sampling of interpretations and performing traditions.

---

[2] My thanks to Peter Manzi for allowing us to use the data for a quantitative analysis. I supervised the thesis together with musicologist Douglas Seaton at the Florida State University.

[3] I am grateful to Elke Schlör, who prepared the data for this paper as part of her thesis.

[4] This assumes that the tunings were standardized to a modern A = 440 Hz and the largest deviation of 3.4% might have been an actual difference in tuning.

Results

The *Arlequin* and its tempo

The range and change of tempo over the years were the first issues to be addressed. There was a large variability in speed, ranging from 208 to 365 beats per minute (bpm) which meant that performances of our short segment lasted between 4.6 and 8.1 seconds. The correlation between year of recording and tempo was not significant. However, an interesting negative correlation (r[49] = −0.33, p <0.05) was observed between tempo and the performer's age at the time of recording (see Figure 15.2). Older performers tended to choose slower speeds than did younger ones, and this effect was enhanced (r[47] = −0.42, p <0.05) when removing the two obvious outliers (Gavrilov, Cherkassky). One might have surmised a gender effect with females playing more expressively and slowly. By weighting the cases by gender and applying a one-tailed test, we discovered a small but significant difference in means (t[62] = 2.0, p = 0.026; x = 265 bpm and 280 bpm for female and male musicians, respectively).

The source of the perceptual metrical peculiarity

When comparing the prescribed notation with the auditory impression, we noted that the odd-numbered measures (1, 3, 5) were lengthened on average by the performers compared

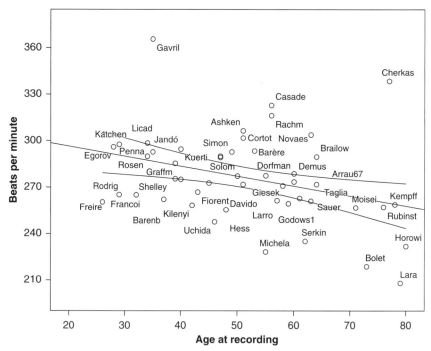

Fig. 15.2 The relation between performance tempo (in beats per minute) and age of performer at the time of recording (regression line with 95% confidence interval included).

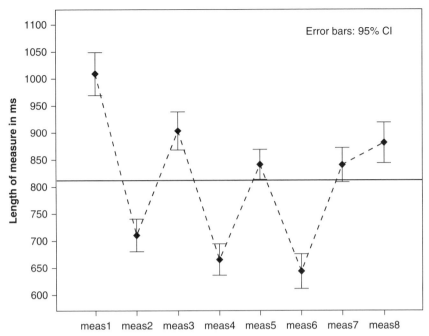

Fig. 15.3 Length of measures demonstrating their unequal durations and the typical arch structure: acceleration toward the middle and phrase final lengthening.

with the even-numbered ones (2, 4, 6, 8; see Figure 15.3). One-sample t-tests with a test value of 812 ms—the theoretical average of all measures—revealed reliable differences at the 5% level in all but one measure (measure 7). Contrasts between durations of adjacent measures were also all significant (measures 1–2, 3–4, 5–6, all p <0.01, t[53] > 10.0; 7–8, t[53] = 2.3, p <0.05). A visually noticeable curvilinear trend from measure 1 to 8 suggested a phrase structure with acceleration toward the middle and a marked phrase final lengthening. There seemed to be considerable agreement about the irregular bar durations. But where did the increase in measure 1 and similarly structured ones arise?

Table 15.1 shows the distribution of note durations for the first two measures. To make durations comparable across performers and thus unconfound performance tempo and note duration, we transformed them to relative beat lengths. This was done by dividing them by the beat durations per minute for the respective performance. The variability in duration of notes of the same nominal value was remarkable (e.g. 8th notes 1, 2[including 16th rest], 4). In fact, note 2 was more than three times as long as note 1. The larger standard errors for notes 2 and 3 (again note 9) suggested that the performers' differing ideas about the 'right' interpretation emanated from this point. The near zero correlation between lengths of notes 2 and 3 (r[52] = 0.064, not significant) disproved my working hypothesis about a simple long–short or short–long relationship at this crucial point in the score (notes 2 and 3). Figure 15.4a shows that all kinds of combinations exist. A similar visualization of the large number of possible options was produced by combining the notes that make up the first beat and the

Table 15.1 Descriptive statistics for the durations of the first nine note events

Position	Min	Max	SE	SD	M (95% CI)
Note 1 (8th)	45	278	6.44	47.36	121 (108–134)
Note 2 (16th + 16th rest)	115	756	15.95	117.19	389 (351–415)
Note 3 (dotted 4)	81	670	12.05	88.52	426 (402–450)
Note 4 (8th)	22	184	3.85	28.29	80 (72–87)
Note 5 (quarter)	157	336	5.36	39.39	234 (223–245)
Note 6 (quarter)	144	333	5.44	40.01	228 (217–239)
Note 7 (quarter)	132	373	7.29	53.60	249 (234–263)
Note 8 (8th)	38	311	6.16	45.26	103 (91–115)
Note 9 (16th + 16th rest)	156	604	10.83	79.56	337 (315–358)

N = 54

following dotted quarter in the first measure (Figure 15.4b). Some interesting outliers emerged, but most performers operated somewhere in a larger central area.

Performers' constraints

Due to the repeating structure of the phrase, the opening gesture will determine how the piece is conceived rhythmically. From the perspective of the pianist, however, the most constraining moment in the excerpt under consideration is the jump from note 8 to note 9, an interval of a 10th, from the E^b to the G above, which requires either a very large hand or a swift motion of the arm. It is, at any rate, advisable to steady the hand in anticipation of note 8 (E^b). That performers in fact hesitated at the note preceding the critical jump was suggested by a significant lengthening compared to a similar note in the next shorter jump (note 15 to 16), $t[53] = 2.3, p < 0.05$ (two-tailed); this estimate is conservative since the phrase arch was not partialled out, obscuring this difference further. The next critical starting point for an interval of a 10th (note 22 to 23) was also longer than the previous one (note 15 to 16), but the differences between notes 22, 15 or 8 were not significant. However, the beat durations of note 8 and 22 correlated reliably, $r[52] = 0.39, p < 0.01$. Finally and most importantly, if the starting point for the jump was a critical technical requirement, we might have even expected an effect of age, which in fact existed. While none of the notes surrounding note 8 showed an effect of age, the duration of this note correlated with the performer's age ($r[47] = 0.37, p = 0.01$). This analysis demonstrated that particular technical difficulties constrained the performer's degrees of freedom in making aesthetic choices.

Seeking support from a music critic's published opinions on the performers

David Dubal, no doubt a great expert in the piano world, has made specific comments about performers and their renditions of the *Carnaval* (1990). His remarks are not

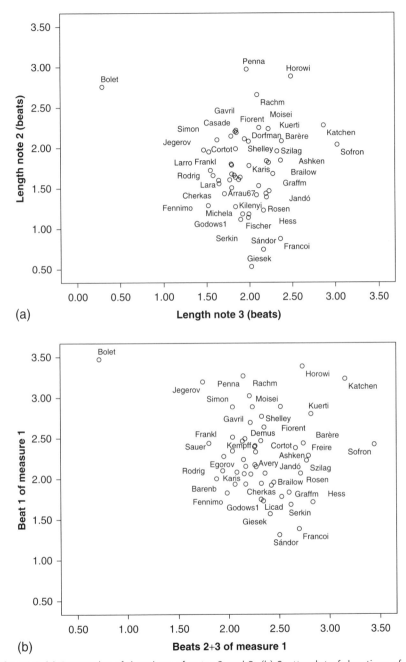

Fig. 15.4 (a) Scatterplot of durations of notes 2 and 3. (b) Scatterplot of durations of first beat and combined beats 2 and 3 of the first measure. Durations are expressed in beats corresponding to each performer's own tempo.

Table 15.2 Comments by music critic David Dubal (1990) about performances of the *Carnaval* (C.) and length of first measure for each performer. A mathematically correct (deadpan) performance would sum up to 3 beats (B) in measure one

Performer	Most specific comments (from Dubal, 1990)	Measure length B1 + (B2 + B3)
Arrau	C. filled with fire, a leaping, soaring spirit	2.15 + 2.17 = 4.32
Barenboim	C. is dull	1.93 + 2.06 = 3.96
Casadesus	Rubato in C. was so subtle that at first it sounded as if he never deviated from the metronome mark ... never sounded tight	2.69 + 2.22 = 4.91
Cherkassky	never remains static, C. sounds spasmodic, and even ill-tempered	1.94 + 2.32 = 4.26
Godowsky	C. is somewhat thin; lacks of comeliness, but winsome style	1.73 + 2.34 = 4.07
Horowitz	Schumann: [earlier] vitality; [later] darker; full of trickery and whimsy	3.38 + 2.74 = 6.12
Kilenyi	at his best in works as Schumann's C.	2.15 + 2.27 = 4.42
Rachmaninoff	legendary C., marvel of control, chiseled phrasing	3.02 + 2.21 = 5.24
Sandor	his best in C.	1.31 + 2.50 = 3.81
Solomon	C. is peerless, orgiastic	2.24 + 2.15 = 4.39

specifically about the *Arlequin*, but it seemed appropriate to include them here to find out if certain interpretations would be favoured (see Table 15.2). At first glance, there seemed to be no systematic relation between the quality implied in Dubal's statements and our measurements, except that more critical comments seemed to coincide with shorter durations of the first beat. Some comments may be misleading, for instance, Dubal does not hold Sandor in very high esteem and Kilenyi receives only a brief entry in Dubal's book; vague remarks such as 'at his best' may thus be politically correct formulae. Although the comment on Horowitz refers to his renditions of Schumann in general, it would certainly apply to the *Arlequin* included here (see Figure 15.4). In essence, while the critic's comments are interesting and even entertaining, they do not offer a suitable point of entry for our understanding of the data.

Discussion

We do not know which score the pianists had used to prepare for their performances and whether or not the recordings were done from memory or with the musical score. We also do not know anything about their ultimate intentions. We assumed that the ambiguity of the notation, typical for Schumann's disregard of barlines, offered pianists vast room for structural and expressive interpretation of the score, in other words creativity. Our analysis showed that in effect Krebs' (1999, p.vii) above mentioned 'pathological metrical states' of the notation do transcend into the performances.

The fastest tempo was 75% swifter than the slowest one in spite of the dynamic marking 'Vivo'! Apparently, the musical description of a whimsical character (Arlequin) allowed different possibilities to express bodily energy and a gay spirit. Although one sometimes hears that tempi have increased over time, this might primarily affect virtuoso pieces and less so character pieces: The recording year made no difference in our case. For mazurka tempi, Cook (2007, p. 188) even found a constant slowing during the age of recording.

Performers try to form gestures of Gestalts. The unduly long duration of note 3 can be explained as a half-bar effect (Sloboda, 1985, p. 85) if we assume that the first beat is performed as the first half of the measure or a run-up to the second beat. It is surprising that the first beat in measure 1 extends to more than twice the duration of the second and third combined. None of the pianists performs the note values as written (which is not surprising); instead, they all add a more or less important hesitation to the first beat, ranging from a 16th note's worth (Sandor, Gieseking) up to a dotted half note (Bolet).[5] This can be gleaned from the empty lower left part of the bottom panel in Figure 15.4. Following the jump-like upswing on the first beat, I would like to call it a 'fermata effect'. It is followed by an equally diverse second half of the measure which is condensed (<2 beats) or extended (>2 beats). My impression and Dubal's statement imply that a lengthening is more pleasing, especially when the first beat together with the following two lasts for at least a theoretical duration of four beats. The combined unit of measures one and two creates a 7/4-type, jumping, frivolous, and arlequinesque impression that Schumann may have had in mind.

Our attempts to analyse teacher–pupil relationships failed. Correlations between timing profiles of teachers with their own students or random colleagues produced an unsystematic range of correlations. Similar results have already been reported in the literature (e.g. by Repp or Gabrielsson). Also, comparing schools of pianists trained in Russia or Germany/France with regard to tempo and timing of critical notes did not yield any useful insights. Looking at phrase arch structure may be a starting point for further analyses (N. Cook, personal communication, January 2009).

If deviating from the exact is at the heart of the art of interpretation, then showing how and where this deviation becomes possible is an important part of performance research that lies between musicology and applied musicianship. One result we dare to draw from the data is that when the musical score offers few firm cues or even ambiguity, 'reproducing' musicians become truly creative, if they want it or not. The big picture certainly may start with the programmatic idea behind the music and associated choices but also includes technical constraints such as those imposed by age. The present analysis on Schumann's metrically ambiguous opening of the *Arlequin* has shown where and how such aesthetic opportunities are actively seized. It is from the performers' reconstructive readings and the ensuing expressive embodiments that true musical experience can emerge for the listeners.

---

5 Jokingly one could claim that this is at odds with Schumann's 'Musikalische Haus- und Lebensregeln', in which he stated: 'Dragging behind and scampering are both bad mistakes' or 'Play in strict time! The way many virtuosi play sounds like a drunkard trying to walk' (Rönnau, 1979).

Acknowledgements

I thank Reinhard Kopiez and Nicholas Cook for comments on a previous version of this paper, my wife Maria for the usual excellent editing work, and especially John Sloboda for the many ideas, inspiration, and friendship since we met in the early 1990s.

References

Appel, B. (2005). Carnaval. Scenes mignonnes sur quatre notes für Klavier op. 9. In H. Loos (Ed.), *Robert Schumann: Interpretationen seiner Werke*, Volume I (pp. 49 56). Laaber, Germany: Laaber.

Clarke, E. (2004). Empirical methods in the study of performance. In E. Clarke, & N. Cook (Eds.), *Empirical musicology* (pp. 77–102). New York, NY: Oxford University Press.

Cook, N. (2007). Performance analysis and Chopin's mazurkas. *Musicæ Scientiæ*, *11*, 183–207.

Dubal, D. (1990). *Art of the piano*. London: Tauris.

Friberg, A., Bresin, R., & Sundberg, J. (2006). Overview of the KTH rule system for musical performance. *Advances in Cognitive Psychology*, *2*(2–3), Special Issue on Music Performance, 145–161.

Gabrielsson, A. (1987). Once again: The theme from Mozart's piano sonata in A major (K. 331): A comparison of five performances. In A. Gabrielsson (Ed.), *Action and perception in rhythm and music* (pp. 81–103). Stockholm, Sweden: Royal Swedish Academy of Music.

Gabrielsson, A. (1999). The performance of music. In D. Deutsch (Ed.), *The psychology of music* (pp. 653–724). New York, NY: Academic Press.

Goebl, W. (2001). Melody lead in piano performance: Expressive device or artefact. *JASA*, *110*(1), 563–572.

Grove Online (2008). In L. Macy (Ed.), *Grove Music Online*. Available at: www.grovemusic.com (accessed 1 January 2009).

Harvey, P. (1932). *The Oxford companion to English literature*. Oxford: Clarendon Press.

Kopiez, R. (2005). Experimentelle interpretationsforschung [Experimental performance research]. In H. de la Motte-Haber, & G. Rötter (Eds.), *Musikpsychologie* (pp. 459–514). Laaber, Germany: Laaber.

Krebs, H. (1999). *Fantasy pieces. Metrical dissonance in the music of Robert Schumann*. New York, NY: Oxford University Press.

Lehmann, A. C., Sloboda, J. A., & Woody, R. H. (2007). *Psychology for musicians*. Oxford: Oxford University Press.

Manzi, P. (1996). *Rhythmic performance practice in Schumann's 'Arlequin'*. Unpublished Master's Thesis, Florida State University, Tallahassee, FL.

Palmer, C. (1988). *Timing in skilled music performance*. Unpublished doctoral dissertation, Cornell University, Ithaca, NY.

Range, H. P. (1964). *Die Konzertpianisten der Gegenwart*. Lahr: Schauenburg.

Repp, B. (1992a). A constraint on the expressive timing of a melodic gesture: Evidence from performance and aesthetic judgment. *Music perception*, *10*, 221–241.

Repp, B. (1992b). Diversity and commonality in music performance: An analysis of timing microstructure in Schumann's 'Träumerei'. *JASA*, *92*, 2546–2568.

Repp, B. (1997). Expressive timing in a Debussy prelude: A comparison of student and expert pianists. *Musicæ Scientiæ*, *1*(2), 257–268.

Rönnau, K. (ed.) (1979). *Robert Schumann: Album for the Young, op. 68*. Vienna: Universal Edition.

Sloboda, J. A. (1983). The communication of musical metre in piano performance. *Quarterly Journal of Experimental Psychology, 35A*, 377–396.

Sloboda, J. A. (1985). *The musical mind*. Oxford: Oxford University Press.

Sloboda, J. A., & Lehmann, A. C. (2001). Performance correlates of perceived emotionality in different interpretations of a Chopin piano prelude. *Music Perception, 19*(1), 87–120.

Wing, A., & Kristofferson, A. (1973). Response delays and the timing of discrete motor responses. *Perception and Psychophysics, 14*, 5–12.

Chapter 16

Quantifying the beat-inducing properties of conductors' temporal gestures, and conductor–musician synchronization

Geoff Luck

Abstract

This chapter summarizes a series of empirical and naturalistic studies which have examined the beat-inducing properties of conductors' temporal gestures. In empirical studies, pre-recorded conductors gestures were presented to participants under laboratory conditions, and relationships between indicated perception of the beat and spatio-temporal features of the gestures explored using statistical methods. In naturalistic settings, live performances of ensembles and conductors were recorded, and similar relationships between the ensemble's performance and the conductors' gestures examined. A key component of both types of study was the use of an optical motion-capture system to make high-quality three-dimensional recordings of the conductors gestures from which spatio-temporal features can be automatically extracted. Laboratory-based studies indicate that, when synchronizing with pre-recorded gestures in isolation, musicians tend to synchronize with periods of negative acceleration along the trajectory, and low position in the vertical axis. Changes in direction alone do not appear sufficient to induce the perception of a beat. These findings are partially supported by the naturalistic studies, in which musicians synchronized with both the conductor and their fellow musicians. Here, ensembles tend to be most highly synchronized with periods of maximal deceleration along the trajectory, followed by periods of high vertical velocity. Thus, it appears that changes in speed (acceleration or deceleration) along the trajectory of a gesture are most likely responsible for the induction of a visual beat.

Musicians playing in a conducted ensemble can utilize both auditory and visual cues to synchronize their performances with each other. Auditory cues are provided solely by the other musicians, while visual cues are primarily provided by the conductor. The musicians, too, may provide some visual synchronization cues to each other, even in a conducted ensemble, but the conductor is the sole visual-only cue-provider. Musicians' ability to pick up and make use of these auditory and visual synchronization cues is, therefore, a necessary skill for a polished ensemble performance (Keller, 2001).

Research has shown that most people, even those with little or no previous experience with conductors' gestures, are able to tap in time with sequences of visual beats produced by a conductor (Luck, 2000), suggesting that the detection of these temporal events appeals to rather basic human perceptual processes. What is less clear is what physical features of a movement trajectory induce the perception of a beat. The analysis of conductors' gestures may be approached in a number of different ways. Conducting manuals, such as those by Prausnitz (1983) and Rudolf (1995) (and many others), for example, offer intuitive descriptions of conductors' gestures based on the authors' training and experience as professional conductors. More theory-driven accounts are provided by Ashley's (2000) application of the philosopher H. Paul Grice's theories to the pragmatics of gestures, and Venn's (2003) model of the semiotics of gestures based on Prausnitz's (1983) intuitive descriptions.

All of the above approaches have their merits. However, they tend to lack the objectivity and generalizability that an experimental and computationally-driven approach can offer. This chapter examines how empirical methods of music psychology can be combined with sophisticated statistical, signal-processing, and motion-capture techniques, to investigate conductors' temporal gestures. Three main areas of research will be discussed: computational feature extraction techniques, the kinematics of conductors' gestures, and musician–conductor synchronization.

Computational feature extraction

When examining the movement of an individual, be it in music, dance, sport, or whatever, there are two basic ways in which the movements in question may be recorded: with a video camera and with a motion-capture system. While video recording captures contextual information, allowing more detailed observational analysis of the movement in question, a more detailed and objective analysis is possible with motion-capture recordings. In particular, the higher temporal and spatial resolution, and three-dimensional (3D) nature of motion-capture data make it particularly amenable to computational analysis. I have used a combination of motion capture and computational feature extraction to examine conductors' gestures in a number of studies, several of which were completed with John Sloboda's guidance (Luck & Nte, 2008; Luck & Sloboda, 2007, 2008, 2009; Luck & Toiviainen, 2006).

In one such study (Luck & Nte, 2008), the spatial position of reflective markers attached to a conductor's right arm was recorded during the production of simple, single beat gestures. The aim was to examine how accurately observers (both musically trained and untrained) could tap in time with a conductor's gestures. These recordings were presented as life-size point-light displays, and the timing of observers' finger taps recorded. The main finding was that individuals who themselves had some conducting experience synchronized more consistently than did any other group of participants. Part of this study involved the development of a suite of software to enable both the presentation of stimuli to participants, and the automatic extraction of movement features for subsequent analysis. This software collated participants' tapping responses, and displayed information regarding the characteristics of the gestures presented to participants as well as characteristics of participants' responses.

The software calculated four spatio-temporal features—instantaneous speed (v), radius of curvature (r), acceleration along the trajectory (a), and rate of change of radius of curvature (r')—for each recorded point along a gesture's trajectory. Gestures could be plotted in a two-dimensional (2D) static form, either with or without indicating v, and information relating to v could be displayed either along the actual trajectory of a gesture, or along a timeline underneath a gesture.

As regards participants' responses, each participant's mean response and its associated standard deviation were calculated for each gesture. In cases where more than one response per gesture was required (such as in multi-beat gestures), the software was able to classify responses according to the beat of the bar they applied to, and generate a mean response and standard deviation for each beat. Individual responses by a participant, or the mean of these responses, could be superimposed onto the 2D trace of a given gesture. In addition, a participant's individual and/or mean response points could be indicated along the v timeline underneath a gesture. Thus, this software allowed any gesture to be plotted in a 2D static form, with or without information relating to v at all points throughout its duration, and with or without information regarding a participant's responses to it. This suite of software has been used in other studies (Luck & Sloboda, 2007, 2008, 2009) to extract and analyse pertinent movement features from conductors' gestures. All of these studies, as well as Luck and Nte (2008), were carried out under experimental conditions since the aim was to observe how people responded in an optimal environment. These studies, as well as a more ecologically valid study by Luck and Toiviainen (2006), are described later in this chapter.

The movement feature extraction approach described above parallels automatic musical feature extraction methods (e.g. Downie, 2003; Leman, 2002). These methods are based on principles of signal processing, music processing, machine learning, cognitive modelling, and visualization. Typical application areas are, for instance, computational music analysis (e.g. Cambouropoulos, 2006; Lartillot, 2004, 2005), automatic classification (e.g. Pampalk, Flexer, & Widmer, 2005; Toiviainen & Eerola, 2006), organization (e.g. Rauber, Pampalk, & Merkl, 2003) and transcription (e.g. Klapuri, 2004) of music, as well as content-based retrieval (Lesaffre *et al.*, 2003).

The movement- and audio-based feature extraction approaches were combined in a study by Camurri, De Poli, Friberg, Leman, and Volpe (2005) (see also Camurri, Lagerlöf, and Volpe, 2003), who used computational methods to analyse expressiveness in audio and movement data. The system described in this study acquired its input from a video camera, and quantified several indicators of expression, including amount of movement, orientation of body parts, and contraction/expansion of gestures. This was not the first systematic analysis of music and movement (see, for example, Krumhansl & Schenk, 1997), but did demonstrate the potential of an automated, computational feature extraction approach to the analysis of both music and movement data.

This combined music and movement approach raises the possibility of moving out of the laboratory and into the real world when investigating conductor–musician synchronization. I have been involved in one such study, in which the gestures of a conductor directing an ensemble were recorded, and the conductor–musician interaction examined (Luck & Toiviainen, 2006). For this purpose, two types of feature were extracted: movement features extracted from motion-capture data of the conductor's gestures, and musical features extracted from audio recordings of the ensemble's performance. Using MATLAB, 12 movement features relating to x, y, z position, their velocity and acceleration components, speed, magnitude of acceleration, and magnitude of acceleration along the trajectory, and a single musical feature, spectral flux, were extracted from the conductor's gestures and the ensemble's performance.

The movement features were extracted using a set of algorithms which were subsequently incorporated into the Motion Capture Toolbox (Toiviainen & Burger, 2010), while the musical feature was extracted with an early version of the Music Information Retrieval (MIR) Toolbox developed by Lartillot and Toiviainen (2007). This latter toolbox permits the automatic extraction of a large number of musical features, similar in scope to the features available in the MIDI Toolbox (Eerola & Toiviainen, 2004). This study, and the main findings, will be described in more detail in the following section.

The research reviewed above has shown that a large number of movement- and music-related features can be extracted computationally from motion-capture and audio data. Adopting a computational approach to movement and musical feature extraction increases the speed and precision of the process, and makes it possible to analyse a large dataset with relative ease. In the next section we will see how a combination of computational feature extraction and statistical modelling can be used to investigate the spatio-temporal properties of conductors' gestures.

Kinematics of conductors' gestures

Given that it is the aim of a conductor to optimize coordination between ensemble musicians using visual cues alone (notwithstanding his or her desire to convey expressive elements of the music), there must be a mutual understanding between the conductor and the musicians as to exactly which features of a gesture indicate a beat, and which features fulfil other functions. By increasing this level of understanding, higher-quality ensemble performances can be achieved. John Sloboda contributed to an understanding of the temporal functions of conductors' gestures in two publications we co-authored (Luck & Sloboda, 2008, 2009).

In the 2008 study, three experiments were carried out, in each of which participants synchronized a single tapping response with the beat communicated in point-light representations of simple, single beat gestures. In Experiment 1, participants synchronized a tapping response with gestures which varied in the amount of curvature with which the beat was defined. In Experiment 2, the curvature component of the gestures was held constant, resulting in stimuli which moved in a straight line, but with the average speed profile of the original gestures. In Experiment 3, the speed component was held constant, resulting in stimuli which followed the paths of the original gestures, but at a constant speed.

In each experiment, perception of the location of a visual beat was investigated by correlating participants' synchronization responses with the four spatio-temporal features calculated by the suite of software described in Luck and Nte (2008), namely instantaneous speed (v), acceleration along the trajectory (a), radius of curvature (r), and rate of change of radius of curvature (r'). A series of regression analyses were used to identify which (combinations) of these features best predicted participants' indication of the location of a visual beat. A key assumption of this method was that each response made by a participant reflected the perception of a visual beat.

Experiment 1, in which participants synchronized with the original gestures, indicated that beat induction was related to periods of negative acceleration (deceleration) and periods of high speed. Specifically, there was a positive linear relationship between v and the number of synchronization responses, and a curvilinear relationship between a and the number of responses, such that synchronizations were positively associated with periods of high acceleration and deceleration, and negatively associated with periods of low acceleration/deceleration. Neither r nor r' appeared to be related to visual beat induction. The relative contribution of these four spatio-temporal variables to beat induction was further investigated in Experiment 2, in which participants synchronized with the constant curvature stimuli, and Experiment 3, in which participants synchronized with the constant speed stimuli. Experiment 2 revealed that beat induction was similarly curvilinearly associated with periods of acceleration and deceleration, but even more strongly associated with particularly high levels of v. Experiment 3, meanwhile, confirmed that neither r nor r' alone were related to visual beat induction.

To summarize, visual beat induction was mediated by (changes in) speed along the trajectory of a gesture. Changes in direction of movement, and/or rate of change of direction, were not responsible for the induction of a visual beat. The lack of an association between r and participants' responses demonstrated in Experiments 1 and 3 supported the notion that visual beat induction is not related to variables that reflect a constant value of a parameter. Meanwhile, the lack of an association between r' and participants' responses shown in these two experiments suggested that changes in the direction of a movement are not in themselves enough to reliably communicate the beat. Thus, not *all* variables which reflect change in a parameter are necessarily related to visual beat induction.

A subsequent study (Luck & Sloboda, 2009) supported these results. Here, participants tapped in time with dynamic point-light representations of traditional conducting gestures in which the clarity of the beat and overall tempo were manipulated.

As before, four spatio-temporal features were computationally extracted from the movement data, and the relationship between the timing of participants' synchronizations and these features examined. A series of linear regression analyses identified absolute acceleration along the trajectory as the main cue for synchronization, while beat clarity and tempo influenced the weights of the variables in the emergent models. Overall, the regression models accounted for 48–73% of the variance in participants' responses.

These results, then, suggest that a visual beat is communicated by periods of acceleration or deceleration, and, as such, support the theory that the percept of a visual beat is created by a variable which reflects a change in the value of one of the parameters that defines a movement's trajectory. These studies were deliberately carried out 'in the lab' in order to examine how people would synchronize with conductors' gestures under optimal conditions. However, the results are largely supported by the more ecologically valid study mentioned in the previous section (Luck & Toiviainen, 2006).

In this study, the gestures of several conductors were recorded 'live' while they directed an ensemble. In addition, auditory recordings were made of the ensemble's performances. Specifically, the 3D position of a marker attached to the tip of the conductor's baton was captured at 120 fps, and a number of movement variables subsequently extracted from the data: x, y, z (position; in this case x = left-right, y = up-down, and z = forward-backward); v_x, v_y, v_z (velocity components); a_x, a_y, a_z (acceleration components); v (speed); a (magnitude of acceleration); and a_t (magnitude of acceleration along the movement trajectory).

The location of beats in the audio track was estimated by calculating the spectral flux of the signal, a reliable feature for beat estimation from audio (e.g. Jensen, & Andersen, 2003). Here, the spectral flux was determined by calculating the Euclidean distance between amplitude spectra determined from two 2048-point windows with 1024-point overlap, the overlapping section being centred at the particular time point. Hamming windowing (see Hamming, 1997) was used. The 12 movement variables were subsequently cross-correlated with the pulse of the ensemble's performance. Results of the analysis indicated that the ensemble's performance tended to be most highly synchronized with periods of maximal deceleration along the trajectory, followed by periods of high vertical velocity (a higher correlation than a_t, but a longer delay).

The results of this study also support the well-known phenomenon whereby the ensemble tends to lag behind the conductor somewhat. The fact that the ensemble's pulse was strongly positively correlated with vertical velocity suggests that the conductor's hand was moving in a fast upward direction, and away from the generally regarded location of 'the beat', when the ensemble played. This is further evidenced by the relatively large lag between the maximum correlation between vertical velocity and the ensemble's performance. The reason for the lag in the real world setting is not clear, but one explanation might be the inertia created by the ensemble—musicians in the laboratory-based studies synchronized in isolation, while those in this study obviously did not. Moreover, the musicians in this study were given no specific instructions to be as accurate as they could with regards to the conductor's gestures, while those in the laboratory-based studies were.

Further support for the finding that beat induction is related to changes in speed along the trajectory comes from a study which employed a temporal adjustment task designed to eliminate temporal lag inherent in the synchronization process (Luck, 2007). Participants were presented with point-light representations of single beat gestures produced by an experienced conductor. Each gesture was presented repeatedly and was accompanied by a short auditory tone with the same periodicity as the visual beat. For each gesture, participants adjusted the temporal location of the auditory tone until it matched the perceived temporal location of the visual beat. The same four spatio-temporal variables were then extracted from the gestures, and their relationship to participants' indicated beat locations examined using multiple linear regression.

Each gesture was analysed separately, and significant models emerged from all analyses, each accounting for 79–88% of the variance in participants' responses. Absolute acceleration along the trajectory was the only significant variable in all models. This study, therefore, demonstrates that, when temporal lag associated with synchronization tasks is removed, beat location in conductors' gestures is related solely to acceleration along the trajectory.

In summary, the research described above suggests that the induction of a visual beat is related primarily to changes in speed of movement, and not to overall speed of movement, direction of motion, or change in direction of motion.

Musician–conductor synchronization

In terms of people's synchronization with conductors' temporal gestures, there is a dearth of relevant literature. The content of conducting manuals tends to focus more on conveying emotional expression rather than temporal information (see Prausnitz, 1983; Rudolf, 1995, for good examples of such manuals), and most research on conductors' gestures has focused on expressive aspects of conducting. For example, classification of expressive gestures has been carried out by Maruyama and Furuyama (2002), while Braem and Braem (2000) undertook a preliminary investigation of the effectiveness of typical expressive gestures to convey the desired emotional message. More general work on the expressive gestures used by conductors includes studies by Holt (1992), who has applied the movement techniques of Rudolf von Laban to the construction of conductors' gestures, and Benge (1996) and Miller (1988), who have used these same techniques to analyse conductors' gestures, and enhance the expressiveness of them, respectively.

Serrano (1994), however, carried out an interesting study in which observers synchronized with point-light computer-generated simulations of conducting gestures. Results indicated that both musicians and non-musicians responded with a high degree of uniformity when the stimuli resembled the kind of motion produced by gravitational forces. Other types of motion, however, received less consistent responses. I examined musicians' synchronization, using pre-recorded, videotaped gestures with which participants had to synchronize a tapping response (Luck, 2000). This study is noteworthy because it marked my first collaboration with John Sloboda: John supervised my master's degree in music psychology at Keele University, UK, and this paper was based on my final thesis. Synchronization accuracy was found to be negatively related to previous synchronization experience, with the most experienced musicians tending to lag behind the beat more than less experienced musicians. Precise recording of the level of conductor–musician synchronization was not, however, possible due to the low frame rate of the recordings.

Temporal issues were also examined by Fredrickson (1994), who found evidence to suggest that the visual cues provided by a conductor were in some cases as important as auditory cues provided by other players in achieving a synchronized ensemble performance. This was despite the fact that, in traditional synchronization tasks, the auditory modality tends to be favoured over visually presented stimuli (Repp & Penel, 2004).

There is also a growing body of work on computer-based interactive conducting systems, such as those described by Ilmonen and Takala (1999) and Lee, Wolf, and Borchers (2005), as well batons and jackets that can be used to control music, and direct virtual ensembles, such as the radio baton and conductor's jacket by Marrin Nakra (see Marrin Nakra, 2001, for an overview), and the 'virtual orchestra' project at Helsinki University of Technology.[1] The main shortcoming of such systems is that they tend to presuppose that the beat is conveyed by the change in direction from downward to upward motion (as was indeed assumed by Luck, 2000), and do not allow for the fact that other features are related to beat induction (Luck & Sloboda, 2008, 2009; Luck & Toiviainen, 2006), thus complicating the investigation of conductor–musician synchronization.

John Sloboda has been involved in two further investigations of musicians' synchronization with conductors' gestures (Luck & Nte, 2008; Luck & Sloboda, 2007), both of which aimed to quantify synchronization with real conducting gestures through the systematic manipulation of relevant variables. In the study with Sol Nte (Luck & Nte, 2008), participants were presented with single instances of simple, single beat conducting gestures in point-light form, and had to tap in synchrony with the beat in each case. Three factors were manipulated: the experience level of the conductor who produced the gesture, the 'clarity' of the gesture,[2] and participants' previous experience. Of these three factors, only participants' previous experience affected the consistency with which they were able to synchronize with the gestures. Specifically, those with both previous synchronization *and* conducting experience (conductors) synchronized more accurately than both those with synchronization experience only (musicians), and those with neither types of experience (non-musicians). Participants with conducting experience themselves were thought better able to make use of the kinematic information contained in the gestures presented to them than the participants who had no such previous experience. Consequently, the participants with conducting experience had a deeper understanding of how the beat was communicated, and, as a result, were able to synchronize more consistently with these gestures. Such performance-facilitating effects of domain-specific experience have been found in other movement-synchronizing activities, such as in relation to tennis players' ability to

---

[1] Available at: http://eve.hut.fi/.

[2] This was accomplished by varying the radius of curvature with which the beat was defined.

return a serve (e.g. Goulet, Bard, & Fleury, 1989), and in squash players' anticipation of ball trajectory and required court position (e.g. Abernethy, 1990; Abernethy, Gill, Parks, & Packer, 2001).

The other study (Luck & Sloboda, 2007) examined synchronization with more complex conducting gestures, namely traditional beat patterns. As in the Luck and Nte study, several pertinent variables were manipulated. Participants were divided into conductors, musicians, and non-musicians, depending upon the type of previous experience they had, and the gestures were produced by two different conductors with different levels of experience. The use of extended beat patterns allowed the investigation of two further factors, namely the tempo at which the sequence of beats was conducted, and changes in synchronization consistency related to beat position in the overall sequence. Synchronization consistency was again positively related to participants' previous experience, with participants who had previous conducting experience being the most consistent overall. Meanwhile, synchronization consistency was negatively related to the conductor's level of experience, with the *novice* conductor eliciting slightly more consistent synchronizations overall. Furthermore, beat patterns conducted at faster tempi were responded to more consistently than those conducted at slower tempi, and the first beat of each measure received more consistent responses than the second and third beats.

The finding that conductor participants achieved the highest level of synchronization, followed by the musicians, while the non-musicians achieved the lowest level of synchronization, is in line with the previously described study (Luck & Nte, 2008). Again, the conductor participants' superior performance may be explained by their better understanding of what exactly characterized a visual beat, and an increased sensitivity to the kinematic information contained in the gestures of other conductors. Thus, it can be seen that when attempting to synchronize with both single beat gestures and traditional beat patterns, it is previous conducting experience that allows participants to achieve the highest level of consistency. The implication here is that a higher level of conductor–musician synchronization could be achieved if all ensemble musicians received (at the very least, basic) conducting tuition. This tuition would lead to a greater understanding of how the beat is communicated, and result in higher-quality ensemble playing when a conductor is present.

As regards the surprising finding that the novice conductor elicited more consistent synchronizations than the experienced conductor, there are at least two plausible explanations. First, the experienced conductor may have deliberately (and perhaps unconsciously) introduced some sort of structure into their beat patterns, emphasizing the downbeats, and relegating the second and third beats to a subordinate status in terms of the accuracy of their production. Participants may thus have responded in a similar manner, maintaining good consistency to the downbeats, but being less concerned with the other two beats, the effect of which was to lower overall consistency. Results of a statistical analysis supported this theory. More specifically, the experienced conductor elicited the most consistent synchronizations on the first beat, but the least consistent synchronizations on the second and third beats. A second possible explanation is that the inconsistency with which the novice conductor produced the gestures may have resulted in participants having to concentrate on synchronizing with every individual beat, as they could not be sure exactly where and when the next beat would be communicated. This increased attention may have resulted in more consistent synchronizations over repeated presentations.

The fact that participants tended to synchronize most consistently with the first beat of each measure provides experimental evidence to support the widely accepted view that conductors and musicians tend to 'come together' on the downbeat. Moreover, downbeats naturally have greater clarity compared to all other beats because of the effect of gravity on their production. Gravity causes higher downward acceleration, necessitating a more marked deceleration as the gesture rounds the corner, due to the negative speed–curvature relationship characteristic of human movement (see Lacquaniti, Terzuolo, & Viviani, 1983). This results in spatio-temporal changes of greater magnitude, and thus greater clarity, for the first beat of each measure compared with all other beats.

As regards the positive relationship between tempo and synchronization consistency, this is in line with Rasch's (1988) finding that that faster tempi tend to be associated with higher levels of synchronization between performers, while slower tempi tend to be associated with less accurate synchronizations. Moreover, it suggests that a similarly positive relationship between speed of presentation and accuracy exists for both auditorily and visually presented stimuli.

Taken together, these findings suggest how one might go about improving the level of synchronization musicians are able to achieve with conductors' gestures. In other words, the transfer of domain-specific corporeal skill in this context highlights the benefit of offering conducting tuition to ensemble musicians to improve their synchronization with the conductor.

Conclusion

This chapter has examined the quantification of conductors' temporal gestures in the context of John Sloboda's contribution to this field as supervisor of my doctoral research. Two major findings emerged from this research. First, in terms of the kinematics of conductors' gestures, communication of the beat is related not to changes in direction, but to periods of acceleration or deceleration along the trajectory. Second, in terms of musicians' synchronization with a conductor, the most important factor in determining synchronization consistency is the previous experience of the musician in question, with previous conducting experience aiding subsequent synchronization the most. It remains to be seen if these results will find their way into music educators' curricula as an aid to increasing the performance level of conducted ensembles.

Finally, I would like to take this opportunity to thank John for supervising my doctoral thesis. I always appreciated John's willingness to grant me a certain latitude in my studies, allowing me to pursue my own interests and find my own direction. He achieved this by offering broad guidance much of the time, focusing on more specific elements if he saw that I was struggling. Certainly, John's many years of supervisory experience were self-evident. Although conducting is not one of John's areas of academic expertise, he is an experienced conductor—John founded the Keele Chamber Choir (later Keele Bach Choir) in 1975, and for 20 years was its principal conductor.

It was perhaps this experience, in combination with his extensive supervisory experience, which enabled him to guide me, and my work on conducting in particular, so expertly.

References

Abernethy, B (1990). Expertise, visual search, and information pick-up in squash. *Perception*, *19*(1), 63–77.

Abernethy, B., Gill, D. P., Parks, S. L., & Packer, S. T. (2001). Expertise and the perception of kinematic and situational probability information. *Perception*, *30*(2), 233–252.

Ashley, R. (2000). The pragmatics of conducting: Analysing and interpreting conductor's expressive gestures. In C. Woods, G. Luck, R. Brochard, F. Seddon, & J. A. Sloboda (Eds.), *Proceedings of the Sixth International Conference on Music Perception and Cognition*. Keele: Keele University.

Benge, T. J. (1996). Movements utilised by conductors in the stimulation and expression of musicianship. Doctoral dissertation, University of Southern California. *Dissertation Abstracts International*, *A54*(3), 18.

Braem, B., & Braem, P. (2000). A pilot study of the expressive gestures used by classical orchestra conductors. In K. Emmorey, & H. Lane (Eds.), *The signs of language revisited: An anthology to honour Ursula Bellugi and Edward Klima* (pp. 143–167). Mahwah, NJ: Erlbaum.

Cambouropoulos, E. (2006). Musical parallelism and melodic segmentation: A computational approach. *Music Perception*, *23*(3), 249–268.

Camurri, A., Lagerlöf, I., & Volpe, G. (2003). Recognizing emotion from dance movement: comparison of spectator recognition and automated techniques. *International Journal of Human-Computer Studies*, *59*(1–2), 213–225.

Camurri, A., De Poli, G., Friberg, A., Leman, M., & Volpe, G. (2005). The MEGA project: analysis and synthesis of multisensory expressive gesture in performing art applications. *Journal of New Music Research*, *34*(1), 5–21.

Downie, J. S. (2003) Music information retrieval. In B. Cronin (Ed.), *Annual review of information science and technology* (pp. 295–340). Volume 37. Medford, NJ: Information Today.

Eerola, T., & Toiviainen, P. (2004). MIDI toolbox: MATLAB tools for music research. Kopijyvä, Jyväskylä, Finland: University of Jyväskylä. Available at: www.jyu.fi/musica/miditoolbox/ (accessed 1 October 2007).

Fredrickson, W. E. (1994). Band musicians' performance and eye contact as influenced by loss of a Visual and/or aural stimulus'. *Journal of Research in Music Education*, *42*(4), 306–317.

Goulet, C., Bard, C., & Fleury, M. (1989). Expertise differences in preparing to return a tennis serve: a visual information processing approach. *Journal of Sport and Exercise Psychology*, *11*(4), 382–398.

Hamming, R. W. (1997). *Digital filters* (3rd ed.). Mineola, NY: Dover Publications.

Holt, M. M. (1992). The application of conducting and choral rehearsal pedagogy of laban effort-shape and its comparative effect upon style in choral performance. *Dissertation Abstracts International*, *53*(2), 437A.

Ilmonen, T., & Takala, T. (1999). *Conductor following with artificial neural networks* (pp. 367–370). Proceedings of the 1999 International Computer Music Conference. San Francisco, CA: International Computer Music Association.

Jensen, K., & Andersen, T. H. (2003). Beat estimation on the beat. In *Proceedings of IEEE workshop on applications of signal processing to audio and acoustics*, 19–22 October, New Paltz, NY, USA.

Keller, P. E. (2001). Attentional resource allocation in musical ensemble performance. *Psychology of Music, 29*(1), 20–38.

Klapuri, A. (2004). Automatic music transcription as we know it today. *Journal of New Music Research, 33*(3), 269–282.

Krumhansl, C. L., & Schenk, D. L. (1997). Can dance reflect the structural and expressive qualities of music? *Musicæ Scientiæ, 1*, 63–83.

Lacquaniti, F., Terzuolo, C. A., & Viviani, P. (1983). The relating kinematic and figural aspects of drawing movements. *Acta Psychologica, 54*, 115–130.

Lartillot, O. (2004). A musical pattern discovery system founded on a modelling of listening strategies. *Computer Music Journal, 28*(3), 53–67.

Lartillot, O. (2005). Multi-dimensional motivic pattern extraction founded on adaptive redundancy filtering. *Journal of New Music Research, 34*(4), 375–393.

Lartillot, O., & Toiviainen, P. (2007). *A Matlab toolbox for music information retrieval.* Paper presented at 31st Annual Conference of the German Classification Society, 10–15 September, Freiburg, Germany.

Lee, E., Wolf, M., & Borchers, J. (2005). Improving orchestral conducting systems in public spaces: Examining the temporal characteristics and conceptual models of conducting gestures. In *Proceedings of the CHI 2005 conference on human factors in computing systems* (pp. 731–740). New York, NY: ACM.

Leman, M. (2002). Musical audio mining. In J. Meij (Ed.), *Dealing with the data flood: Mining data, text and multimedia.* Rotterdam: STT Netherlands Study Centre for Technology Trends.

Lesaffre, M., Tanghe, K., Martens, G., Moelants, D., Leman, M., De Baets, B., De Meyer, H., & Martens, J.-P. (2003). The MAMI query-by-voice experiment: Collecting and annotating vocal queries for music information retrieval. In *Proceedings of the 4th International Conference on Music Information Retrieval (ISMIR'03)* (pp. 65–71). Baltimore: John Hopkins University.

Luck, G. (2000). Synchronizing a motor response with a visual event: the perception of temporal information in a conductor's gestures, In C. Woods, G. Luck, R. Brochard, F. Seddon, & J. A. Sloboda (Eds.), *Proceedings of the Sixth International Conference on Music Perception and Cognition.* Keele, UK: Keele University.

Luck, G. (2007). Identifying beat location in conducting gestures: a temporal adjustment study. Paper presented at the International Society for Gesture Studies Conference 2007: *Integrating gestures*, 18–21 June, Northwestern University, Chicago, IL, USA.

Luck G., & Nte, S. (2008). An investigation of conductors' temporal gestures and conductor-musician synchronization, and a first experiment. *Psychology of Music, 36*(1), 81–99.

Luck, G., & Sloboda, J. (2007). Synchronizing with complex biological motion: an investigation of musicians' synchronization with traditional conducting beat patterns. *Music Performance Research, 1*(1), 26–46.

Luck, G., & Sloboda, J. (2008). Exploring the spatio-temporal properties of the beat in simple conducting gestures using a synchronization task. *Music Perception, 25*(3), 225–239.

Luck, G., & Sloboda, J. (2009). Spatio-temporal cues for visually-mediated synchronization. *Music Perception, 26*(5), 465–473.

Luck, G., & Toiviainen, P. (2006). Ensemble musicians' synchronization with conductors' gestures: an automated feature-extraction analysis. *Music Perception*, *24*(2), 189–200.

Marrin Nakra, T. (2001). *Translating conductors' gestures to sound*. Paper presented at Human Supervision and Control in Engineering and Music. Kassel: University of Kassel.

Maruyama, S., & Furuyama, N. (2002). Functional variations and organisation of gestures by a classical orchestral conductor. *Paper presented at the First Congress of the International Society for Gesture Studies*, 5–8 June, University of Texas at Austin, Austin, TX, USA.

Miller, S. (1988). The effect of Laban movement theory on the ability of student conductors to communicate musical interpretation through gesture. Doctoral dissertation, University of Wisconsin-Madison, USA. *Dissertation Abstracts International*, *49*(5), 1087A.

Pampalk, E., Flexer, A., & Widmer, G. (2005). Improvements of audio-based music similarity and genre classification. In *Proceedings of the 6th International Conference on Music Information Retrieval* (ISMIR'05) (pp. 11–15). London: University of London.

Prausnitz, F. (1983). *Score and podium: A complete guide to conducting*. London: Norton.

Rasch, R. A. (1988). Timing and synchronization in ensemble performance. In: J. Sloboda (Ed.), *Generative processes in music*. New York, NY: Oxford University Press.

Rauber, A., Pampalk, E., & Merkl, D. (2003). The SOM-enhanced jukebox: Organization and visualization of music collections based on perceptual models. *Journal of New Music Research*, *32*(2), 193–210.

Repp, B. H., & Penel, A. (2004). Rhythmic movement is attracted more strongly to auditory than to visual rhythms. *Psychological Research*, *68*(4), 252–270.

Rudolf, M. (1995). *The grammar of conducting: A comprehensive guide to baton technique and interpretation* (3rd ed.). New York, NY: Schirmer Books.

Serrano, J. G. (1994). Visual perception of simulated conducting motion. *Dissertation Abstracts International Section A: Humanities and Social Sciences*, *55*(4–A), 797.

Toiviainen, P., & Burger, B. (2010). MoCap Toolbox Manual. University of Jyväskylä: Jyväskylä, Finland. Available at http://www.jyu.fi/music/coe/materials/mocaptoolbox/ MCTmanual (accessed 4 October 2010).

Toiviainen, P., & Eerola, T. (2006). Autocorrelation in meter induction: The role of accent structure. *Journal of the Acoustical Society of America*, *119*(2), 1164–1170.

Venn, E. (2003). Towards a semiotics of conducting. Paper presented at Music and Gesture, 28–31 August, University of East Anglia, UK.

Chapter 17

Performance cues in singing: evidence from practice and recall

Jane Ginsborg and Roger Chaffin

Abstract

Although long-term recall has been studied for many years, there have been comparatively few investigations of long-term recall for music performance. In the study described in this chapter, we examined an experienced singer's long-term recall for the words and melody of Stravinsky's *Ricercar 1,* for soprano and small instrumental ensemble. The singer recorded nine practice/rehearsal sessions with the conductor as accompanist over four weeks and wrote out the words and music from memory times over a five-year period. The musicians annotated copies of the score to indicate the location of musical features to which they attended during practice and performance cues to which they attended during performance. Comparison with the location of starts, stops, and repetitions during practice showed what the singer paid attention to. For example, attention to the musical structure was signalled by starts at beginnings of sections and phrases; attention to musical expression by the absence of starts at performance cues for expression. Comparison of the annotations with recall showed that these places had become *landmarks.* Recall was better for the first bars of sections and phrases and declined in the following bars, as distance from the cue increased. Other cues became *lacunae*—places that were forgotten, for example, performance cues for preparation where the singer attended to her next entry or to the other musicians. At these cues, recall was worse, improving as distance from the cue increased. The performance cues to which the singer reported attending on stage were prepared during the weeks that preceded the public performance and continued to affect her recall of the piece in the months and years that followed.

Jane Ginsborg writes: 'In this chapter Roger Chaffin and I report a study that directly follows up the research into singers' memorization and recall that I carried out in the course of PhD research at Keele University under the supervision of John Sloboda (Ginsborg, 2000, 2002; Ginsborg & Sloboda, 2007). The first of these studies required singers to provide verbal commentaries while practising and memorizing, and John provided the pilot data for this study, recording his practice sessions as he memorized the bass chorus part for Beethoven's Ninth Symphony. He had heard Roger talking about the research he was undertaking at the time, along similar lines, with the pianist Gabriela Imreh, and put him in touch with me, thus laying the ground for the collaboration that produced the work that we report here.'

The longitudinal case study method, pioneered by Chaffin and Imreh (1994), has been used to investigate how musicians memorize for performance. One important conclusion is that experienced musicians use performance cues, features of the music to which the musician pays attention during practice and rehearsal, and which, as a result, become mental 'landmarks' when the piece is performed. Our study extends the evidence for this conclusion to singing, as opposed to instrumental, performance; and to preparation for ensemble, as opposed to solo, performance. We also provide more extensive evidence of the effects of performance cues on written recall of the score.

Evidence for the use of performance cues comes from case studies in which solo performers video-recorded their practice sessions as they learned new works for performance. Starts, stops, and repetitions during practice indicated places in the music to which the musicians attended during practice. Their post-performance annotations of the musical score identified the decisions they had made in response to specific musical features. Spontaneous verbal comments provided evidence of the practice strategies they used. Written recall of the score after performance revealed the location of the mental landmarks in their memory of the music. Participants to date have included a classical pianist (e.g. Chaffin, Imreh, & Crawford, 2002; Chaffin, Imreh, Lemieux, & Chen, 2003), a jazz pianist (Noice, Jeffrey, Noice, & Chaffin, 2008), and a cellist (Chaffin, Lisboa, Logan, & Begosh, 2010; Lisboa, Chaffin, Schiaroli, & Barrera, 2004; Logan, Begosh, Chaffin, & Lisboa, 2007). In each study, effects of musical structure on practice were pervasive, and different aspects of technique, interpretation, and expression became the focus of attention at various points in the learning process. After the public performance, effects of performance cues on written recall of the score suggested that these places in the music had become landmarks in the musicians' mental map of the piece.

In the present study, we examined a singer (the first author) and conductor preparing Stravinsky's *Ricercar 1* for soprano and small instrumental ensemble for performance. We have previously described how the verbal comments they made during their individual practice sessions and their discussions during joint rehearsals revealed how they negotiated musical goals and established shared performance cues to coordinate their actions (Ginsborg, Chaffin, & Nicholson, 2006a). Here, we summarize behavioural evidence from the same study showing that the singer attended to performance cues during practice and that these cues affected her memory of the piece when she wrote it out from memory. Writing out the score from memory was a normal practice activity for the singer. For the purposes of the study, she wrote it out at intervals over a five-year period, providing an opportunity to observe the effects of performance cues on long-term retention.

Recall from long-term memory has been studied by psychologists ever since Ebbinghaus (1885/1913) pioneered its investigation using himself as his own experimental subject. Retention has normally been studied, however, over relatively short periods—measured in minutes, hours, or days. Relatively few studies have examined retention over months or years, although exceptions include Bahrick (1994) and Rubin (1995, 1977; Rubin & Wenzel, 1996). Most studies of musical memory have likewise focused on retention over relatively short periods. For example, listeners' recognition memory for words and music was studied by Serafine, Crowder, and Repp (1984), Serafine, Davidson, and Crowder (1986) and Crowder, Serafine, and Repp (1990). In contrast, Sloboda and Parker (1985) investigated recall for the melodies of songs by expert and novice musicians learning unfamiliar folk melodies. This showed that recall was far from verbatim, although harmonic and, especially, metrical structure was preserved—see Chapter 9, present volume. Ginsborg and Sloboda (2007), in their study of more and less musically expert singers' recall for words and melody, compared the frequency of *conjoint errors*, where both words and music are recalled incorrectly, and *separate errors*, where errors are made in words or music but not both. Both types of errors occurred, with separate errors being more frequent. This result supported the 'association-by-contiguity' hypothesis proposed by Crowder *et al.* (1990) that words and melody are stored in memory as separate but associated components. The presence of separate errors was contrary to the prediction of Crowder *et al.*'s 'physical interaction' hypothesis that words and melody are fully integrated in memory, which would have resulted in no separate errors.

In the study that provides the model for the present study of long-term musical memory (Chaffin *et al.*, 2002), the pianist Gabriela Imreh prepared Bach's *Italian Concerto* for performance in 33 hours of practice. The pianist's practice was organized in terms of the sections of the musical structure and started and stopped at performance cues more than at other locations in the piece, suggesting that she was thinking of the music in terms of its structure and paying attention to places where performance cues were needed. The effects of this attention were evident in her free recall two years later when she wrote down as much as she could remember of the first page of the score, recalling around 65% of the notes. Her recall was better at section boundaries and at expressive performance cues (places where she had to convey a particular emotion) and declined with each successive bar. Basic performance cues (relating to fingering, technical difficulties, etc.), in contrast, produced a serial position effect in the opposite direction. Recall was *worse* at basic cues and improved with distance from the cue. Similar serial position effects were also found in the study with the cellist who wrote out the 104 bars of the *Prelude* from Bach's Suite No. 6 for solo cello from memory (Chaffin, Logan, & Begosh, 2009).

The serial position effects in both of these studies suggested that beginnings of sections and expressive performance cues served as retrieval cues, providing the musicians with direct, content addressable access to their memory of the music. These places were landmarks in the musicians' mental map of the piece (Chaffin *et al.*, 2002, Chapter 9).

The bars that followed, in contrast, were cued serially by the preceding bar and so recall declined in the bars following the cue, as distance from the cue increased. Recall of an ordered series is generally better for the first item in the series and declines with each succeeding item. At each successive link in the chain there is the possibility that retrieval of the next link will fail. The probability of correct recall, therefore, decreases as distance from the start of the chain increases (Broadbent, Cooper, & Broadbent, 1978; Ebbinghaus, 1885; Fischler, Rundus, & Atkinson, 1970; Lewandowsky & Murdock, 1989; Roediger & Crowder, 1976; Rundus, 1971; Tenenbaum, Tehan, Stewart, & Christensen, 1999)—although it is also true, of course, that for verbal items there is also a recency effect by which the last items of a sequence have higher probability of recall.

In contrast to the positive effect of landmarks, recall at basic cues was *worse* than in other places and improved with distance following the cue. We will refer to such places as 'lacunae'. Lacunae occurred in places where the musician had to pay particular attention to some aspect of the sensorimotor context. For the pianist, many of the basic cues represented technical difficulties or fingerings needed to position the hand for what came next. For the cellist, basic cues represented decisions about bowing, changing string, fingering, shifting the left hand, and nuances of left hand position and intonation. One possible explanation is that attention to these details of execution during practice made them more important in the serial chain of associations cuing what came next. The absence of the usual sensorimotor context during written recall, therefore, resulted in poorer recall at these points (Chaffin & Logan, 2006). Another possibility is that the musicians relied more on the other sensorimotor context to cue their memories at these points. Since the auditory and motor cues produced by playing were not available when writing out the score, recall was poorer (Chaffin *et al.*, 2002, Ch. 7). The two explanations are not necessarily incompatible.

In summary, we expected to find that the singer started and stopped during practice at locations that were structurally important, or contained performance cues or other features requiring practice. Similarly, we expected the singer to avoid stopping and starting in places where a transition needed practice. We expected her to make both separate and conjoint errors in recall and that errors of both types would increase over time. We expected places where the singer started during practice to become landmarks in her memory and places where she needed to attend to details of technique or to the other musicians to become lacunae. We predicted that lacunae would affect recall of the bars that led up to them in addition to affecting those that followed, while effects of landmarks would be confined to bars that followed them.

Learning the *Ricercar*

Jane Ginsborg, the first author, is a former professional singer; she has worked with the pianist and conductor George Nicholson for more than 30 years, performing as a duo and as members of a variety of ensembles. In 2003, the two musicians performed Stravinsky's *Cantata* for two solo singers, women's choir, and small instrumental ensemble. The singer had performed it once before, more than 25 years earlier, and she had not looked at it in the interim. It includes one movement for solo soprano and ensemble, *Ricercar 1* (about four minutes in length). The singer and conductor video-recorded their individual practice sessions and joint rehearsals of this piece. In this chapter we will be concerned with the singer's preparation and recall of the *Ricercar*.

Practice and rehearsal sessions

From mid-November to mid-December 2003, the singer undertook five individual practice sessions lasting four hours and 13 minutes in all (Sessions 1, 2, 3, 5, and 8); the conductor undertook one individual practice session lasting 37 minutes (Session 4). They carried out four joint rehearsals lasting two hours and 47 minutes (Sessions 6, 9, 12, and 15). These 10 practice and rehearsal sessions were video-recorded and transcribed. One brief run-through with the ensemble was video-recorded and transcribed but not analysed (Session 7); three ensemble rehearsals (57 minutes) were not recorded (Sessions 10, 13, and 14). Session 11 was the singer's first attempt to write out the words and rhythms of the work from memory. A public performance of the complete *Cantata*, conducted by George Nicholson, with the first author as solo soprano, was given on 16 December 2003. Sessions were grouped together for analysis as follows: Sessions 1 and 2 (singer learning); 3 (singer memorizing); 5 (singer briefly checking memory alone), and 6 (first of the singer's and conductor's joint rehearsals; Session 8 (individual practice session revisiting technical difficulties, and ensuring that memory was secure); Sessions 9, 12, and 15 (joint rehearsals).

Practice was transcribed by numbering the beats of the piece (1–250) and recording the beat on which each *practice segment* started and stopped. (A practice segment consisted of the uninterrupted performance of a segment of the piece and could range in length from 1 to 250 beats.) For each practice segment, we noted whether the singer's score was open or closed and classified the latter as performed from memory.

Reports

Soon after the public performance, the singer and conductor each independently reported every feature of the music that they had paid attention to during practice and rehearsal and the subset of those features that they were aware of attending to during the performance (i.e. their performance cues). They made their reports by annotating multiple copies of the score. The reports were subsequently categorized as reflecting structural, basic, interpretive, or expressive aspects of the music. The two musicians then compared their reports to identify *shared performance cues* to which they had consciously attended during the performance and to which they knew the other would be attending.

The singer made 12 types of annotation representing features requiring decisions during rehearsal and five types of annotation representing individual performance cues. She and the conductor made seven additional types of annotation representing shared performance cues. These 24 potential predictors were reduced to 16 by grouping annotations that, it was agreed by the musicians, fulfilled similar functions. Figure 17.1 shows an example of how locations were reported for three performance cues for preparation (Prepare-PC) and three for expression (Expressive-PC). The upward arrows on Figure 17.1 indicate the location of the Prepare-PCs; downward arrows indicate

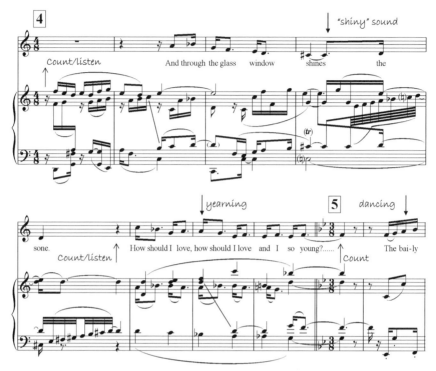

Fig. 17.1 Annotated excerpt from *Ricercar* (beats 92–129).

Expressive-PCs. The performance cues for preparation are the annotations 'count/listen' and 'count' (below the vocal line); the expressive performance cues are the annotations '"shiny" sound', 'yearning', and 'dancing' (above the vocal line). These predictor variables are listed in Table 17.1, which also shows their classification as structural, basic, interpretive, or expressive features or cues. Predictors were coded by dummy variables with '1' representing the presence of the features or cue in question and '0' representing its absence for each beat.

Memorization

The great majority of practice was done from memory. Figure 17.2 summarizes the transcription of practice in Sessions 1 and 2. Each line represents the uninterrupted performance of one segment of the piece. Grey lines indicate that the singer was practising with the score open and black lines indicate when she was practising from memory. The figure should be read from left to right and from bottom to top, with Session 1 starting in the bottom left-hand corner and Session 2 ending in the top right-hand corner. The first half of Session 1 was spent on the first two-thirds of the piece, and the second half on the final third. Most of Session 2 was also spent on the final third of the piece, which contained more new material and was rhythmically more complex than the first two thirds. Reflecting the greater complexity of the music, practice segments were shorter in Session 2 than in Session 1 ($X = 9$ and 21 beats, respectively).

Table 17.1 Singer's and conductor's annotations representing features, individual performance cues (PCs), and shared performance cues (SPCs)

Type of feature/PC	Predictor variable	No. of locations
Singer's annotations		
Structural	Start of section	9
	Switch	7
	Start of phrase	29
Basic	Prepare (count, listen, think, watch)	35
	Basic words (pronunciation)	25
	Technical (including breath)	45
Interpretive	Words (interpretation, i.e. meaning)	29
	Dynamics/tempo	9
Expressive	Expressive	15
Basic PC	Prepare PC (subset of Prepare, above)	20
	Technical (including breath) PC (subset of Technical [including breath], above)	14
Interpretive PC	Stress on words (pronunciation + meaning) PC (subset of Basic words [pronunciation] and Interpretive Words [interpretation i.e. meaning], above)	28
Expressive PC	Expressive PC (subset of Expressive, above)	12
Singer's and conductor's annotations		
Basic SPC	Score SPC (cue entry, coordinate rhythm, cadence)	11
	Arrival/off SPC	8
Expressive SPC	Expressive SPC (subset of singer's and conductor's Expressive PC)	5

Practice from memory began in Session 2. The proportion of practice segments sung from memory increased steadily from 35% in Sessions 1–2, to 64% in Session 3, 97% in Sessions 5–6, 84% in Session 8, and 100% in Sessions 9–15. The singer thus completed memorization of the piece in Session 3, referred to the score occasionally in Sessions 5, 6, and 8, and rehearsed entirely from memory in Sessions 9, 12, and 15.

Comparing reports and practice

Figure 17.3 shows the relationship between what the singer did in practice during Session 3 and her musical understanding of the piece, reported in her annotations of the score (see Figure 17.1). Practice is represented in Figure 17.2 by the horizontal lines and the singer's reports by vertical arrows representing beginnings of sections (bold faced) and phrases (regular case). The singer practised the piece section by

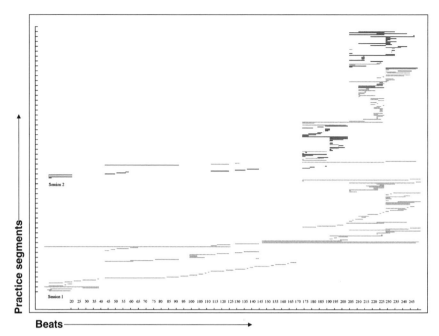

Fig. 17.2 Practice in Sessions 1 and 2 (black, from memory; grey = with score open).

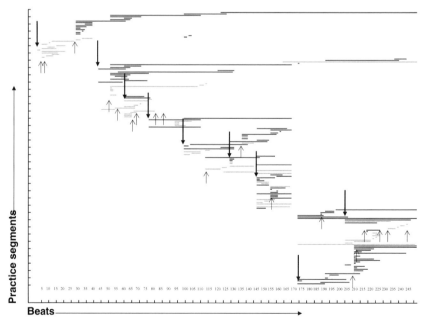

Fig. 17.3 Relating reports to practice in Session 3 (arrows down = starts of section; arrows up = start of phrase).

Table 17.2 Effects of predictor variables on location of starts, stops, and repetitions during practice showing effects across sessions

Type	Predictor variable	Estimate	Standard error	Z
Starts				
Structural	Start of section	2.589	0.360	7.199***
	Start of phrase	4.197	0.369	11.378***
Basic	Prepare	0.802	0.168	4.763***
Interpretive	Dynamics/tempo	1.606	0.320	5.023***
Expressive PC	Expressive PC	−0.983	0.372	−2.641*
Basic SPC	Score SPC	−0.959	0.294	−3.266***
Stops				
Structural	Start of phrase PC	−0.417	0.119	−3.497***
Basic SPC	Arrival/off SPC	2.843	0.184	15.468***
	Score SPC	0.571	0.163	3.509***
Repetitions				
Structural	Start of phrase	1.122	0.216	5.184***
Basic PC	Prepare PC	−0.903	0.246	−3.674***

***$p <.0001$, **$p <.001$, *$p <.01$.

section, starting at the end and working her way forward to the beginning. Within each section, she used beginnings of phrases as starting places. Combining the behavioural record of practice with the musician's self-reports in this way allows us to see how her practice was shaped by her understanding of the piece.

It is impractical to provide graphs for all nine sessions and 16 reports. Instead, Table 17.2 lists those relationships between reports and practice that were strong enough to reach statistical significance ($p <.01$) when we fitted a linear model to the data (Bryk & Raudenbush, 1992; Singer & Willett, 2003).[1] The predictor variables were the musical features and performance cues listed in Table 17.1. The dependent variables were the number of starts, stops, and repetitions for each beat. Sessions were combined for analysis into five sets, as described above (Sessions 1–2, 3, 5–6, 8, 9–15). There were no interactions of predictors with practice sessions and so all of the effects in Table 17.2 represent effects across all practice sessions. Most of the effects are positive, showing that the musicians started or stopped at the features and cues in question *more*, or repeated them more, than other places in the piece. There were three negative

---

[1] The hierarchical model did not assume independence of successive data points and thus modelled the dependence of successive data points in time more appropriately than the kind of standard multiple regression analysis that has been used to evaluate this kind of data in previous studies. The predictors were entered simultaneously as fixed effects. The 250 notes of the piece were divided into nine segments at section boundaries and the reliability of the effects was assessed by their consistency across sections.

effects indicating *fewer* starts, stops, or repetitions. In these cases, the musicians were playing through without stopping, usually in order to practise the feature or cue in context (Chaffin *et al.*, 2002, pp. 183–185). In either case, significant effects show that these locations received more attention and thus more practice than other places.

Table 17.2 confirms our conclusion, based on Figure 17.3, that the singer used the musical structure to organize her practice. She was more likely to start her practice segments at the beginnings of sections and phrases, to avoid stopping at beginnings of phrases, and to repeat these beginnings more (Table 17.2).[2] The analyses also confirm the conclusion drawn by Ginsborg *et al.* (2006a), on the basis of an analysis of the singer's comments during practice, that she practised performance cues including shared cues that ensured coordination with the conductor. Attention to performance cues was reflected in five effects on practice, two for individual and three for shared performance cues.

The singer avoided starting at expressive performance cues where a whole phrase needed to be sung in context in order to evoke a particular feeling, for example, to convey 'dancing' or 'yearning'. Similarly, she avoided starting at shared performance cues involving the score and was also more likely to stop at these cues (Score SPC, Table 17.2). These are places where precise coordination of an entry, rhythmic pattern, or cadential moment with the other musicians was needed. The musicians rehearsed by starting before the critical point and then playing up to or past it in order to rehearse coordinating with each other. When they stopped, it was to allow them to discuss entries or coordination. For the same reason, they were more likely to stop at the locations of the shared performance cue 'arrival/off'. Finally, the singer avoided repetition of performance cues for preparation. Many of these were places where rests were notated for the singer so that she was not singing but listening to the instrumentalists, counting beats and watching the conductor. The negative effect was probably due to the singer omitting these beats strategically to save time during her solo practice.

Starts were also influenced by three types of musical feature that did not become performance cues. The singer practised these features until they became automatic so that they no longer needed attention during performance. Practice started more often at places where she needed to prepare for what came next and where there were changes in dynamics or tempo and expression (Prepare, Dynamics/tempo, and Expressive-PCs, respectively, Table 17.2).

Recalling the *Ricercar*

The singer recalled the piece from memory in four uninterrupted performances: two during the third joint rehearsal (Session 12), with the conductor accompanying the singer on the piano, one during the final rehearsal (Session 15), and the public performance the same day. In Session 12, the singer made one error in one performance

---

[2] The interaction of each predictor with sessions was tested and was significant for the effect of beginnings of phrases on starts. Separate analyses of the five session sets showed that significant effects of this predictor were limited to the singer's solo practice sessions (1–2, 3, and 8) and did not occur in sessions primarily devoted to joint practice or rehearsal (5–6, 9–15).

and two errors in the other. In Session 15, the singer made no errors herself but accommodated to two errors made by the conductor. The fourth, public performance was accurate in all respects.

The singer also recalled the piece from memory on nine occasions when she wrote out what she could remember of the words and melody, notating rhythms above each word, and humming, beating a pulse and conducting as necessary until she had worked through the whole song from start to end. She made the first recall (FR0) between the last two rehearsal sessions in December 2003, as part of her normal preparation for the public performance. She made two more recalls at the end of January 2004 and the end of February 2004. These yielded only one or two trivial errors and we will not report the data. The first time after the performance that the singer made a substantial number of errors was 12 months later, when she recalled the piece in February 2005 (FR1). We will report data for this and the five subsequent recalls in June 2005, August 2006, June 2007, November 2007, and November 2008 (FR2–6). Each of these recalls was made after a period of months of not thinking about the piece, before resuming work on the study. Apart from FR0, recalls occurred 12, 18, 32, 42, 47, and 59 months after the public performance. The mean time interval since last consulting the score was 6.5 months (10, 4, 10, 6, 5, and 4 months respectively for FR1, FR2, FR3, FR4, FR5, and FR6).

The first five times that the singer recalled the piece (FR0 to FR2), she engaged in additional efforts to remember the piece after working through it from start to finish once. She went back through it again, reconstructing as much as she could from memory. For the last four recalls (FR3-6) she did not attempt to reconstruct the piece but simply worked through it once from start to finish.

Scoring accuracy of recall

Each quaver beat was scored for accuracy of recall. Omitted beats were scored '0'; perfectly recalled beats were scored '1'. Beats recalled inaccurately were scored in between '0' and '1' by counting the number of different types of errors made (word, pitch, rhythm/duration.[3] Whole-beat rests were scored '1' if notated, as '0' if omitted. The exception to this rule was if notes were held too long, spilling into rests, in which case the error on the rest beat was deemed a duration error. 'Misspellings' of pitches and rhythms (e.g. $A^{\#}$ for $B^{\flat}$, a semiquaver tied to a quaver for a dotted quaver) and mis-positionings of barlines were ignored.

Accuracy of recall

Accuracy of recall declined steadily over time from 97.1% (FR0) to a low of 66.4% 47 months later (FR5; see Figure 17.4).[4] The decrease is more gradual than the typical

---

[3] Pitches were not recorded in FR0.

[4] A multiple regression analysis was carried out, with time (FR0–6, i.e. five days before and 14, 18, 32, 42, 47 and 59 months after the performance) as the predictor variables and accuracy of recall per beat, as outlined under 'Scoring accuracy of recall' as the dependent measure. Using the enter method, a significant model emerged: $F (7, 242) = 14.09$, $p <.0001$. The model explains 26.9% of the variance (Adjusted $R^2 = 0.269$). While accuracy of recall was not

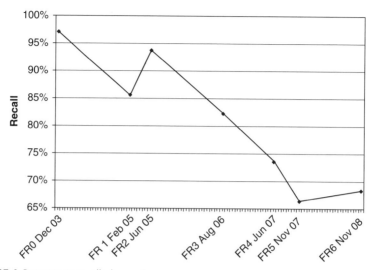

Fig. 17.4 Percentage recalled over time.

J-shaped forgetting curve (Ebbinghaus, 1885). Three factors may account for this. First, FR0 occurred as part of the singer's preparation for performance. Recall had not yet reached the level at which it was perfect, which presumably occurred five days later when the singer performed the piece from memory with complete accuracy. Second, the first three scored recalls involved reconstructions while the last four did not. Third, the singer's intermittent work on the research undoubtedly slowed forgetting. The improvement in recall between February and June 2005 may be attributable, for example, to the comparatively short period of time between the singer's analysing FR1 and undertaking FR2. Despite these factors, the decline in recall approximated the expected course, levelling off at FR5, almost four years after the performance. To our knowledge, this is the first evidence that very-long-term recall of music by a performer follows a similar trajectory of decline as other kinds of memorized material (Bahrick, 1994).

Errors in recall

Figure 17.5 shows the locations of errors in each of the seven written free recalls. The X-axes represent beats of the piece from 1 to 250. The Y-axes represent the degrees of accuracy, with 1 representing complete accuracy and 0 representing complete omission. The top panel (FR0) shows that the singer was able to notate the words and rhythms with considerable accuracy five days before the performance. There were no gaps where the music was forgotten entirely and the piece was recalled with 97.1% accuracy. The majority of errors concerned the recall and notation of rhythms (e.g. at beats 98–99 *And through*) and durations (e.g. at beats 39–40 *wolde*). Errors involving

predicted by FR0–1 or FR5–6, it was predicted by FR2 (B = 64.7, SE B = 21.8, β = 0.196, p = .003), FR3 (B = –87.3, SE B = 14.2, β = –0.41, p <0001) and FR4 (B = –59.6, SE B = 16.7, β = –0.34, p <.0001).

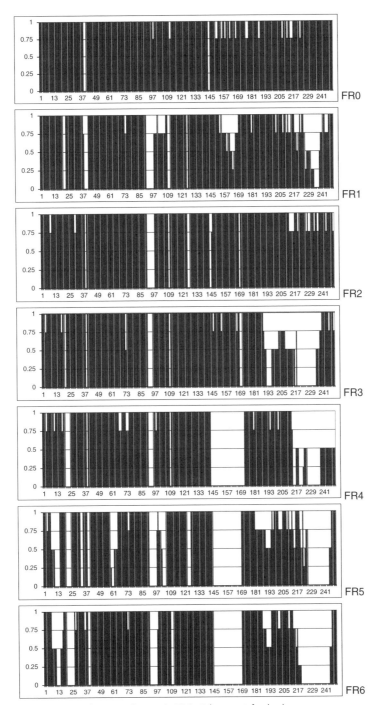

Fig. 17.5 Accuracy and types of error in FR0–6 (see text for key).

the words included the reversal of *now* and *were* at beats 151–152 and the substitution of *shall* for *will* on beat 156.

Fourteen months later (FR1) there was a substantial drop in accuracy, to 85.6%. The majority of errors involved rhythm and duration, although the rests after the second appearance of the refrain were omitted (beats 92–97), as was the phrase *A place e-* (beats 235–238). Four months later, 18 months after the performance (FR2), accuracy increased to 93.7%. Again, rhythm/duration errors predominated and the rests before the third appearance of the refrain were omitted. There was a substantial drop in accuracy to 82.3% after 14 months, 32 months after the performance (FR3). As well as the omitted rests (beats 92–97), the passage *and eke vic-* (beats 193–196) was forgotten. The words *Vertuous and benign* (beats 203–208) were forgotten, although the melody was recalled at first; rhythms were forgotten at *Lett us, lett us pray all, all to* (beats 209–216) before all was omitted between beats 219–234 (*Eternal Which is the hevenly King After ther liff grant them*).

Recall continued its slow deterioration in FR4, 10 months later and 42 months after the performance. Accuracy dropped to 73.5% as the whole of the section following the third appearance of the refrain was forgotten: *For to report it now were tedius: We will therfor now sing no more Of the games joyus* (beats 145–172). The majority of errors were durations, forgetting the melody but preserving the words or omitting words and melody simultaneously. There was one pitch error that had not occurred before (*All*, beat 214), after which the next three words were forgotten (preserving the melody), and then the subsequent melody (preserving the words) before both words and melody were forgotten altogether, as before: *After ther liff grant them A place* (beats 227–237). The words *eternally to sing* (beats 238–244) were forgotten, although not the melody, and the final *Amen* was recalled only with rhythmic errors.

The next recall (FR5), five months later and 47 months after the performance, showed more substantial decline: accuracy dropped to 64.4%. Portions of the very first line were omitted along with the section following the third appearance of the refrain (as in FR4) and the words of *Our quen princis* (beats 182–189), as well as the closing section starting *After ther liff* (beats 227–244). Finally, many of the same passages were forgotten again in FR6, a year later and 59 months after the performance. Accuracy of recall improved slightly, to 68.3%, including recall for two previously forgotten phrases, *And through the glass window shines the sone* (beats 98–109) and *Our quen princis* (beats 182–189).

Conjoint versus separate errors

Errors and omissions were classified as conjoint (errors or omissions in both words and melody, i.e. pitch and rhythm combined) or separate (errors or omissions of words, duration, pitch, or melody). Conjoint and separate errors and omissions were calculated as a proportion of all beats (Figure 17.6). Those involving omissions of both words and melody (conjoint omissions) increased across recalls to 26% of all beats in FR6 (the passages represented as white gaps in Figure 17.5), while conjoint errors peaked in FR3 at 6.8%. The proportion of separate errors declined from a high of 5.6% in FR1 to zero in FR 2 and 5, while the proportion of separate errors involving pitch

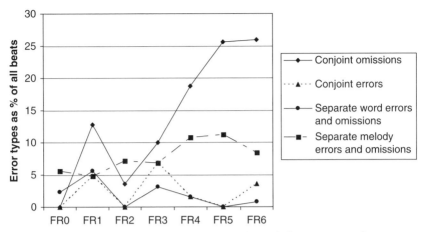

Fig. 17.6 Percentage of all beats constituting conjoint omissions, errors, and separate word and melody errors/omissions in FR0–6.

and rhythm/duration increased to a peak of 11.2% in FR5.[5] Our results are consistent with those of Ginsborg and Sloboda (2007) showing that expert singers make both conjoint and separate errors and that the latter are more numerous. The presence of some separate errors indicates that the singer was able to recall words and music separately. Contrary to the prediction of Crowder *et al.*'s (1990) physical interaction hypothesis, it was not the case that words and melody became inseparable in memory. On the other hand, the preponderance of conjoint errors, including omissions, supported the association-by-contiguity hypothesis that memory for words and music support each other by providing multiple retrieval cues.

Landmarks and lacunae

We found landmarks in the singer's memory—places that she recalled better than surrounding passages. We also found lacunae—places that she recalled worse. Both were indicated by serial position effects in the accuracy of recall. The bar graphs in Figure 17.7 shows mean recall probability as a function of serial position following starts of sections (top left), performance cues for stress on words (top right), and performance cues for preparation (bottom left). The beat where the report was marked was assigned the serial position '0'. For SP-after, any beats that followed in the same bar were also coded '0'. Beats in the next bar were assigned the serial position '1'. Each succeeding bar was numbered successively ('2', '3', '4') up until the next report of the same type, with a maximum value of 4. Serial positions of 4 and greater received the same value to provide the same number of serial positions for all predictors.

---

[5] A multivariate repeated measures MANOVA with one within-subjects factor (time, as above) and seven different dependent variables—the mean of the numbers of errors of each type (none = 0, separate melody = 1, separate word = 2, conjoint error = 3 and conjoint omission = 4) made on each occasion–revealed a significant effect of time: $F(6, 244) = 27.02, p <.0001$ (Pillai's Trace), such that mean scores rose from .1 (SD = .02) in FR0 to 1.3 (SD = .11) in FR6.

Table 17.3 Effects of predictor variables on recall showing effects across sessions

Type	Predictor variable	Estimate	Standard error	Z
Structural	Start of section	−0.038	0.008	−5.02***
Interpretive PC	Stress on words	−0.034	0.009	−3.835***
Basic PC	Prepare	0.017	0.009	1.98*
Interpretive	Dynamics/tempo	1.606	0.320	5.023***

***$p < .0001$, **$p < .001$, *$p < .01$.

The line graphs shown in Figure 17.7 represent the values predicted by the linear model that we fitted to these data representing the effects of serial position. Table 17.3 summarizes the analysis that tested the fit of the model to the data. FR0 and FR2 were omitted from this analysis, and from the data summarized in Figure 17.7, because their low error rates produced negligible serial position effects. We report serial position effects for the three predictors that had significant linear effects. These provide the clearest evidence for the presence of landmarks and lacunae in the singer's memory and were the most similar to those observed in previous studies. Two additional predictors had non-linear effects that are not easily interpreted and are not described here.[6]

At starts of sections and performance cues for stress on words, probability of recall was highest at the cue. Recall decreased stepwise with distance from starts of sections. At performance cues for stress on words, the higher probability of recall persisted for two bars before declining. These effects suggest that these were the main landmarks in the singer's memory, providing direct, content addressable access to these places in the piece. Once the beginning of each passage was retrieved, it cued recall of what followed until, at some point, a link failed and the chain was broken, resulting in poorer recall as distance from the landmark increased (Roediger & Crowder, 1976).

It is not surprising that starts of sections would be landmarks in a musician's memory, since these are the main divisions in the textual and/or musical material and were often used as starting places during practice (see Table 17.2). Performance cues for stress on words, in contrast, were not singled out as starting points for practice. These were places where the singer's interpretation of the composer's intentions required that the meaning of the text be conveyed by stress on a particular word or group of words. At '*prepotent*', for example, the singer made the annotation 'powerful before and after' to indicate the sense of power she wished to indicate as she sang the remainder of the phrase, '*prepotent and eke victorious*'. Apparently, interpretive landmarks of this sort were as distinctive in memory as the starts of sections and their positive effects on recall extended further.

Performance cues for preparation reminded the singer of what came next. The probability of recall was lowest at these basic cues and improved as distance from the

---

[6] Expressive features and dynamic/tempo features resulted in significant but non-linear effects. We are continuing to explore these data by looking at serial position effects both before and after these features and will report the results of these additional analyses on a later occasion.

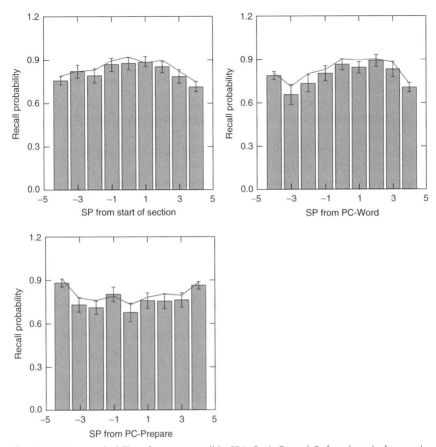

Fig. 17.7 Mean probability of correct recall in FR1, 3, 4, 5, and 6, four bars before and after cues of each type.

cue increased. The serial position effect was thus in the opposite direction from that described for starts of sections and performance cues for stress on words. Many performance cues for preparation occurred in places where the singer needed to watch the conductor and listen to the other instrumentalists. Some of these cues occurred during rests as the singer prepared for an entry. Because rests were generally recalled less well than material that had to be sung, rests were excluded from the analysis. Accordingly, the effect shown in Figure 17.7 is based on recall for sung passages. It is perhaps not surprising that the singer's memory for these passages would be weaker. One explanation is that attention to the other musicians decreased her attention to the music, resulting in weaker memory. Another, not incompatible, possibility is that the singer relied more on the other musicians to cue her memory for the music at these points. Their absence, when she wrote out the score, resulted in poorer recall.

The results are remarkably similar to the two other studies that have looked at serial position effects for performance cues in written recall (Chaffin, Ginsborg, & Dixon, 2009a; Chaffin *et al.*, 2002, pp. 212–216). In each case, there were the same negative serial position effects for structural boundaries (i.e. starts of sections) and positive serial position effects for basic performance cues (i.e. preparation). The instrumentalists in earlier studies did not have any performance cues that were directly comparable with the singer's performance cues for stress on words and in those studies interpretive cues did not produce significant serial position effects. For the singer, places that were critical in determining the meaning of the text played the same role in memory as the expressive turning points in the music played for the instrumentalists in the earlier studies.

Summary and conclusions

Like other experienced soloists who have been studied, the singer engaged in extended practice to ensure that recall occurred with the rapidity and fluency needed for performance (Chaffin & Logan, 2006). The singer had the piece memorized by Session 3, in which she sang 64% of the practice segments from memory. In the following sessions, she continued to practise mainly from memory. In the process, she developed the automaticity and reliability of memory retrieval needed for a secure performance. When she checked her memory by writing out the words and rhythms for the first time (FR0), five days before the performance, there were no gaps; her memory was 97.1% accurate. As she progressively forgot the piece in the months and years that followed, the increasing gaps in subsequent recalls revealed how the music was organized in her memory. Serial position effects identify the location of landmarks in her mental map of the piece and of lacunae, where her memory was weak.

The practice records show how landmarks were established. From the outset, the singer organized her practice by sections and used beginnings of sections and phrases as starting points during practice. In order to start at these places, she had first to think of the words and melody and then start singing. This established a link between the thought and the action. Later, just thinking of the place was sufficient to bring the relevant passage to mind, providing content addressable access to the piece at this point. With further practice, the link became rapid and reliable. In this way, the singer internalized the hierarchical formal structure of the music as a retrieval organization for her memory of the *Ricercar* (Chaffin & Imreh, 2002).

Evidence that the singer's memory for the piece was organized in this way was provided by written recall of the score. Memory was best at starts of sections and performance cues for stress on words and diminished with as distance beyond these landmarks increased. Other performance cues, such as those for preparation, produced lacunae. In these cases, memory was weakest at the cue. The probability of correct recall decreased as the singer approached each cue but increased with distance from it. We suggested that landmarks were recalled better because they could be directly accessed by content address when serial cuing by the preceding context faltered. Serial cuing of subsequent bars then produced the characteristic negative serial position effect as the probabilities of forgetting at each beat accumulate with increasing distance from the cue. Alternatively, landmarks may have been recalled better because they received more attention during practice and were therefore encoded more securely. The two explanations are not necessarily inconsistent.

Lacunae occurred in places where attention to other aspects of the performance distracted the singer's attention. For example, recall was worse at performance cues for preparation and improved linearly as distance from the cue increased. This effect suggests that when the singer needed to think about something else (her next entry, other musicians), her memory for words and music was weakened. Recall was weakest at the focal point of attention, at the cue, and improved progressively as distance from the distraction increased. Similar effects, both positive and negative, have been obtained in two other studies in which performers wrote out the score of a memorized piece. In the case studies of a pianist and cellist mentioned earlier, landmarks were observed at structural and expressive performance cues. Recall was higher at the cue and decreased with distance in the bars that followed (Chaffin & Imreh, 2002; Chaffin et al., 2010). Lacunae were also observed in the same studies, although the authors did not use the term, at basic cues requiring attention to technique. The present study confirms the earlier findings with a much more extensive body of recall data: seven recalls over five years.

Did the singer's expectations about the study shape our findings? The need to record herself undoubtedly affected some aspects of her practice. In the early stages of memorizing, for example, she refrained from moving around the studio while singing because this would have rendered her invisible to the camera, which was in a fixed position. So she confined herself to sitting at the piano in her first four practice sessions. We think it unlikely, however, that the memorization strategies we have described were much affected by the presence of the camera or the anticipation of reporting decisions. Preparation for the public performance was always her overriding concern and for this she needed to rely on well-established practice strategies. We have already suggested that the process of recalling the Ricercar for the purposes of the research and analysing her recall may have slowed forgetting of the piece, even though she followed the instruction always given to participants in her own studies: not to think about the words or melody except during deliberate recall for the purposes of the research.

We believe that our conclusions apply to most experienced performers. To perform reliably from memory requires that memory retrieval be practised. Musicians sometimes find themselves in the position of having to perform from memory without adequate preparation. In these cases, they must rely on serial cuing. Often they get away with it. But most musicians prefer to have a safety net. Performance cues providing content addressable access to memory provide a back-up, just in case. If things go wrong, the musician can jump forward to the next cue and avoid the ignominy of having to go back and start over. The singer in our study, following her normal practice, tested her safety net by writing out the words and rhythms of the melody from memory five days before the performance. Although most performers may not test their memories so thoroughly, we believe that most do set up performance cues and practise their use.

Performance cues differ, of course, as a function of the piece, musical style, instrument, experience of the musician, and demands of the particular occasion. No doubt, there are also individual differences between musicians in the extent to which they establish performance cues rather than relying only on serial cuing. The studies of professional performers to date suggest, however, that most musicians make use of both (Chaffin, 2007; Chaffin & Imreh, 2002; Ginsborg, Chaffin, & Nicholson, 2006b; Noice *et al.*, 2008). This generalization is also suggested by the consistency of the findings from case studies of musicians with general principles of memory (Ericsson & Kintsch, 1995). Musicians' use of musical structure and performance cues is consistent with principles of expert memory developed from the study of experts in other fields, and with principles of memory derived from the study of the general population (Ericsson & Oliver, 1989). There is good reason to expect, therefore, that the same principles generalize to other experienced performers.

References

Bahrick, H. P. (1994). Extending the lifespan of knowledge. In L. Penner, G Batsche, H. Khoff, & D. Nelson (Eds.), *The challenge in mathematics and science education: Psychology's response.* Washington DC: American Psychological Association.

Broadbent, D. E., Cooper, P. J., & Broadbent, M. H. (1978). A comparison of hierarchical matrix retrieval schemes in recall. *Journal of Experimental Psychology: Human Learning and Memory, 4,* 486–497.

Bryk, A. S., & Raudenbush, S. W. (1992). *Hierarchical linear models for social and behavioural research: Applications and data analysis methods.* Newbury Park, CA: Sage.

Chaffin, R. (2007). Learning *Clair de Lune*: Retrieval practice and expert memorization. *Music Perception, 24* (4), 377–393.

Chaffin, R., Ginsborg, J., & Dixon, J. (2009). *Effects of attention during practice on serial position effects in a singer's long term recall.* Paper presented at the Psychonomic Society, November, Boston, MA, USA.

Chaffin, R., & Imreh, G. (1994). *Memorizing for piano performance: A case study of a concert pianist.* Paper presented at the 3rd Practical Aspects of Memory Conference, August, University of Maryland, College Park, MD, USA.

Chaffin, R., & Imreh, G. (2002). Practicing perfection: Piano performance as expert memory. *Psychological Science, 13,* 342–349.

Chaffin, R., & Logan, T. (2006). Practicing perfection: How concert soloists prepare for performance. *Advances in Cognitive Psychology, 2,* 113–130. Available at: www.ac-psych.org/?id=2&rok=2006&issue=2-3article_14 (accessed 28 September 2010).

Chaffin, R., Imreh, G., & Crawford, M. (2002). *Practicing perfection: Memory and piano performance.* Mahwah, NJ: Lawrence Erlbaum Associates.

Chaffin, R., Imreh, G., Lemieux, A., & Chen, C. (2003). 'Seeing the big picture': Piano practice as expert problem solving. *Music Perception, 20,* 461–485.

Chaffin, R., Lisboa, T., Logan, T., & Begosh, K. T. (2010). Preparing for memorized cello performance: The role of performance cues. *Psychology of Music, 38*(1), 3–30.

Chaffin, R., Logan, T.R., & Begosh, K.T. (2009). Performing from memory. In S. Hallam, I. Cross, & M. Thaut (Eds.), *The Oxford handbook of music psychology* (pp. 352–363). Oxford: Oxford University Press.

Crowder, R. G., Serafine, M. L., & Repp, B. H. (1990). Physical interaction and association by contiguity in memory for the words and melodies of songs. *Memory & Cognition, 18,* 469–476.

Ebbinghaus, H. (1885). (Trans. 1913). *Memory: A contribution to experimental psychology.* New York, NY: Teachers College, Columbia University.

Ericsson, K. A., & Kintsch, W. (1995). Long-term working memory. *Psychological Review*, *102*(2), 211–245.

Ericsson K. A., & Oliver, W. L. (1989). A methodology for assessing the detailed structure of memory skills. In A. M. Colley, & J. R. Beech (Eds.), *Acquisition and performance of cognitive skills* (pp. 193–215). Chichester: Wiley.

Fischler, I., Rundus, D., & Atkinson, R. C. (1970). Effects of overt rehearsal procedures on free recall. *Psychonomic Science*, *19*, 249–250.

Ginsborg, J. (2000). Off by heart: expert singers' memorization strategies and recall for the words and music of songs. In C. Woods, G. Luck, R. Brochard, F. Seddon, & J. A. Sloboda (Eds.), *Proceedings of the Sixth International Conference on Music Perception and Cognition*. Keele, UK: Keele University Department of Psychology.

Ginsborg, J. (2002). Classical singers memorizing a new song: an observational study. *Psychology of Music*, *30*, 56–99.

Ginsborg, J., Chaffin, R., & Nicholson, G. (2006a). Shared performance cues in singing and conducting: a content analysis of talk during practice. *Psychology of Music*, *34*(3), 167–194.

Ginsborg, J., Chaffin, R., & Nicholson, G. (2006b). Shared performance cues: Predictors of expert individual practice and ensemble rehearsal. In M. Baroni, A. R. Addessi, R. Caterina, M. Costa, (Eds.), *Proceedings of the 9th International Conference on Music Perception and Cognition*. Bologna: University of Bologna.

Ginsborg, J., & Sloboda, J. (2007). Singers' recall for the words and melody of a new, unaccompanied song. *Psychology of Music*, *35*(3), 419–138.

Lewandowsky, S., & Murdock, B. B. Jr. (1989). Memory for serial order. *Psychological Review*, *96*, 25–57.

Lisboa, T., Chaffin, R., Schiaroli, A. G., & Barrera, A. (2004). Investigating practice and performance on the cello. In S. D. Lipscomb, R. Ashley, R. O. Gjerdingen, & P. Webster (Eds.), *Proceedings of the 8th International Conference on Music Perception & Cognition, Evanston, IL, 2004*. Adelaide, Australia: Causal Productions.

Logan, T., Begosh, K., Chaffin, R., & Lisboa, T. (2007). *Memorizing for cello performance*. Montreal, US: SMPC 07 (Society for Music Perception and Cognition), Concordia University.

Noice, H., Jeffrey, J., Noice, A., & Chaffin, R. (2008). Memorization by a jazz pianist: A case study. *Psychology of Music*, *36*, 47–61.

Roediger, H. L., III, & Crowder, R. C. (1976). A serial position effect in recall of United States Presidents. *Bulletin of the Psychonomic Society*, *8*, 275–278.

Rubin, D. C. (1977). Very long-term memory for prose and verse. *Journal of Verbal Learning and Verbal Behavior*, *16*(5), 611–621.

Rubin, D. C. (1995). *Memory in oral traditions: The cognitive psychology of epic, ballads, and counting-out rhymes*. New York, NY: Oxford University Press.

Rubin, D. C., & Wenzel, A. E. (1996). One hundred years of forgetting: A quantitative description of retention. *Psychological Review*, *103*(4), 734–760.

Rundus, D. (1971). Analysis of rehearsal processes in free recall. *Journal of Experimental Psychology*, *89*, 63–77.

Serafine, M. L., Crowder, R. G., & Repp, B. H. (1984). Integration of melody and text in memory for songs. *Cognition*, *16*, 285–303.

Serafine, M. L., Davidson, J., & Crowder, R. G. (1986). On the nature of melody-text integration in memory for songs. *Journal of Memory and Language*, *25*, 123–135.

Singer, J. D., & Willett, J. B. (2003). *Applied longitudinal data analysis: modeling change and event occurrence*. New York, NY: Oxford University Press.

Sloboda, J. A., & Parker, D. H. H. (1985). Immediate recall of melodies. In P. Howell, I. Cross, & R. West (Eds.), *Musical Structure and Cognition*. London: Academic Press.

Tenenbaum, G., Tehan, G., Stewart, G., & Christensen, S. (1999). Recalling a floor routine: The effects of skill and age on memory for order. *Applied Cognitive Psychology, 13*, 101–123.

Part 7

Music and cultural integration

Chapter 18

Emotions in motion: transforming conflict and music

Arild Bergh

Abstract

In recent violent conflicts around the world, music has often been used to channel emotions and make combatants' fluid identities more explicit and oppositional in order to create or sustain the conflict. In addition, in industrialized countries music is used by groups from different geographical origins to maintain group borders and thus emphasize their differences with other groups. At the same time there is an increased interest in the use of aesthetic materials such as music to attempt to transform these conflicts and tensions, with highly variable results. From an academic standpoint, although there is a lot of high-flown rhetoric about music and its abilities to 'soothe the beast', little empirical work exists on music and its use for reducing conflicts. Rather more is written from speculative and opinionated viewpoints, often by those involved in the projects in the first place. In this article I first discuss the problems involved in writing and researching this highly charged area, even for academics, before drawing on Sloboda's academic work related to music and emotion and music education when discussing empirical data from conflict transformation projects in Norway and Sudan. I end by summarizing some potential real world uses for this new area of conflict transformation, thereby covering both areas that Sloboda has been involved in, first music psychology and now conflict resolution as the Director of Oxford Research Group.

In 2001 a small conference was arranged by the Oxford University United Nations Association, which focused on the conflict in Kashmir (divided between India and Pakistan), and actors from the different sides in the conflict were present. It was a so-called 'Track II' initiative, an unofficial, small-scale event, or 'citizen peacemaking' which attempted to provide impetus to more large-scale diplomatic activities through dialogue between participants from different sides of a conflict. At this event former foreign secretaries from India and Pakistan were present, and during lunch the former Pakistani Foreign Secretary mentioned to me, unprompted, that when they had held official negotiations in the past, they would gather both delegations afterhours and share food and listen to old Hindustani classical music. This, he felt, helped remind them of their shared past before the partition in 1948 and provided relaxation after the tense negotiations.

This short vignette illustrates what is now starting to emerge as a topic for academic investigation: the role of music in conflict transformation[1] and peace building, often analysed through 'folk beliefs' as above.

Soon after the encounter described in the vignette, I started my PhD on music and conflict transformation. As a part of my initial work I contacted the Oxford Research Group, 'one of the UK's leading advocates for the non-military resolution of global conflict'[2] and found it quite a coincidence that their director, John Sloboda, had the same name as the co-author of numerous books and articles I had read on music psychology. So far apart was music and conflict transformation then, that not for a second did I suspect that it was the same person, and in fact, that is how John Sloboda has kept his two interests, music and peace activism, separate. The current volume celebrates both John Sloboda's work as a music psychologist and a peace activist and I hope my contribution will serve to link these two passions in a constructive way.

I will do this by briefly discussing the problems of researching this area before filling in the background on music and conflict/conflict transformation. I will then discuss my empirical work in this area and how it links to John Sloboda's research, before suggesting some ways in which music may 'work' in conflict transformation and how we may fruitfully integrate it in the type of dialogue work that John Sloboda is now engaged in as part of his work with the Oxford Research Group. This reflects the increased interest in music and conflict transformation since our initial meeting in 2002, and points the way forward.

Problems of discussing this topic

One problem I quickly encountered in my research was the amount of hyperbole surrounding music in general, and music and conflict transformation more specifically. These two quotes, with some 120 years between them are illustrative of this problem:

> Music is a moral law. It gives soul to the universe, wings to the mind, flight to the imagination, and charm and gaiety to life and to everything. (Lubbock 1889, frequently attributed to Plato)
>
> Everything a musician plays is an expression of Divine inspiration, and transformative for that very reason. (Youssou N'Dour)[3]

---

[1] 'Conflict transformation' is used in preference to the phrase 'conflict resolution' as the latter implies a complete solution to a conflict, whereas transformation indicates a move away from violence, while the underlying conflict may not be completely resolved, the current state of Northern Ireland would be an example of this.

[2] Available at: www.oxfordresearchgroup.org.uk/about_us/about.php.

[3] SGI Quarterly, 2004. Transformative Power: Interview with Youssou N'Dour. (Available at: http://www.sgiquarterly.org/feature2004Jly-3.html) Accessed 10 January, 2010.

This taking-for-granted of the 'magic' of music, a reluctance to look critically at the issues surrounding this field, the fact that a lot of the writing and/or research is done by either musicians themselves or academics who are music 'fans' often prejudices research: 'writings on music listening often have a penchant for the fascinating and romantic subject of the musical catharsis, or peak experience, self-reported and often sought out by listeners' (Bergh & DeNora, 2009, p. 95). As Sloboda says 'I believe that science has much to offer musicians. One thing that it does is attempt to make theoretical assumptions explicit, and thus open to discussion and test. … Whatever else scientists may or may not do, they can offer people new ways of looking at old issues.' (2005, p.175). One example of this would be to look at the idea in the opening vignette of music bringing back memories of a shared past and allowing relaxation. Of course we academics have to be self-reflexive and acknowledge that for many of us researching music, 'the mystery [of music] is part of the love' (2005, p.175). This, and the fact that modern day peace building and conflict transformation 'are professions afflicted with a proclivity toward the promise of great change. … If constructive social change rolled forward as easily as our words and promises pour out, world justice and peace would have surely been attained by now'. (Lederach, 2005, p. 22). This means that there is a great need, not for critique for the sake of it, or to be 'clever', but to ensure that any tools used, be it music or dialogue workshops, are scrutinized and improved. Because conflict transformation is often a matter of (literally) life and death, we owe it to those involved to hold any attempts to the highest standards of inquiry. I believe the following comment from Sloboda on research into peak musical experiences sums it up well, and points the way forward when he says: '[O]ur attempts to deconstruct need to be constantly held up against the richness of everyday (and peak) musical experience to ensure that it is the full experience we are attempting to explain, and not some conveniently simplified portion of it' (2005, p. 392).

Music and conflict

Any attempt to explain 'the full experience' of music use in conflict transformation must acknowledge the more successful use of music in conflicts. Two overlapping issues are important here, identity and emotion. Many of the wars after 1990 focused on identities, real or perceived, such as Serbs versus Croats versus Muslims in former Yugoslavia. And in any violent conflict, emotions must be controlled (subdued or escalated) for people to be able to kill each other (Kemp & Fry, 2004). Identities and emotions are also important in music: 'When people feel most passionately about music together it is because of its power to mark boundaries…' (Frith & Street, 1992, p. 80). Music is therefore a way not only to affect emotions, but also identities, as Becker has suggested when she says that identities affiliated with music can let listeners experience different emotions as they fit into temporary music-related roles (2001, p. 142). This represents a major problem when music is used to resolve conflicts, and is shown in how music has been used before, during and after conflicts to instigate, continue, or reignite conflict.

Music before conflict

Music played an important role in marshalling the different ethnic groups in former Yugoslavia before the wars there in the 1990s. Pettan (1998) has discussed how independently produced tapes of ultra-nationalistic Croatian music were on sale in stalls long before there was open war and Turbo-Folk[4] was used by Serbians to bolster the myth of the Serbian uniqueness (Hudson, 2003). In Sudan, the *hakamat*, female singers of Darfur who used to praise men who had done some practical feat (Carlisle, 1973), have in recent years used their skills to encourage Jihad.[5] In these circumstances we can see how music has been deployed primarily as a tool, i.e. the aesthetic 'enjoyment' as it were, is of no concern, what matters is how well it works in a given situation— although links to people's identities are important both for those the music is meant to encourage and those it hopes to intimidate.

Music during conflict

Here music has often been used to boost morale among civilians as seen for instance in Britain in the Second Word War (Weingartner, 2006) or in parts of Bosnia in the 1990s (Hadzihusejnovic-Valasek, 1998). In a broad historical view McNeill (1995) suggests that activities that have required humans to keep the same rhythm (such as marching) have been beneficial in building communities and foster strong euphoric feelings among soldiers and others. This has been demonstrated vividly in a documentary from the 2003 invasion of Iraq where US soldiers used loud music, predominantly rap, hardcore and various metal music, while engaging in patrols and attacks inside armoured vehicles (Gittoes, 2005). Music has also been used for torture—prisoners of war in Iraq and Afghanistan over the past few years have been subjected to loud music ranging from Metallica to Barney the Dinosaur (Cusick, 2006).

Music after conflict

Music that commemorates a conflict can appear after the conflict and becomes part of the 'canon' for the conflicting groups. Over time this might cement enemy images of 'the other', and become part of future conflicts. This happened in Northern Ireland during the conflict after the 1960s (McCann, 1995). However, most of the time postwar music may be nostalgic, this can be seen both with refugees who have arrived in countries far away, which may require innovation and changes in their music (McMahon, 2005; Reyes Schramm, 1989) or internally displaced people who are able to continue performing their original repertoire (Bergh, 2008).

Emotions, whether they are basic emotions such as disgust or more cognitive ones such as patriotism (Sloboda, 2005), are in these three periods (before, during, after conflict) enhanced or modified by music with the aim of fomenting conflict. This use of music tends to augment existing feelings, rather than create them from scratch, as suggested by Sloboda (2005).

Music and conflict transformation

Music use in conflict transformation is not a new innovation. For example the Buwaya Kalingga People in the Philippines established peace pacts between different groups

---

[4] A mixture of Eurovision Song Contest style pop with traditional Serbian folk music/themes.

[5] Available at: www.globalaging.org/armedconflict/countryreports/africa/singers.htm (accessed 12 June 2010) and internal report from Practical Action.

and cemented them through feasts which included peace pact-specific songs more than a century ago (Prudente, 1984).

In more recent times music has been used by non-governmental organizations (NGOs) for conflict transformation purposes in contexts such as the Israeli–Palestinian conflict or the various conflicts in former Yugoslavia. In general it has been in small-scale peace building or Track II initiatives that music has been used, and this has taken place within a context of increased attention to the psycho-social issues during and after violent conflicts. This has led to the relatively new human security paradigm as defined by the United Nations: 'Human security is "people-centred", focusing the attention of institutions on human beings and communities everywhere' (Commission on Human Security, 2003). This people-centred approach has become central to the work of NGOs such as the Oxford Research Group, and the desire for such an approach was voiced by one of my informants in Sudan who felt that the West often talked about welfare but ignored family and music, which to him were very important aspects of African welfare.

A complete literature review of this field is not possible here, instead I will mention a few representative examples. Zelizer (2004) has discussed the use of music/arts processes in Bosnia after the war there, including a project that involved a multi-ethnic/multi-faith choir. The focus was on the singing activities, which was what attracted people to the choir, and the conflict transformation was primarily between choir members, whereas for their audiences it was used mainly to show that people from different groups could (again) work together. This is similar work to the West-Eastern Divan Orchestra, the Arab-Israeli orchestra that was set up by the classical conductor Daniel Barenboim and the academic Edward Said to bring young musicians from different parts of the Middle East conflict(s) together (Beckles Willson, 2007).

Another area where music is used is music therapy. This may be as a method in dialogue workshops, as discussed by Jordanger (2008), in connection with a conflict resolution workshop focusing on the North Caucasus conflict that used music following a music therapy technique called 'Guided Imagery' (Bonny, 1997; Summer, 1997). Here a selection of recorded music is played and people are asked to focus on images occurring when listening to the music. The collective experience during this session is described as a musical peak experience which Jordanger felt changed the atmosphere of the entire workshop. Music therapy may also be used to deal with individual traumas arising from war. When describing her prolonged period of work with a Kurdish refugee and torture victim in Berlin, Zharinova-Sanderson (2004) found that music was a valid therapy resource across cultures.

A final example of attempts at using music for conflict transformation is festivals and recordings that feature musicians from different sides of a conflict. For instance in 1995 Palestinian, Israeli, and Norwegian musicians collaborated on a CD under the name *Music Channel* following the Oslo Agreement,[6] and in different parts of the former Yugoslavia there have been many festivals with ethnically mixed bands or Serb, Croat, and Muslim folklore music.

---

[6] Available at: www.discogs.com/Music-Channel-Mantra-For-Peace/release/740387 (accessed 12 June 2010).

Some of the problems with research in this area are listed below:

- A focus on strong (peak) experiences that may be too neat and dramatic, real life conflict transformation is far messier and long-winded.

- An overly romantic view of music's capabilities, with an abundance of phrases such as 'Music ... has the potential to cut across cognitive, emotional, social, spiritual, and physical dimensions of the human experience' (Weaver, 2001, p. 118) or 'The arts by nature hold significant power to transform individuals and societies' (Zelizer, 2004, p. 59).

- The idea that non-rational interventions (i.e. art, music) are capable of resolving conflicts where rational (i.e. negotiated) approaches have failed.

- Power issues are rarely discussed—it is assumed that musicians and NGOs involved have no internal agendas and/or self-interest.

In essence there tends to be a leap of faith from anecdotal/empirical data to general claims about music's power with little grounded discussion. These 'black boxes' are not questioned or inspected very closely and thus present 'some conveniently simplified portion' of reality as I quoted from Sloboda earlier. Although many people have genuine and strong personal experiences where music has affected them to such an extent that it is difficult to find the words to describe it, as has been discussed by several researchers from different academic disciplines (Crafts, Cavicchi, & Keil, 1993; DeNora, 2000; Gabrielsson, 2001), a problem occurs for practical use of music in conflict transformation through extrapolation in two directions: first, the belief that everyone has strong experiences through music; and second, that such experiences can be relied on to occur 'at will'.

Music and conflict transformation, perspectives grounded in data

During my own fieldwork in Norway and Sudan the problems discussed in the previous section and several other themes emerged from the empirical data collected. This has been discussed in more depth elsewhere (Bergh, 2007, 2008; Bergh, Hashim, & Sutherland, 2008). Here I want to provide a brief overview of these themes and link this to Sloboda's work in music psychology and his more recent work in peace building.

The data from Norway come from interviews with former pupils, musicians, teachers, and organizers from a project that took place between 1989 and 1992 in six schools in and around Oslo where the year 4 cohort (11 years old in 1989) attended monthly concerts that presented traditional and classical music and dance from Asia, Africa, and South America. My research took place in 2005–2006, some 13–14 years after the original project finished, which meant the pupils who participated in the project were now adults who felt more at ease in discussing their experiences than was the case when they were children. The data from Sudan focus on the music use in Wau Nour, a settlement of approximately 5000 people, the majority displaced by war, where I interviewed local inhabitants, musicians, and NGO workers. Wau Nour is situated 2–3 miles outside the centre of Kassala and was established in 1988. Music was played by different ethnic groups (there are at least 29 different tribes in the settlement) on most Fridays in a field outside the settlement from the early 1990s until 2003.

The main themes, five in all, that came into view when analysing my data were as follows.

Active musicking

A key point I found (somewhat to my surprise, as I am not a musician myself) was how important active musicking was for the music to have an impact. In Norway the concerts consisted of a mixture of plain performances (especially Asian and South American music) and active dancing/singing/playing by the children (usually for African music). When I interviewed a number of participants, they remembered with a good level of detail the events where they had taken an active part and were positive about them, but were negative or had forgotten about most of the pure listening events. This also showed the importance of casual musicking in a society, as Sloboda (1999) has suggested, it provides a meeting place outside work and school. It also resonates with many of the ideas behind community music therapy (Pavlicevic & Ansdell, 2004). One of the teachers especially praised the African musicians, not as musicians but as educators, which indicates that despite the geographical distance they had a better understanding of the pupils than their own teachers. In fact Sloboda (2001) has pointed out that the changing ideologies in music education may mean that many school music educators have little empathy or understanding for their pupils' musical interests.

Group contact

Changing attitudes to, and perceptions of, out groups is central if conflicts are to be transformed or avoided. If there is no change, then negative views of former enemies are fertile ground for future conflict mongers. The contact theory developed by Allport (1954) suggests that such contact requires equal group status within the situation, common goals, intergroup cooperation and authority support. The contact also has to be of a certain quality or intimacy; superficial contact will leave it worse than before. This was echoed in my findings: in Norway some informants, despite liking African music, had found traditional costumes 'strange' and had discussed participants in terms of coming from 'the jungle'. In Sudan on the other hand, where the contact between the groups was long term and (due to shared displacement) meaningful, the musical encounters resulted in closer relationships and strong reduction in intergroup conflicts. In some ways this ties in with Sloboda's (2005) suggestion that the emotions tied to music can either intensify existing emotions (negative attitudes to African culture) or offer a space for people to see an alternative view of a situation (new views of fellow displaced people).

Thus there is no guarantee that musical experiences move the participants in a certain way—it can be negative or positive, although lengthy/repetitive musical encounters may tend towards the positive. This also underlines the difficulty of using music as representation, that is, to assume that certain types of music are representative of a group of people, and that exposure to the music will improve relations to the out group (Bergh, 2007).

Not for everyone

Although music is (for practical purposes) universally *available*, not everybody is equally interested in music: a Norwegian-Pakistani informant had no interest in the music presented at school, and in Wau Nour some people tried to avoid music for religious reasons. It is therefore important not to assume that there is anything 'universal' about music, neither in its appeal to people, nor in the way it is received and understood (Einarsen, 1998).

Sustainability and community

A key issue when using music for conflict transformation purposes is the sustainability of the immediate outcome. Sustainability is important for any solution that attempts to resolve a root cause of a conflict, rather than just control the conflict (Abbott *et al.*, 2006). In Norway it was clear that interest in the classroom did not translate into any wider change or increased interest. In Sudan on the other hand, changes took hold in the community and positive attitudes generated during musical encounters has resulted in a new, shared, identity of being Wau Nour inhabitants, and not just a disparate collection of tribes. There are a number of issues here. First, the strong emotions that can be evoked by music are temporal, as Sloboda puts it: 'Emotions by their nature are immediate and evanescent: they do not survive long after the triggering event' (2005, p. 218). Second, the impetus for the music use was very different. The Norwegian project was very top-down, run by adults from the governmental agency 'Concerts Norway', who took all decisions without involving the target group, which meant that there was no link between the children's everyday life and the music presented. In Sudan in contrast, music was a naturally occurring and joint activity, thus more of a bottom-up endeavour. And finally, in Norway music was seen as functional, an attitude shared by other music and conflict transformation projects there (Einarsen, 2002), whereas in Sudan it was a process that was allowed to play out over time, something that Zelizer (2004) discussed with regards to music and arts in Bosnia. This meant that music became an important part of the community in Wau Nour. One of my informants who had lost all her family apart from a brother told me that it was her role in the Azande band that was her main link to Wau Nour now. In short, a focus on strong experiences and top-down approaches means that sustainability fails as either the emotional highs cannot be repeated forever, or there are not enough resources available to maintain the professionals who manage the projects.

Music as a space for work

The final theme is that music can provide a space for 'work' (DeNora, 1986), in this case the emotional work involved in adjusting your views of the out group(s) and attempting to understand their views. When interviewing a member from the West-Eastern Divan Orchestra I was told that music was good for conflict transformation because 'First of all you don't have to talk'. In Sudan this was very clear in the way that the Friday concerts allowed different groups to come together and experience (repeatedly) a different side of each other, and my informants were very clear about how they enjoyed these events. One woman said 'even if you do not like someone you can like the music that comes from their radio'. Based on autobiographical work with regards to strong positive music experiences, Sloboda has suggested that such experiences may be difficult when you are in a negative state, 'you can't enjoy the music when you are not enjoying the circumstances in which it takes place' (Sloboda, 2005, p. 183).

This clearly presents a problem in a post-conflict situation with lingering animosity if one assumes that music needs to provide a peak experience for conflict transformation to take place. However, as I will discuss below, this is not really what is required for music to play a role in conflict transformation; clearly many of the displaced people in Wau Nour were in a very negative situation, yet found great enjoyment in music. Sloboda's idea may therefore need to be further tweaked to look at what sort of musicking (active/passive) the listener is engaged in, and what role music plays in the musical experience. Finally, as it is the participants, not the music, that 'work' in these situations, we must be aware that there is no way of predicting what the outcome will be, at least not in short-term projects. In Norway, African musical events, as discussed above, often led to further stereotyping, and did not improve the perception of the out group.

In summary, conflict transformation is about doing very difficult emotional work related to out groups against which there exists strong antipathy, and the role of music has traditionally been seen as a quick working 'magic bullet', but more grounded works indicate that this is a false picture, that the long-term effects are uncertain, and overall the field requires more investigation as well as an understanding of what music really provides. It is for this reason I now want to make some tentative suggestions as to what music can provide in such emotional work.

What role has music in conflict transformation?

In very basic terms we can say that engaging with music can affect you physically or mentally, and that these two realms are often linked. Emotions arising from music listening may affect our bodies or bodily actions in response to music may change our emotions (Gerra *et al.*, 1998). In the mental domain, which I want to focus on here, music may bring out a range of emotions such as sadness or happiness. Emotions that come out of being reminded of specific or general memories, which Sloboda (2005) refers to as episodic and iconic associations, are relatively easy to explain and understand. An episodic association may be a happy feeling that comes when listening to a song that was frequently played on radio when something very positive took place, for instance when we got our first job, whereas an iconic association could occur through music that reminds us of summers and holidays in general.

More difficult to explain are emotions not obviously linked to memories (for a number of cross-disciplinary discussions see Juslin & Sloboda, 2001). DeNora (1986, p.92) and Sloboda (2000, p.221) have both suggested that the 'power' of music may not reside in music as such, but that music acts as a Rorschach ink blot. In other words, music is open to interpretation on the emotional level, and we see in it what satisfies us the most. This does not mean that music is disconnected from everyday life: our personal and social biographies as well as cues linked to the music (DeNora, 1999; Sloboda, 2005) play a big role in how we react to music. Emotions and attitudes are not generated automatically or unidirectionally by music, but by people engaging in a back-and-forth manner with music and within *the spaces afforded by music* and a network the includes other people, objects, and situations as DeNora (2001) and Gomart and Hennion (1999) have suggested.

By describing music as a Rorschach ink blot we allow for considerable agency on behalf of the listener when it comes to emotions. This freedom to project, interpret, and engage in emotional work obviously has important implications for projects that 'use' music to bring people together. But what happens if we take this idea one step further, and see music as a source of diversion, or more precisely, a beneficial interruption? Music then ceases to be a focal point demanding attention, instead it offers a break from tense cognitive processing and/or intense emotions, in this case the emotions that may arise when one focuses on and discusses conflicts. This idea will be anathema to many, especially musicians and academics who specialize in music studies. It therefore requires some careful explanation, in particular as this is an idea where little directly relevant research exists to date.

First of all, I am *not* suggesting that there are certain music styles so simple or banal that they can only be a diversion (in the negative sense of the word), whereas other music styles are more complex and worthy of a listener's careful attention. Nor am I suggesting that this idea applies to any engagement with all styles of music, all of the time. Rather I am suggesting that *at times* any music can provide a form of diversion for those who are involved, and that this function is what makes it powerful in conflict transformation (and similar) contexts. The idea of diversions in conflict transformation work is not new, for instance 'break-time' is a valid, although infrequently used, strategy to deal with problems in mediation and negotiation sessions (Callister & Wall Jr, 2004; Wall Jr & Callister, 1999; Wall & Druckman, 2003).

However, there are two key differences between a break from conflict transformation activities without music and the use of music to provide diversions. First, most societies view music as a worthwhile and positive activity, so engaging with music, even when it acts as a diversion, receives a 'stamp of approval'. On the other hand, simply taking a break to do nothing, or to do other relaxing activities, is seen as non-productive or negative. For example, sitting in front of the television half asleep is 'bad', but doing the same while listening to a recording of classical music is 'good' (Bourdieu, (1986) has discussed such attitudes in terms of social and cultural capital). Second, most listening to or casual performing of music lets us switch our mental focus (voluntary or involuntary) between the music itself and non-musical emotional or cognitive thoughts. So we may focus closely on music for some time, before drifting into thoughts and emotions that may be linked to the music, or may emerge from conflict transformation discussions/interactions. This pattern is very similar to some meditation techniques where a person's focus may oscillate between conscious thoughts and the meditation sound ('mantra') (Holen, 2007).

The aforementioned two points can be illustrated with an example: In a discussion on music therapy and conflict transformation Lopez Vinader discusses a class she is running for expectant mothers where they listen to music. She mentions that 'One woman reported that during the music therapy session it was the first time that she had connected with her baby because otherwise she was under too much stress' (Lopez, 2008, p. 155). Without belittling music therapy we can see that if stress was an issue, requesting time alone to sit and enjoy the pregnancy may be considered self-indulgent, whereas attending a music therapy session is acceptable not only to the woman herself but also to others as it is considered a valued activity (sitting still without music would have been considered inactivity). This I hope explains my first point. The second point is that within this music-based activity, if one is processing negative feelings (in this case guilt for being too stressed to value the baby), one can deal with such feelings, and yet have the opportunity to switch attention back to the music when such feelings are too strong, thus keeping the session overall pleasant.

The first point, music being a valued activity even when providing a diversion, is relatively easy to grasp. The second point, how such a diversion can be beneficial to conflict transformation, requires further exploration. From this point of view the role of music is to *make possible* and to *provide the potential* for interruptions on two levels: the external, social level and the personal, interior level.

Thus music first makes possible interruptions of what may be considered routine, non-reflexive (even embodied) activities that occur in social interactions. In conflict transformation contexts, this may be the presentation of self (Becker, 2001), which make us behave in a certain way in front of others, or instinctively disliking members of the out group. The musical interruption puts a temporary stop to this by providing a liminal space, a space which is temporary and transient, where new and different ways of interacting with the out group can be tried out relatively safely, precisely because of its indeterminate nature. Then music also offers internal micro-interruptions (should we need them) when things become (in)tense emotionally, a frequent occurrence in conflict transformation work. Thus, if a session in a conflict transformation workshop has brought up uncomfortable memories and music is present, the individuals' attention can be switched to the music. This temporary interruption means that the painful process of digesting memories, thinking of or accepting new ideas, thoughts, and emotions can be done in smaller 'chunks', again this echoes ideas present in certain psychology-based meditation techniques (Holen, 2007).

By extension, in this view, different styles of music can provide different spaces that afford different types of work (DeNora, 2000), rather than different emotions being embedded in the music. Any interruption may give positive results as reported by Lesiuk with regards to air traffic controllers: 'Results showed that whether the group sat in silence or listened to music, their stress levels reduced significantly' (Lesiuk, 1992, quoted in Lesiuk, 2005, p. 176). However what music offers in addition is the idea that it is an acceptable activity that does not make participants feel self-conscious.

If we look at what happened in Sudan, we see that the regular, casual, Friday music making in the settlement interrupted the daily interaction between tribes, which initially were very conflict-filled. Within this musical event people could switch between dancing and singing to the music and the emotional and/or cognitive work of viewing their fellow Wau Nour inhabitants in a different light, i.e. the interruptions allowed for new associations to (slowly) emerge. In this way positive changes did not require a single huge and painful readjustment, but could be done in small doses over time.

Viewing the role of music in conflict transformation in these pragmatic terms challenges the idea that 'the power of music' is responsible for major changes in people's attitudes. This understanding is not a rejection of music's possibly unique role, but it implies that a continuous process of interruptions, emotional work and consolidations take place, each in small doses, and that this process requires time and repetition to have an effect. This means that participants in conflict transformation work are not hostages to fortune, waiting for the muse of music to open them up, and conversely that those in charge cannot expect to apply music to transform people and attitudes in an instant.

If the key role of music is to interrupt we may ask why not use any diversion, such as playing games or watching films, instead of music? I suggest that music is useful not because it contains some magic force, but because the real power of music may lie in a range of pragmatic and occasionally unique properties, some of which are as follows:

- Music has a very low threshold for participation, a voice to sing or hands to clap a rhythm is all that is required.

- Music is an easily accessible, worldwide resource in the sense that the basic concept of music is generally understood in most places, although (as mentioned earlier) not everyone enjoys it, and the actual experience of music will differ, depending on a range of local variables such as customs, circumstances, and tastes.

- Music can augment actions, rather than control them, i.e. I can run or talk while enjoying music, whereas most other activities require me to be stationary and/or tend to exclude social interaction beyond the actions required by the activity.

- Music provides a socially acceptable space for admitting to being emotionally affected. Although music may sometimes be banned for religious or political reasons, even the most hardened warrior can admit to being 'moved' by a piece of music. One example of this was seen in the BBC documentary *Killers Don't Cry*, a project with serial killers in South African jails where music was used as part of a workshop.[7]

- The forward temporal movement of music means it invites occasional attention which stops us from being stuck in a single thought, a point highlighted by Lesiuk (2005) with regards to computer programmers who improved their problem-solving technique when listening to music.

An anecdotal example that illustrates the above points was related by Einar Gerhardsen, Labour Prime Minister of Norway for 16 years after 1945, to the music therapist Even Ruud. Gerhardsen described how, occasionally when there was a high level of disagreement at Labour conferences, someone would stand up and suggest a song and the delegates would start singing (E. Ruud, personal communication, 2005). This interrupted the flow of negative feelings due to arguments, required no preparation, created a temporal new space for cooperation, and allowed for both emotions to be expressed and cognitive activities to take place on the side. The Friday music events in Wau Nour also provided similar opportunities for socially sanctioned interruptions. And this is the key point—the musical space has been given a seal of approval by society, it is not seen as strange or suspicious to listen to music, in fact quite the opposite, it gives people social capital and affords changing of mind that seemingly comes about through 'high' aesthetic experiences.

---

7 Available at: http://news.bbc.co.uk/hi/english/static/audio_video/programmes/correspondent/transcripts/1298829.txt (accessed 12 June 2010).

Conclusion

Music is slowly becoming a new tool in small scale conflict transformation projects. As the stakes in such projects can be very high for participants who may face intimidation in their home communities for being involved, it is important that this field is scrutinized and that the discourse around the 'power of music' is replaced by rigorous research even if, as Sloboda has pointed out, stakeholders may feel that it removes some of the magic they connect with music. And this research must pay the same attention to everyday constraints and possibilities in musicking as Sloboda has done in his research.

As I have suggested above, music is no 'magic bullet', and the outcome of music use cannot be predicted, so research may be most fruitful when working on empirical data from different case studies that can give practitioners a range of understandings to build on in this area. In particular it would be interesting to compare music use with other activities to learn more about what is unique to music, and further investigate the notion of music as a sanctioned form of interruption.

Despite the suggestion that music is about interruptions and space, this does not mean that any music can be used under any circumstances. Music may often be counterproductive, especially when it 'confirms' stereotypes of out groups, and this is something practitioners need to acknowledge. This links back to Sloboda's suggestion that music often enhances existing emotions, and the idea presented above that music often augments actions. Organizers of conflict transformation projects must be aware of extra-musical issues, for example, certain types of music may be linked to one of the sides in a conflict. They should involve participants in the music selection to avoid a heavy handed, top-down approach; weaker parties in conflict transformation may agree to use certain music genres they deem 'appropriate' (Hara, 2008), which can affect the outcome. Such power issues need to be addressed both in practice and in research.

Acknowledgements

I thank the editors and anonymous reviewers for useful feedback on this chapter. I also thank Mariko Hara and Tia DeNora for discussing this chapter and helping to clarify some of the points.

References

Abbott, C., Rogers, P., & Sloboda, J. A. (2006). *Global responses to global threats: sustainable security for the 21st century*. Oxford: Oxford Research Group.

Allport, G. W. (1954). *The nature of prejudice*. Cambridge, MA: Addison-Wesley.

Becker, J. (2001). Anthropological perspectives on music and emotion. In P. N. Juslin, & J. A. Sloboda (Eds.), *Music and emotion: Theory and research*. Series in Affective Science. Oxford: Oxford University Press.

Beckles Willson, R. (2007). The west-eastern divan orchestra. *British Academy Review, 10*, 15–17.

Bergh, A. (2007). I'd like to teach the world to sing: music and conflict transformation. *Musicæ Scientiæ, Special Issue*, 141–157.

Bergh, A. (2008). Everlasting love: The sustainability of top-down vs bottom-up approaches to music and conflict transformation. In S. Kagan, & V. Kirchberg (Eds.), *Sustainability: A new frontier for the arts and cultures*. Higher education for sustainability. Frankfurt: am Main, VAS.

Bergh, A., & DeNora, T. (2009). From wind-up to iPod: techno-cultures of listening. In E. Clarke *et al.* (Eds.), *The Cambridge companion to recorded music* (pp. 102–115). Cambridge: Cambridge University Press.

Bergh, A., Hashim, M. J., & Sutherland, I. (2008). Music of the fears: The dialogue between musicking, war and peace. In *ESA Sociology of the Arts Research Network Conference*. Venice: IUAV University.

Bonny, H. L. (1997). State of the art of music therapy. *Arts in Psychotherapy*, 24(1), 65–73.

Bourdieu, P. (1986). The forms of capital. In J. G. Richardson (Ed.), *Handbook for theory and research for the sociology of education* (pp. 241–258). New York, NY: Greenwood.

Callister, R. R., & Wall Jr J. A. (2004). Thai and US community mediation. *Journal of Conflict Resolution*, 48, 573–598.

Carlisle, R. C. (1973). Women singers in Darfur, Sudan Republic. *Anthropos*, 68, 785–800.

Commission on Human Security. (2003). *Human security now*. New York, NY: United Nations. Available at: www.humansecurity-chs.org/finalreport/English/FinalReport.pdf (accessed 12 June 2010).

Crafts, S. D., Cavicchi, D., & Keil, C. (1993). *My music*. Middletown, CT: Wesleyan University Press.

Cusick, S. G. (2006). Music as torture/music as weapon. *Transcultural Music Review*, 10. Available at: www.sibetrans.com/trans/trans10/cusick_eng.htm (accessed 12 June 2010).

DeNora, T. (1986). How is extra-musical meaning possible? Music as a place and space for work. *Sociological Theory*, 4(Spring), 84–94.

DeNora, T. (1999). Music as a technology of the self. *Poetics*, 27, 31–56.

DeNora, T. (2000). *Music in everyday life*. Cambridge: Cambridge University Press.

DeNora, T. (2001). Aesthetic agency and musical practice: new directions in the sociology of music and emotion. In P. N. Juslin, & J. A. Sloboda (Eds.), *Music and emotion: Theory and research* (pp. 161–180). Oxford: Oxford University Press.

Einarsen, H. P. (1998). *Møtet som ikke tok sted*. Unpublished doctoral dissertation. Oslo: University of Oslo.

Einarsen, H. P. (2002). Musikkens roller i kulturmøtet. *Nord Nytt*, 83, 17–34.

Frith, S., & Street, J. (1992). Rock against racism and red wedge: From music to politics, from politics to music. In R. Garofalo (Ed.), *Rockin' the Boat: Mass Music and Mass Movements* (pp. 67–80). Boston, MA: South End Press.

Gabrielsson, A. (2001). Emotions in strong experiences with music. In P. N. Juslin, & J. A. Sloboda (Eds.), *Music and emotion: theory and research* (pp. 431–449). Oxford: Oxford University Press.

Gerra, G., Zaimovic, A., Franchini, D., Palladino, M., Giucastro, G., Reali, N., *et al.* (1998). Neuroendocrine responses of healthy volunteers to 'techno-music': relationships with personality traits and emotional state. *International Journal of Psychophysiology*, 28, 99–111.

Gittoes, G. (Director). (2005). *Soundtrack to war* (DVD). Sydney: Australian Broadcasting Corporation.

Gomart, E., & Hennion, A. (1999). *A sociology of attachment: music amateurs, drug users.* Oxford: Blackwell.

Hadzihusejnovic-Valasek, M. (1998). The Osijek war-time music scene 1991–1992. In S. Pettan (Ed.), *Music, politics, and war: Views from Croatia* (pp. 9–27). Zagreb: Institute of Ethnology and Folklore Research.

Hara, M. (2008). *Rethinking music therapy practice for the elderly in Japan.* Paper presented at Music and health: Current developments in research and practice. Folkstone: University Centre Folkestone.

Holen, A. (2007). *Inner strength: The free mental attitude in Acem meditation*, 2nd edn. Oslo: Acem Publishing.

Hudson, R. (2003). Songs of seduction: popular music and Serbian nationalism. *Patterns of Prejudice, 37*(2), 157–178.

Jordanger, V. (2008). Healing cultural violence: 'collective vulnerability' through guided imagery with music. In O. Urbain (Ed.), *Music and conflict transformation: harmonies and dissonances in geopolitics* (pp. 128–146). London: I. B. Tauris.

Juslin, P. N., & Sloboda, J. A. (Eds.). (2001). *Music and emotion: theory and research.* Oxford: Oxford University Press.

Kemp, G., & Fry, D.P. (2004). *Keeping the peace: conflict resolution and peaceful societies around the world.* London: Routledge.

Lederach, J. P. (2005). *The moral imagination: the art and soul of building peace.* Oxford: Oxford University Press.

Lesiuk, T. (2005). The effect of music listening on work performance. *Psychology of Music, 33*(2), 173–191.

Lopez, M. E. (2008). Music therapy: healing, growth, creating a culture of peace. In O. Urbain (Ed.), *Music and conflict transformation: harmonies and dissonances in geopolitics* (pp. 147–171). London: I. B. Tauris.

Lubbock, S. J. (1889). *The pleasure of life.* Volume 2, Macmillan.

McCann, M. (1995). Music and politics in Ireland: the specificity of the folk revival in Belfast. *British Journal of Ethnomusicology, 4*, 51–75.

McMahon, F. F. (2005). Repeat performance: Dancing diDinga with the lost boys of Southern Sudan. *Journal of American Folklore, 118*(469), 354–379.

McNeill, W. (1995). *Keeping together in time: dance and drill in human history.* Harvard, MA: Harvard University Press.

Pavlicevic, M., & Ansdell, G. (Eds.). (2004). *Community music therapy.* London: Jessica Kingsley.

Pettan, S. (1998). Music, politics and war in Croatia in the 1990s: An introduction. In S. Pettan (Ed.), *Music, politics, and war: views from Croatia* (pp. 9–27). Zagreb: Institute of Ethnology and Folklore Research.

Prudente, F. A. (1984). *Musical process in the Gasumbi epic of the Buwaya Kalingga people of Northern Philippines.* Unpublished doctoral dissertation. Ann Arbor, MI: University of Michigan.

Reyes Schramm, A. (1989). Music and tradition: From native to adopted land through the refugee experience. *Yearbook for Traditional Music, 21*, 25–35.

Sloboda, J. A. (1999). Music-where cognition and emotion meet. *Psychologist, 12*(9), 450–455.

Sloboda, J. A. (2000). Musical performance and emotion: issues and developments. In S. Won Yi (Ed.), *Music, Mind, and Science* (pp. 220–238). Seoul: Seoul National University Press.

Sloboda, J. A. (2001). Emotion, functionality and the everyday experience of music: where does music education fit? *Music Education Research*, *3*(2), 243–253.

Sloboda, J. A. (2005). *Exploring the musical mind: cognition, emotion, ability, function*. Oxford: Oxford University Press.

Summer, L. (1997). Considering the future of music therapy. *Arts in Psychotherapy*, *24*(1), 75–80.

Wall, J. A., & Druckman, D. (2003). Mediation in peacekeeping missions. *Journal of Conflict Resolution*, *47*(5), 693–705.

Wall Jr, J. A., & Callister, R. R. (1999). Malaysian community mediation. *Journal of Conflict Resolution*, *43*, 343–365.

Weaver, H. (2001). *Travellin' home and back, Exploring the psychological processes of reconciliation*. Unpublished doctoral dissertation. Virginia: Union Institute and University.

Weingartner, J. (2006). *The arts as a weapon of war, Britain and the shaping of national morale in the second world war*. London: Tauris.

Zelizer, C. M. (2004). *The role of artistic processes in peacebuilding in Bosnia-Herzegovina*. Unpublished doctoral dissertation. Fairfax, VA: George Mason University.

Zharinova-Sanderson, O. (2004). Community music therapy with traumatised refugees in Berlin. In M. Pavlicevic, & G. Ansdell (Eds.), *Community music therapy* (pp. 233–248). London: Jessica Kingsley.

Chapter 19

The role of music in the integration of cultural minorities

Richard Parncutt and Angelika Dorfer

Abstract

Social, cultural, and political integration involves multiple interactions between and among migrant minorities and the indigenous majority. Measures of integration include frequency of contact, feeling of belonging, and mutual acceptance of other cultural groups. Intercultural exchange and the construction of new cultural identities can both promote and hinder integration. The literature on integration addresses language skills, education, occupation, income, (un)employment, and social capital. What is the role of culture, including music? Twenty-four participants in a musicology course unit interviewed 54 migrants living in Graz, Austria. The interviewees came from Albania, China, Egypt (Copts), Iraq (Kurds), Italy, Nigeria, and Serbia. They spoke about music in their everyday lives, music they perform, their cultural identity and social contacts, the music, customs and traditions of their group, their favourite CDs, and the relationship between music and integration. Qualitative analysis yielded theses such as: migrants identify emotionally with the music of their culture, which helps them to feel at home in a new environment. Music is easier to understand across cultures than language. Music promotes intercultural contact by arousing curiosity and creating a social atmosphere.

This chapter was inspired by John Sloboda's research in two separate areas—music psychology and international politics. We bring them together to address the role of music in the integration of cultural minorities in modern cities. John's early research in music psychology focused on abstract cognitive processes. He later addressed issues of musical meaning and function, and the musical concerns and everyday lives of real musicians and music listeners. While the present contribution focuses on an everyday function of music, it is also inspired by John's political activities within the Oxford Research Group and the success with which he has divided his time and energy between 'pure' research and social/political concerns (cf. Chapter 2).

The analysis by Abbott, Rogers, and Sloboda (2007) of the main problems that face the human race today can also explain why cities are becoming increasingly multicultural. Cultural diversity inevitably leads to intercultural conflict, because different cultures have different values, ways of thinking and ways of going about things, or because differences in language and cultures of communication lead to misunderstandings. Thus, integration is becoming an increasingly important social and political issue.

Our study has implications for both music psychology and international politics. In music psychology, a clarification of the roles of music in cultural integration can feed into research on musical identities (Cook, 1998; Frith, 1996; Hargreaves, Miell, & MacDonald, 2002; Müller, Glogner, Rhein, & Heim, 2002) and the positive psychology of music in everyday life (Bakker, 2003; DeNora, 2000; Kreutz, Bongard, Rohrmann, Hodapp, & Grebe, 2004; Laukka, 2006; North, Hargreaves, & Hargreaves, 2004; Sloboda, 2005; Sloboda & O'Neill, 2001; Sloboda, O'Neill, & Ivaldi, 2001). Regarding international politics, strategies for intercultural conflict resolution can have both local and international implications. Domestic procedures for conflict resolution can be applied to international conflicts—for example, democratic countries may be more able to reconcile competing values and interests and more likely to accept international compromise solutions (Dixon, 1993; Gleditsch, 2002). In the USA, improved communication between Jewish and Arab communities and improved Arab integration (McCarus, 1994) can influence US foreign policy and promote conflict resolution in the Middle East. International conflict resolution can be promoted or hindered by cultural or musical projects; a controversial example is the West-Eastern Divan Orchestra, which its conductor Daniel Barenboim regarded as a 'utopian republic' (Willson, 2009).

Global historical context

Cities in most countries, rich and poor, are becoming more culturally diverse and experiencing the advantages and disadvantages of that development. Cultural diversity expands the palette of cultural activities that a city offers, promotes economic productivity (Ottaviano & Peri, 2006), and *boosts* the leisure and tourism industry (Shaw, Bagwell, & Karmowska, 2004). But intercultural conflict can also increase public support for far-right political parties that exacerbate racist and xenophobic attitudes, challenge the rights of foreigners (e.g. to work or participate in democratic procedures), and strive to curb immigration and asylum (Lubbers, Gijsberts, & Scheepers, 2002). Immigrants often live in neighbourhoods with poor health and educational services and high rates of unemployment, poverty and crime, which further hinders their integration (Kazemipur & Halli, 2002). Since the trend towards greater cultural diversity in modern cities shows no signs of abating, any approach to addressing the problems and raising awareness of the benefits is worthy of consideration.

Migration is a constant feature of humankind (cf. Park, 1928) that has prevented the emergence of genetically relatively homogenous groups ('races'; Owens & King, 1999) and has become more prevalent and rapid in recent centuries (Wakeley, 1999). But modern multicultural cities are also a consequence of increased intercultural communication and mobility: their culturally diverse citizens communicate with and visit their international friends, relatives, and colleagues increasingly easily and often. As multidirectional cross-border flows and transnational networks become stronger, urban multiculturalism is increasingly linked to economic and cultural globalization (Castles, 2006; Hall & Williams, 2002).

Technological progress in communications and transport has enhanced the international mobility of workers and their families (Stalker, 2000). But migration is also driven by international crises and associated climate change, competition for limited resources, poverty, and militarization (cf. Abbott *et al.*, 2007). Climate change is increasing the incidence of storms and famines; these primarily affect poorer countries (Van Aalst, 2006) and generate *environmental refugees*. Environmental problems of all kinds, from earthquakes to nuclear pollution, can provoke migration (Hunter, 2005). The poverty rate in rich nations is increasing (Kazemipur & Halli, 2002), and the gap between rich and poor nations has widened, generating *economic refugees*. Most countries are getting richer, but some poor countries are stagnating, and rich countries are getting richer faster than poorer countries (Seshanna & Decornez, 2003). Reasons include the failure of countries and international markets to tax income and profits fairly (Webb, 2004) and the failure of richer countries to invest 0.7% of their gross national product in international development and poverty reduction (Sachs, 2005). Regarding militarization, international and civil wars and coups produce *refugees of violence* (cf. Barnett & Adger, 2007; Reuveny, 2007). Sixty years after the universal declaration of human rights, fundamental rights are still regularly violated, generating *political refugees*.

These problems reflect a long-term mismatch between technological and psychosocial progress. Historical indicators of psychosocial progress include the French revolution, the abolition of slavery in most countries, and voting rights for women (Sachs, 2005). Nevertheless, 'the human traits that lead to war, environmental disaster, and famine have not improved during recorded history. Our technological advances have increased exponentially over a few centuries, but our intercommunity and interracial skills have improved little' (Shearman, 2002, p. 1468). Evolution has not prepared human beings for problems of planetary dimensions; if we have barely experienced global warming personally, we find it difficult to imagine the ultimate consequences. Moreover, humans tend to go into denial when presented with enormous problems (Cohen, 2001), such as the millions of children and adults who die of hunger each year (Shetty, 2006; Sloboda, 2005).

Since the causes of migration are both complex and massive, the associated problems will grow steadily in coming decades. Cities will be increasingly challenged to address the problems and to perceive and take advantage of the benefits.

Integration, assimilation, acculturation

Cultural minorities that are not consistently discriminated against or persecuted tend to prefer forms of integration in which different cultures live side by side, maintaining and developing their identity (Van Oudenhoven, Prins, & Buunk, 1998). The identities of both majority and minorities are modified, extended, and enriched by interaction with other cultures (*transculturality*: Welsch, 1999). New cultural orientations can emerge when intergroup interactions lead to changes in traditions, behaviours, and preferences. But all parties typically retain and value aspects of their original identity (Kuran & Sandholm, 2007).

The implicit definition of 'integration' depends on the speaker's political agenda, cultural background, and personal experience. While members of majority cultures tend to think of integration as the adaptation of minority groups to a stable majority, members of minority groups are more interested in maintaining minority cultures, which they do not see as contrary to adaptation (Verkuyten & Thijs, 2002). Centre-right governments tend to regard immigrants as responsible for problems associated with migration, expect them to adapt to local conditions, and require them to attend language courses and pass citizenship tests; centre-left governments may instead regard integration as an opportunity to enrich culture and quality of life. But exceptions are frequent: the left may accept xenophobic tendencies among their supporters, while the right may recognize the economic benefits of cultural diversity.

The present approach is biased towards centre-left and liberal-green politics. We consider integration to involve all interactions among all cultural groups, including the majority. All such groups may be either indigenous or international; for example, the majority culture in Australian cities is originally of British origin, and indigenous Australians have become one of a large number of cultural minorities. Minorities can be regarded as 'indigenous' if they have lived in the same area for a long time; indigenous communities in modern Austria include Jews, Roma, and speakers of Slovenian, Croat, Hungarian, Italian, and Czech (Hemetek, 2001).

Integration can be social or individual. Individual integration or acculturation (Ward, Bochner, & Furnham, 2001) can involve language skill acquisition, employment and income, feeling at home, frequency of contact with other groups (meetings, phone calls, events, number of 'foreign' friends and acquaintances), and everyday independence and efficacy (public transport, shopping, cultural activities, contact with authorities). The integration of a social group involves acceptance by other groups, lack of prejudice, and frequency of contact as measured, for example, by rate of intermarriage. It also involves structural integration: representation of minorities in professions, public service and politics, and the incidence, visibility, and stability of institutions such as government and non-governmental organizations (NGOs) that genuinely promote integration. Minorities tend to be regarded by outsiders as homogenous and by insiders as heterogeneous (examples from China and former Yugoslavia are presented by Folkestad, 2002); integration involves feeling at home not only within one's cultural group (in a foreign setting), but also in a wider multi-, inter-, and transcultural setting.

In an increasingly globalized world, familiar categories such as locals and immigrants, integration and assimilation, and settlers and guest workers are becoming blurred. Enculturation (original culture) and acculturation (new culture) cannot always be clearly separated: migrant children simultaneously absorb two different cultures, and while they may be better able to absorb their 'new' local culture than their parents, familiarity with their 'old' culture can enhance their self-esteem and ability to integrate (Auernheimer, 1995). Migrants increasingly have multiple identities and their communities have transnational character (Castles, 2006). Consider for example a Turkish woman living in Graz with two children. Her complex identity includes at least the following elements: Turkish, Muslim, woman, mother, Graz resident. If she is in regular contact by telephone and email with friends and family in Turkey, and occasionally visits Turkey or receives Turkish visitors, her 'community' is international. Today, the term 'international migrant' can be split into several categories or prototypes: *immigrants* (who integrate into a recipient society), *re-immigrants* (who maintain strong links to their society of origin), *diaspora-immigrants* (who maintain strong ties to a well-defined transnational community), and *transmigrants*, who are 'characterized by their durable social, cultural, and economic localization and integration in new and pluri-local Transnational Social Spaces' (Pries, 1998, abstract). Transmigrants have not been uprooted from their original culture; instead, they are world citizens in a globalized economy (cf. Schiller, Basch, & Szanton Blanc, 1997). While the blurring of boundaries may make the conceptualization of integration difficult, it is also positive evidence that integration is occurring.

Integration implies equal rights for settled and mobile cultures. It is often contrasted with *assimilation*, in which minorities are expected to give up their culture (Van Oudenhoven *et al.*, 1998) and *hybridization* into a *melting pot*, in which majority and minorities merge to form a new cultural synergy (Zank, 1998). But since every migrant brings salient, stable habits, memories and constructions of value and identity to a new cultural context, no one is completely assimilated. Besides, migrants often build homes away from home (e.g. Chinatowns) that maintain their identity and culture. African Americans share a strong sense or ethnic identity after centuries of suppression, assimilation, and marginalization (Oyserman, Gant, & Ager, 1995).

Promoting integration

Assuming that integration is the solution—if not the panacea—that modern multicultural cities need and strive for, how can it best be promoted? In general, one can either increase the incidence or salience of positive factors, or decrease the incidence or salience of negative factors. Positive factors include any collective activity that promotes positive intergroup contact (e.g. sport); negative factors, any kind of discrimination, xenophobia or racism. Social and cultural integration can also be promoted by channelling the self-interest of stakeholders (economic relationships among groups), by altruistic projects and activities (NGOs), or combinations (altruistic projects that provide paid work for NGOs). Since all such factors can contribute positively to integration, and social systems are complex and difficult to monitor or model, the combination of different strategies may be greater than the sum of the parts, due to unforeseeable interactions between the positive effects of different strategies and the unforeseeable emergence of new benefits (cf. Mitleton-Kelly, 2003). The best strategy may not, therefore, be to favour one approach at the expense of others, but to promote a diversity of approaches.

What influences integration? Existing literature addresses the role of language skills (Greenberg, Macías, Rhodes, & Chan, 2001); education, occupation and income

(Hou & Balakrishnan, 1996); (un)employment (Gowricharn, 2002); social capital (Jacobs & Tillie, 2004); and the opinions and prejudices of the majority culture (Bobo & Zubrinsky, 1996). On a more abstract level, cultural integration involves *personal identity*—the way an individual describes and understands themselves, which depends directly on culture. *Self-identity* is a form of self-description that may be stable for years or decades; it develops early in life and depends on in-group identification, conceptions of social identities, prejudice, and social context (Bennett & Sani, 2004).

The evaluative aspect of self-identity (How good am I by comparison to other people?) is *self-esteem*. It involves situation- and domain-specific aspects such as coping with stress and musical ability (Hargreaves *et al.*, 2002), and is often founded on group inclusion (Leary, Tambor, Terdal, & Downs, 1995). Self-esteem tends to be weakened by migration: newly arrived migrants may find themselves unable to cope with simple everyday situations due to incomplete knowledge of local language, geography, customs, weather, and so on. Migrant musicians may have difficulty demonstrating their musical ability to local musicians, and in rehearsal may misunderstand local unwritten rules of musical interaction. Both in this specific case and more generally, if music can promote self-esteem, it can promote integration.

Music and integration

Art and music may play an important subsidiary role in integration once existential problems are solved (cf. Maslow's 1943 hierarchy of human needs and motivation). Culture includes shared meanings and behaviours that are variously expressed. Cultures construct different realities and hidden assumptions. Differences are least reconcilable when embedded in fundamentalist political, economic, and religious systems. Thus, intercultural conflicts require attention to and acknowledgement of cultural detail (Marsella, 2005). Art and music can also contribute directly and simply to integration: in everyday social and political settings, foreign artists tend to be accepted when they offer something that locals do not (or cannot), and are not seen as competing for resources (such as employment), but rather creating new resources; the same may apply to foreign sportspeople (cf. Nagel, 1995).

The following everyday example highlights the complexity of music's role in integration. The hypothetical Turkish woman in Graz mentioned above may have limited personal contacts—little more than her husband and two children. Her knowledge of the German language is limited and it is difficult for her to attend German classes. Sometimes she listens to recordings of Turkish music and feels sad and nostalgic. Does this music (or this behaviour) promote or hinder her integration?

Music 'plays an important role in the negotiation, construction and maintenance of identities' (MacDonald, Hargreaves, & Miell, 2009, p. 463). From internationally dominant musical cultures such as Germany (Applegate & Potter, 2002; Folkestad, 2002) to suppressed indigenous cultures such as the aboriginal people of Australia (Gibson, 1998), cultures define themselves through music; 'it may be that the awareness of a common national musical identity independent of social, religious or ethnic background is more prevalent and stronger in countries that have fought for freedom throughout history than in countries which have lived in peace for a long time'

(Folkestad, 2002, p. 155). Greek Cypriot primary school children are exposed to music that carries contradictory ideological messages; they develop 'fluid and often insecure, ambiguous and contradictory national musical identities' (Pieridou-Skoutella, 2007). According to Cook (1998, p. 4–5), 'music ... functions as a symbol of national or regional identity: émigré communities sometimes clung tenaciously to their traditional music in order to preserve their identity in a foreign country... In today's world, deciding what music to listen to is a significant part of deciding and announcing to people not just who you "want to be" ... but who you *are*.' Thus, music not only *reflects* identities—it also *constructs* them.

But self-identity through music does not always promote integration. Although rap music has strengthened the identity of many black Americans, exposure to violent rap can also promote stereotyping of black people (by both white and black people themselves), increasing the probability that black people will be considered violent and unintelligent (Johnson, Trawalter, & Dovidio, 2000). Moreover, identities are never clear-cut, and they seldom correspond clearly to nation-states. Frith (1996) argues 'first, that identity is *mobile*, a process not a thing, a becoming not a being; second, that our experience of music—of music making and music listening—is best understood as an experience of this *self-in-process*' (p. 109).

Several recent empirical studies have addressed the integrative role of culture and music. Sousa, Neto, and Mullet (2005) found that including Cape Verdean songs among songs learned by Portuguese school children reduced black–white stereotyping. In a study of multicultural Stockholm choirs, Pawlig (2003) observed that while relatively few choirs consciously promoted cultural integration, they nevertheless had important integrative functions: they were accessible for immigrants and enabled them to make social contacts, learn about Swedish culture and language, and be socially active and visible. Siegert (2008) studied the role of *maqam* music in the lives and identities of Turkish Germans, and concluded that music promotes integration on a personal level (helping individuals to feel at home in a foreign culture, creating a continuum between the past and the present, maintaining and developing personality and individuality), a social or intersubjective level (helping people to develop authentic relationships within and between heterogenous cultural groups, to overcome prejudice and to open up to outside influences), and a universal level (spirituality and the feeling of establishing a connection between soul and cosmos). Bradley (2006) analysed racialized discourses within multicultural programmes of music education and considered different motivations for engaging in multiculturalism in music education, identifying decolonization as a crucial catalyst for substantive change.

Personal background

This is a preliminary, qualitative study to explore issues and ideas about the role of music in integration. Our approach and interpretations depend on various historical, political, academic, and personal contexts. The study was originally motivated by the first author's political and academic interests and biases. Since these influenced the study from conception, planning, execution, analysis right through to the final conclusions, they will be described in some detail in the first person.

Academically, I am interested in the future development of music psychology, both for its own sake and as a subdiscipline of musicology (Parncutt, 2007, 2008). I agree with Sloboda (2005) that music psychology should more often and more directly address issues of social importance and relevance. To achieve that, music psychology needs a diverse palette of epistemologies and research methods. The discipline is still dominated by empirical cognitive psychology, which like any other epistemology is limited in its scope of application and validity. Of all presentations at the International Conference on Music Perception and Cognition in Sapporo, Japan, in 2008, 75% were reports of empirical and data-oriented studies; only 25% were theoretical studies, reviews, demonstrations, or presentations on research/teaching methods, software development, or music analysis (Parncutt, 2008). Music research can and should aim for a better balance between the humanities and sciences.

As a researcher I have lived in several different countries (Australia, Germany, France, Sweden, Canada, UK) and observed—from the position of an educated, white male—many different forms of racism and xenophobia. I moved from the UK to Austria in 1998 to take up a professorship in systematic musicology at the University of Graz. During my first year, I witnessed a national election campaign in which openly racist or xenophobic public statements were commonplace, which motivated me to contact relevant Graz NGOs and interculturality researchers. Both groups felt powerless to influence the campaign and its negative social effects. I saw this as an opportunity to strengthen the political role of universities and interculturality researchers. Various projects ensued, including documentation of interculturality research in diverse disciplines, a multidisciplinary series of lectures about racism and xenophobia, a project to help the Austrian media avoid racism, and an awareness-raising campaign with catchy, foreigner-friendly slogans.[1]

The data for the present study were collected by students in a master's level seminar. I saw that as a logical and legitimate way to combine my political goals and activities with my music psychology research and teaching. The seminar was politically neutral and no attempt was made to document the political preferences of the students.

The second author of this study was a student on that course. She reports: I grew up in Graz. As a child (aged 6–13), I spent several school holidays travelling in Turkey, Indonesia, Thailand, Egypt, and Uganda (Africa) with my parents. During these trips, which I generally enjoyed, my parents and I made many contacts with local people. I have since then been fascinated by culture and interculturality in the sense of different lifestyles and attitudes. I spent one year studying in Italy. I also spent five semesters working in the Student Union of the University of Graz in the area of international relations, which primarily involved supporting foreign students. In my musicology studies, I was interested in the social and psychological effects of music, which motivated me to take part in this study. Since the problem of integration and the possible role(s) of music are evidently quite complex, I think that it is important to develop ways to individually consider the different aspects and not to over-simplify.

Method

What is the role of music in integration, and how can the role of music in integration be investigated? In this exploratory, qualitative study, we focused on the experiences and opinions of culturally diverse residents of a medium-sized city (Graz, Austria; population 300 000). We wanted to know not only what music people hear and play, and where and when they do that, but also why and how they do that. We aimed not to test hypotheses, but to generate them.[2]

Graz is an interesting location for such a study. The city has a long history of multiculturalism and multilingualism as a central location in the Austro-Hungarian Empire. The extreme racism of Hitler's Third Reich casts a long shadow, and since 1945, Austrians have been alternately addressing and avoiding its consequences and implications (Albrich, 1994). Many who were exposed to Nazi racist propaganda are still alive, and echoes of the past still resonate in the policies of extreme-right political parties. The city recovered politically and economically from the Second World War in a relatively isolated corner of western Europe close to the Iron Curtain. Because Austria was recognized by the Allies as a victim of Nazi aggression, this half-truth was taught to Austrian children in post-war schools, and Austria pursued de-Nazification less seriously and thoroughly than Germany. Moreover, popular support for the dispossession, deportation, and destruction of Jews had been greater in Vienna than in comparable German cities (Tálos, Hanisch, & Neubauer, 2000, pp. 237–259, 767–794). The decade following the fall of communism in 1990 saw a sharp increase in migration and cultural diversity due to the new freedom of movement between the East and West, the refugees generated by conflicts within nearby ex-Yugoslavia, and refugees from more distant conflicts in Africa and Asia. Populist far-right politicians took advantage of the resultant conflicts and xenophobia and in 2000 the Freedom Patry (FPÖ) joined the federal government in a coalition with the centre-right People's Party (ÖVP) (Wodak & Pelinka, 2002). The relationship between the FPÖ and Hitler's National Socialism (Riedlsberger, 2002) was discussed in the European Union, culminating in several months of sanctions that Austrians on both the left and the right considered unfair, reviving anti-European sentiments. Meanwhile, cultural diversity in Graz was steadily increasing and many new NGOs were being established. These NGOs now appear to be the main driving force behind the steady (if slow) progress that is being made towards cultural integration on different levels.

Our approach to the question of music in integration differs in fundamental ways from typical ethnomusicological approaches such as Hemetek (2001). Ethnomusicologists often get involved in the musical activities of foreign culture for an extended period, getting to know its members and gaining their trust (Nettl, 1983). We value and respect this approach but did not adopt it. First, we did not aim to document the music of each group. Instead we asked about its integrative role, and the social and political implications for all minorities and the whole community. To address those issues, we considered and compared a range of different cultures. Second, our study was confined to a university semester. Our student interviewers had only a few weeks to try to get a preliminary insider view of their cultural group and its music. They briefly presented their findings during class before the interviews began. Similarly, our approach also differs from typical approaches in empirical cognitive psychology. Multicultural communities cannot be experimentally manipulated to study cause–effect relationships. Correlations are possible, but did not, in our case, yield significant results (Dorfer, 2009).

Participants

The interviewers were 28 musicology students enrolled in a master's level seminar at the University of Graz in 2006.[3] They had been studying for an average of 2.5 full-time equivalent years and their mean age was 25.6 years. Sixteen were female and 12 were male. All were Austrian citizens and had grown up in Austria; their ethnicity was relatively uniform.

The respondents were Graz residents from seven different migrant groups. They were not randomly selected, nor were they necessarily representative of Graz minorities or even of the minorities that they represented. It is therefore dangerous to attempt to generalize on the basis of our data, and generally not meaningful to count the number or proportion of respondents who answered certain questions in certain ways. The opinions expressed by our participants were primarily personal opinions. The respondents were found by contacting migrant organizations and snowballing. They satisfied the following criteria: residence in Graz, reasonable fluency in German or English, and identification with one of seven specific cultural groups. Of 55 respondents, 14 were excluded from analysis due to communication difficulties (as reported by interviewers in a confidential post-questionnaire) or missing data. In the following, we consider the remaining 41 interviews.

The 41 respondents were associated with seven different countries or cultures: Albania (6 people), China (4), Egypt (Copts; 7), Iraq (Kurds; 5), Italy (9), Nigeria (5), and Serbia (5). Twenty-two were female and 19 were male. They were aged 17–53 years (mean age 30), and had spent between 0.2 and 23 years in the European Union (mean 8 years). Two had grown up in Austria in immigrant families. Further information about the respondents is presented in Table 19.1.[4]

Procedure

At the first seminar session, the students were informed about the main aims and methods of the project. They were then asked to identify cultural groups in Graz with which they had contact or whose music interested them. On that basis, they were divided into seven groups of four members, each of which was assigned to a minority group.

In subsequent weekly sessions, the method of the study was developed. The first author presented a draft interview guideline that was inspired by Höllinger (2004) and Mayring (2002). It included tips on how to contact potential respondents, arrange an interview, put the respondent at ease, encourage the respondent to speak at length without biasing the content, make a sound recording, note the most important points immediately following the interview, and transcribe the interview. It also recommended ways of avoiding tendencies to make socially acceptable statements, answer questions in the affirmative, and invent arbitrary explanations to avoid seeming uninformed. The students commented on the draft and the first author revised it.

Ethical issues were considered in detail. The students discussed intercultural gender issues and were asked to favour same-sex interviews (women interviewed by women, men by men). They discussed possible effects of perceived differences in class or status between interviewer and respondent, and were asked to present themselves not as musical experts, but as individuals who were interested to learn from a specific

Table 19.1 The respondents

Respondent number	Group*	Self-reported identities and corresponding belongingness ratings†	Sex	Age (years)	Years of European residence	Degree of integration‡	Years of regular active music§	Education¶	Occupation**
2	Ch	Chinese 7	F	21	4	2.7	10	2	0
4	Ch	Chinese 7, European 1	F	30	1.5	1.3	22	2	0
6	Ch	Austrian 6, Chinese 6	M	19	9	5.0	0	1	0
7	Ch	Chinese 7, Austrian 6, Religion 1–2	F	27	4	2.7	24	2	0
9	Al	Kosovan 7, Albanian 2 Grazer 5	F	33	8	4.0	5	4	1
10	Al	Albanian Grazer	F	27	7	3.3	0	4	1
11	Al	Austria 6, Albania 5	F	23	23	4.3	4	2	0
12	Al	–	F	27	4	3.0	–	2	0
14	Al	–	F	26	3	4.0	–	4	0
15	Al	Albanian in Graz	F	24	4	2.7	3	2	0
17	It	European, Italian, Christian	M	25	0.7	3.3	–	2	0
18	It	European, catholic	M	23	0.7	2.5	0	2	0
19	It	European, Italian	F	21	0.3	3.0	2.5	2	0
20	It	Italy/Udina/Triestina 7	F	21	0.7	2.0	0	2	0
21	It	Italian/Udina 7	F	23	0.7	2.3	15	2	0
22	It	Southern Italian 7	F	26	0.2	2.7	10	4	0
23	It	South Tyrolean 5	F	22	3	3.0	15	2	0
24	It	South Tyrolean 7, German speaker 5	M	32	0.5	3.3	20	2	0

(Continued)

Table 19.1 (continued) The respondents

Respondent number	Group*	Self-reported identities and corresponding belongingness ratings†	Sex	Age (years)	Years of European residence	Degree of integration‡	Years of regular active music§	Education¶	Occupation**
25	It	myself 7, South Tyrolean 1, Italian 1	F	23	5	5.0	15	2	0
26	EC	Christian 7, Egyptian 7, Austrian 5, Carinthian 5	M	44	17	4.3	–	4	1
27	EC	world citizen 6–7, intellectual 5–6, Copt 3–4	M	43	19	5.0	–	4	1
28	EC	Coptic Christian 7, Egyptian 3.5, Styrian 3.5	M	40	17	4.0	0	4	1
30	EC	Grazer 7, student 3, Copt 2	M	23	18	5.0	8	2	0
31	EC	Orthodox Copt 7, Egyptian 7, Grazer 5	F	29	11	–	–	2	2
32	EC	Copt 7, Egyptian 7, Austrian 4	F	49	15	3.0	10	4	1
33	EC	Copt 6, Egyptian 2, Austrian 6	M	17	17	3.0	–	1	0
34	IK	Kurd 7, European 3	M	35	13	3.7	0	2	1
35	IK	Austrian 4, Kurd 3	M	45	18	5.0	0	–	1
36	IK	Kurd 5, Austrian 2	F	25	4	5.0	0	2	0
40	IK	Kurdistan 7, Austria 5, Persia 4, Ireland 3	M	45	19	4.7	–	2	2
41	IK	Kurdistan 7, German 4, Graz 1	F	32	11	4.3	0	4	–
44	Ni	Afrikan 7, Nigerian 6, Austrian 5	M	39	9	3.7	23	1	1
45	Ni	Nigerian 4–6, Austrian 3–4	M	40	13	4.0	13	3	1

46	Ni	Igbo 7, Nigeria 6, Africa 5, Christian 4	M	34	–	3.3	27	3	0
47	Ni	Christ 7, from Nigeria 7/Ibo 7, live in Austria 7	M	53	10	4.0	46	3	1
48	Ni	Grazer Nigerian	M	22	4	2.7	15	1	2
50	Se	Jugoslavian, Balkan, Serbia, Graz	F	25	6	3.7	8	2	0
51	Se	University 7, Serbia 6, Austria 4	F	23	3	2.3	0	2	0
53	Se	Balkans	F	27	3	5.0	–	2	0
54	Se	Bosnian Serb, Serb	M	26	4	3.3	10	2	0
55	Se	Serb, Grazer	M	25	7	3.7	–	2	0
Mean				**30**	**7.9**	**3.6**	**9.8**		

* Ch, China; EC, Egyptian Copt; IK, Iranian Kurd; etc.
† 1 = I feel I belong very little …. 7 = very much.
‡ 1 = not at all …. 5 = very much.
§ Practice or performance.
¶ 1 = high school; 2 = matriculation; 3 = university degree.
** 0 = training or on leave; 1 = working; 2 = both.
M, male; F, female.

cultural group in Graz about their daily lives and their music. Before the interview, potential respondents received a one-page summary of the main points about the study, including the aims and general direction, reasons for participating, the main things that we wanted, and data security. The time and place of the interview was decided by the respondent and interviewer together; the interviewers had been reminded to be sensitive to issues of privacy, neutrality, and the likelihood of disturbance. The interview began with discussion of the one-page summary. The interviewers checked that participants understood their rights including data confidentiality and then asked for permission to make a sound recording (which was denied in one case).

Interviews took place in a variety of locations, including cafés, university rooms, and private homes. All the respondents were asked to bring three personal favourite CDs (or similar files on hard disc) to the interview (not necessarily music from the respondent's cultural group).[5] Each session began with small talk, after which the recording equipment was checked. The interviews were semi-structured: the interviewers referred to a list of main issues, each of which was divided into several questions. The interviewers were instructed to cover all the main issues and some of the questions for each in any order. The respondents generally did not read the questions themselves. They were encouraged to speak as long as they wished about topics that interested them. If they got side-tracked, the interviewers were instructed to gently redirect the conversation.

Immediately following an interview, the interviewer completed a confidential form to evaluate the ability of the interviewer and the respondent to understand each other (including the effect of any language barrier), the respondent's talkativeness and involvement, the atmosphere (relaxed?, mutual acceptance/liking of interviewer and respondent?), the interviewer's performance (self-evaluation against listed criteria), and disturbances (interruptions, presence of third persons).

Transcriptions of the interviews were prepared by the interviewers and were constructed entirely from words used by the respondents. Grammar was corrected, dialectic variants were transcribed into high German or English, and repetitions were removed. We asked the interviewers to reproduce the respondent's intentions as closely as possible and implicitly accepted interviewers as co-constructors of meaning (Oliver, Serovich, & Mason, 2005). We decided against natural transcriptions that include pauses and their duration, gestures, emphases, facial expressions, stutters, lexically meaningless or superfluous tokens (*aha, yeah, mm*), and incomprehensible speech. We were primarily interested in the shared perceptions and intended meanings of respondents' statements—not in the specific ways in which that content was communicated (conversation analysis).

In the present report, most quotations have been translated by the first author from German into English. The translations are intended to render the essential original meaning and intention in natural English, and tend to be shorter than the originals.

Analysis

The basis for our analysis was the transcripts prepared by the students. Our primary methods of analysis were observer impression, qualitative content analysis, and hermeneutic formulation of hypotheses (cf. Mayring, 2002; Rennie, 2000). The quotations in this report were chosen for relevance (for any specific question, as well as the general question of the role of music in integration) and clarity (comprehensibility and concision), as well as memorability, plausibility and realism. We attempted to balance statements from all seven cultural groups, and from women and men. The number of different respondents who expressed a similar idea was not a criterion for selection; while quantitative studies focus on frequently occurring observations (such as the spontaneous expression of a given idea by different participants in different contexts), qualitative approaches often gain valuable information from isolated, interesting statements. The hermeneutic formulation of hypotheses was inspired by grounded theory, but our analysis was less detailed than that recommended by Glaser and Strauss (1967 and later publications). We combined top-down (or inductive) and bottom-up (or deductive) processes, creatively formulating/revising hypotheses and comparing them with the transcriptions.[6]

Results

The following results are structured according to the written interview guide.

Music in everyday life

How often do you listen to the radio? In what situation? Which stations? Do you prefer music or talking? Do you attend concerts? Listen to CDs? Do you play music or sing? Can you recall a very emotional musical experience in your life?

Consistent with the literature on music in everyday life, the respondents reported diverse musical habits. Some had little time to listen to music, while others listened to the radio whenever they could. The participants who often listened attentively to music, or listened with a specific intention, included students of classical music, a jazz singer, a DJ for electronic music, and a (non-Austrian) wind player in traditional South Tyrol brass ensembles. Two participants were musically active in the Copt community and taught children Copt music.

Musical style preferences varied considerably. Intriguingly, *Musikantenstadl* (a TV show featuring a mixture of traditional, folk and popular music) featured in the selection by a Coptic male (Respondent 28):

> I don't understand it completely, but it is folklore and we Copts feel closer to folklore than modern music.

Musikantenstadl is not archetypical Austrian music: it is well known and clearly part of Austrian culture, but many Austrians do not like it.

The respondent as musician

Do you play a musical instrument? Do you have one at home? Description of instrument? Years of practice? Playing situations? Do you play music of your cultural group? Do you pass this musical knowledge to others?

Twenty-one of the 41 respondents reported playing a musical instrument. For many participants, their musical practice had changed with their change of location. Nine reported playing mainly music of their own culture ('authentic' traditional, original popular or mixtures of the two), 10 reported playing mainly Western music (classical, pop, jazz, or Austrian traditional), and five reported playing a mixture of both. Respondent 45 (Nigerian, male) commented:

> I never played drums at home in Nigeria and played no instrument at all. Here in Graz, I found out that my work, anti-racist projects with children, needs this music and so I started to teach myself this music. So you could say I am self-taught.

Another Nigerian man (Respondent 44) reported the opposite:

> I haven't played for a long time. In Africa I always played.

Respondent 7 (Chinese, female) was studying operatic voice at Graz's music university. She reported:

> In my home country, I learned both these traditional Chinese instruments and we often made music in our family. That is normal for us. I like the music of my culture, but I like singing European classical music and I also like to play music of Mozart or Beethoven on the piano. I can't really decide.

A Coptic woman (Respondent 31) reported singing Coptic music in church services and in religion classes with school children, whom she taught the most important hymns. A Serbian man (Respondent 54) played Serbian music in a wedding band. An Albanian woman (Respondent 9) reported learning to play Western classical piano when she was a child. A Kurdish man (Respondent 40) sang Carinthian traditional choral music.[7]

Cultural identity

Which cultural groups do you belong to? How strongly? Is there a club for your group(s) in Graz? How much contact do you have with this or other groups? With the local majority? Do you feel at home in Graz? Would you like to return to your home country?

The reported identities are summarized in Table 19.1. They reveal interesting differences between reported self-identities and the labels of groups to which respondents were assigned. On the basis of Table 19.1 and the respondents' statements about feeling at home and in contact with other people (of any group including the majority), three independent raters (the second author, a fellow student, and a psychologist) estimated the degree of integration of each respondent on a 5-point scale. Mean ratings are shown in Table 19.1. This tentative and exploratory procedure suggests that our sample was relatively well integrated (the mean was 3.6 on a 5-point scale), but degrees of integration covered a wide range (e.g. seven people were rated as entirely integrated on scale point 5).

Events, ceremonies, traditions

How do you spend your free time? Describe the events and customs of your group in Graz. What roles does music play? Do members of other cultural groups (including the majority) take part? Questions of this kind were asked twice: for the respondent's cultural group and for other cultural groups in Graz.

Respondent 10 (Albanian, female) reported:

We eat and drink. It is rather informal. But you can talk about problems at university or financial problems. We also organize parties; for example for Albania's national holiday ... With loud Albanian music. We go to an Albanian pub, so that we are alone, because we are loud. If you feel homesick and haven't been home for a long time, that's nice.

Respondent 47 (Nigerian, male) enthused:

We have our Independence Day, and everybody gets together to organize it. ... We do that in Nigeria and we do it here, too ... I play with my band or other groups; with a lot of dancing, eating and drinking ... And these are big parties and we also celebrate in Graz ... No matter where they are—every Igbo celebrates—no matter where on earth he is at that moment [*laughs*]. That is our culture. Here in Austria many Austrians have tried it and they all liked it. Yes, we celebrate it in Linz, Innsbruck, Vienna, Graz, and so on, wherever there are Igbos [*laughs*]. Everywhere in the world. Last year and we will also celebrate it next year. Come and see! I invite you to come.

Respondent 40 (a Kurdish man) claimed:

I always organized picnics and invited other people, so that they met each other and then they said: Hey, that was wonderful. We see you and your culture differently now ...

The interviewers assigned to the Kurdish community experienced its openness and generosity directly when they were invited to a picnic and an evening party.

Respondents varied in the roles and importance they assigned to the traditions of their cultural group in Graz. Respondent 24 (Italian, male) pointed out that 'when you are in a different country, your own culture becomes more interesting and important'.

Respondent 10 (Albanian, female) said:

Young people in Albania seem to avoid their traditional music. But when they are away from home, they want that you send them CDs with traditional music ... I have experienced that myself. ... That is because of homesickness.

Respondent 19 (an Italian woman) stated:

At the beginning, when I came to Graz, I spoke a lot to Italians, but now I try not to do that, because we only speak Italian then and I want to learn German.

Respondent 10 (Albanian, female) pointed out that:

We are all students and don't have time to do traditional things ... When I am home, then I enjoy these traditional things. But in Graz I don't miss these traditions.

Respondent 28 (a Coptic man) said:

We celebrate, but it doesn't have the same feeling as at home. Because at home is more about family and food: for us, tradition has a lot to do with eating.

These comments confirm that the new situation in which migrants find themselves causes them to change their personal and cultural orientation and to question and redefine their identity. The new environment offers less comfort and security, so some tend to look for comfort and security in their old familiar traditions.

How do migrants in Graz perceive Austrian culture? Respondent 22 (Italian, female) observed:

> I think that Austrians listen to a lot of classical music ... That's a big tradition in Austria and Germany. I think that people here listen to more classical music than in Italy.

Respondent 15 (Albanian, female) said:

> I have the feeling that in Austria traditional music is less important and so it is not important for integration. In Albania, music is more important. If you know the music, you know the country.

Personal favourite CDs

Respondents had been asked to bring three personal favourite CDs. Here, we asked for details including the importance of the music for them; when, where, and with whom they listened to it, and cultural associations.[8] Five respondents brought three CDs from their minority culture (traditional, popular, or both). Eight respondents brought only Western music (pop, classical, jazz). Four did not bring any recordings. The remaining 24 respondents presented a mixture of music from different cultures. Six included music from other non-Western cultures; for example the favourites of Respondent 21 (Italian, female) were Red Hot Chilli Peppers (US/international pop/rock), Pink Floyd (UK/international pop/rock) and Pjatmizza (Russian pop). Some respondents explained that their favourite non-Western music was similar to the music of their own culture; for others, the music reminded them of a trip abroad. These data are consistent with concepts of multiple identity and blurred cultural boundaries.

Music of the respondent's cultural group

What music do you listen to mainly—both generally and with people from your cultural group? How often? What happened last time? What music is typical for your culture? What is special about it? What role does it play in your life? Do you dislike some of it? It is political? Do you feel free to enjoy it? Does it help you feel at home?

Various opinions were expressed about the music of respondents' own cultural groups. Respondent 7 (Chinese, female) explained:

> We have very many different instruments and directions in our traditional music ... we are all very proud of our music ... it is very beautiful.

But for Respondent 6 (Chinese, male), who had lived in Graz for nine years since arriving at age 10,

> music is mainly for entertainment and relaxation. Chinese music has no meaning for me and I don't listen to it.

Respondents offered contrasting opinions about the social function of music, both generally and in the specific case of integration. The Nigerian respondents tended to see music (including their own) as a human universal that promotes peaceful coexistence. Respondent 45 (male) remarked:

> There is a saying that I read in a book and it says that music is the food of love, and we simply need that.

Respondent 44 (male) observed that:

> For example, if you play some music outside that is good for singing and dancing, everyone will sing, play music, and dance, regardless of where the people come from, from America, Great Britain, Africa, Asia, Europe—they sing and play the music together. It brings people together.[9]

The Copts that we interviewed regarded their music as private—important for their religion and cultural identity. Respondent 31 (female) said:

> Music is an essential part of the church services. The songs reinforce the meaning of the service. ... No belief is possible without Coptic music. Very important.

This respondent did not regard music as playing any role at all in cultural integration. When asked if her music helped her to feel at home in Graz, she replied: 'No. I feel at home in the Graz Coptic community, but that has nothing to do with Graz itself'.

Our Serbian, Albanian, and Italian interviewees tended to regard music as important for cultural identity, but stressed that practical considerations such as employment and language are more important for integration. The different approaches of the different groups were partly based on differing levels of cultural self-organization, which was relatively high for Kurds and Copts and relatively low for Chinese, Albanians, and Italians.

The role of music in the integration of Graz's Serbian minority presents an interesting example of blurred boundaries and complex cultural interactions. Before and during the First and Second World Wars, German literature (e.g. the satirical magazine *Simplicissmus*) presented Serbs as underdeveloped, uncivilized, dirty, and violent (Jörg Becker, 2009). Prejudice was reinforced in the 1990s by events in ex-Yugoslavia. In a recent telephone survey (*Sozialwissenschaftliche Studiengesellschaft*, 2005), 1002 Viennese residents were asked how much Czechs, Hungarians, Sudeten-Germans, Croats, Slovakians, Serbs, and Poles had enriched Austrian culture since the fall of the Austro-Hungarian empire in 1918; Serbs received the highest number of 'not at all' responses (44%), followed by Poles (33%), and Slovaks (32%).[10] Today, many young Austrians frequent nightclubs where Serbian and 'remixed Balkan' jazz and rock is played, and travel abroad to hear Serbian music—for example to the biggest brass orchestra festival on the Balkan peninsula, *Dragacevski sabor trubaca*, held every year in Guca in central Serbia. The festival lasts several days, attracts up to 300 000 visitors and presents up to 50 big bands. Many of the brass orchestras in Serbia are staffed entirely by Roma, although the Roma have long been the target of systematic discrimination (Wippermann, 1997).

Many other musical and cultural contacts between Austria and neighbouring countries appear to promote integration and undermine old stereotypes and prejudices.

Current examples include the Szeged Open-Air Festival in Hungary and the Bosnian Rock musician and film music composer Goran Bregović. More relevant for older Austrians is the Slovenian folk band *Die Oberkrainer* that describes itself as 'Slovenia's music export no. 1' and 'musical ambassadors of Slovenia'.

Music and integration

What is the role of music in your relationships with other cultural groups in Graz? How many traditional Austrians know your music? What happens when they listen to it? What does 'integration' mean for you? Does music contribute to integration—for you personally? Of the various events, projects and institutions that you have experienced in Graz, which promote integration? What role does music play? How could music be used to promote integration? These leading questions, which were deliberately posed near the end of the interview, produced the most interesting responses.

Responses were generally consistent with the assumption that the music of one's culture helps one to feel at home. If such feelings encourage intercultural interaction within Graz, we may regard them as a measure of integration. Four respondents indicated that the music of their own culture makes them feel good, four that it is an important part of their life and cultural identity, three that it made them less homesick, and two that it helps them connect to other people. One respondent (10, Albania) reported getting homesick when listening to music of her own culture, and two thought that there was no connection between music and feeling at home. Two suggested that feeling at home depends more on friends and other factors than on music.

Cultural association

Several respondents mentioned associations between the music of a culture and other knowledge about that culture. Respondent 36 (Kurdish, female) said that:

> The music reminds me of the Kurd's situation, their suffering, the beauty of the country.

Others claimed that the music of a culture tells you something about the people. Respondent 36 (Kurdish, female) said:

> You see the cultures of other people and know why some speak loudly and others quietly. The music helps you to understand that.

Respondent 47 (Nigerian, male) stated:

> Music makes people from other cultures get to know us. Because music is very interesting. Then they say: the Igbos have nice music. Music brings us together—people know more about our culture—they speak well of us.

Respondent 12 (Albanian, female) said:

> Music tells you something about mindsets. We experience foreign cultures from a politically weakened viewpoint. With music you get to know someone differently—not like in conversation. You hear the music and straight away you have an impression of how the Albanians are, for example. That is the quite different from reading about Albanians in a

newspaper and I think it would be good if there were more concerts here in Graz. Not especially for Albanians, but rather for the Austrians. Because based on my husband's experience with a Greek restaurant I can say that Austrians like Greek music very much. More Austrians than Greeks come to the restaurant when Greek music is performed.

Associations between music and other aspects of culture can evidently reduce prejudice. Respondent 40 (Kurdish, male):

> Generally—there is always prejudice, but with music you can somehow succeed in deflecting these prejudices, because many people for example think that the Kurds ... are just Turkish mountain people and nomads. In fact we have a people with a rich culture and we show through our music and culture that we are not nomads but owners and carriers of culture. Yes. We have beautiful voices, beautiful songs, beautiful music and beautiful events.

Some respondents thought that unfamiliar music is difficult to understand and sometimes is not appreciated. Respondent 53 (Serbian, female) said:

> Many ... people don't quite understand our music. At my last birthday the Austrians reacted quite differently to our music than we did.

Respondent 22 (Italian, female) stated:

> I lived for 20 years in Southern Italy and I know the culture, I know the people. But for a foreigner it is difficult. He can have ideas but he can't understand them properly. Perhaps after a while. ... The music of Naples is well known among Austrians, but they don't know the meaning of the songs. That is normal. I don't think I would know the meaning of a traditional Austrian song, either. There are limits.

Respondent 26 (a Coptic man) questioned dominant discourse about the link between music and culture by suggesting that any music can be associated with any culture. He recalled that:

> The music in Austria reminds me of my adolescence in Egypt, e.g. ABBA, Boney M, Bee Gees, Tina Charles ... I have them all on CD.

Language

Is music a universal language that helps foreign cultures to communicate with each other across language barriers? Recent literature in ethnomusicology and music psychology is contradictory. Ethnomusicologists (e.g. Nettl, 1983) have traditionally emphasized the difficulty of understanding the music of foreign cultures without first immersing oneself in those cultures (becoming an 'insider'). More recently, music psychologists have documented an apparently universal ability to recognize basic emotions in the music of foreign cultures (Balkwill, Thompson, & Matsunaga, 2004). Meanwhile, globalization is increasing the rate and prevalence of intercultural communication (Nercessian, 2002).

Several respondents expressed the view that music is easier to understand across cultures than language. Respondent 28 (Coptic, male) stated:

> I think music is very important, because music is a world language. Everyone can understand it.

Respondent 4 (Chinese), when asked whether she listens to music or news on the radio, replied:

> Of course I mainly listen to music. In Austria I also sometimes listen to the news, but unfortunately I understand very little.

Respondent 26 (Coptic, male) commented:

> I can't speak Italian but I like to listen to Italian music. I can't speak Turkish but I can listen to Turkish music.

That music functions as a language can be more true for active musicians, for whom playing together can create a strong bond. Respondent 7 (Chinese, female) said:

> Music is generally very important, because you can communicate even if you don't understand the language. I play a lot of music with student colleagues and we often speak English because we come from different countries and when we play music it doesn't matter because we understand each other. ... You communicate and everyone understands and knows what the other person is thinking. ... Very many students at the music university are not from Austria but they still get along very well and do lots of projects. I think that is very good.

Respondent 24 (a male Italian jazz singer) commented at length on the relationship between music, language and integration:

> Then we can get along well. Because the music is happening, we have a topic of conversation, the song that we play, improvise, and if it is good, then have had a super dialogue, without words—a musical dialogue ... And if they both feel good about the topic, as is often the case in our music, a strong connection can emerge ... If we speak a common language, then we understand each other, like in a relationship. In this case music is the common language and we both go to the concert ... because both of us love that music and because that is our language. ... But to have a relationship after that, music is not so important any more. Only in the beginning, to make the contact. After that I need other strategies to feel okay and to feel good as a Grazer. So that you can get something out of me, so I can be an enrichment for you and you for me.

Emotion

If music promotes integration, what is the role of emotion? Several respondents perceived music of their own culture to be particularly emotional. Respondent 11 (Albanian, female) commented:

> There are so many songs in Albanian that could make me cry because the words are so sad.

Respondent 25 (Kurdish, male) said:

> We are Kurds and we dance to our music, although it is very sad music. If you listen to the words, they are mostly sad and that connects us to our memories. There are some songs, when I hear them, for example about freedom fighters, I start to cry. I only like old music—I don't like modern music at all. I live with my music in the past and not in the future.

Music can be especially emotional if linked with specific personal or historical events. Respondent 24 (Italian, male), remembering the annexation of South Tyrol by Italy after the First World War, commented:

> You know, the Italians came and said: you are no longer allowed to play your own music, you are no longer allowed to speak German. That made the bond with the music much stronger. Of course old people get emotional when they hear that. An example: If someone dies and the musicians play *Ich hatte einen Kameraden*, you can look around and everyone over 60 will go red and cry profusely. ... And among us young people, you can have a look, no-one cries at all. That is because the connection is not so strong.

The emotion evoked by music of one's own culture is often nostalgic and evokes feelings of homesickness. That, it seems, can affect integration either positively or negatively. Respondent 10 (Albanian, female) said:

> I avoid listening to Albanian music when I have not been home for a while because it makes me homesick.

In reply to the question 'How important is the music of your cultural group for you?', Respondent 46 (Nigerian, male) replied:

> I prefer my own traditional music. This music is the best.

Apart from this isolated comment, no other respondent, including those who experienced their own music as particularly emotional, suggested that the music of their culture might be somehow inherently superior. Perhaps the migration experience had taught them that the emotional effect of music depends strongly on cultural background. Another possible explanation is that they, like much of the world, believe that Western high culture is somehow inherently superior to other forms of culture (Judith Becker, 1986). It might have been interesting to ask respondents for their views on this issue, given its relevance for the general question of the role of music in integration.

Context dependence

In general, both migrants and locals were interested in more intercultural exchange, but migrants more often expressed the need to promote their own culture. As noted on p.395, music can be more important for migrants who identify with it than for their friends and family back home.

But not all migrants considered the music of their own culture to be particularly important or emotional. Respondent 2 (Chinese, female), who was studying Western classical music at Graz's music university, said:

> Classical music is very emotional, I often get goose bumps ... pop music is emotional if the text goes well.

Any music? Any culture?

If integration is about feeling good in a new situation, and *any* music can help people feel good, can *any* music (own or foreign) promote integration? Respondent 9 (Albanian, female) said:

> I feel better when I listen to music. But that is true not only for Albanian music but for any music that I like.

Respondent 2 (Chinese, female) commented:

> I sing along with songs from American musicals and lose myself in the music to forget my homesickness.

Respondent 55 (Serbian, male) said:

> Sure, music brings people together. It is easier to celebrate together, to dance, and to talk.

Because Western popular and classical music increasingly dominates world music, it can also have an integrative function. Respondent 18 (Italian, male) said:

> I especially think that concerts can attract people from all cultures. Some artists are famous and loved all over the world.

International music weakens national identification with traditional music, while creating new communities. When asked which cultural groups she identified with or felt she belonged to, Respondent 9 (Albanian, female) replied:

> I like classical music, but there are so many other nationalities that listen to this music.

Younger people tend to feel musical globalization more strongly. Respondent 15 (Albanian, female) said:

> As for music, I think that globalization has had a big effect. Music is now the same for all young people. It doesn't matter whether I live in Austria or Albania, I can listen to the same music.

Perhaps integration may be promoted by any aspect of culture; it is not clear whether music is more important or plays a special role. Respondent 33 (Coptic, male) said:

> Maybe people can understand our food more easily than our music. Many people have come to look at our church because it is so beautiful.

Contact with other groups

Many respondents' comments can be regarded as variations on the contact thesis, according to which contact between cultural groups leads to better communication and hence less conflict and prejudice. Allport (1954) theorized that contact is only beneficial among groups that have equal status, share social norms, and engage in cooperative activities with common goals that involve personal interaction. But some empirical studies (e.g. Wagner, van Dick, Pettigrew, & Christ, 2003) are consistent with contact promoting integration even if Allport's conditions are not met. People may be attracted to musical events, music may be a reason to create networks and clubs, or music may simply be a topic of conversation. But the music of foreign cultures can also be marketed as a exotica, reinforcing racial stereotypes, promoting artistic superficiality, and exploiting economically weaker cultures (Hutnyk, 2000).

Respondent 53 (Serbian, female) commented:

If you are familiar with something, you can understand it better and you are more open to it.

Respondent 48 (Nigerian, male) said:

But there are hardly any social events without music. Music can relax a tense atmosphere.

Respondent 55 (Serbian, male) stated:

Sure, music brings people together. It is easier to celebrate, dance and talk together.

Respondent 14 (Albanian, female) commented:

I met a lot of people through the Salsa dance course. Many students, and older people who are working. I like these people more, because we have something in common. Apart from that I have met many people in Graz who are not so relaxed. In the course there are people whose temperament is similar to mine.

Respondent 45 (Nigerian, male) reflected:

Salsa and samba are in fashion at the moment and people come to learn these dances. In that way they meet new people ... We go to children in schools and kindergartens and try to familiarize them with the music of Africa. In that way we counter racism. The music is a way to reach the children. ... We have to make it clear to those who are in a position to do something that integration means much more than head scarves and language skills. You have to bring people together and music is a good way to do that—as is food.

Curiosity

Music can make people curious about another culture and motivate them to get to know the people and the culture. Referring to a concert of Albanian traditional music on Graz's main square, Respondent 12 (Albanian, female) recalled:

The people stopped to look and were interested. Where do they come from? Oh, that's what it's like in Albania! ... Aha, Albania is real and Albanians live right here among us in Graz.

Respondent 40 (Kurdish, male) said:

I think that without music I would have no need to get to know other cultures.

Acceptance

Integration is promoted by the feeling that others like one's own music—and suppressed by the feeling that others do not like one's own music. Respondent 21 (Italian, female) commented:

I met some Austrians who knew the Italian music and I was so impressed. I was so happy. We sang together.

Respondent 41 (Kurdish, male) said:

We want the others to get to know our culture and music.

Conversely, non-acceptance of music may be unavoidable. Respondent 32 (Coptic, female) reflected:

> The people here accept other kinds of music, but our music is very difficult, rhythmically etc.—it is only for prayer. It helps you meditate. Austria is a land of music and I think they would just find our music boring.

Identity

The music of one's own cultural group can function as a strong reminder of that culture, triggering nostalgic feelings and in that way strengthening cultural identity. Respondent 47 (Nigerian, male) said:

> African music is important for me. The music leads as it were 'back to the roots'. ... Back to my country and my culture. Traditional music takes me back to my 'real' identity.

Respondent 44 (Nigerian, male) also said:

> That piece is not really one of my favourites. I like it because I am very proud of the place where I come from. As I already said, the music gives me meaning. ... It brings my thoughts back home.

Project evaluation

We want to understand the role of music in integration and on that basis to develop new integration strategies. Are those appropriate aims? Are interviews of this kind an appropriate method? Do you have any suggestions or criticism?

Our respondents' practical proposals for using music to promote integration in Graz included the following: public events including different aspects of each culture (various respondents), an entertaining multicultural concert for children (Respondent 9: Albanian, female); a multicultural weekend with folklore, football, music ... (Respondent 26: Coptic, male); financial support for performance of own music (various respondents), and media reports on specific cultures as well as associated economics and politics (Respondent 12: Albanian, female).

When asked whether an Albanian group playing in Graz's main square and other such events can promote integration, Respondent 12 (Albanian, female) replied:

> Yes, if it happens more often. The government should invest more public money in such projects. When that happened, Graz was cultural capital of Europe in 2003 and more money was available for events like that. It was very nice that attention was paid to my own country.

Asked if she had concrete ideas about what such an event should be like and how it should be organized, Respondent 7 (Albanian, female) remarked:

> There are pubs that are run by Albanians. If the managers got support from the city of Graz, it would be easier to stage such events, because if you invite singers from Albania that costs money. It's very hard to finance everything yourself.

Respondent 10 (Albanian, female) stressed that more money was needed to pay musicians.

> We cannot afford musicians for our cultural events. We used to invite folk groups as soon as we heard about them. That stopped a few years ago.

Respondent 35 (Kurdish, male) commented:

> Live music is so expensive that no small group in Graz can afford it. It used to be different ... before 1991, we got support from all sides, from the SPÖ [the main centre-left political party], the Greens, from the Province of Styria, and Caritas (a catholic charity) organization. We could put on big events, but now nothing works. If we ask for help now, they say we should go to our embassy and when they give us 100 or 200 Euros, that is nothing.

Why the emphasis on money? Perhaps our respondents regarded our study as an opportunity to lobby for financial support. Several independently suggested that governments could promote integration by financially supporting the performance and promotion of minority musics.

Conclusions

One consequence of globalization is the increasing importance of cultural integration. Our data suggest that integration is best achieved by combining a range of different approaches. Musical integration is one of those possibilities. Our study highlights intercultural differences regarding the perceived role of music in integration. For example, the Nigerians whom we interviewed regarded music as an integration-enhancing universal language, whereas the Copts had little desire to present their music to other groups.

Bergh (2007), in a retrospective study on the long-term effect of an intercultural school music programme, concluded that music can only positively affect integration if participants (in both minorities and the majority) contribute *actively* to music making or to the organization of events. The findings of the present study are consistent with that finding, which has important implications for the public funding of minority musics. The long-term positive impact on integration may be greater if public money is used to support active music making within minority groups rather than multicultural concerts for passive general consumption. Governments would invite proposals and a multicultural expert committee would evaluate them and financially reward minorities with the most original, creative, promising ideas (given that conformity can be problematic: H. S. Becker, 1982) and the strongest motivation.

A weakness of our study was the limited training of the student interviewers. Additional training in interviewing techniques and intercultural competence would have been beneficial. The social and cultural distance between interviewers and respondents may have biased our conclusions. Important thoughts may not have been articulated if they conflicted with unspoken rules of social interaction. One of the interviewers in each student group should have been a member of the corresponding cultural group, fluent in its main language or dialect. An interviewer with appropriate training should have performed post-interviews with selected respondents.

Can the results of a study in Graz be generalized to other cities that are larger or smaller or situated in different national and cultural contexts? Yes and no. Many of the sentiments expressed by our participants could have been expressed anywhere. But Graz may be atypical in its combination of social openness and political closure. Migrants feel relatively well integrated and free to publicly express their culture, but many non-migrants still harbour strong, deep resentments against migrants and multiculturalism—as reflected by the continuing success of far-right politics.

Acknowledgements

We thank Jane Davidson and an anonymous reviewer for helpful suggestions, and all the students and respondents who took part in the study.

Notes

[1] Further information in German on these political activities can be found on the internet homepage of the Forum for Applied Interculturality Research.

[2] For a more detailed report in German, see Dorfer (2009).

[3] The large number of interviewers is both a strength (diversity) and a weakness (lack of control).

[4] As part of a larger investigation, we also interviewed 28 people who self-identified as Austrians and had grown up in Austria. Their data are not considered here.

[5] We realized later that this may have created difficulties for older participants who listened to cassette tapes or vinyl records, or those who heard their favourite music on audiovisual media such as VHS or DVD.

[6] We assumed that the respondents expressed their opinions spontaneously and honestly, and we did not analyse for Hawthorne effects.

[7] Carinthia (*Kärnten*) is a province of Austria not far from Graz, whose traditional choral style is well known in other provinces. Carinthia is also a traditional stronghold of the far-right FPÖ. The popularity of the FPÖ in Carinthia is based in part on German-speaking intolerance of the Slovenian-speaking minority.

[8] This question aimed to strengthen the connection between respondents' comments and real music. It also maintained interest by varying the interview format.

[9] The authenticity of such statements is questionable given that similar sentiments are promoted by the 'world music' industry.

[10] Presumably, these results would have been similar in Graz and Vienna. They would have been influenced by geographical distance (distant countries make less contribution to culture).

References

Abbott, C., Rogers, P., & Sloboda, J. (2007). *Beyond terror: the truth about the real threats to our world*. London: Random House.

Albrich, T. (1994). Es gibt keine jüdische Frage: Zur Aufrechterhaltung des österreichischen Opfermythos. In R. Steiniger (Ed.), *Der Umgang mit dem Holocaust, Europa—USA—Israel* (pp. 147–166). Vienna: Böhlau.

Allport, G. W. (1954). *The nature of prejudice*. Cambridge, MA: Perseus Books.

Applegate, C., & Potter, P. (2002). *Music and German national identity*. Chicago, IL: University of Chicago Press.

Auernheimer, G. (1995). *Einführung in die interkulturelle Erziehung* (2nd ed.). Darmstadt: Wissenschaftliche Buchgesellschaft.

Bakker, A. B. (2003). Flow among music teachers and their students: The crossover of peak experiences. *Journal of Vocational Behavior*, 66, 26–44.

Balkwill, L. L., Thompson, W. F., & Matsunaga, R. (2004). Recognition of emotion in Japanese, western, and Hindustani music by Japanese listeners. *Japanese Psychological Research*, 46, 337–349.

Barnett, J., & Adger, N. (2007). Climate change, human security and violent conflict. *Political Geography*, 26, 639–655.

Becker, H. S. (1982). *Art worlds*. Berkeley, CA: University of California Press.

Becker, Judith (1986). Is western art music superior? *Musical Quarterly*, 72, 341–359.

Becker, Jörg (2009). Die historische Tradition antiserbischer Vorurteile. *Zeit-Fragen, Special Issue*, 10 years after the Yugoslavian war, April.

Bennett, M., & Sani, F. (2004). *The development of the social self*. London: Psychology Press.

Bergh, A. (2007). I'd like to teach the world to sing: music and conflict transformation. *Musicæ Scientiæ, Special Issue*, 141–157.

Bobo, L., & Zubrinsky, C. L. (1996). Attitudes on residential integration: Perceived status differences, mere in-group preference, or racial prejudice? *Social Forces*, 74, 883–909.

Bradley, D. (2006). Music education, multiculturalism, and anti-racism: 'Can we talk?' *Action, Criticism, and Theory for Music Education*, 5(2), 1–30.

Castles, S. (2006). Migration and community formation under conditions of globalization. *International Migration Review*, 36, 1143–1168.

Cohen, S. (2001). *States of denial: knowing about atrocities and suffering*. Cambridge: Polity Press.

Cook, N. (1998). *Music: a very short introduction*. Oxford: Oxford University Press.

DeNora, T. (2000). *Music in everyday life*. New York, NY: Cambridge University Press.

Dixon, W. J. (1993). Democracy and the management of international conflict. *Journal of Conflict Resolution*, 37, 42–68.

Dorfer, A. (2009). *Die Rolle von Musik in der kulturellen Integration: Eine qualitative Untersuchung in Graz*. Diplomarbeit: Karl-Franzens-Universität Graz.

Folkestad, G. (2002). National identity and music. In R. McDonald, D. Hargreaves, & D. Miell (Eds.), *Musical identities* (pp. 151–162). Oxford: Oxford University Press.

Frith, S. (1996). Music and identity. In S. Hall, & P. Du Gay (Ed.), *Questions of cultural identity* (pp. 108–127). London: Thousand Oaks.

Gibson, C. (1998). 'We sing our home, we dance our land': Indigenous self-determination and contemporary geopolitics in Australian popular music. *Environment and Planning D: Society and Space*, 16, 163–184.

Glaser, B. G., & Strauss, A. L. (1967). *The discovery of grounded theory: Strategies for qualitative research*. Chicago, IL: Aldine.

Gleditsch, K. S. (2002). *All international politics is local: The diffusion of conflict, integration, and democratization*. Ann Arbor, MI: University of Michigan Press.

Gowricharn, R. (2002). Integration and social cohesion: the case of the Netherlands. *Journal of Ethnic and Migration Studies, 28*, 259–273.

Greenberg, E., Macías, R. F., Rhodes, D., & Chan, T. (2001). English literacy and language minorities in the United States. *Educational Statistics Quarterly, 3*(4).

Hall, C. M., & Williams, A. M. (2002). *Tourism and migration: new relationships between production and consumption.* Berlin: Springer-Verlag.

Hargreaves, D., Miell, D., & MacDonald, R. (2002). What are musical identities and why are they important? In R. MacDonald, D. Hargreaves, & D. Miell, D. (Eds.), *Musical identities* (pp. 1–20). Oxford: Oxford University Press.

Hemetek, U. (2001). *Mosaik der Klänge. Musik der ethnischen und religiösen Mindeheiten in Österreich.* Wien: Böhlau.

Höllinger, F. (2004). *Skriptum zur Vorlesung 319.107 Einführung in die empirische Sozialforschung I.* Teaching materials, Department of Sociology, University of Graz.

Hou, F., & Balakrishnan, T. R. (1996). The integration of visible minorities in contemporary Canadian society. *Canadian Journal of Sociology, 21*, 307–326.

Hunter, L. M. (2005). Migration and environmental hazards. *Population and Environment, 26*, 273–302.

Hutnyk, J. (2000). *Critique of exotica: music, politics and the culture industry.* London: Pluto.

Jacobs, D., & Tillie, J. (2004). Introduction: social capital and political integration of migrants. *Journal of Ethnic and Migration Studies, 30*, 419–427.

Johnson, J. D., Trawalter, S., & Dovidio, J. F. (2000). Converging interracial consequences of exposure to violent rap music on stereotypical attributions of blacks. *Journal of Experimental Social Psychology, 36*, 233–251.

Kazemipur, A., & Halli, S. (2002). The invisible barrier: neighbourhood poverty and integration of immigrants in Canada. *Journal of International Migration and Integration, 1*, 85–100.

Kreutz, G., Bongard, S., Rohrmann, S., Hodapp, V., & Grebe, D. (2004). Effects of choir singing or listening on secretory immunoglobulin A, cortisol, and emotional state. *Journal of Behavioral Medicine, 27*, 623–635.

Kuran, T., & Sandholm, W. H. (2007). Cultural integration and its discontents. *Review of Economic Studies, 75*, 201–228.

Laukka, P. (2006). Uses of music and psychological well-being among the elderly. *Journal of Happiness Studies, 8*, 215–241.

Leary, M. R., Tambor, E. S., Terdal, S. K., & Downs, D. L. (1995). Self-esteem as an interpersonal monitor: The sociometer hypothesis. *Journal of Personality and Social Psychology, 68*, 518–530.

Lubbers, M., Gijsberts, M., & Scheepers, P. (2002). Extreme right-wing voting in western Europe. *European Journal of Political Research, 41*, 345–378.

MacDonald, R., Hargreaves, D. J., & Miell, D. (2009). Musical identities. In S. Hallam, I. Cross, & M. Thaut (Eds.), *Oxford handbook of music psychology* (pp. 462–470). Oxford: Oxford University Press.

Marsella, A. J. (2005). Culture and conflict: understanding, negotiating, and reconciling conflicting constructions of reality. *International Journal of Intercultural Relations, 29*, 651–673.

Maslow, A. H. (1943). A theory of human motivation. *Psychological Review, 50*, 370–396.

Mayring, P. (2002). *Einführung in die qualitative Sozialforschung: eine Anleitung zu qualitativem Denken* (5th ed.). Weinheim: Beltz.

McCarus, E. N. (1994). *The development of Arab-American identity*. Ann Arbor, MI: University of Michigan Press.

Mitleton-Kelly, E. (2003). *Complex systems and evolutionary perspectives on organisations: The application of complexity theory to organizations*. Bingley, UK: Emerald.

Müller, R., Glogner, P., Rhein, S., & Heim, J. (2002). *Wozu Jugendliche Musik und Medien gebrauchen. Jugendliche Identität und musikalische und mediale Geschmacksbildung*. Weinheim: Juventa.

Nagel, J. (1995). Resource competition theories. *American Behavioral Scientist, 38*, 442–458.

Nercessian, A. (2002). *Postmodernism and globalization in ethnomusicology: an epistemological problem*. Lanham, Maryland, WA: Scarecrow Press.

Nettl, B. (1983). *The study of ethnomusicology: Twenty-nine issues and concepts*. Champaign, IL: University of Illinois Press.

North, A. C., Hargreaves, D. J., & Hargreaves, J. J. (2004). The uses of music in everyday life. *Music Perception, 22*, 63–99.

Oliver, D. G., Serovich, J. M., & Mason, T. L. (2005). Constraints and opportunities with interview transcription: Towards reflection in qualitative research. *Social Forces, 84*, 1273–1289.

Ottaviano, G. I. P., & Peri, G. (2006). The economic value of cultural diversity: evidence from US cities. *Journal of Economic Geography, 6*, 9–44.

Owens, K., & King, M. C. (1999). Genomic views of human history. *Science, 286*(5439), 451–453.

Oyserman, D., Gant, L., & Ager, J. (1995). A socially contextualized model of African American identity: possible selves and school persistence. *Journal of Personality and Social Psychology, 69*, 1216–1232.

Park, R. E. (1928). Human migration and the marginal man. *American Journal of Sociology, 33*, 881–893.

Parncutt, R. (2007). Systematic musicology and the history and future of Western musical scholarship. *Journal of Interdisciplinary Music Studies, 1*, 1–32.

Parncutt, R. (2008). *Unity in diversity: Bringing together humanities, sciences and practice within musicology and psychology*. Invited presentation, Deutsche Gesellschaft für Musikpsychologie (PowerPoint file available on the internet).

Pawlig, M. (2003). *Chor als Arena für kulturelle Integration. Eine Fallstudie in den Stockholmer Vororten Tensta und Rinkeby*. Magisterarbeit, Berlin.

Pieridou-Skoutella, A. (2007). The construction of national musical identities by Greek Cypriot primary school children—implications for the Cyprus music education system. *British Journal of Music Education, 24*, 251–266.

Pries, L. (1998). Transmigranten als ein typ von arbeitswanderern in pluri-lokalen sozialen räumen: das beispiel der arbeitswanderungen zwischen Puebla/Mexiko und New York. *Soziale Welt, 49*, 135–149.

Rennie, D. L. (2000). Grounded theory methodology as methodical hermeneutics: Reconciling realism and relativism. *Theory & Psychology, 10*, 481–502.

Reuveny, R. (2007). Climate change induced migration and violent conflict. *Political Geography, 26*, 656–673.

Riedlsberger, M. (2002). The freedom party of Austria: from protest to radical right populism. In H. G. Betz, & S. Immerfall (Eds.), *The new politics of the right* (pp. 27–43). Basingstoke, GB: Palgrave Macmillan.

Sachs, J. D. (2005). *The end of poverty: economic possibilities for our time*. New York, NY: Penguin.

Schiller, G. N., Basch, L., & Szanton Blanc, C. (1997). From immigrant to transmigrant: theorizing transnational migration. *Transnationale Migration, 12*, 121–140.

Seshanna, S., & Decornez, S. (2003). Income polarization and inequality across countries: an empirical study. *Journal of Policy Modeling, 25*, 335–358.

Shaw, S., Bagwell, S., & Karmowska, J. (2004). Ethnoscapes as spectacle: reimaging multicultural districts as new destinations for leisure and tourism consumption. *Urban Studies, 41*, 1983–2000.

Shearman, D. (2002). Time and tide wait for no man. *British Medical Journal, 325*, 1466–1468.

Shetty, P. (2006). Achieving the goal of halving global hunger by 2015. *Proceedings of the Nutrition Society, 65*, 7–18.

Siegert, S. (2008). *Integration über Musik am Beispiel der makamhane. Eine kultur- und sozialanthropologische Untersuchung.* Diplomarbeit: University of Vienna.

Sloboda, J. A. (2005). *Exploring the musical mind.* Oxford: Oxford University Press.

Sloboda, J. A., & O'Neill, S. A. (2001). Emotions in everyday listening to music. In P. N. Juslin, & J. A. Sloboda (Eds.), *Music and emotion: theory and research* (pp. 415–429). New York, NY: Oxford University Press.

Sloboda, J. A., O'Neill, S. A., & Ivaldi, A. (2001). Functions of music in everyday life: an exploratory study using the Experience Sampling Method. *Musicæ Scientiæ, 5*, 9–32.

Sousa, M. D. R., Neto, F., & Mullet, E. (2005). Can music change ethnic attitudes among children? *Psychology of Music, 33*, 304–316.

Sozialwissenschaftliche Studiengesellschaft (2005). Einstellungen der WienerInnen zu ZuwandererInnen (Attitudes of the Viennese to migrants; telephone survey no. 161, March–April). *SWS-Rundschau, 45*(2), 233–240.

Stalker, P. (2000). *Workers without frontiers: the impact of globalization on international migration.* Geneva: International Labour Organization.

Tálos, E., Hanisch, E., & Neubauer, W. (Eds.). (2000). *NS-Herrschaft in Österreich. Ein Handbuch.* Vienna: öbv&hpt.

Van Aalst, M. (2006). The impacts of climate change on the risk of natural disasters. *Disasters, 30*, 5–18.

Van Oudenhoven, J. P., Prins, K. S., & Buunk, B. P. (1998). Attitudes of minority and majority members towards adaptation of immigrants. *European Journal of Social Psychology, 28*, 995–1013.

Verkuyten, M., & Thijs, J. (2002). Multiculturalism among minority and majority adolescents in the Netherlands. *International Journal of Intercultural Relations, 26*, 91–108.

Wagner, U., van Dick, R., Pettigrew, T. F., & Christ, O. (2003). Ethnic prejudice in east and west Germany: The explanatory power of intergroup contact. *Group Processes & Intergroup Relations, 6*, 22–36.

Wakeley, J. (1999). Nonequilibrium migration in human history. *Genetics, 153*, 1863–1871.

Ward, C. A., Bochner, S., & Furnham, A. (2001). *The psychology of culture shock.* Hove, UK: Routledge.

Webb, M. (2004). Defining the boundaries of legitimate state practice: norms, transnational actors and the OECD's project on harmful tax competition. *Review of International Political Economy, 11*, 787–827.

Welsch, W. (1999). Transculturality—the puzzling form of cultures today. In M. Featherstone, & S. Lash (Eds.), *Spaces of culture: city, nation, world* (pp. 194–213). London: Sage.

Willson, R. B. (2009). Whose utopia? Perspectives on the West-Eastern Divan Orchestra. *Music and Politics*, 3/2.

Wippermann, W. (1997). *Wie die zigeuner. Antisemitismus und Antiziganismus im Vergleich.* Berlin: Espresso.

Wodak, R., & Pelinka, A. (Eds.). (2002). *The Haider phenomenon in Austria.* New Brunswick, NJ: Transaction.

Zank, W. (1998). *The German melting-pot: multiculturality in historical perspective.* Basingstoke: Palgrave MacMillan.

Postlude

John Sloboda in Conversation with Irène Deliège

The collection of chapters which comprise this volume demonstrate that John Sloboda occupies a pioneering position, being a leader in the field of music psychology. He is someone able to generate unanimous respect in his scientific research as well as in his roles as colleague, mentor, and teacher. But the preceding chapters give little insight into John's own background, training, and emergent interests, and the threads of inquiry he has pursued. For these reasons, we conclude this book by engaging John in conversation and asking him to offer us some explanation about various questions relating to his training and output. We thank John most warmly for being so warm and open in responding to these questions.

When did you begin to learn music?

I started piano lessons at 6 years of age.

How was that initial start decided?

It was my request. When I was young I used to listen every day to a children's radio programme called 'Listen with Mother'. It was a 15-minute programme containing a story, preceded by a short piece of classical music. I was attracted to the music as much, if not more than the story. I am sure this was part of what motivated me to want to play.

In some cases, these musical experiences have had the quality of 'strong' or 'peak' experiences (Whaley, Sloboda, & Gabrielsson, 2008), and my research on memories of childhood peak experiences was in part stimulated by my own memories (Sloboda, 1989).

How did you begin to learn music, did you receive private lessons or did you learn through school?

My parents bought a piano, and found me a local private teacher on a nearby street. By chance she was an excellent teacher, and whose son became a professional musician. Although she died many years ago, we are still family friends with her son.

Do you have any specific musical memories from that period of your childhood/ adolescence?

In the early years of my musical learning, my family did not have a gramophone, nor did we attend many concerts. But I was fascinated to discover new music. The only way to do this was to attempt to play music on the piano from scores. When I was around 9 years old a friend of my parents donated a large number of classical piano scores to us. Some of the music was far too difficult for me, but my curiosity caused me to attempt to sight-read it. I tried everything, and it must have sounded very bad to my parents (and our long-suffering neighbours). I still have some of that music now, for instance a hard-bound copy of Schubert's *Moments Musicaux*.

I was always more interested to sight-read new music than to apply myself to detailed repeated practice on the same piece. By young adulthood I was a very competent sight-reader, a skill that has remained with me. I don't think there is anything very remarkable about my level of skill—it is simply that I did many hours of practice at sight-reading—most weeks, thus conforming to the pattern that was uncovered in my later collaborative research on instrumental practice (Sloboda, Davidson, Howe, & Moore, 1996).

We know that you are a good pianist. Who were your other teachers?

I stayed with my local private teacher for five years. She advised that I should apply to the Royal Academy of Music (one of the main London conservatoires) to be admitted as a junior scholar. From the age of 11 until 16 I attended a special junior school there, which took place every Saturday morning. There I received lessons on two instruments, and also choral and musicianship classes. My first piano professor was John Streets (www.ferrandou.org/tutors.html). When I left the college I continued private lessons until the age of 23 with another professor of the academy, Else Cross, a Viennese lady whose family moved in the same circles as Mahler and Schönberg. She died many years ago, and I am sad that I cannot find any official biography of her. I was very privileged to have such exceptional teachers, but it was their single-minded dedication to music [that] showed me that I could not expect to reach their achievements. I was then, and have always since, been too interested in different activities to concentrate on one.

As you are sight-reading so well, did you receive some particular tuition for that skill development?

No one ever gave me lessons on sight-reading as such, as far as I can remember. I just got better by doing lots of it.

So finally, you didn't choose a career as a performer?

At the same time as learning music, I was also developing a deep interest in science and mathematics at school. When I was 16, the directors of the Junior School of the Royal Academy presented me with a choice: I could increase the amount of time and effort given to daily instrumental practice, or I could leave the college and give my place to someone with more dedication.

I took advice from many people, and the general consensus was as follows. 'If you can earn your living at anything else than music, do it. The life of a performing musician is very hard, and the only possible reason to follow such a life is if music is the only thing that matters to you. Otherwise, take a career in another area, and you will always have music with you, to enjoy for pleasure, with other amateurs'. I am very satisfied that I took this advice, and have never been short of opportunities for rewarding musical activities, done for pleasure, to high quality, but without the need for money from it.

When and why did you decide to study psychology?

In my final years of high school I took Chemistry, Physics, Biology, and Music as special subjects. I had some idea to become a medical doctor. The idea of healing and helping was attractive. But the idea to consider psychology came from a gifted careers adviser at my school, who proposed that psychology might be a better subject to combine my scientific and artistic interests. Another teacher at the same school had an old friend who was a researcher in the Oxford University Psychology Department. He arranged for me to visit Oxford, and as a result of that visit, I applied for, and eventually was successful in gaining a place there to study psychology and philosophy. I began my studies in 1968. At that time, Oxford University did not consider psychology to be a sufficiently well-established subject to be studied on its own. It had to be taken with another subject in equal proportion. I was very pleased to be introduced to philosophical arguments and concepts, although it was psychology which I excelled at most. It was taught in an entirely experimental framework. I don't think we even had a single lecture on Freud. Pavlov, Skinner, Piaget, Broadbent, Hebb, Neisser, Chomsky were the diet of the day. These were the big names who formed my view of the subject! And when I was not studying psychology, I was playing the piano, playing the organ, and singing in several choirs!

I remember when I was finishing my own psychology studies at the University of Brussels in 1985, a symposium on music psychology was organized and you were invited to give a talk. At that time, you had already published papers on general cognitive processes in music: sight-reading, memory. Why did you select those research areas ...?

My initial choice of topic areas was very much determined by the interests and approaches of my main teachers (Patrick Rabbitt, and Neil O'Connor), and the fact that the best early research in the area was indeed being done in cognition (Deutsch, 1972; Longuet-Higgins, 1972). I have written about this at more length in the acknowledgement section of *Exploring the musical mind* (Sloboda, 2005a).

... and later on: child development, music in everyday life, emotion?

For rather contingent reasons, I undertook my PhD studies in a developmental research unit attached to University College London. So from early in my research career, I was surrounded by researchers who gave all their attention to the problems and issues of child development, normal and abnormal. One of my earliest research studies, never published, was on children's cognitive processing. I was deeply impressed by the careful uncovering of unexpected competences in children, through clever experimental methods. This exposure also made me very impatient with the typical adult cognition work, which took a single-time snapshot of a person's capacities. This very static view of human cognition seemed to me to ignore the essential dynamism of human behaviour, which is in constant change and flux.

As soon as one focuses on change and flux in humans, then it becomes clear that the engine of such change are [the] 'hot' processes of motivation and emotion, working on the 'cold' processes of cognition and memory. Both types of process must be studied to understand the whole phenomenon.

When I invited you to the University of Liège to give a presentation of your research, I remember that we received from you a letter informing the organizers that you were no longer doing research in the cognitive domain exclusively. Were you thinking about other options in that period of your life?

The critical shift in my research career came in the late 1980s when I sought to try and understand, for myself, why some events (which included pieces of music) had such a profound and visceral emotional effect on me. This led to one of my most cited studies (Sloboda, 1991) on music structure and emotional response. My interest was very much in the moment to moment events of the music, and how these correlated with (or were responsible) for profound emotional experience.

As far as my personal style, you can see that, even from childhood, if I had the option to choose something new, rather than remain on the same page, I would do so. Although there could be some deeper underlying directions, I am sure that some of the changes I have made in my life are simply motivated by the need for novelty. I think it very important not to 'over-interpret' one's life.

You were, with myself and some other colleagues, part of the foundation group for the constitution of ESCOM [European Society for the Cognitive Sciences of Music]. We met at the University of Liège for the constitution of the society in December 1990. As you have always been one of the most important members of the society, what does ESCOM represent for you?

I feel that the European project [which] began after the Second World War is one of the most important processes of political, cultural, and economic integration that has ever taken place. We have to remember that 65 years ago, Europeans were bombing and slaughtering each other almost without restraint. ESCOM was founded at the moment of great reconciliation, where East and West Germany were reunited and the Soviet Empire collapsed. My greatest joy was to see colleagues from the former Soviet area of influence (e.g. Poland, Estonia) reunited in democratic institutions with their peers from western Europe. Like many in Europe, my family has suffered in many ways from these divisions. ESCOM in a small way represents some healing of those wounds.

In the recent years, you have decided to leave your music psychologist career and, currently, you are working in a completely different area, closer to political, social, and/or environmental problems. Would it be possible for you to explain what you are doing exactly for the moment and why you decided this strong change in your life?

I have written about these matters at great length elsewhere (see particularly Powell, 2005; Sloboda, 2005a). The recent actions of my government, in the Balkans, in Afghanistan, and in Iraq, have been so dangerous for humanity, that I have had no personal option but to devote the majority of my energy to describing what has been done, explaining why it is such a disaster, and helping to propose alternatives (see, for instance Abbott, Rogers, & Sloboda, 2007, www.oxfordresearchgroup.org.uk, and www.iraqbodycount.org). Some people have asked me whether I think that the Obama Presidency means that the West has turned a decisive corner in its dealings with the rest of the world. My view on that at the moment is that we have not yet seen enough real change. There are plenty of good intentions, but results are as yet quite thin. It takes longer than six months to turn around a juggernaut that has been heading in the wrong direction for many decades.

Also, are you doing this full time now, for a short period of time?

I think, in the current state of the world, it makes no sense to plan more than five years ahead. For the next five years I will be devoting 80% of my work time to peace and security, and 20% to other things, including some contributions to music-related research.

As we all observe, you are still busy with publications of articles, editing books, etc. Does this mean that you want to retain a certain part of your work in your previous domain?

My main goals in music psychology are to see through to completion my remaining PhD students, to help them get publications and jobs, and to support in what ways I can the good health of music-science, particularly in contexts where that science can have direct and positive impact on the lives of musicians, those who teach them, and those who benefit from their outputs.

Since I retired from Keele, I undertook some collaborative work with colleagues in the multi-institutional Centre for the History and Analysis of Recorded Music (which has now evolved into the Centre for the Study of Music Performance as Creative Practice). An account of that work is given in Sloboda (2009). At the current moment I have just been appointed Visiting Research Fellow at the Guildhall School of Music and Drama, London, to assist the school in the implementation of its research strategy, and in the development of one or two key projects.

You have a large experience of research and teaching and you have a broad knowledge of the literature in the area of psychology of music. On this basis, what are for you, presently, the most crucial research questions for the future of our domain? Should you like to advise on some particular directions, methodologies, etc.

In the concluding chapter of the *Handbook of Music and Emotion* (Juslin & Sloboda, 2009), we have addressed this issue in a way which has broad relevance to music psychology in general. I think I can do no better than conclude by quoting from that chapter:

> One consideration, which could guide us more explicitly away from 'time-honoured' questions is the notion of benefit: which groups or constituencies stand to benefit from the results of specific pieces of research? There is a tendency, which is by no means confined to music-emotion research, for researchers to define the goals in terms of their own professional worlds—the need to be novel, rigorous, peer-appreciated, and understandable within the institutional and professional constraints and incentives which determine how research resources are allocated. There is nothing unacceptable about any of these factors, but if research is governed primarily by these factors, it will tend to be of primary relevance or interest to other scholars. Maybe emotion researchers could frame more research programmes in light of their potential benefit to a particular constituency within the world of music or within the wider worlds of education, care and healing, business and industry, culture and religion. Although there are some notable exceptions (particularly in the areas of health and therapy), the general impression is that applicability is either not considered at all, or is bolted on at the end in the form of a rather tokenistic afterthought.
> Sloboda (2005[b]) has argued that applicability should be a more explicit factor in strategic research planning, both at an individual and an institutional level. Is there music-emotion research that could be framed around specific practical concerns of composers, performing musicians, audiences, music broadcasters? Can music-emotion research

address important issues of human and cultural development? As Sloboda (2005[b]) noted, the situation is not so much that disputed answers have been given to such questions. Rather, it is the case that most researchers don't even bother to pose or answer them in a serious way.

Retrospectively, it may turn out that the second half of the 20th century was a rather privileged moment in the history of research, where many researchers were left free to 'follow their noses' wherever their individual interests took them. There are signs that the world may be entering a phase of its history when the opportunities and resources for rigorous research become significantly more constrained. As this happens, stakeholders (including tax-payers and governments) may ask more searching questions about the value of particular research domains. Music-emotion researchers perhaps need to be ready with better answers than are currently apparent from most of their outputs! (pp. 945–946)

Note: This interview was conducted in March 2009.

References

Abbott, C., Rogers, P. F., & Sloboda, J. A. (2007). *Beyond terror: the truth about the real threats to our world.* London: Rider, p. 118.

Deutsch, D. (1972). Effect of repetition of standard and comparison tones on recognition memory for pitch. *Journal of Experimental Psychology, 93.1,* 156–162.

Juslin, P.N., & Sloboda, J. A. (2009). The past, present, and future of music and emotion research. In Juslin, P. N., & Sloboda, J. A. (Eds.), *Handbook of music and emotion.* Oxford: Oxford University Press.

Longuet-Higgins, H. C. (1972). Making sense of music. *Proceedings of the Royal Institute of Great Britain, 45,* 87–105.

Powell, J, (2005). How a specialist on the links between music and the emotions became a peace activist: John Sloboda in conversation with James Powell. In T. Zeldin (Ed.), *The Oxford muse: Guide to an unknown city.* Oxford: The Oxford Muse. Available at: www.oxfordmuse.com/selfportrait/portrait57.htm (accessed 5 October 2010).

Sloboda, J. A. (1989). Music as a language. In F. Wilson, & F. Roehmann (Eds.), *Music and child development: Proceedings of the 1987 Biology of Music Making Conference.* St. Louis, Missouri: MMB Inc. Reprinted as Chapter 9 of Sloboda, J. A. (2005) *Exploring the musical mind: Cognition, emotion, ability, function* (pp. 175–190). Oxford: Oxford University Press.

Sloboda, J. A. (1991). Music structure and emotional response: Some empirical findings. *Psychology of Music, 19,* 110–120.

Sloboda, J. A. (2005a). *Exploring the musical mind: Cognition, emotion, ability, function.* Oxford: Oxford University Press.

Sloboda, J. A. (2005b). Assessing music psychology research: values, priorities, and outcomes. In J. A. Sloboda (Ed.), *Exploring the musical mind: Cognition, emotion, ability, function* (pp. 395–420). Oxford: Oxford University Press.

Sloboda, J. A. (2009). *Delineating creativity in music performance* (pp. 3–4). *CHARM Newsletter.* Available at: www.charm.rhul.ac.uk/studies/p6_3.html (accessed 5 October 2010).

Sloboda, J. A., Davidson, J. W., Howe, M. J. A., & Moore, D. G. (1996). The role of practice in the development of expert musical performance. *British Journal of Psychology, 87,* 287–309.

Whaley, J., Sloboda, J. A, & Gabrielsson, A. (2008). Peak experiences in music. In S. Hallam, I. Cross, & M. Thaut (Eds.), *The Oxford handbook of music psychology* (pp. 452–561). Oxford: Oxford University Press.

Index